DREAM
ROUTES
OF THE WORLD

DREAM
ROUTES
OF THE WORLD

Contents

About this book

There is a Far Eastern proverb that says, "You can't see the plains if you don't climb the mountain." People have been traveling for very different reasons since time immemorial, and their rewarding experience was simply discovering another part of the world. Once it was merchants, soldiers, pilgrims and explorers who endured long distances and hardships; today we often track these legendary routes following in their footsteps just for the sheer pleasure of it.

Traveling along these fifty routes of the world, we are taken to the most fascinating travel destinations on earth – to grand natural landscapes, unique cultural sites, vibrantly pulsating cities and quiet dreamy villages. The routes range from the St James' Way in northern Spain and the Romantic Road in Germany to the Friendship Highway in the Himalayas; from the Garden Route in South Africa and the Pacific Highway in Australia to the Alaska Highway and Route 66 in the United States on down to the Inca Trail in Peru and Bolivia.

The route descriptions:

There is an introduction at the beginning of each chapter providing an overview of the travel route and a short preamble about the country and regions in question as well as its specific natural features and historical and cultural sites. In addition, each chapter includes a map and a number of beautiful color photos pointing out important places and sights, charting out the course and roads, describing either specific aspects of nature or culture and hinting at worthwhile excursions.

Important travel information specifying the length of each tour, travel time, local traffic regulations, the climate, best season to travel and useful addresses are all listed in the Travel information box.

The city maps:

These maps include a comprehensive list of the main sights and attractions together with extensive descriptions on special extra pages.

The touring maps:

The course of each route and the most important places and sights are clearly marked on special tour maps at the end of each chapter in addition to an extra supplement reporting on interesting excursions.

Eye-catching symbols (see list opposite) mark the location and the type of attractions along each route. There are short intros in the margins of each map presenting interesting facts and superb color photos highlight particularly fascinating destinations.

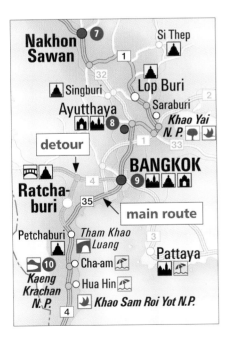

Remarkable landscapes and natural monuments
- Mountain landscape
- Extinct volcano
- Active volcano
- Rock landscape
- Ravine/Canyon
- Cave
- Glacier
- Desert
- River landscape
- Waterfall/rapids
- Lake country
- Geyser
- Oasis
- National Park (fauna)
- National Park (flora)
- National Park (culture)
- National Park (landscape)
- Nature Park
- Cultural landscape
- Coastal landscape
- Island
- Beach
- Coral reef
- Underwater Reserve
- Zoo/safari park
- Fossil site
- Wildlife reserve
- Whale watching
- Protected area for sea-lions/seals
- Protected area for penguins
- Crocodile farm

Remarkable cities and cultural monuments
- Pre- and early history
- The Ancient Orient
- Greek antiquity
- Roman antiquity
- Etruscan culture
- Indian reservation
- Indian Pueblo culture
- Places of Indian cultural interest
- Mayan culture
- Inca culture
- Other ancient American cultures
- Places of Islamic cultural interest
- Places of Buddhist cultural interest
- Places of Hindu cultural interest
- Places of Christian cultural interest
- Places of Jainist cultural interest
- Places of Abor. cultural interest
- Aborigine reservation
- Phoenician culture
- Prehistoric rockscape
- Early african cultures
- Cultural landscape
- Castle/fortress/fort
- Palace
- Technical/industrial monument
- Memorial
- Space telescope
- Historical city scape
- Impressive skyline
- Festivals
- Museum
- Theatre/theater
- World exhibition
- Olympics
- Monument
- Tomb/grave
- Market
- Caravanserai
- Theater of war/battlefield
- Dam
- Remarkable lighthouse
- Remarkable bridge

Sport and leisure destinations
- Race track
- Skiing
- Sailing
- Diving
- Canoeing/rafting
- Mineral/thermal spa
- Beach resort
- Amusement/theme park
- Casino
- Horse racing
- Hill resort
- Deep-sea fishing
- Surfing
- Seaport

North Cape

ICELAND

Reykjavik **1**

Norwegian

Sea

SWEDEN

7

NORWAY **5** FINLAND

Oslo Helsinki

Tallinn ESTONIA

3 *North Sea* *Baltic* **8**

Glasgow Edinburgh LATVIA Moscow

IRELAND DENMARK **6** Copenhagen *Sea* LITHUANIA

2 Dublin UNITED **9** BELARUS

KINGDOM NETHERLANDS

4 London Amsterdam Bremen Berlin

Brugge **14** GERMANY POLAND

15 BELGIUM Würzburg **12** UKRAINE

Paris **10** **11** CZECH REPUBLIC

Nantes Tübingen SLOVAKIA

16 SWITZERLAND Salzburg Budapest MOLDOVA

18 FRANCE Füssen AUSTRIA HUNGARY ROMANIA

San Sebastian Geneva **13** SLOVENIA

Bayonne Venice CROATIA SERBIA *Blac*

PORTUGAL Roncesvalles Menton **22** BOSNIA AND *k*

21 **17** Florence HERCEGOVINA BULGARIA *Sea*

Lisbon **19** Madrid **24** Rome MONTENEGRO

Barcelona **23** ALBANIA MACEDONIA

Sevilla SPAIN Brindisi GREECE

20 *Mediterranean Sea* **25** Messina Athens

26

Alaska
(USA)

Homer **39**

Juneau Istanbul GEORGIA UZBEKISTAN

Prince Rupert C A N A D A **27** TURKEY Buchara

TÜRKMENISTAN

Sault Ste.Marie **40** Tangier TUNISIA SYRIA AFGHANISTAN

35 ISRAEL IRAQ

41 Jackson Portland Halifax MOROCCO Alexandria JORDAN KUWAIT I R A N

U N I T E D Chicago ALGERIA LIBYA **36**

44 S T A T E S **43** **45** Washington EGYPT SAUDI QATAR

42 Amarillo ARABIA UAE

Santa Monica MAURITANIA M A L I Abu Simbel OMAN

Los Angeles NIGER

Tucson CAPE VERDE CHAD SUDAN ERITREA YEMEN

A T L A N T I C SENEGAL BURKINA DJIBOUTI

BAHAMAS GUINEA-BISSAU FASO NIGERIA CENTRAL ETHIOPIA

CUBA GUINEA BENIN AFRICAN

M E X I C O **46** Cancún SIERRA LEONE GHANA REPUBLIC SOMALIA

HAITI DOMINICAN LIBERIA CAMEROON UGANDA

BELIZE REPUBLIC IVORY CONGO KENYA

GUATEMALA HONDURAS COAST GABON RWANDA

EL SALVADOR NICARAGUA BURUNDI

COSTA RICA D.R.CONGO TANZANIA

PANAMA VENEZUELA GUYANA

COLOMBIA SURINAME

Piura ANGOLA

ECUADOR O C E A N ZAMBIA MALAWI

B R A Z I L

47 PERU MADAGASCAR

Lima ZIMBABWE MOZAMBIQUE

48 BOLIVIA NAMIBIA MAURITIUS

Tacna Sucre BOTSWANA

Arica **37** Windhoek

PARAGUAY SWAZILAND

P A C I F I C LESOTHO

49 **38**

Santiago Córdoba Cape Town SOUTH AFRICA

CHILE URUGUAY

O C E A N ARGENTINA

50

Puerto Yungay

Ushuaia

Greenland
(Denmark)

Overview of routes

Iceland ponies in the marshes near Reykholt in the south-west of the island.

Route 1

Iceland

Fire and ice: archaic landscapes on the world's largest volcanic island

This legendary island in the North Atlantic delivers spectacular natural encounters with primordial force: formidable basalt mountains, vast lava fields, mighty glaciers, meandering glacial streams, thundering waterfalls, and much more. All the more comforting, then, when you encounter villages with a centuries-old cultural tradition on the periphery of seemingly infinite, untouched expanses.

Fishing boats in the port at Ólafsvik.

Iceland, the largest volcanic island on earth, is just 300 km (186 mi) from Greenland, but nearly 1,000 km (621 mi) from western Scandinavia. The "wayward end of the world" is what the Vikings called these inhospitable shores close to the Arctic Circle when they settled here in the 9th century and set up one of their first free states.

Today, this 103,000-sq-km (3,976-sq-mi) island has 270,000 inhabitants who live primarily off fishing, sheep farming, cat-

tle and horse breeding, aluminum production, and vegetable farming in greenhouses heated by geothermal energy. Iceland offers visitors unique encounters with nature in its original state, where elemental forces still reign free.

The capital of Iceland, Reykjavík, is full of charm and does boast a number of interesting things to see, but the real destinations on the "Island of Fire and Ice" are outside of the city. The other small towns, such as Akureyri and Húsavík in the north or Egilsstadir on the east of the island, are set in very picturesque locations but their buildings are mostly recent or even totally new. Masonry, concrete and corrugated iron have long since replaced the old peat bricks and traditional thatched roofs of the scattered individual homesteads. Significant cultural monuments are not to be found

anywhere on the island. Iceland's most outstanding attraction is its magnificent landscape. Admittedly, it is no image of pastoral tranquility, but rather one of dramatic activity, extreme wilderness and tremendous diversity.

The four essential elements dominate the island with breathtaking intensity. The air is so fresh and clear that when the weather is good – which is fortunately much more often the case than one would expect here – you can see for over 100 km (62 mi).

Water is available in excess and seems to be absolutely everywhere you look, from meandering rivers, powerful waterfalls, cold and warm lakes located atop hot and cold springs, and of course the famous geysers. More than ten percent of the island is covered in glaciers, with one quarter of the ice surface alone

Massive gurgling mud baths such as this one in Namarskard on Lake Mývatn are typical of Iceland.

On the south coast a 25-m-wide (82-ft) glacial river from the Myrdalsjökull in Skógafoss plunges 62 m (203 ft).

belonging to Europe's largest glacier, Vatnajökull. Indeed, the island owes its name to its numerous glaciers.

Given all of that, however, the earth element is still the most spectacular. Vast areas of land are covered with recently cooled lava, transforming Iceland into an open-air geology museum that reveals how our planet looked during the different phases of its early development.

As a result, however, the inhabitable areas are limited to a few coastal regions. The rest of the island is shaped by steep cliffs and fjords that extend into the interior, which in turn features expansive plateaus, lava fields, deserts of stone, sand and ash, table mountains, glaciers, and active and extinct volcanoes. Today, Surtur, the mythical leader of the fire giants, still leaves fascinating traces of his work all around the island. By stoking the fires deep within the earth, he makes the glowing, viscous magma rise from the depths, melt the earth's crust and erupt in furious explosions. The island itself is actually the tip of a submerged mountain that forms part of the Mid-Atlantic Ridge, where the American and Eurasian tectonic plates drift apart. For visitors, it is a sort of sample gallery of geological shapes, from volcanic craters and cinder fields to tuff cones and countless other whimsical lava formations. Geysers discharge their fountains of scalding water at regular intervals while mud baths bubble away and fumaroles and solfataras smolder. The plentiful thermal springs provide relaxation for Icelanders and their guests all year round and many houses have a bathing pool with volcanically heated water right outside the door.

Steam rises from the boiling hot fumaroles at Haverarond in Lake Mývatn.

Leif Eriksson

Leif Eriksson, legendary Viking seafarer and predecessor of Christopher Columbus, looks out over the rooftops of Reykjavík towards the ocean from his pedestal in front of Hallgríms church. Eric the Red, his father, may not have a statue but he was no less famous. After being banished from Norway, he discovered Greenland from his base in Iceland in 982 and founded its first European settlement. It was from this new colony that the then 30-year-old Leif put to sea in around 1000, with thirty-five men, to begin his famous voyage of discovery. The "Greenland Saga" reports that he landed in North America at around the same latitude as Baffin Island,

Statue of Leif Eriksson in Reykjavík.

which he called Helluland ("flat stone land"). From there he is said to have sailed as far as New England, following the Labrador Current southwards. This he christened "Vinland" because he found vines growing there.

Another contemporary source, however, claims that Leif, "the Happy One", as he was known in his day, had heard from a fellow countryman named Bjarni Herjólfsson about the existence of a foreign land to the west before undertaking his legendary voyage. It was a land that the latter is said to have seen some fourteen years previously after losing his way during a storm.

Ultimately, Leif went down in history as the first European to have set foot on American soil and, in 1930, was posthumously granted this imposing monument in Reykjavík by the U.S. Congress to mark the occasion of the 1,000th anniversary of the first meeting of the Althing.

Iceland's ring road: Anyone circling the island of fire and ice on the roughly 1,500-km-long (932-mi), almost completely paved, coastal road (Route 1) will become acquainted with most of the facets of this unique natural paradise, but a number of detours from the ring road into the interior are certainly worthwhile.

❶ Reykjavík Iceland's capital, which is also the country's cultural, transport, and economic center, is on the northern edge of a peninsula on the south-west coast. Its climate benefits from the mild currents of the Gulf Stream. When it was granted its charter at the end of the 18th century, there were just 200 people settled in the "smoky bay" ("Reykjavík" in Icelandic). Now, including suburbs and outlying towns, the population has grown to around 160,000 – roughly sixty percent of the country's inhabitants.

The city tour begins at the main square, Austurvöllur, which is home to the oldest parliament in the world, a cathedral, and the time-honored Hotel Borg. The city's most prominent feature is the Tjörnin, a small lake in the city center. The new city hall, the National Gallery and some upscale residential villas line its shores. To the south are the National Museum and the Árni Magnússon Institute, home to the medieval saga manuscripts. The council buildings, originally designed as a prison, and the bronze statue of Ingólfur Arnarson, one of Reykjavík's first settlers, are located closer to the port.

On a hill to the south-east of town, Hallgríms church watches over the city with the Leif Eríksson monument standing tall before it. Right next door is the Ásgrímur Jónsson Collection, donated to the state by the Icelandic landscape artist who died in 1958. The Natural History Museum, Einar Jónsson's collection of sculptures, as well as the Árbaer Open Air Museum and the Laugardalslaug swimming pool are also worth a visit.

❷ Hraunfossar Roughly 25 km (15 mi) north of the town of Borganes it is worth taking a detour along the Hálsasveitarvegur (Route 518) to an impressive natural spectacle not far from the Húsafell country estate: the Hraunfossar "lava waterfalls", a multitude of small springs that cascade over a basalt lip into the Hvítá glacial river. Nearby, there is a similar natural attraction called the Barnafoss Waterfall.

❸ Akureyri With 15,000 inhabitants, this "pearl of the north" is located at the end of the Eyjafjördur and is the country's third largest town. It is also the transport center for the north coast thanks to its shipyard, airport and port.

The well-organized local history museum and botanical gardens provide an introduction to the history, flora and fauna of the surrounding region. The Nonnáhús, a monument to local children's book author Jón Sveinsson, alias Nonni, may be interesting for literature fans. The city also serves as a starting point for hiking trips into the

Travel information

Route profile
Length: 1,400 km (870 mi), without detours
Time required: min. 8–10 days
Start and end: Reykjavík
Route: Reykjavík, Akureyri, Mývatnsee, Egilsstadir, Stafafell, NP Skaftafell, Vík, Skogar, Thingvellir

Traffic information:
Many gravel roads. Be careful of varying depths when crossing rivers. The following laws are very strictly enforced for drivers: 0.0 mg alcohol limit for drivers; maximum speed limit in towns 50 km/h (30 mph), on gravel roads 80 km/h (50 mph), on tarred roads 90 km/h (60 mph). The majority of the roads in the interior are first opened in July.

For more information on road conditions call: *0354/17 77* (8am–4pm) or go to: *www.vegag.is*
If you are driving a diesel vehicle you will be required to pay a weight tax on arrival. *www.icetourist.de*

When to go:
Summer is the best time, but don't expect very high temperatures.
Weather in English: *Tel: 0902 / 06 00* *www.vedur.is*

Other information:
Here are a few sites to help you prepare for your trip: www.icelandtouristboard.com www.iceland.org

fascinating interior, for example to the region around the Hlidarfjall at an elevation of up to 1,200 m (3,937 ft).

4 Goðafoss Some 40 km (25 mi) east of Akureyri, the roaring Skjálfandaðfljót River makes its way from the stony expanse of the Sprengisandur plain down toward the ocean over a 10-m (33-ft) escarpment. Despite the relatively short drop, the width and quantlty of water make Goðafoss one of the most impressive and deservedly famous falls in Iceland.

Its name, "Waterfall of the Gods", comes from Thorgeir, the speaker of the Althing. He is said to have thrown the statues of his former house gods into the river here in the year 1000 because the Icelandic parliament decided that Icelanders should convert to Christianity. Norwegian King Olaf had threatened a timber embargo, which would have crippled shipbuilding, an essential industry for the island.

5 Mývatn Located about 30 km (19 mi) east of Goðafoss, Lake Mývatn was formed only about 3,500 to 2,000 years ago by lava discharged during two volcanic eruptions. It is 37 sq km (14 sq mi) in size but only 4–5 m (13–16 ft) deep and fed by hot springs.

The diversity of plant life here is nearly singular on the planet for such northern latitudes. Mosses, grasses, ferns, herbs and birch trees grow along the shore and on the numerous islands. During the summer months, massive swarms of midge flies form over the warm water. Together with the insect larvae, they provide food for the wealth of fish and waterfowl here, thousands of which nest in the many bays, making the region a paradise for birdwatchers.

The Lake Mývatn area is considered one of Iceland's most spectacular landscapes. It is also located in one of the island's most active volcanic zones. Beautiful lava formations are scattered all along the very well-signposted hiking trails. The Dimmuborgir, or "Dark Fortresses", consist of bizarrely shaped formations with small caves and arches. The best view over the pseudo-crater in and around Lake Mývatn can be enjoyed from the rim of the Hverfjall crater, a 170-m-high (558-ft) cinder cone.

6 Krafla The area surrounding the 818-m (2,683-ft) volcano just a few miles north-east of Lake

Mývatn is one of Iceland's most tectonically unstable zones. Considered extinct at the beginning of the 18th century, the 2,000-year-old Krafla suddenly buried the entire region under a thick layer of lava and ash following a violent eruption. The ultimate result was a dazzling, emerald green tuff cone with a crater lake some 320 m (1,050 ft) in diameter.

In 1975, the volcano came to life again for nearly a decade. Its bubbling, steaming sulfur springs have since remained a very popular attraction and are the most visible indication of ongoing volcanic activity.

7 Húsavík/Tjörnes Instead of following the shortest route along the ring road east of Lake Mývatn, it is definitely worth taking a detour around the Tjörnes Peninsula, which is especially fascinating from a geological point of view. A good 30 km (19 mil) after the turnoff near Reykjahlið you will pass Grenjadarstadur, a peat homestead built in around 1870. It was abandoned in 1949 before being turned into a folk museum. The little town of Húsavík, which mainly survives off fishing and fish-processing, has managed to make a name for itself as a tourist destination with a particular focus on whale watching. With commercial whaling

now a thing of the past in Iceland, local fishermen now take seaworthy holidaymakers out on their cutters for a day's worth of whale watching in the summertime.

8 Jökulsárgljúfur and Dettifoss Compared to the rest of Iceland, the climate around Ásbyrgi, the "Fortress of the Gods", is mild and the contours of the landscape quite gentle. A birch forest covers the valley where, legend has it, Odin's six-legged horse shaped a mighty, semi-circular cliff with its hoof. There are the two roads from here that follow the canyon upstream along the edge of the escarpment toward Dettifoss. The eastern of the two is in better condition, while the western one is bumpier and thus

less crowded. Jökulsárgljúfur National Park, founded in 1973, encompasses the canyon-like Jökulsá á Fjöllum valley section between Ásbyrgi and the Dettifoss Waterfall. With a length of

1 The river feeding the Goðafoss begins far to the south.

2 The waterfalls at Hraunfossar, near Húsafell, cascade down from a lava field.

3 The bizarre Dimmuborgir cliff landscape at Lake Mývatn.

4 Volcanic landscape at Reykjahlið, north-east of Lake Mývatn.

5 The Breiðamerkurjökull flows into the Jökulsárlón glacial lagoon on the south side of the Vatnajökull.

Detour

Herðubreið and Askja

Anyone turning off shortly before Grimsstadir, west of the Jökulsá á Fjöllum River, and heading south on the F88 – navigable only with four-wheel drive vehicles – will get a good look at Iceland's interior. The route takes you from the Hrossaborq crater to the southern ring road, the Mývatnsöraefi (or midge lake desert) and the Óðá-

Top: Herðubreið volcano.
Bottom: A view inside the Askja crater.

dahraun desert. The area is lined with vast lava fields, bleak stony expanses, and the occasional shield volcano. You will only seldom come across patches of green vegetation, which grow where water is able to seep through the volcanic soil to the surface. Herðubreið (about 50 km/31 mi) south of Hrossaborg) is one such oasis. A cabin provides somewhat spartan accommodation at the foot of the Herðubreið, imposing, 1,682-m-high (5,519-ft) table volcano.

If the weather is good, you should take a drive to the Dyngjufjöll volcano massif. Just the 40 km (25 mi) jaunt past the magnificent Jökulsa Canyon, the Dragon Gorge (Drekagil), and the Vikrahraun lava flow is worth the extra time.

After roughly a 30-minute walk you get a spectacular the view of the Askja, a 45-sq-km (17-sq-mi) crater with Iceland's deepest lake.

Gullfoss, the "Golden Waterfall", is one of the country's loveliest and most impressive waterfalls in the south-west of the island and is close to a famous geyser. For the last 10,000 years, the waters of the Hvita River, which begins underneath the Langjökull Glacier, have plunged over two 32-m-high (105 ft) precipices to

form an impressive gorge about 35 m (115 ft) deep and 2.5 km (1.6 mi) long. The river's average flow is 109 cu m/sec (3,849 cu ft/sec), but during the spring snowmelt it can increase to 2,000 cu m/sec (70,629 cu ft/sec).

Hekla and Landmannalaugar

Route 26 takes you past Iceland's most famous volcano, the snow-capped Hekla (1,491 m/4,891 ft), on

Top: Hekla Volcano.
Bottom: Landmannalaugar.

the way to Landmannalaugar. The ryolith rock mountains glisten with a range of hues and there are paths leading to a number of spectacular sulfur springs.

Geysir/Gullfoss

You can reach the Geysir thermal area via Flúðir, 15 km (9 mi) before the Selfoss turnoff on Route 30. The geyser, which can blast water up to 60-m (199-ft) into the air, only

A look at Strokkur Geyser.

came back to life in 2000. The Strokkur Geyser is even more active and shoots its boiling stream about 25 m (82 ft) into the sky every five to ten minutes. Just 10 km (6 mi) to the north-east is the Gullfoss, Iceland's most famous waterfall.

206 km (128 mi), the "glacier river from the mountains", as its name translates, is Iceland's second-longest. It is fed from the northern edge of the Vatnajökull Glacier and intersects the ring road at Grímsstadir. About 20 km (12 mi) upstream is where it plunges into the Dettifoss Waterfall over five formidable rock faces into a deep gorge.
Iceland has a number of magnificent waterfalls, but few will make the same impression as Dettifoss. With a span of about 100 m (328 ft), the gray-brown floodwaters of the Jökulsá á Fjöllum drop 44 m (144 ft) into a canyon between vertical basalt walls. In the summer the flow rate reaches up to 1,500 cu m/sec (52,972 cu ft/sec). This makes the Dettifoss Waterfall the mightiest in Europe by a long shot.
A drive from here to the Herðu-breið volcano and the Askja caldera makes for a very worthwhile detour. You'll come to the turnoff about 36 km (22 mi) after Reykjahlið.

⑨ Egilstaðir / Fjorde Eastern Iceland's administrative and commercial center is on the ring road in a mostly agricultural area of the country. It is also a heavily wooded area. A worthwhile destination in these parts is the more than 100-m-high (328-ft) Hengifoss Waterfall on the northern shore of the long and narrow Lake Lögurinn. The ring road follows the coast once you pass Reydarfjördur and affords spectacular views of the wild ocean.

⑩ Stafafell A historical homestead stands on the edge of the Jökulsá á Lóni Delta about 30 km (19 mi) before Höfn, the only port on the entire south coast. Once a vicarage, it now serves as a youth hostel from which you can set off on hikes into the varied landscapes of the Lonsöraefi wilderness region.

⑪ Jökulsárlón About 70 km (43 mi) beyond Höfn, where the impressive ice tongue of the Breidarmerkurjökull Glacier extends to within a few hundred yards of the sea, the ring road takes you right past the island's glacial lake. Glistening a blue-white hue in the lagoon, giant icebergs from the edge of the glacier evoke an atmosphere akin to Greenland.

⑫ Skaftafell National Park Skaftafell National Park, established in 1967, extends from the area around Vatnajökull, Ice-

land's largest glacier, to the south as far as the ring road and provides a multitude of scenic attractions. Within the national park, signposted hiking trails take you into dense forests such as the one in Núpstadaskogar, along extensive wetlands and marshes to dilapidated but intact homesteads, and to the Svartifoss Waterfall surrounded by basalt pillars.
Between Fagurhólsmri and Kirkjubaejarklaustur the ring road now traverses the black sand and scree expanse of the Skeiðar-ársandur. A glacier run here was caused by an eruption of the Lóki volcano below the Vatnajökull Glacier. The melted glacial ice under the Vatnajökull ice cap then surged into the sand in a giant flood wave.

⑬ Vík The big attraction at Iceland's "southern cape" are the bird cliffs at Dyrhólaey, around 20 km (12 mi) away. A number of common North Atlantic seabird species live here at varying levels of the cape. Right at the top are the Atlantic puffins, which hide their tunnels in the grass tufts. On the cliffs beneath them are the kittiwakes and fulmars. You

can take a boat tour from the black sand beach. A lighthouse 100 m (328 ft) up on the cliffs is a popular viewing point.

⑭ Skógafoss The catchment area of the Skógar river, which crosses the road south-east of the mighty Mýrdalsjökull is a good stopover for two reasons. The first is the Skógafoss, a waterfall that is 62 m (203 ft) high surrounded by meadows. You can see the falls from above and below, which is what makes it a special place. Secondly, the meticulously detailed folk museum in Skógar deserves a visit. About 7 km (4 mi) beyond Hella it is worth taking a detour to the Hekla volcano and through the Landmannalaugar thermal region. Back on the ring road, instead of taking the direct return route to Reykjavík, take a detour via Route 30, which passes by the Gullfoss Waterfall and the Strokkur Geyser. Route 35 will then take you directly back to the ring road. Before that, however, you should to take a look at the church in Skál-holt, which was a Viking center in the Middle Ages and boasts lovely glass windows. The main road takes you past Lake þing-

vallavat towards þingvellir, the last stop.

⑮ þingvellir The renowned Thingfeld lies on the northern shore of Lake þingvallavatn. The lava plateau bordering the All Men's Gorge to the west is a very interesting geological area and the historical heart of the country.
It was this "Holy Free State" that became the former Icelandic Free State in the year 930 and it was here that the legendary Althing, the oldest democratic parliament in the world, met annually all the way up until 1798. It was also here that the Icelanders declared themselves a republic on June 17, 1944.

1 Glaciers reflected on a lake in the Skaftafell National Park.

2 The water from Svartifoss, "The Black Waterfall", plunges over an impressive basalt cliff into a basin shaped like an amphitheater.

3 Rock needles in front of the coastal cliffs at Vík, Iceland's southern-most point.

Hraunfossar An underground river appears as if out of nowhere over a 1-km (0.6-mi) stretch on the outskirts of Reykjavík and cascades over a basalt escarpment into the Hvítá, a glacial river. Not far upstream from this "lava rock waterfall" is the equally intriguing Barnafoss ("Child's Waterfall"), the subject of an eerie Icelandic saga.

Goðafoss The Skjálfandafljót River, rising from the edge of the Vatnajökull Glacier, forms the "God's Waterfall" east of Akureyri on its way to the ocean. Its breadth and the volumes of water it drops are impressive.

Mývatn This lake was formed just a few thousand years ago when spring water was dammed by lava. It boasts a surface area of 37 sq km (14 sq mi), is very shallow, and has an unusual wealth of flora and fauna.

Herðubreið/Askja The region to the west of the Jökulsá á Fjöllum River is wild and spectacular but can really only be discovered in a four-wheel drive vehicle. The view of the fire mountains is breathtaking.

Reykjavík The sightseeing attractions in Iceland's small capital city are all close together: the National Gallery, the National Museum, the Árni Magnússon Institute (home to a number of historical manuscripts), the world's oldest parliament and a lively port.

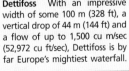

Svartifoss Waterfall It may not be the tallest, but its sensational basalt columns make it one of the most unusual waterfalls in Iceland.

Dettifoss With an impressive width of some 100 m (328 ft), a vertical drop of 44 m (144 ft) and a flow of up to 1,500 cu m/sec (52,972 cu ft/sec), Dettifoss is by far Europe's mightiest waterfall.

The Hekla Volcano Iceland's most famous volcano is 1,491 m (4,892 ft) high and easy to reach. Make a stop at the Leirubakki Information Center where you can learn some fascinating details about the mountain, considered a symbol of evil in the Middle Ages.

Strokkur The Geysir thermal region (after which all such springs are named) is impressive particularly because of the Strokkur Geyser, which shoots its stream of boiling water up to 25 m (82 ft) into the sky every 5 to 10 minutes.

The Skaftafell National Park This national park was founded in 1967, and encompasses parts of the Vatnajökull Glacier. With an area of 1,600 sq km (616 sq mi), it boasts marshes, fens, scree and sand landscapes and birch forests, all against the magnificent backdrop of the Vatnajökull Glacier, which has more ice than all of the alpine glaciers together.

The round Doonagore watchtower on the coast of County Clare.

Ireland

Out and about in the land of the Celts

Ireland is a natural phenomenon in itself. The sandy beaches, striking cliffs, moor landscapes, glistening lakes and green hills are the core of its attractions. But Ireland is more than a natural history museum. It possesses a rich folk tradition that is testimony to the island's vibrant spirit.

Ireland is both an island and a divided nation. The Republic of Ireland (Éire) makes up about four-fifths of the island, while the smaller Northern Ireland is still part of the United Kingdom. As different as they might be, both parts of the island have their very own appeal. The spectrum of landscapes is broad and the natural environment is largely pristine. The central lowlands are surrounded by modest mountain ranges that rise to peaks of more than 1,000 m (3,281 ft) only in the south-west. Despite their relatively small size, however, many of these mountains rise quite strikingly out of the ocean.

The Carrauntoohil (1,038 m/3,406 ft), for example, offers magnificent views of fjord-like bays on the west coast that even appear to change shape in the rapidly shifting light. Lighthouses there defy the relentless pounding of waves on desolate craggy peninsulas. On the flatter coastal sections the sandy beaches provide a contrast to the steep cliffs that surround them. Moorland and countless lakes disappear behind the buttes and green hills of the interior. Indeed, Ireland shows its calmer side on the east coast where the shore is less fragmented, the ocean more tranquil and the surf more placid.

In general, it is not without reason that Ireland has earned epithets like such as "The Green Island" or the more ostentatious "Emerald Isle". Of course, the island does not possess any precious stone mines, but after one of the frequent rain showers, the green appears to take on a special luminosity in the sunlight.

The moors in the interior of the island are scattered with individual fields and meadows. According to a Gaelic saying, the grass in the Irish meadows grows so quickly that if you leave a stick lying in the grass you won't be able to find it again the next day. These fertile areas have been targeted by invaders and

One of the many pubs in the little villages on the Dingle Peninsula.

Cutters waiting to put to sea in the port of Dingle on the peninsula of the same name.

A sensational view of the Cliffs of Moher, one of Ireland's most impressive scenic attractions.

opportunists since the island's discovery. Word quickly reached mainland Europe of the cows in Ireland having enough food in their pastures the whole year round, making winter storage of fodder unnecessary. To be certain, agriculture remains the backbone of the Irish economy today, with statistics attributing one sheep to each of the roughly 5.1 million inhabitants.

Irish lore and music provide a window into the soul of the Irish people. The Irish harp, for example, is the national instrument, hence its appearance on all Irish Euro coins. It is also a very well-read society, in keeping with a long literary tradition. There are libraries and bookshops on almost every street corner. The famous Trinity College Library in Dublin comprises some 2.8 million volumes and one of its greatest treasures is the 9th-century Book of Kells, one of the loveliest medieval Irish manuscripts. Ireland's cultural tradition is also characterized by a wealth of myths and sagas in which fairies and hobgoblins often play starring roles. Even today, the Giant's Causeway, a craggy portion of Ireland's north coast, is shrouded in legend. You can hear all about it over a Guinness or a glass of Irish whiskey in one of the cozy pubs.

Part of Ireland's special attraction also lies in its contrasts. While time appears to stand still in the more remote coastal regions, and the howling wind makes you wonder how those rustic, thatched-roof cottages can withstand the harsh elements, things in Dublin and Belfast are entirely different. There, visitors who are interested in getting a taste of the country's urban culture are certainly in for a treat as well.

In the south and west of Ireland, the coast is rugged and features many secluded bays.

1

The Irish Pub

After fighting through the crowd to the bar, the guest calls out, "a pint of ..." to the man behind the counter. In return he receives the appropriate quantity of his selected "poison", either a Guinness, Harp, Kilkenny or any number of other elixirs. Naturally, a "half pint" also exists,

The Stag's Head, one of Dublin's oldest pubs, is a popular meeting place.

but it is not considered worthy of an Irishman. Some of the more traditional Irish pubs generally tend to be more male dominated affairs that can quite often get loud and raucous. Indeed, it is here in the pubs that the Irish are at their most Irish.

There are a number of basic rules that visitors should attempt to keep in mind when visiting the pub: pay for your beer (or whiskey) as soon as it is placed on the bar for you. Tipping is not expected but it is appreciated. Closing time is closing time, especially if the police station is nearby.

Once around the island: The circular route takes you along wide roads following the coast, from Dublin clockwise around the whole of Ireland, including the counties of Northern Ireland. Fascinating landscapes, lively towns and historical buildings invite visitors to linger a while.

1 **Dublin** (see page 21)

2 **Powerscourt Estate Gardens** An impressive park with lovely Italian and Japanese gardens, areas of untouched nature and man-made lakes directly on the southern outskirts of Dublin. The ambiance here is further augmented by a castle-like country home, which was fully restored following a fire in 1974.

From here, a side trip to the Powerscourt Waterfall is well worth it. The clearly posted signs lead you to Ireland's highest falls, where the Dargle River plunges 130 m (427 ft) over a granite cliff.

3 **Glendalough** About 30 km (19 mi) south of the waterfall, one of Ireland's most wonderfully situated monasteries has stood the test of time amidst the scenic surroundings of the "Valley of the Two Lakes". Known for his reclusive ways, St Kevin founded this isolated monastery in the 6th century. Despite his efforts, other pilgrims followed soon after and the complex grew. The focal point of the former settlement is now the 33-m-high (108-ft) round tower, which is visible from a distance and was both a lookout post and a place of refuge. Most visitors limit their visit to the ruins on the lower

lake, but those on the upper lake are no less interesting and in fact more peaceful to explore. From Glendalough there is a road leading west toward the heart of the Wicklow Mountains, which peak at 924 m (3,032 ft). There are scenic hiking trails leading to the mountain lakes of Lough Dan and Lough Bray. From the mountains you return to the coastal road, then continue southward to Enniscorthy, 50 km (31 mi) away.

4 **Jerpoint Abbey** At Enniscorthy, which features a towering fortress close to the island's southern tip, it is worth leaving the coastal road to take a side road westward into the interior. The Cistercian Jerpoint Abbey (12th century) on the shores of Little Arrigle is one of Ireland's best-preserved monastery ruins. The route then continues to the north-west to what is the interior's loveliest town, Kilkenny

5 **Kilkenny** The 17,000 residents of Kilkenny enjoy life in a medieval jewel of a town featuring narrow alleyways, half-timbered stone houses and myriad historical buildings. The town's landmark is the tower of St Mary's Cathedral (19th century), which stands 65 m (213 ft) tall. Kilkenny Castle, a fortress built by the Normans, towers high

above the River Nore and is one of the most famous in Ireland. The ostentatious Long Gallery has antique furniture and portraits of former lords of the manor. Even the buildings lining Kilkenny's main streets are not short on grandeur, and some of the pubs with their stained-glass windows seem to be in competition with the churches for attention. From Kilkenny the route continues westward to Cashel.

6 **Cashel** The Irish are well aware of the cultural importance of this town of just 2,500 residents. The music and theater events at the Brú Ború Heritage Center are renowned throughout the country.

Most visitors to Ireland, however, are drawn to the Rock of Cashel, an imposing limestone cliff with the ruins of a fortress towering over the broad Tipperary plains. Starting in the 5th century, the fortress was the seat of the kings of Munster whose dominions extended for centuries over large areas of southern Ireland. At the end of the 11th century, the complex passed into the hands of the Catholic Church. It was later plundered by English troops under Oliver Cromwell in 1647 before being

1 The gentle, rolling landscape reflected in the port at Ballycrovane in County Cork.

Travel information

Route profile
Length: approx. 1,200 km (746 mi)
Time required: 2–3 weeks
Route (main locations): Dublin, Kilkenny, Cashel, Cork, Killarney, Ring of Kerry, Limerick, Cliffs of Moher, Galway, Clifden, Westport, Ballina, Sligo, Donegal, Londonderry, Giant's Causeway, Belfast, Dublin

Traffic information:
The Irish drive on the left. Four-wheel-drive vehicles are required only in very remote areas.

Weather:
In keeping with the motto "The only guarantee with Irish weather is that it's constantly changing", you are

advised to take both warm and rain-proof clothing. The mild-Atlantic climate keeps winter temperatures from sinking below 5°C (40°F), while July and August have an average temperature of 16°C (60°F).

Accommodation:
There are myriad options for bed and breakfast establishments in Ireland. They are a popular form of accommodation and are just about everywhere, even in the most remote corners.

Information
Here are a few sites to help you prepare for your trip:
www.discoverireland.com
www.travelireland.org
www.travelinireland.com

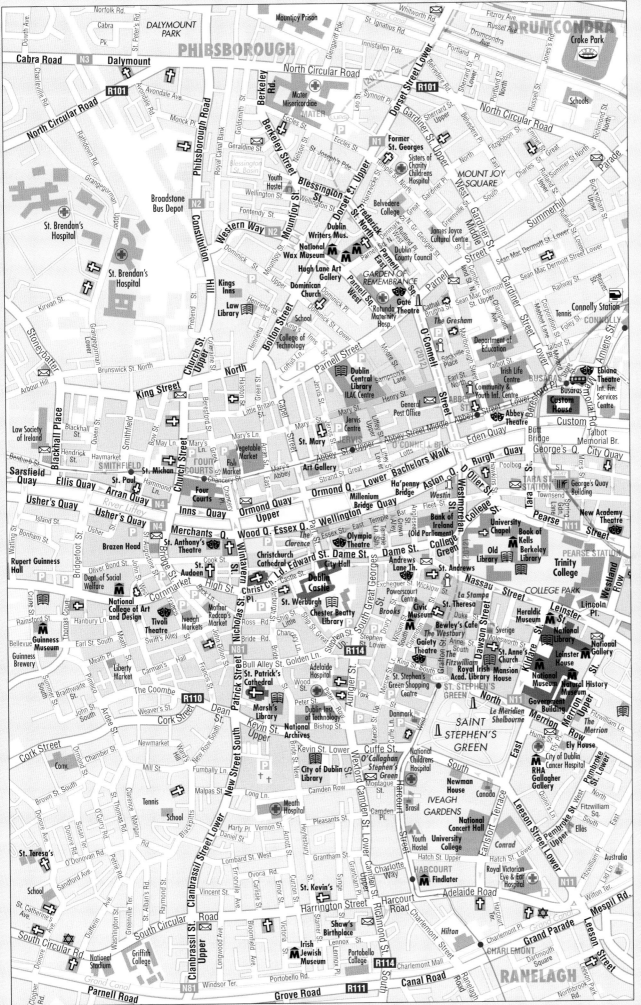

Dublin

The capital of the Republic of Ireland is over 1,000 years old and has always been worth a visit, albeit more for its celebratory flair than for its artistic treasures.

The Vikings, who were the first to settle in what is now Dublin, called their settlement Dyfflin, which basically meant "black puddle". Sound like a bad omen? Well, it must be said that Dublin's long history has indeed been largely determined by outside influences, particularly those of the neighboring English, whose first "colony" was, you guessed it, Ireland. Dublin was selected as the representative center of the Anglo-Irish administration, and yet, despite hundreds of years of rule, the city never fully gave in to British hegemony. Gaelic traditions of music, poetry, storytelling and debate have been ardently upheld in Ireland. It is no surprise, then, that the battle for Irish independence began in Dublin in 1916 with the Easter Uprising. And although today's vibrant, trendy Dublin is no longer Irish enough for some, it is still a very interesting city. The center of the metropolis on the Liffey is characterized by wide shopping

Top: The O'Connell Bridge over the River Liffey in Dublin.
Below: The library at Trinity College, Ireland's oldest university founded in 1592.

streets. A ride on a double-decker bus is a good laugh – preferably outside of the rush hour. Among the other must-see attractions are: the Gothic Christ Church Cathedral; the Gothic St Patrick's Cathedral; the historical Temple Bar nightlife area; Trinity College and lively university district; the National Gallery with a collection of Irish paintings; the National Museum of Irish cultural history; the National Botanic Gardens with 19th-century greenhouses.

Detour

Skellig Michael Monastery

The cells of the Skellig Michael Monastery are a well-preserved example of early Irish architecture. The stone-walled terraces support several stone huts whose domes rise up from square floor plans like beehives. Although the monastery complex was built without the use of mortar, it has withstood the merciless elements of the west coast since the 7th century.

From the mainland it is impossible to see this hidden treasure – a UNESCO World Heritage Site since 1996 – and the island's jagged, 217-m-high (712-ft) cliffs tend to ward off visitors. The 6th-century monks here were searching for a remote location for their sanctuary and their choice fell on Great Skellig, the largest of the Skellig Islands. The conditions on Great Skellig of course demanded a very spartan lifestyle. The monks clambered down from the monastery to the sea every day to catch their daily ration of fish, bartering part of their catch with passing sailors in exchange for corn and tools.

The 670 steps cut into the cliff still allow today's visitors to attempt the exhausting climb up to the

Skellig Michael is a desolate, 17-ha (42-acre) rock island.

complex, which was actually inhabited until the 12th century. The few stone crosses in the small cemetery commemorate the early residents of the monastery, where important manuscripts were produced.

Boots sail to the island between April and September only, and even in those months only when the sea is calm. The roughly 90-min crossing from Portmagee circles Little Skellig island, while the Skellig Experience exhibition on Valentia Island serves as an introduction and preparation for the spectacular Skellig Michael.

abandoned some 100 years later. In addition to the cathedral, its mighty walls also house Cormac's Chapel, a masterpiece of romanesque architecture, and the 28-m (92-ft) round tower. Another of Cashel's attractions is the Folk Village, an open-air museum that documents the region's history.

From Cashel the route continues south-west towards Cork, about 60 km (37 mi) away.

7 Cork The Republic's second-largest city after Dublin has about 125,000 people and is noticeably more "continental" than the capital. It also boasts a range of architectural treasures dating from the 18th and 19th centuries. The old town is situated on an island between two channels of the River Lee. The narrow alleyways, quaint canals and bridges lined with townhouses are reminiscent of Dutch towns.

Cork's landmark is St Ann's Shandon, a church built in 1722. The weather vane in the shape of a salmon on the top of the tower is visible from afar and is a good orientation point. A climb up the tower is rewarded with a panoramic view.

From Cork it is worth taking a detour to the town of Midleton, just 20 km (12 mi) to the east, or to Ballycrovane in the direction of Killarney.

8 Jameson Heritage Center Midleton is known primarily as the site of the island's largest whiskey distillery. A number of famous brands including Jameson, Tullamore Dew and Hewitts are distilled here. On the guided tour you'll learn a bit about the history and techniques of whiskey production.

9 Blarney Castle A second detour takes you along the bypass road north of Cork to Blarney Castle (15th century). Visitors from all over the world flock to the ruins of this castle

10 km (6 mi) north-west of Cork to not just see the legendary Blarney stone but also give it a kiss. According to the legend, anyone kissing the stone will be endowed with eloquence and the power of persuasion, the word "blarney" being a synonym for flattery.

With its many handicraft and souvenir shops, the village of Blarney is quite tourist-oriented. The route back to the main road heading west, the N 22, follows portions of the Lee River.

10 Killarney This town is a popular starting point for exploring south-west Ireland. You won't be able to overlook the many horse-drawn coaches plying the roads inviting visitors to take a tour of the town. Killarney's sightseeing attractions include the National Museum of Irish Transport, with a collection of vintage cars, as well as a lifelike model railway.

Most guests don't linger long in the town, though, for nearby awaits the spectacular landscape of Killarney National Park, which covers an area of approximately 100 sq km (39 sq mi) and features three scenic lakes: Upper Lake, Muckross Lake and Lough Leane, the largest of the three. The many small islands appear like dabs of green paint in the blue water, while the densely wooded hills rise gently from the shores. At a few locations, however, the mountains rise abruptly enough from the lake's edge to create sizable falls. One of these is the Torc Waterfall, which drops 18 m (59 ft) into Muckross Lake, marking the end of the Owengarriff River. Several monasteries and fortress ruins dot the surrounding lake landscape as well, including Muckross Abbey (ca. 1448) and Ross Castle (ca. 1420).

Up until the mid-17th century, some of these buildings formed the last of the Irish bastions in their fight against the English under Oliver Cromwell.

From the lake district, a number of roads lead to the Macgillcuddy's Reeks, a mountain chain that includes the Carrauntoohil, a 1,041-m (3,416-ft) peak.

11 Ring of Kerry In addition to the scenery of the Iveragh Peninsula, there are a number of picturesque locations in County Kerry that are worth a stopover. In Sneem, near the south coast, for example, the colorful houses of this picturesque town make a charming impression.

Only a few miles farther to the west is a 3-km-long (2-mi) road leading from the main road up to Staigue Stone Fort, a Celtic fortification dating from the 3rd/4th centuries.

The 3-km-long (2-mi) Caherdaniel beach has a Mediterranean atmosphere, with scenic sand dunes and boats for hire. The Derrynane House, a feudal country home in the Derrynane National Historic Park, commemorates Daniel O'Connell, an Irish national hero for his efforts in liberating Catholics from oppressive British laws. After the road

takes a turn to the north, a famous postcard scene awaits you behind the Coomakista Pass: a lonely row of houses on a cliff in Waterville that defies the strong winds blowing up from the ocean. From the main road, head westward to the fishing village of Portmagee where boats take you to the monastery island of Skellig Michael. The village is linked by a bridge to Valentia Island off the coast to the north. Accordion music emanating from the pubs is typical of the island's main town, Knight's Town.

Back on Iveragh you soon come to the main town on the peninsula, Cahersiveen, which has retained much of its charm despite the heavy tourism in the area. The village of Glenbeigh boasts the 5-km-long (3-mi) Rossbehy Beach, which seems to never end and proudly flies the sea-blue environmental flag indicating especially clean water. The Kerry Bog Museum nearby has an exhibition on the history of the now defunct peat cultivation trade.

5

6

The town of Killorglin to the north-east nicely rounds off your visit to the Ring of Kerry with a choice of more than twenty pubs.

⑫ Dingle Peninsula A drive around the 48-km-long (30-mi) Dingle Peninsula is equally stunning as the Ring of Kerry, and you'll need to plan at least half a day for it. The alternating craggy cliffs and sandy bays are what

Ring of Kerry

A highlight of any trip to Ireland is the roughly 200-km-long (124-mi) tour around the Iveragh Peninsula, which magnificently displays many of Ireland's most appealing features within a compact area The south coast is more rugged and fragmented into bays than the north coast. The road is good and parking is available at the various points of interest.

make this coastal landscape particularly appealing.
Coming from the south, you leave the main road at Castlemaine heading west. The sandy Inch Spit is a perfect beach for a swim. The main road then continues past several old fortresses

and monasteries. The tiny Gallarus Oratory stone church, with a shape reminiscent of a capsized boat, is one of the best-preserved early churches in Ireland. The Blasket Islands are just off the coast.

⑬ Tralee The main attractions in Tralee are the Kerry County Museum and the Blennerville Windmill, situated just outside of town and the largest still

functioning windmill in Ireland. From Tralee the route heads north to Tarbet, where the road then follows the course of the Shannon River. On the way to Limerick it is worth making a stop in Glin and the Georgian Glin Castle, built in 1780.

⑭ Limerick The mighty Shannon River is spanned by several bridges at Limerick. Although the town does not appear particularly inviting at first glance, it does have a number of sights worth seeing. The oldest building in Limerick, which was founded by the Vikings in the 9th century, is St Mary's Cathedral, built on a hill in 1172.
No less imposing is King John's Castle, from 1200, has five round towers and impressive ramparts. The Hunt Museum has antique relics from all over Ireland.

⑮ Bunratty Castle und Folk Park North-west of Limerick, Bunratty Castle is yet another must for any itinerary. The most famous lords of this manor, from the 15th century, were the O'Briens. The rooms are magnificently furnished with antique furniture and tapestries, creating a unique atmosphere. Medieval-style banquets still take place here in the evenings. From the stout battlements to the dark dungeons, the complex provides a graphic portrayal of aristocratic life in Ireland. An entirely reconstructed medieval Irish farming village has also been erected in front of the castle in the Folk Park.
Continuing north for a mile or so you will come to the 12th-century Augustine Clare Abbey shortly before the town of Ennis. Ennis Abbey (13th/14th centuries) was once one of Ireland's largest and contains some high-quality medieval styling.
The small town is characterized by winding alleys and a lively music scene. Indeed, folk music seems to be everywhere here. From Ennis, the road continues

south-west through the interior before reaching Kilrush, one of Ireland's largest yachting ports, just before the Shannon widens and flows into the ocean. From here you continue along the west coast to one of the region's main attractions.

⑯ Cliffs of Moher The Cliffs of Moher are an absolutely breathtaking feat of nature. These vertical cliffs can be more than 200 m (656 ft) high and stretch over a length of 8 km (5 mi). The spectacular backdrop is accompanied by the cackle of countless sea birds. Visitors can venture up to the edge of the cliffs along the paths but the lack of protective barriers does mean that caution needs to be exercised.

1 County Kerry in the south-west of Ireland is a paradise for botanists and ornithologists.

2 The Macgillcuddy's Reeks mountain range in Kerry is located on the north-east of the Iveragh Peninsula.

3 Fingers of land reach out into the ocean on the Dingle Peninsula.

4 The Blasket Islands are Europe's westernmost point.

5 The Cliffs of Moher are among the many popular attractions in the west of Ireland. They extend over 8 km (5 mi) between Hags Head in the south and Aillensharragh in the north.

6 The town of Limerick is divided into three parts by the Shannon and Abbey Rivers.

Clonmacnoise Monastery

This monastery on the River Shannon is a must for anyone passing through the Irish Midlands. It is especially appealing for the contrast between its ruins and their surroundings. Founded in the 6th century by St Ciaran, the monastery's location was convenient even in the Middle Ages, but at that time the only safe way to reach the site was through the infamous Blackwater Moor.
Between the 7th and the 12th centuries, Clonmacnoise was an important center for scholars and artisans. Numerous valuable manu-

Top: The impressive Clonmacnoise ruins.
Below: Irish crosses in the Clonmacnoise cemetery.

scripts as well as traditional Celtic gold and silver works were written and created here.
Although the monks were long able to withstand attacks from the Vikings and the Normans, in addition to a number of fires, their resistance against English soldiers in 1552 proved futile. The latter ultimately rendered the complex uninhabitable forever.
The site, measuring roughly one hectare (2.5 acres), encompasses the ruins of a cathedral and eight churches as well as copies of a number of high crosses and tombstones. The originals are displayed in the Visitor Center.
An audiovisual presentation provides interesting details on the lifestyle of the monks and on the significance of the individual buildings on the site.

Top: The coastal landscape at Connemara. Part of the peninsula is a national park containing moorlands, swamps, the mountain scenery of Twelve Ben and Glanmore Valley, and the area along the Polladirk River.

Bottom: The scenery at Doo Lough in County Mayo in the north-west of Ireland is breathtaking. The extensive Doo Lough is wedged between the Mweelrea and the Sheffry Mountains and is surrounded by dense forests.

Belfast

The Northern Irish capital has been the subject of largely negative headlines in recent decades but they are quickly forgotten when you arrive in Belfast. The city is situated at the mouth of the Lagan River in a bay known as Belfast Lough.

Belfast is the political, economic and cultural center of Northern Ireland. The lively seaport, with a population of 300,000, has everything that makes a vibrant town into a city – a wealth of shopping opportunities, myriad restaurants, theaters and cinemas, and some architectural highlights.

Belfast was officially founded in the year 1177 with the construction of the Norman fortress, but even after it was captured by England there was no significant development of the settlement. By the mid-17th century, the town comprised no more than 150 houses. Just a few decades later, however, the Huguenots, driven out of France for religious reasons, built up a prosperous linen industry, with tobacco processing and ship-

Belfast's illuminated skyline along Belfast Lough.

building also providing further employment opportunities and economic stimulus. The result was a dramatic rise in the number of immigrants from neighboring England and Scotland. Belfast became the capital of Northern Ireland in 1920.

The most important location in the city center is Donegall Square. It is home to some imposing Victorian buildings as well as the city's most prominent landmark: the grandiose city hall from 1906 with its striking copper dome. The Grand Opera House, which opened in 1894, is one of the most important concert halls in Great Britain. Just a stone's throw away is the famous Crown Liquor Saloon, a Victorian-style pub that is worth a visit just for its stylish stained-glass windows, marble décor and gas lamps.

⑰ The Burren In the town of Lisdoonvarna the R 476 heads south-east toward Leamaneagh Castle (17th century).

You will pass through a unique landscape on the way north known as the Burren, whose name is derived from the Irish word for "great rock" (boireann). In the 17th century, this limestone plateau, with numerous rifts and cleavages, was somewhat grimly described by one English military commander as follows: "No water for drowning, no trees for hanging, no soil for burying". Stone circles and other traces of settlement in this desolate region remain an enigma today.

The excavation of human bones here, however, has proven that the Poulnabrone dolmen, a collection of monoliths, served as a burial ground between 2500 and 2000 BC. The Burren is also known for its caves. One of them, the Aillwee Cave, can be visited and is set back somewhat from the road. Bring a jacket as the temperature in the caves is only 10 °C (50 °F) all year round.

⑱ Galway With a population of about 66,000, Galway is the largest town in western Ireland. It is also a university town and is characterized not only by its cozy alleyways and stone buildings with wooden facades, but also for its pub and music scene. For car drivers the center of the town at Corrib is a nightmare, but it is a paradise for pedestrians and strollers. When the weather is good, street cafés get busy while musicians and artists display their prowess.

The renovated suburbs along the river are testimony to a high standard of living, a result of the high-tech boom of recent years. The town's best-known buildings include the St Nicholas Church, built by the Normans in 1320, and the St Nicholas Cathedral from 1965, on the northern bank of the river.

From Galway, a good road heads east to Clonmacnoise Monastery about 65 km (40 mi) away.

⑲ Aran Islands The ferries to the craggy Aran Islands depart from Galway. The archipelago's main island, Inishmore, is a mountain bikers' paradise, but tours of the island are also offered via minibus or horse-drawn carriage. Recommended stops are the steep cliffs as well as the monastery and fortress ruins like Dun Aengus. The *Men of Aran*, a silent film from the 1930s, portrays the fishermen

doing what would appear even then to have been a tedious job.

⑳ Kylemore Abbey The landscape west of Galway is defined by coastline, mountains and stark moorlands, all protected in part by the Connemara National Park. The route from Galway towards the west and north-west closely follows the coast and features many bays as well as Clifden Castle.

Kylemore Abbey, an enchanting 19th-century Benedictine abbey, is idyllically situated on Kylemore Lough. Part of the present-day national park land actually used to belong to the abbey. En route to the north it is worth taking a detour at Bangor to Blacksod Point.

㉑ Donegal Castle A mighty 15th-century fortress dominates the small town of Donegal. After several renovations, it now looks more like a castle, and the banqueting hall alone is worth the entrance fee. Preserved in the style of the Jacobean era, it boasts a fireplace dating from this time. You leave the coast road at Donegal and head across the northern tip of Ireland toward Londonderry.

㉒ Londonderry You reach the walled town of Londonderry shortly after crossing the border into Northern Ireland. The city is known as Londonderry to Protestants here, while Catholics and residents of the Republic refer to it as Derry, a name derived from the Irish "Daire", meaning "oak grove". Houses in pastel hues characterize the cityscape. The walls of Derry, up to 9 m (30 ft) wide in places, are some of the most intact town fortifications in all of Europe. The Tower Museum details the town's history and the Bloody Sunday Center tells of the Northern Ireland conflict.

㉓ Giant's Causeway The innumerable basalt stones of the Giant's Causeway are the undisputed highlight of the very scenic Antrim north coast. They are also shrouded in legend. One story tells of a giant who built a causeway so that his mistress, who lived on the Scottish island of Staffa, would be able to reach Ireland without getting her feet wet. No one knows the exact number of the mostly hexagonal basalt columns, but some of them measure up to 25 m (82 ft) in height.

The route then continues along the north-east coast of the North Channel, past Dunluce Castle, heading to Belfast and then leaving Northern Ireland again south of Newry.

㉔ Belfast (see sidebar left)

㉕ Bend of the Boyne Before reaching Dublin, it is worth stopping in the Boyne Valley near Slane. The valley features neothlithic passage graves. The grave built near Newgrange in 3200 BC remained untouched until 1960. It has a 19-m-long (62-ft) passage leading to the 6-m-high (20-ft) burial chamber with three side chambers.

1 Giant's Causeway: An estimated 35,000 hexagonal basalt columns rise out of this coastal formation to heights of up to 25 m (82 ft).

2 A prehistoric stone circle at Blacksod Point on the southern tip of the Mullet Peninsula.

3 On a cliff on the north coast of Antrim, Dunluce Castle (13th century) stands exposed to the whims of the rugged coast.

Blacksod Point The Mullet Peninsula is connected to the north-west Irish mainland by a narrow, sparsely inhabited spit of land. On the west, it is a wide rocky plateau with pebble beaches that are constantly pounded by the sea. A granite lighthouse stands at the southernmost tip of the island, at Blacksod Point. Tthe island cemetery here at the "End of the World" is also worth a visit.

Giant's Causeway The roughly 35,000 step-like basalt columns, most of which have a hexagonal shape and rise to heights of up to 25 m (82 ft), are the natural scenic highlight of Northern Ireland. Their origins are shrouded in legend but they are in fact a completely natural form of cooled, slow-flowing lava.

Dunluce Castle The well-preserved 13th-century castle ruins are located on a high cliff on the north coast of Antrim, only about 10 km (6 mi) west of the Giant's Causeway. As defiant as the former headquarters of the lofty MacDonnells and Lords of Antrim may appear today, the castle was in fact powerless in the face of the harsh coastal winds.

Connemara The area in the north-west of County Galway is a barren landscape of stone walls and moors where traditional rural culture has been well preserved. Its white beaches provide a stark contrast, and the Victorian resort town of Clifden is an ideal base from which to explore the area.

Bend of the Boyne Due to its ring-like fortifications, passage graves and cairns, this river valley in the Midlands near Dublin is considered to be the cradle of Irish civilization. The Newgrange passage grave from 3200 BC is particularly striking.

Belfast The numerous Victorian buildings here make the Northern Irish capital and the port at the mouth of the Lagan River well worth a visit. The Grand Opera House and the domed city hall are two main attractions.

Clonmacnoise This especially attractive monastery on the Shannon was founded in the mid-6th century. It has been in ruins since its destruction by English soldiers in 1552.

Dublin Christ Church and St Patrick's cathedrals, as well as Dublin Castle, Trinity College, the National Gallery and the National Museum are all worth a visit in the Irish capital.

Cliffs of Moher The sandstone and shale cliffs, some of which are up to 200 m (656 ft) high, extend over 8 km (5 mi) from Hags Head to Ailllensharagh.

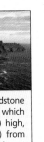

Skellig Michael The monastery shelters on the island of Great Skellig are examples of Irish architecture. The 700 steps give an indication of how tough monastic life must have been.

Rock of Cashel, County Tipperary On the lower reaches of the Shannon, this county is rich in farmland. St Patrick is alleged to have picked three-leaf clover on the Rock of Cashel in 450.

County Kerry This southern Irish county is known for its prehistoric and early Christian sites as well as the panoramic Ring of Kerry. The decrees from Dublin were also willingly ignored here such that the county is also known as "The Kingdom".

County Cork The hinterland of this popular southern Irish resort region is full of lakes and hills. Cork's rocky coastline is very fragmented and richly endowed with islands, peninsulas, bays and idyllic seaports. The city of Cork – the second-largest in Ireland – is situated on an island in the River Lee. It is a typically Irish city with numerous steps, bright cottages, attractive pubs and even a vineyard!

The summit of Buchaille Etive Mor is a challenge for mountain climbers.

Scotland

Clansmen, whisky and the solitude of the Highlands

Whether you're a romantic, a lover of the outdoors or a culture connoisseur, Scotland's raw beauty rarely fails to move the souls of people who make the journey there. Those who choose to experience the rugged, often solitary landscape of the Highlands and the rich history and tradition of this country will be rewarded with unforgettable memories.

Jagged escarpments covered in a lush carpet of green grass, deep lakes in misty moorlands, and torrential rivers tumbling down craggy valleys often typify our image of the Highlands and Scotland in general. But there is more to Scotland than the Highlands in the north, notably the interesting groups of islands to the west and a couple of lovely cities. Glasgow and the capital, Edinburgh, offer modern city living, with cultural events, attractive shopping possibilities and renowned festivals, while idyllic sandy

'Clansmen' in Scottish national costume.

beaches await discovery, for example on the Western Isles. On the mainland, Scotland's first national parks were recently opened around the Cairngorm Mountains and Loch Lomond.

Poets such as Sir Walter Scott and the 'national poet of Scotland', Robert Burns, have written of this country's unique beauty. The modern revival of Gaelic music and language has long since spread beyond Scotland's borders, and Scottish customs like caber tossing and wearing kilts may seem peculiar to outsiders, but to the Scots they are part of their identity. If you take one insider tip, make it this one: Scottish cooking. Once you have tried Angus steak, grouse or Highland lamb, you will no longer limit your praise of the country to single malt whisky. Having said that, there are about 110 whisky distilleries in Scotland, mainly spread

around the Highlands and on the Western Isles. These world-famous single malt elixirs age for up to thirty years in old whisky and sherry barrels.

Scotland's territory covers a total of 78,000 sq km (30,014 sq mi), roughly the top third of the island of Great Britain. Most of its many islands are part of either the Hebrides (Inner and Outer), the Orkneys or the Shetlands. During the last ice age, glaciers formed deep valleys throughout the region. When they melted, they left behind lochs (lakes) and firths (fjords) along the country's 3,700 km (2,300 miles) of coastline.

Among the characteristics of the Highlands, the most sparsely populated area of Scotland, are steep rock faces, heath-covered moors, deep lochs and rushing mountain streams. The Great Glen valley divides the Highlands into two

Eilean Donan Castle lies on Loch Duich in Glen Shiel and is linked to the mainland by a small dam and a bridge. The castle was rebuilt last century from its former ruins.

Kilchurn Castle on the northern edge of Loch Awe dates from the 15th century.

parts. South of the Highlands are the Lowlands, a fertile and densely populated area containing both Glasgow and Edinburgh. The Southern Uplands make up the border with England.

Despite what one might think, Scotland's oceanic climate rarely produces extreme weather conditions – but the weather really can change from sun to rain in a hurry. Wide areas of Scotland are renowned for their characteristic flora (heather, pine trees, ferns) and a wide variety of wildlife.

The Scots are the descendants of a mix of different peoples including the Picts, the Scots, who gave their name to the country, as well as the Scandinavians and the Anglo-Saxons. It was in the 9th century, under Kenneth MacAlpine, that Alba was founded, the first Celtic Scottish kingdom. From then on Scotland's history was plagued with struggles for independence and resistance against the ever-mightier forces of England. In 1707, the 'Acts of Union' created the Kingdom of Great Britain and with that came the end of Scotland's independence.

Things unfortunately went from bad to worse after that. The characteristic solitude of the Scottish landscape was a direct result of the Highland Clearances, a move by their own clan chiefs and aristocratic land owners in the 18th century to run small Highland and island farmers off their plots to make room for more lucrative sheep breeding.

After 300 years, Scotland now has its own parliament again, in Edinburgh, and about 5.1 million people. Although the official language is English, many Scots in the Highlands and on the Hebrides speak Scottish Gaelic, a Celtic language.

Tobemory with its colourful houses lies on the northern end of the Isle of Mull.

Detour

Blair Castle

At Arbroath the A933 makes its way west before you get to Forfar, where the pink-grey walls of Glamis Castle appear through the trees. It is a place steeped in history, from the murder of Duncan by Macbeth to numerous ghost apparitions and the childhood tales of the late Queen Mother, who grew up here.

The trip then continues north-west to Blair Atholl via the Killiecrankie Pass, scene in 1689 of a bloody battle between the English and the Scots.

The origins of Blair Castle date back to the 13th century.

From there an alley lined with lime trees leads to Blair Castle, the residence of the Duke of Atholl. This fabulously equipped, brilliant white castle is among the most beautiful buildings in Scotland.

The Atholl Highlanders, as the Duke of Atholl's private army is called, are a curious band. Every year at the beginning of June an impressive parade is staged in front of the castle with a backing of bagpipe music.

A journey through Scotland: venerable buildings, mysterious stone circles and the occasional whisky distillery line your route, which begins in Edinburgh, takes you through the Highlands and ends in Glasgow.

Detours to the Orkneys and Hebrides are highly recommended and can be easily organized from the various port towns.

❶ Edinburgh (see page 31). Your route begins in the cultural metropolis of Edinburgh, travelling initially north-westward towards Stirling.

❷ Stirling The charming city of Stirling, roughly 58 km (36 miles) west of Edinburgh, is built on the banks of the Forth at the point where it first becomes part of the tidal firth (fjord). It is often called the 'Gateway to the Highlands' and is dominated by a large castle. The oldest part of Stirling Castle dates back to the 14th century. The Church of the Holy Rood (cross), which was built in the 13th century, is historically significant in that it is one of the very few churches from the Middle Ages to have survived the Reformation in Scotland.

❸ Fife Peninsula The Fife Peninsula juts out between the Firth of Forth and the Firth of Tay. In the 4th century the region here made up one of the seven Scottish kingdoms.

The northern coast of the Firth of Forth leads initially to Culross, a small town that blossomed as a trading center in the 16th cen-

tury. Wealthy trade houses have remained intact and make for an enchanting atmosphere here. About 11 km (7 miles) to the east of Culross you'll come to Dunfermline, once a long-standing residence or 'burgh' of the Scottish kings. The ruins of the old castle, abbey and monastery can still be seen atop a hill to the south-west of the town.

A little further east, behind Chapel Ness headland and between the coastal towns of

1 View from the Nelson Monument of the Old Town and castle in Edinburgh.

2 The Scottish national sport of golf was already being played in the 15th century on the sandy beaches of St Andrews.

3 Glamis Castle was the childhood home of the late Queen Mother.

Travel information

Route profile
Length: approx. 1,200 km (745 miles), excluding detours
Time required: 2–3 weeks
Start: Edinburgh
End: Glasgow
Route (main locations): Edinburgh, Stirling, Dundee, Dunottar Castle, Ballater, Inverness, John o'Groats, Durness, Fort William, Inveraray, Glasgow

Traffic information:
Drive on the left in Scotland. Ferries connect the mainland with the various islands:
www.northlink-ferries.co.uk
www.scottish-islands.com

Weather:
The weather in Scotland is generally 'unsettled':

summers are relatively cool, winters on the coast are mild, but in the Highlands bitterly cold, and it can rain at any given moment.

When to go:
Between April and October is the best time. You can check weather forecasts at:
www.onlineweather.com

Accommodation:
An interesting option is a private bed & breakfast:
www.bedandbreakfast scotland.co.uk
www.aboutscotland.com

Information:
wikitravel.org/en/ Scotland
www.visitscotland.com
www.scotland.org.uk

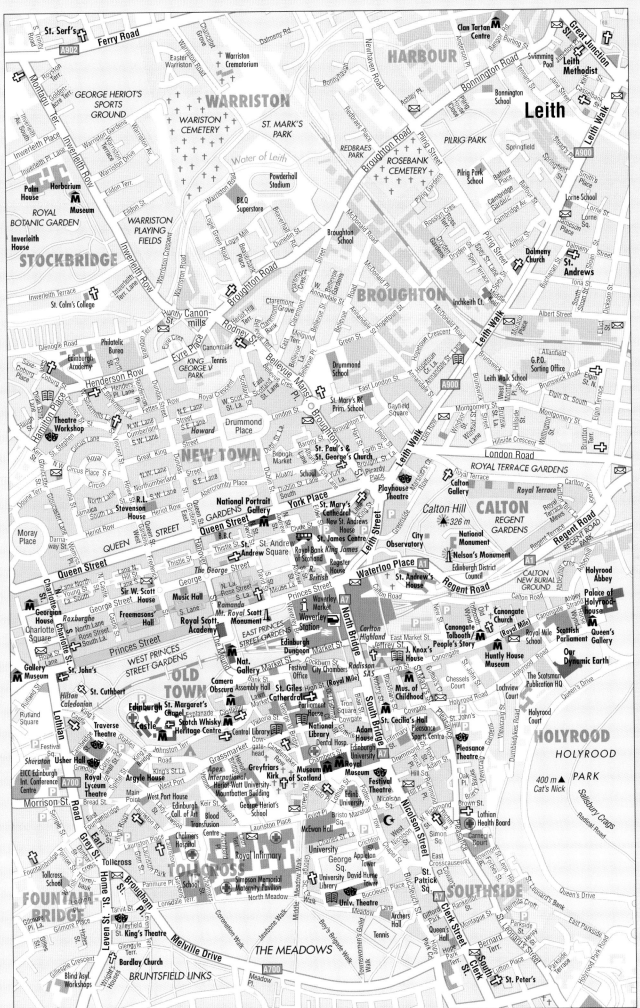

Edinburgh

Both the Old Town and New Town of Scotland's capital have been listed as UNESCO World Heritage Sites, and both are a fascinating display of architectural unity and its exceptional cultural activity. Summer is especially lively during the renowned Edinburgh Festival weeks. The city has been the cultural center of the north since the 18th and 19th centuries, with famous authors such as Robert Burns and Sir Walter Scott making it their home.

The oldest core of the city, inhabited since the Bronze Age, is Castle Rock, a volcanic outcrop upon which King Edwin built the first castle in the 7th century – hence the name Edinburgh. The castle is still the city's eye-catcher but other higher buildings from the 17th century rise up around it like battlements.

The attractions most worthy of a visit in the Old Town include Edinburgh Castle, a large edifice with buildings from numerous eras, of which St Margaret's Chapel (11th century) is the oldest; the Scottish royal insignia in the castle's Crown Room; the Palace

Edinburgh Castle has served as a fort, a royal residence and a prison.

of Holyroodhouse, the Queen's official residence in Scotland; and the Royal Mile between her residence and the castle with its many side streets.

The New Town, built at the end of the 18th century, is home to the National Gallery of Scotland with one of Europe's most important collections of paintings, the Museum of Antiques for early and art history, and the Scottish National Gallery of Modern Art (20th-century art), all of which are worth a visit.

Detour

Balmoral Castle

This royal castle on the River Dee is in the Grampian Mountains, and thus within the limits of the Cairngorms National Park in Aberdeenshire. Prince Albert, Queen Victoria's consort, bought Balmoral Castle in 1846 and later had it replaced with a magnificent granite building in grand Scottish style.

He personally oversaw the interior decoration, which was inspired by Scottish hunting lodges, with large check patterns and floral designs on upholstery that bear witness to the country style. The royal family came here to get away from court ceremonies in London.

Cairngorms National Park, established in 2003, is Great Britain's largest national park and stretches from Grantown on the Spey to Angus Glens near Glamis. Twenty five per cent of Great Britain's endangered species live in the reserve and numerous rare plants

Top: Iconic Highland cattle graze in front of Balmoral Castle.
Bottom: A royal garden party.

grow only at the foot of the central Cairngorms range (Scottish Gaelic for "Blue Mountain"). The various moorlands, heath and forests are typical of the area. Fields and pasture typify the lovely Spey and Dee valleys.

Stone-Age monuments, medieval castles and towns steeped in tradition are testimony to the historical importance of the region.

Elie and Crail, is a series of picturesque fishing villages, castle ruins and old churches.

④ St Andrews Continuing on around the north-east side of the peninsula you will come to the proverbial golfing mecca of the world, St Andrews, about 10 km (6 miles) north of Crail. This, the first ever golf club, was founded here in 1754, and it is still possible to play on the famous Old Course.

The 16th-century ruins of Blackfriars Chapel, at one time Scotland's largest church, are also worth a visit if golf isn't your cup of tea. There is a fabulous view of the grounds from the top of St Rule's Tower.

The route then follows the coast through Dundee to Montrose, about 12 km (8 miles) north of Arbroath. A worthy detour here takes you to Blair Castle, roughly 65 km (40 miles) inland from Arbroath.

⑤ Montrose This port town and 'burgh' is built like a defensive wall on the peninsula of a natural bay. The House of Dun Mansion, built in 1730, stands on the bank of the Montrose Basin. The coastline north and south of Montrose impresses with long sandy beaches and steep cliffs.

⑥ Dunnottar Castle Following the A92 to the north you'll reach one of Scotland's most

fascinating ruins just a few kilometers before Stonehaven – Dunnottar Castle. Built on a rock more than 50 m (60 yds) out to sea, the fortress is connected to the mainland only by a narrow spit of land.

In the 17th century, the Scottish imperial insignia were stored here. Nowadays, only the ruins of the turret, a barrack and the chapel remain of the once formidable construction.

⑦ Aberdeen This town is the capital of Europe's oil industry and one of the largest European ports. Despite its industrial leanings, however, there are a number of historic highlights to visit, including Kings College, St Andrew's Cathedral, St Machar's Cathedral and the Maritime Museum.

From Aberdeen the route leads inland to Ballater. (Here we recommend taking a detour to

Balmoral Castle about 50 km (31 miles) away. The mountain road (A939) then goes from Ballater through Colnabaichin to Tomintoul, the starting point of the whisky trail, before heading to Dufftown and Keith.

You then go west through the Spey Valley to Aviemore where the A9 takes you to Inverness.

⑧ Inverness This modern-day industrial center at the northern

The Orkney Islands

The Orkney Islands, of which only eighteen are inhabited, are around 30 km (19 miles) off the north-eastern coast of Scotland. They are best reached from the ferry ports of John o'Groats and Thurso. Mainland, Hoy and South Ronaldsay are the larger of the islands in the archipelago, with rolling hills formed by glaciers from the last ice age. Despite their northerly location, the islands benefit from a comparatively mild climate caused by the warm Gulf Stream.

along the north coast towards Bettyhill past deserted beaches that are often only accessible by short footpaths. Dunnet Head is the most northern point of the Scottish mainland. The popular holiday destination of Thurso, which is also the ferry port for travel to the Orkney Islands, was the scene of a memorable battle between the Scots and the Vikings in 1040.

To the west of the village of Bettyhill, in the county of Sutherland, the A836 leads over the impressive Kyle of Tongue Fjord and on to Durness. Shortly before Durness is the Cave of Smoo, which was used as shelter by the Picts, then the Vikings, and later still by Scottish smugglers. Organized trips to Cape Wrath, the rocky outcrop on the north-westernmost point of Scotland, are offered from Durness.

1 The once strategic position of Dunnottar Castle is unmistakable: built on a solid rock promontory, a deep ravine separates the castle from the mainland.

2 Inverness is the 'capital' of the Highlands, and its business and administrative center.

3 View from the port over Aberdeen.

4 Mighty waves from the Atlantic crash against the cliffs of Cape Wrath on the north coast of Scotland. The lighthouse was built in 1828.

Top: An historic lighthouse.
Middle: The 'Standing Stones of Stennes', a prehistoric stone circle.
Bottom: Impressive rocky coast.

The inhabitants of the Orkneys, descendants of Scots and Scandinavians, live mostly from farming, fishing and tourism these days. Rock climbers and ornithologists are also fascinated by Britain's highest coastal cliffs (347 m/1,138 ft) on the island of Hoy, while the spectacular landscape and monuments, like the Stone-Age village of Skara Brae or the stone circle of Brodgar on Mainland, are popular with everyone who visits.

The Whisky Trail

The famous 110-km-long (68-mile) Speyside Malt Whisky Trail, which sets off from Tomintoul, is a well-signposted route leading past seven whisky distilleries. Among them are some well-known names such as Glenlivet, Glenfiddich and Glenfarclas.

tip of Loch Ness is the ideal starting point for trips to the home of 'Nessie', Urquhart Castle and into the wild and romantic Highland landscape.

Due to its exposed location, Inverness was regularly involved in military disputes, to the extent that few of its old buildings remain. Most of today's structures were erected in the 19th century.

9 East Coast of the North-west Highlands From Inverness the A9 (and the A99) snake northwards along the striking east coast. Various sites like Dunrobin Castle, Helmsdale Castle or the mysterious Bronze-Age rock lines near Greg Cairns are

worth short visits on your way. One option is to take a long walk from the former fishing village of Wick out to the picturesque cliffs of Noss Head. Nearby are the ruins of Sinclair and Girnigoe Castles.

10 John o'Groats The village of John o'Groats is about 17 km (11 miles) north of Wick on the north-eastern tip of Caithness. Just before you get there, Warth Hill will offer an exceptional view of the area.

Ferries travel between John o'Groats, the Orkneys and the coastal seal colonies.

11 North Coast The A836 then takes you from John o'Groats

Top: Lismore is an island 14 km long (8.8 mi) and only 2.5 km wide (1.6 mi) on Loch Linnhe, north-west of Oban. The Gaelic name lios-mór ("Big Garden") refers to the fertile land on which three hundred types of wildflowers grow. The lighthouse stands at the south end of the isle on the Sound of Mull.

Bottom: The four-storey Castle Stalker in Argyllshire dates from the 15th century and stands proud on a small island in Loch Laich off the coast of Oban in southwest Scotland. Its strategic location made it almost impossible to attack.

The most famous prehistoric construction in Europe – Stonehenge, erected around 3000 BC.

Route 4

England

Magical locations in southern Britain

Ancient trading routes crisscross the south of England, and monumental stone circles bear witness to prehistoric settlements in the region. The Celts, the Romans, the Anglo-Saxons and the Normans came after the original inhabitants of the island and eventually transformed the magnificent natural environment here into a diverse cultural macrocosm with monuments, cathedrals, quaint fishing villages, parks and country houses.

Generally, the 'South of England' refers to the region along the south coast, extending northwards to Bristol in the west and London in the east. For some, however, the south only includes the coastal counties south of London like East and West Sussex, Hampshire and Dorset. Others think of just the south-east including London, while others of the south-west with Cornwall and Devon. In some references, the south even reaches up to the middle of England. Some areas, like Greater London (with around

Bodiam Castle near Hastings.

eight million inhabitants) are densely populated, whereas others like Dartmoor in Devon appear at first glance to be deserted. In the end, the South of England is unspecific, but Britons look at it as an area 'steeped in history' and known for its contrasts: picturesque cliffs and small sailing villages, busy seaside resorts and modern port towns, green pastures and barren moorland.

Indeed, the bustling metropolis of London dominates the south-east, while the more relaxed south-west has a real holiday feel to it. The area has always attracted writers and artists: Shakespeare, Jane Austen, Turner and Constable all lived here, or at least gave the south a recognizable face in their various works. Numerous nature reserves and magical, manicured gardens invite you to take peaceful walks.

Geologically speaking, the British Isles 'separated' from the continent roughly 700,000 years ago. At the time, there had been a land bridge connecting what is now England to the mainland, with a river running through (now the English Channel). The water trapped in the ice at the end of the ice age about 10,000 years ago was then released, causing sea levels to rise and gradually wash away the land bridge. The characteristic white limestone cliffs that we now see in places along the south coast like Dover and Eastbourne are the result of this 'river' flooding through the weakest point between the now divided land masses. The West Country consists mostly of granite, whereas the limestone is typical of the south-east. At the narrowest point in the channel, the Dover Strait, the distance between the United Kingdom and

The natural arch of Durdle Door on the Jurassic Coast of Dorset is the result of erosion by the pounding sea.

The western facade of Wells Cathedral is decorated with countless sculptures from the medieval period.

the European continent is only around 32 km (20 miles).

Demographically, countless generations have created a rich landscape in Britain. Due to the geographical proximity to the continent, the south was always the arrival point for immigrants, invaders and traders. In about 3500 BC, farmers and livestock breeders migrated to the island. The fortuitously warm Gulf Stream provided them and their modern-day ancestors with a relatively mild climate and even some subtropical vegetation. Natural resources like tin and copper also attracted invaders over the centuries.

England has not been successfully subdued by an enemy power since 1066, when the Normans under William the Conqueror emerged victorious at the legendary Battle of Hastings. The vulnerability of the south coast is revealed by countless castles and fortresses, and also by installations from World War II.

The varied history of settlements also features in the endless stories and myths that originate here. King Arthur and his Knights of the Round Table are among the prominent characters in these tales. Castles, cathedrals and grand old universities testify to the historical importance of the south while small fishing villages on the coast have developed into significant port towns that enabled the British Empire's rise to naval dominance. In return came exotic goods and peoples, changing yet again the cultural fabric of the traditional island inhabitants.

'High society' discovered the coast in the 19th century, and from then on vacationed in resort towns like Brighton and Eastbourne. Today the coastal economy relies primarily on services and tourism.

Tower Bridge is a masterpiece of Victorian engineering completed in 1894.

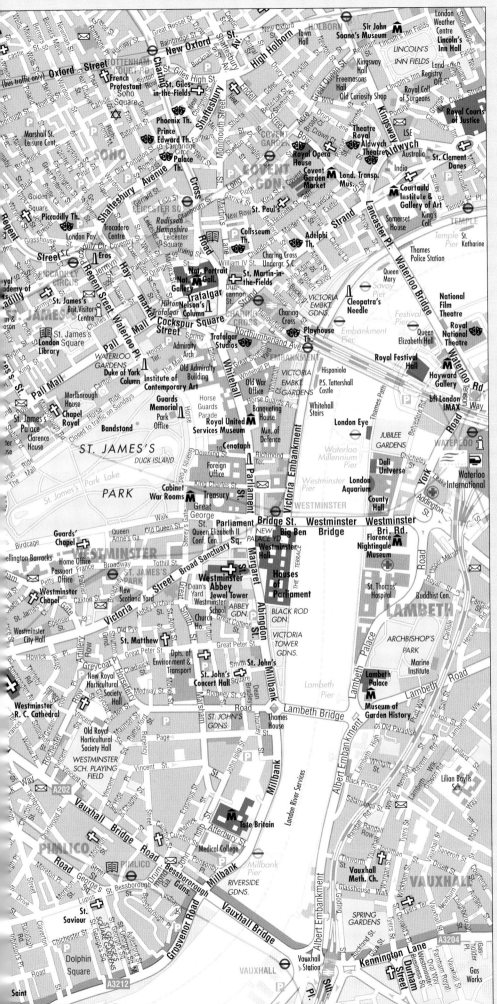

London

England's capital, London, is the seat of British government and an international financial center of massive proportions, but above all it is a cosmopolitan city in the truest sense of the word. For a few centuries, London was the heart of the British Empire, and this is still very much perceptible in its dynamic atmosphere. Due to numerous restrictions for cars in the city center, use of the excellent public transport network or a tour on a red sightseeing double-decker bus is highly recommended.

The western part of central London is typified by diversity – the administrative center of Whitehall in the historic district of Westminster; posh residential and business districts like Knightsbridge and Belgravia; busy squares like Piccadilly Circus and Trafalgar Square; and the fabulous parks like St James's and the Kensington Gardens.

Starting with the district of Westminster, here is a handful of things to see, the first two being UNESCO World Heritage Sites: Westminster Abbey, the mighty Gothic church where English kings are crowned and buried (not to be confused with nearby Westminster Cathedral, a Catholic church from the 19th century), and the neo-Gothic Houses of Parliament on the Thames. Then we have the only remaining part of the original medieval building, Westminster Hall, and next to that the clock tower housing Big Ben (1858). Westminster Bridge crosses the Thames. After that we have Buckingham Palace (early

18th century), the city residence of the Queen, Green Park and St James's Park, and the Tate Gallery with a first-class selection of English art.

In Whitehall you'll find 10 Downing Street, residence of the Prime Minister; the Palladian-style Banqueting House, opposite Horse Guards Parade for the Changing of the Guard; Trafalgar Square with Nelson's Column; the National Gallery with works from the

Top: Buckingham Palace – London residence of the Queen.
Middle: Bustling Trafalgar Square with Nelson's Column.
Bottom: Houses of Parliament with Big Ben.

16th to 20th centuries, the National Portrait Gallery; Hyde Park, a public park from the 17th century with the famous Speaker's Corner; Madame Tussaud's Wax Museum.

In Knightsbridge are the Victoria and Albert Museum, the largest arts and crafts museum in the world; the Natural History Museum, with a famous dinosaur section; the Science and Technology Museum; the legendary Harrods department store with something for everyone; and the younger and less conventional Harvey Nichols department store.

London

In 1851, when Great Britain was at the height of its imperial power and had just celebrated itself in a World Fair, London had around one million inhabitants. Today there are over twelve million people in Greater London and around eight within city limits – the latter makes it the largest city in Europe.

It began modestly almost 2,000 years ago, when the Romans conquered the island that is now England and founded Londinium on the Thames. Many peoples have come to the British Isles, but since William the Conqueror made London his capital in 1066, the city has remained the administrative center of Britain, not least due to its strategic position – near the continent, yet protected in an estuary. The first block of the Tower of London, the city's most venerated building, was in fact laid by William the Conqueror in 1078.

A large fortress and medieval royal residence, the Tower of London complex is centerd around the White Tower (11th century) and it is here that the Crown Jewels are on display. Another one of the most recognizable icons of London's cityscape is the Tower Bridge

center – and the famous London Stock Exchange from 1773.

In the West End you'll find countless theaters, cinemas, pubs and restaurants around Piccadilly Circus, London's most colourful square. Covent Garden, once a market, is now a pedestrian zone in the West End. The Royal Opera House and the British Museum, with a number of world-famous collections, are also here.

Interesting places in the Southwark area include the cathedral of the same name, which is the oldest Gothic church in London. It has a memorial for Shakespeare, whose Globe Theater was rebuilt nearby almost in its original form. The Tate Modern is a striking art museum in a disused power station across the Thames on the Millennium Footbridge. The Docklands and Canary Wharf both feature

Top: St Paul's Cathedral stands in the center of London.
Bottom: Walls from the 13th century protect the Tower of London.

(1894) with its double towers and distinctive bascule bridge.

In the City district of London you should take time to go to St Paul's Cathedral (1674–1710), a Renaissance masterpiece with a walkway that goes all the way around its dome. North of St Paul's Cathedral are the futuristic Barbican towers – a culture and arts

modern architecture – Canada Tower and Canary Wharf Tower, respectively. The latter is the tallest building in the UK at 244 m (800 ft).

In Greenwich is the Royal Maritime Museum with sailing history, the historic Cutty Sark clipper ship, and the observatory, which crosses the prime meridian.

Through Dartmoor National Park

From Torquay, a route leads through Dartmoor National Park, a largely untouched area of moorland and forest on the south-west coast of England that covers approximately 945 sq km (363 sq mi) at an elevation of roughly 500 m (1,640 ft) above sea level. It is one of Europe's largest nature reserves.

Dartmoor is not a primeval landscape, but rather an area that has been cultivated for thousands of years. Numerous archaeological sites – remains of Stone Age villages, stone paths and circles, monuments such as burial sites, and more – testify to the extensive human presence here.

Heather-covered moor landscape in Dartmoor National Park.

An 800-km-long (500-mile) network of footpaths crisscrosses the countryside, and in some places the granite rises out of the earth in formations called tors, or craggy hills. Reddish-brown ferns, heather, windswept trees and shaggy Dartmoor ponies are among the park's simple selection of things to see, especially in the sparse western reaches. Tidy lanes and little villages are common on the more inhabited east side.

From Ashburton, a pretty town near idyllic Widecombe-in-the-Moor, your drive goes through the hilly landscape to Two Bridges, past Princetown with the infamous Dartmoor Prison. Tavistock, an earlier center for tin and copper mining, was famous for hundreds of years because of its rich Benedictine monastery.

has been given this name because of its numerous idyllic bays, palm-littered beaches, mild climate and its urbane atmosphere. Three towns – Torquay, Paignton and Brixham – have become known as Torbay, though they have kept their own individual styles. Elegant hotels, Victorian villas and countless bars and restaurants around the little port give the area a holiday feel.

After the impressive mountain road through Dartmoor National Park (with grades of up to twenty-five per cent), the A390 leads from Liskeard back down towards the coast and St Austell.

⑩ St Austell and the Eden Project Since the discovery of kaolin in the 18th century, the economic welfare of the town has been closely linked to the mining of this important base product used in the manufacture of porcelain. The story of china clay or 'white gold' is retold in St Austell's museum. The Eden Project was constructed over 14 ha (35 acres) on a disused kaolin quarry near Bodelva. In two gigantic greenhouses, gardeners have reproduced two climatic zones – tropical rainforest and Mediterranean. The greenhouses are densely populated with plants from these respective regions in order to allow a natural ecosystem to develop. In another area, a cool zone was set up, in which indigenous plants from Britain and exotic plants from temperate Cornwall flourish. The larger of the greenhouses, the Humid Tropics Biome, is the largest greenhouse in the world covering an area of 1,559 ha (4 acres) at a height of 55 m (180 ft).

⑪ Mevagissey The Lost Gardens of Heligan north of Mevagissy are every bit as fascinating as the Eden Project – strange, prehistoric fallen tree trunks lie amid a subtropical landscape with giant bamboo, ancient tree ferns and mysterious ponds. The gardens were initially planted in the 18th and 19th centuries, but then fell into a long dormant phase.

In 1990, the developer Tim Smit cut through the 5-m-thick (16-ft) thorn bushes and discovered a site that had been forgotten for nearly a hundred years. After a painstaking reconstruction of the original gardens, the microenvironment was saved. The 32-ha (80-acre) site includes a ravine, an enchanting Italian garden, a grotto and ancient

rhododendron bushes. Lost Valley, a jungle environment with a view over Mevagissey, is another highlight of the gardens.

⑫ Penzance The largest town in Cornwall lies 50 km (31 miles) to the west of here. A drive over the Penwith Peninsula to Land's End is definitely recommended. Due to its temperate climate, this striking region is also called the 'Cornish Riviera'.

Penzance was an important tin trading point for the Roman Empire and medieval Europe. The center of town, between Chapel Street and Market Jew Street, is the oldest part of Pen-

zance, where the long since vanished times of the seafarers can still be felt. The Barbican, which is an old storage house, and the Egyptian House (1830) are both worth visiting.

Opposite the town stands the old castle of St Michael's Mount on top of a granite island in the bay of the same name. This former Benedictine monastery came into the Crown's possession in 1535 and was then converted into a fortress. Historians date the founding of the monastery back to the 8th century. At that time Celtic monks had built a monastery on Mont St-Michel in Normandy, which is remarkably,

but not coincidentally, similar to its Cornish counterpart.

At low tide you can cross the bay on foot. At high tide there is a boat service. If you climb to the top of the 70-m-high (230-ft) outcrop, you'll get a fabulous view over Penwith Peninsula. From Penzance, there is a 35-km (22-mile) road that leads round the peninsula to Land's End and on to St Ives.

⑬ Land's End The westernmost point of England is covered with an open moor and heath, and is absolutely riddled with archaeological treasures. Headstones from the ice age and

Bronze Age, Celtic crosses and entire villages that date back to times before the birth of Christ all bear witness to thousands of years of settlement in the area. The continual breaking of the waves from the Atlantic over the mighty rocks led the Romans to christen the place Belerion – Home of the Storms.

⑭ Scilly Isles About 40 km (25 miles) off the coast to the south-west lie the 140 Scilly Isles, which are reachable by ferry from Penzance. The 2,000 inhabitants, who live mostly from tourism and flower exports, are spread over only seven inhabited islands. With their rough granite rocks, white sandy beaches and turquoise bays, the Scilly Isles are best discovered on foot or by bicycle. A collection of the exotic palms and plants that traditionally flourish in this mild climate can be seen in the Abbey Garden at Tresco.

Back on the mainland, the often steep coastal road then follows the Atlantic coast around to St Ives. Ornithologists come here to find rare visitors like thrushes, New World warblers and vireos that have come over from America accidental on the omnipresent Westerlies. Some of the best observation points are the lighthouses.

⑮ St Ives Grey granite houses populate this former fishing village, which also happens to have one of Cornwall's most beautiful beaches. Numerous artists and sculptors have been coming here since the last century, fascinated by the light and landscape. The Tate Gallery has even opened

a 'branch' high above Porthmoor Beach where works by artists from St Ives are on display including paintings by Patrick Heron and Ben Nicholson, who lived here with his artist wife Barbara Hepworth. The village of Gwithian just up the road is also worth a stop.

The tiny fishing village of Port Isaac is near by, just off the A30. It has been spared a lot of the mass tourism that has become rampant in these parts, which makes it a refreshing alternative. The extremely steep streets probably put off a lot of visitors, so the best bet is to park the car above the village, and walk to Kellan Head on the coast.

⑯ Tintagel The legendary ruins on Tintagel Head are said to be the birthplace of King Arthur. Beyond the village of Tintagel a path leads over the cliffs to a green outcrop on the Atlantic that is crowned with crumbling ruin walls and can be reached via the steep staircase. As digs have proven, a Celtic monastery from the 5th century once stood here with a library, chapel, guest house, refectory and even a bath house.

The castle, however, whose ruins are also still visible, only dates back to the 13th century, a fact that would cast a doubt over the speculation of it being the birthplace of the legendary king of England.

And yet he who stands in the fog on the cliffs looking down at waves crashing by the dark entrance to Merlin's Cave can easily feel himself transported back to the times of King Arthur. The Norman church graveyard

has a number of half-buried tombstones telling tales of dead seamen and grieving widows.

The A39 leads further north from Tintagel along the coast, passing between Blackmoor Gate and Dunster across Exmoor National Park. In order to fully appreciate the coast and the moorland here, you should walk a section of the Somerset and Devon Coastal Path, from Bossington for example.

⑰ Glastonbury and Wells At Bridgwater, the coastal road A39 finally turns inland and leads to Glastonbury, a mythical place that attracts countless esoteric types. There are many reasons for the concentration of mystical and supernatural activity here: the remains of King Arthur are thought to be buried under the ruins of Glastonbury Abbey, and Glastonbury is often thought to be the legendary Avalon – a paradise to which Arthur was carried after his death.

Historical facts date the foundation of the first monastery back to the 7th century while the construction of England's largest abbey came around the year 1000 and the dissolution of the monastery in 1539.

The small city of Wells, on the other hand, is known for its glorious cathedral, the first Gothic building in all of England. The main section was completed in 1240, but the western tower and chapel came much later. The western facade was at one time covered with 400 figures, testimony to the skill of the medieval masons here – one picture book carved into the stone relates biblical and world history. Adjacent

to the cathedral is the Bishop's Palace, which is still used by the Bishop of Bath and Wells.

Bath, your next stop, is the cultural center of the county of Somerset and is around 30 km (19 miles) north of Wells on the A367.

⑱ Bath The Romans knew this hot-springs town as Aquae Sulis. They built magnificent swimming pools, Turkish baths and saunas, and turned the town into a meeting place for the Roman elite. Oddly, the unique baths were only discovered in the 18th century.

Bath's rebirth as a health resort began in earnest in the 19th century when the city's grandiose Georgian architecture, concerts and balls enticed London's upper class to enjoy the recuperative benefits of its historic facilities. Visitors could also admire the dignified limestone buildings such as Queen Square, Royal Crescent and Pulteney Bridge.

1 Kellan Head on the striking north-west coast of Cornwall.

2 Street in the picturesque town of St Ives.

3 The West of England begins in the Wiltshire countryside.

4 A great boulder near Lower Slaughter in the Cotswolds.

5 The cove of Port Issac on the west coast of Cornwall.

6 Land's End – in Cornish, Penn an Wlas – the steep, Atlantic-battered cliffs on the westernmost point of Great Britain.

The Romans in England

It's true, the Romans even ruled England, as Britannia, from around 55 BC to AD 410. After Julius Caesar's failed attempt, Emperor Claudius was the first to conquer the island all the way up to what is now Scotland, then called Caledonia, or 'Wooded Land'. Emperor Hadrian had built a wall there in around 122 BC to keep the fearsome Picts (Scottish predecessors) out of the Roman territories in Eng-

Bath: View of the Roman baths and the abbey.

land. The Romans remained on the island for a good 400 years.

The Romans selected Londinium as their capital and founded numerous other cities, with common suffixes like 'caster' or 'chester' being a throwback to the Roman word for fort. Some of their roads are still in use as well, for example the Fosse Way through the Cotswolds. When the Pict resistance grew too strong, the Romans retreated. Their ruins are now monuments.

Today, you can taste the healing waters and take in the atmosphere in the Pump Room.

A short detour of about 12 km (7.5 miles) via Chippenham leads you to the archaeological site at Avebury in Wiltshire. Avebury is home to the remains of England's largest and most impressive stone circle, made up of over 100 stones erected around 3,500 years ago. Nearby, the 40-m-high (130-ft) Silbury Hill looks like a pyramid, but it was not used as a burial site.

19 The Cotswolds The A429 takes you through the deep, wooded valleys and gentle hills of the Cotswolds, an area that has been populated since prehistoric times. After the Romans, the Cotswolds bloomed through the Middle Ages thanks to wool production. The region then sank into a long period of dormancy before being reawakened by tourism.

The typical Cotswolds architectural style and fairy-tale charm can be best seen in places such as Bouton-on-the-Water where golden stone buildings stand side-by-side with little bridges crossing streams in quaint and vivid meadows.

The town of Stow-on-the-Wold with its stone market hall sits atop a hill and was once a thriving sheep market. On the other side of the hill are the tiny villages of Upper Slaughter and Lower Slaughter, whose miniature appearance have made them into much-loved postcard images.

20 Stratford-upon-Avon The birthplace of William Shakespeare (1564) is the northernmost point of your route. In 1594, the famous playwright left for London, where he was able to establish his legendary reputation as actor and writer in one of the leading theater companies of the time. In 1610 he returned to his home town of Stratford, where he died in 1616. Despite thousands of tourists walking in the footsteps of the poet every year, Stratford has been able to retain some of its Shakespearian atmosphere.

Visitors can tour the house where the playwright was born, learn about his life and work in the Shakespeare Center, or watch one of his plays performed by the Royal Shakespeare Company in the Swan Theater. A boat trip on the Avon rounds off the visit.

The A44 towards Oxford passes the impressive Blenheim Palace at Moreton-in-Marsh.

21 Blenheim Palace This impressive palace near Oxford was finished in 1722 and is Britain's largest private home. It was originally a gift from Queen

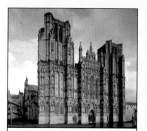

Wells This town was originally founded by the Romans. Its cathedral was begun in AD 700, and the Bishop's Palace is over 800 years old.

Bath 2,000 years ago the Romans established a bath complex that was later rediscovered in 1870. In the 18th century, Bath became a fashionable health resort.

Stonehenge This world-famous prehistoric site was erected between 3100 and 1500 BC by a late Stone-Age people and given some detailed inscriptions in the Bronze Age. Some of the artistically sculpted stones originate from mountains in 'nearby' Wales.

Blenheim Palace This controversial baroque palace completed in 1722 was a gift from Queen Anne to the Duke of Marlborough for winning the Battle of Blenheim (1704). Another famous personage was born here in 1874 – Winston Churchill, a descendant of the Duke.

Scilly Isles Fabulous bays and an exceptionally mild climate make the Scilly Isles a popular holiday destination. Roughly 45 km (28 miles) south-west of Land's End, only seven of the 140 islands are inhabited.

The Cotswolds Typical of this wooded, hilly area are the constructions of Cotswold stone used in bridges, cottages, churches, country houses and walls. Fine examples can be found in Bourton-on-the-Water, Upper Slaughter or Stow-on-the-Wold.

St Ives Two museums in St Ives show works by a group of landscape-inspired artists who 'discovered' the fishing village at the end of the 1920s.

Land's End The stunning scenery from here, the westernmost point of England, has made it into a popular destination for visitors and artists alike.

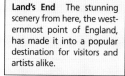

St Michael's Mount Its resemblance to Mont St-Michel in Normandy was the inspiration for this isle's name.

East Devon Coast The lovely coastline of Devon is seemingly endless, quite diverse and littered with holiday resorts.

Shaftesbury Ruins of a cloister and Gold Hill, the most picturesque street in England, make this a charming town.

Anne to John Churchill, the 1st Duke of Marlborough, after his defeat of Ludwig XIV in Blenheim, Bavaria (actually Blindheim near Höchstädt on the Danube). Blenheim Palace is recommended for a relaxing afternoon walk followed by tea. Many garden-lovers come here to visit the palace park, created by landscape gardener Capability Brown in typical English style.

22 Oxford The many spires of Oxford, especially Tom Tower of Christ Church and Magdalen Tower, are visible from the approach road. Oxford is known throughout the world as England's most prestigious university town. Its cathedral and the Picture Gallery, containing masterpieces from the Renaissance and baroque era, are worth a visit. Don't miss the Radcliffe Camera, Sheldonian Theater and the Bodleian Library with its five million books. A coffee break with a book can be taken in the Blackwell Bookshop with a view over Radcliffe Camera.

The college tour is a classic, and leads around the buildings of Merton College, Corpus Christi and New College, among others. Take a relaxing walk through the botanical gardens and its old greenhouses as well.

23 Windsor and Ascot Windsor Castle is in the Thames Valley west of London, and has been the primary residence of the English royal family since the Middle Ages. The fort, built in the 12th and 13th centuries, has been frequently remodelled over the years.

Many sections of Windsor Castle, one of the largest inhabited castles in the world, are open to the public. A trip to St George's Chapel and the Albert Memorial Chapel to view the burial sites of the monarchs is recommended. The Round Tower offers a wonderful view of the castle and the Great Park.

Opposite Windsor Castle is Eton College, founded in 1440–41.

1 Stratford-upon-Avon: the tower of the legendary Holy Trinity Church, site of William Shakespeare's grave.

2 Winston Churchill was born in 1874 in Blenheim Palace (UNESCO World Heritage Site), a baroque masterpiece.

3 The countless spires and towers of colleges and churches give the skyline of Oxford a dignified and unmistakable appearance.

This exclusive private school favours a traditional English education with emphasis on the Classics and sport.

Windsor and Ascot, the famous racetrack, are separated only by a few kilometers. The Hippodrome, built in 1711 by Queen Anne, is among the most famous tracks in the world. From 1825 until 1945, the four-day Royal Meeting race was the only event staged there. Today twenty-five races take place each year.

The last stop now is London, with its historical monuments, impressive museums and world-famous churches.

Oxford This university town is England's education mecca and offers numerous attractions – the Ashmolean Museum, the Bridge of Sighs, the Bodleian Library with the Radcliffe Camera Reading Room, the Sheldonian Theater, thirty-six colleges and the university cathedral of St Mary the Virgin.

Windsor This castle in the Thames Valley was begun in 1070 and regularly extended over the centuries. It has been the principal residence of the royal family since the Middle Ages. Many parts of the castle are open.

London England's capital is at once old-fashioned and modern. A few of the must-sees in London are Westminster Abbey, the Houses of Parliament, Westminster Hall with Big Ben, Buckingham Palace, the Tower of London, St Paul's Cathedral and the British Museum.

Bodiam Castle This moated castle from the 14th century is like a picture from a fairy tale in the heart of south-east England. The castle, though quite large, was built under the guise of protecting the area from French attacks.

Durdle Door This rock formation on the Dorset coast was formed by waves slowly but surely eroding the exposed limestone.

Brighton Despite the destruction of the famous 'West Pier' in 2003, many visitors still go to this now hip seaside resort.

The Seven Sisters At 163 m (535 ft), Beachy Head is Britain's highest limestone cliff. It is to be found in Seven Sisters Country Park, named after the seven distinctive limestone monoliths.

Route 5

Norway

Autumn tundra in the Finnmark Province of Norway's far northern expanse.

Over fjord and fell: the spectacular natural world of northern Europe

Norway shares its borders with Russia, Finland and Sweden and is enveloped by the Norwegian Sea, the North Sea and the Skagerrak. It is a natural realm of truly unmatched beauty – alternately wild and delicate. One tip – make sure you allow plenty of time for the enormous distances.

As you might expect from industrious Scandinavians, the Norwegian mainland has an astonishingly well-maintained road infrastructure. In places where the rugged terrain would have you think the onward journey has come to an end, there appears a ferry, a tunnel or a bridge. Even the smallest hamlets and remote coastal villages are generally easy to reach. And yet progress in this expansive land inevitably takes longer than you've planned, mainly due to the unusual physical geography and strict speed limits. But you won't have to worry much about traffic jams and red lights.

The *Hurtigruten* is Norway's legendary passenger ship, which has been plying the 2,500 nautical miles between Bergen in the south and Kirkenes on the Russian border in the very north for well over a hundred years. It was originally used to transport post and supplies. Nowadays the permanent route, known as 'Imperial Road 1', has become famous as one of 'the world's most beautiful sea voyages'. From a geographical point of view, Norway is unlike any other European country. No other country in Europe is longer (1,752 km/1,089 miles), almost none is as narrow, and despite its odd

Mountain landscape in Kjerringøy in the north.

shape it is (without its polar provinces) three times the size of England.

Almost half of Norway is over 500 m (1,640 ft) above sea level. Its mountains are not particularly high – the highest does not even measure 2,500 m (8,200 ft) – yet nearly a quarter of the country is covered by alpine or high-alpine landscape, glaciers or wide, treeless plateaus at over 1,000 m (3,280 ft) altitude. The generally barren, high plateaus – known as fjells, or fells – are covered in snow for a large part of the year and consist mainly of moors, lakes and rivers.

Above the Arctic Circle and in the highland areas of the interior there is often no sign of human life at all. With the exception of Oslo, Bergen, Trondheim and Stavanger there is no town with more than 100,000 inhabitants in this relatively large country. Four out of five people live on

Historic warehouses in Bergen, member of the Hanseatic League from the 14th to 16th century.

View from the mountain of Aksala over Ålesund past the town center to the port.

the coast or the banks of a fjord. Norway's very craggy coastline, including the fjords and bays, is over 28,000 km (17,398 miles) long – more than half the circumference of the earth.

The country is very sparsely populated and, thanks to the Gulf Stream, free of ice all year. Were it not for these warm ocean currents, the Norwegian mainland would be covered with a crust of ice, as is the case in large areas of the Norwegian polar provinces. On the other hand, the Gulf Stream is also to blame for the high level of summer rainfall, which is common.

Norway's fjords – the most famous of which are Geirangerfjord, Hardanger-fjord and Sognefjord – are the number one tourist attraction here. These former valleys and canyons of various sizes and shapes were carved out by massive gla-ciers and ultimately flooded by rising sea levels following the last ice age.

The short summer months in Norway are quite mild. North of the Arctic Circle – in the 'Land of the Midnight Sun' – summer days actually don't end and the special atmosphere during this time of year often inspires wild parties. The opposite is the case during the cold period, which is snowy and dark in the very north – no sun for two months straight.

Norway is not in the EU and still uses the Norwegian Krone as its currency. After hundreds of years of occupation and inva-sion by the Danes, the Swedes and the Germans, they feel they have earned this 'exclusivity'. But things are going swim-mingly here – fishing and tourism, as well as plentiful oil and natural gas reserves in the North Sea, have made the beautiful 'Land of Utgard' quite prosperous.

Fishing boats in the port of Hamnøy on the Lofoten island of Moskenesøya.

Oslo

At the end of the fjord of the same name, stretching nearly 100 km (60 miles) inland and surrounded by wooded hills, is Norway's capital Oslo, a city dating back to the 11th century. Oslo was called Kristiania until 1925 and had varying political and industrial significance. Although the city is home to a mere half-million inhabitants, it is one of Europe's largest cities in surface area. It is the largest port in Norway and the country's trading and industrial center.

Worth seeing in the center of town: the new town hall (1931-1950), the city's trademark with a sumptuous interior and Europe's highest clock tower; Akershus Fort (from 1300), one of the country's most important

Top: Oslo town hall.
Bottom: Akershus Castle.

medieval buildings; Nasjonalgalleriet, the largest collection of paintings and sculptures in Norway; the royal castle (changing of the guard at 1:30 pm). Highlights outside the city center include Holmenkollen, a winter-sport resort with skiing museum; Munch-Museet; Vigelandpark (Frognerpark) with 200 monumental works in bronze and stone by Gustav Vigeland; Bygdöy peninsular museum with the Vikingskipshuset (three ships from the 9th century); Kon-Tiki Museet with the Thor Heyerdahls Raft (Kon-Tiki, RA I, RA II); Fram-Museet.

North Cape Route: On the 4,000-km (2,484-mile) trip to the North Cape you get to experience just about everything Norway's fascinating natural landscape has to offer: glaciers, waterfalls, mountains, high plateaus, rugged coastline and endless fjords. The cultural highlights include old port and mining towns, interesting stone carvings and charming old churches.

1 Oslo (see sidebar left). From Oslo follow the coast to Kongsberg.

2 Kongsberg The Mining Museum here casts you back to the times of silver mining, which ceased in 1957 after more than 330 years. In the Saggrenda pit you can see what is probably the world's first ever elevator – it consists of ladders that go up and down.

3 Heddal and Eidsborg Norway's first stave church (1147) is in Telemark and has an outer gallery that was used to protect people from the weather and to store weapons.
Road 45 (direction Dalen) splits off towards the Eidsborg stave church at Ofte. The walls of the

church are covered with shingles, which is unusual. About 4 km (2.4 miles) beyond Rødal, Road 13 turns off towards Stavanger.
The E134 also passes through Hardangervidda further on.

4 Hardangervidda Europe's largest plateau is a fascinating area for hiking and is home to rare wildlife. From Skarsmo our route leads north on Road 13. Alongside the road are the wild frothing waters of the Låtefossen. It is definitely worth a short detour (50 km/31 miles) from Kinsarvik, along the Eidfjord to Fossli, to the edge of the Vidda where the Vøringfossen Falls drop 170 m (557 ft) into the depths of Måbø Canyon.
From Kinsarvik, ferries cross the Utne to Kvanndal on the Hardangerfjord. The 'King of the Fjords' reaches far inland at a length of 179 km (111 miles) and a depth of 830 m (2,723 ft). The

Travel information

Route profile
Length: approx. 4,000 km (2,484 miles), excluding detours
Time required: at least 4 weeks, ideally 6–8 weeks.
Start: Oslo
End: The North Cape
Route (main locations):
Oslo, Kongsberg, Bergen, Jotunheimen, Trondheim, Fauske, Narvik, Tromsø, Alta, North Cape

Traffic information:
This route requires some driving skill and good planning as the ferries are often fully booked. Drive on the right in Norway. Customs laws are strictly enforced. Headlights are obligatory even during the day. Bridges, tunnels and

mountain pass roads mostly charge tolls. Mountain roads are often only opened in June/July.

When to go:
The best time to go is from June to August. Even in these months, snowfall is common in the north and on the plateaus.

Accommodation:
Mountain inns, known as fjellstue or fjellstove, and chalets are attractive.

General information:
www.visitnorway.com
www.norway.org
www.norway.com
Customs:
www.toll.no

Detour

Stavanger and Lysefjord

Instead of the E134 south, you can take a spectacular mountain road (13) from Røldal to Stavanger. You will have to cross a good many fjords on this route.

Stavanger, founded in 1125, was still the center of the herring and fish-canning industry in Norway until just three decades ago. In 1970, plentiful oil reserves were discovered in the Ekofisk Field, instantly making Norway's third-largest town the oil capital of the country.

**Top: A colourful port town.
Bottom: Stavanger Oil Museum.**

As a result, some flamboyant buildings were erected, but much of the architecture still recalls the more tranquil times prior to the oil bonanza – the Canning History Museum, for example.

The old town is called Gamle Stavanger and has 173 listed wooden houses in cobblestone lanes. The Gothic cathedral (1125–1300) is noteworthy for being the purest example of medieval church building in Norway. The Kongsgaard, where the Danish kings stayed on their travels between the 14th and 19th centuries, appears spartan in contrast. The Valbergturm, an old fire watchtower and local icon, offers a good view of the town.

The long, narrow Lysefjord is among the prettiest in the country, plunging to a depth of 400 m (1,311 ft) and stretching 40 km (25 miles). Its stone walls rise as high as 1,000 m (3,300 ft).

An impressive suspension bridge spans the fjord at its western end. A boat trip to Lysefjord and the Prekestolen promontory – the Preacher's Pulpit – is a must.

route then leads over the plateau of Kvamskogen on to Bergen.

5 Bergen The most famous street in this old Hanseatic League town is Bryggen, a UNESCO World Heritage Site with picturesque warehouses right on the waterfront. The fishing port, the cathedral, the 12th-century church and the Gamle Bergen open-air museum are also worth visiting.

6 Viksøyri The E16 passes many lakes on the way to Voss, home of the oldest wooden house in Norway – 'Finneloftet' from the 13th century. Further along the route you should take a detour to Viksøyri (with a charming stave church) where you can see the Sognefjord about 40 km (25 miles) away. It is Norway's greatest fjord – 180 km (112 miles) long, in some places only 5 km (3 miles) wide, and up to 1,200 m (3,937 ft) deep.

7 Stalheimskleiva and Nærøyfjord About 13 km (8 miles) past Oppheim, a road leads to the Hotel Stalheim, which has wonderful views. Norway's steepest road leads round thirteen hairpin bends down to the Nærøyfjord. It is the narrowest one in the country with walls up to 1,200 m (3,937 ft) high.

Two impressive waterfalls are also on the route – the Stahlheimfoss (126 m/413 ft) and the Sivlefoss (240 m/787 ft). The main road goes from Gudvangen to Kaupanger and on to Songdal. The fjord route leads past Nærøyfjord, Aurlandsfjord and Sognefjord, among the most beautiful in Norway.

1 UNESCO World Heritage Site: the picturesque wooden houses of Bryggen in Bergen, once a member of the Hanseatic League.

2 An isolated farmstead in the bare fell landscape – Telemark in southern Norway.

3 The Vøringfossen falls cascade from the Hardanger Plateau into the deep and narrow Måbø Canyon.

4 The 800-year-old stave church of Borgund near Borlaug, deep in the Lærdal Valley.

Lysefjord and the majestic rock promontory known as the Prekestolen ("Preacher's Pulpit") is one of south-west Norway's most popular nature attractions. Surrounded by cliff walls up to 1,000 m (3,300 ft) high, the narrow fjord is 40 km long (25 mi) and stretches east from Stavanger. You can reach Prekestolen

on foot or by car; the large viewing platform has no safety railings, so you look 600 m (1,900 ft) straight down into the abyss. Be careful – the height can be dizzying! The hiking trail to the promontory takes you through a pristine boulder landscape and is one of the most beautiful of its kind in Scandinavia.

Detour

Ålesund and the bird island of Runde

This little detour first takes you about 120 km (75 miles) out to Ålesund, an island town with stone buildings (unusual for Norway) that were built by art nouveau architects from all over Europe after a fire destroyed the place in 1904. It is this uniform view of the port town that makes a visit so worthwhile.

The main attractions of the town include a visit to the 189-m-high (621-ft) Aksla Mountain – from its terrace you can enjoy a great panoramic view over the town, the skerry (rock) belt and the Sunnmøre Mountains in the west. From the town park it's about 400 m (1,312 ft) to the viewpoint.

Top: Sheep on the cliffs.
Bottom: A farmstead on the Kløfjellet.

The Atlanterhavsparken Aquarium displays marine flora and fauna local to this Norwegian coastal area. To the east of town is the Sunnmøren open-air museum with more than forty old houses and farms.

The island of Runde, which is only 6.4 sq km (2.5 sq mi), is a must for anyone who loves nature. Although only 150 people live there, up to 700,000 sea birds also call it home. You can get the best view of 'Bird Island', which hosts puffins, uria, razorbills and several varieties of gulls, by booking a boat trip around the island.

Even divers value the area as much as ornithologists – in 1725 a Dutch ship carrying nineteen cases of gold and silver coins sank off the island, as did a Spanish treasure ship in 1588!

Trollstigen

Surrounded by waterfalls, deep valleys and mountains as high as 1,760 m (6,316 ft), Norway's most photographed mountain pass, the Trollstigen, snakes its way from Langdal to Åndalsnes at elevations of up to 850 m (2,789 ft). Eleven hairpin bends with a gradient of ten per cent take some skill to master. The road was built in 1936 and winds along almost vertical rock faces. As a result, it is unfortunately closed to camper vans.

⑧ Borgund The best-preserved stave church in the country can be viewed by taking a short diversion inland after driving through the new 20-km (13-mile) Lærdals Tunnel on the E16.

The church was erected around 1150 and is known for its ornate carvings. The pagoda-shaped bell tower is next to the church.

⑨ Jotunheimen and Sognefjell road Norway's highest and most spectacular mountain pass runs from Sogndal to Lom. It climbs a steep, winding trail into the Jotunheimen Mountains where over two hundred peaks of at least 2,000 m (6,561 ft) form a bizarre ring. The two highest among them are Galdahøppigen

at 2,469 m (8,100 ft) and Glittertind at 2,452 m (8,045 ft).

The Sognefjell is a plateau littered with lakes of all sizes. To the west of the road is Europe's largest mainland glacier, the Jostedalsbree, which is about 100 km (62 miles) long.

⑩ Urnes A small single-lane road now leads from Skjolden on the east bank of the Lustrafjord to the town of Urnes and an 11th-century stave church, the oldest of twenty-nine listed Norwegian stave churches and a UNESCO World Heritage Site. The robust design of the exterior is fascinating and the carvings of fable characters in the interior are lovely.

⑪ Geirangerfjord The route continues through some pretty landscape on its way to the Geirangerfjord, a 15-km (9-mile) arm of the Sunnylvsfjord. Its walls are up to 800 m (2,625 ft) high and many waterfalls feed into the fjord. The panorama from the viewpoint at Dalsnibba before Geiranger is fabulous.

The winding road 'Ornevein' (Eagle Route) leads up into the mountains offering frequent

views over the fjord. After crossing the Nordalsfjord you get your first chance to turn off to Ålesund Island (80 km/50 miles). The main route then continues through the Gudbrands Gorge to the Trollstigen mountain road and on to Åndalsnes. Here you have a second possibility to head towards Ålesund about 120 km (74 miles) down the E136.

The E136 continues east in Romsdalen to Dombås, and from here

Røros

A number of buildings, hangars, pits and slag heaps recall an era when Røros was a great mining center. The oldest copper mine in

The church of Bergstaden Zir, built between 1780–1884.

through the hilly mountainous countryside to the Dovrefjell.

12 Dovrefjell Norway's tallest mountain, Snøhetta, at 2,286 m (7,500 ft) dominates the plateau and you can get a great view from the road's highest point (1,026 m/3,366 ft). The national park is classified as the only remaining intact high-altitude ecosystem in Europe.

The road passes through Drivdalen to Oppdal with its modest open-air museum. On the way to Trondheim (E06) you will be presented with a diversion to the old mining town of Røros (120 km/74.5 miles), with a massive stone cathedral and some charming historic buildings.

13 Trondheim Trondheim was Norway's capital for quite some time. To this day, royal coronations still take place in the mighty Nidaros Cathedral, built in 1070 over the grave of Olav the Holy. The western facade has some particularly interesting sculptures. The Tyholt Television Tower, Fort Kristiansen and the cathedral tower all offer wonderful views over the rooftops of Trondheim.

The scenic E16 leads from Trondheim to Grong, following the banks of numerous fjords along the way. In Grong, Road 760 links up with the R17, the Kystriksveien. The E06 goes north towards Fauske, rolling through the charming Namdalen.

14 Kystriksveien The 560-km (348-mile) Kystriksveien is in effect the mainland counterpart to the legendary Hurtigruten coastal journey – one of Europe's dream routes. Many ferries ply the fjords and lakes in this region and the landscape is varied. But the coastal road requires a lot of time and money, and waiting times are to be expected for the various ferries. The crossing fees can indeed add up to a considerable sum.

A few kilometers beyond Sonja there is a small road to Mo I Rana where you can get back on the E06 to the Saltfjellet-Svartisen National Park.

The section of the coastal road north of the turnoff to Mo I

1 The Jostedalsbreen National Park, the 'Land of the Giants', in southern Norway protects the largest land glacier in Europe, which has four glacial tongues.

2 Picturesque fishing boats reflected in the Lusterfjord, a northern arm of the Sognefjord.

3 South of Oppdal lies the Dovrefjell National Park with Snøhetta (snow cap) in the background (2,286 m/7,500 ft), Norway's highest mountain just outside Jotunheimen.

4 Typical mountainous and fjord landscape in Nordland, the Norwegian province that straddles the Arctic Circle.

town is a UNESCO World Heritage Site dating back to 1644.

The stone baroque church of Bergstaden Zir (1784) in the town center is surrounded by wooden buildings and is worth visiting. With a capacity of 2,000, it is the third-largest church in the country. It was reserved for miners who lived alongside the slag heaps or in the side streets in shacks. Rich citizens, civil servants and mine managers lived in the avenues and pleasant areas of town, as usual.

Detour

Lofoten and Vesterålen Islands

Lofoten and Vesterålen, its northern extension, have been popular holiday destinations for Norwegians since the 19th century. The grandiose scenery of mountains and sea, the colourful villages and the surprisingly mild climate make them exceptional even amid the already spectacular Norwegian landscape. Infrastructure here is excellent, with all the main islands connected to one another as well to the mainland by tunnels or bridges. Ferries take you to the smaller islands.

Both groups of islands reach 250 km (155 miles) out into the Norwegian Sea like a wildly shattered wall of stone, with snow-capped mountains and deep, verdant valleys. Because of the steep cliffs, often only the narrow coastlines are inhabited.

Colourful wooden houses – called Rorbuer – are built on stilts over the water. At places like Austvågøys, wonderful white sandy beaches are hidden in the fjords and bays – not what one would expect this far north. The bird life on the islands is also impressive. In addition to the typical sea and migratory birds, majestic sea eagles are also at home here. The plant life on these once wooded islands is stunted but varied. Mountain, beach and meadow plants grow side by side.

Despite the fact that the Lofoten and Vesterålen are between 150 and 300 km (93–86 miles) inside the Arctic Circle, the air temperature, even in winter, rarely drops below freezing thanks to the warming effects of the Gulf Stream. Due to the constantly warm currents, the Vestfjord has become a preferred spawning-ground for herring and cod, which in turn benefits salmon and trout breeding in the fjords and bays.

Dried and cured cod are considered delicacies. From March to June they are to be found in their masses

drying on wooden racks. Dried fish chips, which like the vitamin C-rich cloudberries are easy to store for long periods, are beloved souvenirs for the 200,000 tourists who visit Lofoten every year.

The detour to Lofoten is a long 587-km (365-mile) drive, but the effort is definitely worth it. The best time of year to visit this stunning archipelago is from the end of May to the middle of July,

when the interplay of midnight sun and mountains will dazzle the uninitiated. Remember to bring your eye masks if you are sensitive to light when you sleep!

Another one of Lofoten's attractions that is worth visiting is Hinnøya, the northernmost medieval church in the world located in Harstad on Norway's largest island. Orcas and porpoises are a very common sight in the Vest-

fjord, but a whale safari is still an unforgettable experience. They are offered from Andenes on the northern point of the northernmost Vesterålen island, Andøya, from June to September and you are likely to see sperm whales in the waters off the shore of the whaling station.

The museum in Stokmarknes on the Vesterålen island of Hadseløya tells of the legendary Hurtigruten liner, which

was 'founded' here in 1881. Hadseløya has no fjords or bays, but is remarkable from a sporting point of view – its circumference is 42.195 km (26 miles 385 yards), precisely the length of a traditional marathon. Naturally, every year in August there is a race around the island.

Svolvær, the capital of the Lofoten on Austvågøya, is overshadowed by a craggy rock that is shaped like a goat,

the Svolværgeita. Don't pass up trips to: the highest peak of the Lofoten islands, the Higravstindan at 1,146 m (3,758 ft); to Raftsund with the second-longest cantilever bridge in the world; and the boat trip to Raftsund in the Trollfjord, which has walls as high as 1,146 m (3,759 ft) in some places and narrow passages that are definitely among the best that the Norwegian landscape has to offer.

From February to April Kabelvåg is northern Norway's cod fishing center. During this time, thousands of fishing boats cast their nets into the waters of the Vestfjord. Around AD 600 there were Vikings living on Vestvågøya. Make sure to pay a visit to the 86-m-long (270-ft) Norman meeting hall in the reconstructed settlement at the Lofotr Museum in the town of Borg.

The 19th-century church in nearby Flakstad on the island of Flakstadøya is considered the prettiest church in the Lofoten Archipelago. Hamnøy, on the beautiful adjacent island of Moskenesøya, is a particularly rustic fishing village.

From Moskenes there is a regular ferry crossing to Bodø on the mainland, and from there you get back on the E06 to Fauske.

1 A scene typical for the archipelago – small fishing villages in front of impressive cliffs on the rare flat areas along the coast.

2 Hamnøy, sheltered at the entrance to the Reinefjord, is one of the oldest fishing villages on the Lofoten island of Moskenesøya.

3 Midsummer's night: from 2 May to 17 July the sun never sets on the north and west side of the Lofoten Archipelago.

4 The fishing village of Reine is surrounded by steep mountain scenery and considered to be one of the prettiest Lofoten villages. The red-painted Rorbuer houses that line the banks have been used by fishermen since the 12th century.

5 The *hjeller*, wooden racks used to dry fish (especially cod), are common sights on the Lofoten Islands.

The classic Norwegian triple: In the unspoilt, uninhabited landscape of the Vesterålen off the north-western coast you will be surrounded by sky, mountains and fjords. The Steinlandsfjord is on the west side of the island of Langøya, which faces the open Atlantic. It is the second-largest island in Norway. The fjord is in

the middle of a vast, treeless mountainous region of breathtaking beauty and is basically the continuation of the Prestfjord, which goes deep into the island's interior. Langøya is one of the most mountainous parts of the Vesterålen region with peaks of up to 1,000 m (3,300 ft). It is also a great whale-watching location.

Flora and fauna in the Finnmark

Long, cold winters with astounding temperatures of -40°C (-40°F) and short but pleasant summers are characteristic of the tundra of northern

Top: Musk oxen.
Bottom: Reindeer run wild here.

Norway. During the few snow-free weeks the small flora in this area seem to explode into berries and blossom, offering direct or indirect nourishment to animals like reindeer, Arctic hares, Arctic foxes, lemmings, snow owls, wolves, bears and lynxes.
In addition, a variety of whale species live in the coastal waters. But the most common encounters are with reindeer and mosquitoes!

Rana is called Helgeland-Salten, the 'Green Road'. A natural tidal spectacle is visible near Løding – every six hours the water trapped behind the 'Eye of the Needle' forces its way through the strait.
From Løding it is a 43-km (27-mile) drive back to the E06 at Fauske. An interesting alternative is the road through the Saltfjellet-Svaryisen National Park. Norway's second largest glacier is high in the Arctic Circle here. The tremendous glacier is hard to reach, however – gravel track turns off at Skonseng towards Svartisdalhytta. Inside the Arctic Circle and above the tree line, only moss and shrubs grow here. The road to Rognan on Saltdalsfjord leads through the high valley of Saltfjells, and then follows the eastern bank to Fauske. The E06 then goes north to Ulsvåg, where you can turn off to Skutvik, the most important Lofoten port.

15 Narvik Swedish iron ore from Kiruna is shipped around the world from the permanently ice-free port of Ofotenfjord here. The warehouses and transport systems are best viewed from the panorama point up on Fagernessfjell (656 m/2,151 ft). Ferries also travel to Lofoten from Narvik. The E08 turns to Tromsø at Nordkjosbotn.

16 Tromsø Northern Norway's largest town ironically benefits from a mild climate. The Polarmuseet has interesting exhibits covering various international polar expeditions. The Tromsøbrua connects the island town to the mainland. Next to it is the town's icon – the pointed Arctic Cathedral (1965). Back on the E06 you drive through some spectacular fjords.

17 Alta This town on the fjord of the same name is a center of Sami culture. The stone carvings of Hjemmeluft, which date back between 2,000 and 6,000 years, are definitely worth a visit. They depict animals, hunting and everyday scenes and are listed as a World Heritage Site. The Alta Canyon is also a must-see, with impressive depths of 500 m (1,634 ft) and a length of 15 km (9 miles).
The route then crosses the tundra landscape of Finnmarksvidda to the port town of Hammerfest. After that, the E06 crosses a plateau before the E69 turns off at Olderford towards the North Cape.

18 North Cape The road then heads past Porsangerfjord to the ferry port of Kåfjord, where ferries travel to Honningsvag on the North Cape island of Magerøya. There is now a tunnel to the island. Across the harsh landscape we reach the North Cape, the end of our trip.

1 The Lyngenfjord is over 10 km (6 miles) wide and one of the prettiest in northern Norway.

2 The Finnmark is characterized by wild, harsh landscape, deep fjords, craggy coastal cliffs and expansive plateaus.

3 The midnight sun shines on the North Cape from May 14 to July 30, yet the Cape is often immersed in thick fog, rain or snow. A globe marks Europe's northernmost point.

Lofoten Typical for the Lofoten are the craggy mountain tops with steep faces, deep green meadows and bright wooden houses on stilts. Here we see winter, but the climate of the islands is actually quite mild due to the warm Gulf Stream.

Lyngenfjord This mountain panorama is one of the most beautiful in Norway. It feels a lot like the Alps.

North Cape Usually foggy and mainly promoted to tourists as the northernmost point in Europe, Magerøya is still worth seeing despite neighbour Knivskjellodden actually being further north.

Ålesund This island, which was rebuilt by Art Nouveau architects from all over Europe following a devastating fire in 1904, is characterized by stone houses, which are unusual for Norway. An aquarium displays Norway's sea life and the view from Aksla Mountain above town is a treat.

Trondheim The Nidarosdom, built in 1070, is Scandinavia's most impressive church, where the coronation of Norwegian kings took place until 1906. You can get a great view of Trondheim from the Nidarosdom tower.

Geirangerfjord About 15 km (9 miles) long and flanked by cliff walls of up to 800 m (2,625 ft), this is truly one of Norway's natural wonders.

Sami Reindeer breeding and fishing are the main activities of Norway's 25,000 indigenous Sami people. The town of Alta is their cultural center.

Finnmark Harsh winters and short summers characterize the almost deserted tundra of northern Norway, which is covered with only stunted vegetation that blossoms quickly and brightly in summer.

Trollstigen Norway's most famous mountain pass takes some handy driving – eleven hairpin bends await you at a gradient of ten percent over an altitude change of 850 m (2,789 ft).

Sognefjord Norway's largest fjord is 180 km (112 miles) long, up to 5 km (3 miles) wide and 1,200 m (3,937 ft) deep. Nearby is the longest car tunnel in the world.

Røros The wooden buildings in the center of town recall a more prosperous era when Røros was a wealthy copper-mining town. The stone church, built in 1784, was reserved for miners.

Bergen The Bryggen road, with numerous historic warehouses nestled together at the fishing port, a charming cathedral, a 12th-century church, the Gamle Bergen open-air museum and one of Europe's largest ocean aquariums all make the old Hanseatic League town of Bergen well worth visiting.

Urnes The oldest Norwegian stave church has ornate wood-carvings and a unique wooden construction. It is located near the Lustrafjord.

Vöringfossen Europe's largest plateau, the Hardangervidda, is the starting point for the 170-m-high (557-ft) Vöringfossen, a spectacular waterfall that plummets into the Måbø Canyon.

Prekestolen This 600-m-high (1,969-ft) promontory, 'Preacher's Pulpit', is one of the must-see attractions in southern Norway.

Oslo World-famous museums, plenty of greenery and water make this sprawling metropolis a fascinating experience. The new town hall on the port is the icon of the Norwegian capital.

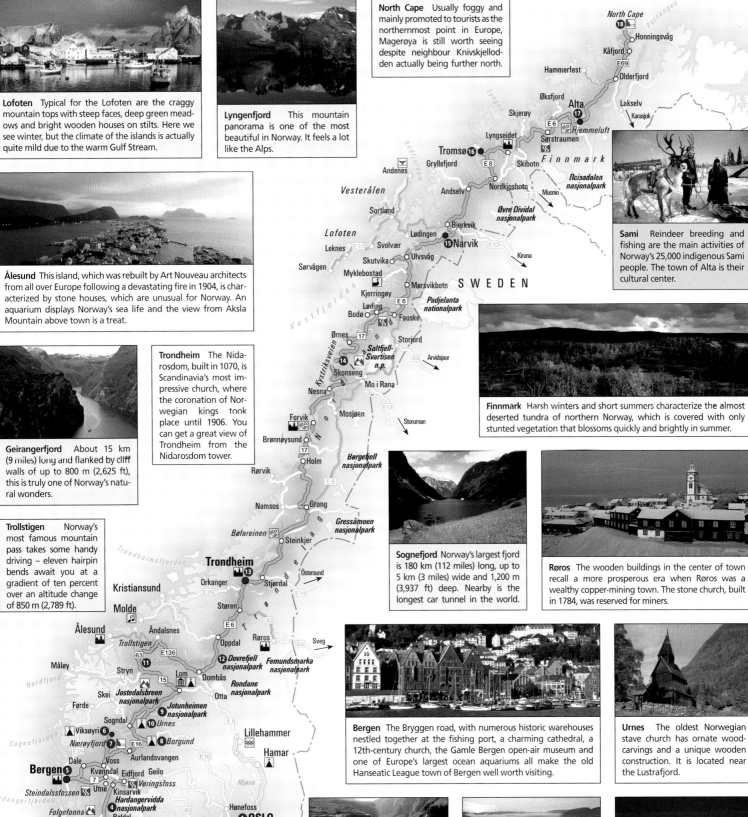

Many Swedes have holiday homes on the skerry coast, as here at Lake

Denmark and Sweden

Where the North Sea meets the Baltic: a journey around the Kattegat

Ever since the bold Öresund Bridge connected Denmark with Sweden, it has been much easier to explore the two "united kingdoms". Indeed, there are many similarities between these Scandanavian countries, but there also many differences to discover. Denmark, the smaller of the two, is known for its seaside holidays, while its larger neighbor features vast tracts of untouched nature.

The most bizarre but perhaps fitting travel recommendation for Denmark came from the royal mouth of its very popular and friendly Queen Margrethe II: "There is no other country in the world that is as much like Denmark as Denmark itself." But what is Denmark? Initially it was an island kingdom comprising the divided Jutland Peninsula, the larger islands of Fünen, Seeland, Falster, Møn, Lolland and Bornholm, and about four hundred smaller islands, of which not even one hundred are inhabited.

Denmark is also a small country that you can cover easily in one day, if you so desire. It is also particularly well suited to those who love the sea. Where else can you choose from 7,400 km (4,598 mi) of largely unspoiled and easily accessible coastlines, from the shimmering blue Kattegat strait and the mild Baltic Sea to the rigged Skagerrak and the tidal North Sea? Denmark's interior, characterized by lakes, fields, forests and moors, is actually quite hilly. The towns and villages, with their whitewashed

Blå Jungfrun National Park west of Öland.

and often slightly dilapidated half-timbered houses, are what the Danes refer to as "hyggelig", meaning cozy. Denmark's cultural assets range from Bronze Age and Viking era archaeological monuments to magnificent manor houses, castles, ground-breaking modern architecture and world-famous museums and art collections.

Beyond the Kattegat strait, the Baltic Sea and the Strait of Öresund, the Kingdom of Sweden – ten times larger than Denmark – offers a breathtaking diversity of landscapes and tranquil expanses. But it also attracts tourists accordingly. The southern part of the country, where little Nils Holgersson's wonderful journeys to the Sápmi region (Lapland) began, will remind travelers a bit of Denmark's meadow and field landscape. North of Gothernburg (Göteborg), however, the

Runn near Falun.

Changing of the guard in front of Amalienborg Palace in the Danish capital, Copenhagen.

Stockholm: Riddarholmskyrka on Riddarholmen. The Swedish church is the final resting place of Swedish kings.

scenery becomes typically Swedish and is more reminiscent of the film adaptations of books by Astrid Lindgren, a Swedish author best known for creating *Pippi Longstocking*. Swedish houses painted "ox blood red" stand in the middle of lush green meadows surrounded by miles of birch and conifer woodlands. Vänern and Vättern, the country's two largest lakes, almost feel like massive inland seas and are also found in this region.

North of Stockholm, nature takes on an increasingly primal feel. Population decreases, the rivers run more wildly and the forests become denser. Sweden's Sápmi region, the northernmost third of the country, is shaped by almost melancholy beauty and pure tranquility. Only the reindeer herds of the Saami people are able to find enough food in the bleak realm of the midnight sun.

Visitors here should do as the outdoor enthusiastic Swedes do and stay a few summer days in a remote *stuga* as part of their adventures in the countryside. They may even encounter one of the 500,000 Swedish moose along the way. There is no need to fear the moose, but you should always be on the lookout for trolls lurking in the forests – Sweden is a land of legends, myths and fairy tales.

This popular cultural strain is also expressed in the numerous festivals and customs here that are unknown in other parts of Europe. The nicest of these is the "magic" midsummer night's festival held all over the country in June. Along with Christmas, this longest day (shortest night) is the most popular holiday in Sweden, when people meet for an evening meal of herring and drink aquavit and "öl" (Swedish for beer).

Egeskov Castle is one of the most beautiful Renaissance water castles in Denmark.

Bornholm

Bornholm, also known as the "Pearl of the Baltic" for its mild climate, is an island about 40 km (25 mi) off the south coast of Sweden, quite far from the Danish mainland. Ferries

Bornholm is popular for sailing.

to the island run from Copenhagen and the Swedish town of Ystad. Roughly 600-sq-km (2312 sq mi) in size, Bornholm is a virtual "Scandinavia in miniature", with miles of sandy beaches, lakes, moors, deciduous and coniferous forests, heaths, dunes and a rocky subsoil not found anywhere else in mainland Denmark.

There are numerous remnants of former settlements on the island. The Hammerhus brick castle from 1260, for example, is the largest and most spectacular ruin in all of Denmark, sitting majestically atop a granite cliff. It makes for a unique experience. Rønne is the largest town on the island and is home to many beautiful old houses, including some charming half-timbered buildings. The whitewashed smokehouses for herring are typical of the picturesque coastal villages.

This tour of southern Scandinavia first heads along the southern Swedish Baltic Sea coast to Stockholm, then passes by numerous lakes and through seemingly endless forests to Göteborg. In Denmark, a fairy-tale journey leads through Jutland, Fyn and Seeland with picturesque ports and trading towns before reaching Copenhagen.

❶ Copenhagen (see page 69) You can get to Malmö from Copenhagen by ferry or via the Öresund Bridge.

❷ Malmö Canals run through the picturesque Old Town here, which can be discovered either on foot or by boat. The Stortorget is lined with some wonderful buildings. The route then continues to Lund, a picturesque

Öresund Bridge

Since 2000, Denmark and Sweden have been connected by the Öresund Bridge. All in all, the project comprises a 4-km (2.5-mi) tunnel from Copenhagen Airport, the 4-km (2.5-mi) offshore island of Peberholm and an 8-km (5-mi) bridge to Malmö, a city on the Swedish mainland. Traveling time across the strait has been reduced from 60 to 15 minutes.

university town where the cathedral is the oldest Romanesque church in Sweden.

❸ Ystad Many imposing half-timbered buildings make Ystad one of the most beautiful cities in Scania. The herring catch brought wealth to the monastery and fishing town back in the Hanseatic era.

After Ystad, it is worth making a detour at Tomelilla to Sweden's only castle complex still to be preserved in its original condition from 1499. Ramparts and yard-thick walls meant it had been previously impregnable. Regular ferries depart Ystad to the Danish island of Bornholm.

❹ Karlskrona Many building complexes in this city were designed for military purposes in the late 17th century and are listed as UNESCO World Heritage Sites. The Karlskrona's Stortorget is among the largest squares in

northern Europe; the admiralty church, built in 1685, and the Trinity church from 1714 are also worth visiting.

❺ Kalmar The Kalmar Union of 1397 united the kingdoms of Denmark, Norway and Sweden. The castle and cathedral of this

❶ The Kalmar Union, which united the kingdoms of Sweden, Denmark and Norway, was signed at Kalmar Castle in 1397. The castle was rebuilt in the Renaissance style by Wasa kings Erik XIV and Johann III in the 16th century.

❷ The cathedral in Lund, Sweden, was begun in 1103. with the help of stonemasons from the Rhineland (Germany). The crypt was completed in 1123, and the cathedral was consecrated in 1145.

❸ The baroque Kalmar Cathedral was constructed between 1660 and 1703. The "Domkyrka" is one of the most important examples of Swedish baroque church archictecture.

Travel information

Route profile
Length: approx. 2,500 km (1,550 mi) without detours
Time required: 4 weeks
Start and end: Copenhagen
Route (main locations): Copenhagen, Malmö, Karlskrona, Stockholm, Falun, Göteborg, Århus, Odense, Copenhagen

Traffic information:
The Green Insurance Card is recommended. "Shark teeth" on the road replace "Yield" signs in Denmark. The Öresund and Storebælt bridges have tolls of up to 50 euros each way for passenger cars. Watch out for deer crossings in Sweden. They are quite common. Low-beam headlights are automatic in both Sweden and Denmark.

When to go:
May to October (Denmark), June to September (Sweden).

Accommodation:
All price categories are available and in demand Scandinavia, particularly holiday homes.
Typically Danish: "Kros" – royally licenced regional guesthouses/hotels (www.dansk-kroferie.dk).

Information:
Denmark:
www.dt.dk
www.visitdenmark.com
Sweden:
Sveriges Rese- och Turistråd, Box 3030, Kungsgatan 36, S-103 61 Stockholm, www.visit-sweden.com and www.sweden.se

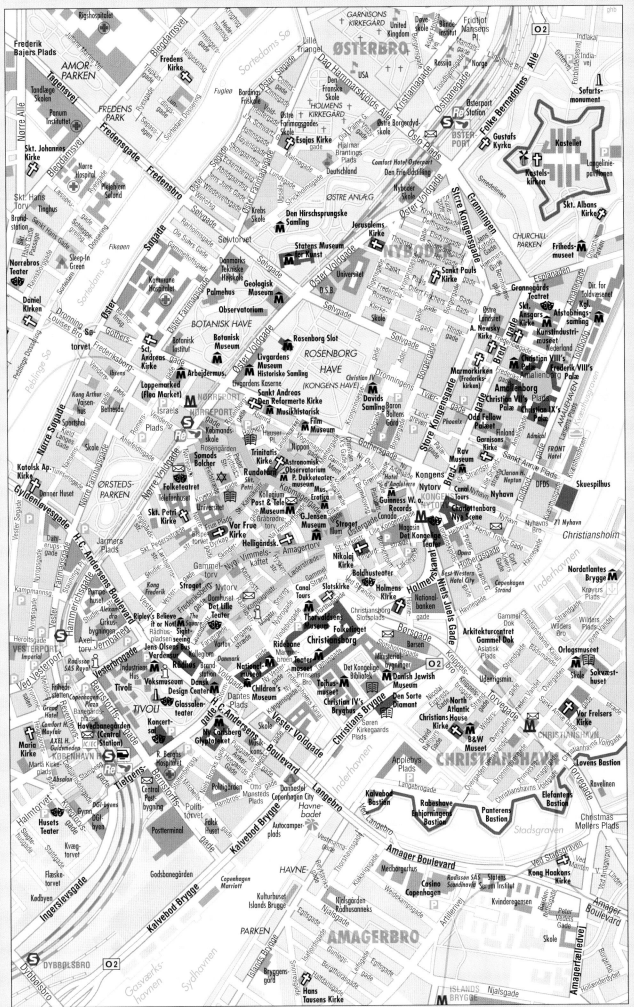

Copenhagen

History and tradition greet travelers at every turn here, the Danish capital and royal residence on the Strait of Öresund. The atmosphere is relaxed and open-minded yet pleasantly introspective, and most tourist attractions can be easily reached on foot.

The city on the Strait of Öresund, which has been the capital of Denmark since 1443, experienced its first heyday in the late Middle Ages as a trading port, and a second boom in the 16th and 17th centuries, particularly under King Christian IV, who greatly expanded and developed the city.

Sights of note here include: the Tivoli Gardens amusement park; the harbor promenade at Nyhavn Canal, lined with old wooden sailing ships and cafés; the canal and harbor tours and boat excursions from here to the popular Little Mermaid statue (Lille Havfrue) on the Langelinie pier promenade are pleasant; the rococo royal residence, Amalienborg Palace; the Zoological Gardens, the green oasis of the city; Slotsholm island with Christiansborg Castle; Thorvaldsenmuseum, with works by famous Danish sculptors; the antique collection of the Ny Carlsberg Glytotek; Rådhus Pladsen, in the heart of the inner city with the

Top: The Little Mermaid.
Middle: Nyhavn, today the oldest port in the city, was constructed from 1671 to 1673.
Bottom: The Tivoli amusement park.

town hall (which offers a spectacular view from its tower); the landmark portion of the Carlsberg brewery; the Nationalmuseet with historical and ethnographic collections and a number of exhibitions.

Detour

Öland and Gotland

Sweden's largest islands were all settled as early as Viking times. During the era of the Hanseatic cities,

Öland: Stone Age cemetery, with a typical windmill in the background

Gotland's capital, Visby, was an important trading hub – briefly even the most important in the entire Baltic region, and much more so than it is today. The cathedral and the mile-long 13th-century city

Top: Rock formations on Fårö beach, Gotland island.
Bottom: The walled town of Visby.

wall, which completely surrounds the UNESCO World Heritage Site, are particularly impressive.
Much praise is given to Gotland's mild climate and landscape, which features lush meadows, forests, beaches and steep coastlines with extremely peculiar rock formations that look like human creations.
Öland, the second-largest island in Sweden, is connected to Småland by a bridge and is the summer residence of the Swedish royal family. As the limestone in the sub-soil drains off rainfall, vast areas of the island are stark grassy with dune steppes, a paradise for many rare species of animals and orchids. Öland also has large deciduous forests and is known for its beautiful beaches and some four hundred windmills.

city on the Kalmarsund is worth seeing, as are the baroque and Renaissance harbor and the buildings in the Old Town. A 6-km (4-mi) bridge spans the sound from Kalmar to the island of Öland.
Your route then follows the coastal road E22 toward Norr-köping. Along the way there are ferry connections to Gotland from Oskarshamn and Västervik. If you have time, be sure to make a detour to the Swedish skerry coast at Västervik, or at Valdemarsvik/Fyrudden or St Anna south of Norrköping.
At Norrköping, the road continues north past the Hjälmaren to the intersection with the E20, where you follow the E20 to Gripsholm, 20 km (12 mi) beyond Strängnäs.

6 Gripsholm Castle Kurt Tucholsky created a literary monument out of this castle at Lake Mälaren. He is buried at the nearby village of Mariefred.
From Gripsholm Castle, the road follows the south-east bank of Lake Mälaren to the Swedish capital, Stockholm.

7 Stockholm (see page 71)

8 Uppsala This city is famous for having the oldest university in northern Sweden, founded in 1477, and Scandinavia's largest cathedral, the Domkyrka, which houses the remains of national heroes, kings Erik and Gustav Wasa. The 16th-century castle and the Carolina Redviva, the largest library in Sweden, are other worthwhile sights in this city on the Frysån River.
To the north is Gamla Uppsala with royal burial mounds and an 11th-century church. It was the country's political center until the 13th century.
From Uppsala, your route leads north to the harbor town of Gävle, marking the start of Highway 80, which you will take west to Falun.

9 Falun The Vikings allegedly mined copper in Falun, but the town's heyday as a center for copper processing ended in disaster: The mine collapse here in 1687 created Stora Stöten, said to be the largest hole in the world at 65 m (213 ft) deep, 370 m (1,214 ft) long and 220 m (722 ft) wide. The town's historic copper mine is a UNESCO World Heritage Site.
On Highway 70, you now head north-west to Lake Siljan, which you will almost completely circumnavigate on your trip.

10 Siljansee Dalarna is a densely forested province known for the carved wooden Dalarna horses. When travelling around the lake, it is worth stopping in Mora on the northern shore.
The town marks the end of the Wasa Track (86 km/53 mi). The "Zorngaarden", a museum by artist Anders Zorn, and the "Zorns Gammelgaarden" open-air museum is worth a visit. From Leksand at the southern end of the lake, you initially follow Highway 70 to Borlänge, where you change to Highway 60 towards Örebro.

11 Örebro In addition to the beautiful sculptures and monuments in this old city in central Sweden, it is also worth paying a visit to the 800-year-old castle on an island in the river, the 13th-century St Nicholas church and the more modern Svampen water tower.
From Örebro, the route now follows the E4 to Vättern via the town of Askersund.

12 Vättern Vättern is Sweden's second-largest lake. Plan a stop at the Göta Canal in Motala, which connects Vättern and Vänern, and in the garden city of Vadstena with its interesting minster and castle.
At the southern end of the lake is Jönköping. From there the route heads directly west to the port city of Göteborg.

13 Göteborg Sweden's second-largest city has a charming Old Town lined with canals. Highly recommended are a stroll down Kungsportsavenyn boulevard, a visit to Lieseberg amusement park and the futuristic new opera, and a boat ride through the ports, canals and islets.
From Gothenburg, it is not far to Bohuslän. Ferries depart Göteborg for Frederikshavn on the Danish Jutland peninsula via the Kattegat. Travel time is around three hours.

14 Frederikshavn The largest city in northern Jutland, Freder-

ikshavn is famous for the Krudt-tårnet, a 17th-century powder tower with a weapons collection spanning three centuries.
Before your journey continues south, it is worth making a small detour to the northern tip of the peninsula in Skagen.

15 Skagen About 150 years ago, a number of artists settled here on the northernmost tip of Jutland, formed an artists' colony and began creating what

1 View of Gripsholm Castle from the beach in Mariefred in Södermanland province. The castle has housed the National Portrait Collection since 1822.

2 Drottningholm Castle (1699) on the island of Lovø in Lake Mälar was modelled on Versailles and has been the residence of the royal family since 1981.

3 A village near Göteborg on the western Swedish coast in Västergötland.

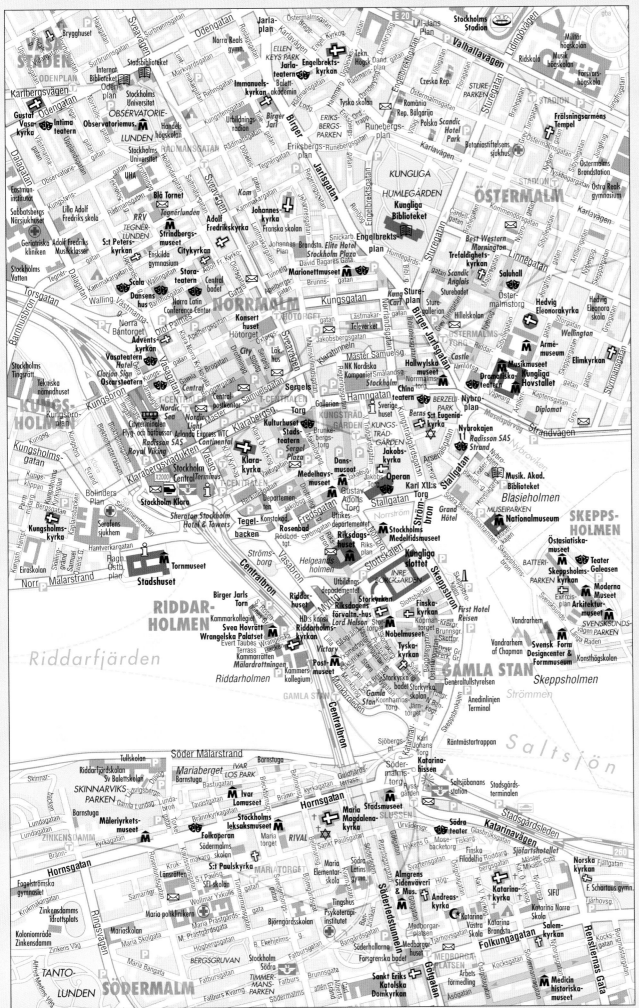

Stockholm

This metropolis, which is home to 1.6 million people, is spread out over fourteen islands at the southern end of Lake Mälar, on the skerry-rich Baltic Sea coast between fresh- and saltwater zones. Founded in 1252 and capital since 1634, Stockholm has developed into a cosmopolitan city, pulsating with diversity. Magnificent buildings, parks, rivers and bridges make it unique among its peers.

Particularly worth seeing in the Swedish capital are: the Royal City Castle (Kungliga Slottet), with around six hundred rooms one of the largest residences in the world; Storkyrkan, Stockholm's oldest church, with Gothic interior; Tyska Kyrkan, church of the German community with an impressive altar; Riddarholmkyrkan, royal burial site since the Thirty Years War; the baroque Reich Chamber of Corporations Riddarhuset; the picturesque harbor quarter between Österlanggatan and Skeppsbron; Stadshus (1911–1923), an icon of the city with a stunning view from the tower; Konserthuset, annual venue of the Nobel Prize ceremony. Some worthwhile museums include: the Nationalmuseet and Moderna Museet (modern art);

Top: Stockholm in winter.
Bottom: 17th-century row houses.

Skansen, the oldest open-air museum in the world; Vasamuseet with the flagship of Gustav II Adolf Vasa, sunk during its launch in 1628. Also worth seeing are the subway stations with artistic decoration ("the longest gallery in the world"); the magnificent Strandvägen boulevard; Stockholm's skerry garden and the residence of the royal family, Drottningholm Castle, with fully functional rococo theater.

Detour

Bohuslän

The region north of Göteborg was named after the 13th-century Bohus Fort ruins near Kungälv. The Bohuslän coast is rich in fjords and skerries and often compared to the coast of southern France because of its picturesque fishing villages and exclusive spa resorts.

One of the most beautiful routes in all of Sweden is the trip to Tjörn and Orust, Bohuslän's largest islands, connected to each other and the mainland by bridges. Animal lovers will enjoy Sweden's largest sea aquarium, Havets Hus in Lysekil, and the Nordens Ark zoo near Smøgen, which specializes in Nordic species. The rock drawings near Tanums-

Top: Coastal landscape near Malmö.
Bottom: Prehistoric rock paintings at Tanumö.

hede are impressive; the only one of Bohuslän's many Bronze Age discovery sites to be included in the UNESCO World Heritage list. The engravings were done between 1800 and 800 BC, and their present-day enhanced tints allow them to be identified more easily.

The climax of the approximately 200-km (124-mi) excursion is the boat-shaped Viking formation near Blomsholm and the 420-m-long (460-yd), 60-m-high (67-yd) Svine-sund Bridge near the border with Norway.

would become icons of Danish painting. Their collective works can be seen in the Skagen Museum and in the Michael and Anna Ancher House. Don't miss the Tilsandede Church, which was ultimately abandoned in 1795 due to the incessant sand that blew onshore here.

16 Sæby The half-timbered fishing houses, cutter port and minster with 15th-century frescos, this spa town is a quaint little bit of paradise. The Saeby-gaard Manor (the oldest part of which dates back to 1576) is also worth seeing. The nearby Voer-gaard Renaissance castle houses a world-class art and porcelain collection.

17 Aalborg The Limfjord and Aalborg are best viewed from the 105-m (345-ft) Aalborgtår-net tower. The Budolfi Cathedral is dedicated to the patron saint of sailors. Jens Bang's Stenhus, the home of a rich merchant built in 1624, and the North Jutland Art Museum should also not be missed.

18 Viborg The cathedral in Denmark's oldest city had to be completely rebuilt in the 19th century. Its ceiling frescos and the medieval quarter are worth seeing, as are the limestone mines, which were shut down in the 1950s after nearly one thousand years of mining. They are in front of the city gates.

19 Århus Denmark's second-largest city was built on a former Viking settlement. The St Clements church, begun in 1200, is Denmark's largest cathedral. The Den Gamle By is the first open-air museum for non-royal Danish culture. Architect, Arne Jacobsen, helped design the Raad-huset, completed in 1942. A 2,000-year-old preserved body

found in the marshland is the main attraction of the Moesgård Museum.

20 Vejle This "mountain town" has a spectacular location on the fjord of the same name. St Nicolai Church is the oldest building in the town and is home to something creepy: a 2,500-year-old preserved body found in the marshland and the walled-in skulls of 23 robbers. The graphic art in the museum and the city's landmark, a wind-mill, are worth seeing. North-west of Vejle is the UNESCO World Heritage Site of Jelling, with impressive burial mounds and two royal rune stones from the 10th century, which are considered to be "Denmark's baptismal certificates".
The Jutland mainland is connected to Fyn island with a railway road bridge and a highway bridge (Storebæltsbro). The island's capital is the next stop.

21 Odense Hans Christian Andersen made this island capital world famous. His childhood home and museum are dedi-

cated to him, while the Carl Nielsen Museum, the Old Town and the Gothic St Knuds Church are other attractions.
From Odense, Highway 9 leads to the next stop, Egeskov.

22 Egeskov This little 16th-century castle with its cemetery and drawbridge is one of the best-known moated castles in Europe. It has an interesting park with baroque landscaping and a nice vintage car museum. From the south of the island it's on to Nyborg on the east coast, where the 18-km (11-mi) Store-bæltbro bridge spans the Great Belt between Fyn and Sjælland.

23 Trælleborg Not far from Slagelse is the Viking fort of Trælleborg, built according to strict geometric theory and dedicated to King Harald Bluetooth (10th century).

24 Roskilde This city's cathedral is a UNESCO World Heritage Site. Thirty-eight Danish regents were buried here. The five preserved Viking ships, discovered in the adjacent Roskilde fjord,

are worth seeing and are presented in the modern Vikinge-skibs Museet.
Finally, you pass Frederiksborg castle to Helsingör at the northern end of Sjælland.

25 Helsingør The main attraction of this city located on the Strait of Öresund is Kronborg castle. Another 50 km (31 mi) or so along the coast and you arrive back in Copenhagen, the end of your journey.

1 The Renaissance Kronborg castle near Helsingør on the strait between Denmark and Sweden.

2 A walk through the open-air museum Den Gamle By in Århus shows you the old Denmark.

3 Roskilde was the summer residence of the Danish kings from the 11th to the 15th centuries. Many Danish rulers are buried in the Romanesque-Gothic cathedral.

4 Frederiksborg castle near Hillerød, north of Copenhagen, houses the National Historic Museum.

Lake landscape near Strängnäs Gustav Wasa was elected king of Sweden in this city on Lake Mälaren in 1523.

Skerry coast off Stockholm The rock islands that stretch along a 150-km (93-mi) belt are a popular weekend refuge for city dwellers.

Stockholm Magnificent buildings, parks, waterways and bridges make Sweden's capital unique. It stretches over fourteen islands between the Baltic Sea and Lake Mälaren.

Vadstena Castle St Birgitta lived in this town on Lake Vättern. The Blue Church is worth seeing.

Drottningholm Castle This castle on an island in Lake Mälaren is the primary residence of the royal family and has a functional rococo theater.

Uppsala This is the oldest university town in the north (from 1477) and is home to Scandinavia's oldest church: 120-m-long (394-ft) and just as high, the Domkyrka, where famous Swedes are buried.

Tanumshede The most remarkable of Bohuslän's Bronze Age discoveries are the rock paintings depicting everyday scenes and cultish activities.

Bohuslän This region stretches north of Göteborg up to the Norwegian border and features a long coastline with numerous bays.

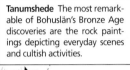

Gripsholm One of the most popular tourist attractions outside Stockholm is the castle on Lake Mälaren. Kurt Tucholsky, whose novel made the castle famous, is buried in Mariefred cemetery.

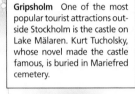

Århus Denmark's second-largest city is home to the country's largest place of worship, the St Clemes Kirke. The Den Gamle By open-air museum is the second-largest of its kind in Europe.

Öland This is the second-largest island in Sweden and is connected to the mainland by a bridge. The beaches are fabulous and the Swedish royal family stays here in summertime.

Gotland Sweden's largest island can be reached by ferry and is popular for its comparatively mild climate. The bizarre rock formations off the coast are a big draw for visitors.

Egeskov Castle This moated castle is surrounded by thick oak forests, from which its name is derived. The castle's park and vintage car museum are also worth a visit.

Copenhagen Denmark's capital is busy yet cozy. Its highlights include the Lille Havfrue (Little Mermaid) and the Tivoli Gardens. Pictured here is the Amalienborg Palace.

Landscape near Ystad Fishing (especially for herring) brought wealth to the region around Ystad, which was traditionally focused on agriculture.

Bornholm The "Pearl of the Baltic" is actually quite far from Denmark. It is home to almost all types of Scandinavian scenery as well as many tourist attractions.

Kalmar Castle The union of Denmark, Sweden and Norway, decreed in the Kalmar Union, took place in Kalmar's magnificent castle in 1397. The cathedral is also worth seeing.

St Petersburg: Smolni Cathedral and Resurrection Monastery.

Finland and Russia

From the empire of the Czars to the land of a thousand lakes

Finland is a quiet country with countless lakes and seemingly endless forests. It is ideal for visitors looking for a bit of peace and seclusion. From Finland's capital, Helsinki, you can also make a detour to St Petersburg, Russia, just a few hours away.

The iconic animal of the Arctic far north, the moose, is very common in Finland. In fact, the very shape of the country is similar to the head of a female elk, and a look at any map of Finland will make it obvious why the "Elk Head" is considered the "Land of a Thousand Lakes": the complex maze of roughly 50,000 to 60,000 bodies of inland water dominates the entire southern half of the country. Approximately 12 percent of "Suomi", the Finnish name for Finland, is covered by freshwater, and nearly 70 percent by forest. The ever-changing landscape of breathtaking waterways, lakes and vast

forests make Finland a dream destination for anyone seeking a quiet, relaxing holiday. Having said that, however, the Finnish Baltic Sea coast along the Gulf of Bothnia and the Gulf of Finland is also a very impressive landscape, with offshore skerry (rock) islands, innumerable bays and long, sandy beaches, picturesque villages perfect for bathing and fishing, and a verdant green hinterland. In addition to that are the slightly more melancholy fjell and tundra regions north of the Arctic Circle.

Finland offers ideal conditions for winter sports between the months of November

19th-century icons of Konevitsa in Kuopio.

and May, but the icy-cold temperatures and the somewhat bleak darkness of the long polar nights may deter. They are also the reason why the Finns are often considered a rather serious and quiet folk. In reality, however, they are a fun-loving and relaxed people who place great value on family and, as soon as summer starts, spend much of their free time outside picking berries, gathering mushrooms, fishing, swimming, boating or just lounging around. They also use the time to "tank up" on light and warmth for the long winters, forgetting time and space and simply enjoying the relief from winter. For 1.5 million music, film, literature, jazz, choir, theater and dance enthusiasts from all over the world, the summer festivals in Finland are the highlight of the year. No other country boasts as many festivals per capita.

Above: the 150-year-old cathedral behind the statue of Czar Alexander II at Senate Square in Helsinki. An imposing staircase leads to the cathedral, whose interior includes a statue of Agricola, Finland's reformer.

St Petersburg: the magnificent baroque building of the Nicholas Naval Cathedral on the Griboyedov canal.

Nearly everyone who visits Finland is there for its natural scenic charm, and less so for its cities. But that is not to say they are without their own charms. And this does not just apply to the neoclassical capital, Helsinki, or Turku, the former capital on the Gulf of Bothnia. Finland's coast is home to plenty of picturesque fishing and holiday towns where, not surprisingly, Swedish culture and language are also widespread. Meanwhile, there is a distinct Russian feel in Karelia, Finland's "Wild East". The Sami settlements beyond the Arctic Circle, like the one on Lake Inari, are also fascinating. Even Finland's unique language should not represent a hindrance as far as pronunciation. Finnish is the one of the few languages in the world to have largely solved the exasperating problem of one sound, one letter. This means you can read "suomalainen" and say it correctly without any overly complex pronunciation rules. Most Finns understand a bit of English and German as well, and only one little Finnish term is actually truly essential: "sauna". Only those who have enjoyed this 2,000-year-old Finnish body wellness ritual have experienced the "true" Finland.

From Helsinki, or one of the coastal towns on the Gulf of Finland, it is also worth taking a trip to the Russian cities of St Petersburg and Novgorod to the south, especially during the "White Nights". Both are Hanseatic cities with unique architectural and cultural treasures. The historic center of St Petersburg, with its beautiful churches, magnificent palaces, museums, canals and bridges, is listed as a UNESCO World Heritage Site, as are the churches of Novgorod.

Most of Finland's lakes are in the south of the country and are connected by rivers and canals.

Helsinki's modern architecture

The fact that Helsinki has a wealth of world-famous modern architecture is mainly due to the devastating blazes that continuously destroyed the city, which was once built of wood: in 1812, after Helsinki was elevated to the status of capital, Czar Alexander I commissioned architect Carl Ludwig Engel (Berlin, 1778–1840), to build stone reconstructions in a neoclassical style, including the cathedral and the university on Senate Square. In the early 20th century, a Finnish version of Art Nouveau architecture known as "National Romanticism" (national museum, main train station) developed. Alvar Aalto's (1898–1976) archi-

Top: National Opera in Helsinki.
Center: Underground rock church.
Bottom: Finlandia Hall, one of Alva Aalto's main works.

tectural style was rational in the 1920s (the parliament buildings) and evolved into aesthetical functionalism during the 1930s. His Finlandia Hall, from 1970, and other buildings throughout the world have indeed influenced entire generations of architects, including the Suomalainen brothers (rock church, 1996). Aalto's principle of "organic" construction, which involves the extensive use of natural materials and shapes, continues to characterize Finnish architecture even today.

The Finlandia Route: the wonders of Finland, St Petersburg and the North Cape on one, albeit long journey. Follow our route through the diversity of southern Finland (Route I) and Lake Saimaa before connecting with Route II, which takes you through Karelia's wild forests toward the northern tip of Europe.

Route I – Southern Finland

❶ Helsinki (see page 77)
Your journey through southern Finland begins in the capital.

❷ St Petersburg For more details, look in the Travel Information box and on pages 78–79.

❸ Ekenäs/Tammisaari The "City of Oaks" is known for the national park just off the coast that features picturesque skerry, or rock, islands. Wooden houses from the 17th and 18th century can be found in the historic center of Ekenäs, while Alvar Aalto's bank building showcases more modern architecture. Raasepori Castle, located outside of town, is a curious place: At the time of its construction in the 14th century, it could only be reached by boat; now it is located in the country's interior.

❹ Hangö/Hanko The Hangö headland sits at the foothills of the Salpausselkä mountains and is mostly covered in dense forest. Finland's southernmost mainland point is a sailing, swimming and fishing paradise for Finns looking to take it easy amidst the skerry gardens or on the

many sandy beaches. The Art Nouveau villas in the park were built at the turn of the 20th century.
Back in Ekenäs, Road 184 leads to Salo on the Lappdalsfjärden. From there it heads back to the unique skerry coast.

❺ Turku/Åbo The skerry garden off the coast of Turku has over 20,000 islands of varying sizes and is one of the Finland's most popular attractions. Only a few buildings in the former capital survived what proved to be Scandinavia's largest fire in 1827: Turunlinna Castle, a solid stone building (built in the late 13th century), and Turku's brick cathedral, consecrated in 1290.

❻ Naantali This town has managed to preserve its late 18th- and early 19th-century architectural charm, the main attraction being the Old Town, the Minster, and the Kultarnata

1 The Uspensky Cathedral towers over the harbor in Helsinki.

2 The skerry gardens off the Finnish coast near Tammisaari.

Travel information

Route profile
Length:
Route I: 1,350 km (839 mi),
Route II (from Juva):
1,400 km (870 mi)
Time required: at least two weeks; do not underestimate the return journey!
Start and end: Helsinki

Traffic information:
The green insurance card is recommended. Video devices must be declared. Vehicle nationality labels are required and low-beam lights during the day are compulsory. Watch out for deer crossings.

When to go:
Route I: June–September
Route II: July–end of August

Accommodation:
Holiday homes, or "mökkis", with sauna facilities are popular of Finland.

Information:
Here are some websites to help you prepare for your trip:
www.visitfinland.com
www.alltravelfinland.com

St Petersburg and Nizhny Novgorod:
The best way to arrive in St Petersurg is to take a ferry from Helsinki or other Finnish port towns, or take a bus from Lappeenranta. There are also good bus or rail connections to Russia from other towns in Finland.

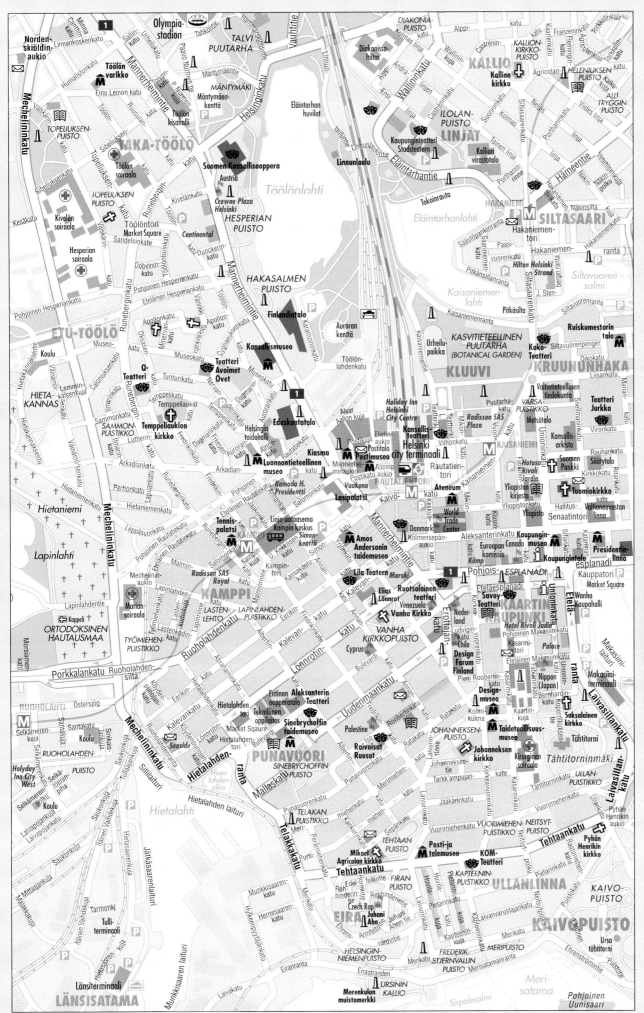

Helsinki

Roughly 500,000 people live in Helsinki, Finland's compact capital, which was founded in 1550 by Swedish King Gustav Vasa. Following devastating fires, Czar Alexander II commissioned Berlin architect, Carl Ludwig Engel, to rebuild Helsinki in the popular neo-classical style of the time. Twenty of the monuments erected between 1820 and 1850 still stand today. Combined with well-known Art Nouveau buildings and other contemporary edifices, the metropolis on the Gulf of Finland offers a unique and enjoyable cityscape.

Amond the attractions in Helsinki, Engel's Senate Square is considered one of the most beautiful plazas in the world. It includes the cathedral, the government palace, the main university campus and the university library. At its center is the statue of Czar Alexander II. The market square and historic market halls at the southern harbor has ferry piers for ships to Suomenlinna, an old Swedish island fort and UNESCO World Heritage Site, and to the skerry islands. The Katajanokka Peninsula has the best panoramic view of the capital. The

View of the cathedral from the harbor.

beautiful Orthodox Uspenski Cathedral (1868) has a lavish interior. Luotsikatu, one of the most magnificent streets in Helsinki has numerous Art Nouveau buildings. The Esplanade, Helsinki's pedestrian zone, is home to Stockmann department store, the largest in Scandinavia.

Museums include the Ateneum (Finnish), the Kiasma (modern) and the Sinebrychoff (foreign). Take a look at the central station with a 48-m-high (158-ft) clock tower, the Suomalainen brothers' rock church (1969), Alvar Aalto's Finlandia Hall (1970), where the last stage of the CSCE act was signed in 1975. The tower at the Olympic stadium provides a fantastic view over Helsinki.

Detour

St Petersburg

Czar Peter the Great planned his city down to the finest detail. First founded in 1703, St Petersburg was meant to be the Russian "window to the West" and it was here on the banks of the Neva that his vision of progress was realized. The entire city was to be built of stone, an innovation in and of itself, and since then, it has developed into one of Russia's most important cultural, political and economic centers. Since its founding, the city's name has changed three times: Petrograd, Leningrad and finally back to St Petersburg, where the October Revolution began. It is well worth paying a visit during the "White Nights" in June when it is still light at midnight.

The square with the mighty Alexander Column (1832) in front of the Winter Palace is a sight along with the mag-

nificently decorated Czars' residence, which has been extended many times. The Hermitage Museum in the Winter Palace is worth a visit including the adjoining buildings. It has a renowned art collection.

Around the palace square you'll find Alexander Park with the architecturally unique Admiralty (UNESCO World Heritage Site), whose golden spire is one of the city's landmarks; Senate Square with the Peter the Great monument; St Isaac's Cathedral (19th century), the largest and most lavishly decorated church in Russia with its golden cupola; Yussupov Palace on the banks of the Moika; St Nicholas' Naval Cathedral with its shiny gold domes (18th century); and the Mariinsky Theater, the world-famous opera and ballet playhouse.

The historic city center (UNESCO World Heritage Site) includes the Peter and Paul Fortress (18th century) with Peter's Gate; the burial site of the czars in the Peter and Paul Cathedral; the crownwork with artillery museum; the Central Naval Museum in the former stock exchange; the art chamber with the rarities collection of Peter the Great and the Lomonossov Museum; the 18th-century science academy; the red and white complex of the twelve councils (1721), today a university; and the baroque Menshikov Palace with a museum on the culture at the time of Peter the Great.

Around the majestic boulevard of Nevsky Prospekt you will find: Kasaner Cathedral; Resurrection Church (1907); Stroganov Palace (1754); Arts Square with the Michaelmas Palace and the Russian Museum; the Ethnography Museum; Anitshkov Palace with Anitshkov Bridge; and the baroque Belosselsky-Belosersky Palace.

Also worth seeing are: the Summer Garden, the city's oldest park with the Summer Palace from 1710, and the Marble Palace; Alexander Nevsky Monastery with its neoclassical Trinity Cathedral; Tilchvin and Lazarus cemetery and Smolni Resurrection Monastery with the baroque Resurrection Cathedral; Pushkin Theater and Pushkin Museum, Dostoyevsky Museum; Sheremetev Palace with the Anna Achmatova Museum.

Don't miss the UNESCO World Heritage Site of Novogorod while you are here. The "New City" is some 200 km (124 mi) south-west on Lake Ilmen, on the main road to Moscow. Despite its name, Novgorod is one of Russia's oldest cities, founded in the 9th century with close ties to the Hanseatic League, which had a branch office in Novgorod. The walled Kremlin of the former city state, which existed from the 12th to the 17th centuries and is protected by nine towers, is indeed imposing. Novgorod's churches, built between the 12th and 14th centuries in a great variety of styles, are also famous. At the time, almost every residential street and guild had its own ornate church.

1 The Winter Palace: a masterpiece of Russian baroque.

2 St Isaac's Cathedral is the largest and most magnificent church in St Petersburg.

3 The Grand Palace, summer residence of the czars, is in Pushkin (Tsarskoe Selo) near St Petersburg and was built in 1724, for Catherine the Great, wife of Peter III.

4 The lavishly fanciful focal point of Peter I's summer residence is the great baroque palace near St Petersburg.

Savonlinna

Savonlinna is located at the heart of a complex maze of a thousand lakes in what is known as the Saimaa lake district. The main attractions of this charming area include the provincial museum, located in a former granary on Riihisaari Island in front of the castle gates; the Mikko, Savonlinna and Salama museum ships, the market square with a pier for boat excursions into the Saimaa lake district, and the 100-year-old Rauhalinna wooden villa, which is just outside of town.

The Olavinlinna fort, built in 1475, and reached via a pontoon bridge, is considered one of Finland's most beautifully preserved medieval castle complexes and has hosted the

Olavinlinna was the first Finnish castle to be built during the time of firearms.

Savonlinna opera festivals for more than thirty years. This festival is the largest regular cultural event in Finland. The town of Savonlinna, located about 330 km (205 mi) from Helsinki, is also happily known as the "Bayreuth of the North", a German city with a lovely Old Town and a very popular opera and music festival. The event is also often likened to the Salzburg Festival.

Many performances are held in the castle's inner courtyard under a canvas tent or in the Savonlinna concert hall, famous for its wonderful acoustics. The festival takes place from July to early August. For more detailed information, visit the official Internet site at: www.operafestival.fi

Castle, which is the summer residence of Finland's president. Anyone wishing to experience the skerry garden up close can follow a small access road to Pulkkalla. The N8 leads to Rauma at the Gulf of Bothnia.

7 Rauma Finland's third-oldest city is an important center for top bobbin lace making. The historic Old Town, which has been completely unaffected by any fires over the last 320 years, has been declared a World Heritage Site: 600 wooden buildings form the largest inner city complex of this kind in all of Scandinavia. From Pori take the N8 to the N2, which leads to Forssa and from there head to Hämeenlinna.

8 Hämeenlinna The birth house of composer Jean Sibelius (1865–1957), the Häme brick castle from the 13th century, and Aulanko Park are all among the attractions here.

9 Lahti This famous winter sports town is situated on an impressive moraine tuffet with two lakes. It impresses visitors with its six ski jumps and a small ski museum. The Church of the Cross (built in 1978, designed by Alvar Aalto) and the Sibelius Hall are considered architectural gems. Lahti is also the gateway to Finland's lake region, while the Salpausselkä mountains and Vesijärvi and Päijänne lakes offer a variety of leisure options.

The landscape along the N5 to Mikkeli affords visitors everything they would expect of the "Land of a Thousand Lakes".

10 Mikkeli This city is situated in a rolling hills landscape and was built on orders from Czar Nicholas I in 1838. It had already become an important center in eastern Finland during the Middle Ages. A small stone chapel from 1320 in the market square dates back to this time as well. The largest wooden vicarage in Finland – Kenkävero — is in the town center. Roughly 700 lakes and ponds surround the city, and marshlands stretch off toward the north. Dark-green forests, shimmering lakes, a few villages and some remote summer homes are scattered along the way to Savonlinna and Kerimäki. Those wanting to travel up to the North Cape must initially stay on the N5 and not turn off toward Savonlinna.

11 Kerimäki The world's largest wooden church is located in the small town of Kerimäki, north of

Savonlinna. Its benefactor – an emigrant who found wealth in America – provided the building plans in feet, but the Finnish architect built it in metres, hence its unintended dimensions (27 m (89 ft) high with a capacity of 5,000). The tiny village only has about 6,000 people!

12 Retretti and Punkaharju Beyond Savonlinna, it is worth making a stop at the Retretti art center – partly above ground and partly in caves – and at the mile-long moraine hill Punkaharju, which stretches between Lakes Pihlajavesi and Puruvesi. The rest of the journey on the N6 from Sääkjsalmi runs between the lake district and the Russian border.

13 Imatra on Lake Saimaa Imatra, a lively garden city on the Russian border, is located in the main basin of Lake Saimaa, the largest in Finland. The "Lake of a Thousand Islands" is known for its ringed seal population living in freshwater. In Imatra, it is worth visiting the community center, designed by Alvar Aalto, in the Vuoksennista district, and the Vuoksa waterfalls, mostly "subdued" for a power plant.

14 Lappeenranta This old garrison city is located on the Saimaa canal, which runs for 50-km (31-mi) from the lake district past the Russian border to the Gulf of Finland. All kinds of

cruises are available on Lake Saimaa and they depart from Finland's largest inland port. Most of the city's attractions are located outside the old fortress section of Lappeenranta, whose ramparts have been partially reconstructed.

The Orthodox church is the oldest in the country (1785) and is worth a visit. Near Luumäki, Route 25 takes you to Haminia on the Gulf of Finland.

15 Hamina/Vehkalahti The Swedish ramparts here from the early 18th century are worth seeing. They were designed to replace the Vyborg fort that fell to the Russians, but they were again seized by the Russians before their completion. Hamina's charming octagonal market square, in the center of which is the town hall from 1789, is an urban gem.

16 Kotka The main attractions in Finland's largest export harbor are the Orthodox St Nicholas' Church (1795), a simple edifice with an ornately decorated wall, and the grand buildings from the 19th century (trade union house, town hall, savings bank). The coastal road to Porvoo affords breathtaking views of the deep fjords and the skerry coastline.

17 Porvoo/Borgå This town has two old quarters: the Old Town plastered in header brick

with a Gothic brick cathedral, and a "younger" Old Town with neoclassical stone buildings. The red warehouse sheds on the shores of the Porvoonjoki are from the 18th and 19th centuries and worth seeing. The best view of the country's second-oldest city is from the old bridge. Helsinki, the final stop on the Route I section, is another 51 km (32 mi) from here.

Route II Juva – North Cape

18 Kuopio The city's Orthodox Church Museum shows you how deeply Russian Orthodox beliefs are rooted in the Karelian community. It has one of the most famous collections of its kind in Western Europe.

Not far from the museum, a trailhead leads you up to the Puijo at 232 m (761 ft), where you get a spectacular view of the university town and the lakes and forests of Karelia from the 75-m-high (246-ft-) tower.

19 Kajaani This industrial city on the Oulujärvi is particularly worth seeing for its Kajaaninlinna Castle (17th to 20th centuries) and the minuscule town

1 The historic center of Rauma, declared a UNESCO World Heritage Site in 1991.

2 An attractive rapeseed field on the way through southern Finland.

Looking out over the lake district near Kuopio in the province of Savo. Finland's nickname, "Land of a Thousand Lakes", is rather an understatement around here: more than 50,000 lakes, of all sizes and often connected to each other, cover approximately one-tenth of the country.

The old trading city of Nizhny Novgorod and its port on the ice-covered Volga River.

Russia

Moscow and the Golden Ring

The Golden Ring is really a must-see for enthusiasts of Russian art and architecture. The name itself actually refers to a ring of charming old towns north of Moscow – gems of Old Russia. They are localities that could easily be the setting for Russian novels, and the historic monasteries and churches are indeed testimony to a bygone era.

The term Golden Ring, which was first coined in Russia at the start of the 1970s, refers to a series of Old Russian towns north of Moscow, the main ones being Vladimir, Suzdal, Yaroslavl, Rostov Velikiy, Sergiev Posad, Pereslavl-Zalessky and Kostroma. Moscow itself is also included. These Old Russian centers originally evolved from former medieval fortresses built as protection against the Mongolians. Their mighty kremlins – defensive complexes – monasteries and churches were endowed with magnificent mosaics,

icons and valuable treasures and represented a stark contrast to the misery of everyday life in these rural towns. While the term "Golden" refers to the striking, gilded domes of the medieval churches, the word "Ring" denotes the close cultural and historical links between the individual towns. Today they still stand as testimony to the "Old Russia" that existed until the October Revolution and which was a deeply religious nation.

The towns of the Golden Ring are spread out across the broad, undulating plains

The New Virgin Convent in Moscow

which, shaped by the forces of multiple ice ages, extend to the south-east from the Gulf of Finland. The predominantly continental climate is characterized by warm summers and cold winters. Average temperatures in January are -11 °C (14 °F), while July reaches an average of about 19 °C (65 °F). Annual rainfall measures roughly 530 mm (209 in). The landscape along the upper reaches of the Volga and its tributaries, the Oka and Kama, is dominated by sizable rivers and lakes.

What most people would consider Russian history begins in the 10th century on the banks of the Dnepr, in Kiev, home to the Slavic tribes who traded with the passing Varangians from the north. It was only in the mid-11th century that the Russian heartland shifted towards the north-east, to the Golden Ring. The relatively mild climate, navigable rivers and

Red Square is Moscow's largest and most famous square. St Basil's Cathedral at the southern end draws everybody's attention.

Moscow: the Kremlin with the Great Kremlin Palace, the Cathedral of the Dormition and "Ivan the Great" bell tower.

existing trade routes that traversed the region led settlers to establish a series of towns during this period (9th–11th centuries). The population quickly rose to between 10,000 and 20,000.

With the collapse of the first Russian Empire, Vladimir became the successor to Kiev in the mid-12th century. During the same period, many residents of Kiev left the city for the Golden Ring region. The towns there became the capitals of powerful principalities. Rostov, Suzdal and Vladimir, for example, had already become trading centers as well as hubs of secular and religious power even before the founding and rise of mighty Moscow. At that time, Moscow was part of the principality of Vladimir-Suzdal. In the 13th century, the Mongolians subordinated the Russian Empire and forced substantial tributes from its inhabitants.

Moscow, at that time of minimal significance, eventually spearheaded the battle against the "Golden Horde", leaving the other principalities of the Ring to sink into obscurity after the end of the 14th century. Although chased out of the European zone, the Mongolians continued to leave their mark on Russia's Asian territories until the late 15th century.

An important ally of the Russian state at this time was the Orthodox Church, whose churches, monasteries and monasticism created a unified front.

A trip around the Golden Ring usually begins in Moscow, then continues through the large towns described on the following pages. However, there are also other interesting small towns to be found off the beaten track, such as Pushkino, Bratovscina, Rachmanowa, Muranovo or Abramtsevo.

Rostov Velikiy: A mighty wall encloses the kremlin and its picturesque churches.

The Kremlin

The word "kremlin" actually refers to the fortified sections of Old Russian towns. At the end of the 15th century, Italian architects built a 2-km-long (1.2-mi) wall around Moscow's Kremlin. It was between 15 and 20 meters (49 and 66 ft) in height and crowned with 19 towers. The wall forms a scalene triangle with one side running along the Moskva River. The Kremlin served as the residence of the Czars

The Moscow Kremlin complex covers around 28 hectares (69 acres).

and the Patriarchs of the Russian Orthodox Church until the 18th century. Its most important buildings include the Grand Kremlin Palace, the Armory Chamber housing Czarist treasures, the Patriarch's Palace, the Terem Palace, the Faceted Chamber, the Senate, the Arsenal and the barracks with the stables. The magnificent churches include the Annunciation, the Assumption and the Saviour's Cathedrals, as well as Ivan Veliky's bell tower dating from 1600.

Moscow and the Golden Ring: This poignant journey through the history of Old Russia begins in Moscow, continues via Rostov northwards as far as Kostroma, and then brings you back to Moscow via Ivanovo. During the trip you will be constantly confronted with the feeling that time has indeed stood still.

1 Moscow (see pages 88–89) Your route begins in Moscow before heading north towards Sergiev Posad, known as Zagorsk between 1931 and 1991.

2 Sergiev Posad The Monastery of the Holy Trinity and St Sergius (1340) is without doubt one of Russia's most important religious sites and serves as a pilgrimage destination for Orthodox Christians. It is encircled by a 1,600-m-long (1750 yard) wall that was breached once, albiet ultimately in vain, by Polish troops for sixteen months from 1608–1610.

Sergiev Posad was a national sanctuary even during the Czarist era and enjoyed unfettered support from the ruling class, who had their own residence in the complex, the Chertogi Palace (17th century). Large enough to accommodate a royal entourage of several hundred during official visits, the state converted the monastery into a museum in 1920 and it became a UNESCO World Heritage Site in 1993.

The Monastery of the Holy Trinity and St Sergius contains wonderful examples of paintings from Old Russia. The iconostase in the cathedral, for example, is decorated with works done by famous icon master Andrei Rublov and his assistants. The Holy Trinity was finished by the master himself.

The complex also displays outstanding examples of Russian architecture from the 14th to the 18th centuries. These defensive monasteries originally had several functions, as hospital wards, poorhouses, orphanages and schools. For a long time they were in fact the only institutions of their kind in all of Russia. The hospital building dates from the early 17th century, as do the adjoining churches St Zosima and St Sabbatius.

3 Pereslavl-Zalessky This Old Russian trading town is actually one of the oldest towns in the country and has a wealth of lovely churches and wooden houses. Located on the shores

of Lake Pleshchcyevo, the town was founded in the 10th/11th centuries, and its ramparts also date from this time.

The outer walls of the white cathedral from 1152, on the Red Square behind the walls of the town's kremlin, are decorated with semicircular ornaments called "zakomaras", important stylistic features typical in Old Russian architecture.

A few of the older remaining kremlin buildings include: the Church of the Metropolitan Peter from 1585; the 17th-century Annunciation Church with its spacious nave; the Goritsky Monastery dating from the first half of the 14th century; and the Danilov Monastery, located in the lower-lying south-western part of the town, which is from the 16th century.

Travel information

Route profile
Route length: 760 km (472 mi)
Time required: 8–10 days
Start and end: Moscow
Route (main locations):
Moscow, Sergiev Posad, Pereslavl-Zalessky, Rostov Veliky, Yaroslavl, Kostroma, Suzdal, Vladimir, Moscow

Special note:
There is a range of operators offering organized tours along the Golden Ring route. If you prefer to travel according to your own schedule, however, you have the option of hiring a car with a driver from Moscow.

Traffic information:
Entering Russia by car is possible, in theory, but it can be very complicated and time-consuming.
Entry visas require a passport, application and passport photograph.

Visiting the monasteries:
There are strict rules of conduct that apply in the various monasteries. Women need to wear a headscarf and a skirt; shorts and bare shoulders are taboo.
A film and photography permit is also required.

Further information:
Here are some websites to help you plan your trip:
www.thewaytorussia.net
www.russia-travel.com
www.geographia.com/russia
www.visitrussia.com
www.moscowcity.com

The Czars

Starting with Ivan IV (16th century), Russian rulers bore the title Czar, derived not from the Latin "Caesar" but from the oriental "Sar" (prince). For a long time it was the Rurikids who occupied the Czarist throne, but they were eventually succeeded by the Romanov family in the early 17th century.

Czar Peter the Great, who ruled from 1689–1725, was intent on reviving the Russian nation by means of sweeping reforms and wanted to bring the country more in line with its Western European counterparts. He also liked to refer to himself as "Emperor and Absolute Ruler". Following Peter's death, Russia was ruled

Top: Catherine II lays trophies from the Russian-Turkish War (1787–1792) at the tomb of Peter the Great. Below: The last Russian Czar, Nicholas II, and Czarina Alexandra Fyodorovna, were crowned in the Church of the Assumption in Moscow in May 1896.

4 Pereslavsky National Park This national park protects Lake Pleshcheyevo, the surrounding forest areas and wetlands, and the churches and cathedrals of Pereslavl-Zalessky. The lake is a breeding ground for 180 indigenous and thirty migratory bird species, and is home to brown bears as well. There is also a museum detailing the history of the Russian fleet and it was here that Czar Peter the Great built the first small battleships for mock warfare. It is the birthplace of the Russian navy.

5 Rostov Velikiy This city affords a panorama of stunning beauty, with its cathedral of seven silver roofs, a kremlin and the towers of the Monastery of Our Savior and St Jacob rising up beyond picturesque Lake Nero. The name Rostov Velikiy has special historical significance here: In Czarist Russia, only Novgorod and Rostov were entitled to use the adjunct "Velikiy", meaning great. The town, founded in 862, had already developed into a flourishing trading center by the Middle Ages.

The large kremlin in Rostov Velikiy is protected by a wall over 1 km (0.6 mi) long with eleven towers. Silver and gold domes crown the palace here. When Prince Andrei Bogolyubsky conquered the town in the 12th century, it became the largest and most beautiful town in his principality. He had the Cathedral of the Dormition built in 1162. Only fragments of the 12th-century frescoes survived. The five domes of the Church of the Assumption rise opposite the cathedral. The lovely Church of St John (17th century) on the banks of the Ishna River is also worth a visit as it is one of the very few surviving wooden churches in the region.

6 Yaroslavl Prince Yaroslav founded this fortified town at the confluence of the Kotorosl and the Volga rivers in the year 1010, and many of the original historical buildings have been preserved despite the ravages of war. The town enjoyed its golden age in the 17th century and the buildings from this era are among the loveliest in Russia.

1 Moscow's St Basil's Cathedral comprises eight small chapels, each with a tower, grouped around the central church tower.

2 The Monastery of the Holy Trinity and St Sergius in Sergiev Posad is considered a unique gem among Russian monasteries.

3 One of the loveliest monasteries in Pereslavl Zalessky is the Gorizky Monastery founded in 1328.

4 Rostov is one of the smallest towns along the Golden Ring.

by a numbers of Czarinas, or female Czars including Czarina Elizabeth and Czarina Catherine. Czar Alexander I was elemental in the victory over Napoleon in 1812/13, while his successor Nicholas I ultimately lost the Crimean War of 1853–1856. His successor Alexander II, however, was a reformist who put an end to Russia's serf-based society in 1861. Nicholas II, who reigned from 1894 to 1917, led Russia in World War I.

Of the last six Czars, three of them met with violent deaths: Paul I was strangled in 1801; Alexander II was killed by a terrorist bomb in 1881; and Nicholas II was shot together with his entire family in 1918 by the Bolsheviks. His death brought an end to the reign of the Russian Czars.

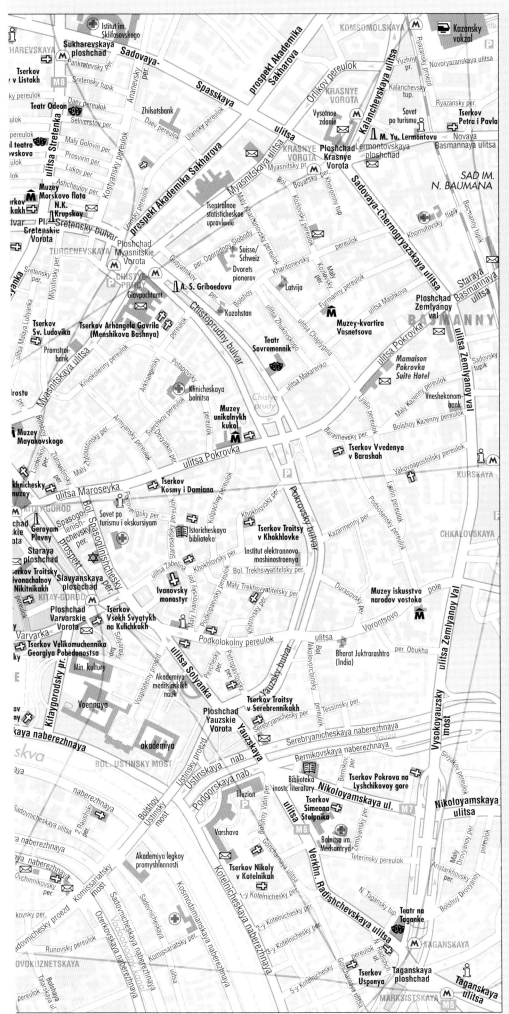

Moscow

Russia's capital lies on the Moskva River, which is a tributary of the mighty Volga. Mention was first made of Moscow in 1147, and it became the residence of the Grand Prince in 1325. In 1713, under Czar Peter the Great, Moscow lost its capital city status to the newly founded St Petersburg. In 1918, it was the Bolsheviks who once again made Moscow the political center of Russia's massive realm.

Moscow has been plundered repeatedly during its history, and has suffered a number of major fires. At the beginning of the 20th century, Moscow had 450 churches and twenty-five monasteries as well as 800 charitable institutions. Even after the decline of the Soviet Union, this city of 10 million still boasts impressive cultural statistics. Indeed, with roughly sixty theaters, seventy-five museums, over 100 colleges and 2,300 listed buildings, it is one of the world's top-ranking cities. The sights near Red Square include the enchanting St Basil's Cathedral (begun in 1555 under Ivan the Terrible in memory of the conquest of Kasan, consecrated in 1557, and completed in 1679), the Kremlin (citadel, former coronation venue, seat of power, and a

Vladimir Ilyich Lenin (1870–1924), as well as the tombs of numerous political figures and artists, the former artisan district of Kitaigorod and the GUM department store (1889–1893). Other attractions around Red Square include the Yelisseyev deli, the Duma, and the Bolshoi Theater.

Interesting sights near Arbatskaja Vorota Square include the seat of the Russian government (the "White House"), the Church of Christ the Savior (rebuilt 1994–1997), and the "Stalin high-rise buildings".

Other sights worth visiting include: the palatial Moscow subway stations (begun in the 1930s), the Tretyakov Gallery (Russian and Soviet art), the museums and the former artists' district of Arbat, the Pushkin Museum

Top: One of seven gingerbread style high-rises.
Bottom: Evening on the Moskva in the historic city center.

former prison) with twenty towers, the Great Stone Bridge, the Kremlin cathedrals (including the Uspenski Cathedral), the Alexander Garden, the remains of the Manege (former indoor riding arena that almost completely burned down in 2004) and the History Museum, the Kremlin Wall, the mausoleum with the mummified body of

of Fine Arts (also includes Western European art, the Priamos Treasure), the New Virgin Monastery including the "Celebrity Cemetery", the Lomonosov University (the oldest in Russia), Gorky Park with its sculpture garden and the lovely Kolomenskoye Church of the Ascension (southern outskirts of the city).

The twin towers of the Holsten Gate in Lübeck

Route 9

Germany, Poland, Baltic States

In the footsteps of the Hanseatic League

The Hanseatic route along the Baltic Sea from northern Germany through Poland and into the Baltic States is unique for its tranquility, impressive scenery and dreamy qualities. Time seems to stand still here, creating a magic that is singular to this coast and the villages and cities that line it.

During the last ice age, the Baltic Sea and the Baltic states were actually buried under a thick sheet of ice. After it melted away, the land, now free from the pressure of the ice, slowly began to rise. The Baltic land ridge – a hilly moraine landscape filled with lakes on the southern coast of the Baltic Sea – is a glacial rockfill region from this last ice age, and the Baltic Sea of course has added its own features to the coastal outline. It created impressive spits, the Courland Spit being one of the most beautiful, and carved out lagoons with tranquil inland bodies

of water like the Szczecin or Vistula lakes. The famous white chalk cliff coasts, owe their current appearance to the surging, post-ice age Baltic Sea.
The Baltic Sea is often known by its Latin name of Mare Balticum. "Balticum" is derived from "baltas", meaning "white" in Lithuanian and Latvian. Indeed, the beaches, dunes and craggy coastal cliffs practically sparkle in brilliant white. The Vorpommersche Boddenlandschaft, Jasmund, Slowinsky and Courland Spit national parks protect some of the most beautiful stretches of the Baltic coast.

Old Town alleyways in Estonia's capital, Tallinn.

Because the coastlines in Poland and the Baltic states are only sparsely populated, there is still enough room in the forests and marshlands for animals that have long been extinct in other parts of Europe: elks, bears, lynxes and wolves still have a natural habitat here. Storks nest in the countless church towers, while cranes brood in the marshlands.
Your journey passes through six of the countries lining the Baltic Sea. In addition to Germany and Poland, these include Lithuania, Latvia, Estonia and Russia – more specifically, Kaliningrad, a Russian exclave actually separated from Russia proper. The histories of these countries are closely intertwined with the Teutonic Order, and many of the castles and cities in the region were also members of the Hanseatic League. Since the collapse of the Soviet Union, the Baltic States have

The Dornbusch lighthouse is located at the northern tip of the sprawling Baltic Sea island of Hiddensee. It is much sandier than Rügen in the east and has no steep banks.

were built in the mid-15th century and modelled on Flemish bridge gates.

gained independence and are once again asserting their own cultural traditions.

A journey along the Baltic Sea coast is therefore in some ways a journey through time: back to before World War II – a period that is still tangible in the countryside – and the time of the Hanseatic League.

The League was an association of merchants established in the 12th century as a Germans response to the increasing risk of Baltic Sea trade. It quickly developed into a mighty urban and trading league that eventually ruled northern Europe economically for over 300 years. Many cities received their town charters in the 13th century, and the revolutionary Lübeck Law was adopted by over 100 Hanseatic cities. The Hanseatic League owes much of its success to its organization and vast capital, but also to the design of efficient ships such as the cog.

It had a wide hull, was initially oarless and intended as a sailing ship, and had high superstructural parts that allowed it to transport loads over 550 tons. Confident merchants and municipal rulers then built magnificent churches, palaces and town halls in the brick Gothic style now typical of the Baltic Sea region, and their robust Hanseatic ships used the church towers as orientation points along the coast. Many churches in the various Hanseatic cities are dedicated to St Nicholas, the patron saint of sailors and fishermen, or the pilgrims' patron saint, St James the Elder.

The decline of the Hanseatic League began in the 15th century as decreasing numbers of Germans chose to migrate east, and the Hanseatic League finally lost its supremacy to the increasingly powerful kingdom of Poland and Lithuania.

Sunrise over Gdańsk: The brick building of St Mary's Church towers over the Rechtstadt area.

The Roland Column (1360)

The Roland Column on Bremen's market square is the port city's oldest monument. The 5.5-m-tall (18-ft) figure represents freedom from market and import tariffs as well as high court jurisdiction and municipal law. Originally, a wooden statue stood at this site but it was set ablaze in 1366 by soldiers loyal to Archbishop Adalbert II. The second Roland, once again made of wood, was eventually replaced by the current stone version in 1404.

In 1513, the dais was added along with the two-headed eagle plaque and transcript, which urges the good

Roland in Bremen's market square.

citizens of Bremen to thank God for the freedom that Emperor Karl gave the city.

Over the centuries, the Roland Column has become a general symbol of freedom and can actually be found in a number of northern German cities, particularly in those with the Magdeburg city charter. Roland is usually depicted as a warrior holding a shiny sword but not wearing helmet.

Roland is the hero of the *Song of Roland* in which, in 778, as margrave of Brittany and in conjunction with Emperor Charlemagne, he fought against the Muslim Moors who had conquered the Iberian Peninsula during the early 8th century. Roland was killed that same year in the Battle of Roncesvalles in the Pyrenees. The *Song of Roland*, which made the protagonist into one of the emperor's nephews, and which enjoyed a huge revival in popularity in the 13th century, keeps the memory of his heroic feats alive.

The Hanseatic route: Passing through the lowlands of northern Germany, along the Bay of Mecklenburg and the Baltic Sea coasts of Poland, Lithuania, Latvia and Estonia, your path mirrors the trading routes of the Hanseatic League, where ports and merchant cities characterized by traditional brick architecture line the road like pearls on a necklace.

❶ Bremen (see page 96) The journey begins in the Free Hanseatic City of Bremen which, with Bremerhaven 50 km (31 mi) north, forms the smallest of the federal German states. On the way to Stade, the B74 leads past Teufelsmoor, north-west of Bremen.

❷ Stade This small town on the lower Elbe was an important trading port more than 1,000 years ago, but Vikings destroyed the castle in 994. Stade became a Hanseatic League member in the mid-13th century, but nearby Hamburg soon challenged its dominance.

On the way to Hamburg, the road passes through the Altes Land (Old Country). In Germany's largest fruit production region, it is worth seeing the traditional farming villages, particularly in spring when the trees are in bloom. It was not until the 12th and 13th centuries that an elaborate drainage system allowed the once marshy lower Elbe to be cultivated.

South of Hamburg you can take some interesting detours to Lüneburg and the Lüneburger Heide (see margin on page 95).

❸ Hamburg (see page 97) Those not wishing to drive into Hamburg's city center should take the A1 to the port city of Lübeck.

❹ Lübeck This merchant settlement founded in the 12th cen-

tury was given the status of Free Imperial City by Emperor Friedrich II in 1226. The city became the voice of "foreign affairs" for the German Hanseatic League when it was founded, and the first General Hanseatic Day was held in Lübeck in 1356. At the end of the 13th century, Lübeck was the most densely populated city in Germany after Cologne and, with 25,000 inhabitants by 1500, it was one of the largest cities in Europe.

Some of Lübeck's most important attractions are in the medieval Old Town, which was extensively rebuilt after the destruction of World War II and which is completely surrounded by moats and the Trave River. It was declared a UNESCO World Heritage Site as a main location for German Gothic brick buildings.

A series of churches have been preserved or renovated including the cathedral, begun in 1173 and completed in the 13th century, St Mary's parish church, built by the people of Lübeck, St Catherine's Basilica and the brick Gothic churches of Saints Jakobi and Petri. The city's main landmark, however, is the 15th-century Holstentor gate, part of the once-mighty fortifications. The Gothic town hall is evidence of the city's wealth and the confidence of its sponsors. A highlight of any stroll through the Old Town are the medieval burgher houses, the most attractive of which are located on Mengstraße (also home to the

Buddenbrookhaus of the Mann family), Königstraße, the Große Petersgrube and on Holsten Harbour. Your journey continues east from the city on the Trave through the Klützer Winkel to Wismar on the Bay of Wismar.

❺ Wismar The picturesque old port in this merchant settlement

and Hanseatic town is just a fishing port these days. As an international port, Wismar was of national significance for Baltic Sea trading for over 750 years, and the walled city has largely been able to preserve its beautiful medieval look. Wismar has numerous gabled houses from the Renaissance and baroque

Travel information

Route profile
Route length: approx. 1,700 km (1,056 mi)
Time required: 3–4 weeks
Route (main locations): Bremen, Hamburg, Rostock, Rügen, Sczeczin, Gdańsk, Olsztyn, Kaliningrad, Klaipėda, Riga, Tallinn

Traffic in formation:
Check the validity of the vehicle's liability insurance before driving into any of these countries!

Visas:
Russia: You need your visa, international driver's licence, vehicle registration, and an

international green insurance card.
EU countries: All you need for the EU are a valid passport or ID card.

Information:
Here are some websites to help you plan your trip.
Poland:
www.polen.travel/en
Russia:
www.waytorussia.net
Estonia:
www.visitestonia.com
Latvia:
www.latviatourism.lv
Lithuania:
www.tourism.lt

Detour

Lüneburg and the Lüneburger Heide

The foundation of Lüneburg's wealth and the reason for the city's acceptance in the Hanseatic League was the Lüneburg salt mines, which contained one of Germany's strongest and most effective natural healing sols. In the days of the League, salt was a highly sought-after commodity across the entire Baltic Sea region. Lüneburg, still very much intact today, has a wealth of northern German brick architecture and was one of Ger-

Top: Reed-covered houses in the Lüneburg Heath.
Center: The Old Crane, Lüneburg.
Bottom: 14th-century court alcove in the Lüneburg town hall.

periods (16th to 18th centuries) and a Gothic residential home from 1380. The oldest burgher house in the city, the "Old Swede", is located on the market square where you will also find the fountain house, the "Wasserkunst" (1602), in Dutch Renaissance style. The fountain provided the city with water until the end of the 19th century. The royal court from 1555 is modelled on Italian styles and the sculptures can be traced back to Dutch influences. The Gothic St Mary's Church, with its slender tower, was modeled on the church of the same name in Lübeck.

A 30-km (19-mi) detour takes you south to Schwerin, capital of Mecklenburg-Vorpommern.

6 Schwerin Slavic tribes built a castle here in the "City of Seven Lakes" on the shores of Lake Schwerin in the 11th century. As a royal residence town of the Mecklenburg dukes, the castle, situated beautifully on an island, and large parts of the Old Town were given their current look back in the 15th century by royal architect, Georg Demmler. He

used Chambord Castle in the Loire Valley as a model and created one of the most famous works of historicism. The cathedral, which dates back to the 13th–15th centuries, is a masterpiece of German brick Gothic. From Schwerin, a road leads back to Wismar through Cambs, and then the B105 follows the old trading route between Lübeck and Gdańsk. On the way to Rostock you can make detours to the Cistercian monasteries of Sonnenkampf (13th century) and Bad Doberan (14th century).

7 Rostock This city was established by German merchants and craftsmen at the end of the 12th century, and experienced its heyday as part of the Hanseatic League in the 14th and 15th centuries. The University of Rostock (est. 1419) is one of the oldest in the Baltic Sea region. Today, the metropolis on the Lower Warnow River mostly survives off its lively port. The Thirty Years War left Rostock in ruins, as did heavy bombing during World War II, and most of its late-Gothic, baroque and classicist homes were destroyed, but

many have been carefully restored or rebuilt. The late-Gothic town hall, which actually comprises three buildings, is unique, and the city's two parish churches are dedicated to St Peter and St Nicholas. St Mary's Church, with its famous astronomical clock, towers over the north-west corner of the central market square.

From Rostock there are numerous possible detours to Warnemünde on the coast or to the beautiful Mecklenburg lake district farther inland.

The Rostock Heath (Rostocker Heide), east of the city, is a pristine moor and woodland. The western part was felled to build "cog" ships during the time of the Hanseatic League, while the eastern section was kept as a ducal hunting reserve.

Nature lovers should visit the fishing town of Wustrow on Fischland, the narrow spit that leads over to the Darss Peninsula in the Vorpommersche Boddenlandschaft National Park.

A lovely road between Bodstedter Bodden and Barther Bodden goes to Barth via Zingst and back to the B105 at Löbnitz.

8 Stralsund This city's former significance as Hanseatic League member is still reflected in the buildings today. It has a network of medieval streets, primarily with brick Gothic architecture, and many of the burgher houses originate from the 15th–19th centuries. This "Venice of the North" is located on the Strelasund, a strait between the mainland and Rügen. In the center of the city, which is a UNESCO World Heritage Site, the town hall towers over the Old Market, while just next door is a late-

1 View of the St Pauli piers on the dry docks in the internationally sigifi-cant Port of Hamburg.

2 The town hall and St Peter's Cathedral on Bremen's market square.

3 Merchant houses and sailing ships at Holsten Harbour in Lübeck.

4 A baroque garden surrounds Schwerin Castle on an island in Lake Schwerin.

5 The "Wasserkunst" fountain house on Wismar's market square.

many's richest cities in the 15th and 16th centuries. Many half-timbered houses testify to this dazzling era. The main attractions of the city on the Ilmenau include the Gothic complex around the Platz Am Sande, the town hall and the Old Crane at the Stintmarkt.

Vast oak, birch and pine forests west of the city were felled to exploit the Lüneburg salt mines (956-1980), leaving behind a unique heath landscape.

The Free Hanseatic City of Bremen

The name Bremen probably derives from "on the edge" (of the water). The mighty fishing and merchant city on the Weser River was founded in the early Middle Ages, and Bremen's bishop's see and cathedral have stood close to the Weser on the fortified dune hill since 787.

Bremen's economic significance originally emerged due to its location on the Weser and proximity to the sea just 60 km (37 miles) away. The city had a port and a ford, and was also an important diocesan town. In the mid-12th century, Bremen came into conflict with Duke Heinrich the Lion,

Beautiful view over patrician houses and Bremen's Roland Column.

who seized the city on two occasions. The wealth from foreign trade during the 13th century financed the town hall, important religious buildings and a city wall (1129) enclosing residential towers built by wealthy merchants. It was not until 1358 that the city became a Hanseatic League member, and in the 17th century it became a Free City. The plagues that began in the mid-14th century haunted Bremen several times. In the 15th century, the city was a booming commercial center, but large parts of the old town were destroyed in World War II.

Attractions here include: the market square with the Roland Column (1404); Schütting, the merchants' guild house (16th century); the town hall (15th century) with its renaissance façade; the Gothic Church of Our Lady (13th century); the hall church of St Martin on the Weser; St Peter's Cathedral (begun in the 11th century) with its cathedral museum; Böttcherstraße with the Roseliushaus museum and the Paula Becker Modersohn House with works by the artist; the Schnoorviertel, formerly a residential quarter for fishermen and craftsmen; and the wall complex with a moat. Museums: Overseas Museum with folklore collection; the art gallery with its famous graphic design collection; and the Universum Science Center Bremen.

The Free Hanseatic City of Hamburg

Thanks to its location on the Elbe River and its proximity to the North Sea, Hamburg rose to significance as a trading and port town in the 12th century. The most important German port city is now a cosmopolitan metropolis.

Hamburg was an early member of the Hanseatic League and in the 14th century became the most important transshipment center between the North and Baltic Seas. The old and new town were united in 1216, and just sixty years later Hamburg was ravaged by fire. The same happened again in 1842, and large parts of the city were destroyed in World War II.

Attractions here include: St Michael's Church with Michel, symbol of the city; St James (14th century); St Catherine (14th/15th century); St Peter (14th century); St Nicholas; the homes of the Shopkeepers' Guild (17th century); the stock exchange (19th century); the old town with town hall (19th century) and town houses (17th/18th century); Inner Alster Lake with the Jungfern-

Top: St Nicholas Church and the town hall from the Lombard Bridge on the Jungfernstieg promenade.
Bottom: The Gruner+Jahr publishing house and "Michel".

stieg promenade; the warehouse district of the Old Free Harbour; St Nicholas Fleet (17th/18th century); St Paul's pier (1907-1909); the Kontorhaus district with the Chile House (UNESCO). The Ethnology Museum, the Hamburg Art Gallery, the Planten un Blomen Park, and the zoo are worth visiting too.

In about 1818, Caspar David Friedrich immortalized the Wissower Klinken formations with his painting "The Chalk Cliffs of Rügen". Seen here from the Victoria viewpoint, the plateau, which is over 100-m (328-ft) high in parts, falls away steeply into the Baltic Sea on the eastern side of island of Rügen. During the

Cretaceous period, some seventy million years ago, lime platelets were deposited in a deep strait and developed into a 100-m (109-yds) solid layer of chalk. Since 1990, the Jasmund National Park in northern Germany has protected this geological outcrop as well as the Stubnitz beech forests.

Detour

Cammin Lagoon and the Wollin Island

Although the southern Baltic Sea coast is pretty flat, it is full of pockets and peninsulas. Over the millennia, spits (long strips of sand often covered in vegetation) have isolated the numerous bays from the open sea, creating Stettin and Cammin Lagoons, for example, in

Top: Fishermen on the beach at the Miedzywodzie resort on Wollin.
Center: The cathedral of Kamień Pomorski (built 1176–1385).
Bottom: Sunset over the Cammin Lagoon.

the delta region of the Oder River. Holiday resorts on the lagoon include the Hanseatic city of Kamień Pomorski and Miedzywodzie on the island of Wollin. Parts of the island are protected as part of a national park.

big and little mills as well as the old castle. A detour to the northern edge of Gdańsk brings you to the lovely Cathedral of Oliva, with its baroque interior, as well as to Sopot, once the most glamorous seaside resort on the Baltic Sea coast.

South of Gdańsk is the Gdańsk River Isle, the northernmost part of the Vistula Delta. This landscape, which is partly submerged in the sea, was partially dried out in the 15th century and then reclaimed in the 17th century. Crossing the river island heading south-east you will soon arrive in Malbork.

⑮ Malbork St Mary's Castle, destroyed in World War II and rebuilt starting in 1961, is on the right bank of the Nogat, which flows north-east at this point. The mighty castle complex comprises two parts separated by a trench and protected by a common moat. Malbork's old German name – Marienburg – refers to its Christian founders: In the second half of the 13th century, the grand master of the Teutonic Order moved his seat of government here from Venice. South-west of the castle is the late-13th-century city of Marienburg, whose center is dominated by the impressive

town hall. St John's Church is just to the north.

Heading north-east from Malbork you arrive in yet another Hanseatic city.

⑯ Elbląg When the Teutonic Order began its fight against the "heathen" Prussians, it established a Hanseatic city here in 1237 to help their cause. Until 1370, it was of greater importance in the area than even Gdańsk. When the medieval Old Town became too small, a new town was designed.

The Elbląg River connects the city to the Gdańsk bay and therefore to the Baltic Sea, and wheat and wood exports originally made the city rich. Some of the many burgher homes from the 16th and 17th centuries have been restored and attest to the former wealth of Elbląg, which was a Free Imperial City starting in the early 16th century. In January 1945, shortly before the end of World War II, it was heavily bombed.

Attractions include the Market Gate, the Gothic Dominican church, the St Nicholas Church with its 96-m (315-ft) tower, and the Ordensburg ruins.

From Elbląg a detour south on the E77 leads to the important medieval city of Olsztyn.

⑰ Vistula Lagoon Route 503 heads north-eastward along the Vistula Lagoon to the town of Frombork. The road, which closely skirts the lagoon, is surprisingly diverse, with sudden climbs to the highlands near

Suchacz followed by stretches of forest before the road falls dramatically back down to the lagoon. Further along you'll see impressive green of the Vistula Spit. This headland stretches north-east, parallel to the coast,

The Masuria lake district

Very few visitors can resist the charming landscape of the Masuria lake district. Whether on foot, on bicycle or in a canoe, the roughly 30,000 lakes in this area are loosely connected with each other by creeks, rivers and canals flowing through stunning forests. Gnarled trees shade the cobblestone lanes where horses and carts still ride, while storks build their nests high up in the church spires. A visit to Masuria is a journey through time to the early 20th century.

Top: A birch grove in Masuria.
Center: A "Panjewagen" or small horse-drawn cart.
Bottom: Copernicus is buried in the Gothic cathedral of Frombork.

and is home to villages whose former names included Vogelsang and Schottland (German for birdsong and Scotland).

The town of Tolkmicko, back on the 503 to the west, is at the northern end of Butter Mountain, the highest peak in the Elbląg Highlands: 197 m (646 ft). It has a pretty beach with fine, white-grey sand and a cute little marina with sailboats.

The onward journey takes you down some splendid avenues; gnarled old trees line the road and provide shade from the glaring sunlight. Some of the lanes have such dense treetops

that the road even stays dry in light rain.

The town of Frombork is culturally the most interesting city in the Ermland region because of the historic hilltop cathedral complex. The museum, as well as the cathedral itself, is dedicated to the works of Copernicus, who studied astronomy here. The water tower affords a wonderful view over the lagoon and port. The route continues along the lagoon to the Hanseatic city of Braniewo, former residence of a prince-bishop.

The St Catherine's Church, which was only rebuilt a few years ago,

dates back to the 14th century. The Polish-Russian (Kaliningrad) border is just a few miles further north-east.

You'll cross a few borders before arriving in Lithuania, since the Russian exclave, Kaliningrad, lies between the new EU states.

18 Kaliningrad Kaliningrad was the last major city founded by the Teutonic Order, in 1255. Having already been a refuge for Slavic Prussians, with whom the crusading German Catholics had long been in conflict, the newly designed city comprised three central components: the

Old Town between the castle and the Pregel River; Löbenicht in the east; and the Kneipphof (1327) on Pregel Island in the south. The city became a member of the Hanseatic League in 1340. Kaliningrad is the former capital of East Prussia and the home of Imannuel Kant. He taught at the university from 1755 to 1796. Today, the Königsberg Cathedral glistens in its new splendor after being renovated in the 1990s – mostly with German money. Other worthwhile sights include the old German city manor houses on Thälmann and Kutusow Streets, while parts of the warehouse district have also remained intact. The New University, constructed from 1844 to 1862, has been rebuilt as well.

The coast near Kaliningrad is known for its amber deposits. If you are luck, you may even be

1 The Crane Gate on the Mottlau in Gdańsk was both a city gate and a port crane.

2 The Renaissance castle of the dukes of Pomerania in Stettin.

3 The famous astronomer, Copernicus, is buried in the Gothic brick cathedral of Frombork.

Olsztyn is the capital of Masuria. From the capital, it is worth going to see some of the sights in the area. Lidzbark Warminskj, with its impressive castle, was once the residence of the Ermland bishops. The castle of Reszel dates back to the 13th century. The Teutonic Order built a fort in Ketrzyn in 1329. Beyond Ketrzyn, a sign will direct to the north-west to the "Wolfsschanze" or "Wolf's Hole", a bunker Hitler built in 1939 that became one of his favorite hideaways towards the end of the war. The pilgrimage church of Święta Lipka is a baroque gem.

Mighty walls and bastions surround the fort complex of Malbork, residence of the grand master of the Teutonic Order from 1309 to 1457. The middle castle with its grand master palace (left half), is a unique architectural gem of the northern German brick Gothic style. The high castle (center) contained meeting, living

dining and sleeping quarters as well as a church (the highest tower of the complex in the background). The Dankertsturm tower (front, right) was both a watch-tower and an outhouse. The fort, half of which was destroyed in 1945, was restored and declared a UNESCO World Heritage Site in 1998.

Teutonic Order

In 1190, during the third crusade, some citizens of Bremen and Lübeck who were temporarily based in the Holy Land established the Teutonic Order, also known as the Order of the Brothers of the German House of St Mary in Jerusalem, or the Order of German Knights, German Masters and Crusaders. It has always been symbolized by a straight, symmetric black cross on a white background. After the emperor and the Pope had guaranteed that successfully evangelized regions would be assigned to the Order, what had originally been a hospice order became an military order of knights beginning in 1198. It then shifted its range and region of activities from Palestine to the non-

Once a base of the Teutonic Order, today a UNESCO World Heritage Site: the Marienburg.

Christian Baltic. Numerous forts and roughly 100 cities, including the exclave of Kaliningrad, were founded during this period. Gdańsk and Pomerelia were also conquered. In 1231, the Order established its own clerical state in eastern Prussia, but its land was never a contiguous territory, but rather a conglomeration of scattered land possessions. By 1309, the eastern Prussian city of Malbork became the Order's capital, and the Marienburg defence complex built there was the residence of the grand masters of the Order for nearly 150 years. In 1466, the western lands of the Order were lost to the Prussians and the Order's headquarters were relocated to Kaliningrad. As of the 16th century, the Order's numbers began to decline, but it resumed clerical activities in 1929 (in Germany it restarted in 1945). The approximately 1,000 members primarily work in the pastoral and care-giving fields. The grand master's residence is now in Vienna.

able to find a piece of this beautiful stone for yourself!

19 Courland Spit National Park "The Courland Spit is a narrow strip of land between Memel and Königsberg (now Klaipèda and Kaliningrad), between the Courland Lagoon and the Baltic Sea. The lagoon contains fresh water, which is unaffected by the small connection to the Baltic Sea near Memel, and is home to freshwater fish." These were the words of author Thomas Mann, who owned a house in this area in the 1930s that is now open to the public, to describe the unique natural paradise here that has been declared a UNESCO World Natural Heritage Site.
The Courland Spit National Park protects the forests rustling in the sea breeze, the dreamy towns with their traditional wooden houses, and the pristine dune and beach landscape along the Baltic Sea and the lagoon. The southernmost town in the Lithuanian part of the Courland Spit is Nida. The dune landscape, with dunes up to 60 m (197 ft) high, is also jokingly known as the "Lithuanian Sahara".

20 Klaipèda A series of seaside resorts make this coast the most attractive holiday spot in Lithuania. The Baltic town of Klaipèda, located at the mouth of the lagoon and which appeared to still be in slumber until just a few decades ago, is today one of the country's important industrial centers. Its history also began with the Teutonic Order, and Klaipèda adopted the Lübeck city charter in 1254.
Just a few miles further north is the popular spa resort of

Palanga, with its fine white-sand beaches, dunes and vast pine forests. With a bit of luck, you can experience some spectacular sunsets here after visiting the botanical garden and the interesting amber museum.
From Klaipèda, the A1 takes you through Kaunas to Vilnius, the capital of Lithuania, 300 km (186.5 mi) away. If you would rather head to Riga, Latvia, take the A12 east for 100 km (62 mi).

21 Rīga The Latvian capital on the mouth of the Daugava became a member of the Hanseatic League in 1282, and is one of the most beautiful cities in the Baltic region. The Old Town itself was declared a UNESCO

World Heritage Site. Within its walls are buildings dating back to numerous eras in European architecture including medieval patrician homes, twenty-four warehouses in the Old Town, and some art nouveau houses, which in some cases line entire residential streets. Apart from the former palace of Czar Peter the Great, it is also worth visiting St John's Church (14th century), which is on the ruins of a diocesan town and was burned to the ground in 1234. The castle of the Teutonic Order, built in 1330, features the Sweden Gate and is home to many museums. The Saints Peter and Paul Cathedral was built at the end of the 18th century.

German merchants began unifying here in what was called the Great Guild back in the mid-14th century and even constructed their own Great Guild building. The locals were excluded here and in the Small Guild, where German craftsmen held secret meetings in the Small Guild building. The Schwarzhäupterhaus, or House of the Black Heads, built by merchants from Riga in 1341, is one of the most beautiful buildings in the city. The red brick construction has several storage levels.
Riga's icon is the 137-m (450-ft) wooden tower of St Peter's. The Latvian parliament building is a replica of the Palazzo Strozzi in Florence. The Arsenal, Riga's old

4

5

The Baltic Sea region has always been an important source of amber, a fossil resin that originates in ancient pine trees and hardens due to lack of oxygen. By flooding ancient amber forests, the 30- and 50-million-year-old amber was dug out of the earth and transported to the Samland coast of Kaliningrad.

The world's largest source of amber is still found on the Baltic Sea coast of Samland, and the amber from here often has interesting fossil imprints (entombments) of animals, typically insects, and parts of plants. The stone is extracted through a process of open-cast mining or it is fished out using nets.

Amber was extremely popular as jewelry and in amulets as early as the Stone Age, but has also been traditionally used in medicine. In the Hanseatic territory, it played an important role as a trading commodity, and was distributed as far afield as the Islamic world. The collection of amber on the coast became the fran-

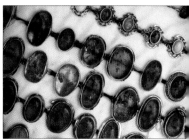

Top: Amber with an embedded insect.
Bottom: Amber, cut and mounted into jewelry.

river of the same name. This quaint old city, which dates back to the 13th century, is an important Estonian port city but is also famous as a health resort because of the healing mud from the area. Homes from the 16th and 17th centuries, as well as the Orthodox St Catherine's Church and the baroque St Elizabeth Church, are also worth seeing. The last stop on your journey along the Baltic Sea coast is the Hanseatic city of Tallinn.

㉓ Tallinn In the 13th century, the knights of the Teutonic Order advanced as far as the northern reaches of the Baltic territories, right up to the entrance of the Gulf of Finland. Tallinn itself was first documented in 1154. Its Hanseatic League membership, which began in 1284, indeed inspired the city's rapid economic rise, but the collapse of the Order in the 16th and 17th centuries marked the start of a decline for Tallinn. After 1945, the capital became Estonia's most important industrial city.

The many churches on cathedral mountain and in the lower part of town, as well as the Gothic church spires soaring toward the heavens like giant needles, all make Tallinn a fantastic architectural destination. The towers of the city wall and the baroque domes on the patrician houses are also interesting relics of a world gone by. Many of the quiet, narrow lanes are still paved with cobblestones.

The Gothic Old Town is a UNESCO World Heritage Site and has the oldest town hall in northern Europe (14th/15th centuries). The nearly intact city walls are adorned with twenty-six towers. Cathedral mountain, which falls dramatically toward the sea, is the site of the cathedral and Toompea Castle. The view over the rooftops to the historic Old Town is magnificent. The 13th-century Cathedral of the Virgin Mary is one of the oldest churches in Estonia, while the baroque Kadriorg Palace, with its beautiful park, was designed by Nicolo Michetti for Czar Peter the Great in 1718. The Dominican monastery was built in 1246, and is the oldest existing monastery in Estonia.

1 The Courland Spit is 98 km (61 mi) long and in parts only 400 m (0.25 mi) wide. It lies between the Baltic Sea and the Courland Lagoon.

2 Looking out over the distinctive skyline of Rīga's Old Town.

3 Rīga: The tower of the 13th-century St Peter's Church.

4 With its imposing city walls and watchtowers, Tallinn had one of the best northern European defense complexes of the 16th century.

5 The cathedral – the main church of Kaliningrad – was completely destroyed in 1944, and was not rebuilt until the 1990s.

chise of the sovereign princes, initially controlled by the dukes of Pomerelia and later by the Teutonic Order. The latter also created the post of amber master within the organization and held onto a monopoly of the trade from the High Middle Ages. Amber collectors had to surrender their findings to this master, and even in the late 19th century it was not easy for outsiders to gather amber on Baltic Sea beaches. Following the collapse of the Hanseatic League, Gdańsk and Kaliningrad became centers for amber mounting.

customs house (1828–32), is also worth seeing. For those interested in architecture and rural lifestyles of the 16th to 19th centuries, be sure to visit the open-air museum.

West of Rīga is the spa resort of Jūrmala, on a headland in the Gulf of Rīga. Fine sandy beaches stretch over 30 km (19 mi) and a handy railway connects the capital with the town.

From Riga, it is worth making a small detour to Sigulda, located in the idyllic Ganja National Park about 50 km (31 mi) to the north-east. The main attractions

in the park include a toboggan run, Turaida Castle, and the numerous interesting caves and wells that can be discovered along the hiking routes.

From Rīga , the E67 leads north along the Gulf of Rīga to the Estonian capital, Tallinn. You'll cross the border at Ainazi.

㉒ Pärnu The Estonian west coast is similarly appealing, with picturesque forests, shimmering water, simple thatched houses, stout castles and old ruins. About 180 km (112 mi) north of Riga is Pärnu, located on the

Detour

Kaunas and Vilnius

Kaunas was the capital of Lithuania between the world wars. The old city center and the castle are located on a peninsula at the confluence of the Nemunas and Neris Rivers. The Hanseatic League had a branch office here from 1441 until 1532, before the fire of 1537 destroyed large parts of the Old Town.

From Kaunas it is roughly 100 km (62 mi) to Vilnius, the current capital on the Vilnia river. That city's landmarks are the many watchtowers scattered through the picturesque Old Town. The "Rome of the Baltic", as this picture-book town used to be called, still contains remnants of its former masters, the Jesuits, champions of the Counter-Reformation in the kingdom of Poland and Lithuania. Vilnius was first documented in 1323, and even then it was already a prosperous trading and merchant settlement. Vilnius surprises most visitors with its magnificent baroque churches and buildings. The narrow, pictur-esque cobblestone lanes zig-zag through the Old Town, at the center of which is the university, a Renaissance building with a number of courtyards influenced by Italian styles. The Vilnius cathedral was rebuilt several times before being given its current classicist makeover in the 18th century. The city's main road is formed by the Gediminas Prospekt, lined with lime trees. Extensive baroque and classicist palaces attest to the wealth that once flowed through the city.

Lübeck The entire Old Town of the "Queen of the Hanse" and "City of Marzipan" is beautiful, primarily its churches and brick buildings including the town hall, Hospital of the Holy Spirit and the Holstentor gate.

Wismar This walled Hanseatic city has done an outstanding job of preserving its medieval Old Town.

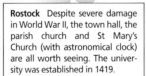

Rügen Since 1937, Germany's largest island has been connected to the mainland via the Rügen Dam. The stunning chalk cliffs have made the Baltic Sea island famous.

Usedom The eastern tip of the island, connected to the mainland by bridges, is part of Poland. The German side has a series of well-known seaside resorts like Zinnowitz, Bansin, Heringsdorf and Ahlbeck (here).

Rostock Despite severe damage in World War II, the town hall, the parish church and St Mary's Church (with astronomical clock) are all worth seeing. The university was established in 1419.

Hamburg The "Gateway to the World" with "Michel", town hall, the Jungfernstieg, the Blankenese quarter, St Pauli piers, the warehouse quarter and the port.

Bremen A busy port once made the Weser city rich. The market square with the Roland Column is particularly nice.

Schwerin This city is located on Lake Schwerin, the second-largest lake in the state of Mecklenburg-Vorpommern.

Stralsund Brick Gothic buildings and burgher houses from the 15th to 19th centuries are typical of this city on the Strelasund.

1 A romantic location: The picturesque town of Trakai with its impressive medieval fortress set on the lakeshore.

2 The neoclassical cathedral of Vilnius, built in the 18th/19th centuries, has a remarkable, free-standing tower.

3 Interior view of the magnificent Church of the Holy Spirit in Vilnius, the "Rome of the Baltic".

Tallinn Estonia's capital is home to a Gothic Old Town and the oldest town hall in northern Europe (1400s). Its landmark is the cathedral mountain, which drops off steeply into the sea.

Sigulda The main attractions of this small town in a densely forested area are Turaida Castle and the nearby "Folk Song Hill" with sculptures depicting traditional Latvian songs.

Rīga The Latvian capital displays some important European architectural styles, from medieval to Art Nouveau, and is one of the most beautiful cities on the Baltic Sea.

Courland Lagoon This nature paradise is home to dunes, forests, fairy-tale towns and a choice of Baltic Sea or freshwater beaches. Famous artists and literary figures (Corinth, Schmidt-Rottluff, Pechstein, Thomas Mann) spent many a holiday here. The narrow headland was restricted territory during the Soviet era.

Gdańsk Gdańsk was completely destroyed in 1945, but extensive reconstruction work has ensured that the Crane Gate (above) as well as 650 other buildings again shine in their "former glory".

Vilnius Lithuania's capital is peppered with baroque buildings and is located near the border with Belarus. Here: the neoclassical cathedral and its bell tower.

Kaliningrad This city, founded by the Teutonic Order in 1255, was a member of the Hanseatic League from 1340. The cathedral has been restored after being severely damaged in World War II. The former capital of East Prussia and home of Immanuel Kant, a professor here from 1755 to 1796, is rather unsightly, but is located near the Samland coast, which is worth visiting.

Masuria Tiny alleyways and cobblestones, village ponds and migrating storks' nests. A visit to this region is a journey back in time. Dense forests, gentle hills and the beautiful Masuria lake district, home to more than 3,000 lakes, characterize this subtle moraine landscape in north-eastern Poland.

Malbork The Marienburg castle, which was rebuilt after World War II, was the residence of the grand master of the Teutonic Order in the 13th century. The town of Malbork is located near the castle.

Frombork This 14th-century cathedral, located on an impressive embankment, is a model of northern German brick architecture.

The vineyard town of Löf. The tall hills of the Upper Mosel Valley taper off a bit just before the

Germany

Wine, culture and the rolling hills of the Rhine, Mosel and Neckar

The Rhine is the subject of countless songs, the "most German of all rivers" and without doubt one of the most beautiful rivers in Europe. The Mosel, which flows into the Rhine at Koblenz, is smaller but no less alluring. The Neckar, which joins the Rhine from the east at Mannheim, is a worthy rival on all counts. All three rivers boast enchanting valleys bound by lovely hills dotted with castles, vineyards and quaint villages.

The Rhine, known as Rhenus by the Celts and the Romans, is 1,320 km (820 mi) long, making it one of the longest rivers in Europe, and one of the most important waterways on the continent.

The Rhine originates in the canton of Graubünden (Grisons), Switzerland, flows into and out of Lake Constance, nips over the Rhine Falls at Schaffhausen, then continues on toward Basel as the Upper Rhine. The Upper Rhine then turns northward across the Upper Rhine Plain where

Ladenburg on the Neckar.

it enters its most familiar "German" manifestation. The Neckar joins the Rhine at Mannheim where the latter becomes the Middle Rhine, which cuts spectacularly through the low mountains of central western Germany, accompanied on the left bank by the "peaks" of the Hunsrück and on the right by the Taunus foothills. The Mosel flows into what is now the Lower Rhine at Koblenz and enters the Lower Rhine Basin near Bonn. After passing through Cologne, Düsseldorf and Duisburg, it leaves Germany just after Kleve and flows into the North Sea in the Netherlands a few river miles later.

In 2002, the Middle Rhine from Bingen to Koblenz was declared a UNESCO World Heritage Site, in recognition not only of its natural beauty but also the cultural, historical and, not least, economic significance of this stretch of the river.

This stretch of the valley is inextricably linked with the "Rhine Gold" of Wagner fame and epic Nibelung legend, and on both sides of the meandering river are steep hillsides with exquisite vineyards and defiant medieval castles.

It seems every castle and every rock formation on the Rhine is linked with a myth or a legend, whether it is of the beautiful Loreley, who is said to have lured many a boatsman to his untimely death with her songs, or of the two estranged brothers in Burg Katz (Cat) and Burg Maus (Mouse).

But perhaps all of these myths and legends were merely inspired by centuries of delectable Rhine wine, whose vineyards are as much a part of the culture here as the numerous castles that line the river's banks. Whatever the case, the wine is most certainly influential in creating the

One of Germany's most famous picture-postcard views: Heidelberg on the Neckar.

river converges with the Rhine.

View over the Rhine of the much fêted Loreley rock, which rises 132 m (433 ft) above the river.

conviviality of the people in the region, which reaches its climax during Carnival, especially in Cologne. A more recent festivity on the Rhine is the spectacle "Rhein in Flammen" (Rhine in flames): five times a year, fireworks soar over the river between Rüdesheim and Bonn.

Wine also plays an important role along the longest and largest of the Rhine's tributaries, the Mosel. Known for its romantic meandering course, the Mosel originates in the southern Vosges Mountains in France and flows into the Rhine at Koblenz after 545 km (339 mi). With the exception of Trier, which is located on a comparatively broad section of the Mosel, no other large cities have developed on its banks because the river's valley is so narrow. This makes the surrounding countryside, especially between Bernkastel-Kues and Cochem, particularly

charming with its vineyards, wine-growing towns and medieval castles. The Mosel Valley is a unique cultural landscape with thousands of years of history started by Celtic and Roman settlers.

Farther upstream from where the Mosel joins in, "Father Rhine" has already collected one of his other sons: the Neckar, yet another of the German "wine rivers". The Necker originates at 706 m (2,316 ft) in the Schwenninger Moos and flows into the Rhine 367 km (228 mi) later at Mannheim. Along its course, it twists and turns through steep valleys like the one at Rottweil, or meanders through broad meadows like the ones where Stuttgart and Heilbronn are now located.

Below Neckarelz, the river cuts through the red sandstone formations of the Odenwald, and from Heidelberg it passes through the Upper Rhine Plain.

The Reichsburg above Cochem on the Mosel is one of Germany's most attractive castles.

The Romans in Trier

Emperor Augustus founded Trier, Germany's oldest town, back in 16 BC, and gave it the name Augusta Treverorum. Augustus built the town on a strategically clever location where the Mosel River valley (in Latin Mosella) widens, the same spot where Caesar had defeated the Celtic Treverers – another reason for the Treverorum name.

In about 100 AD, an amphitheater with capacity for 20,000 spectators was built here. Its ruins can still be visited today. In 117 AD, Augusta Treverorum became the capital of the Roman province of Belgica prima,

Top: Imperial baths (ca. 360 AD).
Bottom: Porta Nigra Roman gate.

administrative seat of the prefecture for the provinces of Gallia, Britannia and Spain as well as the emperor's residence.

During the 3rd and 4th centuries, Trier was a sort of ancient world metropolis, with remarkable 70,000 inhabitants. Today, in addition to the amphitheater ruins, the Aula Palatina (once the residence of Constantine the Great), the imperial baths and the Barbara thermal hot springs still bear witness to Trier's ancient Roman heyday. The icon of the city, however, is the Porta Nigra, the 2nd-century Roman gate that was never quite completed. (The gate was remodeled as St Simeon's Church under Frankish rule in the 11th century.) The Franks had conquered the city in 475, and for centuries defended it against attempts at recapture. By the 6th century, Trier had become an archbishopric.

Your route along Germany's enchanting rivers begins in Trier and follows the course of the Mosel down to its confluence with the Rhine at Koblenz. It then heads back up through the Middle Rhine Valley past countless castles and vineyards to Mannheim. From there you will travel parallel to the Neckar River to Tübingen.

❶ Trier Framed in by the forested hills of the Hunsrück and Eifel, Trier sits in one of the few broad valleys along the Mosel. It is a city of superlatives: Northeast of the Roman Porta Nigra is the church of St Paulin (18th C.), designed by Balthasar Neumann and the region's most significant baroque structure. The Cathedral of St Peter was begun in the 4th century, making it the oldest cathedral in Germany. The Liebfrauenkirche next door (13th C.) is one of the oldest Gothic churches in the country. And the Hauptmarkt with its Marian cross and the St Peter's Fountain is one of Germany's most attractive fairy-tale squares.

From Trier to Koblenz you skirt both sides of the Mosel among the enchanting hillside vineyard towns.

❷ Bernkastel-Kues The half-timbered houses and the Marktplatz here are dominated by the

Detour

Maria Laach and the Southern Eifel

The Southern Eifel, part of the Rhenish Slate Mountains, is bordered on the south by the Mosel River. Its highest peak is the basalt hilltop of the Hohe Acht at 746 m (2,448 ft). Typical features of the Southern Eifel are its maars, small crater lakes of volcanic origin. The largest of these is Laacher Lake, which reaches a depth of 53 m (174 ft) and covers 3.3 sq km (1.3 sq mi). A strong groundwater current feeds the lake, and rising gas bubbles are indicative of the fact that the volcanic activity in the area has not entirely stopped. Other well-known maars in the area are the Dauner Maare, the so-called "blue eyes of the Eifel".

The mighty Benedictine Maria Laach Monastery

The famous Benedictine Monastery of Maria Laach, dating from the 12th century, is situated near Mendig on the shores of Laacher Lake. The monastery (consecrated in 1156), has a total of six church steeples and is considered a gem of Romanesque architecture for its strict geometric lines and extraordinary beauty. It was the last monastery in the Rhineland to be founded by the Benedictine order. The most fascinating sights inside the complex include the tomb of Heinrich II (11th century), the canopied high altar, the crypt, the arched portal and especially the famous "Laacher Paradies", a stonemason's work on the west façade's balcony that symbolizes the Garden of Eden.

ruins of Landshut Castle, with vineyards climbing up to its stone walls. A bridge connects Bernkastel with Kues, the birthplace of philosopher Nikolaus von Kues (1401–1464).

❸ Traben-Trarbach This charming vineyard town straddling the Mosel is distinguished by attractive half-timbered houses and patrician villas. Fans of Art Nouveau architecture will find some unique specimens here, including the Brückentor, the Huesgen Villa, the small Sonora Villa and the Hotel Bellevue, all reminders of a golden age in the wine trade at the turn of the 20th century.
Towering above the small town is Grevenburg Castle. On Mont

Royal, enclosed by a wide loop in the river, are the ruins of a fortress planned by Vauban.

❹ Zell This vineyard town on the right bank of the Mosel boasts remnants of very old town walls, the church of St Peter and a former electors' palace.
On the road to Bremm you can take a scenic detour to Arras Castle (9th C.) near Alf.

❺ Mosel Loop at Bremm Among the most famous of the Mosel's many hairpin turns is the one around the wine village of Bremm, whose vineyards on the Bremmer Calmont are among the steepest Riesling vineyards in Europe. The village itself is lovely, with picturesque narrow

alleyways and the usual half-timbered houses. Heading downstream, take a trip to legendary Burg Eltz castle.

❻ Cochem This town is one of the most attractive in the Mosel Valley. It is dominated by the Reichsburg, built in 1070, destroyed in 1688 and built once again in the 19th century in neo-Gothic style. The Marktplatz is surrounded by lovely old row houses and the town hall from 1739. Before the vineyard town of Kobern-Gondorf you will see the ruins of Ehrenburg castle near Löf-Hatzenport and in Alken the twin towers of Thuant Castle rise above the Mosel.
From Kobern, it is worth taking the time to visit Maria Laach (see

box to the right), culturally perhaps the most important sight in the southern Eifel mountains.

1 View from Calmont of the wide arch in the Mosel near Bremm.

2 The main square in Trier with Gangolf, the market cross and Steipe, which also functioned as the town hall until the 18th century.

3 Bernkastel-Kues, a medieval vineyard town on the Middle Mosel.

4 View across the Mosel towards Cochem and the Reichsburg castle.

5 Burg Landshut, nestled among the vineyards above Bernkastel-Kues, has been a ruin since 1692.

Burg Eltz is one of Germany's most beautiful medieval castles. Built on top of a 70-m-high (230-ft) rock formation and enclosed on three sides by the Elz River, the castle was damaged in battle. In 1268, it became a "Ganerben" castle, meaning it was in the possession of three lines of the same family dynasty living under

the same roof. In the course of 500 years of construction, a fortified castle complex was created with eight residential towers grouped around a small central inner courtyard. Thanks to the centuries of construction, architectural styles from romanticism to baroque can be seen here.

Mathildenhöhe Artists' Colony in Darmstadt

In the eastern part of Darmstadt lies Mathildenhöhe, a park created by Grand Duke Ernst Ludwig in 1899, that became the Darmstadt Artists' Colony until 1914. At the time, Art Nouveau was the style in fashion,

Top: Mathildenhöhe with exhibition building and tower.
Bottom: Mosaic in Wedding Tower.

and the grand duke became its most enthusiastic patron. Initially he invited seven young architects, painters and sculptors to the city, and on the Mathildenhöhe he encouraged them to pursue and realize their ideals, which were considered revolutionary at the time. The 48-m-high (157-ft) Wedding Tower by Joseph Maria Olbrich stands out among the Art Nouveau edifices here. Anyone wishing to explore Art Nouveau more thoroughly should pay a visit to the artists' colony museum in the Ernst-Ludwig-Haus.

An odd contrast to these buildings is the nearby Russian-Orthodox chapel with its gilded domes and lavish decorations. It was built for Czar Nicholas .

which has nine glass windows painted by the artist between 1978 and 1985, depicting scenes from the Bible.

17 Wiesbaden The capital of the state of Hesse is located at the foot of the wooded Taunus Mountains. Thanks to its twenty thermal hot springs here, Wiesbaden has been a popular spa resort since the Romans built a fort here in the year 6 AD. The main thoroughfare in town is the stately Wilhelmstrasse, at the northern end of which is the spa district with the imposing neoclassical Kurhaus (1907) and the Kurhauskolonnade, the longest colonnade in Europe. Diagonally opposite the Kurhaus is the impressive Hessian State Library. West of the spa district you come to the Kochbrunnen, a fountain combining fifteen of a total of twenty hot springs,

as well as the Kaiser Friedrich Baths, beautifully decorated in Art Nouveau style.

In the center of the city is the Stadtschloss (municipal palace), completed in 1841, and the seat of the Hessian Landtag (regional government) since 1946. Opposite that is the impressive old town hall from 1610, and the square is dominated by the red neo-Gothic Marktkirche church from 1862.

18 Frankfurt am Main (see pages 120–121)

19 Darmstadt This former Hessian imperial residence town is distinguished by remnants of life at the royal court. In the city center is the ducal palace, which was built over the course of more than six centuries. The last extensions were added in the 18th century.

Up on the Mathildenhöhe, evidence of the regional rulers' passion for hunting is on display in the Kranichstein Hunting Lodge. The market square and the old town hall from 1598 testify to the fact that bourgeois life has always played an influential role here. A weekly market takes place on the square around the 18th-century fountain. If you want to go for a stroll, head to the Herrngarten, formerly a park for the regional counts that was transformed into an English-style landscape garden in the 18th century and finally opened to the public in the 19th century.

From Darmstadt, the detour to Lorsch is a must. The Königshalle, or royal hall, is a jewel of Carolingian architecture and one of the oldest completely preserved medieval structures in the country. A slightly longer

detour goes to the former imperial city of Worms (see page 119).

20 Heidelberg This idyllically situated university town on the Neckar is considered one of the birthplaces of German romanticism. Towering over the Old Town are the famous castle ruins. The expansive grounds, which are laid out in terraces, were remodeled and extended several times between the 13th and the 16th centuries. To the modern eye it is a fascinating jumble of castle and chateau, with Gothic as well as Renaissance elements, the latter of which are of particular interest, especially the Ottheinrichsbau from 1566) and the Friedrichsbau from 1607. Superb views of the Old Town below unfold as you make your way around.

At the heart of the Old Town, directly on the market square

Detour

The Imperial Cathedrals of Worms and Speyer

For centuries, the icon of the imperial city of Worms has been the late-gothic St Peter's Cathedral from the 11th/12th centuries. With four spires, two domes and five ornate sandstone reliefs in the northern nave, it is a highlight of Romanesque architecture.

Over the years, the cathedral has undergone a series of internal transformations, during which it received a baroque high altar by Balthazar Neumann as well as

Top: The cathedral in Worms.
Bottom: The Staufer crypt in the cathedral in Speyer.

magnificent choir stalls (both from the 18th century).

The old imperial city of Speyer is also on the west side of the Rhine and, like Worms, likewise enjoys a long history. Witness to this is the six-towered, triple-naved and exceptionally tall cathedral of Saints Martin and Stephan. At the time of its consecration in the year 1061, it was the largest place of worship in the world. It houses the tombs of eight German emperors, among other figures of note. The large stone dish on the square, the so-called cathedral bowl (1490), was filled with wine whenever a new bishop was being chosen.

with its historic fountain, is the late-Gothic Heiliggeistkirche (Church of the Holy Spirit), which houses the tombs of the regional electors.

The Old Bridge, with its lovingly preserved medieval bridge gate, is another of the city's most recognizable icons. Once you get to the other side, it's just a short stroll to the famous Philosophers' Walk on the slopes of the Michelsberg. It is from here that you get the most attractive views of the Old Town, the Neckar and the castle.

We recommend another detour while in Heidelberg: the former imperial city of Speyer.

After returning, continue along the B37 through the Neckar Valley. From Neckargemünd, the road runs through the narrow valley via Hirschhorn up to Bad Wimpfen past picturesque villages and stout castles.

㉑ Bad Wimpfen This town is divided into two parts: Wimpfen im Tal (lower) and Wimpfen am Berg (upper). In the former, enclosed by old city walls, sights include the early-Romanesque Ritterstiftskirche (13th C.) and its adjacent monastery.

The landmark of Wimpfen am Berg are the Staufen towers of the Kaiserpfalz (imperial palace). Half-timbered houses such as the Bügeleisenhaus, a former bourgeois hospital, the Krone Inn, the Riesenhaus, (the manor house of the lords of Ehrenberg) all combine to create a charming medieval atmosphere in the upper town. Also worth a visit are the sumptuously decorated municipal church and the Parish Church of the Holy Cross. The best views of the old town and the Neckar Valley are from the western donjon of the former imperial palace.

㉒ Heilbronn This town is best known as the center of one of Germany's largest wine-growing regions. The Renaissance-style town hall on the market square has an astronomical clock from the 16th century. Construction of the nearby St Kilian's Church began back in 1278. South-west of the market square you'll find the Deutschhof, former headquarters of the knights of the Teutonic Order.

㉓ Ludwigsburg This city's founder, Duke Eberhard Ludwig, felt most cities lacked creativity. This inspired him in 1704, to fashion one according to his own personal designs.

Ludwigsburg's most lavish building, the Residenzschloss (palace), is still the focal point of the city today. The "Swabian Versailles" is one of the largest baroque chateaus in Germany, further

enhanced by the magnificent gardens, for which Ludwigsburg is famous. During the annual Blossoming Baroque festival, thousands of visitors flock to the 30 ha (74 acres) of beautifully

1 "Mainhattan": the impressive skyline of Frankfurt am Main.

2 The royal hall of Lorsch Monastery, a "jewel of the Carolingian Renaissance".

3 Hirschhorn: the "Pearl of the Neckar Valley" is just east of Heidelberg.

4 The Kaiserpfalz palace in Bad Wimpfen was built in the 12th century by the Staufer.

5 Ludwigsburg Palace is one of the largest baroque palaces in all of Europe.

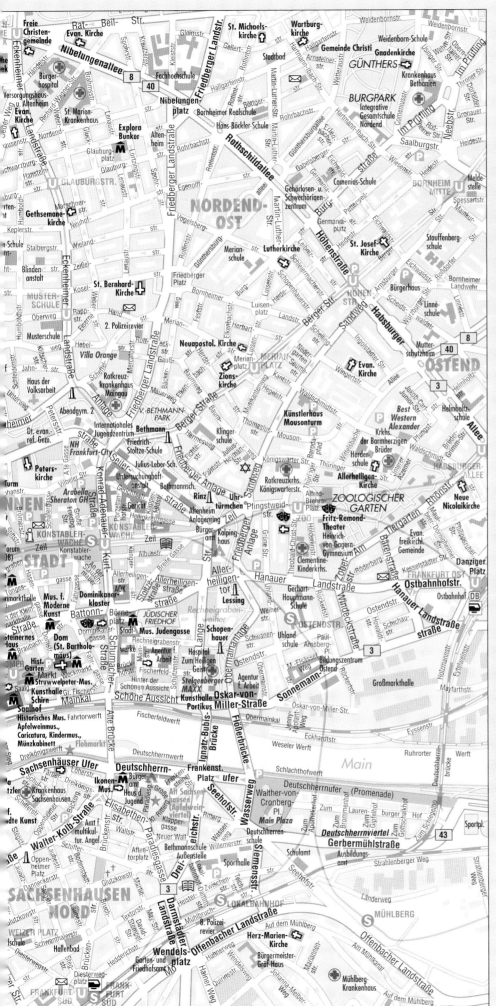

Frankfurt

"Mainhattan" or "Bankfurt" are nicknames often used to refer to Germany's metropolis on the Main. It is not entirely without reason, for the city's numerous skyscrapers do indeed resemble its North American counterpart.

Frankfurt is not just Germany's financial center, but second only to London in European finance. The 258-m-tall (846-ft) Commerzbank skyscraper is Europe's tallest office building, and Frankfurt's airport is one of the largest on the continent. The city is also a major international trade fair and publishing center. As the birthplace of Goethe, it is not unjustifiably the host of the world's largest book fair.

Indeed, Frankfurt has played an important role throughout Germany's history. Its Kaiserpfalz (imperial palace) was first mentioned in 794. In 876, it became the capital of the Ostrogoth empire. From 1356 to 1802, German kings and emperors were chosen and crowned here. In 1848/49, the German National Assembly met at St Paul's Church to defend the merits of democracy before the German court.

As "Mainhattan", Frankfurt has often had a dubious reputation – but unjust-

Sights in the Old Town include: Römerberg with the Römer Old Town hall (with corbie gables from the 15th–18th centuries); the imperial hall, once a venue for coronation banquets; the Ostzeile, opposite the town hall, featuring six half-timbered patrician houses; the old St Nicholas Church (consecrated in 1290); the Domplatz and the Kaiserdom cathedral from the 13th–15th centuries, a coronation church from 1562; Paulsplatz and the neoclassical church of St Paul (1796–1833), where the Goethe Prize and the Peace Prize of the German Book Trade are awarded by the City of Frankfurt; the baroque Hauptwache (1729/30); Goethe's birthplace and the Goethe Museum; the neoclassical Börse (stock exchange, 1879) building; the Eschenheimer Tower (with remains of the old town walls); and the late-neoclassical Old Opera House from 1880.

Past and present in close vicinity: view of the Römer, the Paulskirche and the Frankfurt skyline

ly so. Despite widespread destruction during World War II, and booming construction since, the city has managed to preserve much of its Hessian charm. This is especially evident in the historic Old Town around the Römerberg. On the other side of the Main River are half a dozen museums of world renown as well as the Sachsenhausen nightlife district.

Important museums in Frankfurt include: Kunsthalle Schirn (German painting from the Renaissance on); Museum for Modern Art; the Jewish Museum in the former Rothschild mansion; Nature Museum Senckenberg; the German Architecture Museum; Städelsches Art Institut with paintings from the 14th century to the present.

1

Detour

Lake Constance

Lake Constance is the second-largest lake in the Alps, and the largest in Germany. In the northern half, the Überlinger Lake, is Mainau, the "Island of Flowers", with its almost subtropical vegetation. Between Unter Lake and Zeller Lake is Reichenau, the "Island of Vegetables". From the Hoher Pfänder (1,063 m/3,488 ft) between Lindau and Bregenz, superb views unfold across the "Swabian Sea", the Old Town of Lindau, on an island in the lake, and the pictur-

Top: The Old Castle in Meersburg.
Center: Pilgrimage church of Birnau.
Bottom: View of Wasserburg.

esque villages of Wasserburg and Langenargen.

Friedrichshafen, on the German northern shore, is associated with zeppelins. In Meersburg stands the oldest lived-in castle in Germany. Near Unteruhldingen you can go visit two reconstructed prehistoric Pfahlbauten, or pile dwelling villages, which remind us of the early settlers in the area. Nearby in Birnau is one of the most beautiful baroque churches of the Lake Constance region.

landscaped gardens, which also boast an attraction for kids – the fairytale garden. Everyone from Hansel and Gretel to the witch, Sleeping Beauty, Snow White and the frog prince reside in this charming little park.

There are a number of other castles in Ludwigsburg as well. Not far from the imperial palace, in the middle of a vast nature and wildlife park, is Favorite, a baroque hunting lodge and maison de plaisance. It was constructed on the orders of Duke Eberhard Ludwig between 1713 and 1723. The Monrepos Palace on the lake was completed in 1768, a rococo building that features an attractive Empire interior and is often used as a venue for concerts, for example during the Ludwigsburg Castle Festival. From Ludwigsburg, a detour to the north-west to the Maulbronn monastery is worthwhile. This Cistercian monastery is the most completely preserved medieval monastic complex north of the Alps and has been a declared a UNESCO World Heritage Site. The triple-naved basilica was consecrated in 1178, while the chapter house dates from the 14th century.

24 Stuttgart The capital of Baden-Württemberg is charmingly nestled into a valley that opens out towards the Neckar. The historic city center and the rows of houses seem to climb up the often steep slopes.

Originally built around a 13th-century moated castle on the Neckar, Stuttgart quickly developed into a very important trad-

ing city. The magnificent Königstraße runs from the impressive, 58-m-high (190-ft) tower of the Stuttgart central station to the grand Schlossplatz. In the middle of the square are the Jubilee Column (1842) and some modern sculptures by Alexander Calder and Alfred Hrdlicka. The square is dominated by the Neues Schloss (new castle, 1807) with three separate wings, expanisve gardens and the neoclassical Königsbau (1860) opposite, which houses the Stuttgart Stock Exchange.

The Altes Schloss (old castle) was completed in the Renaissance style in 1578. Today, it houses the renowned Württembergisches Landesmuseum (state museum). Also on Schillerplatz, one of Stuttgart's most attractive squares, is the Gothic collegiate church with two towers (12th–15th centuries), the old chancellery, completed in 1544, and the "Fruchtkasten" (fruit box), an old grain silo from the 16th century.

Other interesting sights include the Akademiegarten next to the new castle, the Staatstheater (state theater) and the Staatsgalerie (state gallery). Roughly 10 km (6 mi) south-west of the city center is Solitude, an extravagant rococo palace built on a hill in 1767, on the orders of Duke Karl Eugen.

North of the city center, not far from the Killesberg with its 217-m-high (712-ft) television tower, is the Weissenhof artists' colony, designed by renowned architects including Le Corbusier, Mies van der Rohe, Walter

2

Gropius and Hans Scharoun. In the present district of Bad Cannstadt stands the Wilhelma, one of the most attractive and diverse botanical and zoological gardens in Germany.

25 Tübingen A university town since 1477, the "Athens on the Neckar" is still defined by the overwhelming student culture and the accompanying vibrant bar scene. Tübingen's picturesque and meticulously maintained Old Town, which climbs up in terraces from the banks of the Neckar, has a number of half-timbered houses surrounding a charming market square. From the 16-century Schloss Hohentübingen, which you can reach via the delightfully scenic Burgsteige lane, you get magnificent views of the Old Town and the Hölderlin Tower on the opposite side of the river. The famous poet lived here from 1807 until 1843.

Other sights worth visiting include the nearby Alte Burse

(1478–1482), Tübingen's oldest university building, as well as the Evangelisches Stift (1536). From Alte Burse you will also be able to see the Collegiate Church, built around 1470, the old auditorium and the town hall, dating back to the 15th century. Tübingen has always had a hint of Venice about it, especially when the "Stocherer" (pokers) punt on the Neckar with their longboats.

From Tübingen, a detour to Lake Constance brings you back to the Rhine, which flows into the lake west of Bregenz, Austria, and leaves it again near Stein, where it is referred to as the Upper Rhine.

1 View across the Neckar to Tübingen and its Stiftskirche with the remarkable spire.

2 Villa Solitude in Stuttgart was built between 1763 and 1767 on the orders of Duke Carl Eugen.

Mosel Loop at Bremm The slopes on the loop are the steepest Riesling vineyards in Europe. Bremm delights visitors with its alleyways and half-timbered houses.

Cochem To see the main feature of this town on the Lower Mosel you have to look up: Reichsburg Castle was built in 1070 and renovated in the 19th century.

Eltz Castle This picturesque fortified castle with fairy-tale towers and decorative balconies was built back in 1160.

The Rhine near Kaub This small romantic town on the right bank of the Rhine is surrounded by a medieval town wall and is one of the most important wine-growing villages on the Middle Rhine. Kaub is dominated by Gutenfels Castle from the 13th century. On an island in the river is the former Pfalzgrafenstein toll tower from 1326.

Trier Germany's oldest city boasts buildings dating from Roman times to the present. The market square is a charming centerpiece.

Mainz This bishops' town was founded by the Romans and is one of Germany's oldest cities. Sights include the Gutenberg Museum, the cathedral and the half-timbered houses in the Old Town.

Bacharach Situated on the left bank of the Rhine, this little half-timbered wine village is enclosed by turreted town walls from the 16th century and dominated by Stahleck Castle.

Bingen Among the sights here at the confluence of the Nahe and the Rhine are Klopp Castle and the Mouse Tower.

Frankfurt Europe's tallest office building distinguishs the skyline of "Mainhattan". The airport is one of the largest on the continent too. Goethe's birthplace is also importance for its international trade fairs and many banks. In addition, it boasts a very attractive Old Town.

Heidelberg This venerable university town is the epitome of German romanticism. The castle ruins (13th–16th centuries) rising high above the beautiful Old Town and the Old Bridge (1786–1788) are the most recognizable icons of Heidelberg. The best views are from the Philosophenweg.

Tübingen This old university town (since 1477) boasts a picturesque and almost entirely preserved Old Town.

Speyer Located on the high banks of the Rhine, Speyer Cathedral was begun in the year 1025. It is Germany's largest Romanesque building. This is a view of the crypt, built in 1041.

Ludwigsburg This county seat is known for its ducal palace, the largest baroque palace complex in Germany, also known as the "Swabian Versailles".

Stuttgart Baden-Württemberg's capital city is situated at the bottom of the Neckar River valley. The elegant Königstraße leads up to Schlossplatz and the New Palace. Also worth seeing are the Königsbau and the Old Palace.

Lake Constance With an area of 538 sq km (207 sq mi), Constance is the second-largest lake in the Alps. Romantic villages, orchards and vineyards thrive on its shores. The mild climate even supports subtropical plant life on Mainau. Constance, Meersburg and Lindau are cultural gems.

Germany

A fairy-tale journey – the Romantic Road

Four city gates and fourteen towers surround the medieval fortress town of Dinkelsbühl.

From the vineyards of Mainfranken through the charming Tauber Valley, to the geologically unique meteor-crater landscape of Ries and along the Danube, into the foothills of the Alps and the limestone mountains of Bavaria, the Romantic Road leads past myriad cultural sites from different centuries while giving you a glimpse of Germany's diverse natural landscape.

For the millions of visitors who travel the Romantic Road each year, it is a route that makes the cliché of charming and sociable Germany a reality. The stress of modern living seems to have had no effect in towns like Rothenburg ob der Tauber, Dinkelsbühl or Nördlingen, where the Middle Ages are still very much a part of the atmosphere. Yet they are dynamic towns that have understood the value of preserving the relics of their great past and carefully rebuilding those that were destroyed in World War II.

Plenty of culture awaits the traveller along this route. Alongside the well-known highlights there are numerous architectural gems that are also worth viewing if time permits. Some examples of these are Weikersheim Castle, the small church in Detwang with its Riemenschneider altar, Schillingsfürst Castle, the old town and castle at Oettingen, Harburg high above the Wörnitz Valley, the convent in Mönchsdeggingen, the churches in Steingaden and Ilgen, the little church of St Koloman near Füssen and other

King Ludwig II by Ferdinand von Piloty.

treasures along the way that have – perhaps luckily – not yet been discovered by the tourist hordes.

And yet the natural highlights should not be forgotten either as you cruise the Romantic Road to places like Würzburg, Rothenburg, Dinkelsbühl, Nördlingen, Donauwörth, Augsburg, Landsberg, the Wieskirche or Füssen, whose unique beauty is underscored by their rustic settings in romantic valleys, enchanting forests or impressive mountains.

Two of the most visited buildings on the route have been classified as UNESCO World Heritage Sites: the Würzburger Residenz and the Wieskirche, important baroque and rococo works. A trip to Munich, the charming and cosmopolitan capital of Bavaria, or to the Werdenfels region with its famous sights such as Oberammergau, Linderhof Castle, Ettal

Donauwörth with its Gothic parish church and 15th-century Tanzhaus. The once 'free city' has an incredible medieval old town.

The St Koloman Pilgrimage Church stands in a field against the backdrop of the Schwangauer Mountains.

Monastery and the twin villages of Garmisch-Partenkirchen enhances this aspect of your German experience.

For those who have the time, a visit to one of the numerous festivals that take place along the Romantic Road is highly recommended. Some are based around regional history like the Meistertrunk in Rothenburg ob der Tauber, a re-enactment of a drinking contest from the 17th century, or the Kinderzeche in Dinkelsbühl, a children's festival originating in the 17th-century Thirty Years War.

Classical music lovers should try to obtain tickets for the Mozart Festival in Würzburg, the Jeunesses Musicales concerts in Weikersheim, the Mozart Summer in Augsburg or the Richard Strauss Days in Garmisch. The Cloister Theater performances in Feuchtwangen are staged before a magnificent backdrop.

In addition to all this, there are festivals where anybody can participate, like the Free Town Festival in Rothenburg ob der Tauber or the Peace Festival in Augsburg. All these events take place in summer. Then of course there is the world-famous Oktoberfest in Munich, unmatched on the entire planet in its degree of debauchery and its sheer size. In winter the Christmas markets set up stalls that invite you to stroll, shop and drink a mulled wine with gingerbread cookies and other delicacies.

To sum it up, the Romantic Road has myriad attractions throughout the entire year, and takes you through the prettiest regions of Bavaria and Baden-Württemburg. Like no other road in Germany, it connects regional history with broad cultural landscapes, and brings the country's rich past to life.

The majestic throne room in Neuschwanstein Castle.

Johann Balthasar Neumann and Giambattista Tiepolo

Johann Balthasar Neumann was born in 1687 in Eger. Following an apprenticeship as a cannon founder, he went to Würzburg in 1711 to work in this trade. But his passion lay in architecture and he took every possible opportunity to learn more, supported by Prince-Bishop Johann Philipp Franz of Schönborn.

In 1720 he began his greatest work as royal architect of the Würzburger Residenz. Other important works by Neumann include the Würzburg Chapel, the pilgrimage churches in Vierzehnheiligen and Gößweinstein, Weißenstein Castle in Pommersfelden, Augustusburg Castle in Brühl and the Bruchsal Castle. When the master builder died in 1753 in Würzburg he was buried with military honours.

Top: Staircase in the Würzburger Residenz.
Bottom: Self-portrait of Tiepolo in the ceiling fresco over the staircase.

Most of the works of the Venice-born painter and etcher Giambattista Tiepolo can be found in Italy and in the royal castle in Madrid. Yet his principal works were the ceiling frescoes in the staircase and emperor's rooms of the Würzburger Residenz.
Tiepolo died in 1770 in Madrid. In the ceiling fresco of the staircase in Würzburg the painter immortalized himself and Neumann. Neumann is sitting upon a cannon.

The Romantic Road – The fascinating route between Würzburg and Füssen is lined with picturesque towns, forts, castles and priceless works of art. The road starts in the Main River Valley on its way through the charming Tauber Valley into the Wörnitz Valley and then crosses the Danube to follow the Lech towards the impressive Alps.

① Würzburg The Romantic Road begins with a sensation: the majestic Würzburger Residenz (1720), a baroque masterpiece. Despite the devastating bombings of 16 March 1945, which left even the most optimistic people with little to be optimistic about, this city on the Main offers many sights: the late-Gothic chapel of Mary and the rococo Haus zum Falken blend nicely on the market square.
The cathedral, which was consecrated in 1188, has unfortunately lost some of its character due to war damage. Near the baroque Neumünster lies the tranquil Lusamgärtlein, where the minstrel Walther von der Vogelweide lies buried. And all of this is dominated by the mighty fortress (13–18th centuries) on the Marienberg with its Main-Franconia Museum containing many works by Tilman Riemenschneider.

② Tauberbischofsheim This town in the Tauber Valley is famous for its history in the sport of fencing. It is distinguished by the Kurmainzisch Castle, whose storm tower is a masterpiece from the turn of the 16th century. The Riemenschneider School altar in St Martin's Parish Church is also worth seeing.

③ Bad Mergentheim The Old Town in this health resort is dominated by the Castle of the German Knights (16th century). Don't miss the baroque castle church designed by B. Neumann and François Cuvilliés. A small detour to see 'The Madonna' by Matthias Grünewald in Stuppach Parish Church is worth it.

④ Weikersheim Continuing through the Tauber Valley, Weikersheim invites you to visit its Ren-aissance castle and baroque gardens, which are among Germany's prettiest. The small former royal capital is surrounded by numerous vineyards.

⑤ Creglingen The Tauber Valley houses many of the works of

Travel information

Route profile
Length: approx. 350 km (217 miles), excluding detours
Time required: 7–10 days
Start: Würzburg
End: Füssen
Route (main locations): Würzburg, Tauberbischofsheim, Bad Mergentheim, Rothenburg ob der Tauber, Dinkelsbühl, Nördlingen, Donauwörth, Augsburg, Landsberg, Schongau, Füssen

Traffic information: Drive on the right in Germany. There is a 420-km (261-mile) cycle path that runs parallel to the Romantic Road. More information about this route can be found on the

Internet at:
www.bayerninfo.de.

Information:
There is a lot of information available on the Romantic Road but no definitive site for the entire route. The following sites might help you get an idea of how to organize your trip.

General:
www.romantischestrasse.de
en.wikipedia.org/wiki/Romantic_Road

Town sites:
www.rothenburg.de
www.dinkelsbuehl.de
www2.augsburg.de
www.fuessen.de

Augsburg: Fuggerei

Jakob Fugger, known in his day as simply 'the Rich', lived from 1459 to 1525. As financier and creditor to Habsburg emperors Maximilian I and Charles V, he almost had more power than the rulers themselves since they were dependent on him for capital. But as a man of faith Jakob Fugger also wanted to do something for his salvation, so with his brothers he founded the Fuggerei in 1516, the world's first social housing project.

People who found themselves in need through no fault of their own were provided with accommodation in one of the 67 buildings containing 147 apartments. The 'town within the

Top: The apartment blocks of the Fuggerei, the oldest low-income housing estate in the world.
Bottom: The Fuggerei Museum, showing an original sleeping area.

the wood sculptor Tilman Riemenschneider. The altar in the Creglingen Herrgottskirche is among the most beautiful. The Old Town here is a lovely mix of half-timbered houses and medieval fortresses.

6 Rothenburg ob der Tauber
This small town is synonymous around the world with German medieval Romanticism. A walk along the well-preserved town walls offers an overview of the place and great views across the Tauber Valley. The market square is dominated by the town hall, which has Gothic and Renaissance wings. You can also view more works of Tilman

Riemenschneider here. In fact, the triple-nave St Jakob Basilika houses his Holy Blood Altar. Further along the route heading south you'll cross the Frankenhöhe, the European watershed between the Rhine and Danube.

7 Feuchtwangen This one-time collegiate church, part Romantic, part Gothic, is worth a visit any time of the year. The marketplace has an attractive mix of bourgeois town houses.

8 Dinkelsbühl The main attraction of this town in the idyllic Wörnitz Valley is the perfect medieval town center with its town walls. Other highlights include the Deutsches Haus, a fabulous half-timbered house, and the St Georg Parish Church (second half of the 15th century). The town is more than 1,000-years-old.

9 Nördlingen Ideally you would approach fabulous Nördlingen from above in order to fully appreciate the nearly perfectly circular city center. Its original town walls have been masterfully preserved and its five town gates are still in use today.
St Georg is one of the largest late-Gothic German hall churches, its icon being 'Daniel', the 90-m (295-ft) bell tower. On a clear day from the tower you can

make out the rim of the Ries crater, especially towards the south-west, the south and the east.

10 Donauwörth This 'free town' developed from a fishing village on the Wörnitz island of 'Ried' at the confluence of the Wörnitz and the Danube. Most of its attractions are located along the main road, the Reichsstrasse: the Fuggerhaus from 1536, the late-Gothic Maria Himmelfahrt Parish Church, the Tanzhaus from around 1400, the town hall and the baroque Deutschordenshaus. The baroque church of the old Benedictine monastery Heiligkreuz is also worth visiting.

11 Augsburg 'Augusta Vindelicorum' was the original name given to Augsburg by its Roman founders. By the 16th century the 'free town' was one of the most important cultural

1 View of the Würzburger Residenz from Residenzplatz with the Franconia Fountain (1894).

2 The town hall in Augsburg with its remarkably symmetrical facade and 78-m (256-ft) Perlach Tower.

3 View from 'Daniel' over the Nördlingen market square.

town' even had its own church and a well. Indeed, the flats in the Fuggerei are still available to Augsburgers in need. And the rent is still one Rhine Taler as it was when it was built – the equivalent of 0.88 euros.

House rules still oblige the daily recital of the Lord's Prayer, Hail Mary and 'believe in God for the founder'. The site is run by the Royal Fugger Foundation. It is impressive that people in the 21st century profit from Fugger's prosperity in the 16th century.

The former imperial city of Rothenburg ob der Tauber has what is considered one of the best-preserved medieval Old Towns. Its countless half-timbered houses and labyrinthine alleyways are encircled by a 3-km-long (2-mi) city wall with forty-three towers and tower gates that transport visitors back to 14th-century

Germany. One of the most romantic spots in the city is the fork in the road at the Plönlein, near the Siebersturm tower and the low-lying Kobolzeller Gate from around 1360, on the south side of town.

Beer gardens

The Munich beer gardens were born from the need to store the beer in a cool place. To do this the brewers built large cellars, usually right next to their breweries. In order to protect them from the heat, they planted the area with chestnut trees. And because a rest in the shade of the

Beer garden at the Chinese Tower in the Englischer Garten.

trees became popular, they set up tables and benches.

King Ludwig I allowed them to serve beer there but the breweries were forbidden to sell food. And so it came about that the citizens brought their own snacks with them – often meatloaf, cheese, radishes and pretzels. This custom has survived to this day, although now many beer gardens serve snacks or even full meals alongside their beer.

So, Cheers!

Detour

Munich

There are many ways to discover Munich – by bike through the different quarters, a museum tour or shopping in Old Town. Or you can do it by theme.

The Munich of artists

Important paintings and sculptures are on display in the large and impressive Munich museums: the Alte and Neue Pinakothek, Pinakothek der Moderne and Haus der Kunst. The Lenbachhaus and the Villa Stuck show how successful artists lived in Munich at the end of the 19th century. The Lenbachhaus was designed by the architect Gabriel von Seidl in 1887 for the painter Franz von Lenbach and is a fantastic little museum with a wonderful variety of art and photography.

Today it is home to a municipal gallery and contains major works by the Blaue Reiter group. The Villa Stuck was designed by the aristocratic painter Franz von Stuck in 1897–98 and hosts a variety of exhibits. A wander into the heart of Schwabing is also part of any trip on the trail of artists – at the beginning of the 20th century, 'bohemian Munich' used to gather near Nikolaiplatz. Schwabing has been able to preserve some of its old flair.

Green Munich

For those who have had enough of the city it is also easy to find a bit of nature in this wonderful city. The first and foremost of the green oases is of course the Englischer Garten. At 4 sq km (1.5 sq mi) it is the world's

largest city park – even larger than Central Park in New York. Beyond the vast lawns and brooks that flow through this wonderful park there are a few architectural highlights as well: the Chinese Tower, the Monopteros and the Japanese teahouse. The best way to explore the Englischer Garten – and Munich in general – is by bike. Take a break along the way at one of the beer gardens.

The Isar River runs straight through Munich and on a summer day can be a nice way to cool down. To get there just walk to the Deutsches Museum. There are stony riverbanks to stroll and dip your feet in the water, and even a few places to jump right in!

In the center of town, just a few steps from Karlsplatz (also known as Stachus), is the old botanical gardens park. The of Nymphenburg porcelain statues spread around the park are beautiful. Take a tram to Nymphenburger Park, another oasis of relaxation where you'll find landscaped gardens and a baroque castle.

Munich theater town

For theater lovers, Munich offers interesting shows and fantastic theater architecture. The majestic Cuvilliés Theater is part of the former royal Residenz. François Cuvilliés designed the fabulously ornate rococo structure. A second building that attracts theater lovers and architecture enthusiasts is the Kammerspiele in the Maximilianstrasse. Architects Richard Riemerschmid and Max Littmann allowed their art-nouveau

fantasies free rein here in 1900–01. A lengthy restoration was finished recently.

Another building with a bit of history is the Prinzregenten Theater, which was badly damaged during World War II and not reopened until the renovation was completed in 1996. It was built in 1901 to celebrate the works of Richard Wagner. You can see international operas in the Prinzregenten Theater and in the classical National Theater. Munich also has a lively free theater scene, some of which moves around regularly.

1 Munich by night: View over the Frauenkirche with its imposing spires and the neo-Gothic town hall tower. To the far right is the Olympia Tower.

2 The Siegestor gate in Schwabing separates the two great avenues of Leopoldstrasse and Ludwigstrasse.

3 The Cuvilliés Theater is the city's oldest surviving opera house. Only the interior remains of the original building.

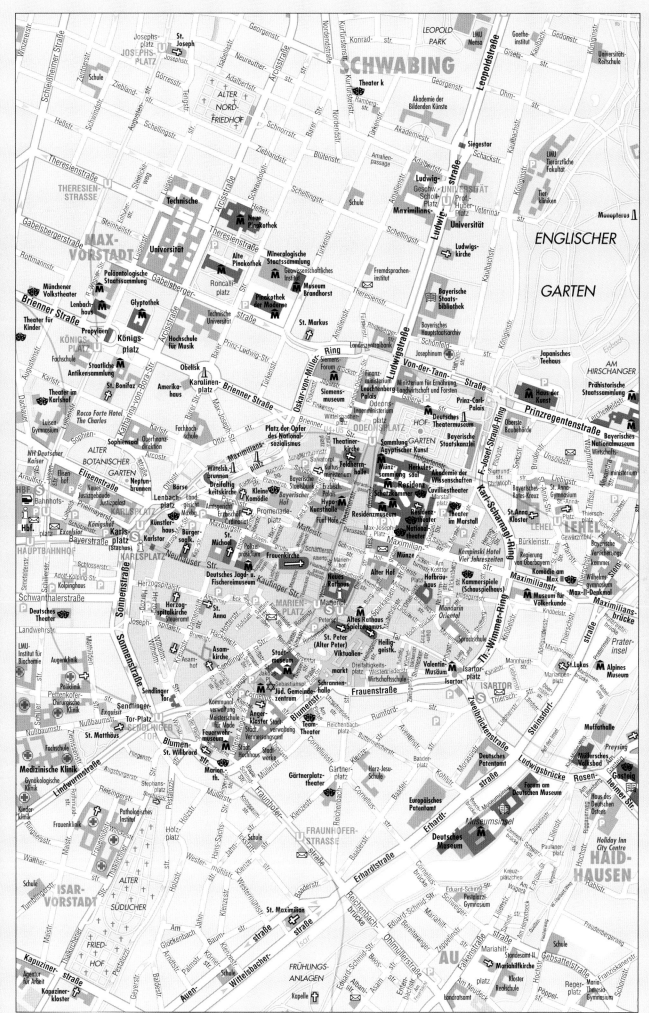

Munich

Munich exudes the magic of an old city that still manages to remain youthful, multicultural and very much itself.

Munich was originally founded by Guelph Heinrich the Lion, but the royal Wittelsbacher family controlled the city until 1918 and played a much greater role in its history. They are to be thanked for most of the city's monuments and works of art and the prettiest stretches of road. Ludwig I was particularly energetic, claiming that he wanted to build 'Athens on the Isar'. The Old Town lies between the Isartor, Sendlinger Tor, Karlstor and the Feldherrnhalle. Schwabing, the university and museum district, gives Munich its reputation for being a fun-loving and cultured city of the arts.

Attractions in the historic city center include Marienplatz with the new town hall from the 19th century, the old town hall from the 15th century and the baroque Mariensäule; the late-Gothic Frauenkirche with its two iconic spires; Asamkirche, a rococo masterpiece; the Residenz with the treasure chamber, Residenz theater (rococo) and court garden, which was expanded during the Renaissance; the National Theater; the baroque Theatinerkirche; the Renaissance church of St Michael's; the

Top: National Museum, on Max-Joseph-Platz.
Bottom: Nymphenburg Castle.

Hofbräuhaus and Viktualienmarkt and the bronze Bavaria on the Theresienwiese.
There is also the Nymphenburg Castle and Park and the Olympic Park from 1972. Don't miss the museums: Deutsches Museum, the Alte Pinakothek, the Neue Pinakothek, the Pinakothek der Moderne, Lenbachhaus, Glyptothek, Bayerisches Nationalmuseum; Stadtmuseum in the old Zeughaus and the Villa Stuck.

1

King Ludwig II

In 1864 Ludwig II ascended to the Bavarian throne. He soon withdrew into a dream world, where fantasies of Louis XIV's palace took over and Richard Wagner's operas influenced the architecture of the Linderhof, Neuschwanstein and Herrenchiemsee

King Ludwig II's *Night time Sled Ride*, by Rudolf Wenig.

castles. Wagner would not have been able to create the Bayreuther Festival had it not been for financial support from Ludwig. Yet the king's passions tore great holes in the state's finances and so he was certified insane in 1886. A few days later he drowned in mysterious circumstances in Lake Starnberg and thus became a popular myth.

and financial metropolises north of the Alps. The town hall was built between 1615 and 1620 and was designed by Elias Holl, as was the Zeughaus of 1607. Stained-glass windows depicting the five prophets in St Maria Cathedral are among the oldest in the world. The streets are lined with many patrician houses like the Schaezler and Gignoux palaces. A few towers and gates (such as the Red Gate) are left over from the old town defenses.

From Augsburg it is a quick half-hour drive to Munich (see pp. 130-131). From there you can take the Lindau motorway straight to Landsberg.

⑫ Klosterlechfeld This monastery was built on the site of an historic battlefield from the year 955. Elias Holl was the architect of this pilgrimage church, which was erected in 1603. It was based on the Pantheon in Rome.

⑬ Landsberg am Lech The first wall surrounding the Old Town between the Lech River and the Lech bluff was built in the 13th century. It included the Schmalzturm at the top end of the triangular main plaza, which

2

is dominated by the town hall. The stucco facade of the town hall was designed by Dominikus Zimmermann in 1719.

The Bayer Gate, built in 1425, is part of the third wall and is one of the most beautiful of its kind in southern Germany. The four churches in Landsberg am Lech are especially noteworthy: the Gothic, late-baroque Maria Himmelfahrt; the Johannis-kirche by Dominikus Zimmermann; the Ursuline Convent Church by J.B. Gunetzrhainer (begun in 1740) and the Heiligkreuz Monastery church. Portions of the 15th-century

Landsberg town wall are also quite well-preserved.

⑭ Altenstadt St Michael's is one of Upper Bavaria's most significant Romantic churches. It was built in the early part of the 13th century and is surrounded by a mighty protective wall. It houses frescoes from the 14th and 15th centuries as well as the 'Grosser Gott von Altenstadt', a Romanesque crucifix from around 1200. Because of its enormous size, it is one of the most important works of art of its type, radiating an expressive calm in the church.

⑮ Schongau The drive to Schongau follows the Lech River through Claudia Augusta. The Gothic Ballenhaus of 1515 bears witness to its previous importance as a trading town.

The town walls with their battlements are still conserved in part, as are five towers and the Frauen Gate to the west (14th century). The Maria Himmel-fahrt Parish Church, which was remodelled by Dominikus Zimmermann in 1748, has frescoes by Matthäus Günter and is well worth a visit.

If time permits, you can continue from here into the Werdenfels

charming baroque church after another. Add the natural environment of the area and you've got a delightfully attractive combination for walks such as the one leading through the Ammerschlucht to Wieskirche.

17 Wieskirche One of this route's best highlights is the Wieskirche, built by Dominikus Zimmermann in 1745. Against the backdrop of the Trauchberge Mountains, the ceiling frescoes and a large part of the stucco here were done by Johann Baptist Zimmermann. The white and gold interior appears light and cheerful, as if music had been turned to stone. The Wieskirche near Steingaden is visited by hundreds of thousands of tourists every year. It is considered to be a complete work of art.

18 Hohenschwangau and Neuschwanstein These two royal castles are picturesquely set in a striking mountain scene. Crown Prince Maximilian gave Castle Hohenschwangau (12th century) a neo-Gothic facelift in 1833 – Ludwig II, the man behind nearby Castle Neuschwanstein, had spent part

of his youth here in Hohenschwangau. Neuschwanstein is the idealized image of a medieval castle with towers, battlements and majestic rooms.

19 Füssen The Romantic Road comes to an end in this small town on the Lech River. Don't miss the St Mang Monastery or the baroque St Magnus Parish Church. The medieval edifice here was also given a generous baroque remodel. The trompe l'oeil on the facade of the Hohen Schloss castle courtyard is particularly noteworthy. The facade of the Heilig-Geist-Spital Church (1748–1749) is sumptuously painted. To finish off the trip, how about a wild nature experience: take a gander at the nearby Lechfall.

1 Neuschwanstein Castle with the Allgäuer Alps as a backdrop.

2 The pilgrimage church of the Gegeißelter Heiland auf der Wies lies in the Pfaffenwinkel and is a UNESCO World Heritage Site.

3 The two-tiered choir in the Wieskirche with the painting of Christ in the center.

Dominikus Zimmermann

Born in 1685 in Wessobrun, this trained carpenter actually reached his masterful heights as a builder and stucco artist. He became rich and famous thanks to his trade and even became mayor of Landsberg am Lech

View from the ornate pulpit above the choir stalls in the Wieskirche.

from 1749 to 1754. In 1756 he moved into the house he had built next to his masterpiece, the Wieskirche near Steingaden, and lived there until his death in 1766. His other works include the Steinhausen Pilgrimage Church and the Frauenkirche in Günzburg.

area to enjoy some wonderful mountain scenery (see Detour, p. 134).

16 Rottenbuch The old Augustine canonical church in Rottenbuch was remodelled

between 1737 and 1742 and now shines with baroque cheerfulness. Stucco artist Joseph Schmuzer and painter Matthäus Günter were responsible for the wonderful interior. In this area it isn't hard to stumble over one

The Oberammergau Passion Play

In 1633 a plague epidemic occurred during the Thirty Years War that inspired the people of Oberammergau to inaugurate this 'play of suffering, death and the resurrection of our Lord Jesus Christ', which they would perform every ten years.

The play was enacted for the first time in 1634 at the cemetery where the victims of the plague had been buried. This location was then used until 1820. In 1830 it was moved to its current venue where, in the year 2000, the play was performed for the 40th time.

Over 2,000 people from Oberammergau – all amateurs – took part in the most recent Passion Play, as actors, musicians, singers or stagehands. The story lasts around six hours and the text has been modified numerous times over the years. It is a regular source of dispute.

The people of Oberammergau are not always in agreement when it comes to the Passion Play. For example, the decision as to whether or not to allow married or older women to participate had

Top: Backdrop of the Passion Play in 2000.
Bottom: Crucifixion scene in Oberammergau.

to be decided by the Upper Regional Court. The result was that they are allowed to participate.

The current open-air stage was originally built in 1930 but was fully renovated between 1997 and 1999. As the theater was brought up to date with technology, the town can now host other events, such as operas, in the years between the Passion Plays.

Detour

Werdenfelser Land

A small detour from the Romantic Road takes you into the Werdenfelser Land, a magnificent mountain landscape with numerous romantic towns and villages. To take this detour, do not continue on to Füssen from the Wieskirche. Instead turn east towards Unterammergau and Oberammergau.

Oberammergau

The prettiest house in this picture-book village is the so-called Pilatushaus, which is richly decorated with paintings by Franz Seraph Zwink. The outside wall on the garden side of the house depicts the Judgement of Jesus by Pilate, hence the name of the house. Today Pilatushaus is home to a gallery and 'live-work studio' where you can watch local wood-carvers ply their trade. Oberammergau has been renowned for its wood-carving tradition since the Middle Ages and there are around 120 of them here. When the Passion Play is not scheduled you can take a tour of the theater.

Linderhof

After a short drive through the romantic Graswang Valley you reach Linderhof Castle, the only castle built by Ludwig II that was actually finished during his lifetime. The baroque construction is surrounded by large grounds containing other odd and interesting buildings, for example the Venus grotto, which was built to resemble the Hörselberg grotto in Wagner's *Tannhäuser*. Other sites include a Moorish Kiosk, a Prussian pavilion from the 1867 World Exhibition, which Ludwig II had majestically redecorated to his tastes, and the Hundinghütte, a perfect Germanic log cabin based on Wagner's Valkyrie.

Ettal Monastery

Standing in front of the majestic church of Ettal Monastery, you have the feeling of having stumbled across a little piece of Italy in the middle of the Bavarian Werdenfelser Land. The painting of Christ, the centerpiece of

the church, was donated in 1330 by Emperor Ludwig of Bavaria. There was initially a Gothic abbey here that was remodelled in 1710 in a majestic baroque style. The building, erected by the Italian Enrico Zucalli, was decorated with stucco by artists J.B. Zimmermann and J.G. Ueblherr, and a magnificent ceiling painting by J.J. Zeiller and M. Knoller. The layout, a twelve-sided central construction is unique in Germany and was actually necessary for the facade. The Benedictine monks had not only God in mind when they built their monestary, but also the awe it would inspire in its visitors.

Garmisch-Partenkirchen

In 1935 the two villages of Garmisch and Partenkirchen were joined into a market town. Many houses here are decorated with frescoes. Haus zum Husaren is a particularly well-known example. In Garmisch the old Gothic parish church of St Martin, with its

well-preserved frescoes, and the new baroque parish church of St Martin are worth visiting. In Partenkirchen the pilgrimage church St Anton, built on the Wank, the local mountain, dates back to the middle of the 18th century. Music lovers should head for the Richard Strauss Institute and the Strauss Villa, where the composer spent a large part of his life.

You shouldn't miss taking the gondola up to the Zugspitze (2,962 m/9,718 ft), Germany's highest mountain.

1 The golden cross marks the eastern peak of the Zugspitze, which offers a great panoramic view.

2 The north facade of Linderhof Castle reflected in the lake.

3 The town of Garmisch-Partenkirchen, one of the most renowned health resorts at the base of the Wetterstein Mountains.

Bad Mergentheim The Old Town here is dominated by the Castle of the German Knights (16th century). Its church was designed by B. Neumann and F. Cuvilliés.

Weikersheim This precious royal town in the Tauber River Valley has a Renaissance castle and a baroque garden, one of Germany's prettiest.

Dinkelsbühl More than 1,000 years of history bless this town in the Wörnitz Valley, perhaps the best example of medieval architecture. Surrounded by formidable walls, its main attractions are the Deutsches Haus and St Georg Cathedral.

Augsburg The Renaissance town hall and Perlach Tower are highlights in this 2,000-year-old city.

Wieskirche This pilgrimage church is considered in its entirety entity to be one of the major works of Bavarian rococo art.

Linderhof Castle The only one of Ludwig II's three castles to be finished during his lifetime is surrounded by a park with unusual buildings, some of which are derived from Wagner's operatic fantasy world.

Füssen/Neuschwanstein The old city between the Ammergau and Allgäu Alps awaits you with two royal castles: Hohenschwangau (12th century, transformed to neo-Gothic in 1837) and the world-famous fairy-tale castle of Disney fame, Neuschwanstein (1869–86).

Würzburg Despite the bombings of 1945, this wine city on the Main offers a number of attractions. The most important of these are St Kilian Cathedral (opened in 1188), the old Main bridge and Fort Marienberg (13th–18th centuries).

Würzburger Residenz The majestic construction, started in 1720, was supposed to replace Fort Marienberg. Its scale is amazing, both inside and out.

Feuchtwangen This former 'free town' with rows of pretty houses has a collegiate church that is part Romantic and part Gothic. There is also a handful of museum collections worth seeing.

Rothenburg Once a Franconian 'free town', Rothenburg has hardly changed since the Thirty Years War. The town offers spectacular views over the Tauber River Valley.

Nördlingen St Georg is one of Germany's largest late-Gothic hall churches. From the bell tower 'Daniel' you can get a good view of this almost perfectly circular town.

Nymphenburg This baroque castle in Munich is a majestic site indeed. The expansive grounds make for a lovely walk or picnic. The state porcelain factory is next door.

München A detour into the Bavarian capital should be part of any trip along the Romantic Road. With the Old Town and the Schwabing district, the Viktualienmarkt, the Englischer Garten, the impressive Olympic Park as well as churches from almost 850 years ago and world-famous museums, this 'international village' has much more to offer than just the 'Oktoberfest'.

Map labels:
Schweinfurt · Frankfurt · Main · ❶ WÜRZBURG · Nürnberg · Kist · Kitzingen · Tauber-bischofsheim ❷ · Ochsenfurt · Lauda-Königshofen · Röttingen · Creglingen ❺ · Bad Mergentheim ❸ · Welkersheim ❹ · Stuppach · Heilbronn · Rothenburg o.d.Tauber ❻ · Naturpark Frankenhöhe · Blaufelden · Schillingsfürst · Ansbach · Nürnberg · Heilbronn · ❼ Feuchtwangen · Crailsheim · ❽ Dinkelsbühl · Wilburgstetten · Fremdingen · Naturpark · Oettingen · Wallerstein · Wemding · Ulm · Bopfingen · ❾ Nördlingen · Altmühltal · Möttingen · Harburg · Donauwörth ❿ · Dillingen · Danube · Wertingen · Pöttmes · Naturpark · Meitingen · Ulm · Augsburg- · Aichach · Zusmarshausen · ⓫ AUGSBURG · Westliche · Friedberg · Bobingen · Königsbrunn · Wälder · Schwabmünchen · MUNICH · ⓬ Klosterlechfeld · Kempten (Allgäu) · Buchloe · ⓭ Landsberg a.L. · Ammersee · Kaufbeuren · Altenstadt · Hohenfurch ⓮ · Starnberger See · ⓯ Schongau Peiting · Marktoberdorf · ⓰ Rottenbuch · Kempten (Allgäu) · Wildsteig · Steingaden · Nesselwang · ⓱ Wieskirche · Schwangau ⓲ · Halblech · Oberammergau · Füssen ⓳ · Neuschwanstein · Linderhof · Ettal · Oberau · Garmisch-Partenkirchen · Zugspitze 2962 · Innsbruck · AUSTRIA

In the heart of Europe

Schönbrunn Palace in Vienna – a former Habsburg summer palace with

The Route of the Emperors: Berlin – Prague – Vienna – Budapest

On this journey along the ancient European transport and trade arteries of the Elbe, Vltava and Danube rivers, Europe presents itself in all its historical and cultural diversity. On the various riverbanks, cities like Dresden, Prague, Vienna and Budapest show off their abundant monuments of art, and everywhere along the route are palaces, castles and urban gems surrounded by unique natural scenery.

No emperor could ever have imagined that at the beginning of the 21st century you would be able to travel all the way from the Spree River (Berlin) to the Danube without any complicated border checks, particularly after the centuries of mini-states in the region and the tragic rift of the 20th century. What happened to the days when autocratic despots jealously erected border checkpoints and threw up 'iron curtains' to protect their territories? When the Viennese

knew nothing of Budweis or Bratislava, and to the people of West Berlin, Dresden might as well have been further away than the Dominican Republic? Gone indeed are those days. These days, the road is free to explore what is so close and yet still quite unfamiliar, and there really is a lot to discover.

Berlin, Germany's old and new capital, is its very own unique tourist cosmos. It would take weeks to see even a fraction of its museum treasures, its continuously

The landmark of Vienna: St Stephen's Cathedral.

changing skyline with so much contemporary architecture, an art and restaurant scene that is just as dynamic as that of any other cosmopolitan city, and its large green parks. On this route, however, Berlin is but the starting point of a fascinating journey across Europe.

In Brandenburg and Saxony, both core regions of German intellectual history, one highlight seems to follow the next. Potsdam, the royal residence of the Prussian kings, provides a magnificent overture to the Lutheran town of Wittenberg, to Weimar, the focal point of German classicism, and to the porcelain metropolis of Meissen, your next stops.

Dresden is simply irresistible as a tourist destination. The capital of Saxony, which rose like the proverbial phoenix from the ashes (and from the floodwaters in 2002), enchants with its baroque and rococo

extensive gardens.

Charlottenburg Palace in Berlin, the summer residence of Sophie Charlotte, wife of Frederick I.

Hradčany Castle above the Charles Bridge, Prague's most famous bridge, on the Vltava River.

buildings and its art galleries. Music lovers flock to highlights like the Semper Opera, the Staatskapelle orchestra and the famous Kreuzchor choir.

Attempting to describe in words the exquisite beauty of Prague is often an exercise in futility. The views across the Vltava River towards Hradčany Castle are some of the most unforgettable city sights anywhere on earth. And just like one of Mozart's melodies, the magic hovering above the picturesque alleyways in the Small Quarter and around the Old Town Square will leave no soul untouched.

From the splendidly restored spa towns of Karlovy Vary and Mariánské Láznů, to Litoměřice, Hrad Karlštejn, České Budějovice and Český Krumlov – the number of five-star attractions in Bohemia is just incredible.

There are just as many amazing sights on the journey through Upper and Lower Austria – Freistadt, Linz, Enns, Grein and Krems, not to mention the Melk and Klosterneuburg monasteries.

Away from urban attractions, nature will also spoil you along the route – the heathlands of lower Fläming and Lower Lausitz, the sandstone mountains on the River Elbe, the Vltava Valley, the Bohemian Forest, the Mühl Quarter, Wachau and the Viennese Forest. Between city tours and museums you can tank up on oxygen everywhere on this trip. On top of that, you can always sample the tasty delicacies that the local cuisine has to offer.

An almost exotic piece of scenery awaits you at the end of your tour, east of Budapest across the River Tisza – the Hortobágy National Park, a real piece of the idyllic Hungarian Puszta.

East of Budapest's Matthias Church is the Halászbástya, the Fisherman's Bastion.

Following in Luther's footsteps

Wittenberg, the town of Luther and one of the focal points of German intellectual history, is located 30 km (18 miles) west of the impressive medieval town of Jüterbog. To get there, take the B187.

As a university town, the cradle of the Reformation and the 'workshop' of seminal humanists, Wittenberg was one of the intellectual centers not only of Germany in the 16th century, but of Central Europe. It was here that the influential scholar Martin Luther came in 1508 to hang his famous ninety-five Theses fulminating against the clerics on the Castle Church door, thereby kicking off the Reformation.

Memories of him and of the theologian Philipp Melanchthon are still very much alive. In the house where

Wartburg Castle near Eisenach.

Martin Luther lived from 1508 to 1546, there is a museum on the history of the Reformation. The house where Melanchthon lived, studied and died is also open to the public, and is also the only private home remaining from the 16th century. The town church of St Mary where Luther used to give his sermons is also worth seeing.

Despite it being off your route, a visit to Wartburg castle is highly recommended. About 250 km (160 miles) from Dresden you'll find Eisenach, where Luther went to school. Southwest of Eisenach, atop the Wart Mountain, in the middle of the Thuringian Forest, is the medieval Wartburg Castle, built in 1150. It was in this castle that Luther translated the New Testament from Greek into what was then the first-ever German version of the bible in 1521–22. The rest, as they say, is history.

From the Spree in Berlin to the Danube in Budapest – a journey through the European heartland of old empires is now possible without border checks, through five countries from the German capital to the Hungarian capital. It will give you a comprehensive overview of its cultural depth and scenic beauty.

❶ Berlin (see pp. 140–141).

❷ Potsdam Our first stop outside the city limits of Berlin is Potsdam, the state capital of Brandenburg. It is famous mainly for the beautiful baroque and neoclassical buildings and its magnificent parks dating from the era of the Prussian kings.

The best-known attraction of this town, which is 1,000 years old and has been partially declared a UNESCO World Heritage Site, is Frederick III's pompously decorated summer palace. Its park covers 300 ha (740 acres) and was designed by Lenné. It is an architectural gem in itself, full of statues and monuments such as the neighbouring park of Charlottenhof.

In Potsdam's Old Town, the Old Market with the St Nicholas Church and the former town hall, the Marstall stables, the Dutch Quarter and the old Russian colony of Alexandrowka are all worth a visit. Another must-see is the New Garden with its Marble Palace and Cecilienhof Castle.

From Potsdam, drive to the old town of Beelitz, and from there east to the B101 south towards Luckenwalde.

❸ Luckenwalde At first glance, this medieval market town may seem dull and industrial, but its interesting historical center has been well preserved. Its landmark is the steeple of St Johannskirche with its Gothic frescoes and important altar statues. A former hat factory, built at the beginning of the 1920s by Erich Mendelsohn, is also remarkable.

❹ Jüterbog This town, located 15 km (9 miles) further south at the edge of the lower Fläming heathlands, still has most of its original fortifications, including three beautiful gates. Sites here include the Liebfrauenkirche, the Nikolaikirche and the town hall, but the main attraction is really 5 km (3 miles) to the north: the ruins of the Cistercian monastery of Zinna, with important Gothic wall paintings.

Driving along the edge of the Lower Lausitz heathlands for

Travel information

Route profile
Length: approx. 1,100 km (700 miles), excluding detours
Time required: at least 2 weeks
Start: Berlin, Germany
End: Budapest, Hungary
Route (main locations): Berlin, Potsdam, Dresden, Prague, České Budějovice, Linz, Krems, Vienna, Bratislava, Komárno (Komárom), Budapest

Traffic information:
Drive on the right in all the countries on this trip. Speed limits are signposted. If not, 50 km/h (35 mph) in built-up areas, 90–100 km/h (55–60 mph) outside of towns. Autobahns in Germany have no speed limit

unless otherwise indicated. In the other countries, 130 km/h (80 mph) is usually the limit. Roads are typically good in all five countries.

When to go:
Central Europe is typically quite warm in summer, cold in winter, and inconsistent in spring and autumn. Always have a rain jacket, regardless of season.

General travel information:
Here are some sites that may help get you started with planning:
wikitravel.org/en/Berlin
www.saxonytourism.com
www.czech.cz
www.aboutaustria.org
www.oberoesterreich.at
www.hungary.com

Detour

Weimar

This Thuringian city with wonderful museums and monuments attracts visitors from far and wide. You reach Weimar from Dresden via the A4 Autobahn. In 1990 it was the European Capital of Culture and it certainly dressed itself for the occasion. Luther, Bach and Cranach all worked here; Goethe, Schiller, Wieland and Herder took German classicism to its peak; and Walter

about 100 km (62 miles) on the B101, you will pass Elsterwerda and Großenhain before you reach the Elbe River and the porcelain center of Meissen.

5 Meissen In the 12th century, this 'Cradle of Saxony', where the German emperors founded the first settlement on Slavic soil, was a royal residence of the House of Wettin. Until the devastations of World War II it was able to preserve its medieval imprint, with the Gothic cathedral and Albrecht Castle representing both religious and worldly power. These are still visible from the historic Old Town with its market square and half-timbered buildings.

Today the town is more famous for its 'white gold' than for its 1,000 years of history. Home of Europe's first hard porcelain, Meissen has produced this valuable product since Augustus the

Strong founded the factory in 1710. It continues to be exported all over the world.

Past Radebeul, the route along the B26 takes us to Dresden, the Saxon state capital 25 km (16 miles) away.

6 Dresden This former elector's residence, which has also been praised as the 'Florence of Germany' or the 'Baroque Pearl', is doubtless one of Europe's major cultural centers. In 1485 it became the seat of the Albertinian government, and during the 17th and 18th centuries, Augustus the Strong and his successors turned it into one of the most magnificent baroque residence cities in all of Germany.

The devastating bomb raids in February 1945 were unfortunately fatal for the city, destroying the Old Town almost beyond recognition. However, many of the famous buildings have either

already been restored or are still works in progress, chief among them being the Zwinger, housing the 'Old Masters' art gallery; the Semper Opera; the castle; the Frauenkirche; the Japanese Palace; the Albertinum, housing the 'New Masters' art gallery; the Green Vault; and the Brühl Terraces high above the riverbank. You should definitely visit the important attractions in the surrounding area, above all Pillnitz Castle, Moritzburg Castle and the so-called Elbe Castles.

If you are not intending to do the detour to Weimar and Wartburg Castle, you now follow the B172 upriver from Dresden. You'll pass Pirna, with its picturesque center and the interesting Großsedlitz baroque gardens, and enter the spectacular Elbe Sandstone Mountains.

7 Elbe Sandstone Mountains In order to get the best possible

views of these bizarre sandstone rock formations, you would really have to do a boat trip on the meandering river. Barring that, you can get some magnificent views from the road. Most of the area is now included in the 'Saxon Switzerland' National Park, with its monumental plateaus. Königstein Castle and the bastion in the spa town of Rathen are quite popular. Bad Schandau is the starting point for hiking and climbing tours to

1 Dresden owes its nickname, the 'Florence of Germany', to its baroque cityscape, which includes the Semper Opera and the Frauenkirche Church.

2 View of Sanssouci Palace, Friedrich II's summer residence, considered a rival to Versailles.

3 Moritzburg Castle was used by the Elector Friedrich August II of Saxony as a hunting lodge.

Top: Goethe and Schiller in front of the National Theater in Weimar.
Middle: Weimar Castle, home to the state art collection.
Bottom: Lucas Cranach House on Weimar Market.

Gropius started Bauhaus architecture here. Attractions are the Goethe House and Schiller House, the Bauhaus Museum, the Duchess Anna Amalia Library, the historic cemetery and the castle with its collection of art.

Karlovy Vary and Mariánské Lázně

Just over 40 km (25 miles) south of the German-Czech border, near Ústí nad Labem, follow the N13 west via Most and Chomutov to the Karlovy Vary, formerly the German Karlsbad ('Charles Bath'). Legend has it that it was actually Emperor Charles IV himself who found the hot salty springs in the area when he was out hunting deer in the 14th century.

Top: Town center of Karlovy Vary. Bottom: Health spa facilities at Mariánské Lázně.

Over the next 500 years, Bohemia's most famous and most glamorous spa town developed around these springs, with European elites from politics, art and society all making their way here to see and be seen. After fifty years of drabness during the Communist era, a glittering rebirth followed in 1989. Most of the Wilhelminian buildings, including the Mühlbrunn Colonnades, the town theater and the Grandhotel Pupp, now radiate again with all their former glory.

From the densely settled banks of the Tepla River, take the turnoff onto the N21 just outside Cheb and drive just 60 km (37 miles) to the second legendary spa town of Mariánské Lázně ('Mary's Bath'), where Goethe wrote his 'Marienbad Elegies' in 1823. Its stucco facades were completely restored in the original Schönbrunn imperial yellow. Especially magnificent are the 120 m (131 yds) of cast-iron colonnades.

the Schrammsteine rocks and through Kirnitz Valley up to the Lichtenhain waterfalls.

⑧ Děčín The rocky sandstone scenery continues in all its grandeur here on the Czech side of the border. From the town of Hřensko, for example, there is a beautiful 4-km (2.5-mile) walk to the spectacular Pravčická Gate stone formation. An ideal starting point for trips into the park area is Děčín, where the famous 'Shepherd's Wall' towers 150 m (492 ft) over the river.

On the way to the Ústí nad Labem region you'll find another magnificent rock formation, crowned by the ruins of Strekov castle. From here you can take a detour heading west on the N13 via Most and Chomutov to the renowned spa towns of Karlovy Vary and Mariánské Lázně.

⑨ Litoměřice At the confluence of the Eger and the Elbe (Labe), where the Bohemian hills flatten out towards the plains, is the ancient town of Litoměřice surrounded by vineyards and orchards. Its Old Town is among the most beautiful in Bohemia. At its center is the market square, which is around 2 ha (5 acres) in size. Don't miss the 'Kelchhaus', the town hall and St Stephen's Cathedral on Cathedral Hill.

About 4 km (2.5 miles) to the south, Terezín invokes memories of darker times. In World War II, the German occupation was not good to this town, which was originally built by Joseph II as a fortification against Prussia. There was a large concentration camp here.

⑩ Mělník High above the junction of the Vltava and Elbe Rivers is the much-visited town of Mělník, with its market square surrounded by beautiful stately houses. The town's most eye-catching sight, however, is its castle, a cherished possession of the local nobility for more than 1,100 years. The terrace of the castle restaurant has some fantastic views over the idyllic river valley.

From Mělník it is 40 km (25 miles) to Prague, the fairy-tale city on the Vltava River, and only 30 km (18 miles) to what is considered Bohemia's most famous castle.

⑪ Prague For detailed information see p. 143.

⑫ Karlštejn After 16 km (10 miles) on the R4, you head westbound at Dobřichovice for around 40 km (25 miles) until you get to this monumental castle perched majestically on a limestone rock 72 m (236 ft) above the Berounka Valley. It was built in the mid 14th century by Emperor Charles IV as his royal residence and a depository for the treasures. Its highlight in terms of art history is the Chapel of the Cross in the Great Tower with its gold-plated arches.

Back on the R4, you go to Příbram, which is located 50 km (31 miles) south-west of Prague, just off the main road.

⑬ Příbram This industrial and mining town, where silver has been mined since the 14th century and uranium since 1945, would not be worth mentioning if it were not for one of the Czech Republic's most visited pilgrimage destinations at its south-eastern edge – the Church of Our Lady of Svatá Hora with its baroque additions.

South-east of Příbram, not far from the B4, are two imposing castles on the bank of the Vltava River, which actually forms a reservoir more than 100 km (62 miles) long in this area. One of them is Zvíkov Castle, built in the 13th century on a towering rock outcrop; this former royal residence is worth a visit for its Chapel of St Wenceslas and the late-Gothic frescoes in its Great Hall. Orlík Castle, owned by the Schwarzenberg family for more than 700 years

1 View over Prague's Charles Bridge with the Old Town bridge tower and the church of St Franciscus in the background.

2 Hrad Karlštejn was used as a summer residence by Charles IV.

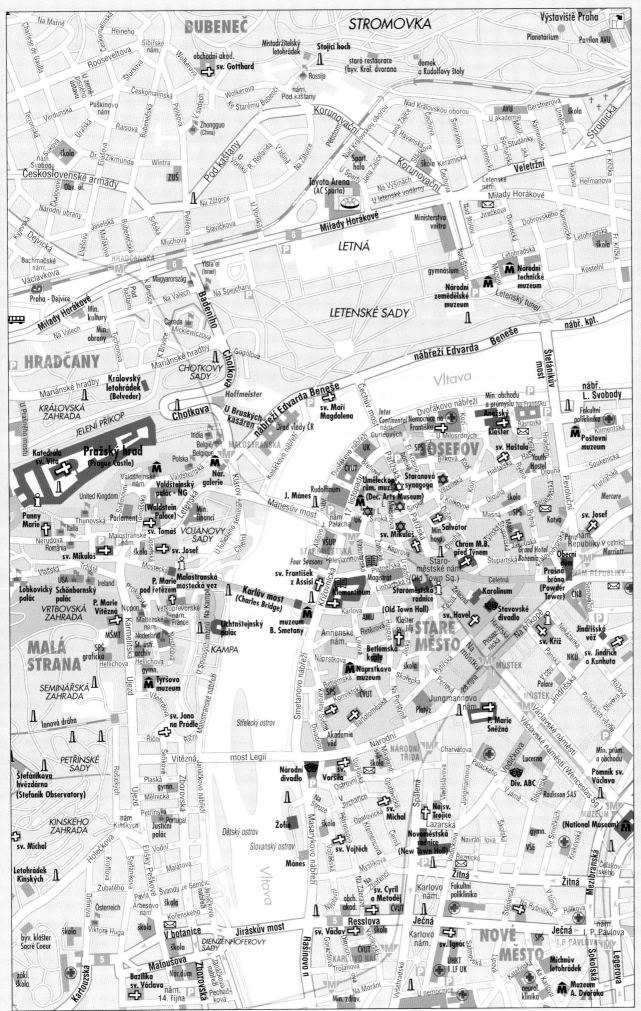

Prague

For centuries, the 'Golden City' has been an important intellectual and cultural center, characterized by unique and beautiful architecture throughout the entire city.

Although Prague escaped destruction in World War II, time has still taken its toll on the city's buildings over the centuries. Thanks to an expertly managed restoration, however, Prague can once again show off the magnificence of more than 1,000 years of history.

The Czech people can be proud of their capital, which is the former residence of Bohemian kings and Habsburg Emperors. Hradčany Castle, where they used to reside, provides you with the best views of this masterpiece of historical urban architecture – the entire city is designated a UNESCO World Heritage Site.

In the Old Town go see the Altstädter Ring with rows of historic houses; the baroque Týn Church and Jan Hus Memorial; the art-nouveau Representation House; St Wenceslas Square with buildings from the 19th and 20th centuries; the Gothic town hall with its astronomical clock; and the late-Gothic gunpowder tower.

In the Castle Quarter on the Hradčany visit the castle (royal residence since the 10th century); the Golden Alleyway; the King's Palace with Renaissance Hall; the St Veit's Cathedral, with relics from

Town hall and Týn Church, Prague.

St Wenceslas, the national saint; St George's Basilica (12th century).

In the Josefov district see the Old Jewish cemetery, the Old New Synagogue, and the Pinkas Synagogue.

In the Lesser Quarter visit the Charles Bridge (14th century); St Nicholas Church, Prague's most important baroque church and the Waldstein Palace of the commander Wallenstein.

The castle of Český Krumlov

There are many good reasons why the castle of Český Krumlov, located high above the Vltava River, is a UNESCO World Heritage Site – it comprises forty buildings and palaces with a total of 320 rooms and halls, as well as five courtyards and castle gardens measuring 7 ha (17 acres), with some very interesting detailing.

The castle buildings, erected on different rock formations, are connected by a three-storey viaduct with a canopied three-level walkway. The entrance is dominated by the tower, painted in 1590. The rococo castle theater dating from 1767 still has its original, and still functional, stage engineering. This open-air stage in the castle park is unique because it is the audience – not the stage – that turns when there is a change of scene.

The gigantic castle of Český Krumlov rises up high above the city.

The Masque Hall is also worth seeing. It is painted with figures from polite society and the *Commedia dell'Arte* (completed by J. Lederer in 1748). Also worth mentioning are the four bears guarding the entrance to the compound.

and reconstructed in neo-Gothic style in the 19th century, captivates with its richly decorated interior.

14 Písek On your way south on Road 20 you'll cross the Otava River after 50 km (31 miles). The well-manicured center of this little town used to be an important stopping point on the so-called Golden Path, the trade route between Prague and Passau. Deer Bridge recalls the town's importance as an ancient traffic hub. The bridge, which was built in the second half of the 13th century, is Bohemia's oldest stone bridge.

15 České Budějovice Another 50 km (31 miles) on, you come to České Budějovice, which is world-famous for its breweries. Since Ottokar II founded the town in 1265, its center has been the market square. The most dramatic sight on this huge square, which covers an area of 133 by 133 m (145 by 145 yds) and is surrounded by arcades on all sides, is the Samson Fountain. From the viewing platform of the steeple (72 m/236 ft), you can easily spot the other sights of the town – the baroque cathedral

of St Nicholas, the town hall, the Dominican Monastery and the Church of Our Lady, as well as the Salt House.

Around 10 km (6 miles) to the north, the battlements of Hluboká Castle appear on the horizon. Considered 'Bohemia's Neuschwanstein', this lavishly furnished castle was also owned by the Schwarzenberg family until 1939.

16 Český Krumlov Upriver from České Budějovice, it is another fifteen minutes by car along the Vltava River to the famous town of Český Krumlov. UNESCO certainly had its reasons for declaring this gem of more than 700 years as a World Heritage Site. Its location on both sides of a narrow hook in the river is incredibly scenic, and the labyrinthine alleyways of the Old Town and the Latrán with its shingled roofs are almost unsurpassably quaint. Highlights of every city tour are the Gothic St Vitus Church and the Schiele Center. The painter Egon Schiele worked and lived in Český Krumlov in 1911.

The defining attraction of the town, however, is its castle. It is Bohemia's second-largest,

and is surpassed only by the Hradčany in Prague. It was originally owned by the Rosenberg family for 300 years, then by Emperor Rudolph II before landing in the hands of the counts of Schwarzenberg in the early 18th

century. A guided tour of the castle shows you the living quarters, gallery, chapel, the Masque Hall with frescoes and a fine rococo open-air theater. It has been a designated UNESCO World Heritage Site since 1992.

17 **Freistadt** Right across the border in Austria you'll come to the next delightful example of medieval town planning. The center of the northern Mühl District, developed under the Babenberg Dynasty, quickly became the most important trading post between Bohemia and the Danube. To this day it has kept its 14th-century fortifications. Take a stroll through the narrow alleyways between the Linz Gate and the Bohemia Gate, past the town's handsome mansions and the huge town square to the church. Make sure not to miss the Mühl District House in the castle, which has a superb collection of reverse glass painting.

Your next stop is Linz, the capital of Upper Austria, and from there our route follows the northern banks of the Danube (B3) towards Vienna.

18 **Linz** (see sidebar on the right).

19 **Enns** This attractive town near the Danube dates back to a Roman fort called Lauriacum and is one of the most ancient towns in Austria. Its landmark is the city's free-standing tower, which measures 60 m (197 ft). Antiquity is brought to life in the Museum Lauriacum, which is located on the town square. On the left bank of the Danube, some miles north of Enns, lies the market town of Mauthausen. A monument in the local granite quarries commemorates the fact that the Germans ran a concentration camp here, where

1 View of Český Krumlov castle and the Old Town.

2 Samson Fountain on the square in České Budějovice, also known as Budweis of Budweiser fame.

3 The old cathedral on Linz's central square.

Linz

In the last couple of decades, Linz, which had long endured a bad reputation as an unattractive industrial town, has radically polished up its image. Contemporary art, using the most modern media and technology available, now defines Linz's cultural identity.

The Lentos Museum of Modern Art, the Ars Electronica Festival and the Design Center all pay their tribute to modern times. Every year, the bigwigs of computer art turn up for the Ars Electronica Festival, and a multimedia wave of sound and light descends on the city.

Beyond all this modernism is also the neatly restored historic center around the town square, which includes the Renaissance Landhaus (house of the provincial government), the castle, the Church of St Martin, the parish church and the old and new cathedrals, as well as a number of interesting galleries and museums.

An integral part of any sightseeing trip should also be a boat ride on the Danube with the Linz City Express, or a journey up the Pöstlingberg mountain on the ancient mountain railway.

The Melk Abbey – a spiritual center on the Danube

As far back as AD 976, Margrave Leopold I had established Melk Castle as his residence. Over the years, his successors equipped it with valuable treasures and relics. Then, in 1089, Margrave Leopold II handed the castle over to the Benedictine monks of the nearby Lambach Abbey. To this day, the monks continue to live at

The monastery library, decorated in shades of brown and gold, houses roughly 100,000 books.

the abbey according to the Rule of St Benedict.

Over the course of centuries, the monks not only collected but also produced valuable manuscripts for the abbey's vast library. In many areas of the natural and social sciences, as well as in music, the members of the Melk Abbey have chalked up some outstanding achievements during the establishment's illustrious history.

To this day, the monks continue to be active in the areas of counselling, economy, culture and tourism. Ever since it was founded, Melk Abbey has been an important spiritual and religious center in Austria.

around 100,000 people lost their lives.

Around 30 km (18 miles) downriver, at the start of the 'Strudengau', a stretch of river that is feared for its strong currents and dangerous sandbanks, is the little town of Grein. It originally became wealthy because local mariners would guide voyagers through the dangerous waters. It also has a very delightful rococo theater. Close by, the castle ruins of Klam are also worth seeing.

20 Ybbs This traditional market and toll location marks the beginning of the next section of the valley, the so-called 'Nibelungengau'. North of the power station (1958), the historic castle of Persenbeug keeps vigil over the valley. The castle remains the property of the Habsburg family and can only be viewed from outside.

A little further east, there are two reasons for a short excursion up to Maria Taferl, a Lower Austrian market town with no more than a thousand inhabitants. In addition to the baroque pilgrimage church, whose exuberant hues and shapes are truly beguiling, it is mainly the view from the terrace that is so captivating – the entire Nibelungengau of Burgundian legend sprawled out at your feet. In

good weather, you can even see large parts of the Eastern Alps.

21 Melk A real baroque icon salutes us from a rock outcrop 60 m (197 ft) above the south bank across the river, around 10 km (6 miles) east of the pilgrimage church. It's the Benedictine abbey of Melk with a church, two steeples and a facade of more than 360 m (393 yds) – undoubtedly one of the most magnificent of its kind in the world. This religious fortification, which was built in the

early 18th century, impressively symbolizes the euphoria among the clerics and the nobility after their dual triumph – over the Reformation and over the Turks. There is exuberant splendour everywhere in the edifice: in the Emperor's Wing with the Emperor's Gallery, which is nearly 200 m (219 yds) long; in the marble hall with its frescoes by Paul Troger; in the vast library with approximately 100,000 volumes; and also in the church, with ceiling frescoes by Johann Michael Rottmayr.

Back on the northern riverbank, the B3 takes us past the Jauerling Nature Park via Aggsbach, Spitz, Weißenkirchen and Dürnstein to the spectacular transverse valley of the Wachau River. Many of these places have an interesting history, like the Aggstein Castle on a rock outcrop high above the Danube. It is said that a series of unscrupulous men abused the castle's position on the river to rob passing Danube boats and charge exorbitant tolls. The ruin of Dürnstein tells the tale of the capture

Wachau

The transverse valley of the Danube, between Melk and Mautern and Emmersdorf and Krems, is the very image of a central European cultural landscape. No surprise, then, that it has been listed as a UNESCO World Heritage Site.
Blessed with a sunny climate and surrounded by picturesque, painstakingly terraced vineyards, it is just as famous for its good wines and fruit, especially its apricots, as for its history and stone memorials.

Danube, it takes just under thirty minutes to get to Tulln.

24 Tulln This town on the Danube, which started out as a Roman fort called Comagenis, has an impressive architectural ensemble of parish churches and a former charnel house. A visit to the mighty salt tower with its Roman core is also worth doing, and can easily be combined with a stroll along the riverside promenade. A museum with around ninety original paintings commemorates Egon Schiele, the town's beloved son and groundbreaking expressionist.

1 The Melk Abbey, founded c. 1000 AD, received its distinguished baroque makeover between 1702–39.

2 The icon of Wachau – the baroque monastery at Dürnstein contains a Renaissance castle, a former Augustinian monastery and a former Clarissan nunnery, all forming a unique ensemble on the bank of the Danube.

3 High above the Danube, not far from Aggsbach, is the Schönbühel Castle dating from the 12th century.

4 Impressions of Wachau – Weißenkirchen, the local wine-growing center, with its mighty Gothic parish church.

Top: Aggstein Castle ruins, Aggsbach.
Bottom: A lovely vineyard near Weißenkirchen.

In addition to the historic treasures of Krems, Stein, the old Kuenringer town of Dürnstein and the monasteries at Göttweig and Melk, the many small towns with their Gothic churches, covered arcades on the vineyards and medieval castles are among the highlights of a drive through this region 'wrapped in the silver band of the Danube'.
Must-sees along the northern river bank are Spitz with the Museum of Navigation, St Michael with its bizarrely decorated filial church, Aggsbach, the wine-growing towns of Weißenkirchen, Joching and Wösendorf, and last but not least, Dürnstein with its monastery and legendary castle.

of Richard the Lionheart and Blondel, the singer, who recognized him.

22 Wachau (see sidebar right).

23 Krems This town is located on the exact spot where the Danube trade route meets one of the main routes between the Alpine foothills and the Bohemian Forest, and where traders and mariners as far back as the early Middle Ages came to exchange their goods. This mercantile center at the eastern entrance to

the Wachau is not only one of the oldest, but also one of the most beautiful towns in the whole area. As a way into its restored alleyways, take the Steiner Tor ('Stone Gate'). From here, there is a circular walk across Corn Market to the Dominican Church, which houses the wine museum, and on to Gozzoburg on the High Market. From the gunpowder tower you have a beautiful view onto the more modern districts, the port and the Danube over to Göttweig Monastery. On the way

back you go along the road, past such architectural gems as the Bürgerspitalkirche, Gögl House and the town hall.
At the western end of Krems is the town of Stein. Must-sees here are the Minorite and St Nicholas Churches and a number of magnificent buildings as well as a former monastery which now houses the 'House of Lower Austrian Wines'.
Driving along the Wagram, a steep slope where lovely vineyards drop colourfully and abruptly down towards the

Budapest by night – Left: The west side of the city is dominated by the castle district with the palace (a domed structure rebuilt in 1945), St. Matthew's Church (rebuilt 1874–1896), and the Fisherman's Bastion from 1905. Foreground: The Elisabeth Bridge was the longest bridge in the world when it was built between

1897–1903. Center: The most famous Danube bridge of the city, however, is the suspension bridge built between 1839–1849. Two towers support the 380-m-long (495-ft) structure, which connects with Roosevelt Square on the Pest side.

Puszta – the central European steppe

Driving east from Budapest on the M3 motorway and then from Füzesabony on the N33, you reach Hortobágy, Hungary's oldest national park. Here, ancient prairie lands stretch out between the Tisza and Debrecen Rivers, the last vestige of the puszta landscape that once covered the entire steppe.

Crossing this grassland by car (it was designated a UNESCO World Heritage Site in 1999), you can hardly see anything but flat, monotonous

Top: The Puszta's landmarks are draw wells and herdsmen's huts. Bottom: Field of sunflowers in the Puszta.

countryside. Therefore, in order to see it in all its beauty you need to go exploring on foot, by bike, by boat or by horse-drawn carriage.

Right next to the famous Bridge of Nine Arches in Hortobágy Village, a museum takes you back to the everyday life of the Puszta herdsmen, a lifestyle that has all but disappeared. You can encounter old animal breeds in this area such as grey cattle, woolly boars and Raczka sheep.

Riding performances and bird watching or a visit to a pottery and a meal of the local savoury pancakes round off your visit.

a 'city of fortifications' like no other in the monarchy. After Ferenc I, King of Hungary, had found shelter from Napoleon's army in Komárno in 1809, it was made the central defense post of the Habsburg Empire.

Ever since the Treaty of Trianon (1920) marking the Danube as the border of the realm, the city has been divided into two parts. The former Old Town on the northern shore is now part of the Slovakian town of Komárno. On the Hungarian side, three fortifications are an interesting attraction for military history enthusiasts.

Monostor, the largest of the forts with 640 rooms and 4 km (2.5 miles) of underground shelters, is sometimes nicknamed 'Gibraltar of the Danube' and there are guided tours around it. The Igmánd fort, which is significantly smaller, houses a museum with findings from Roman times.

32 Tata This spa town at the bottom of Gerecse Hill gives off an atmosphere of cosiness and charm with its lakes and complex labyrinth of rivers and canals. But its location and its history have not been kind to the 'City of Water' – for 150 years it was situated on the border between the territories of the Habsburgs and the Ottoman Empire, which resulted in consistent large-scale devastation of its buildings

But every cloud has a silver lining. In around 1730, the Esterházy princes, then rulers of the town, initiated the reconstruc-

tion of the Tata, whose myriad baroque architectural ensembles shape the town to this day. Be sure to visit the ruins of the castle, built in the 14th century and later expanded into a magnificent Renaissance Palace by Matthias Corvinus. Don't miss Esterházy Castle and the former synagogue, which houses about 100 plaster-of-Paris copies of famous antique sculptures.

Halfway between Tata and Budapest – you can see it from the M1 motorway – is an apogee of Hungary's Romance architecture reaching high up into the sky. The Zsámbék Church itself actually collapsed in the middle of the 18th century, along with the adjacent Premonstratensian priory. Even as ruins, though, the colossal dimensions of the building are truly spectacular.

33 Budapest The Magyar metropolis has around two million inhabitants on a location where the Romans had already founded a town called Aquincum. Like many others, the two medieval communities of Ofen and Pest were devastated by the Mongols in 1241.

After the reconstruction, Ofen became Hungary's most important city, but was overtaken in the early 19th century by its sister town of Pest. The two cities were finally united in 1872. In the early 20th century, Budapest was considered the 'Paris of the East', a reputation it is still hoping to regain despite the devastation of World War II and more than four decades of Soviet rule.

The first thing on a long list of things to do just has to be the castle mountain. It is here on this limestone rock, nearly 1.5 km (0.9 miles) long, above the right bank of the Danube that the country's historical heart has been beating ever since the first king's castle was constructed upon it by Béla IV. Combining the Matthias Church, the Fisherman's Bastion and the castle, which houses several first-rate museums, this quarter has some of the most important sights in the city. And there are also some unforgettable panoramic views down to the city and to the river. The view from the neighbouring Gellért Mountain is just as scenic. The majority of the city's sights are located on the left bank of the Danube, in the Pest district. Once you leave behind the narrow Old Town center, the cityscape is typified by extensive Wilhelminian ring and radial roads.

You can visit St Stephen's Basilica, the National Opera, the National Museum, the Grand Synagogue and, directly by the river, the large market hall and the even larger houses of parliament. Out in the city forest are Vajdahunyad Castle, the Széchenyi Baths and the Museum of Fine Arts.

A must-see is, of course, the baroque palace in Gödöllő 30 km (18 miles) north-east of the city center, where Emperor Franz Joseph I and his wife Elizabeth ('Sisi') lived.

1 Budapest – the Houses of Parliament on the banks of the mighty Danube. In the foreground is the city's suspension bridge.

2 Hungarian grey cattle in Hortobágy National Park.

Sanssouci The rococo ensemble, whose name means 'Carefree', is the most visited attraction in Potsdam, capital of Brandenburg, where you can take a carefree stroll through the summer residence of Friedrich II.

Berlin The old and new German capital has become even more attractive since the Berlin Wall came down. Located on the Spree and Havel rivers, it has a lot of greenery, vibrant nightlife and myriad cultural highlights both in the former east and in the west. Pictured is the Charlottenburg Palace.

Meißen The center of this porcelain town and 'Cradle of Saxony' has a medieval atmosphere. Above it is the towering cathedral and the Albrecht Castle.

Wartburg Legend has it that the castle was founded in 1067. Located at the edge of the Thuringian Forest it was probably the site of the German minstrels' contest. Luther translated the bible into German here.

Dresden Buildings like the Zwinger and the Semper Opera House, as well as precious collections like the Old Masters Gallery, have made Dresden a leading European cultural metropolis.

Saxon Switzerland Whether you prefer hiking or a boat trip on the Elbe River, the bizarre plateaus, rock outcrops and gorges of the Elbe Sandstone Mountains near Dresden are fascinating. Most of the area has been made into a national park.

Prague The Czech capital is located on the Vltava River and has an unusual skyline. Hradčany Castle, Charles Bridge and the art-nouveau buildings of this 'Golden City' are unique. This photograph is of Týn Church.

České Budějovice The center of this world-famous city of breweries and beer is the market square with Samson Fountain.

Karlovy Vary This spa town on the Eger River has some healing springs as well as historical and modern spa facilities.

Český Krumlov Its location on a curve in the Vltava River, its dreamy Old Town, and the huge castle on the hill make the Bohemian town of Krumlov a real gem.

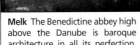

Wachau The forest and wine-growing area of Wachau extends from Melk to Krems – a transverse valley of the Danube that is 30 km (18 miles) long.

Melk The Benedictine abbey high above the Danube is baroque architecture in all its perfection.

Vienna The Austrian capital is always worth a visit. The number and quality of the sights in this metropolis on the Danube is simply overwhelming. Pictured here is the Austrian Parliament Building.

Fertőd, Esterházy Palace The 'Hungarian Versailles' in Fertőd used to belong to a family of princes. There is even an opera house and a puppet theater inside.

Budapest One of the landmarks of the Hungarian capital is the mighty suspension bridge (1839–1849). The list of further sights in the metropolis on the Danube is a long one – from Fisherman's Bastion and the crown of St Stephen in the National Museum to the neo-Gothic Houses of Parliament and the terrific art-nouveau bath houses.

Switzerland's most photographed icon: the Matterhorn, at 4,478 m (14,692 ft).

The Alps

Spectacular mountain scenery between Lake Geneva and the Salzburg region

Looking at any map, it is immediately clear that the Alps form a sort of backbone for the European landmass. This route will take you on a journey of exploration through every facet of this complex terrain, from the shores of Lake Geneva to a world of rock and ice around Zermatt and Grindelwald, from glamorous winter resorts to the fairy-tale scenery of the Dolomites, and from the Grossglockner High Alpine Road to the Salzburg region and the birthplace of Mozart.

For many, the Alps are the "most beautiful mountains in the world". All told, this high Central European range covers an area of 200,000 sq km (77,200 sq mi). The western section alone is home to about fifty peaks rising over 4,000 m (13,124 ft). There are many more in the 3,000 and 2,000 m (9,843 and 6,562 ft) range – nearly 2,000 in Austria alone.

The range features the jagged limestone spikes of the Dolomites, bulky gneiss and granite massif, and lower layers made of sandstone, slate and flysch. It stretches from mighty Mont Blanc, at 4,810-m (15,782-ft) the tallest peak in the Alps, to the gentle knolls of the Wienerwald (Vienna Woods).

Famous rivers such as the Rhine and the Rhône, the Po and the Save, the Drava and the Inn originate in the Alps, and vast lakes such as Lake Constance, Lake Geneva and Lake Lucerne are all nestled in their valleys. Immense waterfalls like the ones in Krimml, Lauterbrunnen,

Salzburg: Residenzplatz with fountain.

Gastein or on the Tosa thunder down granite faces, while glistening glaciers continue to hold their own in the highest and more remote areas – though the effects of climate change can be seen.

The main charm of the area lies in the juxtaposition of contrasts; the Côte d'Azur is just a stone's throw from the foothills of the Maritime Alps, and the glaciers of the Bernese Oberland are not far from the Wallis (Valais) wine region. An hour's drive will take you from the rocky peaks of the Dolomites to the cypress-lined lanes of Lago di Garda, and it wouldn't take much longer to get from the icy cold cirque lakes of the Hohe Tauern to the warm swimming lakes of Carinthia.

The mightiest mountain ranges in the world, such as the Himalayas or the Andes, might have more exalted reputations and are more sparsely populated,

The distinctive hallmark of South Tyrol: the Three Peaks, in the Sexten Dolomites. The highest peak rises to 2,999 m (9,840 ft).

Evening ambience in Salzburg: Looking out over the Salzach to the Old Town with Hohensalzburg Fortress.

but what sets the Alps apart is indeed their human dimension. Extreme mountaineers do not need permits, visas or porters to indulge in their passion. When it comes to infrastructure, accommodation and dining, people seeking a more comfortable experience will be delighted by the ease of travel and the plethora of options. Even the desire for a more urban environment can be satisfied in cities such as Grenoble, Bolzano and Innsbruck. And yet those seeking temporary refuge from civilization will also find more than enough solitude on hikes, climbs or just relaxing in a meadow all day long – all without bumping into another single person.

However, what makes the journey along the backbone of Europe so fascinating is not just the spectacular scenery, but rather the distinctive and diverse cultural traditions that seem to change as often as the landscape, and the undeniable natural charm of the Alps. Rural architecture, customs and handicrafts form an "alpine heritage" that is once again being enthusiastically promoted in many places – without necessarily being motivated by tourism.

Aside from the dominant peaks like the Matterhorn, the Jungfrau, the Eiger, the Mönch, Bernina, Marmolada, the Tre Cime di Lavaredo and the Grossglockner, mention should certainly be made of the fruit and wine growers along the Rhône or Adige, the anonymous architects of the Engadine or East Tyrolean manors, the thousands and thousands of alpine dairy farmers and dairymaids, and the creators of all the frescos, sgraffiti, shingle roofs, and carved altars in the village churches, castles and manors.

Rustic farmhouses are still common in the high valleys of Switzerland.

Funes Valley is one of the most beautiful in the South Tyrol, surrounded by the impressive mountain scenery of the Geisler range, the western part of the Puez-Geisler Nature Park. At 3,025 m (9,925 ft), the Saas Rigais is the highest mountain in the Geisler cluster. The valley behind it is known by the locals as "in Berge".

Located here, at an altitude of 1,340 m (4,397 ft) above sea level, is St Magdalena, whose church, sacristan house, old schoolhouse and Obermesnerhof farm form an interesting architectural ensemble in front of the Geisler peaks. You can access the Funes Valley through the Eisack Valley north of Klausen.

Detour

Müstair Benedictine Monastery

Where the B38 from Stilfser Joch reaches the Adige Valley, a detour heads along the B40 towards the Resia Pass as far as Schluderns. From there, it climbs over the Ofen Pass back to Zernez in the Lower Engadine region.

Müstair, located just 1 km (0.6 mi) over the border at an altitude of 1,240 m (4,068 ft), welcomes its guests with a monument known throughout Europe: the St John's Benedictine Monastery. The building, which gave the town its name (Müstair means minster and is derived from the Latin monasterium), was founded by the bishop in Chur at the end of the 8th century and was subsequently expanded on several occasions. The complex's main attraction is the nearly 1,200-year-old minster.

Not very imposing on the outside, the monastery houses a treasure

The statue of Charlemagne and frescos in the Müstair Minster.

that prompted UNESCO to declare it a World Heritage Site back in 1983: around ninety frescoes from the 8th to the 12th centuries, which two art historians unearthed rather accidentally under a new painted surface at the start of the 20th century. The oldest of these date back to the time of Charlemagne and depict scenes from the life and passion of Christ, as well as the Last Judgement. They are considered the world's most extensive cluster of frescos preserved from Carolingian times. Roughly 400 years newer, but just as impressive, are the Romanesque paintings depicting the martyrdom of St Stephen and other religious themes.

and Lake Sils), it offers a wide range of outdoor sporting options in both winter and summer. The Cresta Run, or "skeleton sled run", and the bob run to Celerina are legendary.

A varied programme of nightly entertainment meets the needs of the guests, who are as famous as they are wealthy.

From St Moritz, the B27 takes you down the Inn River through Samedan and Zuoz to the Lower Engadine region – a worthwhile detour for those who appreciate the old-world charm of Graubünden villages.

The main route now heads from St Moritz over the Pontresina and Bernina Pass at 2,323 m (7,622 ft), past the dream-like panorama of the glaciated Bernina Group, into the valley of the upper Adda, the Veltlin, and into Italy. From here, the spectacular Stilfser Joch pass rises to 2,578 m (8,458 ft) at the foot of the Ortler (Ortles) peak and heads to Bormio before taking you through the Trafoi Valley down to the Etsch (Adige), where it is worth making a detour through Schludern (Sluderno) to St John's Monastery in the Val Müstair. Continue east to Merano in the Vintschgau Valley.

⑬ Merano This city on the Passer River blossomed under the rule of the counts of Tyrol until the mid-14th century. After the Habsburgs took over co-rule in South Tyrol and moved the residence to Innsbruck, Merano's significance waned. It did not return to the spotlight until the 19th century, when word spread about the healing effect of the local springs and mild climate.

Reputable figures began coming in droves from all over Europe to seek rest and recuperation.

The main sites in the Old Town, with its narrow lanes, quaint arcades and old burgher houses, include the Gothic St Nicholas Church (with the St Barbara Chapel), the Hospital Church and the sovereigns' castle with 15th-century frescos in the chapel. It is also worth taking a walk through the elegant residential area of Obermais.

Indeed, they contain the very epitome of Dolomite magnificence, the Tre Cime de Lavaredo, which come into view as you make your way toward Misurina. The next stops are Schluderbach and Toblach. You are in the Drava Valley here, but will soon cross into Austria and arrive in Lienz just under 40 km (25 mi) away.

16 Lienz The capital of East Tyrol is surrounded by splendid mountains and is home to a number of charming buildings including St Andreas Parish Church, with the tomb of the last count of Görz, and the baroque St Michael's subsidiary church. Bruck Castle has Tyrol's largest homeland museum, and the city's Roman roots are evidenced by the graveyards of its predecessor, Aguntum.

17 Heiligenblut Over the Iselsberg at 1,204 m (3,950 ft) and

1 Evening ambience at the Langkofel Massif (3,181 m/10,437 ft), west of the Sella Group.

2 After the Tre Cime de Lavaredo, the Vajolet Towers are the most beautiful in the Dolomites and are part of the Rose Garden at the Karer Pass.

3 The Grossglockner High Alpine Road affords spectacular views of the Alp summits.

Merano: Tyrol Castle

Perched high above Merano and the Vinschgau is a castle that is a detailed reflection of Tyrol's eventful history and gives the entire region its name. Tyrol Castle, built by local counts in 1140–60, experienced its golden age in the 14th century under Margarethe Maultasch, when it resisted the siege

Tyrol Castle above Merano

by King Charles of Bohemia. Once the royal residence had been moved to Innsbruck, the castle began to fall into a state of disrepair. After extensive restorations, the castle, which can be reached on foot in just twenty minutes, is now home to a regional museum. The Romanesque entrances at the forecourt of the great hall and the chapel entrance are gems of art history.

14 Bolzano The capital of South Tyrol is located at the confluence of the Isarco and the Adige rivers and is not only the economic center of the region, but also a hub of alpine art and culture. A stroll through the nar-

row lanes between Lauben, the Kornplatz and the Obstmarkt reveals a charming Old Town that dates back to the Middle Ages. Highlights include the Dominican and Franciscan monasteries, Maretsch Castle, Runkelstein Fort, the City Museum, and the old parish church in the Gries district, with part of an altar by Michael Pacher.

South-east of Bolzano, the SS241 takes you into the dreamy landscape of the Dolomites, littered with breathtaking limestone towers and peaks. The Karer Pass (with a view of the Rose Garden), the Fassa Valley and Passo Sella are the next stops, and the jagged rock formations here never fail to impress.

The road heads along the twisting SS242 with a view of Sassolungo toward the Val Gardena through Ortisei until you reach

the vast Val d'Isarco. Continuing north, you will arrive in Klausen. From there you can take a short detour to get a stunning view of the Funes Valley. On the way back through the Isarco and Gardena valleys, turn off on SS243 after the town of Plan and head towards the Passo Gardena. A breathtaking backdrop of giant rock walls unfolds as you pass the Sella Group via Colfosco and Corvara. As you cross the Passo di Campolongo you will be further delighted by the geological wonders here before reaching the "Great Dolomite Road" which leads to Cortina d'Ampezzo.

15 Cortina d'Ampezzo This famous spa and winter sports resort is surrounded by some of the most beautiful 3,000-m-high (9,843 ft) peaks in the region.

The Keizersgracht canal in Amsterdam is

Netherlands, Belgium

Medieval guilds and burgher cities from Amsterdam and Bruges

Flatlands, canals, dykes, windmills, clogs, and medieval houses reflected in the canals and waterways – these are all the things we associate with the Netherlands and Belgium, along with charming landscapes covered in vibrant fields of tulips, famous sea ports and bustling cities with old markets, squares and town halls.

When we think of the Netherlands, there are certain pictures that come to everyone's mind: world-famous Dutch cheeses; the stately old windmills that were once used to drain the countryside and now dot the landscape like beautiful gems; or the countless dykes that have become an essential element in protecting the country against ocean tides. For centuries, the Dutch have been trying to conquer new land from the North Sea: they build levies and embankments, pump it dry, and then settle and farm it. In fact, two-thirds of all Dutch people today live in the "lower" lands, which are up to 7 m (23 ft) below sea level. This is made possible by canals and drainage ditches that are often located higher than the roads, fields or villages.

In contrast to "life on the seafloor", the sprawling metropolitan areas are home to six million people – 40 percent of the total population. However, the cities at the edge of the "Randstad" chain, which includes Amsterdam, Leiden, Haarlem, The Hague and Rotterdam, only make up a mere tenth of the country's area and are surrounded by a wonderfully

Rembrandt, self-portrait from 1669.

green landscape of croplands, marshes and moors.

In many cities, it is still easy to get a sense of how successful the Netherlands was over the centuries as a world trading power whose colonies brought great wealth to the country. That wealth is reflected in the ornate buildings of the Old Towns, which line the quaint canals. Today, more than 55,000 houses in the Netherlands are listed buildings.

The wealth of earlier times has also naturally also benefited the arts. Painters like Rembrandt, Franz Hals, Jan Vermeer and Piet Mondrian are synonymous with the Netherlands. Ultimately, this historically seafaring nation's experiences with distant lands and foreign cultures has created an atmosphere of open-mindedness that has been preserved until the present day.

The network of windmills in Kinderdijk is a listed UNESCO World Heritage Site. The successful technical innovation was developed in the 18th century.

spanned by fourteen bridges.

Ghent, with its medieval townscape of proud patrician houses on the Graslei.

There is also an extra special ambience in the land of the Flemings and Walloons, who united to form the kingdom of Belgium some 160 years ago. Although Belgium has some first-class references in men like George Simenon and Jacques Brel, and is loved for its Brussels lace, Ardennes ham and a highway that is lit up at night, it is not a classic holiday destination – but that is short-sighted.

The coastal resorts along the North Sea, the wide sandy beaches and the spectacular dune landscapes alone are worth making the trip. And it's not just romantics who go into rapture over the ornate façades and wonderful buildings that reflect off the canals and waterways, or the church spires that soar high above the historic Old Towns of Bruges and Ghent. Brussels, which proudly calls itself the Heart of Europe, is home to one of the most beautiful market squares in the world – the Grand' Place – and the stunning Museum of Fine Art displays works by masters from Rubens to Magritte.

On an unusual note: no other country has a higher population of comics illustrators per square mile – which means that comic strips, along with Brussels lace, Antwerp diamonds and Belgian pralines, are among the most commonly exported Belgian products.

At every turn, it is apparent that Belgians know how to live. Surprising as it may seem, no other country in Europe has as many award-winning restaurants. The most popular drink in Belgium is beer, and there are almost five hundred types produced in over hundred breweries. And as far as snacks go, well, pommes frites (french fries or chips) are said to have been invented here.

Every two years in August, a spellbinding carpet of flowers covers the Grand' Place in Brussels.

Detour

Zaandam and Alkmaar

Zaandam was once the center of the Dutch shipbuilding industry and is located just 15 km (7 mi) from the city of Amsterdam. Czar Peter I (1672–1725) studied the latest in shipbuilding technologies at the time, and his house has been made into a museum.

Further to the north-west, the old mills, pretty houses and exhibits of the Zaanse Schans open-air museum display everyday village life from different eras.

Top: Windmills on the Zaan.
Bottom: Cheese market, Alkmaar.

From April to mid-September, the town of Alkmaar comes under the influence of its cheese culture. In the picturesque Old Town quarter, which is home to a number of interesting buildings, farmers sell their delicious cheese balls and cheese wheels on the open-air market.

Along the Dutch and Belgian coast: In Holland, the route heads through the "nether lands", with their seemingly endless fields of flowers, and then to the bustling metropolises. In Belgium you visit cities with charming, medieval Old Towns and priceless works of art.

❶ Amsterdam (see pages 170–171) Your journey begins in Amsterdam. From there, you can initially take a day trip to Zaandam just 15 km (9 mi) north to the Zaanse Schans open-air museum and the cheese town of Alkmaar a bit further north.

❷ Haarlem This city is about 20 km (12 mi) west of Amsterdam and was officially mentioned in the 10th century. It has a picturesque Old Town quarter whose Grote Markt was once a sports arena. The beautifully decorated 17th-century gabled houses are evidence of the wealth the city once achieved as the stronghold of the drapery and fabric bleaching guild.

At the south end of the square is the Grote or St Bavokerk, a late-Gothic cruciform basilica. The nursing home where painter Frans Hals spent his final years was converted into a museum in 1912, with important works by the great artist.

❸ Keukenhof The Bollenstreek between Haarlem and Leiden takes you through a sea of flowers. It is home to the fields of around 8,000 nurseries that specialize in wholesale flowers.

The Tulip Route leads to the most important of these nurseries; the mecca among them for all flower lovers is the world-famous Keukenhof.

The information center was jointly founded by a community of flower growers in 1949.

❹ Noordwijk aan Zee In the height of summer, this seaside resort after the turnoff at Sassenheim attracts tens of thousands of beachgoers with 13 km (8 mi) of strand and vast sandy dunes. Just like Katwijk ann Zee a few miles further south, Noordwijk has a style that is reminiscent of English seaside resorts. From here it's another 20 km (12 mi) to Leiden.

❺ Leiden The oldest university town in the Netherlands was already home to 11,000 students back in the mid-17th century.

Travel information

Route profile
Length: approx. 400 km (249 mi)
Time required: at least 8–10 days
Start: Amsterdam
Finish: Bruges
Route (main locations): Amsterdam, Leiden, The Hague, Rotterdam, Breda, Antwerp, Mechelen, Brussels, Ghent, Bruges

Traffic information:
Speed limit in the city is 50 km/h (30 mph); on rural roads it's 80 km/h (50 mph) (in Belgium it is 90 km/h (56 mph)); and on highways 120 km/h (75 mph). The legal alcohol limit for drivers is 0.05, and it is strictly enforced. Remember to

bring a warning triangle in case of emergencies.

When to go:
Generally from May to October. Holland is typically at its most beautiful in late spring when everything is in bloom.

From June to late August, southerly winds bring sunny and mostly dry days. At that time, the average maximum temperature is around 20°C (68°F). Only in high summer is swimming really an option.

Information:
Holland:
www.holland.com
www.traveltoholland.org
www.visitbelgium.com

The most beautiful view over the town and its canals can be seen from the Burcht or fort, a mound fortified with brick curtain walls over 1,000 years ago that was built to protect against Holland's most persistent enemy: flooding. The Pieterskerk, a Gothic cruciform basilica with five naves, is worth seeing and, of course, the city's most famous native son is Rembrandt Harmensz van Rijn, born here in 1606. A few of his works are on display in the Stedelijk Museum de Lakenhal.

6 Scheveningen The center of this North Sea coastal resort is the magnificent old Art Nouveau health spa establishment that is today a luxury hotel. The 3-km-long (2-mi) beach boardwalk and the Scheveningen Pier, which extends 400 m (437 yds) out into the North Sea, are also

well-known features of the town. The International Sand Sculptures Festival is held here every year in May.

7 The Hague The third-largest city in the Netherlands is the seat of government as well as the headquarters of the International Court of Justice with the UN War Crimes Tribunal. The city's history goes back roughly 750 years and began with a few houses built around the hunting grounds of the Count of Holland. One of these houses, the Binnenhof or "Inner Court", was built in the 13th century and is still home to the nation's politics – it is the seat of government and the Parliament. The city's most important tourist attraction is the Mauritshuis, a neoclassical building with an art gallery featuring priceless works by famous Dutch painters from

the "Golden Age" as well as Flemish Masters.
The Mesdag Panorama, a cylindrical painting created by Hendrik Willem Mesdag in 1881, is 120 m (131 yds) long and 14 m (46 ft) high and hangs in a building at Zeestraat 65. It gives visitors the impression of standing in the middle of the Scheveningen dune landscape.
The nearby Mesdag Museum has additional paintings from the Hague School of the late 19th century. Another building that constantly makes headlines is the Vredespalais in the Carnegieplein. This half neo-Gothic, half neoclassical Peace Palace is the venue for the controversial meetings of the International Court of Justice.

8 Delft Halfway between The Hague and Rotterdam is Delft, with its historic Old Town and

charming canals. It is particularly famous for its pottery.

9 Rotterdam Container terminals, trans-shipment centers, warehouses and silos all line up beside one another over 20 km (12 mi) along the Nieuwe Waterweg at the world's largest port. All kinds of goods are moved through this port at the mouth of the Maas and Rhine rivers.
It is not difficult to see that emphasis is placed on modern high-rise architecture in "Maashattan". One of the most amazing sights is the Erasmusbrug, a suspension bridge over the Nieuwe Maas constructed by Ben van Berkel in 1996.
The city museum, which has an interesting display of the history of Rotterdam, is in the Het Schielandshuis, a former administrative building that managed the 17th-century dyke systems. The Boijmans van Beuningen Museum at the Museumspark is home to a sizeable collection of Old and New Masters. A variety

1 Around 1,300 bridges span Amsterdam's countless canals.

2 The Gravenstenenbrug bridge in Haarlem spans the Spaarne River.

3 A tulip field near Keukenhof, also known as the Garden of Europe.

4 Night view of the port city of Rotterdam.

5 The Binnenhof or "inner court" (13th century) in The Hague is seat of Parliament and other governmental institutions.

6 Beach boardwalk in Scheveningen, a seaside resort in front of the gates of The Hague.

Detour

Lake IJssel

The cities around Lake IJssel still evoke the time of the explorers. It was from Hoorn, for example, that Captain Willem Schouten set off for the southern tip of South America in 1616, now Cape Horn. Abel Tasman, the first European to discover New Zealand and Tasmania in 1642, also set sail from here. The West Frisian Museum has

Top: Hoorn with its port tower.
Bottom: Enkhuizen, spice center.

exhibits on other colonial adventures that originated from Hoorn. Enkhuizen was the spice-trading center of the East India Company. The Zuiderzee Museum, in a former warehouse in the historic center, has interesting exhibits on shipping and fishery, while an open-air complex with farmhouses and handicrafts gives you an idea of life in the old days.

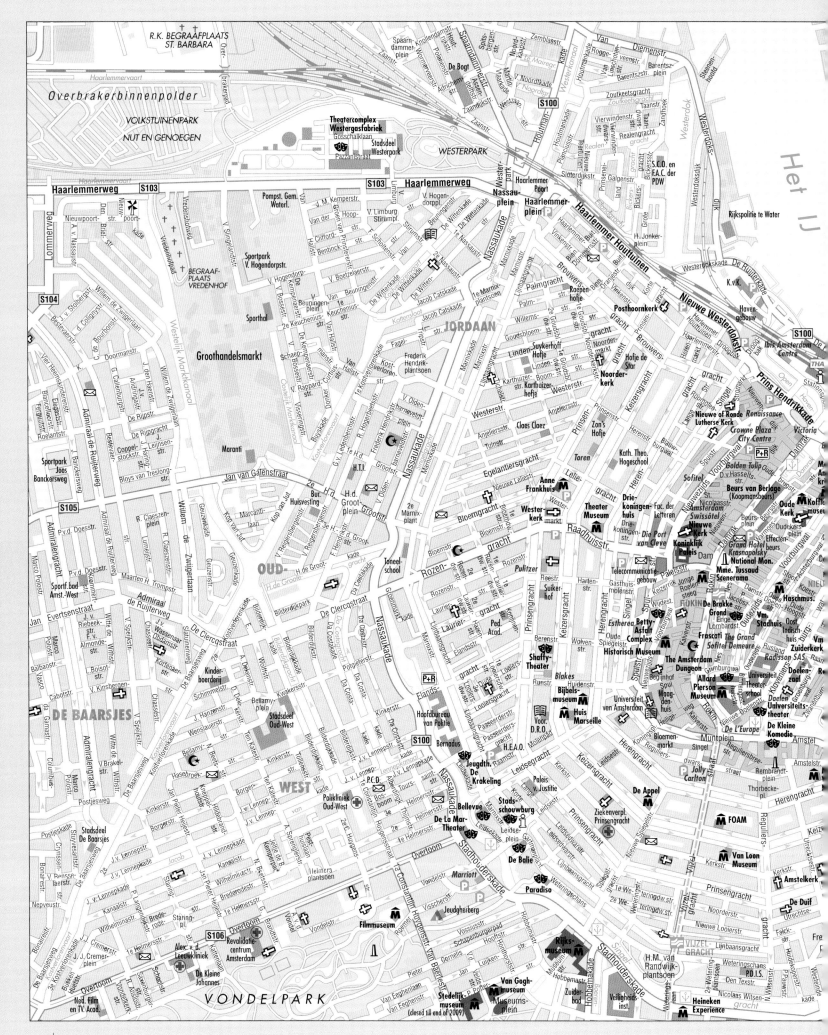

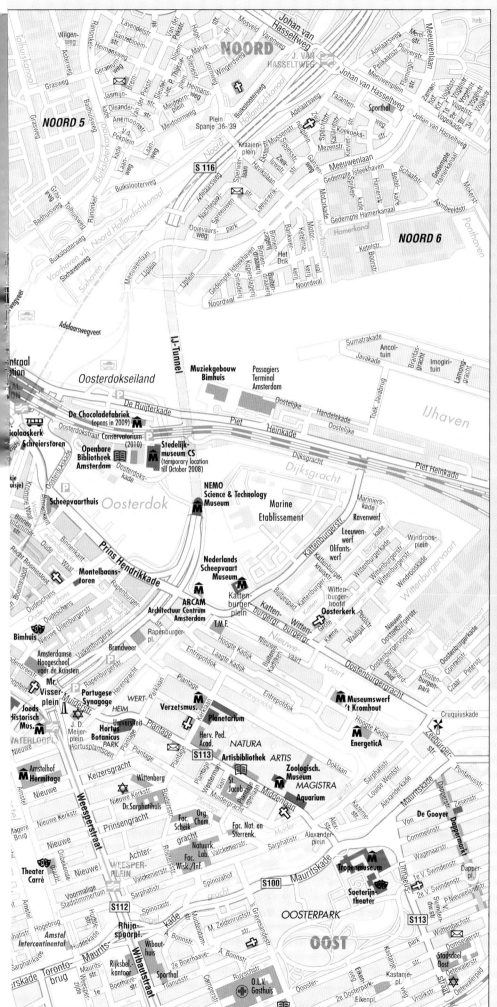

Amsterdam

The capital of the Netherlands is one of the smallest and most manageable metropolises in Europe. It is tolerant and cosmopolitan, but also characterized by a rich history, so it is no coincidence that Amsterdam, the headstrong city at the mouth of the Amstel, is a popular tourist destination.

Amsterdam is the world's largest pile-dwelling settlement. The foundations for the buildings in the entire Old Town district are formed by countless logs beaten up to 30 m (98 ft) into the ground, creating some seventy man-made islands – and the romantic flair of a city on water.

Amsterdam's Golden Century, which roughly equates to the 17th century, marked the beginning of construction on the crescent-shaped Three Canals Belt. In the historic center alone, four hundred bridges span the canals. Water levels are maintained at a constant height using a system of locks and pumps, and some goods are still transported through the city by water even today.

Hundreds of houseboats are moored at the docks of the 160 canals in the Canal Belt and are just as much part

The tourist attractions in the Old Town include: the oldest church, the Oude Kerk (14th century, rebuilt in the 16th); the late-Gothic Nieuwe Kerk where Queen Beatrix was crowned; Dam, once a market place with the Nationaal Monument; the 17th-century town hall, Koninklijk Paleis, whose façade frieze is dedicated to sea trade; Museum Amstelkring, an original canal house used by ostracized Catholics as a secret church in the 17th century; Beurs van Berlage, the 19th-century merchants' stock exchange; Montelbaanstoren, the former city tower (1512); the seven-towered Waag, formerly a city gate and part of the mighty fort; and the Rembrandt House, the master's home with a modern museum wing.

In the former Jewish quarter: the Portuguese synagogue (1675) and Joods

Top: Patrician houses along a romantically lit canal.
Bottom: The Magere Brug is the most famous of Amsterdam's bridges.

of the townscape as the numerous cyclists, flower stands with "tulips from Amsterdam", and the beautiful barrel organs that play the world-famous popular song.

Amsterdam's cityscape resembles a bustling open-air museum, and its open-mindedness, cultural diversity, international cuisine, and the countless options for all types of accommodation suit every budget and every standard. All of this makes the capital of the Netherlands one of the most popular destinations in Europe. Amsterdam is also a very youthful and tolerant city, often leading the way in areas such as fashion and design. It is also easy to get to from just about anywhere.

Historisch Museum; a museum complex housed in four former synagogues; the neo-Gothic Central Station (19th century); Amsterdam's historic museum in the complex of the former orphanage; and the Begijnhof, a former Beguine convent.

In the Canal Belt: Westerkerk (17th century); the Anne Frank House, preserved in its original state; and the historic working quarter of Jordaan with the beautifully renovated Hofjes, historic residential complexes.

In the museum quarter: The Rijks-museum, the world's most famous collection of Dutch Masters; the Van Gogh Museum; Stedelijk Museum for Modern Art; and the Vondelpark landscaped gardens.

Top: The northern end of the Grand' Place in Brussels shows the Hotel de Ville (1401–1459) on the left. The middle of the picture is taken up with several guild houses: second from the left is the mariners' guild house and the last house on the right is the domed Maison des Boulangers. The right side of the picture is

dominated by the Maison du Roi (1536). Bottom: The southern end of the square is characterized by the neoclassical Maison des Ducs de Brabant in the middle of the picture, while on the left is the Maison du Roi, with the historic town hall again on the right.

The picturesque fishing ports of Saint-Guénolé

France

Limestone and granite: natural and cultural landscapes of the French Atlantic coast

The territory extending out into the Atlantic and the English Channel in north-western France is not exactly hospitable in terms of weather, but the romantic windswept coast and the luscious green interior radiate a sense of magic that captivates even the most unsentimental visitors. Indeed, across the entire region between Le Havre and Nantes, every stone seems to have a story to tell.

Powerful Atlantic surf, jagged windy bluffs, and shimmering white limestone cliffs scattered with the long, deserted sandy beaches. These are the elements that define the coastlines of Normandy and Brittany, where dynamic forces of nature are unfettered and the aesthetic is that of an ancient world. Augmenting the scene are sleepy fishing villages and busy port cities, elegant seaside resorts and cozy holiday towns.
Thousands of years of human history here have left so much behind that the entire

Fort La Latte on the Brittany Côte d'Armor.

region could be considered an open-air museum. Castles and manors, abbeys and cathedrals, meticulously preserved Old Town centers, half-timbered row houses and stone buildings all attest to eras of power and wealth.
Stout fortifications and sentry towers are reminiscent of darker times. Normandy was ruled by the Celts, Romans and Germanic tribes until the 5th century, before the Vikings and Normans claimed the area as theirs. The war between England and France lasted for centuries before the Huguenots devastated the land. But all of this was nothing compared to the German occupation in 1940. Within four years, all of Normandy had become a battlefield until allied troops landed on Calvados and Cotentin beaches on June 6, 1944, "D-Day". The territory was eventually liberated in September of

1944, but many of the cities lay under soot and ash.
Today, Normandy is experiencing what is arguably the most peaceful era in its long history. The roughly 30,000-sq-km (11,580-sq-mi) region is primarily involved in agriculture, and is characterized by grasslands with stone walls, fields of grain and apple plantations.
The coast, which is about 600 km long (373 mi), transforms Normandy a popular holiday destination in July and August, when not only the French come to the lovely resorts and stunning beaches in droves. From here, it is possible to make interesting detours to places such as the famous rock island monastery of Mont Saint-Michel.
Before the Common Era, Brittany was home to a culture that continues to mystify the scientific world: Who were the

The impressive limestone cliffs (falaises) of the Normandy coast near Étretat, north of Le Havre. It is definitely worth seeing the Falaises d'Amont and the Falaises d'Aval not far from the city.

on the Bigouden Peninsula form the south-western tip of Brittany.

people of the megalith culture? Were the menhirs, the stone monuments from between 5000 and 2000 BC, used as solar or lunar calendars? Were they fertility symbols, cult sites or processional avenues? There are still no explanations for any of these exciting questions.

After 500 BC, the history becomes clearer. Around this time, the Celts came and settled in the area, which they called "Armor" or "Land by the Sea". Although they were evangelized around AD 500, they preserved many of their "pagan" customs and legends, as well as their Breton language. Certain Celtic elements still thrive here: fantasy and defiance are particularly defined, fuelled on by a healthy dose of pride. Brittany, which covers an area of roughly 27,200 sq km (10,499 sq mi), is one of France's most important agricultural regions. It is a

fishing center and almost every sea bass (loup de mer) or monkfish you eat in Europe comes from its waters. It also specializes in early vegetable exports as well as meat and dairy processing. With its 1,200-km (746 mi) coastline, it is second only to the Côte d'Azur among tourism regions in Europe.

The wind and the stones, the green the meadows and the wild Atlantic ocean spray – Brittany is defined by all of this. That said, it did not achieve true international fame until the emergence of the comic book, *Asterix and Obelix*. Indeed, they are the best-known Bretons after King Arthur and have delighted readers around the world since the first strip by René Goscinny and Albert Uderzo appeared in 1959. The only downside is that their village unfortunately does not exist anywhere Brittany.

Saint-Malo on the northern coast of Brittany is situated on an island of granite.

Cotentin Peninsula

The Cotentin Peninsula is the most impressively primeval landscape in Normandy. The coastline here is mostly craggy and wild, but there are long, sandy beaches that occasionally stretch between the jagged rocks. In the south, for example, the peninsula separates a vast moorland area from the interior, while in the north the landscape is reminiscent of Ireland or southern England, with rolling hills, verdant green meadows and rustic stone walls.

The storming of the beaches in Normandy by Allied troops on June 6, 1944, is remembered in many local towns here. At La Madeleine, for instance, a museum commemorates the soldiers who landed at "Utah Beach". Massive fortifications, which were built by

Fishing boats in the port of Barfleur in the north of the peninsula.

the Germans as part of the Atlantic wall to protect against a British invasion of the continent, can be seen near Crisbec. A memorial skydiver hangs from the church spire of Sainte-Mére-Église, and there is also a war museum.

The most important city in the area, Cherbourg, emerged from World War II virtually unscathed, and the streets and narrow rows of houses still emanate the charming atmosphere of the 18th and 19th centuries. The umbrellas of Cherbourg, which were the inspiration in 1963 for the title of the award-winning film, *Les parapluies de Cherbourg*, are still produced.

A tour of the Norman-Breton coast takes you first from the urban jungle of Paris to the wildly romantic limestone cliffs of Normandy and the beaches where Allied forces landed in 1944. Brittany then offers a unique natural and scenic experience and confronts visitors with the mysteries of prehistoric cultures and myths.

1 Paris (see Tour No. 16) Highway N 15 is a good way to get to Normandy from Paris, and leads you along the impressive Seine River valley.

2 Rouen This Norman city is home to one of France's largest sea ports, despite its inland location. However, what really fascinates visitors is the historic Old Town, with its quaint alleyways snaking between crooked half-timbered houses, churches with extravagant ornamentation, the magnificent Notre-Dame Cathedral and the rest of the massive fortifications.

3 Fécamp This is where the road meets the Côte d'Albâtre, the Alabaster Coast, where the bizarre limestone cliffs drop more than 110 m (361 ft) down to the sea. Fécamp was once famous for two things: its booming fishing port and its tasty Bénédictine cordial. The Sainte-Trinité Church of the Benedictine abbey has been lovingly preserved.

4 Étretat This village was one of the fishing villages that was particularly popular among artists in the 19th century. It is situated in a bay enclosed on both sides by romantic cliffs. The Notre-Dame Church from the 13th century is astonishingly large for such a small town, and is well worth visiting.

5 Le Havre This city at the mouth of the Seine was occupied by the Germans in World War II and bombed by the Allies for an entire week in an attempt to win it back. The important port and center were rebuilt, but it is more modern and functional than it is picturesque. The most impressive site is Europe's longest suspension bridge, inaugurated in 1988. The art museum houses a collection of impressionist and cubist works.

6 Honfleur This port city is steeped in tradition and considered the most beautiful city on the Côte Fleurie, the Floral Coast. The architectural gems of the old port, the wharfs lined with narrow row houses, and the steep, hilly Ste Catherine quarter exude fishing village romanticism and an artistic flair.

Travel information

Route profile
Length: approx. 1,400 km (870 mi)
Duration: 10–14 days
Start: Paris
Finish: Nantes
Route course: Paris, Rouen, Le Havre, Honfleur, Caen, Brest, Quimper, Lorient, Nantes

Traffic information:
The blood-alcohol limit for drivers is 0.05 and it is strictly enforced.
The speed limit in cities is 50 km/h (30 mph), on rural roads 90 km/h (55 mph), on expressways 110 km/h (70 mph) and 130 km/h (80 mph) on the motorways. Motorways require tolls.

When to go:
Spring and autumn are ideal, because it the peak season at most resorts is in high summer. Extreme heat is not an issue in this region. Temperatures average around 15°C (59°F) in May and October, while June to September you can expect about 18-20°C (64-68°F). Regardless of the season, the weather here is very active and it can rain at any time.

Information:
Here are some websites to help you plan your trip.
www.franceguide.com
www.brittanytourism.com
www.discoverfrance.com

Dinan

Dinan, perched high above the Rance Valley, is one of the most impressive walled cities in Brittany. It is dominated by a mighty fort that contains the residential tower of Duchess Anne and dates all the way back to the 14th century. The wall, which is 3 km long (2 mi), still contains sixteen towers and gates, and to

Top: View of Dinan with the Gothic bridge over the Rance. Bottom: An alleyway in Dinan.

this day completely encircles the picturesque Old Town.

The Old Town quarter itself has lovingly preserved its medieval character, with narrow alleyways, half-timbered houses, patrician row houses and quaint churches. It is clear that the city was wealthy in its day and that the trade in products like fabrics, canvas, wood and grains was lucrative, particularly in the 18th century.

The sites that are worth seeing include the St Sauveur Church, which was partially built in the 12th century and has a late-Gothic gable, and the St Malo Church, built in the 15th-century with window panes telling the history of the town. Also worth a visit is the Franciscan monastery, which today houses a school, but the Gothic cloister can also be viewed. Walkers will find rest and relaxation in the English Garden near the Tour Ste Catherine view point.

The Musée de la Marine is housed in the oldest church of St Étienne, dating back to the 14th century.

❼ Deauville This town is the epitome of sophisticated seaside resorts. In the mid-19th century, the rich and famous came in droves to the expensive luxury hotel, part of which still exists today. Deauville's town center comprises the casino, which served as inspiration for Ian Fleming's *Casino Royal*, and the stylish squares include the Promenade de Planches, which is constructed of wooden planks.

❽ Caen Nearly completely destroyed in World War II, Caen is now a modern city. Its historic features are the two abbeys of Abbaye-des-Dames and Abbaye-aux-Hommes.

It is worth making a detour out to the Cotentin Peninsula, which includes Cherbourg and other villages such as Barfleur. From Coutances at the south-western end of the peninsula, continue south on the D971.

❾ Granville The "Monaco of the North" is today a mix of medieval city and fishing village. The impressive Old Town is perched high above the center on a cliff. As in Deauville, one of the most famous buildings is the casino, opened in 1910. Couturier, Christian Dior, spent his childhood in the pinkish house with exotic garden. Today, it is the Dior Museum.

Heading towards Avranches on the D911 you will get magnificent views of the Bay of Mont Saint-Michel, which runs right along the coast.

❿ Mont Saint-Michel France's most frequently visited attraction is not necessarily a place of peace and quiet, but you can still feel the magic of this town. Its location on a conical mountain in the middle of a tidal bay renders the monadnock either isolated as an island in the ocean or as a rock island surrounded by sand. It is simply sensational. Hermits lived in the first houses of worship in the area until, according to lore, Saint Aubert was charged in the 8th century by Archangel Michael to build a sanctuary on the mountain. Further development on the structure began in the 13th century. The church of Notre-Dame-sous-Terre, the new abbey church, the three-levelled monastery complex, the cloister and the Salle de Chevaliers are the most interesting areas.

The D155 heads out of the Bay of Mont St-Michel towards the Côte d'Emeraude, the Emerald Coast, which is home to probably the most beautiful town of the Breton north coast.

⓫ Saint-Malo This medieval city of the corsairs was badly destroyed in World War II but was rebuilt to its original condi-

1 Six-storey row houses from the 17th century line the beautiful port of Honfleur.

2 Mont Saint-Michel, an icon of Normandy and a famous abbey, is an unrivaled synthesis of monastery and fortress architecture.

3 Looking out over the city wall of St Malo, which encloses the restored Old Town quarter.

Pointe de Saint-Mathieu is a unique complex atop a 30-m-high (98 ft) headland, approximately 20 km (12 mi) west of Brest. The complex includes a 36-m-high (118 ft) lighthouse, a square signal tower, the ruins of a former Benedictine abbey church, Notre-Dame de Grâce, whose western façade is from the 12th century.

(the rest was built between the 13th and 16th centuries), and the village church of Saint-Mathieu. The lighthouse itself was built in 1835, using the stones from

The "calvaires" of Brittany

Among Brittany's most famous tourist attractions are the ornate granite calvaries, or calvaires. Some of the most beautiful ones are found in the Elorn Valley between Morlaix and Brest, and a well-signposted "Circuit des Enclos Paroissiaux" connects the most interesting of them.

Calvaires typically depict the apostles and saints of the Passion story grouping around Christ on the cross with other biblical figures. They were primarily created by Breton artists during the time of the plague. All of the calvaires are in "enclos paroissiaux", or walled churchyards, and the faithful enter through an impos-

The calvaire of Saint-Thégonnec.

ing gate, or "porte triumphale". The church and ossuary (ossuaire) were built with the calvaires to create a grandiose church complex. Local communities actually competed with each other to design the most beautiful vicarages.

One of the most impressive is the Saint-Thégonnec village calvaire built in 1610. It portrays an enthralling version of the Passion story of Jesus Christ and includes Saint Thégonnec. According to legend, the saint had his cart drawn by a wolf after his donkey was eaten by the pack to which the wolf belonged. The pulpit in the church of Saint-Thégonnec is also worth seeing.

tion after 1945. The Ville Close, the Old Town with its granite houses from the 17th and 18th centuries, as well as the promenade along the ramparts are but a few of the highlights.

The road to Dinard heads over the 750-m-long (0.5 mile) dam cum bridge of the tidal power station over the Rance. Its lock is 65 m (213 ft) long.

12 Dinard The second-largest seaside resort in Brittany is a garden city nestled neatly into a hilly landscape. A walk along the Promenade du Clair de Lune is a must. Dinard was and still is a favorite meeting place for the international jet set.

A great detour from here takes you 22 km (14 mi) south towards Dinan, a picturesque little town perched high above the Rance River. Anyone wishing to skip this side trip can head along the scenic coastal road past Cap Fréhel to the capital of the Côte d'Armor, St-Brieuc, some 3 km (2 miles) inland.

13 St.-Brieuc This city has a nicely preserved Old Town with gorgeous half-timbered houses, including the Hôtel des Ducs de Bretagne. The twin-spired cathe-

dral from the 13th century, which was modified over the 18th and 19th centuries, looks almost like a fort.

14 Côte de Granit Rose Off the coast from the fishing port of Paimpol is the Ile-de-Bréhat, a birdlife reserve with red granite rock formations like the rest of the neighboring eighty-six islands. It is of course this stone that gave the entire coast the name Côte de Granit Rose. Also worth seeing is the fishing town of Ploumanach just a few miles

further north, as well as Plougrescant at the mouth of the Jaudy River north of Tréguier. The chapel in the small seaside resort of Perros-Guirec is also made of red granite.

From Lannion, the road continues along the coast to Finistère, the "end of the earth", and it is here that Brittany showcases its most attractive side: the Atlantic crashing along the wild, craggy cliffs, and lighthouses balancing precariously on promontories and islands surrounded by the ocean. The picturesque

fishing villages feature houses of solid stone and walled church courtyards.

15 Morlaix This port city is home to an Old Town that is well worth seeing for its carefully preserved medieval houses, but the townscape is actually dominated by a massive railway viaduct.

Those interested in the vicarages and calvaires should turn off here onto the N 12 into the Elorn Valley and head towards St.-Thégonnec (see left margin).

16 Roscoff There is a regular ferry connection to England and Ireland from this heavily frequented spa resort. The town has a number of beautiful old fishermen's houses, and the laboratory for oceanographic and marine biology research here is world renowned.

17 Brest This city was transformed into France's largest naval port by Cardinal Richelieu in the mid-17th century, and it remained so until being reduced to rubble during World War II. Since its reconstruction, it has become one of the most modern cities in the country and is once again an important naval base. The Pont de Recouvrance, with pylons 64 m (210 ft) high and a total length of 87 m (285 ft), is the longest drawbridge in Europe. Brest's research center and Océanopolis maritime museum are located at the Moulin Blanc yacht harbor.

A short detour west takes you to the Pointe de St-Mathieu, famous for the lighthouse located within the ruins of an old monastery. From Brest, take the N165 along the Bay of Brest to Le Faou, a town with interesting medieval houses made of granite. The D791 will take you to the Crozon Peninsula with its stunning coatal cliffs.

18 Crozon The main town on the peninsula of the same name is a popular holiday destination. Gorgeous beaches are tucked between breathtaking cliffs, and you can take boats to explore the picturesque coastal grottos. Four headlands extend out into the sea here. Perched atop one of them is Camaret-sur-Mer, at one point the most important lobster and crayfish port in France. It is worth going to see the Château Vauban, a fort built according to designs by Louis XIV's master military engineer, the Marquis de Vauban.

West of Camaret-sur-Mer are the Alignements des Lagatjar, quartzite menhirs arranged in a U-shape in three rows. You can get a spectacular view of this prehistoric wonder from the peninsula's most beautiful cape, Pointe de Penhir.

19 Douarnenez This city has an interesting Old Town and is one of the most important fishing ports in Brittany. The maritime museum displays a collection of boats and all sorts of information on shipbuilding. Popular spa resorts in the area invite you to spend a day on the beach.

20 Pointe du Raz This cliff drops 70 m (230 ft) to the sea and is the westernmost point of France. It is also one of the most visited places in Brittany. Countless holidaymakers do the half-hour climb over the rocky ridge every day. And for good reason: the view of this rugged landscape amidst the surging waves of the Atlantic is spectacular.

Offshore is the small tiny Ile de Sein. It is flat and has hardly any vegetation, but the charming white houses shimmer invitingly. Far out at sea, the mighty lighthouse of Phare d'Ar-Men, built on a ledge in 1881, helps ships navigate the dangerous waters from up to 50 km (31 mi) away.

1 View from the 72-m-high (236-ft) coastal cliffs of the Pointe du Raz in Finistère, looking out over its most striking imagery, the storm-swept lighthouses.

2 Ile-de-Bréhat on the Côte de Granit Rose, the Pink Granite Coast, far away from the holiday resorts and crowds.

3 A Breton stone house at the northern tip of Brittany near Plougrescant, not far from Tréguier.

4 The natural harbor in Brest, with the mighty Château de Brest from the 12th–17th centuries. The city is one of the most important naval bases in France.

5 A remote Breton house on the Pointe du Raz – an abode for individualists.

Detour

Quiberon

Millions of years ago, the stunning Quiberon Peninsula was an island. Now, it is connected to the mainland by a narrow isthmus and is home to an upscale holiday paradise with a wide range of spa resort and watersport options.
The Côte Sauvage is a series of craggy rock cliffs that is intermit-

Quiberon at dusk.

tently broken up by small, sandy bays. The east coast is home to wide, sandy beaches that are perfect for relaxing family holidays as well as sports like wind surfing and land sailing. Analgesic Thalasso therapies are also on offer in the town of Quiberon, and St Pierre-Quiberon has a stone formation with twenty-two menhirs.

21 Quimper The capital of Finistère is a pretty old town with pedestrian zones, quaint medieval row houses and towering church spires.
It is definitely worth seeing St-Correntin Cathedral with its magnificent 15th-century Gothic windows and twin 76-m-high (249 ft) spires. Local history and culture is exhibited at the Musée Départemental Breton.
Point-l'Abbé, south of Quimper, is a small town whose ornate lacework and embroidery made it famous well beyond Brittany. On the way to Quimperlé you will pass Pont Aven, where Paul Gauguin painted and developed his unique expressionist style with Emile Bernard between 1886 and 1889. The Musée de Pont-Aven provides an insight into this time. A well signposted footpath heads from the banks of the Aven River to the painters' favorite spots.

22 Quimperlé This small town has a lower section as well as an upper section picturesquely situated on a headland between the Isole and Ellé rivers. It has some charming old houses and

the circular Ste-Croix Church is also worth seeing.
Your route now heads into the southern part of Brittany. The port city of Lorient has no less than five ports, including one of the most important fishing ports in France. In Auray, roughly 18 km (11 mi) before Vannes, you should not miss the detour to the approximately 3,000 menhirs of Carnac. From there continue along the peninsula to Quiberon.

St. Thégonnec The pulpit and calvaire of the village church here are masterpieces of 17th-century Breton art.

Côte de Granit Rose Picturesque pink and reddish rocks characterize the northernmost tip of Brittany. They have been beautifully shaped by the wind and waves.

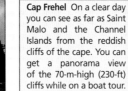

Cap Frehel On a clear day you can see as far as Saint Malo and the Channel Islands from the reddish cliffs of the cape. You can get a panorama view of the 70-m-high (230-ft) cliffs while on a boat tour.

Brest France's largest naval port was almost completely destroyed in World War II. Today, Brest is one of the country's most modern cities.

Pointe de Saint Mathieu Looks can be deceiving: the lighthouse 20 km (12 miles) west of Brest is not on top of the old monastery walls (12th–16th centuries), but behind them.

Pointe du Raz This dramatic lighthouse is on a 70-m-high rock formation in the Atlantic. The climb takes about thirty minutes.

Quiberon This peninsula is popular among watersport enthusiasts, while families prefer the more sheltered east coast.

Carnac Now a spa resort, this location was even popular in prehistoric times: 3,000 menhirs (from 4000–2000 BC) and other stone monuments attest to human settlements.

In the realm of the menhirs

Carnac and the surrounding area are home to the largest megalith field in the world. Roughly 3,000 megaliths, also known as menhirs, are spread over several areas, all fenced in for their protection. The largest and most beautiful of them is the Alignement de Kerzhero, stony witness of a history dating back to between 4000 and 2000 BC. There are also prehistoric burial mounds, the most interesting

Carnac: Alignement de Kerlescan.

Vannes The capital of Morbihan is a worthwhile destination for anyone with a romantic streak. The medieval alleyways, the partially preserved Old City wall with its quaint towers, and the charming half-timbered

houses attract thousands of visitors every year.

Archaeological relics from the region are displayed in the Musée d'Árchéologie du Morbikau, in the 15th-century Château Gaillard. Anyone who does not want to go directly to Nantes from Vannes on the highway should take the 30-km (19 mi) detour to the French coast, for example to Le Croisic, at La Roche-Bernard.

Nantes The journey ends in Nantes, which vied for centuries with Rennes to be the capital of

Brittany, It eventually lost in the late 19th century.

This city at the mouth of the Loire River was once the most important port city on the Loire, and magnificent buildings in the Old Town attest to this. The Château des Ducs de Bretagne is an impressive fort surrounded by a moat.

In addition to the impressive cathedral, the Old Town's Art Nouveau plazas and elegant 18th-century arcades enchant visitors to Nantes.

1 The coastal landscape on the Quiberon Peninsula is breathtaking: the shimmering cliffs, electric blue-white skies and the crashing waves are conducive for a stroll.

2 Half-timbered row houses in front of St Corentin Cathedral in Quimper. This capital of the Département Finistére is also a bishop's see.

3 Hundreds of yachts bob up and down in the marina of Le Croisic on the headland west of St Nazaire. The popular holiday resort offers a wide range of watersports in summer.

of which is the 12-m-high (39 ft) St Michel tumulus with chapel. From above, you can get a wonderful view over the landscape of menhirs. If this doesn't satisfy your passion for prehistory, don't worry: you can also visit the dolmens (tomb chambers) in the surrounding area.

Honfleur The city on the Côte Fleurie, the Floral Coast, emanates port romanticism. The Musée de la Marine is inside Honfleur's oldest church, while the Musée Satie remembers the city's great composer.

Limestone coast near Étretat This village lined with glorious cliffs ("falaises") was a favorite among artists like Monet and Courbet in the 19th century.

Deauville This elegant seaside resort was already popular in the mid-19th century. Luxury hotels, casinos and the Promenade des Planches still prosper here.

Paris The capital of France is also the country's cultural center. If you want to explore the city's numerous museums and enjoy its special flair, make sure you allow plenty of time.

Dinan A mighty castle towers over Dinan, considered one of the most idyllic towns in Brittany. Miles of walls with sixteen gates surround the Old Town quarter on the left bank of the Rance River.

St. Malo The granite houses in the Old Town quarter and the boardwalk on the ramparts are impressive here. The city has been restored to its original state.

Mont St Michel This cone-shaped monadnock with its magical location in a tidal bay, is one of the country's most popular attractions. Additions were made in the 8th century, and again from the 13th century onwards. Three million visitors come to the small monastery island every year.

The old port of La Rochelle and the watchtowers of St-Nicolas and Tour de la Chaîne.

France

Via Turonensis – on the old pilgrimage route from Paris to Biarritz

The Via Turonensis was mainly travelled by pilgrims from the Netherlands and northern France on their way to Santiago de Compostela in Galicia, the far north-west corner of Spain. They mostly went on foot to their imminent salvation. Today, there are still pilgrims who follow the Camino de Santiago (St James' Way) and its various 'side streets' for religious purposes, but most people these days are simply interested in seeing the wonderful sights along the way.

Four different trails originally led pilgrims through France to the tomb of St James in Santiago de Compostela – the Via Tolosana from Arles through Montpellier and Toulouse to Spain; the Via Podensis from Le Puy through Conques, Cahors and Moissac to the border; the Via Lemovicensis from Vézelay through Avallon, Nevers and Limoges; and finally, the fourth route, the Via Turonensis, known as the 'magnum iter Sancti Jacobi' (the Great Route of St James).

The route's name comes from the city of Tours, through which it passed. The pilgrims started at the tomb of St Dionysius in St-Denis before heading through Paris, down the Rue St-Jacques to the church of the same name, where only the tower still stands on the right bank of the Seine. The tomb of St Evurtius was the destination in Orléans, while the tomb of St Martin, who was often compared to St James, awaited pilgrims in Tours. In Poitiers, there were three churches on the

Jeanne d'Arc Arriving at Orléans, a painting by Jean Jacques Scherrer.

intinerary: St-Hilaire, Notre Dame la Grande and Ste-Radegonde. The head of John the Baptist was the object of worship in St-Jean-d'Angély, and pilgrims would pray at the tomb of St Eutropius in Saintes. Bordeaux was also the custodian of important relics like the bones of St Severin and the Horn of Roland.

The pilgrims of the Middle Ages would most certainly have been amazed and would have shaken their heads at the buildings that the modern pilgrims along the Via Turonensis today find so fascinating. While the largest and most beautiful buildings in the Middle Ages were erected to honour and praise God, modern man seems obsessed with himself and his comforts. 'Pilgrims' nowadays are most interested in visiting the castles along the Via Turonensis, drawn to the extravagance as if by magic.

The modern glass pyramid by I.M. Pei in front of the magnificent Louvre building has been the museum's main entrance since 1989.

Château de Chambord, in the middle of a large forest, is a structure of fairy-tale proportions.

Perfect examples of this absolutism are just outside Paris in the Île-de-France – the enormous palace complex of Versailles and the castle of Rambouillet which, as the summer residence of French presidents, continues to be a center of power. Many other magnificent buildings are scattered along the Loire River and its tributaries, the Indre, Cher and Vienne, including the colossal Château de Chambord, a dream realized by King Francis I, the Château de Chenonceaux, and others like Beauregard, Chaumont, Valençay, Loches, Le Lude and Langeais.

The area around Bordeaux is home to a completely different kind of château. Médoc, Bordeaux and Entre-Deux-Mers are names that make the wine-lover's heart skip a beat. This region is the home of myriad great wines, in particular red wine. The wineries around Bordeaux, most of which look like real castles in the middle of vast vineyards, are referred to as châteaus and include internationally renowned names such as Mouton-Rothschild, Lafitte-Rothschild and Latour.

Last but not least, today's 'car pilgrims' are attracted to destinations that are far off the beaten track and would have seemed rather absurd as a detour to the pilgrims of the Middle Ages – namely, those on the Atlantic coast. The sandy beaches and coves of the Arcachon Basin and the sections of coast further south on the Bay of Biscay provide wind and waves for windsurfers and surfers. The elegant life of the 19th century is celebrated in the charming seaside resort of Biarritz and, from here, it's not much further to the Aragonian section of the Camino de Santiago, which stretches along the northern coast of Spain.

The Médoc on the left bank of the Gironde is one of the best red wine regions in the world.

Detour

Chartres

Even from a great distance, Chartres Cathedral is an impressive edifice, soaring like a mirage above the vast expanse of cornfields in the Beauce region. Up close, any doubts of its stature vanish immediately. This masterpiece of Gothic architecture, a large portion of which was built in the second half of the 12th century, simply overwhelms with its dimensions and design.

Chartres Cathedral

The facade and, in particular, the entrance area are a dazzling sight full of lavish ornamentation, but the cathedral's greatest treasure is inside: glass paintings unsurpassed in their number and beauty anywhere else in the world. The vivid stained-glass windows depict both biblical and historical scenes, and thus provided literate and illiterate believers alike with their wealth of information.

The rose windows are also stunning, and their engraved tracery contains an extensive range of images. The southern and western rose windows illustrate the Last Judgement, while the eastern rose window is dedicated to the Virgin Mary.

Chartres Cathedral, a UNESCO World Heritage Site since 1979, should definitely not be missed.

The Via Turonensis follows one of the four major French routes of the St James' pilgrimage trail. Starting in the Île-de-France, you'll head to Orléans on the Loire, continue downstream past some of the most beautiful and famous Loire châteaus and then, from Saumur onwards, make your way south into the Gironde to Bordeaux. Prior to arriving in Biarritz, you stop in St-Jean-Pied-de-Port, the former last stop for pilgrims before crossing the Pyrenees.

❶ St-Denis The actual pilgrim route begins in St-Denis, north of Paris. During the heyday of the Camino de Santiago (St James' Way) pilgrimages, this town was located north of the former city border and was the meeting place for the pilgrims coming from Paris. The French national saint, Dionysius, is buried in the city's cathedral. The basilica, where almost all of France's kings are entombed, is considered the first masterpiece of Gothic architecture.

❷ Paris (see pp. 194–197). South-west of Paris is Versailles. The name of the palace is intrinsically tied to the Sun King, Louis XIV, and is a symbol of his display of absolutist power.

❸ The Palace of Versailles Louis XIII first had a small hunting lodge built on the site where this magnificent building now stands. Under Louis XIV, the lodge was gradually expanded to the immense dimensions we know today, followed by some 'insignificant' extensions like the opera, built under Louis XV. During the reign of the Sun King, Versailles was the place where anyone who wanted to have any sort of influence in the State had to stay. Apart from the large, opulent reception rooms such as the Hall of Mirrors, the Venus Room, the Hercules Room or the Abundance Salon, there were also the king and queen's lavishly furnished private chambers. The opera is a real gem, completed in 1770.

Beyond the water features of the Bassin d'Apollon is the vast park complex, which is home to the Grand Trianon, Petit Trianon and Le Hameau. The Grand Trianon was built under the orders of Louis XIV – one wing for him and the other for his beloved, Madame de Maintenon. The Petit Trianon was built for Louis XV's mistresses. Le Hameau is almost an absurdity – a small village with a homestead, dairy farm, mill and pigeon loft, where Marie Antoinette played 'peasant', a game that did not win her any fans among supporters of the revolution – she wound up under the guillotine on the Place de la Concorde.

❹ Rambouillet Although the palace is the summer residence of the French president, it can be visited most of the time. The building consists of wings designed in different architectural styles including Gothic, Renaissance and baroque.
This castle only became royal property in 1783, when Louis XVI

Travel information

Route profile
Length: approx. 1,100 km (684 miles), excluding detours
Time required: 10–14 days
Start: Paris
End: Bayonne
Route (main locations): Paris, Versailles, Orléans, Blois, Tours, Saumur, Poitiers, Saintes, Cognac, St-Émilion, Bordeaux, St-Jean-Pied-de-Port, Bayonne

Traffic information:
Drive on the right in France. The speed limit in built-up areas is 50 km/h (31 mph), 90 km/h (56 mph) on rural roads, 110 km/h (68 mph) on expressways and 130 km/h (81 mph) on highways. Headlights are required when driving in foggy, rainy or snowy conditions.

Weather:
The best seasons to visit the Île-de-France and the Loire Valley are spring and autumn, when the Loire Valley shows off its most beautiful side and is ablaze with all shades of yellow and red. For more information go to:
www.meteofrance.com

Information:
General
www.francetourism.com
www.franceguide.com
www.theviaturonensis.com
Paris
en.parisinfo.com
Loire Valley
www.westernfrancetourist board.com
Bordeaux
www.bordeaux-tourisme. com

The town revolves around its castle, where the individual building phases are very easily recognized. The oldest section is Louis XII's wing, constructed in red brick with white limestone decorations. The Francis I wing is far more lavish, built in Renaissance style with traces of French Gothic in parts. The king would often have his heraldic animal, the salamander, displayed in certain areas. What really catches your eye is the Renaissance-style staircase tower in the interior courtyard, where the royal family could attend events.

Noble palaces such as the Hôtel Sardini, the Hôtel d'Alluye and the Hôtel de Guise are proof that, apart from royalty, numerous other aristocrats also had their residences along the Loire. The St-Louis Cathedral is not Gothic and only dates back to the 17th century, the previous building having been extensively destroyed by a hurricane. An

Ludwig XIV and Absolutism

L'état c'est moi – I am the State. This statement by Louis XIV aptly characterizes his understanding of power. The 'Sun King' was born in 1638 and, following the death of his father in 1643,

Louis XIV – a painting by H. Rigaud, 1701, Louvre, Paris.

acquired it as a hunting lodge. The park and the adjacent Rambouillet forest are ideal places to take a relaxing stroll. On the way to Orléans to the south of Paris, it's worth making a detour to Chartres, whose name is automatically associated with its Gothic cathedral, the largest in Europe.

⑤ Orléans This city's cathedral, Ste-Croix, is built in Gothic style, though only very small parts of it date back to the Gothic period. The original building, destroyed during the French Wars of Religion, was rebuilt under Henry VI, and the architects of the 18th and 19th centuries continued to use the Gothic style.

The city's liberator lived in the house named after her – the Maison de Jeanne d'Arc. The half-timbered house, which was destroyed in World War II, was reconstructed identically to the original. Only very few of the

beautiful old houses and noble palaces were spared from the severe attacks of the war, but the Hôtel Toutin, with its gorgeous Renaissance interior courtyard, is one that was. Of course, Orléans wouldn't be complete without the statue of Jeanne d'Arc, erected on the Place du Martroi in 1855.

Before heading on to Blois, it's well worth making a detour to the beautiful moated castle of Sully-sur-Loire, some 40 km (25 miles) south-east of Orléans. From Orléans, you have two options for reaching Chambord, which is somewhat outside of the Loire Valley – either along the right bank of the Loire to Merand and across a bridge, or along the left bank of the Loire on small rural roads.

⑥ Chambord King Francis I had this château built on the site of an older hunting lodge. Lost among the vast forests,

the result was a vast dream castle with an incredible 440 rooms, seventy staircases, corner towers, a parapet and a moat. Leonardo da Vinci was apparently involved in its construction as well, designing the elaborate double-helix staircase whose two spirals are so intertwined that the people going up cannot see the people going down, and vice versa.

One of the château's real charms is its unique roof silhouette with its numerous turrets and chimneys. Francis I did not live to see the completion of his château, and work was not continued on it until the reign of Louis XIV. Louis XV gave it as a gift to the Elector of Saxony, who had it gloriously renovated. The château fell into temporary neglect after his death.

⑦ Blois In the first half of the 17th century, Blois was the center of France's political world.

1 View of the Eiffel Tower lit up at night from one of the many bridges along the Seine.

2 The Palace of Versailles – the Cour de Marbre courtyard is paved with marble slabs.

3 The oldest bridge in Paris, the Pont Neuf, spans the Seine on the north and south sides of the Île de la Cité. Despite its name 'New Bridge', the Pont Neuf was opened in 1607 and connected the city to the island in the river, its medieval center.

proclaimed king at the tender age of five. His reign was subsequently defined by his love of all things opulent and gaudy, and the Palace of Versailles is the most impressive and repeatedly copied example of this.

After the death of Cardinal Mazarin, Louis XIV limited the rights of parliament and the aristocracy and strengthened the army. He ruled with absolute power until his death in 1715.

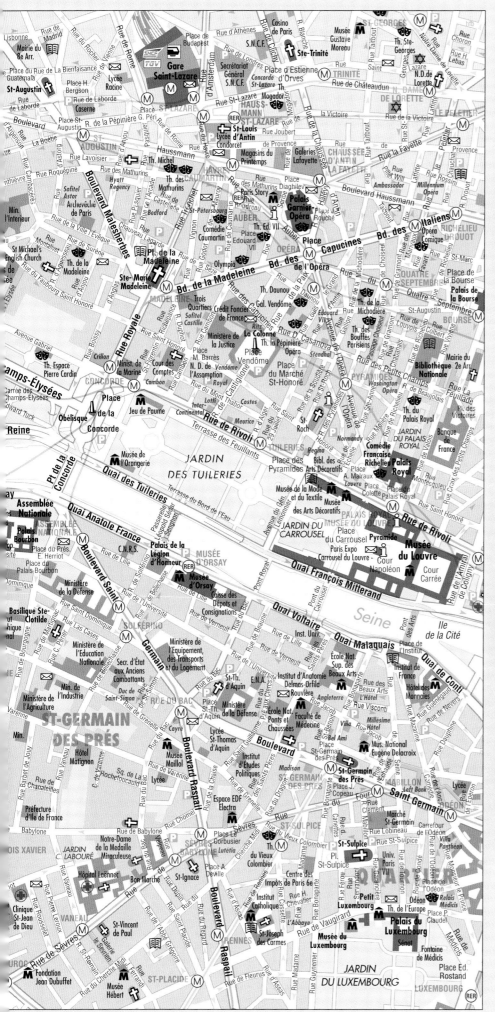

Paris

The French capital is a city of thrilling contrasts – rich in tradition and at the same time avant-garde, enormous in size and yet captivatingly charming. Paris is also a university city and the place of government, a global center for fashion and art, incredibly multicultural and yet still very much the epitome of all things French.

Throughout its long history, Paris has continually been in a state of expansion. The city always appeared to be bursting at the seams. Today, greater Paris covers an area of about 105 sq km (40 sq miles) and is home to some twelve million people – more than twenty percent of the entire population of France. This city's non-stop growth is not least due to the fact that Paris does not accept any rivals. The nation's capital has always been unchallenged in its political, economic and cultural significance.

On the south side of the Seine you won't be able to miss the Eiffel Tower, the symbol of Paris built for the World Fair in 1889. The iron construction, towering 300 m (984 ft) over the city, took engineer Gustav Eiffel just sixteen months to completed. The viewing platform, accessed by

Be sure to see the Place de la Concorde, an excellent example of wide boulevards and geometric plazas that gave the French capital its 'big city' look during its renovation in the 19th century. Also visit the park complex Jardin des Tuileries, which leads up to the Louvre; the Place Vendôme with its upmarket shopping; the Palais Garnier, an opulent 19th-century opera house; and the 17th-century Palais Royal.

Montmartre, on the north side of town, is great for exploring both day and night. Things to see include the historic Moulin de la Galette with its outdoor garden restaurant; the Sacre Coeur basilica up on the hill, with fantastic views of the city; the Père Lachaise Cemetery (east, outside city center), one of three large cemeteries built around 1800 with the graves of numerous celebrities (Oscar Wilde, Jim

Top: Place de la Concorde, one of the most magnificent plazas in Europe.
Middle: The striking Arc de Triomphe on the Champs-Elysées by night.
Bottom: The Eiffel Tower was erected in 1889 for the World Fair.

elevator, is one of the city's major attractions. The Hôtel des Invalides, a complex crowned by the Dôme des Invalides, was built by Louis XIV for the victims of his numerous wars.

North of the Seine is probably the most magnificent boulevard in the world, the Champs-Elysées, with the Arc de Triomphe providing a great view of the streets emanating from its center.

Morrison, Edith Piaf, Eugène Delacroix and Frédéric Chopin, for example). All the cemeteries have detailed maps available at the main entrance.

In the northern suburb of St-Denis you will find the early-Gothic church of St-Denis, the burial place of the French kings, and the Stade de France, a massive football stadium with capacity for 80,000, built for the 1998 World Cup.

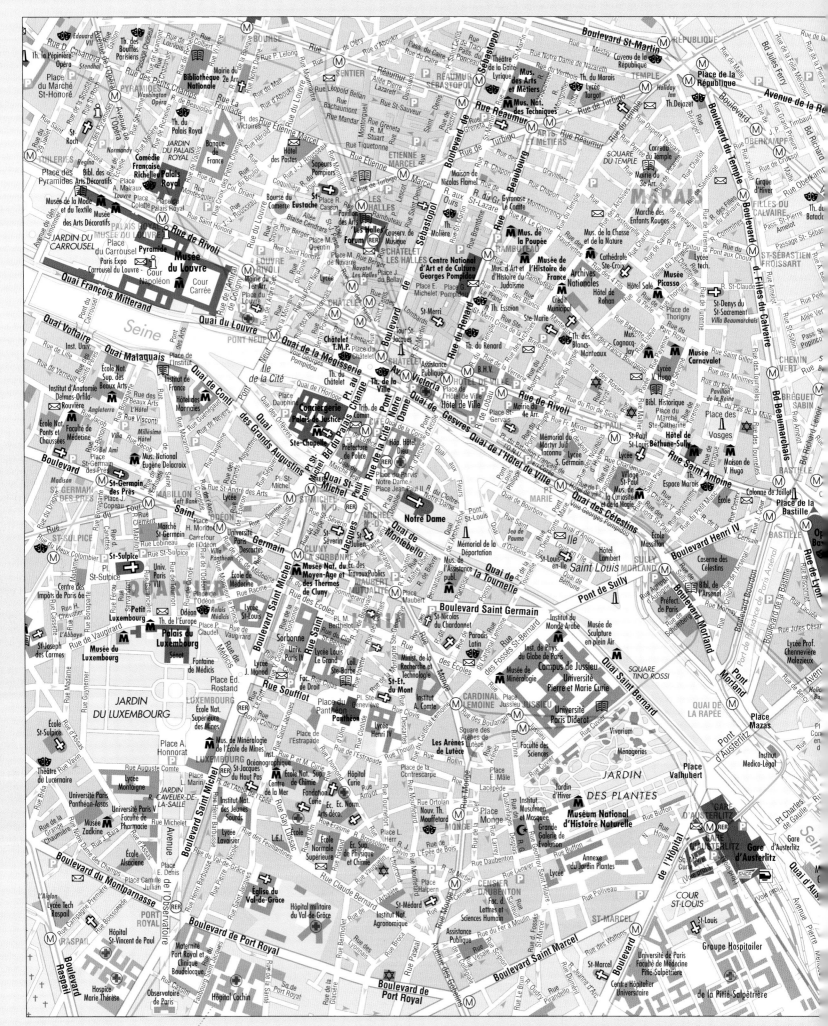

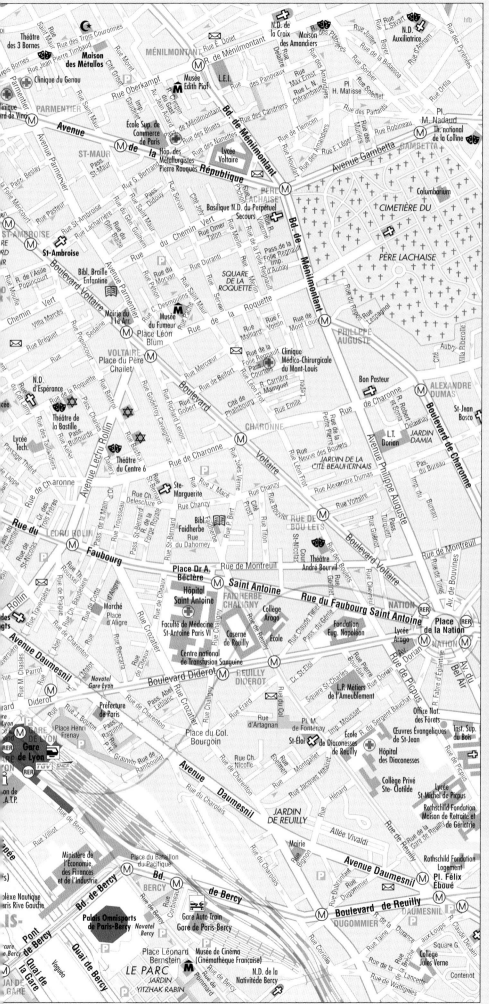

Paris

The historic center of the 'City of Light' is relatively easy to navigate, and many sights can be reached on foot. However, you should allow yourself copious amounts of time – after all, if you fancied it, you could spend days just wandering around the Louvre.

During the Middle Ages, when Paris was arguably the most important city in Europe, three factors determined the city's development and status – the church, its royalty and the university, all of which have left their mark on the historic city center. Out on the Île de la Cité – the city's oldest core settlement where the Romans, Merovingians and Carolingians based their dominions – stands one of France's most splendid cathedrals: Notre Dame.

As of 1400, medieval royalty focused their power on the northern banks of the Seine at the Louvre, which was begun in 1200 as part of a first ring of fortifications and developed into a magnificent residence over the centuries. On the other side of the river, in the Latin Quarter, professors and students united to establish the Sorbonne at the end of the 12th century. The riverbank, with its grand buildings, is a UNESCO World Heritage Site.

the former palace chapel of Ste-Chapelle, a high-Gothic masterpiece; the Conciergerie, part of the medieval royal palace; Pont Neuf, one of the most beautiful bridges on the Seine; and the idyllic Île St-Louis, south-east of the Île de la Cité, with its Renaissance buildings.

North of the Seine visit the Louvre, first a medieval castle, then the royal residence until the 17th century, then rebuilt and made into one of the largest art museums in the world; the Centre Pompidou, a cultural center with exemplary modern architecture; the Hôtel de Ville, the 19th-century town hall at the Place de Grève; the Marais quarter with the romantic Place des Vosges, the avant-garde Opéra National de Paris, the Gothic church of St-Gervais-et-St-Protais, the Picasso museum, and the Hôtel Carnavalet's museum on the city's history.

Top: The illuminated Louvre pyramid was built at the end of the 20th century as part of the costly modernization of the largest art museum in the world.
Below: From the 12th to 14th centuries, the Gothic Notre Dame Cathedral was built on the Île de la Cité in the medieval city center.

On the Île de la Cité, don't miss the early-Gothic Cathédrale Notre Dame (12th/13th centuries), where you can climb both 68-m-high (223-ft) towers;

South of the Seine go to the famous Latin Quarter; the St-Germain-des-Prés and Montparnasse Quarters and the Jardin du Luxembourg park.

Jeanne d'Arc (Joan of Arc)

Jeanne d'Arc was born in 1412, the daughter of a rich farmer in Domrémy in the Lorraine region. At the time, France had been heavily involved in the Hundred Years War with England since 1337, and the English had advanced as far as the Loire.

At the age of thirteen, Jeanne began hearing voices in her head telling her to join forces with the French heir apparent, Charles VII, and expel the English from France. After she recognized him in Chinon, despite his disguise, people started believing in her divine mission. She was then given his support and went with the French army to Orléans, which was occupied by the English. With

A golden statue of Jeanne d'Arc on the Place des Pyramides in Paris.

her help, the city was liberated on 8 May 1429.

Jeanne was also able to persuade Charles VII to follow the dangerous road to Reims to be crowned. The ceremony took place in July 1420 in the Reims cathedral. However, the farmer's daughter from Lorraine, who was now France's heroine, had enemies too. In 1430, the Burgundians, who were allied with England, succeeded in imprisoning and handing Jeanne over to the English. She was accused of heresy and witchery in Rouen in 1431 and, as Charles VII thought it to be politically incorrect to help her, condemned to be burned at the stake on 30 May 1431. The conviction was overturned in 1456, and in 1920 Jeanne d'Arc was granted sainthood.

especially lovely half-timbered house, the Maison des Acrobates, is located on the cathedral square. If you are interested in Gothic churches, pay a visit to the 12th-century St-Nicolas.

8 Cheverny This castle, built between 1620 and 1634, is still owned by the family of the builder, Henri Hurault. It is also probably thanks to this fact that the castle still contains a large part of the original, opulent interior decor. The ceiling frescoes in the dining hall and bedroom are particularly worth inspecting.

9 Chenonceaux Powerful women played a large role in the history of this romantic pleasure palace. For example, Cathérine Briçonnet supervised its construction in the early 16th century while her husband was in Italy. After Thomas Bohier's death, the building fell into the hands of the king and Henry II gave it as a gift to his beloved, Diane de Poitiers, who extended it to include a bridge over the Cher. Following Henry's death, his wife, Catherine de Medici, kept the castle for herself, and it is thanks to her idea that the Florentine-style bridge was built, including its own gallery.

After Catherine de Medici, the widow of the assassinated Henry III, Louise de Lorraine, proceeded to live a life of mourning in what was actually a very

bright and cheerful-looking castle. This spirit returned in the 18th century with the arrival of middle-class Louise Dupin, who saved the castle from the destruction of the revolution. Only very little remains of the original decor, but Renaissance furnishings have been used to give an impression of what the interior may have been like.

Located on the bridge pier is the gorgeous kitchen, where copper pots and pans still hang in an orderly fashion.

10 Amboise Perched on a hill sloping steeply into the Loire is France's first major Renaissance château. Although only parts of the construction have been preserved, they are still very impressive in their size and grandeur.

Following an expedition to Italy in 1496, Charles VIII brought back with him Italian artists, craftsmen and works of art to decorate the palace. The interiors of the mighty towers were constructed in such a way that a rider on a horse could reach up into the storey above. The Chapelle-St-Hubert is a good example of Gothic architecture. Not far from the château is the Le Clos-Lucé mansion, where Leonardo da Vinci spent the final years of his life. Francis I had originally arranged for the Italian universal genius to come to France, and a small museum displaying models of Leonardo's inventions pays homage to this influential man.

The small town located below the château, a row of houses,

and the clock tower all date back to the time of this region's heyday. From Amboise, a small road leads through the middle of the Loire Valley to Tours.

11 Tours This is the town that gave the Via Turonensis its name, and the tomb of St Martin here was an extremely important stop for St James pilgrims. Revolutionaries demolished the old St-Martin Basilica at the end of the 18th century. The new St-Martin Basilica, in neo-Byzantine style, contains the tomb of the saint, consecrated in 1890. It is an example of the monumental church architecture of the time, one that made use of many different styles.

The St-Gatien Cathedral is the city's most important historic

The Romanesque style of the Poitou region is typified, for the most part, by rich sculptural decorations. The facade of the former collegiate church

Top: The western facade of the Notre Dame Cathedral in Poitiers.
Bottom: A look inside the church.

church. The two-storey cloister provides a great view of the towers' tracery and the finely carved flying buttresses.

In some parts of the Old Town, like the Place Plumereau, you could be forgiven for thinking you were back in the Middle Ages. Charming half-timbered houses with pointed gables and often ornately carved balconies are proof of the wealth of the traders at the time. A waxworks cabinet is located in the historic rooms of the Château Royal (13th century).

⓬ Villandry The last of the great castles to be built in the Loire during the Renaissance (1536) fell into ruin in the 19th century and its Renaissance gardens were then made into an English-style park. The Spanish Carvallo family eventually bought it in 1906 and it is thanks to them that the castle has been renovated. More importantly, the gardens were remodelled in the original Renaissance style. This explains why a lot of the people who visit the castle today are lovers of historic landscaping. Whether it be beds of flowers or vegetables, everything is laid out artistically and trees and hedges are perfectly trimmed into geometric shapes.

⓭ Azay-le-Rideau This castle on the Indre, built between 1519 and 1524, captivates visitors with the harmony of its proportions and its romantic location on an island in the river. However, it did not bring its builder, the mayor of Tours, Gilles Berthelot, much luck. Like other French kings, Francis I could not tolerate his subjects openly displaying their wealth. Without further ado, he accused the mayor of infidelity and embezzlement, and seized the castle.

⓮ Ussé The Château d'Ussé was built on the walls of a fortified castle in the second half of the 15th century. With its turrets and merlons, as well as its location at the edge of the forest, it's easy to see how it was the inspiration for authors of fairy tales. The Gothic chapel houses an important work of art from the Italian Renaissance, a terracotta Madonna by the Florentine sculptor Luca della Robbia.

⓯ Saumur Horse lovers around the world should be very familiar with the name Saumur. The cavalry school, founded in 1763, is still France's national riding school. The castle was built in the second half of the 14th century and is located on a hillside above the city.

Today, it houses two museums, an art museum and the Musée du Cheval. In the Old Town, half-timbered houses like the town hall on the Place St-Pierre, which was created in 1508 as a patrician palace, and the numerous 17th-century villas are all worth a look. In the Gothic church of Notre Dame de Nantilly, the side aisle, which Louis XI had built in a flamboyant style, is home to a prayer chapel that an inscription identifies as being the royal oratorio. On rainy days there are two interesting museums worth visiting: a mask museum (Saumur produces a large quantity of carnival masks) and a mushroom museum. These

1 After Versailles, the fantastic 16th-century water palace in Chenonceaux is the most visited château in France.

2 A stone bridge crosses the Loire in Amboise, home to the grand château of the same name.

3 Located on the left bank of the Indre, the 15th-century Château d'Ussé is like a fairy-tale castle made into reality.

4 Saumur – a view over the Loire to the Château de Saumur and the church tower of St-Pierre.

of Notre Dame la Grande in Poitiers, completed in the mid 12th century, is a particularly good example of this. Above the three portals, as well as to the left and right of the large second-floor window, is an ornately sculptured series of images depicting themes from the Old and New Testament such as Adam and Eve, the prophet Moses, Jeremiah, Josiah and Daniel, the Tree of Jesse, the Annunciation, the birth of Christ, the twelve apostles and, in the gables, Christ in the Mandorla with two angels.

The church of St-Pierre in nearby Parthenay-le-Vieux was built in the late 11th century. The most striking part of this building is the eight-cornered transept tower, but the most beautiful features are the decorative figures on the facade. Samson's battle with the lion is depicted here, as well as the horseman, which is typical for the Romanesque style in Poitiers. The image of the Melusine fairy, which appears more than thirty times, is an original element.

La Rochelle and Île de Ré

A detour to Île de Ré first takes you to La Rochelle, an important port town since the 11th century and considered one of France's most beautiful cities. In 1628, Cardinal Richelieu seized the town, which had for too long taken the wrong side in the political debate of the day – over 23,000 people died during the brutal occupation.

Today, its main attraction is the Atlantic port, where yachts bob up and down in a picture-perfect

Top: An aerial photo of Île de Ré.
Bottom: A view of the port at St-Martin-de-Ré.

scene. The city's best-known tourist sites are down by the Old Harbour – the Tour St-Nicolas and the Tour de la Chaîne. In times of war, an iron chain was stretched between the two towers to protect the port from enemy ships. The town hall (1595–1606) is built in Renaissance style with a gorgeous arcaded interior courtyard.

The Île de Ré – also known as the 'White Island' – is connected to the mainland by a 4-km-long (2.5-mile) bridge. Vineyards and salt marshes dominate the scene and are surrounded by pretty villages whose houses are decorated with lush flowers. The main town on the island is St-Martin-de-Ré, with a citadel that was constructed in the 17th century by the famous fort builder, Vauban.

St-Clément-des-Baleines near the north-western tip of the island is also interesting – it has two lighthouses worth seeing.

precious fungi are grown in the surrounding area in numerous limestone caves.

From Saumur, the westernmost point of the journey through the Loire, the road heads 11 km (7 miles) back towards Fontevraud-l'Abbaye.

16 Fontevraud-l'Abbaye This abbey was founded in 1101 and existed as such until the 19th century. In the tall, bright church (consecrated in 1119) is the tomb of Eleonore of Aquitania. Southwest France 'wedded' England when she married Henry Plantagenet, later Henry II of England. Eleonore's husband and their son, Richard the Lionheart, are also buried in Fontevraud.

The 16th-century cloister is the largest in all of France. However, the abbey's most original building is the monastery kitchen, which almost looks like a chapel with six arches.

17 Chinon This castle-like château high above the banks of the Vienne played an important role in French history. This is where Jeanne d'Arc first met Charles VII and recognized him despite his costume, his courtiers, who were hiding him, and the fact that she had never seen him before. It is for this reason that the large tower, the Tour de l'Horloge, houses a small museum dedicated to her. Other

parts of the castle, originating from the 10th to 15th centuries, are only ruins now. A highlight of any visit to the castle is the view over the Vienne valley.

18 Châtellerault This town, no longer of much significance, was once an important stop for pilgrims on the Camino de Santiago. Pilgrims would enter the town, as did Jeanne d'Arc, through Porte Ste-Cathérine. The church of St-Jacques, the destination of all pilgrims on the Camino de Santiago, was furnished with an ornate set of chimes. Some of the houses, such as the Logis Cognet, enable you to imagine what life was like in the 15th century.

19 Poitiers This old city, which was an important stop for pilgrims on the Camino de Santiago, found an important patron in Duke Jean de Berry. In the second half of the 16th century, it became a center of spiritualism and science and its churches still show evidence of this today.

20 Marais Poitevin The marshland located west of Poitiers and stretching all the way to the coast seems to have remained stuck in time. The most important and often the only means of transport in the 'Venise Verte' (Green Venice) is one of the flat-bottomed boats.

The Romanesque churches of Parthenay-le-Vieux, some 50 km (31 miles) west of Poitiers, are well worth a visit. You have to return to Poitiers before continuing on to St-Jean-d'Angély.

21 St-Jean-d'Angély Although it has now paled into insignificance, this town was once an important destination for St James pilgrims as it was here that they had the opportunity to pay their respects to John the Baptist. Only ruins remain of the Gothic church, but a row of beautiful half-timbered houses, the Tour de la Grosse Horloge (clock tower) dating from 1406, an artistic fountain (1546), and the 17th-century abbey enable modern visitors to take a trip back in time.

From here, it's worth making a detour to the port town of La Rochelle on the Atlantic, where you can make an excursion out to the Île de Ré.

22 Saintes The capital of the Saintonge looks back on a long history, traces of which can still be seen today. The Arc de Germanicus, which was originally the gateway to a bridge, dates back to Roman times. When the bridge eroded, it was saved and rebuilt on the right bank. The ruins of the amphitheater, dating back to the 1st century and today overgrown with grass,

once seated 20,000 people. There are also some impressive remains from the Middle Ages. The Abbaye aux Dames, for example, was founded in 1047, and the Romanesque church was built in the 11th and 12th centuries. The Gothic St-Pierre Cathedral was constructed in the 13th and 14th centuries and the tower was added in the 17th century. The church of St-Eutrope, dating from the late 11th century, was one of the destinations of the St James

Château Mouton-Rothschild

In the Bordelais wine region, château does not mean castle, but rather a large vineyard. One of this region's world-famous vineyard abodes is the Château Mouton-Rothschild in Pauillac on the Gironde. Predominantly upmarket Cabernet-Sauvignon grapes are grown here, on a piece of land covering about 80 ha (198 acres).

Baron Philippe de Rothschild came up with the idea to make his wine bottles into small works of art. As a result, for over half a century artists have been creating labels for the property's top red wines. The list of contributing painters reads like a 'Who's Who' of modern art – Jean Cocteau (1947), Georges

Top: Vineyards as far as the eye can see.
Bottom: The château's wine cellar.

Braque (1955), Salvador Dalí (1958), Juan Miro (1969), Marc Chagall (1970), Pablo Picasso (1973), Andy Warhol (1975), Keith Haring (1988). You can admire these artworks, as well as many other exhibits, in the château's wine museum.

to the St-Émilion appellation, which produce very high quality wines, is the small town whose beginnings trace back to a monastery. The sizeable rock-hewn church here (9th–12th centuries), whose understated facade faces towards the pretty market place, is a special attraction. The collegiate church was built in the 12th century and its main aisle is Romanesque. By no means should you miss having a look at the very well-preserved cloister. The donjon, a relic from the royal fort, towers high above St-Émilion where the 'Jurade' wine confrèrie meets to test the new wines. Every year, from the tower platform, the members ceremoniously declare the grape harvest open.

26 Bordeaux This old city on the Garonne has long been dominated by trade – predominantly the wine trade. An historic event had a profound effect on the city – in 1154, Bordeaux fell under English rule

1 Storm clouds over the port of La Rochelle with its 15th-century Tour de la Lanterne.

2 With its medieval houses, squares and streets, St-Émilion is a charming little town in the middle of the lovely wine region of the same name.

pilgrims. They prayed here in the spacious crypt at the tomb of the city's saint, Eutropius.
From Saintes you head southeast towards Cognac.

23 Cognac This town, on the banks of the Charente, today very much revolves around the drink of the same name, which expert noses will be able to catch whiffs of as they stroll through the town. The Valois Castle, from the 15th and 16th centuries, has a cognac distillery.

An exhibition at the town hall allows you to get a better understanding of the history and production of the precious brandy, which takes between five and forty years to mature. Some of the distilleries offer interesting tours of their facilities.
You head south-west from here to Pons before continuing on to Libourne.

24 Libourne This small town is a typical bastide, a fortified town, built at the time when

South-West France was an apple of discord between England and France (1150–1450). Every bastide is surrounded by a wall and has a grid-like layout and a large market square. Libourne was founded in 1270 and was for a long time a very important port for shipping wine out of the region. Today, it's worth taking a stroll around the Place Abel Surchamp.

25 St-Émilion Soaring out of the sea of vineyards that belong

Côte d'Argent and Côte des Basques

The Côte d'Argent refers to the stretch of coast between the Bassin d'Arcachon and Biarritz, where it turns into the Côte Basque, straddling the French-Spanish border. Apart from excellent swimming, the Côte d'Argent also hosts a unique natural landscape.

The Dune de Pilat is Europe's highest dune, fluctuating between 105 m and 120 m (345 ft and 394 ft), with a width of 500 m (1,640 ft), and a length of 2.7 km (2 miles). The

The romantic coast of Biarritz.

Parc Ornithologique du Teich is also worth a visit.

The Côte Basque is home to one of few swanky seaside resorts in the region – Biarritz. It experienced its heyday during the Belle Époque, when Napoleon III and his wife, Eugénie, spent their holidays here. The Rocher de la Vierge (Rock of the Virgin) and its statue of the Madonna have a charming location out in the sea. A footbridge leads you out to the isolated formation. The casino and many of the hotel palaces are evidence of the glitz and glamour of Biarritz' golden age. St-Jean-de-Luz is a picturesque old town and several of its houses display the typically Basque half-timber style.

The Sun King met his bride, the Spanish Infanta Maria Theresa, for the first time here in the Maison Louis XIV. Her house, the Maison de l'Infante, is located just a little further on.

and, thanks to their huge interest in the region's wines, trade boomed. Even when Bordeaux was again part of France, it still maintained a close relationship with the British Isles.

The Place de la Comédie, with the classical columned facade of the Grand Théâtre, is an ideal place to start a stroll through the city. The Esplanade des Quinconces here is considered the largest square in Europe. You shouldn't miss seeing the city's churches. The St-André Cathedral was built between the 13th and 15th centuries and fascinates visitors with its Porte Royale, a magnificent door lavishly decorated with sculptures. Apart from the church, there is the Tour Pey-Berland, a free-standing tower. St-Michel was constructed somewhat later, in the 14th/16th centuries, and is furnished in 17th-century baroque style.

Those following in the footsteps of Camino de Santiago pilgrims should pay a visit to St-Seurin. Worshipping St-Severin (St-Seurin) was an important part of the route. The early-Romanesque crypt dates back to this time.

Bordeaux has a lot more to offer than just St James relics – the city gates of Porte de Cailhau, Porte d'Aquitaine, Porte de la Monnaie and Porte Dijeaux, for example. The Pont de Pierre (a stone bridge) and the tall, modern bridge, Pont d'Aquitaine, dating from 1967, are also worth a look.

Those interested in seeing the region's world-famous vineyards should make the 50-km (31-mile) journey along the Gironde to the Château Mouton-Rothschild in Pauillac.

27 Les Landes This is the name given to the landscape typical of the area south of Bordeaux – flat, sandy earth with sparse pine forests. The forests are planted by hand and are still used for their lumber by-products, predominantly for the extraction of resin.

The region's capital is Mont-de-Marsan, located somewhat off the beaten track in the southeast and home to some interesting Romanesque houses, the 15th-century Lacataye donjon and some very pretty parks.

28 Dax This small town on the Adour is one of France's most frequently visited thermal baths. Water at a temperature of 64°C (147°F) bubbles out of the Fontaine de la Néhé.

The 17th-century cathedral here is also worth seeing. The apostle gate from the earlier Gothic building is significant in an art-history context.

A visit to the Musée Borda in a beautiful city palace and a stroll along the banks of the Adour round off the visit.

If you want to go to the seaside, you can can drive 40 km (25 miles) from Dax to the southern end of the Côte d'Argent and then further on to the Côte des Basques around Biarritz.

On the other hand, those wanting to get a whiff of the mountain air in the Pyrenees should continue south-east along the spectacular route to Orthez.

29 St-Jean-Pied-de-Port In the Middle Ages, this mountain

town was already an important stop for pilgrims – and the last before the strenuous crossing of the Pyrenees over the Roncesvalles Pass and across the Spanish border. 'Saint John at the Foot of the Pass' manages to preserve its medieval character even today. The banks of the Nive River are lined with houses from the 16th and 17th centuries and the Gothic church of Notre Dame du Bout du Pont.

30 Bayonne The capital of the Pays Basque is a densely settled area but it has managed to retain much of its charm in its center with bridges on two rivers, large squares and rows of houses packed closely together around the Gothic cathedral of Ste Marie. Its city festival is famous, held every year on the second weekend in August.

1 The Bay of Biarritz with its tiny port and the main beach.

2 The Pont du Pierre crosses the Garonne in Bordeaux, with the striking tower of the Cathédrale St-André in the background.

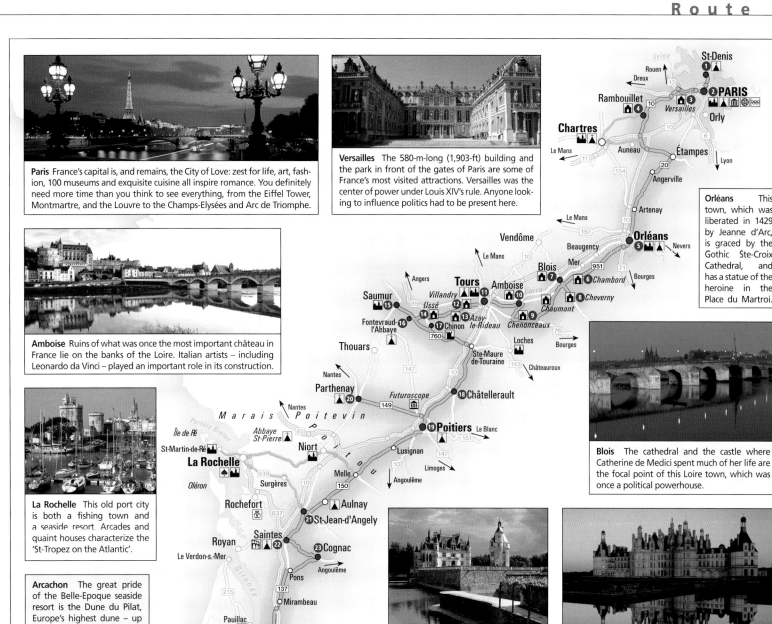

Paris France's capital is, and remains, the City of Love: zest for life, art, fashion, 100 museums and exquisite cuisine all inspire romance. You definitely need more time than you think to see everything, from the Eiffel Tower, Montmartre, and the Louvre to the Champs-Elysées and Arc de Triomphe.

Versailles The 580-m-long (1,903-ft) building and the park in front of the gates of Paris are some of France's most visited attractions. Versailles was the center of power under Louis XIV's rule. Anyone looking to influence politics had to be present here.

Orléans This town, which was liberated in 1429 by Jeanne d'Arc, is graced by the Gothic Ste-Croix Cathedral, and has a statue of the heroine in the Place du Martroi.

Amboise Ruins of what was once the most important château in France lie on the banks of the Loire. Italian artists – including Leonardo da Vinci – played an important role in its construction.

Blois The cathedral and the castle where Catherine de Medici spent much of her life are the focal point of this Loire town, which was once a political powerhouse.

La Rochelle This old port city is both a fishing town and a seaside resort. Arcades and quaint houses characterize the 'St-Tropez on the Atlantic'.

Arcachon The great pride of the Belle-Epoque seaside resort is the Dune du Pilat, Europe's highest dune – up to 120 m (394 ft) high, 3 km (2 miles) in length and 500 m (1,640 ft) wide, it's like a small desert. The Cap Ferrer headland and the fishing towns of the Arcachon Bay are also worth seeing.

Château de Chenonceaux It was mainly women who influenced the tone of this Renaissance building on the banks of the Cher in the Loire Valley.

Château de Chambord With 440 rooms, a wide moat, and scores of towers, chimneys and gables, this dream castle is truly one of a kind. Leonardo da Vinci created one of the château's seventy staircases, an intricate double-helix spiral.

Poitiers Numerous churches and the cathedral are evidence of this town's location on the Camino de Santiago.

Bordeaux This wine, trade and port city on the Garonne is home to a multitude of tourist attractions including the Place de la Comédie with the Grand Théâtre; Europe's largest square, the Esplanade des Quinconces; the ornate St-André Cathedral (13th–15th centuries).

The vineyards of the Médoc This region north of Bordeaux is dominated by vineyards. More than 130 wineries, often called châteaux, produce red wine.

Biarritz Winter guests made this former whaling town on the Basque coast popular in the 19th century. Its beaches and promenades still enjoy huge popularity.

Bayonne This town is the heart and soul of the French Basque region. Its Gothic cathedral, famous for its folk festival in August, is definitely worth a visit.

St-Émilion Amid the vineyards are the fortress complexes of St-Émilion, with its famous cathedral and rock-hewn church.

Lavender fields – a symbol of Provence. The plants are cultivated for their scented oil.

Route 17

France and Spain
The 'Land of Light' – from Côte d'Azur to Costa Brava

The coastline along the Côte d'Azur, the Golfe du Lion and the Costa Brava could hardly be more diverse or enticing. At the southern edge of the Alps, the Côte d'Azur showcases a landscape of breathtakingly unique beauty. Provence is a paradise for nature lovers and culture enthusiasts, while the Camargue is a near pristine delta landscape. The Costa Brava gets its name from the mountains which drop away steeply into the sea.

An incredibly varied stretch of coast between Menton on the Côte d'Azur and Barcelona on the Costa Brava greets visitors with all the beauty the French Midi and the north-eastern Spanish coast have to offer.

Directly behind Monte Carlo's sea of houses and apartments are the captivating mountains of the Alpes-Maritimes, which only begin to flatten out near Nice, allowing trendier cities like Cannes and Antibes to sprawl a bit. The foothills of the Massif des Maures once again straddle the coast beyond St-Tropez where there is really only enough room for small, picturesque villages – your search for sandy beaches will be in vain. But not to worry, you'll find them again around Hyères and the offshore islands in the area.

Wine-lovers will get their money's worth between Toulon and Cassis – the wines grown between Bandol and Le Castellet are some of the best in the Midi. Marseille then presents itself as the port city with two faces. Founded by the Greeks, and

The Calanques cliffs near Cassis.

later a stronghold of the Romans, its cultural history dates back 2,500 years. At the same time, it was long the gateway to the cultures on other Mediterranean shores – Europe, North Africa and the Near East are all represented in Marseille's multicultural population.

West of Marseille, in the delta between the two mouths of the Rhône, sprawls a breathtakingly beautiful wetland of ponds, marshes, meadows and plains abundant with springs, grass, and salt fields – the Camargue. North of here is where you'll discover the heart of Provence. Cities such as Arles, Avignon and Nîmes are strongholds of European cultural history with their unique examples of Roman architecture.

The Languedoc-Roussillon region begins west of the Rhône delta and stretches to the Spanish border with a mix of long

Isolated bays along the rocky coast of the Costa Brava near Cadaqués.

St-Tropez: The international jet set discovered this idyllic fishing town in the 1950s and since then there have been more yachts than fishing boats anchored in the port.

beaches and mountainous hinterland. The Languedoc is home to the troubadours, and the Roussillon was part of Spain until the 1659 Treaty of the Pyrenees. The Catalán legacy in this region can still be seen at every turn. Even bullfights are still held here. The Languedoc was also home to the Cathars, who broke away from the Catholic Church in the 13th century.

Between Narbonne and Carcassone in the hills of Corbières, where an invitation to taste wine should never be refused, are numerous ruins of the proud castles that once stood here. With its fortress complexes, Carcassonne takes you back in time to the Middle Ages. South of Narbonne, near Leucate, marks the start of long, brilliantly white sandy beaches stretching to the Franco-Spanish border and the eastern foothills of the Pyrenees.

The last of the French villages before reaching Spain are self-assured fishing villages virtually embedded into the mountains. The Costa Brava, as this coastline is called, owes its name to the steep seaside cliffs at the eastern end of the Pyrenees. Bravo also means 'brave' or 'outstanding' in Spanish, so travellers should expect much more than just a wild coast.

The further south you go, the bigger the beaches become and the more towns and villages appear. The Catalán capital, Barcelona, is Spain's second-largest city. Carthaginians, Romans, Visigoths and Moors have all left their legacy here, making the city into a European metropolis with a special Catalán charm. The numerous art-nouveau buildings by Gaudí and Domènech i Montaner are quite spectacular. Life pulses day and night on the Ramblas, Barcelona's pedestrian zone.

The Old Town of Carcassonne enclosed by a double wall.

Top: View from the far side of the Rhône across to Avignon, capital of the Département of Vaucluse. All that remains of the famous Pont St.-Bénézet are the arches. The medieval city is encircled by a 4.5-km-long (7-mi) city wall.

Bottom: The centerpiece of Marseille is the Vieux Port (old port), which is protected by two mighty forts: St.-Jean (here) and St.-Nicolas. The imposing new-Byzantine Cathédrale de la Major to the left of the fort dates from the 9th century. It is 140 m (460 ft) long with a 70-m-high (230-ft) dome.

The horses of the Camargue

Covering a marsh, meadow and grasslands area of roughly 140,000 ha (345,940 acres), the delta between the two main forks of the mouth of the Rhône is one of the largest wetlands in Europe. Agriculture – predominantly rice cultivation – is concentrated on the northern part of the Camargue, while salt is extracted in the flat lagoons of the south-eastern section.

The southern part, on the other hand, is a nature paradise not found anywhere else in Europe. The delta's grassy meadows are home to not only the well-known Camargue horses and Camargue bulls, but also to numerous water and marsh birds – around 10,000 pairs of flamingos breed in the marshes, the largest of which is the Etang de Vaccarés. Twice a year, more than 350 species of

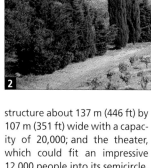

Wild Camargue horses.

birds stop at the Parc Ornithologique du Pont de Grau in the Camargue's south-west.

The black Camargue bulls are distinguished by their lyre-shaped horns. The white Camargue horses, semi-white thoroughbreds found in the Solutré cave paintings, often frolic among the bulls. Their physical characteristics include a compact body, angular head and thick mane, and they are born black or dark brown in color only growing their white coat after the age of five. If the wild horses are broken in to saddles and bridles at a young age, they can be perserving riding animals and very useful to herdsmen for controlling herds of cattle. A number of guided tours offer even amateur riders the chance to go for a gallop into the marshes, to the beaches or to see the bull herds, allowing people to experience many parts of the Camargue that would be otherwise inaccessible.

structure about 137 m (446 ft) by 107 m (351 ft) wide with a capacity of 20,000; and the theater, which could fit an impressive 12,000 people into its semicircle. The tidy Romanesque Church of St-Trophime is a masterpiece of Provencal stonemasonry, with a portal that dates back to 1190. The Romanesque-Gothic cloister adjacent to the church is considered the most beautiful in all of Provence.

From Arles, a rural road heads north-east to one of Provence's best-known villages, Les Baux.

 **Les Baux-de-Provence** This stone village is perched on a 900-m-long (2,953-ft) by 200-m-wide (656-ft) rocky ridge that rises dramatically out of the modest Alpilles range. In the Middle Ages, troubadours performed their courtly love songs in the once proud fort of Les Baux. The fort's unique location on a rock combined with the gorgeous view over the expanses of the Camargue and

the Rhône delta draw countless visitors to this car-free town every year.

From Les Baux, the road crosses the Alpilles to St-Rémy, a 24-km-long (15-mile) mountain range between Rhône and Durance.

St-Rémy-de-Provence Nostradamus was born in this quintessential Provencal town in 1503, and van Gogh painted his picture of the cornfield and cypresses here in 1889. St-Rémy's predecessor was the old city of Glanum, about 1 km (0.6 miles) south of the present-day center. An 18-m-high (59-ft) mausoleum dates back to this time and the Arc Municipal traces back to the time of Emperor Augustus.

Avignon This former papal city dominates the left bank of the Rhône and is still surrounded by a 4.5-km-long (3-mile) city wall. The Rocher des Doms and the enormous Palais des Papes (Papal Palace) are an impressive sight even from a distance.

Seven French popes resided here between 1309 and 1377, the time of the Papal Schism. The last 'antipope' did not flee his palace until 1403. The mighty fort-like Palais des Papes was built during this century-long schism, but next to nothing remains of the once ostentatious interior decor.

The famous bridge, Pont St-Bénézet (also known as Pont d'Avignon), was built in 1177, and four of its original twenty-two arches still stand today. From Aix, the journey heads north to two more of Europe's most beautiful Roman constructions. Near Sorgues, the D17 turns off towards Châteauneuf-du-Pape. The popes of Avignon built yet another castle here in the 14th century. Today, the wine from this region is one of the best in the Côtes du Rhône region. If you have enough time, you should make a detour into the Luberon or Villeneuve-les-Avignon on the way to Orange (see p. 211).

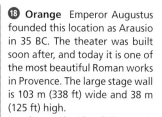 **Orange** Emperor Augustus founded this location as Arausio in 35 BC. The theater was built soon after, and today it is one of the most beautiful Roman works in Provence. The large stage wall is 103 m (338 ft) wide and 38 m (125 ft) high.

On the north side of the city is the third-largest triumphal arch of its kind, with a height of 22 m (72 ft), a width of 21 m (69 ft) and a thickness of 8 m (26 ft).

Driving south-west along the A9 you reach the Pont du Gard, a famous Roman aqueduct.

Nîmes This city of temples, public baths and theaters was founded in AD 16, also by Emperor Augustus. The Romans' most impressive building is the amphitheater, with an oval arena and tiered stone benches that seated 25,000 guests. The Maison Carrée, from the second and third centuries AD, is one of Europe's best-preserved Roman temples, with columns and decorative friezes. Many public baths,

Canal du Midi

The dream of connecting the Mediterranean to the Atlantic existed for many years but wasn't made a reality until Paul Riquet, an engineer from Béziers, took on the task between 1666 and 1681. With the 240-km-long (149-mile) Canal du Midi he connected the Mediterranean port town of Sète to the industrial city of Toulouse, which he in turn connected to the Atlantic via the Garonne River, navigable from Toulouse onwards.

The canal, with its countless dams, aqueducts, bridges and locks, was an engineering masterpiece for the 17th century and, with regard to trade, became the backbone of goods transport in the Languedoc region. Today, the canal is a romantic waterway for leisure skippers for whom the French way of life is more important than a quick journey.

The Canal du Midi is a UNESCO World Heritage Site.

Houseboats can be rented in Sète, Béziers, Narbonne, Castelnaudary, Carcassonne and Toulouse, and they indeed make for some interesting excursions. The journey is done at a leisurely pace and in some parts passes beneath long avenues of sycamores, through impressive landscapes and grand vineyards, and near cultural attractions.

Along the way, there is still time for fishing, swimming or simply relaxing. A boat licence is not required to charter a boat, as all important instructions are given at the start.

㉔ Narbonne This town was once the most significant Roman port in the area. The Horreum, an underground granary built in the first century BC, is visible evidence of this time.

The Cathédrale St-Just, with its beautiful sculptures and vivid stained-glass windows, dates back to the 13th century. The Palais des Archevêques is a fort-like complex with massive towers (14th century). Some 60 km (37 miles) west of Narbonne is Carcassonne, a prime example of medieval fortress architecture.

㉕ Carcassonne This city on the steep bank of the Aude is visible from quite a distance. Its double walls with distinctive merlons and towers date back to King Louis IX, who began construction in the 13th century. Porte Narbonnaise takes you to the Old Town, where the most

1 Along with the Cathédrale St-Nazaire, the historic fort town of Carcassonne has been listed as a UNESCO World Heritage Site.

2 Some of France's best wines are grown in the mountainous hinterland of the Languedoc.

3 Visible from a distance – the Cathédrale St-Nazaire, the landmark of Béziers on the Canal du Midi. This Romanesque-Gothic church was built between the 12th and 14th centuries. In the foreground is the Pont Vieux (13th century) over the River Orb.

Pont du Gard

This 2,000-year-old bridge at 49 m (161 ft) in height is the highest bridge ever built by the Romans and probably the best example of Roman bridge construction. The 'bridge' was actually also an aqueduct carrying water from Uzès to Nîmes. It was in operation for about 500 years.

temples and a theater (today a park) are concentrated around the Jardin de la Fontaine. About 20 km (12 miles) north-east of Nîmes is the Pont du Gard. From Nîmes, the route heads along the north-western edge of the Camargue to Aigues-Mortes.

⑳ Aigues-Mortes This town impresses visitors with the mighty walls of its fort, which are still completely intact. Aigues-Mortes, or 'Place of Dead Water', was constructed by Louis XI in the 13th century to consolidate his power on the Mediterranean coast. One part of the city wall can still be accessed. The Tour de Constance provides the best view over the city and the Camargue.

㉑ Saintes-Maries-de-la-Mer A 30-km-long (19-mile) road heads through the Camargue to the département capital, Les Saintes-Maries-de-la-Mer, well-known for the gypsy pilgrimage held every year in May. The Roman church here looks like

a medieval castle with its battlements and crenellated platform.

㉒ Montpellier The capital of the Département Hérault is home to France's oldest Botanic Garden, among other things. The focal point of the city is the Place de la Comédie, with a 19th-century opera house. Its most important attractions include the 17th-century patrician houses.

㉓ Béziers The route now heads through Montepellier to this lovely city on the Canal du Midi. The town's most recognizable landmark is the massive Cathédrale St-Nazaire (14th century), which is perched like a fort on a mountain above the city.

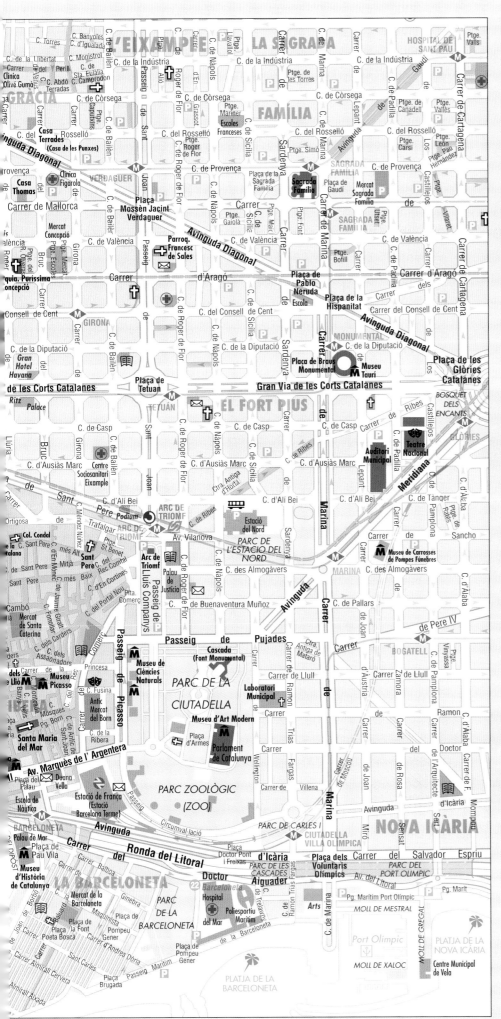

Barcelona

The capital of Catalonia, with its striking monuments, exciting nightlife and beautiful walks along the port and the sea, combines cosmopolitan flair with independent local tradition. Of course, it is also the city where Antoní Gaudí erected his largest and most compelling architectural feats.

Madrid's eternal competitor has a history that spans more than 2,000 years. Founded by the Romans, it was later conquered in 236 BC by the Carthaginian Hamilka Barcas, who named it Barcino. Control over this Mediterranean city changed hands between the Visigoths in 415, the Arabs in 713 and the Franks in 803.

When the kingdoms of Catalonia and Aragon were united (1137), it rose to become an important Spanish port and trading city. It unsuccessfully tried to become independent from Spain in the 17th century, and during the Spanish Civil War in the 20th century, Barcelona sided with the Republicans – against the eventual victor, Franco.

Towards the end of the 19th century, a completely new style of art and architecture developed in Barcelona – Modernism, the Catalán version of art nouveau, which has shaped the city's contemporary image like no other. Apart from Antoní Gaudí, the most important figures in this movement were architects Josep Puig i Cadalfalch and Lluís Domènech i Montaner. Many of their buildings are found in the Eixample quarter.

The best views of the city are seen from Montjuic in the south, or the 532-m-high (1745-ft) Tibidabo in the west, both of which are accessed by cable car. Particularly worth seeing are the Barri Gòtic, the oldest, elevated part of the city; the medieval square; Plaça del Rei with the palace of the Catalán and Castilian kings; Palau Real Major; the mighty Gothic cathedral; La Seu with its crypt and cloister where geese traditionally guard the tombs; Plaça del Pi, a square full of atmosphere; Las Ramblas, Catalonia's most famous pedestrian and shopping strip; the nostalgic market hall of La Boqueria (the 'gorge') with a wide range of products; Museu Nacional d'Art de Catalunya, whose collection of Romanesque frescoes and altar paintings is internationally reputed; Museu Picasso, with 3,600 works by the artist, who studied in Barcelona; and the Museu Maritim, a maritime museum in old shipbuilding halls.

The city's most magnificent building, and Antoní Gaudí's (1852–1926) masterpiece is the huge, still-incomplete church of La Sagrada Familia with its flamboyant, deeply symbolic design. Gaudí's other works include the counts' private residence of Palau Güell in the Barri Xines; the apartment blocks of Casa Milà, with bizarre sculptural decorations and a magical roof landscape; Casa Calvet and Casa Batlló in the modernist Eixample; and the Avinguda de

Gaudí, with its wide avenues very much in keeping with the great architect's style. Palau Güell and Casa Milà are UNESCO World Heritage Sites.

Domènech i Montaner has various works throughout the city, including:

Top: La Sagrada Familia by Gaudí.
Middle: Palau de la Música Catalana.
Bottom: Las Ramblas, Barcelona's 'pedestrian mall'.

Casa de l'Ardiaca, Casa Lleó Morera, Palau de la Música Catalana, Fundació Antoni Tàpies, Illa de la Discòrdia, Hospital de la Santa Creu i de Sant Pa and Museo de Zoologia.

A picturesque village crowned with a pilgrimage church along the Camino de Santiago in Galicia.

Spain

Camino de Santiago and Costa Verde – a journey through verdant Spain

Since the Middle Ages, pilgrims from all over the world have been drawn to the shrine of the apostle St James in Santiago de Compostela. Picturesque villages and towns, monasteries and castles, and the mighty cathedrals of Burgos and León line the 'Camino', which stretches from the Pyrenees on the border with France to Galicia in the north-western corner of Spain. The return journey skirts the rugged northern Spanish coast.

Legend has it that the apostle St James was beheaded in Palestine in the year AD 44 and his remains were sent by boat to the extreme north-west of Spain, where he had previously taught the gospel. It was not until much later, after the apostle's grave was discovered in the early 9th century, that the first St James' Basilica was built.

Subsequently, in 950, Gotescalco, the Bishop of Le Puy, became one of the first to make the pilgrimage to Compostela with a large entourage. Cesareo, the

Abbot of Montserrat, followed suit in 959. The stream of pilgrims grew so much that in 1072 Alfonso VI suspended the toll for the Galician Trail. Just one century later, Aymeric Picaud, a priest from Poitou, wrote the first guidebook for the pilgrimage to Compostela, which was published throughout all Europe's monasteries as *Codex Calixtinus*.

Paris, Vezelay, Le Puy and Arles became the main meeting points from which the groups of pious travellers would continue on their way. Before starting their jour-

The bulls entering the arena of Pamplona.

ney, the pilgrims and their equipment – a hat and coat to protect against the weather, a gourd for water and a staff for defence – were ceremoniously blessed. The seashells that the first pilgrims brought back from Galicia quickly became the symbol for future pilgrims. Those who arrived in Santiago and could prove the pilgrimage by showing their pilgrim book to the cathedral's secretary received the 'compostela', an official pilgrim certificate. To this day, every pilgrim who travels along the Camino de Santiago for at least 100 km (62 miles) either by walking or riding a bicycle or a horse also receives such a certificate.

Picaud described the meeting points in France: the two trails over the Pyrenees and the main trail from the Puente la Reina. Pilgrims coming from Paris, Vezelay and Le Puy would go over the Puerto

Every pilgrim's goal – the Cathedral of Santiago de Compostela.
According to legend, the remains of the apostle St James were brought
to Galicia from Jerusalem and were later found in the city on this site.

The Cuevas del Marbei Llanes beach lies on the Costa Verde at the foot of the Sierra de Cuera.

de Ibaneta (1,057 m/3,468 ft), and those coming from Arles would go over the Puerto de Somport (1,650 m/5,414 ft). In his trail guide, Picaud even describes the townships, hospitals and accommodation options along the way in great detail – the classic pilgrim trail still follows these today.

Nowadays, the thousand-year-old trail is signposted with blue signs depicting hikers or yellow St James shells. You can also experience the beauty along the way as an 'independent pilgrim', perhaps learning even more about the country, the people, the art and the culture of this stunning area. The rugged mountains stretch from the western Pyrenees to the Cantabrian Mountains, over the plateaus of the northern Meseta, mostly moorland, to the semi-desert area of the Navarran Bardenas Reales.

While the pilgrims' destination is Santiago, you have the option of heading back along the northern Spanish coast, which partly corresponds to the Aragonian pilgrim route, and experiencing the charming interplay of mountains and sea on the rugged, craggy Atlantic coast between Galicia and the Basque country (País Vasco).

On the way to the Basque country, the tour passes through the historic province of Asturias, with its mountain pastures, and Cantabria, with its impressive Atlantic coniferous forests. The mountains then go east into the Pyrenees. Both routes also offer a multitude of art and culture, with historical relics dating back 1,500 years. From the treasures hidden in the tiniest of village churches to the lavishly filled chambers of major cathedrals, St James' Way will not disappoint.

Chaparral scenery along the Camino de Santiago, from the Pyrenees to Galicia.

About half of the 1,600 km (1,000 mi) of Galicia's coastline comprises cliffs, some of them the highest in Europe. Rías such as this one are river deltas that are subject to tidal movements and are also typical of the wild coast. Comparable to fjords but much flatter, they are distributed throughout the

north-western Rías Baixas and northern Rías Altas regions. The majority of Galicia's population lives along the coast where fishing is still the most important commercial industry.

Palacio Real de Aranjuez, the king's summer residence south of Madrid.

Route 19

Spain

Castile: On the road in Don Quixote country

Castile is not only the geographical center of Spain, but also its historical heartland and the birthplace of Castilian Spanish. Vast, ochre-colored plains, magnificent cities and monumental castles distinguish the region surrounding Madrid.

In modern-day Spain, the Castilian highlands contain two of the country's autonomous regions: Castilla y León in the north-west and Castilla-La Mancha in the south-east. This political division largely reflects the natural geography, with the Cordillera Central, or the Castilian Dividing Range, running straight through the two regions and separating them from each other.

On either side of the mountain range extends the Meseta Central, an expansive, slightly arid plateau where vegetation is sparse and only solitary pine and eucalyptus trees dot the landscape. Despite the relative aridity, however, the ground is fertile and supports the cultivation of grains, sunflowers, chickpeas (garbanzo beans) and wine grapes. In winter, the predominantly treeless landscape is more or less fully exposed to the strong winds and cooler temperatures, while in the summer the sun beats down mercilessly on the hot plains.

The large La Mancha plateau to the south-east of the meseta owes its name to the Moors, people of Arab and Berber (North African) descent who conquered much of Iberia for several hundred years. They named it manxa, meaning "parched

Easter processions ("Semana Santa") in Zamora.

land", but in present-day Spanish mancha simply means "spot".

In the Middle Ages, Castile was actually still densely forested, but the former world power needed every available tree to build its extensive fleet of ships. In the bare countryside that resulted, grassland fortunately took hold in some areas and is able to sustain a modest living for goat and sheep farmers. The animals supply milk for the region's best-selling export product – savory and rich Manchego cheese. Some parts of the countryside here seem almost uninhabited. While the landscape is often monotonous at first glance, however, this is what makes it so fascinating. The sunsets are unique, the sky dowsed in a range of reddish hues.

The most important chapters of Spanish history were written in the heart of this

Iconic windmills and a castillo near Consuegra overlooking over the plains of La Mancha.

Built onto a rock, the Alcázar defiantly stands guard over the Old Town of Segovia.

region. In the 11th century, for example, it was here that the Reconquista gained momentum and Christian forces massed in order to reclaim the southern half of Iberia from the Moors. It is as such the birthplace of the Spanish nation, a fact that is reflected in the seemingly non-stop historical sites. Generals and kings erected great fortified castles that became monuments to their victories in the Christian reclamation of the area.

On a journey through Castile, it is these old cities that receive the lion's share of your attention. Some Old Towns, such as those in Ávila, Salamanca, Segovia, Cuenca and Toledo have been declared UNESCO World Heritage Sites due to their historical importance. The city of Salamanca is home to the oldest university in Spain; the charming Plaza Mayor in Valladolid became the model for similar squares in other cities. Few other cities possess such perfectly preserved medieval town walls as Ávila; and stunning Toledo awaits visitors with countless architectural treasures from the Convivencia (coexistence), a period when Jews, Christians and Muslims lived peacefully together and the city experienced a period of unrivalled prosperity.

Not only the larger cities, but in particular the smallest villages proudly celebrate their cultural treasures and landmarks, be they architectural, in the form of majestic castles, old churches or "simply" windmills, or cultural in the form of festivals. One literary figure of the region gained world-wide fame through his struggle with the windmills – Don Quixote de la Mancha. He mistook the windmills for giants, wildly flailing about, and he rode to attack them with his lance drawn.

The library of the Monasterio San Lorenzo de El Escorial, north of Madrid.

The Rio Tajo (Tagus River) forms a natural boundary on three sides of the Old Town of Toledo, where the Alcázar and cathedral dominate the cityscape. Like most castle palaces in central Spain, the Alcázar of Toledo is also of Moorish origin: its name goes back to the Arabic al-qasr, roughly "fortified village". Initially the

capital of Visigothic Hispania, Toledo enjoyed a long period of prosperity known as La Convivencia (the coexistence) that began in the 8th century under the rule of the Caliphate of Cordoba. The mixed Gothic and Moorish styles here date back to these periods. Toledo was also briefly the residence of the Castilian kings.

Córdoba: view of the Puente Romano bridge and the Río Guadalquivir across to the Mezquita, the most important attraction in the city. The Mezquita represents 1,200 years of architecture from both Islam and Christendom. The prayer house was begun by Abd ar-Rahman I in the 8th century and was expanded in the 10th

century by caliphs al Hakam II and Al Mansur into the largest mosque in the Muslim West. In the 16th century, a cathedral was built in the middle of this unique Moorish structure. From the outside the building seems austere, but the interior has a bewildering 850 columns.

The Santa Maria da Vitória monastery in Batalha was built partly in the Manueline style.

R o u t e   2 1

Portugal

The land of fado and peaceful matadors: a journey to the "edge of the world"

When it was still a province of the Roman empire, what is now Portugal was once called Lusitania. In the sixth century it was part of the Visigothic empire. In the 8th century the Moors took over, but as a result of the "Reconquista" to take back Iberia, it became a kingdom separate from Galicia and León. Portugal finally gained independence in around 1267, and takes its name from the port city of Porto (Latin: porto cale).

Portugal was known in Antiquity and in the Middle Ages as the "edge of the world" and, even in the 20th century, its location on the edge of the continent had both advantages and disadvantages. It is a relatively narrow country, roughly 150 km (93 mi) wide and 550 km (342 mi) in length, but it has 832 km (517 mi) of coastline characterized by steep cliffs and miles of glorious beaches.

The mighty Tagus River (Tejo) divides the mountainous north, the Montanhas, from the rolling south known as Planícies,

Armação de Pera beach near Albufeira.

or plains. In the north you journey through what is still largely an untouched forest and mountain landscape with abundant water resources, the Costa Verde with its pine groves, the fertile Minho region with the vineyards of the Douro Valley, and the remote "land behind the mountains", Trás-os-Montes. Central Portugal has a very different character, with the Serra da Estrela range rising to an altitude of almost 2,000 m (6,562 ft), with vineyards dotting the river valleys and the flood plains of the Tagus. Southern Portugal is dominated by Alentejo, Portugal's "breadbasket", with its vast landed estates that were dissolved after the "Carnation Revolution" of 1974. It is a flat, open region extending as far as the Serra de Monchique. Portugal's best-known region, of course, is Algarve, with its rocky cliffs and sandy beaches.

The population distribution is uneven throughout the country. While the sparse mountain regions are largely empty, there are almost three million people in Lisbon and almost one million in the greater Porto region. Cork is one of Portugal's best-known agricultural products: the country has more than eighty-six million cork oaks and they have to be twenty years old before the bark can be peeled for the first time. Today one in three of the world's wine corks still comes from Portugal.

As with most European countries, Portugal, too, has a diverse historical and cultural heritage to look back on. Unique throughout all of Europe, however, is the Manueline architectural style, which enjoyed its heyday during the reign of King Manuel I (1495–1521), arguably Portugal's "golden age". The Manueline is

The dream destination for many holidaymakers is situated in the south of Portugal: the Algarve, with its magnificent beaches and deep blue ocean.

Bragança Citadel enjoys a strategic location on top of a knoll and once served as a place of refuge.

a mixture of Gothic and Renaissance elements, supplemented with frenzied decoration inspired by exploration.

The cultural influence of the Portuguese voyages of discovery saw the development of exotic, maritime ornaments that were utilized in abundance everywhere. The azulejos, the usually blue and white tiles that can be found almost everywhere in Portugal, are a Moorish legacy and, in addition to their aesthetic function, they protect against heat, provide sound insulation, reflect light and liven up surfaces. Those hoping to immerse themselves in the world of the Portuguese will not be able to avoid *saudade*, a word that somehow defies translation because it denotes a sentiment that seems to exist only in Portugal and that is also intricately linked to the language's long development. The word derives from the Latin "solus",

meaning loneliness, and therefore also expresses feelings such as solitude, yearning, melancholy, mourning, pain, and a restrained joy of life. *Saudade* is best expressed in *fado*, the traditional Portuguese folk song alleged to originate from Lisbon's Alfama district and from Coimbra. They are tristful songs mostly concerned with unfulfilled longing, lost love or despair. In Lisbon, *fado* is primarily performed by female singers accompanied by two guitarists, while in Coimbra it is typically young men who convey this sense of "fatum" (fate) deriving from social and political circumstances, like Jose Afonso with his fado number "Grandola", which accompanied the 1974 Carnation Revolution leading to the overthrow of the Salazar dictatorship.

It is a telling reflection of Portugal – a beautiful country with a hint of sadness.

On the outskirts of Lisbon, in Benfica: the Palacio Fronteira boasts magnificent gardens.

Sintra and the Palácio Nacional da Pena

This former Moorish town and later summer residence of the Portuguese kings and aristocracy lies at the base of a rocky outcrop with dense vegetation. It is characterized by winding alleyways, picturesque street corners and charming quintas. In the town center is the Paço Real, the Manueline city palace (15th/16th century) that offers a mixture of diverse architectural styles. Its oversized chimneys are the landmark of the town. The Palácio is visible from a distance and dominates the town of Sintra from atop the highest of its rocky promontories.

Sintra: The remarkable Palácio Nacional da Pena was built in 1840.

This Portuguese fairy-tale creation is a pseudo-medieval fortified castle with a truly bewildering mix of styles, from Gothic doors, Manueline windows, Byzantine ceilings and minaret-like towers to Moorish azulejos and other Romanesque and Renaissance elements. The whole thing is fascinatingly bizarre.
It was built between 1840 and 1850 by the Baron of Eschwege on behalf of Prince Ferdinand of Saxe-Coburg.

This circuit of Portugal begins in Lisbon and takes you west from the capital as far as Cabo da Roca before heading north to the culturally exciting cities of Porto and Braga. After a detour to the ancient town of Bragança, it then turns to the south passing through the Ribatejo and Alentejo regions on the way to Faro in the Algarve before returning to Lisbon along the coast.

1 Lisbon (see page 259)

2 Cascais The long beaches here have transformed this fishing village into a popular destination with plenty of cafés and boutiques. The daily fish auction provides something of a contrast to the main sightseeing attractions, which include the Parque da Gandarinha as well as the ornate azulejos in the old town hall and in the Nossa Senhora de Nazaré chapel.
A scenic coastal road takes you to Europe's western-most point north of Cascais. Cabo da Roca rises up 160 m (525 ft) out of the pounding Atlantic.

3 Sintra (see sidebar left)

4 Mafra North of Sintra is Mafra, home to a colossal palace completed in 1750, with which King João V once aimed to overshadow the Spanish El Escorial. Behind the 220-m-long (241-yd) façade are 880 rooms, a chapel the size of a cathedral and a sizable basilica.

5 Óbidos From Mafra, you continue north along the coast as far as Peniche, one of Portugal's largest fishing ports. Situated on a prominent headland jutting out into the sea, Peniche has an 18th-century maritime fort that is worth visiting before heading inland toward Óbidos. Óbidos, also known as the Queen's Village, is a must-see in Portugal. The fortified hilltop village boasts charming alleys with tidy white houses decorated with flowers, all contained within a picturesque medieval town wall that is up to 15 m (49 ft) high in places.

1 The view over the old part of Lisbon from Largo das Portas do Sol.

2 The picturesque village of Azenhas do Mar is north of Praia das Maçàs near the Cabo da Roca.

3 You can walk around the town wall in Óbidos in around 45 minutes.

Travel Information

Route profile
Length: approx. 1,250 km (775 mi)
Time required: 14–16 days
Start: Lisbon
End: Setúbal/Lisbon
Route (main locations): Lisbon, Cascais, Sintra, Peniche, Óbidos, Leiria, Coimbra, Porto, Braga, Guimãres, Vila Real, Guarda, Marvão, Estremoz, Évora, Moura, Mértola, Faro, Portimão, Lagos, Sagres, Setúbal, Lisbon

Traffic information:
The speed limit on the motorways is 120 km/h (75 mph), on national roads 90 km/h (55 mph), in towns 60 km/h (35 mph). The legal blood alcohol limit is .05 and it is strictly enforced. Seatbelts are compulsory.

The motorways are also subject to tolls.

When to go:
The best times to visit Portugal are spring and autumn. Summer can be gruellingly hot.

Accommodation:
State-run hotels, or pousadas, in historic buildings and/or scenic locations, are a popular form of accommodation in Portugal. Check this site for more information:
www.pousadas.pt

Further information:
Here are some websites to help you plan your trip.
www.justportugal.org
www.travel-in-portugal.com
www.portugal.com

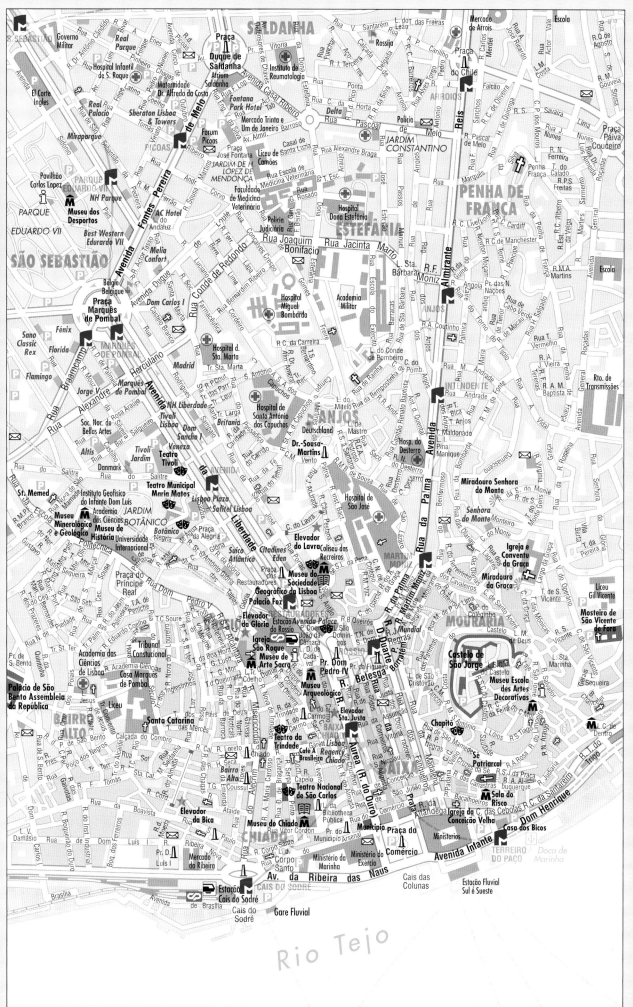

Lisbon

The sea of buildings in the "white city" extends from the wide mouth of the Tagus River up the steep hills of the Barrio Alto. Lisbon's wonderful location attracts visitors from all over the world who, like the locals, navigate the hilly city in eléctricos, creeky old trams.

Sights particularly worth seeing in Lisbon include: Alfama, the oldest and most picturesque district with labyrinthine streets on a fortified hill, dominated by the ruins of the Castelo de São Jorge; the two (of many) lovely miradouros, or viewing terraces, that make Lisbon so enjoyable, are tucked between the ruined fortress and the medieval Sé Cathedral; the Avenida da Liberdade, a 90-m-wide (98-yd) boulevard from the 19th century; the Barrio Alto (upper town), an entertainment district with countless bars, restaurants and fado taverns; Baixa, the lower town rebuilt in a regimented fashion following the devastating earthquake of 1755, today a banking and shopping district; Chiado, the former intellectuals' district in Belle Époque style; the Elevador de Santa Justa (1901) between the upper and lower town; the Museu do Azulejo in the Madre de Deus monastery; the Museu Calouste Gulbenkian, an oil magnate's founda-

Top: Rossio, the center of the Baixa.
Middle: Old Town buildings decorated with azulejos.
Bottom: The Torre de Belém, built in the 16th century.

tion with top-ranking European art; the Museu de Arte Antiga, the largest museum of Portuguese art; the Oceanário, a magnificent aquarium; and the Palácio dos Marqueses da Fronteira, a castle complex with a magnificent baroque garden.

Detour

Fátima and Tomar

Fátima is in fact an unassuming place on the Cova da Iria plateau north of the Tagus, but it has also been one of the most important Catholic pilgrimage destinations since 1917. The Virgin Mary allegedly appeared before three shepherd's children on a total of six occasions. At the last appearance, 70,000 people witnessed the "Milagre do Sol", when the sky is said to have darkened and the sun, blood red, circled around itself.

Following an eight-year period of research, the Vatican ultimately recognized the apparition of the Virgin and had the Rosary Basilica built at the site in 1928, which attracts hundreds of thousands of pilgrims every year. The square in

Tomar's town center resembles an open-air museum.

front of the basilica is twice the size of St Peter's Square in Rome.

Not far from Fátima is the small town of Tomar, which is dominated by the fortress-like former convent belonging to the Order of Christ, an order of medieval knights founded in 1314, following the suppression of the Knights Templar (founded in 1119) and which was subject to the will of the king and not that of the Pope. The order's red cross was long resplendent on the sails of Portuguese caravels.

The former Templar fort was later converted to a monastic castle in the Manueline style and is now a UNESCO World Heritage Site. At the center of the complex is the rotunda, built by the Templars in 1160. Be sure to see the high choir, the chapter house and the inner cloister.

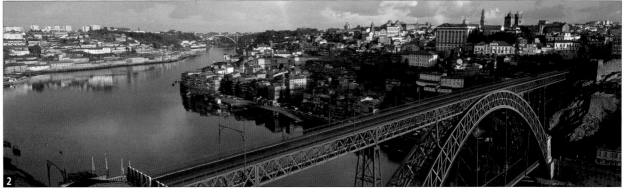

6 Alcobaça It is hard to believe that one of Christianity's largest sacral buildings – the former Cistercian Mosteiro de Santa Maria de Alcobaça – was built in this town of just under 6,000 inhabitants north of Caldas da Reinha. Founded in the late 12th century and completed in about 1250, it was the first Gothic edifice in Portugal.

The three-storey baroque façade (18th century) is 220 m (241 yds) wide and 42 m (138 ft) high. The three naves of the Gothic interior are also impressive due to their unusual dimensions: 106 m (16 yds) long, 20 m (66 ft) high, but just 17 m (19 yds) wide.

Many of the visitors here are pilgrims visiting the tombs of King Pedro I and his murdered mistress Ines de Castro, who is buried directly opposite him so that, "at the resurrection, each of them should see the other first of all". The complex is a UNESCO World Heritage Site.

7 Batalha This simple country town is on the way to Leiria and is also a UNESCO World Heritage Site for the world-famous Santa Maria da Vitoria monastery. Construction began in 1388, following João I's historical victory at Aljabarrota (1385), but it was not completed until 1533. The complex has become a kind of national shrine for the Portuguese as a symbol of the country's independence from Spain.

A 15-m-high (49-ft), elaborately decorated Manueline portal invites you to enter the cathedral, which is nearly as long as a football field and 32 m (105 ft) high. It is adjoined by the "royal" cloister and contains the tomb of King João I.

8 Leiria Portugal's coat of arms contains the images of seven castles. One of these is in Leiria and it is one of Portugal's most beautiful. The history of its construction begins with the Romans, is influenced by the Moors, and continues through to the crusaders. The complex is now a mix of Gothic and Renaissance styles and affords a magnificent view of Portugal's largest pine forest.

From Leiria it is worth taking a detour to the south-east, first to Fátima, a pilgrimage site about 30 km (19 mi) away, and then to the Templar castle in Tomar.

9 Coimbra This town on the steep banks of the Rio Mondego is one of Europe's oldest university towns (12th century) and in fact was the only one in Portugal until 1910. The center boasts a fortress-like cathedral (Sé Velha, the largest Romanesque church in Portugal), also dating from the 12th century. Behind the cathedral you then continue up to the old university, which is the former royal palace. The highlight here is the library (1716–1728), Portugal's loveliest

riques make up the heart of the Ribeira district, where wealth and poverty collide – the stock exchange is juxtaposed with narrow, dingy alleyways.

⓫ Braga This old episcopal city is inland and to the north-east of Porto and is home to twenty churches closely packed together. The originally Romanesque cathedral was frequently remodeled over the centuries and has two massive towers.

Other sites include the 18th-century Palácio dos Biscainhos, surrounded by a magnificent

baroque construction featuring gilded wood and fresco ceilings by Portuguese artists. Not far from the library, in the former bishop's palace, is the Museu Machado de Castro, with the Sé Nova (new cathedral), a former Jesuit church (1600) high on the slope above it.

A short walk takes you through a maze of alleys to the Mosteiro de Santa Cruz, a former Augustinian monastery. Take a break in the Parque de Santa Cruz, part of the monastery grounds. The Quinta das Lágrimas estate was the setting for the love story between Spanish Crown Prince Pedro and his mistress Ines that ended in such tragedy. The Fonte las Lágrimas (Fountain

of Tears) supposedly originated with Ines' tears after her death. Life in Coimbra is heavily influenced by the 20,000 students who still wear the traditional *capa* gown, and not just for special occasions like the Queima das Fitas festival.

❿ Porto It was no coincidence that Portugal's second-largest town on the Costa Verde was the European Capital of Culture in 2001. The port at the mouth of the Rio Douro has a great deal to offer visitors. Five bridges now link Porto with Vila Nova de Gaia, where a majority of the port wineries are based.

The streets and rows of houses in Porto's Old Town seem to cling

precariously to the steep granite cliffs. At the lower end of the Avenida dos Aliados is the Praça Liberdade with the Torre dos Clerigos, the highest church tower in Portugal at 75 m (246 ft). At the other end is the town hall with its 70-m-high (230-ft) bell tower. The huge azulejo scenes on the wall of the São Bento railway station are especially worth seeing as well.

En route to the Ponte de Dom Luis I you come to the cathedral with its sacrament altar made from 800 kg (1,764 lbs) of silver. From here you can go down into the Bairro da Sé district, the oldest part of Porto, or to the Largo do Colegio. The Praça da Ribeiro and the Praça Infante Dom Hen-

1 The "royal cloister" in the Santa Maria da Vitória Monastery, Batalha.

2 The Ponte de Dom Luís I in Porto was designed in Gustave Eiffel's office. To the left of the picture is the former bishop's palace; behind it to the right is the Torre dos Clérigos and the cathedral.

3 The University of Coimbra is located on the Alcácova and is the oldest in Portugal.

4 The monumental baroque stairway up the Bom Jesus do Monte pilgrimage church in Braga.

Detour

Bragança

This town in the somewhat spare, north-eastern reaches of Portugal was once the ancestral seat of the last Portuguese royal family. The

The citadel of Bragança

castle, which dominates the town, was built in 1187, has eighteen towers and a mighty keep, the 15th-century Torre de Menagem. In front is a 6.4 m (21 ft) pillory (pelourinho) on a granite wild boar. In the town itself is the Domus Municipalis, a type of Romanesque style town hall. The cathedral was originally Romanesque, but later converted to the Renaissance style in the 16th century.

The area north of Siena is the traditional wine growing region for Chianti Classico.

Italy

From Riviera di Levante fishing villages to famous Renaissance cities

From golden rolling hills, aromatic pine forests and stylish cypress boulevards to extraordinary art treasures and mouth-watering cuisine – Tuscany is a perfect holiday destination for nature lovers, art connoisseurs and gourmets. With rustic villages, a rich history and unique landscapes, this attractive region presents itself as one of Europe's 'complete artworks'.

Travelling in Tuscany is simply an intoxicating experience for the senses. Your eyes feast on the magnificently cultivated landscape, the delicate hints of rosemary and lavender please the nose, and your palate is spoilt for choice with world-famous Chianti wines and a cuisine that, with great help from the Medici family, had already begun conquering the world during the Renaissance. If that were not enough, nearly all Tuscany's charming ancient towns offer abundant art treasures as well.

Historically, central Italy is a region that has been inhabited for thousands of years, and proof of that fact is not hard to find. The ubiquitous remains of Etruscan necropolises, ruins from Roman settlements or the medieval town of San Gimignano make the point clear enough. Tuscany reached its zenith primarily during the medieval and Renaissance periods, and rightly regards itself as the 'Cradle of European culture'. Modern art, including painting, sculpture and architecture, can be traced back to this region.

Michelangelo's *David* in Florence.

The most important role in the region's rise to glory was played by the Medici, a Florentine family of vast wealth and influence that decisively dictated politics and the arts in that city for almost three hundred years, between 1434 and 1743. The pronounced cultural interest of the Medici drew the renowned artists of the time into their fold and, as patron of the arts, the family commissioned some of the most important works of the Renaissance period.

The cultural bounty of Tuscany attracts a great number of tourists every year. But a visit to Tuscany should include not only the well-known towns but also the countryside, as Tuscany is as famous for its ancient rural aesthetic as it is for its urban culture. This extraordinary countryside was planned in incredible detail and cultivated for centuries, with the landed

Cypresses, wine, an isolated farmhouse in the rolling hills – Tuscany presents a unique cultural landscape.

View from Pienza across the Tuscan plain with the cathedral tower in the background.

gentry as well as the farmers playing a part in the development. The farms, with a geometrical layout unchanged over the years, were placed on hilltops and all boasted a cypress-lined drive to their entrances. These splendid, centuries-old cypress lanes indicate their penchant for precise planning here.

Geographically, Tuscany stretches from the Apennine Mountains in the north to the Monte Amiata in the south, offering a varied landscape with rugged mountains, gentle rolling hills, the fertile coastal area of the Maremma and the green valleys of the Arno river. Southern Tuscany differs considerably from other Tuscan regions, being much hotter and having a less lush vegetation, dominated by maquis – dense, evergreen shrubs.

Industry and tourism are the economic backbones of Tuscany. Agriculture's main product is olive oil, but agriculture nowadays only supports a small part of the population. As a holiday destination, Tuscany is almost perfect all year round – between May and June an abundance of plants blossom in an extraordinary range of colours, while summer is dominated by the radiant red of the poppies and the glowing yellow of sunflower fields. Autumn is the time of the grape harvest, when the chestnut trees and the beeches change colour in late October and transform the landscape into a sea of mellow golden and red.

Your tour also enters the Emilia, a region between the river Po and the Apennine Mountains where Bologna is the city of note. On the west coast you reach Liguria with the Riviera di Levante and the tourist mecca, La Spezia. And from the hills of eastern Tuscany you finally reach Umbria.

Built on cliffs, the coastal village of Rio Maggiore in Cinque Terre.

View from the south over the red rooftops of Florence. The Arno River is spanned by a number of bridges, the most famous of which is the Ponte Vecchio on the far left. The apartments on the bridge are still used for commercial purposes and shops. The campanile (bell tower) of the Palazzo Vecchio on the

Piazza della Signoria (middle of picture) rises above the sea of buildings along with the 85-m-high campanile and the red dome of the Santa Maria del Fiore cathedral by Brunelleschi.

The cathedral of Santa Maria Assunta, built between 1136 and 1382, rises high above the medieval rooftops of Siena. It is one of the most beautiful Gothic structures in Italy. The façades of the cathedral and its campanile (bell tower) are striped with black and white marble from the region. The richly-adorned

south-west façade is particularly impressive. To the right is the façade of the unfinished nave. The campanile of the Palazzo Pubblico (left of the dome) is the second-highest medieval tower in Italy at 102 m (320 ft).

Assisi

A short trip to Assisi in nearby Umbria is highly recommended. The famous basilica in Assisi is entirely dedicated to St Francis (1182–1226), who was born here. Everywhere you will find churches and memorials

Frescoes in the Basilica di San Francesco.

erected in honour of this worldly saint, also known as the 'Patron Saint of Animals and Ecology'.
Since the time of Francis, the impressive layout of the small village on the flank of Mount Subasio has hardly changed. One event, however, was far-reaching – the construction of the basilica, three years after the saint's death. The upper church houses works by many of Italy's renowned late-Romansque and early-Gothic artists. Nowhere else in Italy can you find a collection of this calibre. The lower church, where the saint is buried, is the pilgrimage site. Damage from the earthquake in 1997 has been almost completely repaired.

Tuscan countryside. A diocesan town in the 12th and 13th centuries, Massa Marittima boasts magnificent medieval buildings such as the Duomo San Cerbone (1228–1304).
Stay on the SS441 and SS73 for 75 km (46 miles) to Siena.

19 Siena Siena's red-brick palaces and extraordinary flair often give this town a more authentic ambience than its great rival Florence. The 'Gothic City' stretches over three hillsides in the heart of the rolling Tuscan countryside. Its historic center has long been designated a UNESCO World Heritage Site. Siena is also home to what is arguably Italy's most beautiful square, the shell-shaped Piazza del Campo, surrounded by Gothic palaces. Twice a year it hosts the legendary Palio horse race, which attracts up to fifty thousand spectators and causes total chaos throughout the city.
The Duomo (12th century) is Siena's cathedral and one of the jewels of the Gothic period. It should not be missed. Other architectural treasures include the Palazzo Pubblico (1288–1309) and the slim 102-m (334-ft) Torre del Mangia, one of the most daring medieval towers.
The center of the Chianti area is north of Siena. From here, small roads lead to the domain of Chianti Classico, carrying the emblem 'Gallo Nero' (black cockerel) as proof of its outstanding quality. The vineyards advertise 'Vendita diretta' for wine tasting and direct sales.
Follow the S222, S249 and S408 in a clockwise direction to visit a number of quaint villages – Castellina in Chianti, Radda in Chianti, Badia a Coltibuono, Moleto and Brolio with its castle Castello di Brolio.

20 Montepulciano About 70 km (43 miles) south-east of Siena is Montepulciano, a Renaissance town of outstanding beauty on top of a limestone hill. The small town, with its lovely brick buildings, is a Mecca for wine and art connoisseurs. Just outside Montepulciano you'll find San Biagio, an architectural treasure dating back to the 16th century. The pilgrimage church is laid out in the form of a Greek cross and is surrounded by cypresses – in perfect harmony with the landscape.
From Montepulciano the S146 leads to Chiusi and south-east to the junction of the S71, which runs along the west side of the Lago Trasimeno before bringing you to Cortona 40 km (25 miles) away. From the lake we recommend a detour of about 75 km (46 miles) to visit Assisi on the S75 – birthplace of the legendary St Francis of Assisi.

21 Cortona Cortona, one of the oldest Etruscan settlements, is another Tuscan hill town situated above the plains of Chiana. We recommend a stroll through the maze of the Old Town, full of alleyways and steps. The Piazza Garibaldi offers a spectacular view of the Lago Trasimeno.

22 Arezzo Arezzo, 80 km (50 miles) south-east of Florence, is the last port of call on your journey. The palaces of rich merchants and influential families dominate the scene, along with the ubiquitous religious buildings. The town is wealthy, partly due to its worldwide gold jewellery export industry.
The Gothic Basilica of San Francesco has become a Mecca for art lovers. The main attraction is the *History of the True Cross*, a series of frescoes by Piero della Francesca. *La Leggenda della Vera Croce*

(The Legend of the True Cross) is also one of Italy's most beautiful frescoes. Its theme is the wood from the tree of knowledge in the Garden of Eden that became the cross on which Christ was crucified. The colour and the perspective are extraordinary.

1 The pilgrimage church of Tempio di San Biagio (1518–34) is a masterpiece by architect Antonio da Sangallo just outside Montepulciano.

2 The Duomo and the 102-m (334-ft) bell tower of the Palazzo Pubblico dominate the modest skyline of Siena.

3 Because they grow so straight and tall, cypresses are the local favourite for delineating recreation areas or a landmark.

Parma This town is famous for its food – the delicious prosciutto di Parma and of course Parmesan cheese. After being destroyed during World War II, the Old Town was not restored. The Lombardian-Romanesque Duomo (12th century) and the Palazzo della Pilotta are the only remains.

Módena A Duomo (1184) with an 88-m-high (29-ft) bell tower and leafy arcades are the prominent features of this town.

Bologna This university town in the province of Emilia-Romagna is steeped in history and well worth a visit. The Church of San Petronio, with its two famous leaning towers, and the interesting alleys and palaces keep you wandering.

Prato The historic part of this textile industry hub is surrounded by medieval fortifications. Prato is home to its own Duomo and the Castello dell'Imperatore, built by Emperor Frederick II from 1237 to 1248. The rest of the Old Town is an interesting mix of ancient and modern buildings.

Portofino This seaside town in the Gulf of Rapallo is surrounded by olive and cypress groves. The quaint fishing village has long attracted the rich and famous, who have built luxury villas here.

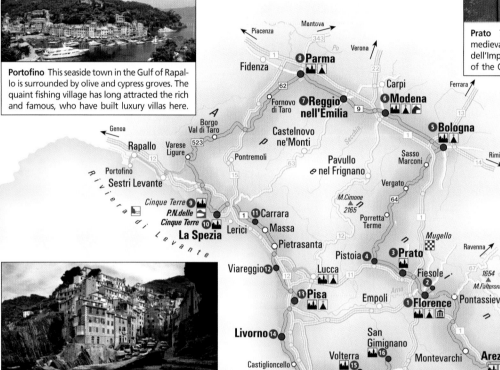

Florence A trip to Florence should start at the Piazzale Michelangelo, to get a perfect view of the 'Birthplace of the Renaissance', before visiting the other main attractions – the Duomo Santa Maria del Fiore (1296–1436), the Uffizi, the Ponte Vecchio and the Palazzo Vecchio.

Cinque Terre The villages of Monterosso, Vernazza, Corniglia, Manarola and Riomaggiore on the Riviera di Levante are among Italy's most photographed.

Assisi This town on the western flank of Monte Subasio is the birthplace of the famous St Francis (1182–1226).

Lucca Seven arches open onto the historic center of this walled town, to the Duomo San Martino (11th century) and to many merchants' houses, towers and villas.

Volterra This ancient city is still very well preserved and surrounded by medieval ramparts. Volterra is famous for its alabaster products, and its History and Etruscan Museum ranks among Italy's best.

Elba Italy's third-largest island offers an amazingly varied landscape with mountains, lowland plains, olive groves, pine forests and bays for swimming. In the northern part of the island is Napoleon's summer residence, the Villa Napoleonica – a must-see.

Massa Marittima The upper part of town offers a breathtaking view over the historic center's red roofs, with the Duomo San Cerbone (1228–1304), and the surrounding Tuscan countryside.

San Gimignano Many of the medieval buildings here have been expertly preserved, among them fifteen of the original seventy-two medieval towers, which offered shelter against enemy attack.

Pisa Not only the Leaning Tower, but all the buildings on the Campo dei Miracoli (the Field of Miracles), including the Duomo and Baptistry, are worth visiting. Although these edifices in elegant Carrara marble were constructed at different times, they convey perfect architectural harmony.

Siena Florence's eternal rival is defined by the Gothic period. The Piazza del Campo, one of Italy's most beautiful squares, is a perfect example. Also visit the Duomo and the bold Torre del Mangia.

The Temple of Hera in Paestum, also known as the 'Basilica', was built around 530 BC.

Route 23

Italy

On the Via Appia from Rome to Brindisi

In the time of the Imperium Romanum, the motto of the day was 'All roads lead to Rome', when Romans saw their capital as the cradle of not only their own empire but of the civilized world. Large parts of Europe and the entire Mediterranean were ruled from here, and military roads ensured the necessary logistical infrastructure. Probably the best known of these ancient roads is the Via Appia Antica, the basis for your journey.

Relatively little remains of the brilliant splendour of ancient Rome, but what is left is indeed impressive enough – the Colosseum, the Baths of Caracalla, the Pantheon, Domus Aurea, the Arch of Titus, Forum Romanum, the emperors' forums and the Capitol. Contemporary Rome, on the other hand, is defined more dramatically by the unremitting desire of the popes to build magnificent churches, palaces, squares and fountains using the best architects of their times. The popes

were particularly active during the Renaissance and baroque periods. To this day, St Peter's Square and St Peter's Cathedral remain the heart of the city and of the Catholic Christian world.

The ancient Via Appia began at what is today Porta Sebastiano, and originally only went as far as Capua. It was then extended past Benevento and Taranto to Brindisi in 190 BC. Around AD 113, Emperor Trajan added yet another ancillary road that led through Bari.

Statue of Emperor Marcus Aurelius in Rome.

The 540-km-long (336-mile) basalt route, lined as it is by countless ancient tombs, temples, villas, ruins and even early Christian catacombs, can still be driven today and is considered 'the longest museum in the world'.

The road initially takes you out of Rome and into the hills of the Colli Albani where, in the Middle Ages, popes and Roman nobles had numerous villas and castles built – collectively known as the Castelli Romani. From Velletri, the Via Appia continues in almost a dead straight line to what is today Terracina on the Tyrrhenian Sea, then through Gaeta and inland towards Cápua.

From here, there is still an access road to the former Greek city of Neapolis, known today as Naples. This is home to the infamous Mount Vesuvius, a still-active volcano that once destroyed Pompeii and

The Ponte Sant'Angelo bridge in Rome leads over the Tiber to the Castel Sant'Angelo, built in AD 139 as a citadel, prison and papal residence.

The 13th-century Cathedral of Matera (Apulia) is maintained in the late Romanesque style.

Herculaneum, and whose next eruption remains a concern for some geologists. For the time being, the view from the crater's rim provides a wonderful view of the bustling city of Naples and the Island of Ischia in the Gulf of Naples.

From Naples, the journey continues along the sea around the Gulf to Sorrento. Since the time of the Roman emperors this picturesque area has been a meeting place for aristocracy. The southern side of the Sorrento Peninsula is where the steep cliffs of the Amalfi Coast begin, with its quaint, pastel-coloured villages nestled between the azure sea and the brilliant yellow lemon trees. At the end of the famous Amalfitana coastal road lies Salerno, where the actual Mezzogiorno begins. The stunning coastal road then continues on to Paestum, with ancient golden-yellow Greek temples that are some of the most beautiful examples of their kind in Europe. Indeed, the Greeks settled in southern Italy long before the Romans and left some magnificent relics of a blossoming civilization.

After Sapri the route leaves the coast and heads east through the inland province of Basilicata towards the Gulf of Taranto. At Metaponto on the gulf, the route again swings inland towards Matera, whose 'sassi' – former ancient cave dwellings – are a UNESCO World Heritage Site. Taranto marks the starting point for the journey through the 'Land of the Trulli', whose capital is Alberobello.

After passing through Ostuni you finally arrive in Brindisi, where one of the two ancient port columns is a reminder of how important this city at the end of the Via Appia once was for the mighty Imperium Romanum.

Remains of a colossal statue of Constantine the Great in the Palazzo dei Conservatori in Rome.

The Imperium Romanum

History teachers of every generation will tell their students that 'Rome was born in 753'. However, the creation of Rome more likely took place around the turn of the 6th century BC. It began with the merging of several towns into a municipality (still) under Etruscan rule.

In 510 BC the citizens chased away Tarquinius Superbus, their Etruscan king, and created an aristocracy from which the Roman republic eventually emerged. This officially lasted until 31 BC when Emperor Augustus came to power.

The expansion of Rome initially proceeded very slowly and was hardly noticed by the Greek colonists in southern Italy or the Carthaginians in North Africa (present-day Tunisia). However, after the three Punic Wars

Stairway to the Palazzo Senatorio.

(264–241 BC, 218–201 BC, 149–146 BC), almost all of Italy, including the surrounding islands, was under Roman rule. Victories over the Etruscans, Greeks and Carthaginians further guaranteed Roman dominance in the western Mediterranean and the Imperium Romanum was born.

The advances of Roman legionnaires were highly visible throughout almost all of Europe, sections of North Africa and in the Near East. At its largest, under Emperor Trajan (AD 98–117), the Imperium Romanum stretched all the way from the British Isles to the Persian Gulf. It had reached its zenith, which in turn marked the beginning of the end.

By AD 395 the no-longer governable western Imperium and the East Roman Empire were divided, with Byzantium as the capital of the eastern part. Germanic tribes then invaded the West Roman Empire and in AD 476 the Germanic ruler Odoaker dethroned the last West Roman emperor, Romulus Augustulus.

On the trail of the ancient Via Appia: this route begins in Rome and follows the famous highway of classic antiquity to Cápua, where it was later extended to Benevento, Taranto and then Brundisium (Brindisi). The stations recall the country's important historic periods.

① Rome For a detailed description of the myriad attractions here, see pp. 284–285.

Porta Sebastiano used to be known as Porta Appia because this ancient city gate marked the start of the Via Appia. The area around the porta includes the burial site of the Scipios, the famous Temple of Mars and the tomb of Cecilia Metella on the cypress-lined road to Frascati.

② Frascati This is the most famous town of the Castelli Romani. Its glorious location, numerous patrician villas (e.g. the 17th-century Villa Aldobrandini), its exceptional white wine

and 'porchetta', crispy grilled suckling pig, all contribute to this renown. And the popes enjoyed it all, which is why Frascati was their long-time summer residence before they moved to Castel Gandolfo. Roughly 5 km (3 miles) east of the city are the ruins of the ancient Tusculum, the favourite abode of Cicero, one of Rome's greatest orators and philosophers.

A few smaller places around Frascati are also worth a visit. The main attraction of the Grottaferrata, 3 km (2 miles) south of Frascati, is the castle-like monastery of San Nilo, founded in 1004, with frescoes from Domenichio (17th century).

Travel information

Route profile
Length: approx. 650 km (404 miles), excluding detours
Time required: 10–12 days
Start: Rome
End: Bríndisi
Route (main locations): Rome, Frascati, Velletri, Latina, Terracina, Gaeta, Cápua, Naples, Sorrento, Salerno, Paestum, Rotondella, Metaponto, Matera, Taranto, Martina Franca, Bríndisi

Traffic information:
Drive on the right in Italy. Speed limit in built-up areas is 50 km/h (31 mph), on highways 130 km/h (81 mph). International licences are required unless you have a new photocard licence from a European nation. Spare bulbs and warning triangle required.

When to go:
The best times to travel are spring and autumn, as temperatures are pleasant. In summer, temperatures can rise to over 40°C (105°F), though by the sea it is often cooler with the breezes. For current weather conditions at many holiday destinations visit:
www.italy-weather-and-maps.com

Information:
www.italiantourism.com
www.justitaly.org
For accommodation and events:
www.slowtrav.com/italy

St Peter's Basilica

Until a larger replica was built on the Ivory Coast in the 1990s, San Pietro in Vaticano was the world's largest Christian church. San Pietro was built under the auspices of master architect Giovanni Bernini between 1656 and 1667, and towers above St Peter's Square (Piazza San Pietro). This absolutely massive plaza is in turn lined with four semicircular colonnades containing a total of 284 columns and 88 pillars. In the middle of the square is the 25.5-m-high (84-ft) Egyptian obelisk, to which two fountains were added, one in 1613 and the next in 1675.

St Peter's Basilica was originally built in 1506, on the site where Constantine the Great had previously placed a basilica over the tomb of Petrus in 320. The most reputable Renaissance builders and artists helped construct the church, including Bramante, Raffael, Michelangelo and Bernini.

The enormous double partition cupola, started by Bramante and finished

The light-filled altar area with Bernini's altar canopy.

It's worth taking a small detour into the Alban Hills (Colli Albani – 740 m/2,427 ft) to see the township of Rocca di Papa, some 8 km (5 miles) south-east of Frascati. Monte Cavo at 949 m (3,114 ft) provides a wonderful view out over the province of Lazio.

The town of Marino is also located roughly 8 km (5 miles) away to the south of Frascati. During the wine festival on the first weekend of October, wine flows from the Fontana dei Mori instead of water!

❸ Castel Gandolfo This small town, idyllically located on Lake Albano (Lago Albano), has been the summer residence of the popes since 1604. The Papal Palace (1629–69) and other impressive homesteads like Villa Barberini and Villa Cyco, are the defining buildings in the area. The Piazza, with the Church of

San Tommaso and a stunning fountain by Bernini, is also worth seeing.

❹ Albano Laziale High above Lake Albano, the legendary Latin Alba Longa is said to have once been located here before the rise of Rome even began. The remains of a villa belonging to the famous general Pompeius is still open to the public. In Arrica, the neighbouring town designed by Bernini, it's worth visiting the Palazzo Chigi and the church of Santa Maria dell' Assunzione (1665) at the Piazza della Republica.

❺ Genzano This small town between the Via Appia Antica and Lago di Nemi is famous for its annual 'Infiorata' – on the Sunday after Corpus Christi a carpet of flowers adorns the Via Italo Belardi all the way up to the church of Maria della Cima.

The flowers come from the neighbouring town of Nemi, which is also a local strawberry-growing center.

❻ Velletri The southernmost of the Castelli Romani communes is Velletri, located at the edge of the Via Appia Antica. Like Frascati, it is known for its excellent wines, but apart from this there are architectural attractions including the Piazza Cairoli with its 50-m-high (164-ft) Torre del Trivio from 1353, the Palazzo Communale from 1590, and the cathedral, which was completed in 1662.

The Via Appia then continues from Velletri to Latina.

❼ Latina This township is a good starting point for a day trip to the lovely forests and lakes of the Circeo Nature Park, which stretches over the mountainous promontory of Monte Circeo. At

the tip of the peninsula is the alleged grotto of the sorceress, Circe, from Homer's *Odyssey*. From Latina, the route leads into the coastal town of Terracina.

❽ Terracina This town, which is today a famous spa resort,

1 The impressive complex of St Peter's Square, Rome, a masterpiece created by Bernini between 1656 and 1667. The obelisk in the middle of the square was erected in 1586 with the help of horses and winches.

2 The Arch of Constantine in Rome, constructed in AD 315, is next to the Colosseum, the largest amphitheater of ancient times and the scene of countless gladiator battles.

3 An icon of Rome and a popular meeting place – the Spanish Steps. They get their name from the Piazza di Spagna.

by Michelangelo, is 132 m (433 ft) high. Michelangelo also created the famous Pietá statue in the aisle.

St Peter's itself is 186 m (610 ft) long and 136 m (446 ft) wide, with a height in the main aisle of 45 m (148 ft). It has capacity for up to 60,000 people. The papal altar stands over the tomb of Petrus and beneath the Confessio, which is vaulted by Bernini's 29-m-high (95-ft) bronze canopy.

Over the centuries, the faithful have kissed the right foot of the bronze statue of Petrus at the Longinus pillar so often that it is now shiny. Bernini's Cathedra Petri lies in the Apsis while left of the main altar is the papal treasury and the Vatican grotto, a crypt with the tombs of many popes.

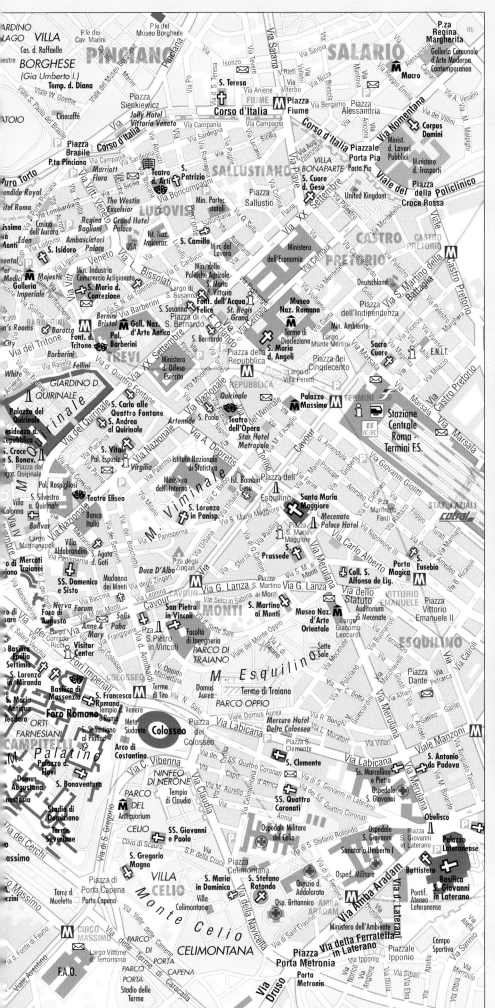

Rome

The 'Eternal City', with its unparalleled artistic treasures and architectural monuments from basically every period of Western culture, is the center of the Catholic world and at the same time the lively and vibrant capital of Italy - you just have to see Rome at least once in your life!

Rome, built on seven hills around the Tiber River, obviously has a long and eventful history that has left endless marks on the city. Its neighbourhoods, squares, monuments, buildings and architectural treasures have been built in every style imaginable.

Today, not all seven of the ancient hills are recognizable in the sea of houses, but from the Piazza del Quirinale on the Quirinal, the highest of these hills, you can get a fantastic view over the entire city. It is said that Rome was founded in 753, but the first traces of

the city eventually regained political importance in the 19th century when Italy was reunited and Rome was made the capital of the Kingdom of Italy.

Ancient Rome includes the Forum Romanum, the main square of the Old City; the Colosseum with its four storey arena; and the Pantheon, the domed masterpiece of ancient architecture. In the Vatican City is St Peter's Basilica, the domed, Renaissance-style monument; the Vatican museums and galleries, probably the largest collection of art in the world; the Sistine Chapel;

Top: Nicola Salvis' masterpiece, the Trevi Fountain, was completed in 1762.
Bottom: The view of Ponte Sant'Angelo and the Castel Sant'Angelo.

settlement are clearly older. In fact for centuries before that there was significant activity here. The year 509 BC, for example, was a dramatic one in which the Roman Republic was established – and one oriented towards expansion. Rome soon became the mistress of the Mediterranean and ultimately, during the time of the emperors, the ruler of the known world. The Age of the Popes began after the fall of the Roman Empire. Rome then became primarily a religious center. However,

and the Santa Maria Maggiore with original mosaics from the 5th century (exclave of the Vatican). Be sure to visit the Villa Giulia, once a papal summer residence with the national Etruscan museum.

The baroque square of Piazza Navona, the baroque fountain Fontana di Trevi, and the Spanish Steps are great meeting places.

For day trips, take the Via Appia to the catacombs of San Callisto and San Sebastiano, or go to Tivoli.

Rome, "the Eternal City", was the center of the Roman Empire and later the Christian world. Impressive ruins testify to the former might of the empire, and the countless religious buildings are evidence of the former power of the popes. Seen here: the portico of the Pantheon, with its many granite columns, built in

25 BC in honor of the "many gods". The building was given its present form under Emperor Hadrian, and its interior is unique for the single light portal (oculus) in the middle of the dome that provides daylight for the 43 m-high (140 ft) circular structure. The dome's diameter is also 43 m (140 ft).

The frescoes of Pompeii

On 24 August in AD 79, the enormous plug that had sealed the cap of Mount Vesuvius for centuries exploded out of the mountain into the sky above the volcano. A huge cloud of cinders, stone and ash obscured the sun and glowing red magma spilled over the edge of the crater into the valley, burying the Roman cities of Pompeii and Herculaneum.

It all happened so quickly that some people could not get away. Like their cities, they were buried under 6 m (20 ft) of ash, lava and cinders – virtually mummified. Due to the sudden nature of the event and the quickness with which it engulfed these towns, it actually preserved homes and people in precisely the positions they were in when the eruption happened. As a result, much of what we know today

The portrait of Terentius Nero and his wife (1st century BC).

about ancient Roman life was discovered in the ruins of the towns.

Following the disaster, Pompeii was subsequently forgotten until the 16th century. Excavations only began in 1748 and gradually uncovered an almost completely preserved ancient city – not only temples, theaters and forums, but also houses and many other aspects of everyday Roman life – shops, kitchens, hostels, latrines, tools, public baths and, of course, the famous Pompeii Red Frescoes.

The most beautiful and best-preserved of these are in the Casa del Menandro, the Casa dei Vettii and the Villa dei Misteri, including a 17-m-wide (56-ft) series of images depicting the mysteries of the cult of Dionysus.

It is no wonder that Pompeii has long been designated a UNESCO World Heritage Site. However, the hordes of visitors and vandalism mean the excavation site is unfortunately in disastrous condition.

was once an important Roman trading town. Evidence of this can still be seen here.

The devastating bomb attacks during World War II actually had one fortuitous result – they uncovered a number of ancient sites, including a section of the Via Appia and the original foundation of the Roman Forum.

The cathedral is from the Middle Ages and is located on a former temple site. It contains some artistic treasures such as a mosaic floor dating back to the 13th century. The spectacular coastal road leads from here to your next coastal town.

9 Gaeta The Old Town, whose silhouette is dominated by the Aragonian fort and the Church of San Francesco, has a picturesque location on a small peninsula. However, the town is particularly worth visiting for the unique bell tower in the 12th-century cathedral – its bricks are fired in bright colours. The small Church of San Giovanni a Mare, dating from the 10th century, also contains a small oddity – the builders wisely designed the floor on a slope so that the sea water could run off again at high tide. For a long time Gaeta was a fortress for the kingdom of Naples.

After a few kilometers, the road leaves the coast and heads inland towards Cápua.

The ancient Via Appia

The most famous of ancient Rome's legendary roads was named after its builder, Appius Claudius Caecus, and was designed using large hexagonal blocks laid on an extremely solid foundation. First constructed as a military transport route, it was later used more heavily for trade. It originally led from the Porta Sebastiano in Rome to Cápua, but was extended through Benevento and Taranto to Brindisi in 190 BC. As Roman road archtiects mainly preferred straight lines, the road actually runs 'perfectly straight', despite steep rises in the Alban Hills and the Pontine Marshes. The Via Appia is 4.1 m (13 ft) wide, enough for two large transport wagons to pass each other at the time. You can still drive its complete length of 540 km (336 miles).

10 Cápua When it was initially built, the first 'section' of the Via Appia ended here in Cápua. This former Etruscan center, with its enormous amphitheater from the 1st century AD, was destroyed after the collapse of the West Roman Empire and rebuilt by the Lombards in the 9th century. The cathedral's bell tower dates back to this time. The Museo Campagna on the nearby Palazzo Antignano houses numerous discoveries from the city's ancient burial sites.

The tour now leaves the Lazio landscape and continues on towards Campania.

11 Caserta Just a stone's throw away from Cápua is the town of Caserta, sometimes boastfully called the 'Versailles of the South' – Bourbon King Karl III built the monumental French-style Palazzo Reale here. The palace is grouped around four large interior courtyards and is

Vesuvius

Mount Vesuvius is the youngest and only remaining active volcano in mainland Europe – it's 12,000 years old and last erupted in 1944. It is unknown how long its current dormant phase will last, but one thing is for certain – the pressure is rising inside. At present, a 3-km-deep (2-mile) plug is blocking the crater hole, and the magma continues to bubble up from a depth of 5–7 km (3–4 miles).

In the event of another eruption, more than 600,000 people living around Mount Vesuvius are potentially in harm's way. Since the last eruption, the volcano now has two peaks – Vesuvius itself at 1,281 m (4,203 ft) and Monte Somma at 1,132 m (3,714 ft). The main crater has a depth of up to 300 m (984 ft) and a diameter of about 600 m (1,969 ft).

The crater of Mount Vesuvius.

church of Gesù Nuovo, dating from the 16th century. The Old Town of Naples, with its 300 churches, castles and town houses, was declared a UNESCO World Heritage Site in 1995.

In addition, there are three castles in the center of the city: Castel dell'Ovo from 1154, the residence of the Normans and Hohenstaufen of Swabia; Castel Nuovo (1279–82) in the port area; and the star-shaped Castel Sant'Elmo (14th–16th century) on Vomero Hill, just opposite the former Carthusian monastery of Certosa di San Martino. The Palazzo Reale and the Teatro San Carlo (1737) are also worth visiting.

Next to the Gothic Duomo San Gennaro (13th century) is the Gothic church of Santa Chiara (14th century), burial place of the Anjou kings with an interest-

For those adventurous enough to climb the mountain, the view over the Gulf of Naples from the edge of the crater is gorgeous. These cinder cones and their most recent lava layers have virtually no vegetation, but halfway up are some sturdy oaks and chestnut trees making a go of it. Below 500 m (1,640 ft) there are even oleander, gorse, silver lichen, olive and fruit trees as well as the vines of the 'Lacrimae Christi' wine region. Despite its deadly outbursts over the millennia, the fertile soil on the slopes of Vesuvius continues to draw people back after every eruption.

There are a number of options for getting right up close to Vesuvius. The simplest is taking a ride on the Circumvesuviana, a train ride around the volcano that takes about two hours. Alternatively, there is a bus ride from Ercolano that takes you to the former chairlift station. From there, it takes about half an hour to climb to the top.

1 The view over the Bay of Naples with the yacht port and Vesuvius in the background.

2 One of the important country villas of the ancient city of Pompeii – the Villa dei Misteri. Its wonderfully colourful paintings (80–30 BC) depict occult celebrations.

3 The church of San Francesco di Paola in Naples was modelled after the Roman Pantheon. Its cupola is 53 m (174 ft) high.

an impressive five storeys high. The whole complex – declared a UNESCO World Heritage Site – is 247 m (810 ft) long, 184 m (604 ft) wide and has 1,200 rooms with 1,800 windows.

No less extraordinary are the 120-ha (297-acre) baroque gardens with statuaries and water features including the Great Waterfall, which are a mighty 78 m (256 ft) high!

Somewhat in contrast to this extravagance here is the modest medieval mountain town of Caserta Vecchia 10 km (6 miles) to the north-east. There is a Norman cathedral here that was consecrated in 1153.

From Caserta, it's roughly 40 km (25 miles) to Naples, originally founded as Neapolis by the Greeks in the 7th century BC.

12 Naples Italy's third-largest city is often considered the 'most Italian' in the country. It is probably the noisiest and most hectic, but also the most likeable of Italy's big cities, where washing lines still hang over the narrow alleys and the gap between rich and poor provides a somehow fascinating cultural mix.

The Spaccanapoli (literally 'split Naples'), a boulevard that cuts right through the city, widens at the turn-off to the north-south axis, Via Toledo, and leads you into the Piazza del Gesù Nuovo. At the center of the square is a 34-m-high (112-ft) baroque column dedicated to the memory of plague victims from the 17th century. Opposite this is the

The view from the road along the Amalfi Coast, one of Italy's steepest coastlines, alternates between breathtaking views of the blue Mediterranean, magnificent coves, picturesque towns and the island of Capri. This is the land of lemon trees and sunshine, of spectacular cliffs plunging into the sea and lush vegetation.

The highlights of any trip here are Positano and Amalfi. Although tourism has long roots in these former fishing villages, the now world-famous seaside resorts still possess a nostalgic flair that cannot be taken from them.

Piran, Slovenia, is a sailing port that juts into the Adriatic with buildings from the Venetian era.

Around the Adriatic

The Realm of the Winged Lion

Sometimes rather sparse, sometimes lush Mediterranean vegetation – but always a view of the sea. Journeying along the Adriatic through Slovenia, Croatia and Italy you will encounter medieval towns, art and culture in spades, as well as tiny rocky coves and beaches stretching for miles.

The northern reaches of the Mediterranean were originally named after the ancient Etruscan town of Adria on the Po Delta, which today is a good 40 km (25 mi) inland to the south-west of Chioggia and is now only linked to the sea by a man-made canal. The town was taken over by the Greeks after the Etruscans, and since that time the mouth of the Po has moved eastwards at a rate of up to 150 m (164 yds) per year. The Adriatic is actually a shallow arm of the Mediterranean, reaching depths of no more than 1,645 m (5,397 ft) between Bari and the Albanian coast.

Venice, the first stop on your journey around the Adriatic, is a trip in itself. The gondolas, palaces and unique cultural monuments of the lagoon city are the result of its rise to power in the 13th century, when influential patrons attracted the greatest artists of the age. It was the Renaissance in particular that shaped not only the city but also the entire look of coast's culture. For it is not only at the start of the journey through the autonomous region of Friuli-Venezia Giulia that you will encounter Venetian towns. Venetian architectural jewels are also scattered along the adjoining coastline

Fresco in the Capella degli Scrovegni in Padua.

of the Istrian Peninsula as well as along the entire Croatian coast.

Many foreign cultures have laid claim to Istria over the centuries due to its fortuitous geographical position. With 242 km (150 mi) of coastline and idyllic medieval towns, the peninsula has now developed into a popular holiday destination, with tourism providing the coastal residents with a lucrative livelihood.

Between Istria and the mainland is the Kvarner Gulf, which includes the islands of Cres, Lošinj, Krk, Pag and Rab, but the lively port city of Rijeka is the starting point for our journey along the Croatian coast. The coastal road is lined by relatively barren landscape, an intense mix of light, sea and limestone. All the more surprising, then, that the valleys behind the ridge are so fertile, protected from the infamous *bora*, an icy autumn wind.

The Church of San Giorgio Maggiore in Venice, built between 1559 and 1580 and designed by architect Andrea Palladio.

The port of Vieste in the north-east corner of the Gargano Peninsula in Apulia, southern Italy.

Vineyards and lush Mediterranean vegetation are pleasing to the eye and provide a refreshing contrast to the lunar landscape of the limestone cliffs. With its steep coastline, the Adria Magistrale is considered one of the most dangerous stretches of road in Europe. On the other hand, there are many interesting destinations and worthwhile attractions that can only be reached via this route. And, with the Serbo-Croatian War having left very few scars along the coast, tourism has undergone a revival in recent years. As a result, the service sector has also become the most important economic engine for the whole coastal region.

The ferry from Dubrovnik to Bari links the Croatian and Italian coastlines, which are at once similar and different. The section along the Italian side of the Adriatic covers a total of five regions: Apulia, Abruzzi, the Marches, Emilia-Romagna and Veneto, each with an individual culture and landscape.

The settlement of the area goes back a long way. The Etruscans, the Greeks, the Venetians and the Romans all established towns throughout this coastal region. And the coast itself is as diverse as the region: the cliffs of the Gargano Peninsula rise dramatically from the water while south of Ancona the foothills of the Apennines protrude into the ocean. The tourist centers beyond Rímini are very different again. There, sandy beaches stretch for miles and have mutated into centers of mass recreation.

Veneto, on the other hand, paints a very different picture with canals, lagoons and tidy little islands off the coast at about the same latitude as the university town of Padua.

The defiant St. Nicholas Monastery on the island of Korčula off the Dalmatian coast.

Murano and Burano

For centuries, Murano glass was considered the best in the world and the small island has served as the headquarters of the Venetian glass industry since the 13th century. A museum provides interesting insights into the art of glass blowing.

In addition to the quality glass products, the triple-nave Maria e Donato Basilica from the 12th century is also worth visiting. The building with its wonderful apse design is a mixture of Venetian-Byzantine and Early Romanesque elements and boasts a fine mosaic floor dating back to 1140. Venetian nobility discovered the island in the 16th century and made it their their summer holiday location of choise, the elegant villas and parks bearing witness to this golden era.

The high church tower is the icon of Burano.

Burano paints a different picture. This lively little fishing island has wonderfully vibrant cottages and is the center of the Venetian lace industry. A small museum proudly displays a collection of the finest lacework covering two centuries and includes veils, dresses and fans.

An incomparable landscape combined with cultural diversity are what characterize this tour around the Adriatic, but a number of things remain constant as you pass through Italy, Slovenia and Croatia: the idyllic nature of the coastlines and clear seas, dramatic rock formations and cliffs, the gentle valleys and the tantalizing coves with magnificent beaches.

❶ Venice (see page 299) Following one of the undisputed highlights of this tour right at the outset, namely a visit to Venice, you continue along the B14 as far as the intersection with the B352.

❷ Aquiléia Aquiléia was one of the largest towns in the ancient empire of Augustus, but today it is home to just 3,400 inhabitants. The remains of the Roman town as well as the Romanesque Basilica of Our Lady, with its magnificent 4th-century mosaic floor, have both been declared a UNESCO World Heritage Site.

❸ Udine It was only in the late Middle Ages that this former Roman settlement developed into the region's main city. The influence of Venice can be seen throughout the town, as well as on the Piazza Libertà, whose loggias and the splendid clock tower (1527) truly make it one of the loveliest squares in the world. The Renaissance Castello di Údine towers over the Old Town and the Santa Maria Annunziata Cathedral (14th century) features masterful altar pieces and frescos by Giambattista Tiepolo.

With its high limestone cliffs dropping sharply to the ocean, the Riviera Triestina has very little in common with the rest of the Italian Adriatic. Continuing from Údine via Monfalcone to Trieste along the B14 you get a taste of the craggy, bizarre landscape that awaits in Dalmatia.

❹ Trieste This Mediterranean port was part of Austria for

1 The imposing baroque church Santa Maria della Salute on the Grand Canal has a foundation of more than one million piles.

2 A spectacular sunset near Grado over the Gulf of Trieste, the northernmost part of the Adriatic.

Travel information

Route profile
Length: : approx. 2,125 km (1,320 mi)
Time required: at least 3 weeks
Start and end: Venice
Route (main locations): Venice, Trieste, Pula, Rijeka, Split, Dubrovnik, Bari, Pescara, Ancona, Ravenna, Padua, Venice

Traffic information:
The motorways in Austria, Switzerl and Italy all require a vignette. You also need to carry the Green Insurance Card with you.
Warnings of live landmines have been issued in Croatia; these warnings should obviously be heeded when making excursions into the coastal hinterland between Senj and Split as well as in

the mountains south-east of Dubrovnik!
Information regarding the ferries from Cres and Rab as well as to Bari:
www.croatia-travel.org
www.croatiatraveller.com

Entry requirements:
Slovenia, Croatia, Bosnia-Herzegovina require a valid personal identity card or passport. In Bosnia-Herzegovina you need to register with the police for a stay of over 24 hours.

Information:
Here are some websites to help you plan your trip:
www.traveladriatic.net
www.slovenia.info
www.croatia.hr
www.ciaoitaly.net
www.venetia.it

Venice

A visit to the magnificent lagoon city is simply unforgettable, regardless of the time of year.

If you can somehow avoid the high season when thousands of tourists jam the narrow alleys around Piazza San Marco, you are lucky. But Venice (a UNESCO World Heritage Site) is so extraordinarily beautiful that it is a treat all year round.

As a maritime power, Venice was once the queen of the eastern Mediterranean. The city is unique, and not least because of its medieval architectural design that is an amalgamation of Byzantine, Arab and Gothic elements. This capital of the northern Italian province of Venezia includes over one hundred islands in a sandy lagoon in the Adriatic. The city is linked to the mainland via causeways and bridges, and was built on piles. There are over 150 bridges and 400 canals.

Originally, Venice was a refuge built after the invasion of the Huns, and its inhabitants actually remained independent for centuries in what was then a remote location. They even managed to take over the legacy of

The Doge's Palace in Venice was the residence of the Doge from the ninth century as well as the seat of the Venetian government.

Ravenna in the eighth century, but by the 15th century, the flow of world trade had shifted, leaving the former queen without its foundation. Venice stagnated thereafter, stuck in the early stages of becoming a metropolis.

Sights here include: the Piazza San Marco, city center for the last thousand years; the Basilica di San Marco with its priceless décor (11th century); the Doge's Palace, a masterpiece of the Venetian Gothic; the Grand Canal with the Rialto Bridge; the Church of Santa Maria Gloriosa dei Frari; the Scuola Grande di San Rocco, the Galleria del L'Accademia with collections of Venetian paintings from the 14th to 18th centuries; and the other islands of Murano, Burano and Torcello.

The lion of San Marco guards the Molo San Marco above the Grand Canal. On the other side of the canal is the Santa Maria della Salute, one of the most impressive churches in this lagoon city at the confluence of the Grand Canal and the Canale di San Marco.

Top: Gondolas bobbing on the Canale di San Marco with the monastery island of San Giorgio Maggiore in the background. Middle: The Grand Canal is 3.8 km (2.4 mi) long and lined with magnificent palaces. Bottom: The Piazza San Marco, the Basilica di San Marco and the sun shining through the Doge's Palace.

Rab and Cres

Whether you are a fan of culture or the sea, Rab island will not disappoint. Revealing all of its magic behind a protective row of cliffs, Rab is an oasis with forests and a wealth of agriculture.

A former Roman colony, the island has been under Croatian, Venetian, and even Austrian rule. The picturesque Old Town of Rab, with the unmistakable silhouette of its four

The Old Town of Rab.

bell towers, is tiny, its waterfront and the medieval alleyways inviting visitors for an easy stroll. For swimmers, the road continues to Suha Punta with its oak and pine forests and numerous small coves.

The neighboring island of Cres has a more rugged charm of its own. Journeying along the main road you get the impression that you are in the mountains but then every now and again you get a breathtaking view of the ocean. Cres is also linked

Top: Coastal landscape on Cres.
Below: Cres' idyllic port.

by a small spit of land to the nearby island of Lošinj. The port of Mali Lošinj, with its vibrant late baroque buildings, is a popular stop with magnificent yachts from all over the world anchoring here.

over five hundred years, from 1382 until 1918, when the city was annexed by Italy after World War I. Open squares and cozy cafes are testimony to the former presence and influence of the Austro-Hungarian monarchy, before it lost influence as a center of trade and culture. The atmosphere of the Grand Canal with its small boats is dominated by the imposing Sant' Antonio Church (1849).

5 Koper und Piran The Slovenian coast is only 40 km (25 mi) long and yet three towns here offer you virtually all of the aspects of the sea and seafaring you could want: Koper, the country's trading port, Izola the fishing port and Piran, where the beachgoers sun themselves. Formerly an island, Koper is now linked to the mainland by a causeway. The center of the historic Old Town has a Venetian flair and is dominated by the Titov trg and the Praetorian Palace, the cathedral and the bell tower. One palace loggia on the square has been converted into a relaxed coffee house. Izola was also built on an island and before being later linked to the mainland. There are ample signs of a Venetian past here

too, but Izola is primarily a fishing village and port.

Piran, on the other hand, is one of the loveliest towns along the Adriatic, and lives primarily from tourism. The town's focal point is Tartini Square, lined by a semi-circular row of old buildings on the one side and with views of the small fishing port on the opposite side. In Piran, the best thing to do is go for a stroll and let yourself be enchanted by the delightful details of the loggias, fountains and wells.

The onward journey now takes you onto Croatian soil.

6 Umag The craggy west coast of Istria, from Savudrija to Rovinj, has lively coastal resorts, fish-

ing villages and small Venetian towns on the seaside that feature a varied landscape. The road initially travels through reddish, open countryside where you arrive in the "breadbasket" of Istria, the focal point of which is the lovely town of Umag. This former Venetian port on a spit of land has a historic Old Town that is surrounded almost completely by the sea. In the Middle Ages, Umag – then still an island separated from the mainland – belonged o the Bishop of Trieste. The route then continues along small, scenic roads along the coast to Poreč.

7 Poreč Headlands covered in pine forests, lagoons with crystal-clear water and craggy

cliffs of marble are the hallmarks of the 70-k-long (43-mi) riviera between Poreč and Vrsar, and it is no surprise that the little town of Poreč, originally settled by the Romans, has developed into Istria's tourism center. The main attractions include the towers of the former town walls, the 15th-century bell tower and the Euphrasian Basilica with its elaborate décor and fine mosaics – the most significant monument to Byzantine sacral architecture from the 3rd to 6th centuries.

In order to reach the medieval coastal town of Rovinj by car you will need to round the Limski zaljev bay on the E751 and, after a very short drive through the interior, turn off to the west of the peninsula.

Detour

The Plitvice Lakes

An unforgettable natural spectacle awaits visitors to the Plitvička jezera National Park in the north Dalmatian hinterland. The waters of the Korana River plunge down a total of 156 m (512 ft) into a series of stepped lakes and waterfalls over dolomite and limestone terraces. There is a total of sixteen lakes in the park, each one as beautiful as the last, glistening in shades of deep blue and green. The unmistakable hues come from the limestone, which is the dominant type of stone in the region. The ninety waterfalls and cascades are located in what is largely still pristine mixed forest, which has a particular appeal in autumn.

The national park's most impressive waterfalls are the Plitvice Falls where the waters of the Plitvice River plunge 72 m (236 ft) down into the canyon. One of the park entrances is located conveniently

There are more than ninety waterfalls in this national park.

8 Rovinj
Insiders know that this coastal village, with its Venetian bell tower, numerous brightly painted houses, charming alleyways, and myriad swimming options is one of the country's loveliest. The rocky island has been settled since antiquity and was a prosperous fishing and trading center under the Venetians.

A stroll through the Old Town should begin at the waterfront promenade with its lovely views. The unique flair of Rovinj's center is formed by the Trg Tita Square, which opens out onto the waterfront with welcoming cafés, a town museum and a splendid late-Renaissance clock tower. The imposing St Eufemija baroque church (1736) with its bell tower is also worth visiting. The route now returns to the E751 in order to reach the next stop. After passing through the very impressive limestone landscape you ultimately reach the southern part of Istria in a wine-growing area interspersed with stone walls.

9 Pula
This port and industrial town with its imposing Roman arena is located at the southern end of the peninsula. Pula had developed into a prosperous provincial capital even during the era of Emperor Augustus. With its 62,400 residents, it is today still the peninsula's cultural and economic center.

Visitors are drawn by the museums and the ring-shaped Old Town laid out around the castle hill, but the most impressive sight remains the amphitheater, a huge structure with arcade arches up to 33 m (108 ft) in height. Pula's undisputed landmark is of course also a UNESCO World Heritage Site.

10 Labin
The journey now takes you along the east coast of Istria to the north-east.

The E751 crosses the Raša Valley, which is a steep canyon in places, and then climbs rapidly up to the delightful medieval town of Labin, high above the sea. The stretch along the winding east coast is now dominated by Ucka, Istria's highest mountain at 1,400 m (4,593 ft). This is the beginning of the Opatijska Rivi-

iera, with the charming 19th-century seaside resorts of Lovran and Opatija. Brestova marks the end of the Istria region, which is now Kvarner Bay.

11 Opatija
Belle Époque styles, blossoming gardens and elegant coffee houses are all traces of the Austro-Hungarian monarchy here in Opatija. After being designated as a spa in 1889, this seaside resort developed into an urban work of art.

In addition to the obvious beach pursuits, Opatija offers splendid walks along the 8-km (5-mi) waterfront promenade. European high society used to meet in Angiolina Park (1885) in the town center, and the glamour of those days can still be relived with a walk under the acacia, cedar and lemon trees.

1 Sailing yachts with the historic town of Trogir in the background. The medieval Old Town is enclosed by an impressive town wall.

2 Old Town Rovinj, dominated by the 60-m (199-ft) campanile.

3 The port of Piran has charming townhouses dating from the Venetian era.

close to the falls while another gate opens at the largest of the Plitvice lakes, the Kozjak jezero. The idyllic landscape is easily accessible on the many miles of boardwalks and the 40 km (25 mi) of hiking trails. Electric boats and a mini tourist railway also help to ensure that the longer distances can be negotiated comfortably. Caution: brown bears, wolves and wildcats roam through the forests and canyons, with otters living in the lakes.

The lake landscape has countless whitewater sections and crashing waterfalls. They have been used in a number of films. The wild landscape around the Plitvička jezera covers an area of 295 sq km (114 sq mi) and was made into a national park back in 1928. It was then declared a UNESCO World Heritage Site in 1979.

Detour

Korčula

There are only a few places along the Adriatic coast where an island is this close to the mainland, in this case Korčula and the Pelješac Peninsula.

Top: The Venetian fortress in the island's capital.
Bottom: View of the picturesque island of Korčula.

Korčula, a mountainous island with comparatively lush vegetation, covers 276 sq km (107 sq mi) and has a good variety of activities to offer visitors. Legend has it that the famous Moreška sword dances, performed only on specific feast days, derive from the threat posed by the Ottoman Empire. The island's capital has Venetian-style architectural gems combined with a walled medieval Old Town, a triumphal arch, St Mark' Cathedral and the bishop's palace.

12 **Rijeka** The port and industry town of Rijeka often serves only as the starting point for a drive along the coastal road. But that would not do the city justice. One of its attractions is the 33-m-high (108-ft) bell tower of the St Marija Cathedral (13th century, façade from the 19th-century), known as the "Leaning Tower of Rijeka" due to its angle. There are also a number of museums and the pedestrian zone lined with boutiques and shops. Be sure to visit the Trsat fortress (13th century), which towers above the town affording a fantastic panoramic view of the mountains and the sea. The journey continues along the Croatian coast on the E65, also known as Adria-Magistrale, a 600-km (373-mi) stretch between Rijeka and Dubrovnik that follows the coastline almost the whole way, passing through a unique landscape comprising limestone mountains, shimmering, crystal blue water and – typically – bright sunshine.
Anyone with time for a longer detour should turn off at Kraljevica towards Krk and cross over at Valbiska to the island of Cres with its impressive, barren lunar landscape.

13 **Crikvenica** This seaside resort is situated about 30 km (19 mi) away from Rijeka. In the summer it attracts tourists with a wide sandy beach and the 8-km-long (5-mi) waterfront promenade, which extends as far as Selce.
A visit to the aquarium is also worthwhile and provides an insight into the wealth of Mediterranean fish and plant life. About 30 km (19 mi) further on is

the town of Senj. From there it is worth taking the detour to the Plitvice lakes, roughly 90 km (56 mi) away.
Back on the coastal road this stretch is lined with small towns inviting you to stop over. The ferry port of Jablanac is located halfway between Rijeka and Šibenik and from here it is worth taking a detour to the scenic island of Rab – the crossing only takes ten minutes.

14 **Zadar** The Dalmatian capital boasts some historic buildings from the Venetian era such as the circular St Donatus Church and the campanile of St Anastasia's Cathedral dating from the 12th and 13th centuries. The ruins of the medieval town fortress and the Roman forum are also worth visiting.

15 **Šibenik** This charming port is dominated by the glistening white cathedral by Jura Dalmatinác (1441). The talented builder spent most of his life working on

his masterpiece, which is a unique embodiment of the transition from the Gothic to the Renaissance style. The apses contain a row of seventy-four heads, each of which displays an individual vitality and are especially intriguing.
The surrounding landscape is a bit more hospitable here than the northern section of the coastal road. The vegetation also becomes more Mediterranean. Close to Šibenik is the start of the Krka National Park, a singular landscape of natural springs, babbling brooks and tumbling waterfalls – the realm of Croatian fairies and water sprites. The route continues via Primošten. Wine has been produced in this area for centuries, with elaborate walls of white stone built to protect the vines from the cold winds of the bora.

16 **Trogir** The charming Old Town of Trogir is situated on a small island. The winding alleys and a cathedral by the famous

master builder Radoan transport visitors back to the Middle Ages. The town, which only has 7,000 residents, was once a Greek and then a Roman colony before becoming Croatia's political and cultural center from the 9th to 11th centuries, as is evidenced not only by the very impressive cathedral (13th–16th century), but also by the many splendid churches and palaces.
The magnificent Old Town has since been declared a UNESCO World Heritage Site.

17 **Split** The stunning port of Split, with 188,700 residents, is the cultural and economic center of Dalmatia and has numerous museums and theaters. It is out on a peninsula dominated by Marjan hill. The Old Town has a curious mixture of Roman, medieval and modern buildings, with the impressive Diocletian Palace (built at the turn of the 4th century) and the 13th-century cathedral – the entire Old Town was declared a UNESCO

Detour

Kotor, Budva and Sveti Stefan

You can make a very interesting detour now from Dubrovnik into Montenegro. Awaiting you in the quaint coastal town of Kotor are narrow, labyrinthine alleyways, charming little squares and a number of well-preserved medieval buildings. The fortress, which was intended to protect against attacks from the sea, has a wall around it measuring 4.5 km (2.7 mi) at a height of 20 m (66 ft). Of the three city gates still standing, the ninth-century south gate is the oldest.

The Cathedral of St. Tiphun, completed in 1166, has magnificent 14th-century frescoes and is an important example of Romanesque architecture. In fact, Kotor is one of the best-preserved medieval towns in the region.

In Budva, situated on a small island linked to the mainland by a cause-

World Heritage Site. Unfortunately, it suffered significant damage during the Serbo-Croatian War, but that is slowly being repaired.

18 Makarska-Riviera This stretch of the Croatian coast becomes narrower and narrower as the journey progresses, until there is only the Biokovo mountain range separating the coast from Bosnia-Herzegovina. This is home to the once popular seaside resort area known as the Makarska Riviera, which was a passenger liner stop back in the 19th century. Sadly, a great many of the historic buildings from that era were destroyed by an earthquake in 1962.

The high mountain ridge results in a mild climate that has inspired wine grape and olive cultivation. The picturesque fishing villages, pleasant pebble beaches and pine forests invite visitors to stop in.

A few miles before Donta Deli there is a turnoff leading to the Pelješac Peninsula. You can catch ferries from here to the island of Korčula. In order to provide Bosnia-Herzegovina with access to the sea, Croatia had to surrender a tiny piece of its coast. The road to Dubrovnik therefore passes through another border crossing.

19 Dubrovnik Viewed from the air, this town looks as if it is clinging to the rocks like a mussel. In the Middle Ages, Dubrovnik was known as the seafaring republic of Ragusa. The Old Town, which features a mix of Renaissance and baroque buildings, winding alleys and a wide main street lined with cafés, is surrounded by mighty walls that open up toward the sea in only a few places. Basically impregnable for centuries, the town nevertheless faced near complete destruction on two occasions: from a strong earthquake in 1667, and from shelling by the Yugoslavian army in 1991. Fortunately, the bombed-

out roofs of the public buildings were rebuilt with a great deal of effort, such that the townscape has largely been restored.

Other attractions include testimonies to the golden 15th century when Ragusa vied with Venice for power. The Rector's Palace with its arcades, harmoniously round arch windows and baroque staircase dates from this era, as does the completely intact town wall with a total length of 1,940 m (2,122 ft). Kotor, Montenegro, is roughly 90 km (56 mi) from Dubrovnik, but the small medieval town is worth the detour. Bari, on the east coast of southern Italy, can be reached from Dubrovnik on a 16-hour ferry crossing.

20 Bari The capital of Apulia (331,600 residents) was initially founded by the Romans and was long subject to changing rulers. Foreign trade with Venice and the Orient brought wealth to the city, which still has a historic Old Town of Byzantine origin.

Large parts of the region surrounding Bari are used for agriculture, in particular olive cultivation.

The onward route takes you along the Autostrada 98 for a few miles before turning off at Ruvo di Púglia onto a smaller road towards Castel del Monte.

21 Castel del Monte This hunting castle from 1240, also known as the "Crown of Apulia", towers up from the plain and can be seen from quite a distance. The castle was built according to the laws of numerical mysticism by the German Staufer Emperor Frederick II (1194–1250) who had a passion for science and magic. The symmetrical, octagonal castle has a ring of octagonal towers, so that the only variations are those brought about by the changing daylight, an impressively active design element within the building.

The route continues along an equally small road to Barletta and from there 39 km (24 mi) along the coast to Manfredónia. A few miles further on it continues up to Monte S. Angelo.

1 The Biokovo Mountains form a wonderful backdrop for sailing yachts in one of the coastal resorts on the Makarska Riviera.

2 The Old Town of Split from the marina.

3 Sveti Ivan fortress is one of Dubrovnik's most popular photo motifs. The Old Town and the port create a picturesque backdrop.

4 View over the sea of buildings in the Old Town of Dubrovnik looking toward Lovrijenac fortress.

Top: The Old Town of Budva.
Bottom: The tiny but luxurious island of Sveti Stefan.

way, visitors are also immersed in the Middle Ages. The historic Old Town with its narrow alleys and valuable cultural monuments such as St Ivan's Church (17th century) and St Sava's Church (14th century), is surrounded by a fortress boasting gates and towers.

The medieval fishing village of Sveti Stefan lies in the middle section of the Budvanska Riviera. The 15th-century town, originally built on an island to protect it against pirates, has today become a comfortable seaside resort.

Detour

Urbino

Urbino, the cradle of humanism and the birthplace of Rafael, lies amid a graceful landscape of rolling hills, fields and forests. It was here that Duke Federico di Montefeltro lived, a patron of the arts and sciences in the mid-15th century who turned the town into the center of humanist philosophy. The magnificent brickwork buildings of the Old Town are protected by a medieval wall and are entirely dominated by the gigantic Palazzo Ducale. This imposing building is a UNESCO World Heritage Site.

All of the main streets lead to the Piazza della Repubblica. From there the Via Vittorio Veneto leads up the

Top: Palazzo Ducale (1444–1482).
Bottom: Piero della Francesca painted this portrait of Federico da Montefeltro who built the Palazzo.

hill to the Palazzo Ducale. The ducal palace is considered one of the most important Italian Renaissance buildings and, with its elegant courtyard lined with round arched arcades, it is an absolute highlight in the history of architecture.

The journey now takes you past two lagoons: Verano and Lesina. At Térmoli the route joins the N16. Térmoli itself holds little appeal, but the road now twists through the hilly, coastal landscape, revealing consistently good views. Inviting coves and picturesque villages like Vasto or Ortona perched on the cliffs tempt a stopover.

㉒ Vieste and the Gargano Peninsula The spur of the Italian boot consists of a wild limestone massif (1,000 m/3,281 ft) that is mostly uninhabited. Monte San Angelo is the highest town on the Gargano Peninsula at 850 m (2,789 ft). You have a wonderful view of the plateau and the Gulf of Manfredónia from the town, which has been an important southern Italian pilgrimage destination ever since the apparition of the Archangel Michael in a nearby grotto at the end of the 5th century. A 12th-century bishop's throne and other valuables adorn the grotto, which is shielded by bronze gates from Constantinople (1076).

Vieste is on the eastern tip of the peninsula. It has splendid beaches and a lovely medieval Old Town where the traditional outdoor *mignali* (staircases) are linked by narrow archways.

㉓ Pescara The largest town in the Abruzzi region always seems to be bustling. Large sections of the town were sadly destroyed in World War II but they have been rebuilt with generous, open architecture. Only a very small historical Old Town still exists now around the Piazza Unione. The town's attractions include its fine sandy beaches and the annual jazz festival in July, where legendary musicians like Louis Armstrong have performed. Pescara is at the mouth of the river of the same name.

㉔ S. Benedetto del Tronto Italy's largest fishing port is a lively and vibrant place. The town's icons include the splendid, palm-lined promenades, the

elegant villas and a long sandy beach. The fishing museum and the fish market are also worth a brief visit.

The steep Riviera del Conero, with the Monte Conero promontory, features stunning limestone cliffs, forests and narrow pebble beaches. It is worth taking some detours inland from here, for example to Loreto, perched like a fortress on a hill above Porto Recanati.

㉕ Ancona The foothills of the imposing Monte Conero drop down to the sea in steps while Ancona, the attractive regional capital of the Marches, sits down at sea level on the natural port. Although the port and industry town with 98,400 residents was originally founded by the Greeks

and boasts a rich history as a seafaring republic, its historical monuments unfortunately tend to be second rate.

In Ancona you should immerse yourself in the port atmosphere, which actually might be a welcome change from all the beach time and medieval towns. The San Ciriaco Cathedral (dating from the 11th 14th centuries) is perched high above the town. The Byzantine-influenced building is one of the most impressive Romanesque churches in Italy. En route to Pésaro there are a number of historical villages inviting you to stop a while, including Senigallia, the first Roman colony on the Adriatic coast. The Old Town there features the imposing Rocca Roveresca fortress.

Detour

San Marino

On the eastern edge of the Apennine Mountains, which form the spine of Italy, is Monte Titano with its towering fortresses built on a promontory to protect the world's smallest republic, San Marino, from potential harm. The republic comprises the capital of the same name and eight other villages.

The stonemason Marinus, thought to be from the island of Rab in what is now Croatia, originally sought refuge here in around AD 301 after fleeing persecution as a Christian in Diocletian times. The inhabitants drew up their own

The La Guaita fortress on Monte Titano from the 10th/11th centuries.

constitution in the 13th century and declared themselves an independent commune – and so it has remained to this day. San Marino's livelihood is based on stamps and coins as well as on handicrafts, agriculture and tourism.

Parking is available in the lower town of Borgo Maggiore. From here you continue either by foot or via the Funivia, a cable car with wonderful views. The historic Old Town has tiny alleys and surrounded by a wall. There is a fantastic panoramic view from the Piazza della Libertà and the Palazzo del Governo. In addition to the Old Town, it is also worth visiting the San Francesco Church (1361) with a collection of paintings. The three fortresses of Monte Titano are also worth seeing and are reached via the Salita alla Rocca steps.

From Pésaro it is worth taking an excursion to the Old Town of Urbino 35 km (22 mi) to the south-west.

㉗ Cattólica to Rímini This is where you will find the tourist strongholds of the Adriatic, coastal resorts which, with their sandy beaches stretching for miles, a diverse range of sporting opportunities and vibrant nightlife are focused on entertaining the masses. Rímini's history goes back a long way, however, so make sure you enjoy that aspect too.

Having first gained major significance as an Etruscan port, Rimini is divided into two districts that could hardly be more different. While the site of the Roman town is still recognizable

1 Castel del Monte is visible from a distance, rising up from the plain. The two-storey castle was built in 1240 by the German Staufer King Frederick II and is one of the most fascinating buildings from the Middle Ages.

2 Typical for the Apulia region, the labyrinthine Old Town of Vieste is dominated by white stone buildings.

3 The Gargano National Park also protects the high, rocky coastline of the peninsula of the same name. There is a series of caves and grottos to be visited.

4 Cervia, around 15 km (9 mi) south of Ravenna, is a small fishing village from the 18th century. The charming houses of workmen from the nearby salt works line the bay.

㉖ Pésaro At the exit from the Foglia Valley is the industrial town and port of Pésaro. The Old Town, with its Palazzo Ducale (15th–16th centuries) on the Piazza del Popolo is worth visiting. Continuing now toward Rímini the, coastal strip becomes noticeably narrower and the hinterland more mountainous.

Remains of ancient civilizations: the amphitheater in Taormina.

Italy

Sicily: in the footsteps of the Greeks, Normans, Arabs and Staufers

Italy's largest island offers such great cultural diversity that it seems to embody an entire continent. Classic Greek temples, Norman cathedrals and baroque palaces have transformed the island into a larger-than-life open-air museum of art and cultural history. Nature in turn provides a powerful complement to the scene, offering dramatic rocky coasts and superlatives like the home of Europe's largest volcano.

On the edge of Europe, yet at the center of the Mediterranean world – there is no better way to describe Sicily's role in history. For lovers of antiquity, this island between the Ionic and the Tyrrhenian seas is a piece of Greece. For the good citizens of Milan and Turin, it is a stumbling block in front of the Italian boot that is dominated by shadowy powers and slowing down the pace of the country's progress. For Sicilians, despite the fact that many of its people suffered under the feudal conditions and were forced to emigrate due to the pressures of poverty, it will always remain "terra santa" – their sacred homeland – and it is all too often being kicked around by the Italian boot.

Historically, when so-called "world" politics revolved more or less around the Mediterranean, Sicily was the strategic crown jewel at the heart of the battle for dominance of this preeminent domain. In early antiquity, it was the Greeks, virtually dragged along by the Phoenicians, who colonized the island and made Syracuse

Mosaic of Christ in Monreale Monastery.

the center of the ancient world – before the era of the Roman empire. They were then followed by the Romans, Vandals, Byzantines, Arabs, Normans, Staufers, Aragonese and Neapolitans. Many of these conquerors ruthlessly plundered the country and fought bloody wars on its soil. By contrast, the Arabs cultivated growth between the 9th and 11th centuries by planting citrus and mulberry trees, sugarcane and date palms. They made the island into a gateway for Europeans to experience their more highly developed civilization.

Almost all of them, however, left behind stone reminders of their presence. The result is that, in terms of cultural and art history, Sicily now presents itself not as just an island, but as a continent in miniature, a rich fabric of tradition contained in one island. From the classic Greek tem-

Mount Etna is one of the most active volcanoes in the world today. It has more than 1,000 minor craters as well as eruption points that regularly spew lava. It is closely monitored from a dedicated observatory.

The Concordia Temple in the Valle dei Templi near Agrigento dates back to the 5th century BC.

ples at Agrigento, Segesta and Selinunt to the Norman-era cathedrals of Monreale, Palermo and Cefalù, or the baroque Old Towns of Noto, Ragusa and Modica: Sicily has all these styles in their purest forms. Of course it is not only these and other civilizations that fascinate today's tourists on a visit to the "Continente Sicilia". The land and the people leave an equally inspiring impression. Whether you come in the spring, when a paradisical sea of flowers cloaks the entire island with its aromas, or in the summer, when the gruelling heat parches the soil, Sicily rarely fails to enchant. Its ancient beauty, which neither earthquakes, volcanic eruptions nor outbreaks of human violence have been capable of destroying, looks destined to remain.

The juxtaposition of contrasts, passions and an almost fatalistic lethargy; the either–or, friend or foe, love or hate, life or death attitude is an essential element of the Sicilian mentality. On the piazzas of Palermo or Catania, life pulsates chaotically and yet elegantly. The other side of the coin, however, can be seen in the economy and politics. The spirit of the Mezzogiorno, the Mafia, the bureaucracy and the corruption forms an unholy alliance, exercises a painful lack of consideration for nature.

But one thing is certain: This small piece of land nearly equidistant from the African and European continents, will undoubtedly awaken the senses of any visitor and enchant them with its exotic fragrances, vibrant hues and unique light. It will inspire a desire in you to return before you even complete the journey back across the Straits of Messina at the end of your trip.

Solitude can still be found on the Isola Salina, the second-largest of the Aeolian Islands.

The remote location of the temple of Segesta creates an impressive and mystical atmosphere. It was built opposite Monte Barbaro, where the ruins of the ancient city of Segesta and its theater can be seen. The ancient Greek peripteros, a temple surrounded by a portico with columns, was built in the 5th century BC.

It has thirty-six well-preserved Doric columns, six on its narrow sides and fourteen on its long sides, and covers an area of 61 x 26 m (200 ft x 86 ft). The temple was never completed, and the cella that is typically found at the center of this type of temple is also missing.

The Parthenon on the Acropolis was built under Kallikrates and Iktinos in 447 BC.

Greece

Classics of antiquity up close

Greece is the cradle of western civilization, and it is no surprise that the legacy of the ancient Greeks and its classic antiquities have inspired waves of fascination in the country. But a trip to *Hellas* is more than just a journey back through time: Greece is also a place of great natural beauty, with impressive mountainous landscapes, idyllic islands, wild coasts and pristine white-sand beaches.

One-fifth of Greece's total area comprises islands. No place in the entire country is farther than 140 km (87 mi) from the sea, and the 14,000 km (8,700 mi) of coastline offer endless possibilities for spectacular hiking, swimming, sailing or just relaxing on the beach.

On the mainland and the Peloponnese, less than one-third of the land is suitable for farming. Agriculture is therefore concentrated on the plains of the country's north-east. The national tree of Greece, for example, the olive tree, can thrive up to elevations of around 800 m (2,625 ft), and does so on the mainland as well as on the islands.

Greece's mountainous landscape and its proximity to the sea have obviously shaped civilization here for millennia. The most significant evidence of this is that, throughout the country's long history, the combination of mainland and archi-

The Virgin Mary in a Meteora monastery.

pelago prevented the formation of a central power. Instead, small city-states were the natural entities created here since ancient times, despite the fact that these were more easily conquered and ruled by foreign powers than a centralized structure might have been.

When the Roman Empire broke up in AD 395, Greece was part of the Eastern Roman Empire (Byzantium). It became Christian very early on. After the Crusades (11th–13th centuries), and in some cases well into the 16th century, large parts of the country fell under the rule of the Venetians, whose legacy can still be seen in various place names and architecture. In 1453, the Ottomans seized Constantinople and later large parts of Greece. When it came to beliefs, the Turks were tolerant, and their Greek subjects enjoyed religious freedom. The Orthodox Church

The spectacular "Shipwreck Beach" on the north-west coast of Zákinthos. This southernmost island in the Ionic Sea was called the "Flower of the Levant" by the Venetians.

The island fort of Bourtzi protected Nauplia from enemies attacking from the south.

thus became a unifying and protective force for all Greeks during the Ottoman era. Isolated from the important cultural and intellectual developments in the rest of Europe, Greece remained untouched by the Renaissance, Reformation and Enlightenment.

National pride, which emerged in the late 18th century, finally led to revolution in 1821, but it was quashed by the Turks. It was not until 1827 that the Greeks, with help from the British, French and Russians, were able to shake off Turkish rule and proclaim a sovereign state. After independence in 1830, the Greeks made Bavarian Prince Otto von Wittelsbach the king of their nation as Otto I, after which a number of German architects worked in Athens to ensure the nation was transformed into worthy capital of the new Greece after centuries of decline.

At the time, however, some areas of Greece were still under Turkish rule, which again led to wars with the Turks – with varying success – and it was not until the early 20th century that Crete and a number of other Aegean islands were returned to Greece.

As a travel destination, Greece is often presented with deep blue skies above a turquoise sea, with whitewashed houses on a hillside above a quaint port – and not incorrectly. Regardless of whether you are hopping around the more than 2,000 islands or exploring the mainland, Greek hospitality is an exceptional national quality here.

A word of warning, however: their driving can be rather "adventurous" at times. Some think the middle of the road belongs to them, even on curves, so make sure you drive with caution!

Such vibrantly colored fishing boats are typical of many Greek port towns.

Detour

Euboea

A bridge connects the mainland with Greece's second-largest island, which has still somehow remained largely untouched by mass tourism. Long stretches of the two main roads in the north and south head alternately along rugged cliffs and sandy beaches, passing picturesque fishing villages and small seaside resorts. The mountain roads and between remote villages provide spectacular views of the island. Halkida is the capital of Euboea, and its main attractions include the Turkish-Venetian Kastro quarter with an imposing mosque, an aqueduct and a fortress.

Heading north, Route 77 initially skirts the west coast. After Psahná , however, it becomes more mountainous, and the scenery is characterized by olive groves and pine forests before you are taken into the narrow Kleisoura Gorge. The mountain village of Prokópí lies at

A monastery on an island between the ferry ports of Skala and Euboea

the foot of Kandillo, the highest peak in the northern half of the island at 1,246 m (4,088 ft).

Anyone not wanting to miss out on seeing the sandy beaches on Euboea should continue on to Agriovótano on the northern tip.

The interior of Euboea is similarly rugged, and from Sténi Dírfios you can climb Dírfis, the highest mountain on the island at 1,745 m (5,725 ft) in about four hours.

Expressway 44 connects you with the south of the island along the west coast to Erétria. The few ruins of the ancient city include the theater, the acropolis and a temple of Apollo. Following the Gulf of Euboea you reach Alivéri, with its interesting Venetian tower. The nearby mountain village of Stíra is known for its "dragon houses". The journey ends in Káristos, which is dominated by the mighty Venetian fort Castello Rosso.

This journey through the Greece of antiquity will take you through majestic mountains and glorious coastal landscapes to the most important remnants of this ancient civilization, as well as to the legacies of Roman, Byzantine and Venetian eras on the southern mainland, Attica and the Peloponnese peninsula.

1 Athens (see pages 324–325)

2 Cape Sounion From Athens, you initially head about 70 km (43 mi) south along Highway 91 to the outermost point of the peninsula. The lovely beaches at Voúla and Vouliagméni are worthwhile spots to stop along the Attic Coast between Piréas (Piraeus) and Soúnio. At the bottom of the cape is an amazing temple dedicated to Poseidon, god of the sea, from 444 BC. It provides stunning views down to the Saronic Gulf.

From Cape Sounion, the route continues north along the eastern side of the peninsula. Then, east of Athens, you take Highway 54 toward Marathón. The Marathón Plain was where the Greeks defeated an army of Persians in 490 BC. On the day of the battle, a messenger in a full suit of armour brought news of the victory to Athens and the 42-km (26-mi) stretch became the reference distance for the modern marathon.

Following the coastal road to the north, you can make a

detour to Évia (Euboea) Island near Halkída.

3 Thebes From Halkída, Highway 44 heads to Thíva, the new name of ancient Thebes, which is today an insignificant provincial town. The few historic remnants from what was once the mightiest city in Greece, in the 4th century BC, are on display in the Archaeological Museum. Continuing north-west you will pass the tower of a 13th-century fort built by Franconian crusaders.

Heading towards Delphi, you initially take Highway 3 and then turn onto Route 48. The city of Livádia lies in the middle of vast cotton fields. After Livádia you will get some spectacular views over Mount Parnassus to the north-west.

4 Ósios Loukás After about 13 km (8 mi), a road turns off southward toward Distomo, and a 13-km-long (8-mi) street leads to the Ósios Loukás Monastery, considered one of the most beautiful Greek Orthodox monasteries from the Byzantine era

Travel information

Route profile
Length: approx. 1500 km (932 mi)
Time required: 3 weeks
Start and finish: Athens
Route (main locations):
Athens, Cape Sounion, Thebes, Delphí, Corinth, Nauplia, Sparta, Máni, Methóni, Olympia, Patras, Corinth, Athens

Traffic information:
Greece has a good network of well-maintained roads. You should have a green insurance card with you. Speed limits are as follows: highways 110 or 120 km/h (70 or 75 mph), rural roads 90 km/h (55 mph), in town 50 km/h (30 mph).

When to go:
The best seasons in Greece are spring between March and May, or autumn from October to November. Summers are extremely hot and dry.

Accommodation:
Greece offers a wide variety of accommodation, from domátias (guestrooms for rent) to expensive luxury hotels. For more information check out: *www.gnto.gr*

Information:
Here are some websites to help you plan your trip.
www.gogreece.com
www.in2greece.com
www.greeka.com

Oracle of Delphi

The Oracle of Delphi began having a significant effect on the fates of many Greek city-states in the 8th century BC. Rulers would address their questions to Apollo, for whom priestess Pythia then communicated his replies. She sat perched over a crevice, out of which hot steam rose, presumably sending her into a trance.

The ruins of the Temple of Apollo in ancient Delphí

(10th century). It houses some magnificent mosaics from the 11th century.

Another 24 km (15 mi) down the often steep and winding Highway 48 and you arrive in Delphí.

5 Delphí Evidence of Delphí's magic can be seen in both its mythology and in its beautiful natural setting. Located amid a picturesque mountain landscape on the steep slopes of Mount Parnassus, the town was considered by the ancient Greeks to be the center of the world. The Oracle of Delphí in the Sanctuary of Apollo was a regular center of consultation between the 8th century BC and AD 393.

The most famous sites of ancient Delphí include the amphitheater from the 2nd century BC, with a stunning view of the Temple of Apollo from 200 years earlier; the Holy Road; and the Sanctuary of Athena Pronaia with the Tholos, a famous circular temple. The Archaeological Museum's many sculptures and a recon-struction of the sanctuary is also worth a visit. The highlight is the life-size bronze charioteer, which had been dedicated to Apollo as a reward for a victorious chariot race in 478 BC.

From Delphí, it is worth making a 220-km-long (137-mi) detour to the Metéora monasteries (see pp 326–327) in the mountainous heart of northern Greece.

Anyone wanting to omit the detour north will initially follow the same route back to Thíva, then continue along Highway 3

1 The icon of Athens: a view from the south over the Acropolis, with the imposing Parthenon in the center of the complex and Mount Lykabet-tos on the right in the background.

2 The ceiling of the Caryatid Porch at the Erechtheion on the Acropolis is supported by columns in the shape of young women, so-called caryatids.

3 Three of the twenty columns were rebuilt at the Tholos, a round building at the Sanctuary of Athena Pronaia in Delphí.

The wisdom of the oracles was often ambiguous and therefore required interpretation by a priest of some ranking. Roman emperors tried to resurrect the cult in the 2nd century, but the oracle fell silent in AD 393 and the sanctuary was eventually shut down.

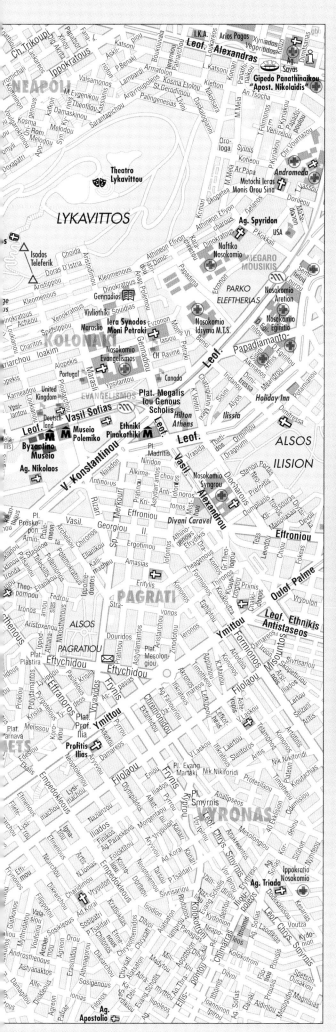

Athens

The Greek capital is a pulsating, modern metropolis with three million inhabitants, approximately one third of whom live in the greater Athens area. The city's most recognizable icon is visible from afar and is the epitome of ancient Greece: the Acropolis.

Athens is a city of contrasts: chaos on the roads, traffic jams, complicated environmental problems and oppressive smog polluting the entire valley, while the greatest ruins from antiquity, especially the Acropolis, still stand tall on the south side of city center.

Athens' most famous site is the mighty Acropolis – a UNESCO World Heritage Site –, the castle hill of the ancient city that was converted into a holy district around 800 BC and mainly used to worship the goddess Athena, the city's patron saint. The Acropolis sits atop a steep, rugged, 156-m-high (512 ft) pale limestone plateau and was an important place of refuge for the population in times of need. The early beginnings of a castle wall already existed in the 13th century BC. After the old temple was destroyed by the Persians in 480 BC, the complex of

the dramas of Aeschylus, Euripides and Sophocles premiered in front of an audience of 17,000; and the Roman Odeion (AD 160), a construction commissioned by the wealthy Athenian, Herodes Atticus.

The Acropolis project ultimately required a huge sacrifice from the Athenian taxpayers: the total costs were more than 2,000 ancient gold talents, an enormous sum of money for a city-state the size of Athens.

Clustered around the Agora, the ancient market place from 600 BC and the center of public life for centuries, you will find the Doric Temple of Hephaistos, or Theseion (449–440 BC); the Attalos Stoa portico, once an artisans' center with discoveries from the ancient Agora, now reconstructed as a museum; the octagonal Tower of the Winds (1st century BC), formerly a clep-

the Roman Library of Hadrian at Monastiraki Square.

Around the bustling Syntagma Square in modern Athens, you should see the Parliament building (Vouli), built by the architect Friedrich von Gärtner in 1842; the national garden created in 1836 with exotic plants; the Numismatic Museum in the home of Heinrich Schliemann; the ruins of Hadrian's Gate and the Temple of Zeus (Olympieion) dating back to Roman times; the ancient Kallimármaro Stadium, reconstructed for the first modern Olympic Games in 1896; the National Archaeological Museum with a unique collection of ancient Greek art; the Museum of Cycladic Art; the Byzantine Museum; and the Benáki Museum (Byzantine works, Coptic textiles).

The surrounding area features: the Kaisariani Byzantine monasteries with

In the 5th century BC, Pericles was able to gain support from the citizens Athens for the city's most ambitious building programme: the construction of the Acropolis, initially with three temples.

monumental marble buildings with the Propylae gate construction, the small Temple of Nike, the imposing Doric Parthenon (447–432 BC), and the Ionic Erechtheum with its Caryatid Porch were all created in the first half of the 5th century BC, the time of Pericles. The most extensive damage to the Parthenon dates back to the 17th century when a Venetian grenade hit the Turkish powder warehouse in the Parthenon and sent the roof flying into the air. Important sculptures and reliefs are also on display in the Acropolis Museum.

The main attractions below the Acropolis are the Theater of Dionysus, where

sydra and sundial with a weather vane; the Roman Agora, from around the birth of Christ; and the adjacent Fethiye Mosque (15th century).

In the Plaka, the picturesque Old Town quarter with narrow alleyways, small shops, cafés and taverns, are several Byzantine churches, such as the beautiful Little Mitropolis (12th century) and Athens' oldest Christian church, the 11th-century cross-in-square Kapnikarea church on the fashionable Ermou shopping street. Also worth seeing is the Panagía Geogoepíkoòs cross-in-square church (12th century) at the Plateía Mitropóleos, as well as a small bazaar mosque and the ruins of

the St Mary's Church, built around 1000, and 11th-century Dafni, which has some ornate gold leaf mosaics in the main church, UNESCO World Heritage Site.

It is worth taking a day trip out to Piraeus, Athens' port since ancient times, with the Mikrolimano fishing port, Hellenic Marine Museum and Archaeological Museum. Also visit the Poseidon Temple on Cape Sounion, 67 km (42 mi) away, and the islands in the Saronic Gulf, home to Aegina with the Temple of Apollo and the Temple of Aphaia, the island of Poros with its charming scenery, and the artists' island of Hydra.

Detour

Metéora Monasteries

The name Metéora means "floating rocks" – and the literal sense of the term becomes apparent to any visitor as soon as they arrive at this vast monastery complex. The Metéora monasteries are some of the most beautiful and impressive attractions in all of Greece.

From Delphí, the road initially heads west as far as Ámfissa, where you turn onto Highway 48 towards Brálos. From there, Highway 3 passes through Lamía to Néo Monastíri, and continues along Highway 30 through Tríkala to Kalambáka.

The first sandstone towers can be seen on the horizon from quite a distance. The monastery buildings sit atop high cliffs, which soar up vertically out of the Thessalia Plain to heights of 300 m (984 ft). The roughly 1,000 sandstone formations are deposits from a large lake whose waters eroded out the pillars before the sea level dropped.

After the 9th century, when foreign invaders began their conquest of the region, some hermits sought refuge in this remote world of rock towers. One of them was a recluse named Barnabas, who settled here at the end of the 10th century. Many others soon followed suit on the nearby towers. The monasteries themselves were not built until the 14th and 15th centuries, when the Serbs threatened with invasion. In 1336, the monk Athanásios from Athos established the first monastery, which was followed by twenty-three others. The buildings on the cliffs were used by the recluses as both places of refuge in the face of foreign invaders, as well as places of worship. The foundations were financed by wealthy private individuals looking to secure themselves a place in heaven; some monasteries still even bear the names of their founders. The monks lived according to strict monastic rules that prohibited women from entering the monasteries. Even in times of need, they were not allowed to accept food from women.

The monasteries were built in places out of the military's reach and could only be accessed in a very circuitous

route using rope-ladders or other climbing aids. If a situation appeared unsafe, the monks could retract their ladders; or they could receive welcome guests, drop down a basket or net and pull the visitors up. Everyone visiting Metéora for the first time will automatically ask themselves, when looking at the steep cliffs, how the first hermits climbed these tall, sharp rocks, which can today only be mastered by sport climbers.

One supposes they beat pegs into narrow crevices and worked their way up. The paths quarried into the rock were only created in more recent times. The architectural construction of the individual monasteries is largely a function of their varying positions on a crag or over an abyss. The internal structure of the monasteries is relatively uniform, and they have all the essential facilities required by occidental monasticism: a prayer chapel, a kitchen, a refectory (dining hall), a cistern, monk cells, a library and a treasure chamber.

The Metéora monastery frescos

Even in ancient times, painting the walls was a common form of artistic and spiritual expression. Indeed, these colorful murals fulfilled an important role in the Byzantine Empire (Eastern Roman Empire) and the form even experienced a sort of heyday in the 9th century.

Frescos (from the Italian "fresco", meaning fresh) were created by applying fresh watercolors to wet lime surfaces. The mineral dyestuffs penetrated the fresh rock and bonded chemically with the lime and sand to form a hard surface.

Top: Agíos Stephanos Convent
Bottom: Fresco with Jesus and saints

Built by Eastern Orthodox monks hoping to escape the imminent conquest of the Turks, some of the Metéora monasteries are still home to rich murals from the 14th to 16th centuries. Due to their natural inaccessibility perched on top of dramatic limestone towers, many of the frescos have in fact been very well preserved, for example the ones in the small Stéfanos Chapel, which date back to the early 16th century.

The Ágios Nikólaos Monastery, built in the late 14th century and expanded in 1628, also houses a vast collection of frescos. A monk named Theophanes painted some of the most beautiful frescos here around 1527. The nuns of the Ágios Stéfanos Convent continue to operate an icons workshop even today.

Rousánou Monastery, perched atop a crag and founded by two brothers from Epirus in 1545. For a long time the location was only accessible using rope-ladders and was often used by the people from the surrounding area as a place of refuge. The oldest preserved monastery in Metéora bears the name Moní Hypapante.

Three monasteries are particularly worth seeing: Várlaam was founded in 1518 and its church (Katholikón) is home to beautiful frescos. Perched 623 m (2,044 ft) up, Megálo Metéoro is the highest and largest monastery, and the hermit caves of its founder can still be visited today. Ágios Stéfanos is a convent and was founded by Byzantine Emperor Andronikos III in 1332.

From 1490, all monasteries were subordinate to the abbot of the Metamórfosis Monastery, built between 1356 and 1372, and one of the oldest monasteries in Metéora. The monks stayed in their monasteries even after the Turkish conquest of northern Greece and new monasteries were still being founded in Metéora in the late 15th

century. Some of the monasteries were large properties and were thus subject to tribute to the Turkish rulers.

The 16th century was the heyday of monastic life in Metéora, but also a time of fierce conflicts between the various monasteries. Towards the end of the 18th century, the first monastery complexes had already fallen into ruin

because of difficulty in maintaining their basic structures. Today, there are still thirteen monasteries that are in parts completely impoverished and have largely fallen into disrepair, but some of them still have valuable libraries. In total, six monasteries can still be visited. The most spectacular of these is undoubtedly the little Moní

1 The view from the Metéora monasteries stretches far into the Thessalia Plain.

2 The Metéora monasteries were inaccessible to unwelcome guests.

3 An impressive fresco in the Várlaam Monastery, founded in 1518.

Built in 444 BC, the fifteen gleaming white columns of the temple on Cape Sounion create an ideal location for a sanctuary to worship Poseidon, god of the sea. Looking out over the Saronic Gulf, this temple on a cliff soaring 60 m (197 ft) above the sea was used by seafarers as an orientation point even in ancient times.

Because of its strategically favourable location, the temple district was later developed into a fort complex around 431 BC. Ruins of the fortress walls, as well as the tower and gate complexes, are evidence of this today.

Mycenae

The present-day village of Mikínes (Mycenae) is home to the Orea Eleni guesthouse, where German treasure hunter and amateur archaeologist Heinrich Schliemann lived in 1876 during his groundbreaking excavations here. It was primarily thanks to his efforts that Mycenaean culture from the late Greek Bronze Age (1100 BC) was discovered at all. From the village of Mikínes, a road leads you about 2 km (1.2 mi) to the fortified palace area.

According to legend, the founder of the ancient Mycenae was Perseus, the hero who killed Medusa. The civilization's first heyday was between 1600 and 1500 BC, and the second between 1400 and 1200 BC.

The Treasury of Atreus, built without any mortar, is a monumental domed tomb. You enter the most important shaft tomb from early Mycenaean times through a 9-m-long (30 ft) and

The golden Mask of Agamemnon

120-tonne (132-ton) lintel (the crown of a doorway). The "cyclopic" walls of the palace, where only Mycenae's upper class lived, are joined together with solid blocks of stone. The famous Lion Gate with its lion relief forms the entrance.

Just behind here is where Schliemann (whose discoveries are subject to ongoing controversy) found the mask that has since been known as the "Mask of Agamemnon". Out of the seven other large shaft tombs, the tomb of Clytemnestra, Agamemnon's wife, is in the best condition.

toward Athens as far as Asprópirgos before finally turning off west onto a small road that runs parallel to the coast. The route follows Salamis Bay, where the Greeks defeated the Persian fleet in 480 BC. Past Mégara, you will get some spectacular views of the Gulf of Aegina.

❻ Corinth Some 25 km (16 mi) down the road you see the first glimpses of Corinth, considered Greece's most beautiful city in its heyday during the time of Emperor Hadrian in the 2nd century AD. Apart from the breathtaking Corinth Canal, the main attractions include the Temple of Apollo (44 BC), the Temple of Octavia and the Lechaion Road. A number of excavations document the sheer size of this ancient city, which was leveled by an earthquake in 375 and again in 551.

From Corinth, take Highway 70 along the north-eastern coast of Peloponnese to Epidauros.

❼ Epidauros Ancient Epidaurus was a sanctuary of Asklepios, the god of medicine, and a city famous for its imposing amphitheater (4th century BC), which

is very well preserved and well known for its unique acoustics.

❽ Nauplia About 40 km (25 mi) further west is Nauplia. After the Greek War of Independence, this was temporarily the capital of the Kingdom of Greece, from 1829–1834. The port for centuries the constant target of enemy attacks, which prompted the construction of the two forts of Akronafplía and Palmídi in the north, and the island fort of Bourtzi in the south. The stylish Venetian quarter was built at the end of the 17th century.

❾ Tiryns This fort dates back to the 14th or 13th century BC and perches atop an 18-m-high (59-ft) cliff above a once swampy plain. The imposing walls of the fort are made of blocks of stone that are 2 to 3 m long (7-10 ft) and weigh up to an impressive 12 tonnes (13.2 tons). According to Homer, only giants – cyclopses in this case – could have built the 700-m-long (2,297-ft), 8-m-thick (26-ft) wall. The town of Árgos is 13 km (8 mi) away.

From there, it's worth making a detour north to Mycenae. A

small road turns off at Fihtí. Back in Árgos, the route heads west through Arcadia to Trípoli, and from there 60 km (37 mi) through the historic Laconia landscape to Sparta.

❿ Sparta Ancient Sparta was a city-state that once superseded Athens in importance. By contrast, the modern 19th-century Spárti has little to offer. Apart from its acropolis (outside the city center), it's worth visiting the Archaeological Museum with Roman mosaics from the 4th and 5th centuries.

⓫ Mistrás The neighbouring town of Mistrás at the foot of

Taygetos peak (2,404 m/7,888 ft) was founded near ancient Sparta in 1249, and is said to have had a population of 50,000 in its heyday, around 1700.

The unique Byzantine ruins of the city, which is located on a steep hillside, display impressive buildings from the 13th to 15th centuries, including some interesting churches, a monastery and the Despot's Palace. Above the town, clinging to the mountainside, is a fort from the 13th century (Kástro) built by crusaders from Franconia.

Back in Sparta, take Highway 39 to the town of Hania 47 km (29 mi) away and from there, it's 75 km (47 mi) to Monemvassía.

Monemvassiá

A fortified, seemingly impregnable city that has actually been an island since an earthquake in AD 375, Monemvassiá still presents itself as the "Gibraltar of Greece". Its name – monem vassia means "single entrance" in Greek – can be traced back to the town's location where a dam provides the only access to the mainland. Even today, the island has no cars and can only be reached on foot.

For a long time, Monemvassiá was ruled by the Venetians, who built a castle here in the decades following 1464, which they then heavily modified in around 1700. During the city's heyday in the 15th century, 50,000 people lived on the island. Today there are about fifty. From their port, the inhabitants once controlled maritime trade between Italy and Constantinople and the sea around the southern Peloponnese.

The little Agía Sophia church is the only preserved building in the upper town.

A 16th-century wall 900 m (2,953 ft) in length and up to 16 m (52 ft) in height protected the city on both the land and sea sides, and a rock staircase led from the lower town to the ruins of the upper town, which had been created as a refuge in the 6th century. It was the most densely settled part of the island during the Middle Ages.

The icon of Monemvassiás is the modest Agía Sofia Church from 1328. The ruins of the fortress and a large cistern have been preserved from the 13th century.

Some beautiful churches still stand in the restored lower town, including Panagía Myrtidiótissa (18th century), Christós Elkómenos (13th century), Agíos Nikólaos (1703) and Panagía Chrysafítissa, whose church bell hangs in a tree.

Monemvassiá is a popular daytrip destination for Greeks and it is precisely this which gives the village its particular charm – there are very few tourists.

From the intersection, it's downhill to Gythio, the gateway to the Mani Peninsula, the middle of the three fingers of the Peloponnese peninsula.

⑫ **Máni Peninsula** This peninsula south of the route from Gythio to Areópoli is also known as Deep or Laconian Máni. The trip around Máni is about 90 km (56 mi) and initially heads past the Castle of Passavá (13th century) on the largely uninhabited mountainous eastern side. The peninsula itself remains largely in its original state, but many of the villages are deserted today. From Páliros, on the southern tip, the route heads north to Vathia with its tower houses. The village has the most impressive location on the west coast, and the 17-km-long (11-mi) stretch between Geroliménas and Pígros Diroú is famous for its Byzantine churches from the 10th to the 14th centuries.

In the north-west near Kíta and Mamína are some interesting stalactite caves, the most impressive of which is Pírgos Diroú, which can be explored by boat. In Areópoli, old residential towers have been converted into guesthouses.

⑬ **The west coast of the Peloponnese** From Areópoli, you continue to follow the coast north to Kalamáta. This city is located at the Bay of Navarino, where a united English, French and Russian fleet defeated the Ottomans in 1827. The beaches here are lined with dunes that stretch along the west side of the western finger of the peninsula. A small detour branches off from here to the port town of Methóni 13 km (8 mi) away. The route heads north along the coast for 15 km (9 mi) before Pírgos, where the picturesque but very winding Route 76 turns off and heads through mountainous Arcadia to Andrítsena, with the Temple of Bassae from the 5th century, and Karitena, with a bridge over the Alfíos, from the 15th century. This same road takes you back to Kréstena and over the Alfioó River to Olimbía (Olympia).

⑭ **Olympia** Traces of earlier settlement here date back to as

1 The tower houses of Vátheia, not far from Cape Ténaro on Máni.

2 One of Mistrás' Byzantine churches.

3 Limeni, the port of Areópoli on Máni.

The Corinth Canal

Corinth was Greece's most important trading city in ancient times thanks to its various points of access to the Aegean and the Ionic seas. To avoid sailing around the stormy southern

The 6-km-long (4-mi) Corinth Canal.

cape of the Peloponnese, people began early on searching for ways to cross the narrow isthmus. In some places, ships were hauled over a 6-km-long (4-mi) cobblestone road. Work on a navigable channel started at the narrowest point even in ancient times, but the canal was eventually only completed in 1893. The resulting waterway is 23 m (75 ft) wide, 8 m (26 ft) deep and is cut through walls that are 52 m (171 ft) high.

early as the 2,000 BC. In ancient times, the town was a religious sanctuary of Zeus and a sporting cult site. It was here that the first Olympic Games were held no later than 776 BC.

All of Olympia's significant religious sites are found within the "Altis", a walled holy district. The sporting competitions took place outside the Altis, and the sites include a stadium for runners, the hippodrome (for chariot races) and the training sites of Gymnasion and Palaestra.

Other attractions are the Pryentaion, where the Olympic torch was lit and the Heraion, a temple dedicated to the goddess Hera. The Olympic torch is still lit in front of this temple before all Olympic Games. The Echo Hall, a foyer with two naves, was famous for its sevenfold echo. Columns at the ruins of the Temple of Zeus from 450 BC testify to the vast size of the former building. Olympia's Archaeological Museum is one of the best in Greece.

North of Pírgos you will drive along a road lined with olive trees, vineyards and sugar cane plantations.

⑮ Zákinthos Ferries to this, the southernmost of the Ionic Islands, operate from the port town of Kilíni on the north-west coast of the Peloponnese. you can easily drive around the island in one day. Almost all of the Venetian buildings in the main town were destroyed in an earthquake in 1953, but the Agios Dionísos Church (1925) and the traditional Arcadian houses are worth seeing.

The Blue Caves on the North Cape can be accessed by boat from Agios Nikólaos. Another of the island's attractions is the beach shipwreck on the north-west coast, while Laganás Bay in the south is a breeding ground for loggerhead turtles.

⑯ Patras From Lehená, take Highway 9 to Patras. It is worth making a detour here to the

lagoons along the coast. Stretching through this area is one of Europe's largest wetlands where swamps, stone pines and dunes are used by migratory birds as a stopover point. There is a visitors' center at Lápas.

The naval Battle of Lepanto took place in the strait north-east of Patras, the third-largest city in Greece with no notable attractions. This was where Don Juan d'Austria defeated the Ottoman fleet in 1571.

⑰ Diakoftó Rather than taking Highway 8, we recommend you follow a small rural road along the coast. For a little diversity along the way, it is worth taking a ride on the cog railway from Diakoftó some 40 km (25 mi) east of Patras to Kalávrita at a height of 700 m (2,297 ft). The journey over this 22-km-long (14-mi) stretch with fourteen tunnels and a number of bridges takes approximately one hour and travels through some picturesque mountains. If

you choose to drive between these two towns, you will see the Méga Spíleo Monastery perched up in the mountains as if clinging to a rock face. The monastery, which is said to be the oldest in the country, was where the Greeks began their revolution against the occupation of the Ottomans. From Diakoftó, the road that runs parallel to the Gulf of Corinth will take you back toward Corinth and eventually back to the capital, Athens.

1 The octagonal fortress tower on the island of Boúrtzi near Methóni dates back to the 16th century.

2 Ruins of the former sporting grounds in ancient Olympia.

3 A few Doric columns of the former Temple of Apollo in Corinth are still standing.

Metéora These monastery buildings are perched atop rock towers up to 300 m (984 ft) high, date back to the 14th/15th centuries, and sure live up to their name, "Floating Rocks". Five of the complexes are still inhabited.

Delphi The city of the Oracle perches on the steep slopes of Mount Parnassus with an amphitheater, the Temple of Apollo and an archaeological museum.

Aráchova In summer, this village near Thebes and Delphí attracts hordes of visitors with its wine, cheese and woven products.

Pindos Mountains This unique massif has two impressive national parks that are home to silver wolves, brown bears, the second-highest peak in Greece, Oros Smólikas at 2640 m (8,662 ft), and Europe's deepest gorge, the Vikos Gorge (900 m/2,953 ft).

Athens One-third of all Greeks live in the metropolitan area of their capital (since 1834). Athens hosted the 2004 Olympic Games. Numerous antiquities on the Acropolis plateau and in the National Archaeological Museum attest to Athens' former importance.

Corinth This port city, which has been fortified for 2,700 years, has impressive ruins, including the temples of Apollo and Octavia, and a famous canal that opened in 1893.

Euboea A diverse coast and a mountainous interior with numerous gorges characterize Greece's second-largest island, large parts of which have still barely been discovered by tourism. The bustling island capital of Halkida (Chálkis) is home to a 15th-century mosque.

Marathon A museum and the sizable burial mound of fallen Athenians recall the ancient battle of 490 BC between the Greeks and the invading Persians. The Greeks were the victors here.

Zákinthos The main attractions here are the breeding grounds for loggerhead turtles in Laganás Bay – and of course the pristine beaches.

Temple of Poseidon One of the most famous landmarks of the Aegean is Cape Sounion, adorned with a sanctuary for the god of the sea since 445 BC.

Epidaurus The highlight of this ancient cult site and healing town is Greece's best-preserved amphitheater from the 3rd century BC. It seated 12,000 people.

Methoni This former Venetian port city is one of the largest on the Peloponnese and was protected by this fortress tower.

Máni Pensinsula This rugged mountainous area has no noteworthy ports or beaches, but interesting watchtowers characterize many of the region's old villages such as Váthia, pictured here.

Mistras Numerous monasteries, walls, houses and palaces in a wild, romantic setting make the ruins here a highlight of any trip on the Peloponnese. The peninsula's most important city during the Middle Ages, Mistras was established 5 km (3 mi) west of ancient Sparta and was built at the foot of the 2,404-m-high (7,888-ft) Taygetos.

Monemvassia The "Gibraltar of Greece" is a fortified island town characterized by medieval and Venetian architecture that can be reached by a bridge.

The tombs of Hasan Pasa Kümbet at Ahlat, on the northern shore of Lake Van.

Turkey

Temples, mosques and gorgeous coves

Olive orchards, beaches and the snow-capped peak of Mount Ararat – Turkey welcomes visitors with an enormous wealth of scenery and landscapes. Beyond that, cultural landmarks and monuments of numerous empires spanning more than nine thousand years play a huge role in making your trip to Turkey an unforgettable experience.

Your journey through the Republic of Turkey begins in a surprisingly rural setting. Istanbul's lively arterial roads are full of all sorts of businesses, but they soon give way to the green fields of East Thrace, a totally different landscape where traditional tearooms, bazaars and caravanserais coexist with modern highways, cargo vessels, Roman ruins and monuments like those in Gelibolu (Gallipoli) National Park.

It was here that Turkish troops managed to defeat the British and Australian Armies after months of fighting in 1915 – all under the command of Mustafa Kemal Pasha, later to become known as Atatürk, 'Father of the Turks', founder of modern Turkey.

All along the Mediterranean shores of western Anatolia, the 'Coasts of Light', there are historical sites of ancient Greek and Roman culture in all their breathtaking beauty. Among them are Pergamon, Ephesus and Milet, some of the most incredible examples of art and architecture from those times. The Hellenic mathematicians and philosophers living in Ionia, on Asia Minor's western

Head of Medusa in the ancient city of Didyma.

frontier, transformed that city into one of the cradles of European civilization.

On the south coast between Marmaris and Alanya you will be delighted by the plentiful beaches where water sports and relaxation are high on the agenda. For more adventurous travellers, there is also rafting, paragliding, cave excursions and mountain climbing. With a bit of searching you can find secluded coves and pristine natural settings.

Between the Olympus Mountains and the coast, a region of fishing villages, farms and winding pathways has been converted into a holiday destination where sensitive infrastructure and environmental considerations were taken into account right from the beginning. The project, known as the 'South Antalya Project' or 'Kemer project', has been called a 'total success'. The motto was 'Less is More', and

A strange sight – wind and rain have exposed these tuff pillars near Göreme in Cappadocia.

The Hagia Sophia in Istanbul is a masterpiece of Byzantine architecture. The building is no longer used for religious purposes, but as a museum.

it seems to have worked with the upmarket boutiques and hotels.

East of Anamur Castle, built on a magnificent location above the sea, your 'Turkey adventure' can really finally begin. Very few people come this far to see the wide horizons of eastern Anatolia. For hours, and over considerable distances, the land appears completely empty, with low-lying, dust-coloured villages barely standing out from the surrounding countryside. Yet this easternmost region of Turkey is where you find the country's largest lake, Lake Van, and its highest peak, Mount Ararat. Due to Ararat's remote location, however, we recommend you visit Nemrut Dagi in the Taurus Mountains, a man-made mountain with a 2,000-year-old king's tomb.

Lake Van and the town of Van, on the other hand, are worth a longer visit.

In central Anatolia you can experience Muslim culture at its most intense, especially in the highlands between the Taurus Mountains to the south and the Pontic Mountains at the Black Sea. Towns like Sivas or Konya are centers of Islamic mysticism.

Cappadocia, a must-see, is home to the bizarre erosion landscape around Nevsehir and Göreme. The tuff formations are a truly fantastic experience, both in terms of nature and culture. Byzantine monks once sought shelter here from Muslim Arab attacks. Today the cave dwellings and churches form a giant open-air museum.

An even older culture exists near Ankara, Turkey's modern capital. The Hattusas ruins are now a UNESCO World Heritage Site – one of a total of nine UNESCO Cultural and Natural Sites in Turkey.

The Celsus Library in Ephesus with its restored facade.

Sultan Ahmet Camii in Istanbul is the only mosque in the world with six minarets. They are juxtaposed with an ensemble of domes and half-domes and afford an impressive silhouette against the evening sun. Built in 1616, this sacred building was given the nickname "Blue Mosque" by Mehmet Ağa, a student of the

renowned Ossman architect, Sinan, because of the almost twenty thousand predominantly blue tiles that cover the domes and walls. Of particular interest from an art history perspective are the faience details with traditional motifs illustrating plant life on the bottom section of the walls.

Istanbul

Its fairy-tale location on the Bosporus Strait and the Golden Horn makes Istanbul worth a visit. There is a lot to see and do in this historically charged city so perfectly placed between East and West, and its friendly people will not disappoint.

This city of three names – Byzantium, Constantinople, Istanbul – was the mistress of two empires that both decisively shaped the history of the Mediterranean for almost two thousand years – the East Roman or Byzantine Empire and its direct successor, the Ottoman Empire. Art treasures from every era of its history as well as the variety and vitality of modern Istanbul make the city an ideal destination for lovers of art and culture.

In the Old Town between the Golden Horn, Bosporus and the Marmara Sea there are a few things you shouldn't miss – Hagia Sophia, the religious center of ancient Byzantium built by the emperor Justinian I from 532 to 537. It has a magnificent dome and some beautifully preserved mosaics. Hagia Eirene goes back to pre-Constantine times, the current building having

the 'Blue Mosque' (17th century); the Hippodrome, an antique carriage race track; the Museum of Turkish and Islamic Art; the Sokollu Mehmet Pasa Mosque (16th century); the Mosaic Museum; the beautiful ancient steam baths of Haseki Hürrem Hamam (1557) and Cagaloglu Hamam (18th century); Sogukcese Sokagı, a road lined with restored timber buildings from the Ottomans; and the High Gate, a rococo gate.

In the Old City check out: the Grand Bazaar, the world's largest indoor market; the Egyptian Bazaar, a book bazaar; the New Mosque (17th century); the Rüstem Pasa Mosque dating from the 16th century with its colourful tiles; the Beyazit Tower, a fire tower from 1828; the Beyazit Mosque (16th century); Nuruosmaniye Mosque (18th century); the Constantine Col-

Top: Hagia Sophia was originally used as a Byzantine coronation church.
Bottom: The Grand Bazaar is the world's largest indoor bazaar.

been erected in the 8th century. The Archaeological Museum has an interesting collection of antique exhibits. In the Ottoman city center be sure to visit – Topkapi Sultan's Palace, a spacious compound with magnificent buildings structured by courtyards and gates; the well of Sultan Ahmed III (1728); the Sultan Ahmed Mosque –

umn from AD 330; and the Sultan Süleyman Mosque.

At the edge of the Old City visit the Hagios Georgios (1720), the cast-iron Church of St Stephen (1871), Tefur Palace (11th century), some ruins of the Theodosian wall (5th century), the Mihrimah Mosque (16th century), the Chora Church and the Victory Mosque.

Detour

Hierapolis and Pamukkale

The gleaming white sinter terraces above the valley are something right out of a fairy tale – albeit a recent one. Concerns for both tourism and the environment were fortunately taken into account when the greying terraces were restored over the past few years. The reason for this bizarre landscape is the high concentration of lime in the steaming hot water (36°C/96°F) that cascades down from mountain springs. As it cools, layer upon layer of lime is deposited onto the terraces.

Top: Monument of the apostle Philippus in Hierapolis.
Middle: View of Hierapolis above Pamukkale.
Bottom: Ancient ruins of Hierapolis.

The extensive ruins of the ancient town of Hierapolis are also part of this UNESCO World Heritage Site. In around 190 BC, these hot springs were probably an important reason that Eumenes II of Pergamon founded this town here, which was later to become an important Roman spa complex.
Besides the Roman baths and Nymphaeum (a huge fountain), the theater is particularly impressive with its 15,000 seats and a stage house. South-west of Pamukkale are the ruins of Aphrodisias.

The parks, promenades and baths of Balcova provide a charming Mediterranean atmosphere, along with the lovely beaches of the Çesme Peninsula. From Izmir, there are two ways to reach the sinter terraces at Pamukkale – through the mountains via Sardes and Salihli (210 km/130 miles) or more quickly via Aydin on Road 320 (270 km/168 miles).

10 Ephesus This city of ruins near the town of Selçuk really defines the concept of ancient – the Lydians and Carians worshipped the mother goddess of Kybele here long before Greek traders and settlers arrived on the Ionian coast and built their own temple to Artemis in the tradition of the mother goddess. In approximately AD 129, Ephesus became the capital of the Roman province of Asia. At the time it had about 200,000 inhabitants. Archaeologists have been able to reconstruct more of Ephesus' temples, streets, baths and living quarters than any other site in Turkey. The city port, however, has silted up over the centuries and the sea is now several miles away.
Not far from Kusadasi is the important Ionian town of Milet.

11 Milet Like Ephesus and Priene, the trading town of Milet had to be relocated several times because its port was threatened by silt buildup. Today the former port is hardly visible among the ruins, which nearly disappear into the flood plains of the Meander River (Büyük Menderes). Only one field with a mighty theater, an agora (square) and the walls of the baths have survived.
The area that was once the largest town in ancient Greece is now home to frogs and storks. Historically, however, the cities of Thales, Anaximander and Anaximenes formed the center of philosophy and mathematics in the empire.
Road 525 first takes you to the forested region around Lake Bafa before reaching the well-preserved temple of Euromos. South of Milas you take National Road 330 to Bodrum, a pleasant drive with plenty of opportunities for excursions and breaks.

12 Bodrum This former fishing village is now a tidy white-washed town on a striking blue bay. Its center is the Castle of the Knights of St John (1413). If you want, you can hire a gulet, one of the traditional sailing vessels from these parts, to take you out to a secluded bay for a picnic.

13 Knidos/Datça The road now takes a sweeping curve along Gökova Bay, which is almost 80 km (50 miles) long, through Milas, Yatagan, Mugla and Marmaris, and out onto the 'pan handle' of the Datça Peninsula.

Only late in the 20th century did tourism strategists set their sights on the Turkish south coast, a coastline once visited only by traders, crusaders and pirates. In the early 1980s they worked out how many holidaymakers would be enticed by a trip to sunny Turkey given available flight capacity. The target area was 'within six hours' by plane to the holiday destination. This radius made Turkey available to people from Oslo, London or Kuwait. At the edge of Antalya, planners brooded over road maps near Konyaalti Beach, nowadays home to one luxury hotel after another. The final hour had struck for the small orange groves along the coast.

But with the establishment of the Olimpos and Termessos National Parks and other national parks further upcountry, some grand scenery was saved from the scramble to develop

Top: The lagoon near Ölü Deniz is now a protected area.
Bottom: The castle of the Knights of St John is the icon of Bodrum.

A national park here covers an area of roughly 1,500 sq km (580 sq mi) and protects the local forests and bays from the sadly unbridled development taking place in the area.

From the fishing and holiday village of Datça you can take a boat across to Knidos, a town founded in 400 BC at the end of the peninsula. Among the sights of this important antique trading and military post are an acropolis and the temples of Aphrodite and Demeter.

Leaving Marmaris behind we now drive through forested landscapes, over mountains and rivers, back along the coast, and then past Lake Köycegiz and some antique sites (Kaunos Rock Tombs) to the small town of Fethiye. National Road 400 starts here and follows Turkey's south coast. The rock tombs at Fethiye are well worth a climb at sunset. Ölü Deniz has attractive clear waters and an 'almost' white sand beach. It is the most famous bay south of Fethiye.

⑭ Phaselis On your way to Olimpos National Park you will be amazed by the antique Lycian town of Xanthos, miles of hotel-free beaches around Patara, the ancient towns of Kalkan and Kas, and the island world of Kekova with its submerged city. All of these are worth a visit.

A short detour from National Road 400 then takes you to Phaselis, an ancient port with a unique atmosphere. The ruins of three ports, an amphitheater, an agora and bath

houses make this town, situated at the foot of an impressive mountain range, a worthy stop.

⑮ Antalya This town has been called 'Smiling Beauty of South Turkey'. In only two decades, this lovely place has become the undisputed tourist destination of southern Turkey. From the terrific mountain backdrops, city beaches and bustling nightlife to lively bazaars and outstanding museums, Antalya has everything the tourist's heart desires. In springtime you can go skiing in the mountains and take a plunge in the sea later all in one day, or you can take trips to Termessos National Park or the ancient town of Termessos. Golfers are drawn to nearby Belek, Turkey's upmarket golf center.

⑯ Manavgat/Side Just one hour east of Antalya is the ancient port of Side, now home to idyllic sandy beaches. In Side and the provincial town of

1 Sunset over the sinter terraces of Pamukkale.

2 Kaunos: Lycian rock tombs near the holiday destination of Dalyan.

3 Beautiful beaches for bathing and snorkelling near Fethiye.

the land. Care was also taken to provide adequate water and electricity, install a waste disposal system and effectively combat forest fires. It didn't take long for investors to start arriving in droves, followed by guests – initially in their tens of thousands, and soon after in their millions.

The South-East Anatolian Project

Ever since the giant reservoirs of the 'South-East Anatolian Project' began helping to irrigate large stretches of land and providing hydroelectric power, the Euphrates River has turned the steppes of Turkey's far east into fertile agricultural lands. The 'world's largest water pipes' – as Sanliurfa locals proudly boast – are part of one of the most extensive irrigation projects on the planet.

From Atatürk Dam, water flows through 26 km (16 miles) of pipes measuring almost 8 m (26 ft) in diameter onto the Harran Plains. Some farmers in the area continue to live in

The Euphrates south of the Keban Dam near Elazig.

old-fashioned beehive-like houses. Behind the dam is the Atatürk Reservoir, the world's sixth largest and only one in a series of massive reservoirs that have submerged several rocky gorges on this formerly wild river. Places like Kahta on the way to Nemrut Dag, which used to be in the middle of a dry plain, are now located right on the lake shore.

Turkey's reserves of hydroelectric power are enormous, and the conditions for its exploitation are very favourable. There are many large rivers that flow from the mountains and highlands, cutting through the coastal mountain ranges in narrow valleys.

When it comes to the Tigris and Euphrates, however, Turkey's Arab neighbours are suspicious of the country's intentions. How much water will be left downstream if the Anatolian cotton fields are harvested three times per year? Indeed, the battle for water in this region is far from over.

Manavgat a little further inland you have a vast range of accommodation to choose from.

Using this area as a base, there are interesting trips to Köprülü Canyon National Park and the Manavgat waterfalls. Thrill-seekers can take organized rafting tours on the Köpru River.

17 Alanya This is the third holiday destination on the south coast after Side and Antalya. The impressive red Seljuk castle on a steep rock outcrop above the town has 146 towers, stunning views and offers romantic sunsets. It's definitely Alanya's biggest attraction.

The town's palm-lined alleyways and subtropical flora are wonderful for relaxing strolls, and Alanya's extensive beaches are well-suited to all kinds of sports and activities. Not long ago, one of Turkey's most beautiful stalactite caves – Dim Magarsi – was made accessible to the public.

18 Anamur From here, the distances between towns will start getting longer. Blasted out of coastal cliffs, National Road 400 is made up of a never-ending series of breathtaking sea views. Spiny, fragrant scrubland dominates the landscape while trees are rare in the area. The town and castle of Anamur, however, are strikingly different – on the

flood plain of the Dragon River you'll find lush green fields.

Greek settlers established the port of Anamurium as far back as 400 BC at this southernmost point in Asia Minor, and for a long time their trade with Cyprus flourished. The remains of a palestra (sports stadium), an odeon (theater) and baths several floors high still bear witness to these times.

The inhabitants of Anamurium were eventually driven out by Arab invasions in the 7th century. In the 12th and 13th centuries the town was resettled. Soon thereafter, Anamur Castle was built by a ruler of the Karaman principality. With its battlements and gallery, thirty-six towers and three courtyards, this is one of the most impressive medieval fortifications in all of Anatolia. Its location also makes it unforgettable – right above the coastal rocks, the waves crash against the castle walls. Later Ottoman rulers added a mosque, a bath and a well to the courtyards.

19 Silifke In 1190, Frederick I Barbarossa ('Red Beard') wanted to take this town during the third crusade, but one day in June a few miles outside of it he drowned in the Göksu River. Silifke, which was founded around 300 BC by Seleukos I Nikator, is the most unchanged of any

town on Turkey's south coast. It is set against the majestic backdrop of the Cilikian Mountains close to the sea and makes a good base for a handful of day trips and excursions to islands, caves and ancient sanctuaries. Among the town's sights are the Roman ruins of Olba and Diocaesarea (Ura/Uzuncaburç) set in some terrific scenery; the Byzantine monastery of Alahan; and also Cennet ve Cehennem ('Heaven and Hell'), two deep, round rock valleys.

20 Adana This area is dominated by the nearby Taurus Mountains, which rise to an impressive 4,000 m (13,000 ft). Between Adana and the sea are the

Çukurova Plains with their endless fields of cotton. Turkey's largest mosque was recently constructed on Adana's Seydan River. In recent decades, 3,500-year-old Adana has grown to become Turkey's fourth-largest city. Its thousands of shops, bazaars and minarets are typical of the historical Old Town while the new city is home to tree-lined boulevards, modern banks and high-rise buildings.

After passing Kahramanmaras, Adiyaman and Kahta, your route ascends the desolate mountain regions of the Taurus Range.

21 Nemrut Dağı The monumental eagles and statues sitting curiously at 2,150 m (7,050 ft)

Göreme Cave Churches

The translation of Göreme means 'thou shalt not see'. This landscape of volcanic tuff extends from Kizilirmak ('Red River') in the north to the underground cities of Kaymakli and Derinkuyu in the south. It is hardly imaginable these days that more than a thousand years ago local people carved extensive tunnels and living quarters several storeys high into the crumbling rock, often as a refuge from repeated attacks by Muslim fighters. The systems often went to depths of over 85 m (273 ft) and giant millstones were used to seal off the entrances on each individual level. The designers integrated narrow shafts to circulate air, and water was taken from large cisterns.

Top: Rock Church near Göreme.
Bottom: Tokali Kilise, 'Buckle Church'.

above sea level have become the leading icon of adventurous, exotic Turkey. The tomb monuments, which continue to baffle scientists to this day, were erected by King Antiochos I of Commagena (an Anatolian state around the birth of Christ). Today there are only ruins where cities once thrived. Two of the tomb's three original terraces have been well preserved, with fragments of statues seemingly randomly placed around the site. Their heads gaze out over the land towards the rising sun. Greek as well as Oriental gods were worshipped here.
Road 875 now takes us via Adiyaman west of the Atatürk Reservoir to Şanliurfa.

22 Şanliurfa On the vast plains of Upper Mesopotamia, a rock promontory bears the ruins of an ancient fortification. Soldiers serving under Alexander the Great founded this city and gave it the Macedonian name Edessa. Şanliurfa was an important place for early Christianity as well as for Arab scholars. Its spring was already sacred to the Greeks and to this day there are sacred Muslim carp swimming in it ('Abraham's Pond').
From Şanliurfa, National Road 360 takes us to Diyarbakir, the largest town in eastern Anatolia.

23 Diyarbakir To this day, the Old Town here is surrounded almost completely by the origi-

nal Roman-Byzantine walls of basalt rock. East of these walls is the legendary Tigris River. Palaces, mosques and madrasahs (Koranic schools), caravanserais, churches, lively bazaars and modern boulevards all give this city its many faces. You reach Lake Van in the east by taking a winding mountain road for about 250 km (160 miles).

24 Van Lake Van covers an area of 3,750 sq km (3,225 sq mi), is located at an altitude of 1,600 m (5,250 ft) and is surrounded by mountain ranges more than 4,000 m (13,000 ft) high. Roughly 3,000 years ago, the town of Van on the south-eastern shore was called Tuspa. It was the capital of the Urartu Kingdom, famed for its highly skilled metalworkers and grand fortifications. The Armenian church (915–921) on Ahtamar Island sits amid quaint olive groves and is definitely worth a visit for its stucco work and frescoes.
Your route to Sivas circles Lake Van and goes through some wonderful mountain scenery past Elazig, the Keban Reservoir to the north and Divrigi, whose large mosque is a UNESCO World Heritage Site.

25 Sivas This town's architecture is impressive, above all the intricately decorated gates of

the Gök Madrasah. The 'Mukarnas', little niches in the building, are decorated to look like stalactites. Depictions of plants and animals cover the walls of these niches, giving them a labyrinth feel. The financial means for such intricate ornamentation were provided by Sivas' fortuitous location – the main trade routes to and from Russia, Egypt, Iran and south-eastern Europe all pass through here.

26 Kayseri In ancient Rome, Kayseri was called Caesarea. At the time it was the capital of Cappadocia. The modern town sprawls out onto the plains at the foot of the Erciyes Dagi Mountain, whose mighty summit reaches 3,916 m (12,848 ft) and is always covered in snow. The Old Town of this industrial city has a lot to offer to lovers of art and architecture. The buildings from the heyday of the Seljuk Empire (11th–12th centuries) are worth seeing, along with those from later centuries. The mosque of Huand Hatun, a Seljuk princess, is well worth a

1 Panorama of Cappadocia with bizarre tuff towers near Göreme.

2 The impressive, 1,000-year-old Armenian church on Ahtamar Island in Lake Van.

Visitors to Cappadocia can explore not only the narrow tunnels of this fascinating underworld, but also the bizarre canyons, semi-arid lunar landscapes and wide, green valleys above the surface. The now abandoned rock churches of Christian hermits and monks are well worth seeing too. Imitating church buildings, the monks carved vaults and cupolas, arches and pillars out of the tuff rocks. There are around 150 of these churches, many of them with beautiful frescoes.
After severe and long-term depredation, UNESCO finally got involved. Since the 1970s it has been aiming to secure and restore what has not yet been completely lost. Among the most beautiful churches are Elmali Kilise ('Apple Church'), Carikli Kilise ('Sandal Church'), Tokali Kilise ('Buckle Church') and Yilanli Kilise ('Snake Church').

A perfect peak in the shape of a flat cone, adorned with small round stones (top right) and remnants of monumental heads of humans and eagles (left) from statues that were originally much larger than life size – that is what you see when you arrive in Nemrut Dağı after the long drive through the Taurus Range

There are two more terraces built by King Antiochos I of Commagene (d. 38 BC), one of which still contains remnants of a temple oriented toward the rising sun. The burial chamber that is presumably hidden below the cone has not yet been excavated due to fears that it might collapse.

Whirling Dervishes

If you want to see whirling dervishes dancing in their bell-shaped white gowns, go to Konya in Central Anatolia or, during the summer, to the ancient theater of Aspendos on the south coast. In 1925, the order of the dancing dervishes or 'Mevlevî' was forbidden in Atatürk's secular republic.

Whirling dance of Mevlevî dervishes.

In 1990, however, the 'Mevlana Culture and Art Foundation' was founded. Known as 'Mevlana' among his followers, hence the name of the order, the mystic and meditative teachings and ecstatic poetry of its founder, Celâleddin, may be alien to most Westerners. Yet it is hard to resist the magic of the whirling dances: '... they were spinning with such surprising speed that I could do nothing but admire them', wrote the Briton Samuel Purch in 1613.

visit with its madrasah, large baths and the mausoleum of the benefactress.

27 Nevsehir/Göreme The former is a predominantly modern town, but its Seljuk castle on the local mountain and its mosque and madrasah (Koranic school) are worth seeing. These were donated by a Grand Vizier of the Ottoman Empire in the 18th century, who was initially lauded but later decapitated.

For many visitors, however, the town is simply a good starting point for excursions to the picturesque lunar landscape of Cappadocia. The cones, obelisks and tuff pillars here are the result of erosion over millions of years as well as extensive use by local people as cave dwellings, monks' habitations and lookout posts. Cappadocia is basically one big open-air museum with a terrific setting for this unique 'natural architecture' and some good hiking.

28 Konya The crusaders marvelled when they arrived in Konya in the Middle Ages, and modern Konya keeps up the tradition of beauty with wide boulevards and more parks than any other town in central Anatolia. Lovers of historic architecture and sculpture will find many precious stone carvings on

the mosques and madrasahs of this former Seljuk capital.

The monastery of the Mevlevî dervish order (Mevlânâ Tekkesi) has been a museum since the order was outlawed by Atatürk back in 1925. For centuries this was a center of the Mevlânâ sect. The Huzuri Pir Hall ('Presence of the Saint') is always filled with crowds of visitors wanting to touch their hands and lips to the sarcophagi of Celâleddin and his closest followers. The founder of the order came from Persia, lived in Konya for almost half a century and died in 1273. There are several museums in Konya with outstanding collections. Don't miss them if you have enough time.

The road across the Anatolian highlands to Ankara 300 km (185 miles) away is well developed and easy to drive. You cross a deserted, dry plain with some impressive mountain scenery. From March to May the plains are in full bloom and the colourful carpets of wild tulips are one of the most popular themes of Turkish art.

Between Cihanbeyli and Kulu, you drive along the Tuz Gölü salt lake (1,500 sq km/580 sq mi). In the summer it shrinks to a bog with salty white edges.

29 Ankara This town was crucial in the Turkish National War

of Liberation, which saved the country from being divided up among the victorious powers of World War I. At the time, around 1920, this small town only had about 30,000 inhabitants. By 1980, there were two million and today there may be as many as four million. Only a fraction of this city actually dates back more than eighty years.

Atatürk's decision to move the capital into the Anatolian plains 600 km (375 miles) away from the Aegean coast at first seemed absurd to many people, but it was a way to make Ankara (the Roman Ankyra) the instrument and symbol of a new orientation for the country. The move was designed to bring not only the Aegean Coast but the whole of Turkey closer to Europe. The ploy seems to have worked, at least in this young metropolis. The German architect Hermann Jansen was responsible for much of the town planning in modern Ankara. For an encounter with the 9,000 years of Anatolian history, be sure to visit the Museum of Anatolian Civilization.

Allow at least two days for an excursion to Hattusas (Turkish: Bogazkale), the almost 4,000-year-old capital of the Hethitan kingdom, which has a number of palaces and temples.

Heading north, a winding road takes us into the Köroglu Daglari

and Ilgaz Daglari forests. The route to the Black Sea coast then ends among some gentle, hilly scenery in Kastamonu on the northern slopes of the Pontic Mountains.

30 Kastamonu Numerous terraces and the well-proportioned Ottoman mosques dating from the 15th and 16th centuries are among the town's noteworthy sights. Sultan Suleyman the Magnificent's chef and storehouse overseer was the architect of Yakub Aga Külliyesi, a stately mosque with a central dome and neighbouring madrasah.

Even more impressive than its mosques, however, are Kastamonu's two-and three-storey timber-framed houses, or 'Konaks'. The ground floors were made of stone, with bays and mostly flat roofs and they give the city an attractive provincial feel. The small river in the valley terminates in the Kizilirmak River a little to the east, which in turn flows into the Black Sea.

31 Safranbolu Since its Old Town was designated a UNESCO World Heritage Site in 1994, this town has been more famous than Kastamonu, its neighbour to the east. The 'Saffron City' had its heyday in the 18th century, at a time when it was the trade hub for this much sought-

2

3

Atatürk

After the disaster of World War I, Mustafa Kemal Pasha became the saviour of Turkey. His people called him Atatürk, 'Father of the Turks'. In other parts of the world very little is known about this man, who instilled new confidence into a downtrodden, under-developed country and also opened the door for Turkey's social and political shift towards the 'West'.

He introduced Western legal principles and constitutional systems, separated church and state, created new schools, supported women's rights and gave up the previously used Arabic letters in favour of Latin script.

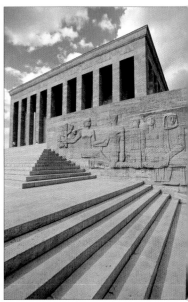

An eternal remembrance of modern Turkey's founding father: the Atatürk Mausoleum.

Born in 1881 in Saloniki, Mustafa Kemal Pasha eventually decided to pursue a career in the military. In 1915, when the Ottoman Empire was pushed into World War I by Germany, the Allies under British command landed at the Dardanelles in an attempt to take Istanbul. With large numbers of casualties on both sides, Mustafa Kemal Pasha forced the attackers to retreat.

Four years later, when the victorious powers divided the Ottoman Empire among themselves, Kemal Pasha founded a government in Ankara and organized the resistance. Skilful in military and diplomatic matters, he abolished both the Sultanate and the Caliphate. The modern Republic of Turkey was established in 1923.

monuments have been well preserved in park-like settings amid the urban surroundings. The former inhabitants of Prusa ad Olympum, its ancient predecessor, had long ago learned to appreciate the local hot springs. The town received its nickname from Mount Uludag, the 'Mystical Olympus'. In 1326, Bursa became the capital of the Ottoman Empire.

Bursa is now a large city, but in winter Mount Uludag provides respite with ski resorts and a gondola that takes you to the top. Some pastel-coloured houses adorn the Old Town, and there are some babbling fountains beneath green cypresses. Due to its elevation the climate is pleasant even in summer, making Bursa a nice final stop on your way back to Istanbul.

Taking National Roads 575 and 130 you will pass through Gemlk. From Kocaeli (Highway 04), it is only 240 km (150 miles) back to Istanbul.

1 The Mevlânâ Monastery in Konya has been the destination of pious pilgrims for centuries.

2 Traditional houses on the slopes of Safranbolu.

3 The Kocatepe Mosque in Ankara was consecrated in 1987.

after yellow plant dye that was used as a spice, medicine and, above all, dye for various foodstuffs. The 'Konak' houses here have been lovingly maintained and restored; most of them are built with two storeys around a central courtyard and brick roofs. The Old Town (Carsi) is easy to explore on foot, and a little further out on a hill in Baglar are the summer residences of some wealthier families. In the Carsi there are a few worthwhile

museums as well as crafts workshops, a lively bazaar, typical tearooms and hotels – almost all of them located in historic buildings.

Taking National Road 755 south from Safranbolu you'll arrive at National Road 100 (E80) at Eskipazar after about 60 km (37 miles). When you get to Gerede, the road becomes Highway 04. At Sakarya, take National Road 650 south towards Bözüyük. After roughly 120 km

(75 miles) you follow National Road 200 (E90) north-west, which takes you to Bursa (another 120 km/75 miles), your last stop on the tour before we head back to Istanbul.

32 Bursa Its location on the slopes of Mount Uludag combined with the magnificent architecture of its palaces, mosques and mausoleums all make Bursa one of the most beautiful towns of the former sultanate. The city's

An impregnable rock face – Fort Meherangarh in Jodhpur on the edge of

Route 28

India

Rajasthan and the 'Golden Triangle'

Rajasthan means 'Land of the Kings', yet many villages in this region of India live in extreme poverty. Exploring the land of the Rajputs, you very quickly realize one irony about this 'desert state' – there is a lot more green than you might think. And where else does India dazzle with such vivid colours and magnificent palaces as in Rajasthan?

Due to Rajasthan's size and diversity, it can be difficult to decide what to do first after arriving in Delhi. Despite being the capital of the state, the glorious Maharaja city of Jaipur is not always the first stop. Instead, many visitors are initially, and naturally, drawn to the Mughal city of Agra in the state of Uttar Pradesh, which makes up the other corner of India's 'Golden Triangle' (Delhi-Agra-Jaipur). After all, it is the home of the immediately recognizable Taj Mahal, the white marble mausoleum built by Mughal Emperor Shah Jahan for his

favourite wife Mumtaz Mahal. The Islamic building has ironically become the most visible icon of India despite Hinduism being the dominant religious and ethnic identity factor in this culturally multifarious country. About eighty-two percent of the people living in India are Hindus – the rest are a mix of Muslims, Christians, Sikhs, Buddhists and Jains.

Continuing westwards to Jaipur, now the capital of the whole of Rajasthan and barely four hours away from Delhi on the new motorway, you pass through

Vivid colours and ornaments – that's Rajasthan!

Mathura, the legendary birthplace of the god Krishna and a holy pilgrimage destination for Hindus. Again, though, one is struck by the number of large mosques here. You will see this type of religious coexistence almost everywhere in Rajasthan, not just in the so-called 'Golden Triangle'. The mighty walls of the Maharaja's fort bear witness to the centuries of power struggles between the Rajput dynasties and the Mughal emperors.

Part of the legacy of the Rajputs are their former hunting grounds, which are now some of India's most beautiful national parks and reserves. East of the long Aravalli Range near Bharatpur, for example, are three fabulous ones – Keoladeo Ghana, Sariska and Ranthambore. In the latter two it is possible to witness tigers in the wild, especially in the 400-sq-km (154-sq-mi) Ranthambore National Park.

The Taj Mahal: a monumental marble grave built by Shah Jahan on the Yamuna River in Agra not far from the 'Red Fort'. The mausoleum took twenty-two years to complete and houses the sarcophagus of the Mughal emperor's favourite wife, Mumtaz Mahal, who died giving birth to their fourteenth child in 1631. His own sarcophagus followed in 1666.

the Thar Desert, residence of the Maharajas of Marwar.

West of the Aravalli is the semi-arid Thar Desert, which extends far into Pakistan. Former caravan routes through the Thar have become tourist tracks in recent decades. The camel safaris to the sand dunes around Jaisalmer and Bikaner are a whole new riding experience and visits to desert villages, carpet weavers and potters are interesting. The indigenous population of this region, the Bishnoi, have been carefully cultivating native flora and fauna for 600 years.

Rajasthan is not all rustic – the engineering feat of the century, the Indira Ghandi Canal, brings water from the Himalayas and the Punjab into the Thar. Stony desert soil becomes farmland and the desert shrinks. Modernity has also changed transportation – instead of running on a narrow gauge, trains are now rolling into the desert on standard Indian gauge.

Looking for remnants of the magic of 'a thousand and one nights'? You'll find it in more than a few places – Rajasthan tempts visitors with bazaars, temples and palaces from Alwar to Jaipur, from Udaipur to Jodhpur, from Bikaner into the Shekhawati land of 'painted cities'. Rajasthan also provided the model for Heritage Hotels, which are now all over India but nowhere as prevalent as in Rajasthan. Heritage Hotels are opulent palaces, glamorous merchants' houses (havelis) or relaxing country houses that have been turned into hotels by their owners. In some of them, royal personages stay under the same roof as normal hotel guests. From a comfortable bed to extreme luxury, every taste is catered for at Heritage Hotels – again a piece of 'a thousand and one nights' in Rajasthan.

A camel safari is almost a must – campfires under the starry sky included.

Jaipur's most photographed sight is the five-storey "Palace of the Winds" – Hawa Mahal – from the late 18th century, part of the giant City Palace built for the women of the court. Because they were seldom allowed to leave the palace, the countless oriels on the east side of the palace allowed the women to watch the

activities and resplendent processions in the street below without being seen, especially on festival days. The ornate stone lattice windows provide good air circulation and visitors can get a good view of the Old Town from the upper floors.

Keoladeo Ghana National Park

About 100 years ago, Maharajas irrigated the bushland south of Bharatpur using dams and canals in order to attract birds, which were subsequently shot in their thousands by Anglo-Indian hunting parties.

A family of storks in the Keoladeo Ghana National Park.

In 1983 the area was declared a national park covering 29 sq km (18 sq mi). It is home to more than 370 bird species, among them the Siberian Crane. The best time to visit the park is during the months of October to March.

5 Alwar Set into the rocky Aravalli Mountains, Alwar is an old trading center with a royal palace and relatively few foreign visitors. Agra, Jaipur and the nearby national parks provide more of a draw for tourists than the ancient royal residence of Alwar, a town that received mention in India's great Mahabharata Epic from the 2nd century BC. All of this makes the city and the Rajput palace and gardens even more authentic.

Oddly, many of the palace's rooms serve the banal purpose of storing government files, which are stacked to the ceiling in places. Only the fifth floor has a museum with some of the hunting trophies, silver tables, meter-long scrolls and works of the Bundi school of painting.

6 Sariska National Park This reserve covers an area of about 800 sq km (308 sq mi) roughly 37 km (23 miles) south of Alwar, and was made a national park in 1979 with a focus on conserving the tiger. There is plenty of space for the tigers to live peacefully in the jungle here – they are actually rather afraid of people.

Failing a tiger sighting, you may catch a glimpse of beautifully spotted Chital deer, Chowsingha antelope, hyenas, a pack of wild boar or very likely a pack of rhesus monkeys.

There are also Mughal forts and temples both within and around the park. Take Highway 8 via Shahpura 100 km (62 miles) to Jaipur where you will be greeted first by magnificent Fort Amber.

7 Jaipur This old town, also known as the 'Pink City' for the colour of its facades, was planned on a nine-part rectangular grid in 1727 – very rational and geometric town planning. At the same time, the nine old-town quarters of Jaipur symbolize the Brahmin Hindu cosmos. The open-air observatory Jantar Mantar at the palace also fits in

well with this cosmic association and is one of the main attractions here. You can even walk on some of its 'instruments', which are made of brick.

Jaipur, which is the western point of the 'Golden Triangle' (Delhi-Agra-Jaipur), is home to over two million people and is thus the only town with over a million inhabitants in Rajasthan. To this day the city is full of palaces.

The first Maharaja of Rajasthan to convert Rambagh, his summer palace, into a hotel was Sawai Man Singh II in 1957. Since then his aristocratic brethren all over

India seem to have adopted the 'Palace and Heritage Tourism' concept.

Jaipur is also a center for jewellery, jewels, precious inlaid marble and all sorts of other arts and crafts.

1 A symbol of India – tigers in the Sariska National Park.

2 The magic of an old town on the edge of the mountains – the 19th-century city palace of Alwar sits above the temple pond.

In Jaipur's mountainous surroundings there are numerous palaces, temples, gardens and forts to entice visitors, like here in the Galta valley. Hundreds of pilgrims worship the Sun god in the Surya Temple above a natural swimming pool in the rock (top) and below is the recently renovated Gaitor Palace.

The Jains

Much like the Hindus, the faith of the Jains theoretically leads them through a series of reincarnations to 'Moksha', a sort of liberation from earthly existence. The Jains worship the 'Tirthankaras', the twenty-four

Head of Buddha in the Jain temple in Ranakpur.

forerunners, as their teachers, the last of which was Mahavira who lived in the 6th century BC.
Apart from 'Ahimsa' (peacefulness), Jains also preach 'Asteya' (not taking from others), 'Brahmacharya' (moderation as far as food, drink and sexuality are concerned) and 'Aparigraha' (inner distance from worldly possessions).

8 Ajmer A defiant fortress built upon a stark rocky plateau overlooking a walled city, the model for many cities in this area where for centuries it was necessary to defend against the repeated attacks of ambitious conquerors. At Fort Taragarh in Ajmer, there is not much left of the often 4-m-thick (13-ft) walls built by a Hindu ruler some 900 years ago.
But Ajmer presents itself as a lively, pulsating city in many respects. It is home to many schools and universities and a pilgrimage destination for pious Muslims and Jains. In fact, about a quarter of the more than 400,000 inhabitants are Jains. Following the example of British public schools, the still highly regarded Mayo College in Ajmer was founded in 1873 for the sons of the Rajputs.
The Dargah Sharif Mosque Center is even older and was developed around the tomb of Khwaja Moinuddin Chisti, who was a friend of the poor. In memory of his works, two enormous iron vats of food are still provided for the needy at the entrance to the holy district.

Even Emperor Akbar made a pilgrimage to Ajmer.
A more recent building that is worth a visit is the Nasiyan Temple from 1864, built by the Jains. A two-storey hall fantastically depicts the heavenly cosmos of the Jains, including golden temples and the airships of the gods. About 11 km (7 miles) from Ajmer you'll come to Pushkar.

9 Pushkar The name Pushkar means 'lotus blossom'. But in this case we are not talking about just any lotus blossom. It is the one that Brahma allegedly dropped to the floor to create Pushkar Lake. That is why the little town of Pushkar with its 15,000 inhabitants is one of the holiest sites in India.
Half surrounded by mountains, this little town with tidy white houses and the fresh green fauna of a nearby oasis possesses a majestic beauty. Unfortunately, it has been so overrun by tourism in the last few years that Pushkar's priests, beggars and numerous self-appointed Sadhus ('holy men') have developed a business sense to accompany their piety.

They constantly invite travellers to the 'Puja', the washing ceremony, which takes place at the fifty-two ghats, the steps down to the lake. Then without delay they demand payment with rupees or, even better, dollars. The 'Little Varansi' at Pushkar Lake is therefore best visited in

the morning – the temples open early. The view from the hill with the Savitri Temple, dedicated to Brahma's wife, is especially beautiful. It can be reached after a good half-hour hike.
From Pushkar you'll need a day of driving through winding mountain landscapes to get to

Ranakpur. On the way, you'll be tempted to take a detour to one of the biggest forts in Rajasthan – the 15th-century Fort Kumbhalgarh. The 36-km (22-mile) wall around the perimeter of this fort is said to be second only to the Great Wall of China in length and protects a total of 360 temples – 300 Jains and the rest Buddhist. You get a splendid view of the Aravalli Mountains from atop the wall.

⑩ Ranakpur Completely different from Pushkar, this holy temple town of the Jains typically allows you to enjoy its treasures in peace and quiet. It is set back from any larger neighbours in a forested valley with family farms, two reservoirs and a handful of hotels.

One of these is the Maharani Bagh Orchard Retreat, a former fruit garden and picknicking spot of the Maharaja of Jodhpur. It is just an hour's walk from the Jain temples and the pilgrim hostels. Before climbing the steps to the temples you will be required to remove anything you have that is made of leather or other animal products. The four temples here date from the 15th and 16th centuries. Three of them are dedicated to the 'forerunners' Adinath, Parsvanatha and Neminath, and the fourth is dedicated to the Sun god Surya. Take a look at the unique stonework on the hundreds of columns and domed prayer halls. Flowers are placed before the pictures of Jain saints and music echoes through the rooms.

It is now a good 80 km (50 miles) to Udaipur, the biggest city in the south of Rajasthan.

⑪ Udaipur Also known as the 'Queen of the Lakes', Udaipur is considered by many to be the most beautiful city in Rajasthan. Today it has 400,000 inhabitants, and from its founding in the year 1568 it was constantly under the rule of the Sisodia Maharanas until Indian independence in 1947.

The title Maharana ('Great King') is equivalent to Maharajah. In the old realm of Mewar, the Sisodias took the top position in the royal hierarchy of India, and their influence is still felt today. Nearly 500 years ago they were responsible for many of the reservoirs and artificial lakes that were built in the area. In the midst of the most beautiful of these, Lake Pichola, summer palaces were built on two islands opposite the mighty towering complex of the city palace. The bigger of the two island palaces became world famous as the Lake Palace Hotel. The list of celebrated guests is endless. The nightly spectacle of the lake bathed in lights is best enjoyed from one of the roof terrace restaurants in the old town.

Parks like the 'Garden of the Ladies of Honour' (Saheliyon ki Bari) contribute not only to the charm of Udaipur when the lotus ponds and roses are in bloom, but also reveal the artistic sense and craftsmanship present here. Behind the city palace and in the small side streets are countless studios and shops where you can witness hundreds of indigenous artists and craftsmen that still specialize in the miniature paintings of the old academies and the skilled carpet weaving of the region.

⑫ Chittaurgarh Seven mighty gates once secured the ascent to the plateau over the Berach River 100 km (60 miles) to the east of Udaipur. On the plain below is a city of 75,000 inhabitants founded in the 8th century and once the capital of Mewar.

1 In 1567 Maharana Udai Singh ordered the creation of Lake Pichola when he declared Udaipur the capital of Merwar. The Lake Palace Hotel is on an island in the lake.

2 Pushkar: India's holiest of lakes is supposed to have developed from Brahma's lotus blossom.

The Thar Desert

The only great desert on the subcontinent stretches from the foothills of the Aravalli Mountains to the Indian-Pakistani border to the Indu Valley, and occupies nearly half of Rajasthan, an area of 250,000 sq km (155,000 sq mi). But the Thar Desert is not like the Sahara desert. Sand dunes without vegetation are only found in small areas to the west and south of Jaisalmer. Geologists consider it a semi-arid region.

The journey from Jodhpur to Jaisalmer and from Jaisalmer to Bikaner takes hours. You'll see sand swirling in the hot wind, green, withered, thorny acacia bushes on the horizon, and maybe a tree, but only few villages.

But the Thar is not devoid of human life. Women by the side of the road balance all manner of supplies on their heads as they walk along the road – water jugs, or sand and stones for a building site. And they wear brightly coloured dresses threaded with silver.

Camel caravan in the Thar Desert.

Adolescents herd their goats and men drive colourfully painted trucks over the sandy road or journey on camels with turbans of yellow or red.

If you take the time for a detour from Highway 15, ideally with a guide, you'll come to a few farms and villages in the middle of the stony landscape where the stone or mud buildings are surrounded by thorny bushes to protect the sheep and goats from dogs and hyenas.

West of the Thar the landscape of the desert changes to green fields thanks to the Indira Ghandi Canal. Though it is not without its environmentally damaging effects, this 'engineering feat of the century' in India pumps water from the Punjab into Rajasthan and gives many farmers a chance to cultivate crops in an otherwise wasteland area.

The steep walls of the rocky plateau rise to 150 m (492 ft), but despite its formidable gates and walls it was still conquered three times by Mughal armies. Each of these invasions culminated in a 'Jauhar' by the women and children – the heroic ritual of collective suicide by throwing themselves onto burning pyres. The men then committed 'Saka': battling to their last breath.

Dozens of sprawling palace and temple ruins, a narrow 15th-century 'victory' tower, which you can climb, and some pavilions and ponds are all that is left of the glory and decline of this medieval residence.

Back in Udaipur the journey continues via Som straight through the Aravalli Mountains to the north-west in the direction of Abu Road. When the heat begins to hit the plains in April, the hotels in Rajasthan's 'hill station' Mount Abu begin to fill up. Close to the border to Gujarat, Abu Road winds its way to 1,200 m (3,937 ft) where you can live comfortably in this mountain village (20,000 inhabitants) even in the summer.

⑬ Mount Abu The hilly forest and hiking areas, Nakki Lake, the splendid view from 'Sunset Point' and a protected wildlife area for leopards, bears and red deer, all quite close to the center of town, make Mount Abu an enjoyable diversion for tourists, particularly if you've come in hotter months. The Dilwara temples outside of Mount Abu are well-known among art lovers.

On a par with the Jain temples of Ranakpur, the skilful stone carvings and sculpture in the five main temples here (11th–18th centuries) are even considered by some to be the best Jain work ever done.

To the left and right of Abu Road heading towards Jodhpur there are a number of Rajput residences, small country palaces with gardens usually near a village, and some former 'havelis' in their modern guise as 'Heritage Hotels'. Among the 'havelis' are the Ghanerao Royal Castle, Karni Kot Sodawas, Bera, Bhenswara, Sardasamand, Fort Chanwar Luni and Rohet Garh.

⑭ Jodhpur In stark contrast to the rural landscape along the road, Jodhpur is Rajasthan's second-largest city and has more than 800,000 inhabitants. It is also the south-eastern point in the great 'Desert Triangle'.

Once you are in town, the streets of Jodhpur are dominated by hectic traffic and lively trade in the bazaar. But high above it all stands the mighty Meherangarh Fort, built by the Rathore rulers, more than 120 m (393 ft) above

the Old Town alleys in the north-west of the city. The fort's palaces are known for their superb filigree stone patterns and spacious courtyards.

Across the city on Chittar Hill is the magnificent Umaid Bhawan Palace, the last of the monumental residences built by the Rajput (1929–43). Museums, markets, arts and crafts and antiques await you here.

⑮ Jaisalmer For many people, the most lasting impression of their desert travels in Rajasthan is the moment the honey-gold walls of Jaisalmer appear above the sandy plains. Since the 12th century the ninety-nine bastions of these fortifications have dominated the hills of the city of Jaisalmer.

Even until far into the 19th century, the caravans of the spice

and silk traders travelled in and out of the city. Ironically, it was the faraway Suez Canal that made the difference. By boosting sea trade with Europe it more or less put an end to the overland business. As a result, Jaisalmer's wealthy traders and their fairy-tale mansions with opulent facades, bay windows and balconies became a thing of the past virtually overnight.

After the tumultuous division of India and Pakistan in 1947, Jaisalmer's strategic location on the western border gave it renewed significance and India soon invested in streets and railways. Yet the conversion from the narrow-gauge railways to the Indian wide-gauge system is actually a recent development, and one that greatly benefited tourism. Since the 1990s the

industry has grown dramatically, and the population of Jaisalmer has doubled to 40,000 in the last decade. Jaisalmer is now the center of desert tourism in India and a main gathering point for camel drivers and thousands of souvenir sellers.

The adventure is not all lost, however, on a trip to Desert National Park west of the city, which includes oases and deserted medieval cities like Kuldhara and Kabha. The Akal Wood Fossil Park, located 17 km (11 miles) south of Jaisalmer on the road to Barmer, has fascinating fossilized tree trunks 180 million years old.

In just two hours from here you can also reach Pokaran, a small desert town with only 20,000 inhabitants.

16 Pokaran The name of Pokaran went through the international press in 1998 when the Indian government demonstrated its status as a nuclear power by carrying out several test detonations near the neighbouring town of Khetolai. But what is also worth seeing in Pokaran is the fort built in the 14th century, whose imposing walls are an example of a private restoration initiative.

The family of the Thakur Rajputs has been living in this fort for thirteen generations and has

installed not only a Heritage Hotel but also a small museum, which specializes in archaeology and folklore. When the owner can spare the time, he willingly explains to his guests how the neglected rooms of the palace are being restored to former glory.

17 Gajner Wildlife Sanctuary This well-preserved old palace on the lake is surrounded by old trees and almost seems haunted. The grounds, which are only 30 km (18 miles) west of the large city of Bikaner, were once used by their owner as hunting territory until India's conservationists and biologists pressed for the creation of a nature reserve under the auspices of 'Project Tiger'.

The primary objective of the reserve was obviously to protect and increase the number of species living here. The secondary objective was to increase tourism in the area. The Gajner Wildlife Sanctuary is now a paradise for birds and wild animals, and the Gajner Palace itself was turned into a Heritage Hotel.

1 The Meherangarh Fort towers high above Jodhpur.

2 The Indira Ghandi Canal flows into the Gadi Sagar, the temple lake of Jaisalmer.

Desert fortresses

There is hardly a city in the Thar Desert that doesn't have an accompanying fort. Peaceful times were rare in this wild region all the way up until the 19th century, and protective walls were a necessity. Some fans of Rajasthan travel exclusively from fort to

Jaisalmer's upper city has ninety-nine mighty bastions.

fort, inspecting the wooden gates crowned by iron spikes and reinforced with iron bands, climbing steep steps and marvelling at the collections of weapons and opulent chambers.

Khimsar, one of the most romantic forts, lies by the side of a small road between Jodhpur and Nagaur south of Bikaner. It was restored by its owners and not only has an attractive dining room and a refreshing pool, but also a cosy private cinema.

Shekhawati

As long as their caravans crossed the country, the merchants in Shekhawati in the north-east of Rajasthan were rich. Well, they are still wealthy but have long since moved their houses

Typically painted facade in the Shekhawati region.

and businesses to Kolkata or Mumbai. The 'havelis', their opulently decorated town houses, are mostly deserted now. But it is with amazement that you behold the colourful facades of these mansions, which depict stories of gods, dancers, railways and the first motor cars, all with a seemingly naive delight.

The rooms are decorated with antiques and enjoy a view of the bird-lake activities including boating, golf, cycling and hiking. However, during longer stretches of drought or a non-existent monsoon, there is nothing to be done – the lake dries out and the birds move on.

18 Bikaner The main roads to Bikaner, an old city of the Maharajas with a current population of about 500,000, have improved over the years as more and more palaces have recently converted to hotels. But the contrast between the present and the past, between bazaar alleys and shanty towns is more stark than in Jaipur or Udaipur.

The forward-planning Maharaja Dungar Singh had an electricity network installed comparatively early, in 1886. His successor then had schools, hospitals and canals built. A mighty ring of walls surrounds Junagarh Fort, which was built towards the end of the 16th century. Its mirrored cabinets, delicately decorated chambers and its opulent coronation hall make it one of the high-

lights of Indian palatial architecture in the region.

Away from the city on a visit to India's only state camel-breeding farm you get to see first-hand why 750,000 of the five million camels worldwide live right here in Rajasthan.

A slightly unusual facet of Hindu culture presents itself to visitors about 30 km (18 miles) south in Deshnok at the Karni Mata Mandir, a temple with silver doors and marble reliefs. Rats are worshipped here as holy animals and run around uninhibited. According to legend, they are the souls of dead poets and singers.

19 Mandawa There are no big cities in the Shekhawati region east of Bikaner and north of Jaipur. Mandawa, founded in 1790 and now the tourist center of the area, is accordingly modest in size. Comfortable accommodation is limited here. The best option is the former Rajput palaces where the owner often lives in a separate wing. The Roop Niwa Palace in Nawalgarh is an option, or try the 18th-century Castle Mandawa.

Desert sands blow around the walls of the former fort of Mandawa (begun in 1760), behind which the Rajput Rangir Singh continues to restore the decaying splendour of palace halls and boudoirs to provide space for more visitors. No room here is the same as another. Exploring Mandawa you can find several large 'havelis' (Gulab Rai and Saraf, for example), a deep well with steps leading down to it, or a few antiques and arts and craft shops.

Mandawa is a convenient starting point for excursions into the partly green, partly desert landscape around the city and to a dozen other typical Shekhawati villages. The neighbouring village of Nawalgarh about 25 km (15 miles) away has more 'havelis' than any other town in the Shekhawati region. Several open their doors to visitors. The Poddar Haveli Museum from the 1920s has around 750 images on its facade, not counting the painted passages in the inner courtyard, as well as collections of musical instruments and historical photographs.

The drive to our last destination, Neemrana, takes around six hours (225 km/140 miles). Take the turn-off about 15 km (9 miles) north of Behror on Highway 8 between Jaipur and Delhi.

20 Neemrana For those who enjoy castles and exotic living, Neemrana is a very desirable destination. Some years ago a Frenchman and an Indian turned medieval Fort Neemrana above the village into a Heritage Hotel. With a sure sense of style and every detail of attention to the needs of their guests, they created an array of terraces, balconies, rooms and suites that spoil you without overdoing the decadence.

From the city of Neemrana it is another 120 km (74 miles) via the Delhi-Jaipur Highway back to the starting point, Delhi.

1 The 'Pushkar Mela' is not the only big camel market in Rajasthan. Nagaur, north of Jodhpur, is also famed for its own gathering, which takes place once a year in January or February.

Jaisalmer With ninety-nine bastions, Jaisalmer towers 80 m (263 ft) above the Thar Desert. It was the residence of the Bhati Rajputs, a contested headquarters for caravan trade.

Fort Amber One of India's most beautiful, the Amber Palace (17th/18th century) in the fort of the same name is adorned with mirrors, marble halls, imposing gates and grand views of the stark mountains outside. The Mata Temple has a black marble depiction of Kali.

Delhi Mughal Emperor Shah Jahan had the Red Fort (Lal Quila) built between 1639 and 1648. The most beautiful of its buildings is the reception hall Diwan-I-Khas. Also worth seeing in Delhi are the Jama Masjid Mosque, the tomb of Mughal Emperor Humayun, the Lodi graves and the Qutb Minar minaret.

Jodhpur In front of the steep rock of Meherangarh Fort sits the 'Jhaswant Thada', a white marble palace built in memory of Maharaja Jhaswant Singh II to honour his progressive policies.

Fatehpur Sikri This city was founded by Akbar the Great in 1569 at the zenith of Mughal power in India. The Jama Masjid (Friday Mosque) is the center of the city's holy district.

Desert National Park This national park in the Thar Desert is a superb example of the ecosystems here and the rich variety of species (Dorkas gazelles, desert lynx, giant Indian bustards).

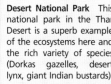

Sariska National Park Formerly the hunting ground of the Maharaja of Alwar, this region is alive with tigers and dense forest. Located in the Aravalli Range, it became a national park in 1979. The Maharaja's summer palace near the grounds is now an hotel.

Agra The Red Fort (1565–73), built as a fortification with deep and broad trenches, soon became an example of imperial luxury and prestigious architecture. It is accentuated with large courtyards, palaces, and opulent columned halls like the triple-nave marble hall of Diwan-I-Am shown here.

Ranakpur The 15th/16th-century temples built by the Jains contain unique halls with superb stone-carvings and domes considered among the most important masterpieces in all of India. They belong to a well-educated subculture in India.

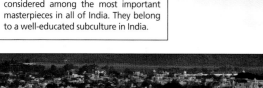

Udaipur The city palace of the Maharanas of Mewar, the oldest dynasty in Rajasthan, has been continuously expanded since it was built in the 16th century. It is still inhabited by the family.

Jaipur The 'Palace of the Winds' was built with stone lattice windows to allow the ladies of the court to see without being seen.

Gwalior Fort The enormous walls of this mighty fortress rise high above the town. It contains the Man Singh Palace, built around 1500, and four other palaces.

Taj Mahal Tomb and monument of a great love: the great Mughal Emperor Shah Jahan had this mausoleum built in Agra for his wife Mumtaz Mahal, who died giving birth to their 14th child.

Map labels: Saharanpur, Meerut, Moradabad, Hapur, Ludhiana, Hisar, DELHI, Ghaziabad, New Delhi, Gurgaon, Faridabad, Palwal, Neemrana Fort Palace, Dharuhera, Hodal, Hathras, Bareilly, Kanpur, Ganganagar, Churu, Shekhawati, Behror, Alwar, Nagar, Dig, Mathura, AGRA, Taj Mahal, Sri Dungargarh, Ratangarh, Mandawa, Kot Putli, Bharatpur, Fatehpur, Nawalgarh, Kanwat, Tal Chhapar Wildlife Sanctuary, Gajner Wildlife Sanctuary, Bikaner, Sikar, Shahpura, Sariska National Park, Rajakhera, Sujangarh, Keoladeo Ghana N.P., Mahwa, Fatehpur Sikri, Deshnok, Kanwat, Jaigarh Fort, Dholpur, Nokhra, Nagaur, Amber Fort, Dausa, Morena, Sambhar Salt Lake, Gwalior, Bap, Phalodi, Khimsar, JAIPUR, Dabra, Bhikamkor, Kishangarh, Dudu, Indore, Sonagiri, Jaisalmer, Desert National Park, Pokaran, Pushkar, Ajmer, Bhopal, Akal Wood Fossils Park, Jodhpur, Beawar, Bandanwara, Shergarh, Shiv, Dhawa Doli Wildlife Sanctuary, Rohat, Sojat, Bhim, Bhilwara, Balotra, Pali, Kumbhalghar, Deogarh, Bhopal, Radhanpur, Sanderao, Rajsamand, Chittaurgarh (Chittor), Sadri, Ranakpur, Nathdwara, Nimbahera, Sirohi, Mangarwar, Mount Abu Wildl. Sanc., Mt.Abu 1722, Udaipur, Mount Abu, Abu Road, Salumbar, Jaisamand Sanctuary, Som, Radhanpur, Kherwara, Ahmadabad

The stupa in Boudhanath is 40 m (131 ft) high, the tallest in all of Nepal.

Nepal and Tibet

On the Road of Friendship across the Roof of the World

The path over the main crescent of the Himalayas easily makes it into our list of dream routes. After all, you cross part of the highest mountain range in the world, passing turquoise-coloured lakes and endless high steppe regions that are still traversed by nomads with yak, goat and sheep herds. Add monasteries perched on impossible bluffs and you've got an unforgettable journey. Our route begins in Kathmandu, meanders through central Nepal and ends in Lhasa on the Kodari Highway.

Foreigners have only been allowed to visit the previously sealed-off country of Nepal since 1950. Much has changed culturally since then, but fortunately the fascination that the country inspires has not. About a third of the country is taken up by the Himalayas, the highest point of which lies on the border to Tibet – Mount Everest, at 8,850 m (29,037 ft).

Between the protective Mahabharat Range in the south and the mighty main crest of the Himalayas in the north lies the valley of Kathmandu, which contains the three ancient and royal cities of Kathmandu, Patan and Bhaktapur.

Even in the age of the automobile the spirit of times past is palpable in the capital, and Kathmandu continues to impress visitors with its royal palace and the hundreds of temples, statues and beautiful wood-carvings on the facades and monuments. The second of the ancient royal cities, Patan, lies on the opposite shore of the Bagmati. Once again, a former royal

Buddha statue Amithaba/Tashilhunpo Monastery.

palace and over fifty temples remind us of Nepal's glorious past. South-east of Kathmandu lies Bhaktapur, where the alleys and streets are dominated by Newari wood-carvings.

Before you start off from Bhaktapur towards Lhasa, it is worth undertaking a journey to Pokhara in the north-west, on the shore of the Phewasees at the bottom of the Annapurna Massif. Via Lumbini, the birthplace of Buddha, and Butwal the round trip leads you to Bharatpur, the gate to the Royal Chitwan National Park, and eventually back to Bhaktapur.

The Kodari Highway then brings you over the main ridge of the Himalayas into Tibet. Along this panoramic route you are constantly under the spell of 7,000 to 8,000-m-high (22,967 to 26,248-ft) mountains. In Tingri, for example, you finally experience Everest as an impressive single

'Om mani padme hum' – Tibetan monks gather for communal prayer in the Sakya monastery near Lhaze.

Sagarmatha National Park with its grandiose mountain landscape is listed in the UNESCO World Heritage register.

entity. The journey here can become arduous at times, as the highway leads over passes where the air is rather thin – over 5,000 m (16,405 ft) above sealevel on the Lalung-La Pass, for instance.

Tibet, 'The Land of Snow', has been closely linked to China since the 13th century. The current Tibet Autonomous Region (TAR) of China has an extremely low population density – roughly 2.5 million Tibetans, and 350,000 Chinese live on 1.2 million sq km (463,000 sq mil) of land. The Chinese dominate the economy, politics and government. Since the 9th century, Tibetans have followed Lamaism, a Tibetan variant of Buddhism whose religious and political head is the Dalai Lama.

The route through Gutsuo, Tingri, Lhaze, Yigaze, Gyangze and Nagarze into the city of Lhasa, which was once forbidden to foreigners, is lined by Lamaist monasteries –

at least, the ones that weren't destroyed by the Chinese cultural revolution. Sakya is one of the oldest monasteries in Tibet and the 15th-century Buddhist monastery of Tashilhunpo has also been preserved – the latter contains a 26-m-high (85-ft) bronze Buddha. It is unlikely that anybody wouldn't be fascinated by the Kubum monastery in Gyangze, a monumental complex of temples with pagodas, stupas and palaces.

Lhasa, the 'Place of the Gods', lies at an elevation of 3,700 m (12,140 ft) and was chosen by Songsten Ganpo (620–49), the first Tibetan king, as his royal residence. Where today the famous red and white Potala Palace looks down on the city, Ganpo had built a fortification that later became Tibet's theocratic center of power, including all pictorial works and national treasures – the icon of Tibetan religiosity.

Prayer flags on the Road of Friendship near Xigaze.

The 40-m-high (130-ft) *stupa* in Bodnath is the largest in Nepal. It was built on a semicircular dome that rests on three pedestals that can be accessed via stairs from three sides. The *stupa* itself is rectangular and adorned with the "all seeing eyes of Buddha", which face the four points of the compass. The

geometric shapes symbolize the elements of fire, water, earth, air and spheres, and the five divine Buddhas that are assigned to them. The dome is encircled by statues of the 108 Amithaba Buddhas.

Chitwan National Park covers about 930 sq km (360 sq mi) in the Terai lowlands south-west of Kathmandu near the border with India. It was founded in 1973 and is the largest jungle region in Nepal with more than fifty mammal and four hundred bird species. Among them are elephants, rhinos, the rare Gavial

crocodile, Bengal tigers, leopards, water buffalo, and monkeys. From the lodges in the park you can either go on an elephant safari or take a boat to look for the different animals. Beware of snakes and scorpions if you do venture out.

The Potala is a majestic 13-storey palace that dominates the city of Lhasa and is the traditional winter residence of the Dalai Lama. There are thought to be 999 rooms behind the 360-m-long (1,200-yd) façade made of walls up to 5 m thick. The whitewashed section of the palace together with the two smaller yellow

buildings houses primarily the administrative and storage rooms. The Red Palace at the center is the actual residence of the Dalai Lama and has been a pilgrimage destination for Tibetans for centuries. The palace was begun in 1645 and finished in 1694. Until the end of the 19th century it was the highest building in the world.

West of the modern city is the UNESCO World Heritage Site of Old Sukhothai. In the middle of the 13th century, this became the center of the powerful Kingdom of Sukhothai and contains a total of forty temple complexes on an area of 70 sq km (27 sq mi), with the imperial city in the middle. Here, the temple complex is

reflected in the man-made lakes with its lotus-shaped main *chedi*, the small *chedis* surrounding it and a massive statue of the sitting Buddha. The bell-shaped *chedi* with the lotus bud on the top was typical for the era between the 13th and 15th centuries.

Detour

Batu Caves

The Batu Caves are among the most visited attractions in the Kuala Lumpur area. They are located 15 km (9 miles) north of the city on Highway 68 to Kuntan.

These giant limestone caves are part of a huge labyrinth of rock openings and tunnels. Because of a shrine inaugurated in the main cave in 1892, this is one of the most important pilgrimage destinations for Malay Hindus.

Top: Hindu shrine in the central cave at Batu.
Bottom: A Hindu pilgrim.

Every year in January and February thousands of Hindu faithful come to the Batu Caves during the festival of Thaipusam, celebrated here for two days. Its highlight is a procession of penitents with metal hooks poked into their backs and chests.

13 Krabi Most visitors come here because of the dream beaches and limestone cliffs in the area to the south and west of town. These are the 'beach images' that most people have come to associate with Thailand nowadays and some are truly spectacular.

Krabi, which is surrounded by karst cliff formations, has 21,000 inhabitants and is a good jumping-off point for boat trips into Phang Nga Bay; the famous Phi Phi Islands 40 km (25 miles) south with their magnificent beaches, steep karst rock faces and good diving; and a host of other white sand beaches and islands.

The temple compound of Wat Tham Sua with its beautiful view of the bay and the surrounding countryside is located on a rock outcrop 8 km (5 miles) north of Krabi.

From here we carry on across the southern Thai plains, which are among the most fertile in the country.

14 Hat Yai For many Thais this city is a shopping paradise because there are a lot of goods smuggled from Malaysia in the shops and markets.

West of the town center at Wat Hat Yai Nai is the world's third-largest reclining Buddha at 35 m (115 ft) long and 15 m (50 ft) tall. From Hat Yai you can do a little detour to Songkhla

about 25 km (16 miles) and the lakes on the east coast north of town.

A short drive south to Sadao takes you to the Malay border where the road turns into Malaysia's Highway 1. As an alternative to the North-South Highway, which is a dual carriageway, you can take the old road, which mostly runs parallel to the new one.

15 Alor Setar The state capital of Kedah is located in the middle of a wide, fertile plain with picturesque rice paddies. The region is known as 'Malaysia's rice bowl'.

The town landmark, the Zahir Mosque (1912), is one of the largest and most beautiful in Malaysia. With its very slender minarets and onion domes it embodies beautifully everyone's mental image of an oriental mosque.

16 Penang Island The tropical island of Penang, which is up to 700 m (2,300 ft) high in places, is located in the Gulf of Bengal and connected to the mainland by a bridge. Visitors from around the globe are attracted to the beaches at its northern end and to Georgetown, its lively capital. With Chinese shopping streets, narrow alleyways, numerous temples, magnificent clan houses (such as Khoo Kongsi) and colonial buildings such as Fort Cornwallis (18th century) it always makes for a pleasant stroll.

17 Kuala Kangsar For more than 150 years Kuala Kangsar, located 110 km (68 miles) further south, has been the residence of the Sultans of Perak. This pleasant town on the wide Perak River has two cultural monuments worth seeing – the former sultan's palace of Istana Kenangan built in 1926, and Masjid Ubudi-

ah, which was built 1913–17 and whose golden domes and minarets make it one of the country's finest mosques.

18 Ipoh The state capital of Perak has 500,000 inhabitants and owes its economic rise to the profitable tin deposits in the area. These were exploited well into the 1980s. Ipoh seems quite provincial for a city its size. The Kinta Valley to the north and south of the town is dominated by steep, partly

1 The temple of Kek Lok Si, also known as the Temple of a Thousand Buddhas, is in Georgetown on the island of Penang. Construction began in 1890.

2 Tea plantations in the Cameron Highlands in Malaysia at 2,000 m (6,500 ft). These highlands are renowned for their pleasant climate.

At 452 m (1,483 ft), the Petronas Towers are among the highest buildings in the world and have certainly become Kuala Lumpur's most recognizable landmark. A 'sky bridge' 58 m (64 yds) long connects the two towers at a height of 170 m (558 ft). The towers were designed by Cesar Pelli and inaugurated in 1998.

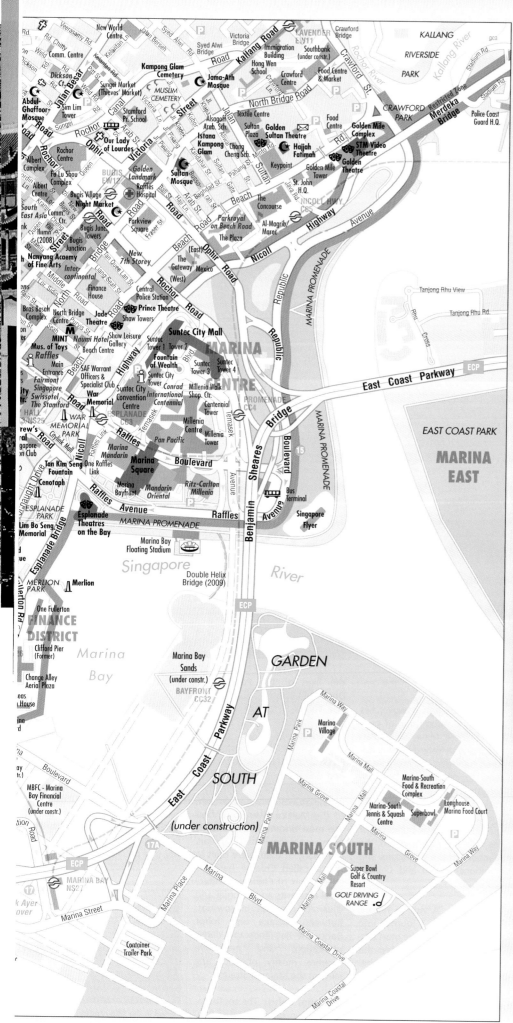

Singapore

The city state of Singapore is located on a small island in the Malacca Straits at the southern tip of the Malay Peninsula. It was founded as a trading post in 1819 and in the space of only a few years became South-East Asia's most important traffic hub as well as a major financial center.

Singapore is Asia's cleanest city and it has the best air quality of any of the world's large urban centers. The city charges high fines for environmental offences such as throwing away cigarette ends, and there are also high road tolls, horrendous car taxes and strict limits on registration quotas for new vehicles. With this draconic set of measures, the local government has long since managed to effectively ban cars from the city. Its outstanding public transport network makes it very easy to get to any point within the city limits quickly.

Singapore's population of roughly 4.5 million people is two-thirds Chinese, while the remainder is a mix of mostly Indian and Malay people. During the colonial period each of these ethnicities had its own neighbourhood, each of which has been meticulously reconstructed in recent years. Their markets, shops and restaurants are particularly full of atmosphere in the evening. The most colourful markets are in Little India.

Present and future coexist peacefully in this city. The commercial center is home to one skyscraper after another, the airport is one of Asia's busiest and the container terminal is the largest in the world. But quite a number of historic buildings survive to keep Old Singapore alive.

Many of the colonial buildings in this neighbourhood along the Singapore River, where the city was founded in 1819, have also been meticulously restored over the years. They now house government buildings as well as a handful of museums and a small concert hall.

Sentosa Island, located just off the main island, is one of Singapore's most popular tourist destinations. In fact, its countless leisure attractions make it really quite similar to Disneyland.

If you are seeking some peace and quiet in nature, you can retreat to the heartland of Singapore Island. It is hard to believe but even in this modern city there is still a small area of the island's original tropical rainforest. Bukit Timah Nature Reserve protects that last remnant very strictly.

At Sungei Buloh Nature Park there are more than 120 species of birds living in the mangrove swamps. Singapore Botanic Gardens and Singapore Zoological Gardens enjoy good reputations around the world.

Sights in the Colonial Core include Padang with the Supreme Court, the Victoria Theater (1862), the Old Parliament House (1826–27) and City Hall (1929), the famous Raffles Hotel (1887) and Fort Canning Park.

A Singapore's view of Orchard Road, central street.

Chinatown also has a number of interesting sights to behold – Sri Mariamman Temple with its seventy-two Hindu gods, the Jamae Mosque (1830), Boat Quay with its romantic seaside promenade, and Thian Hock Keng Temple (1839), the oldest of the Chinese temples in Singapore.

Sights in Little India and Kampong Glam include the Sultan Mosque, the city's largest mosque; Istana Kampgong Glam, the former sultan's palace; Arab Street; several temples, including Leong San See Temple (1917), Sakya Muni Buddha Temple (Temple of a Thousand Lights), and Sri Srinivasa Perumal Temple (1855); and Orchard Road, a lively shopping street.

The Terracotta Army about 30 km (19 mi) east of Xi'an is one of China's most popular sightseeing attractions. Roughly seven thousand figures make up the clay army that includes soldiers, officers, archers and even horses. They are arranged in battle formation and are guarding the tomb of Qin Shi Huangdi (259–210 BC), who

actually had the chamber built during his own lifetime. About 700,000 workers, architects and artisans are said to have been involved with the construction of the underground burial palace and the army. The figures, which were originally painted, are over 180 cm (6 ft) tall and each one is unique.

Maijishan Shiku is a grotto 25 km (16 mi) south-east of Tianshui that is also known as the Museum of Chinese Stone Sculptors. Since the 4th century, more than 1,000 caves and sculptures have been pounded out of these walls; ceramic figures have been shaped, and walls painted. Art connoisseurs are able to recognize

the connection between Chinese and foreign style elements as well as the development of a national sculptural style. About 195 grottos contain several thousand figures and more than 1,000 sq m (10,760 sq ft) of paintings. The galleries and staircases were erected to help visitors view the amazing site.

Giant kangaroos

If you follow the Stuart Highway north towards Darwin you will regularly come across signs warning you of kangaroos crossing the road. These marsupials are the continent's national animal with an estimated population of about twenty-five million. Despite their cuddly popularity with tourists, these vegetarian creatures are viewed by local farmers as pests because they graze uncontrollably on valuable sheep pastures.

In Australia there are fifty-six kangaroo species, divided into two families – the 'real' kangaroos and the 'rat' kangaroos, a newer species. During your trip, you will mostly come across the 'real' kangaroos, the hopping kind with extremely short forearms and powerful legs and tails.

Giant red kangaroo.

Some are as small as large rabbits while others, like the giant red kangaroo, can reach 2 m (6.5 ft) standing on their hind legs. Cape York is home to two species of tree kangaroo.

Kangaroo offspring are actually born during a late phase of embryonic development, the rest of which is completed from within the mother's pouch. Females have only one baby per year, which then feed for seven to ten months in her pouch while she feeds another offspring with milk outside the pouch.

Kangaroos' long and powerful tails are used as counterweights for hopping and jumping, but their soft leathery feet do not damage the ground below them. In the open grasslands of the dry center, you regularly come across giant red kangaroos which, like all kangaroos, live in herds.

Shortly after starting out from Adelaide, the Stuart Highway leads straight into the outback. Ayers Rock and Alice Springs lie at the halfway point of the route. The landscape turns into savannah in the far northern sections, and numerous national parks give travellers an idea of the Northern Territory's flora and fauna.

❶ Adelaide With more than a million inhabitants, Adelaide lies on the north and south sides of the Torrens River. The city's many parks, gardens, historic arcades and churches give it a very European flair. Yet despite all this, Adelaide is often considered a bit of a backwater by people from other Australian cities, or is even called 'wowserville', but this seems off the mark.

Every two years one of the world's most important cultural festivals takes place here – the Festival of Arts, held in the Adelaide Festival Centre. It is a tolerant and multicultural city with several museums along the 'Cultural Mile', including the Art Gallery of South Australia, the Ayers House Historical Museum (one of the most attractive colonial buildings in Australia), the Migration Museum on the history of immigration, and the South Australia Museum, with a good collection of Aboriginal tools, weapons and everyday items.

For a great view of the city go up to Montefiori Hill. Then take a break in the enchanting Botanic Gardens. If you feel like a swim, take one of the nostalgic trams down to Glenelg or Henley Beach. A worthwhile day trip is the drive into the Adelaide Hills or to the Barossa Valley. The first vineyards were planted here in 1847 by a German immigrant, Johann Cramp. Today in the Barossa Valley, 40 km (25 miles) long and 10 km (6 miles) wide, there are over 400 vineyards producing wines that have slowly but surely gained recognition around the world. One of the year's cultural highlights is the Vintage Festival with music, sauerkraut, brown bread, apple strudel, and of course wine.

Another interesting detour takes you to Kangaroo Island, 113 km (70 miles) south-west of Adelaide, which can be reached via the Fleurieu peninsula with its inviting sandy beaches. Australia's third-largest island is 155 km (96 miles) long and 55 km (34 miles) wide. You will come face to face here with the kangaroos that gave the island its name.

In the Seal Bay Conservation Park, thousands of sea lions bask on rocks in the sun. In Flinders Chase National Park, koalas lounge in the eucalyptus trees.

Travel information

Route profile

Length: approx. 3,200 km (1,987 miles), excluding detours
Time required: 3 weeks
Start: Adelaide
End: Darwin
Route (main locations): Adelaide, Port Augusta, Coober Pedy, Alice Springs, Wauchope, Tennant Creek, Katherine, Pine Creek, Darwin.

Accommodation:
Aside from signposted campsites, it's always possible to spend the night in a highway 'roadhouse'.

Traffic information:
Drive on the left in Australia. The Stuart Highway is completely tarmac from Adelaide to Darwin. In general, the driving conditions on auxiliary roads east and west of the highway are good. International driving licences are required for some nations. If you want to explore the outback, a four-wheel drive vehicle is recommended. There are service stations and rest areas about every 200–300 km (124–186 miles) along the highway. Speed limits are 50 km/h (30 mph) in town and 100 km/h (62 mph) outside towns. The blood alcohol limit is 0.05 percent and there are severe penalties if it is exceeded.

Information:
Australian Government
www.dfat.gov.au
General information:
www.australia.com
National Parks:
www.atn.com.au/parks

Detour

Flinders Ranges National Park

From Port Augusta take scenic Highway 47 through Quorn and Hawker to the mighty wall of the Wilpena Pound. Gravel roads then lead to the most important sights of the 950-sq-km (370-sq-mi) Flinders National Park, one of the most beautiful in South Australia. It protects the 400-km-long (240-mile) Flinders Range, which extends like a wedge between the salt lakes of Lake Torrens, Lake Eyre and Lake Frome and continues far into the outback, providing life support to many of the animal and plant species in this arid region.

The often bizarre rock formations come in red and violet hues, especially at sunrise and sunset. Bright,

Flinders National Park is one of the earth's oldest geological formations.

The real trip to the far north begins on Highway 1 from Adelaide. On the northern banks of Spencer Gulf is the industrial port town of Port Pirie, 250 km (155 miles) from Adelaide. Enormous grain silos bear witness to the extensive wheat farming in this region. Zinc and silver ore are processed here too, as is lead.

About 65 km (40 miles) further north, on the way to Port Augusta, it is worth taking the scenic detour into Mount Remarkable National Park at the south end of the Flinders Range. From the 959-m-high (3,146-ft) Mount Remarkable you can get a fabulous panoramic view of the entire region.

After another 70 km (43 miles) along Spencer Gulf, the indus-

trial port town of Augusta awaits you and marks the actual starting point of Stuart Highway (Highway 87).

❷ Port Augusta This town is often called the 'Gateway to the outback'. In preparation for the trip, a visit to the Wadlata Outback Centre is highly recommended. A few historically important buildings including the Town Hall (1887), the Court House (1884) and St Augustine's Church, with lovely stained-glass windows, are worth seeing. The Australian Arid Lands Botanic Gardens north of town familiarize you with the flora and fauna of the outback.

A short detour to the nearby Flinders Ranges National Park is an absolute must.

❸ Pimba This little town is right next to the enormous Woomera military base. Interestingly, the 'restricted area' on the base contains the largest uranium source in the world.

Australia's largest natural lakes can also be found outside of Pimba. These salt lakes are only periodically filled with water and are the remnants of what was once a huge inland sea. In the dry season they transform into salt marshes or salt pans.

To the east of Stuart Highway is Lake Torrens, in the national park of the same name, which covers an area of 5,800 sq km (2,240 sq mi). Frome Lake and Eyre Lake are also in the park. Further west is Lake Gairdner, another salt lake that is part of a separate national park.

❹ Coober Pedy In 1915, fourteen-year-old Willie Hutchinson and his father discovered Australia's first opal completely by chance, about 270 km (168 miles) north of Pimba. The name Coober Pedy originates from the Aborigine 'kupa piti' (white man in a hole). Since then it has been overrun with pits up to 30 m (98 ft) deep and giant slag heaps that, due to consistent demand for opals, are constantly being expanded. In fact, 70 percent of the world's opal mining takes place in the Coober Pedy area. The raging sandstorms and intense heat in the area have compelled nearly half of the 3,000 inhabitants to live in 'dugouts', underground homes built in decommissioned opal mines. The often well-furnished apartments maintain consistent temperatures between 23°C and 25°C (73°F and 77°F) and can be up to 400 sq m (4,305 sq ft) in size. There is even an underground church in Coober, as well as underground bed and breakfast accommodation. Be sure to pay a visit to the lovingly restored Old Timers Mine while you are here.

1 Road signs warn of kangaroos.

2 The night skyline of Adelaide reflected in the Torrens River.

3 At the base of the Stuart Range lies Coober Pedy, the 'Opal capital of the world'.

colourful flowers also grow in the valleys and gorges of the mountains in springtime. Giant red kangaroos live here, as do yellow-footed rock wallabies and other smaller species of rock wallabies. Bearded dragons (a type of monitor lizard) sun themselves on the hot rocks while broad-tailed eagles and brown falcons circle in the sky above.

The highlight of a trip into the national park is the Wilpena Pound, one of Australia's greatest natural wonders: a 17-km (10.5-mile) by 7-km (4.3-mile) crater-like 'cauldron' that resembles a natural amphitheater with its ring of high, pointed rocks. A small passage is the only way into the bowl, which is an Aboriginal sacred place. You will get the best view from the scenic outlook point.

Visitors here can immediately sense why Uluru – commonly known by its "white man's" name of Ayers Rock – is a holy place for Aboriginal people. Since 1985, the holy mountain has actually been back in their possession, but not without a condition: that the rock can still be climbed. The Kata Tjuta – also commonly

known by their "white man's" name, the Olgas – comprise thirty-six monoliths that are also located on holy ground. Only two hiking trails lead to the ochre-colored canyons and crevices. The more spectacular of the two sites is located on the 6.4-km-long (4-mi) Valley of the Winds Walk.

Thousands of Aboriginal rock paintings dot the spectacular landscape of Kings Canyon in Watarrka National Park. A lush oasis has developed in the Garden of Eden (illustrated here), providing ancient cycad palms and river eucalyptuses with plenty of water.

Eventually, the Lasseter Highway makes its way west at Erlunda towards the Yulara Resort and the Visitor Centre of the Uluru and Kata Tjuta National Parks (1,325 sq km/511 sq mi).

If you are looking for outdoor adventure, turn left off the highway onto a track towards Chambers Pillar, a 56-m-high (184-ft) sandstone monolith that early settlers used as a point of reference and in which many explorers have carved their names and dedications.

5 **Ayers Rock** The Aborigines call this massive rock mountain Uluru (863 m/2,831 ft above sea level) and cherish it as a sacred place. Subsequently, since the path to the top is one of sacred significance, they 'kindly ask' that people do not climb it – but they do not forbid you to do so. Instead, they ask you to admire it from below as you stroll along the 9.4-km (5.8-mile) 'base walk'.

The rock itself measures 3.5 km (2.2 miles) by 2.4 km (1.5 miles), and extends several kilometers down into the earth. It rises to 348 m (1,142 ft) above the steppe landscape like a whale stranded on a deserted beach. Due to its high iron content it changes colour with the movement of the sun – from crimson, rust, pink, brown and grey to a deep blue. After rainfall it even goes a silvery shade – a perpetu-

ally impressive show that will dazzle any visitor.

6 **The Olgas** Known as Kata Tjuta by the Aborigines, the Olgas (1,066 m/ 3,497 ft above sea level) are a similarly spectacular sight. Kata Tjuta, meaning 'many heads', is 32 km (20 miles) to the north-west of Uluru and comprises a group of thirty geologically similar, mainly dome-shaped monoliths that spread over an area of 35 sq km (13.5 sq mi), the highest point peaking at 546 m (1,791 ft).

It would appear that the Olgas were once a single mountain that eroded over time into individual hills. The Valley of Winds traverses a stark mountain range through which either seasonal icy winds blow or burning hot air turns each step into a torturous affair.

7 **Henbury** Back on Stuart Highway the journey continues to the north. Approximately 2,000–3,000 years ago a meteor impacted not far from Henbury, leaving twelve distinct craters. The largest has a diameter of 180 m (560 ft) and the smallest just 6 m (20 ft).

At Henbury, the Ernest Giles Highway splits off towards Watarrka National Park. It is a dirt track until it joins the Laritja Road where it becomes tarmac

and eventually leads to the Kings Canyon Resort.

8 **Watarrka National Park and Finke Gorge National Park** The centrepiece of the Watarrka National Park is Kings Canyon on the west end of the George Gill Range. With walls that rise to 200 m (656 ft), the canyon looks as if it were man-made. A number of Aboriginal rock paintings and carvings adorn the rugged canyon facades. The Aborigines aptly call the beehive-like eroded sandstone dome the 'Lost City'. Kings Canyon is best visited on foot by taking the Kings Creek Walk.

From the resort, the Meerenie Loop (a dirt road) leads to the Aborigine town of Hermannsburg. On this slightly daunting stretch of road you'll cross low sand dunes that lead up to the base of the Macdonnell Range. East of the old Hermannsburger Mission, Larapinta Drive turns south and for the last 16 km (10 miles) it runs through the dried-out Finke riverbed to Palm Valley. This last section is only really accessible with four-wheel

1 Chambers Pillar rises 56 m (184 ft) over the Simpson Desert.

2 The Finke River eroded the steep ravine in Finke Gorge National Park.

Roadtrains

The infamous Australian roadtrains are lorries that can measure up to 53 m (174 ft), have as many as fifteen axles

'Roadtrains' ensure the supply of provisions to isolated areas.

and sixty-two tyres and supply the outback with basic necessities. Without them, life on an isolated farm or an inland mine would be impossible. These monsters of the road have 400–500 horsepower and barrel down highways, gravel roads and sand tracks brushing aside any possible obstacles. The tractors are fitted with large grilles designed to protect the radiator from collisions with animals.

Roadtrains run mostly across the sparsely populated outback. They can carry up to 80 tonnes of freight and regularly travel 4,000 km (2,484 miles). Overtaking a roadtrain can be dangerous: airborne gravel can destroy a windscreen, and they tend to swerve due to heavy winds and massive loads.

Aboriginal people have been living on the fifth continent for roughly fifty thousand years. Over this long period they have adjusted seamlessly with their arid surroundings becoming excellent observers of nature and outstanding trackers. Material possession is a foreing concept to these people, whose social structure

is organized into tribes and clans. The central element of their spiritual-mystical world is "dreamtime", a time when humans and animals rose from the earth, and their countless rock paintings and body art are related to this concept.

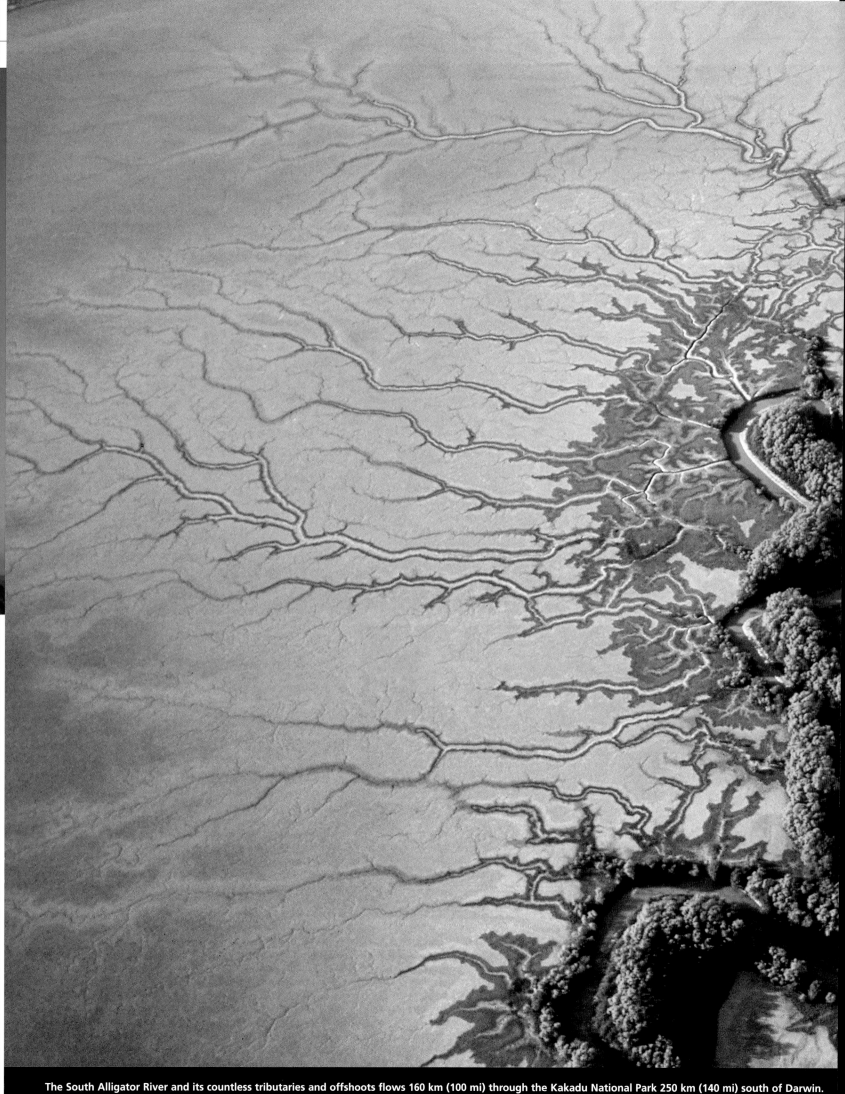

The South Alligator River and its countless tributaries and offshoots flows 160 km (100 mi) through the Kakadu National Park 250 km (140 mi) south of Darwin. On its way to the Pacific Ocean it passes through rainforest, eucalyptus forests, mangroves and marshlands – and allows saltwater crocodiles the chance to

travel far into the interior. Due to the unique nature of this swampland and the significant cultural heritage of forty thousand years of Aboriginal settlement here, the park has been decalred a UNESCO World Heritage Site.

Aborigines

When the European settlement of Australia began at the end of the 18th century, they saw the country as 'terra nullius' or unknowed land, but at least 350,000 Aborigines (from the Latin 'ab origine', meaning from the origin or the beginning) had lived on the continent for more than 50,000 years. The Aborigines were organised in kinships, clans and tribes and roamed the continent as hunters and gatherers. What they needed to live, they found in the desert or the rainforest.

The Aborigines' totemic and magical beliefs have been around for thousands of years: mountains, rocks, rivers, lakes and trees all have souls.

One of the many X-ray-style rock drawings in the Kakadu National Park.

Their perception of the world is influenced by the 'Dreamtime' in which past, present and future are permanently interlinked.

In the beginning, the world was a flat disk shrouded in darkness until the giants came with light, water, clouds and rain and created all forms of life. The giants then turned into mountains, rivers, lakes, trees and animals. Nature as a whole is therefore divine in Aboriginal 'Dreamtime'.

All of these concepts feature heavily in Aborigine rites, traditions and customs such as body painting, magical songs and rock paintings. The indigenous Australians have been fighting hard for the return of their lands and social recognition from European descendants for more than fifty years.

display here. Nature lovers in particular stop in Katherine because the Cutta Cutta Caves Nature Park is just 24 km (15 miles) away to the south-east. The stalactite and stalagmite formations in the caves are an important refuge for rare bats and tree snakes.

16 Nitmiluk National Park This impressive network of canyons formed over thousands of years by the Katherine River is one of the greatest natural wonders of Australia – Katherine Gorge. Red-brown limestone canyon walls rise up to 100 m (328 ft) above the river. The best way to view them is from a sightseeing boat that embarks in Katherine, or you can explore the river by canoe when it is not the rainy season. During the rainy season the otherwise calm river turns into a raging torrent and is not really navigable.

Biologists often marvel at Katherine Gorge for its unbelievable variety of wildlife – freshwater crocodiles live here, along with more than 160 species of birds and numerous butterfly species. All in all, nine of the thirteen gorges in the park are open to visitors.

Edith Falls is a particularly spectacular natural phenomenon. You can reach the falls by either taking the rough 75-km (48-mile) track, or the more comfortable Stuart Highway. Smaller pools and waterfalls invite sun-weary visitors to take a refreshing swim.

17 Pine Creek This town, 90 km (56 miles) north-west of Katherine, was once a hot spot for gold diggers. Today it's a supply station for those on their way to Darwin, or the starting point for excursions to the Kakadu National Park to the east.

If you would like to visit that world-famous national park, leave the Stuart Highway at Pine Creek and take the Kakadu Highway towards Jabiru. You will find the park visitor centre there and can plan your trip.

18 Kakadu National Park Covering an area of 20,000 sq km (7,800 sq mi), this national park in Arnhem Land is one of the largest and most attractive in Australia. The scenery shifts from the tidal zone at Van Diemen Gulf and the flood plains of the lowlands to the escarpment and the arid plateaus of Arnhem Land. The most impressive attraction is the escarpment, a craggy 500-km-long (310-mile) outcrop with

spectacular waterfalls such as the Jim Jim Falls, Tain Falls and Twin Falls, which are at their best towards the end of the rainy season. The name of the park comes from 'Gagudju', which is the name of an Aboriginal language originating in this flood-plain region.

Biologists have counted 1,300 plant, 10,000 insect, 240 bird and seventy reptile species, including the feared saltwater crocodile. The rare mountain kangaroos, wallabies and one-third of the country's bird species are also native to this area. Due to its diversity, this impressive park has been made into a UNESCO World Heritage Site.

There are over 5,000 Aborigine rock paintings here, the most famous of which are on Nourlinge Rock, Ubirr Rock and in Nangaluwur. The paintings,

The wildlife of Kakadu National Park

This national park is renowned for its animal diversity. The park is made up of a tidal zone, flood plains, a steppe and the Arnhem Land Plateau. Alone 240 bird species have been counted by ornithologists here, including the Jaribu. The crocodile is the best-known among seventy reptile species here. Daily almost fifty mammal species meet at the watering hole.

The Arnhem Highway leads back through Cooinda and Jabiru to the Stuart Highway. From Noonaman the road leads south before heading west through Batchelor into Litchfield National Park.

⑲ Litchfield National Park The main attractions of this park are immediately visible – the open eucalyptus forests, the thick rainforest around the escarpment, and the massive, skilfully crafted gravestone-like mounds of the magnetic termites can reach heights of 2 m (6.5 ft). Due to the extreme midday heat the termites have cleverly aligned the long side of their mounds with the north-south axis in order to warm their homes in the morning and evening sun while protecting them from the midday sun.

The Tabletop Range escarpment is a spectacular sight where waterfalls like Sandy Creek Falls, Florence Falls, Tower Falls and Wangi Falls cascade down the ridge even in the dry season. The unique environment around the falls has developed its own unique spectrum of monsoon rainforest wildlife.

⑳ Darwin Due to its proximity to the South-East Asian countries to the north of Australia, Darwin has developed into a culturally very diverse city, which is reflected in its numerous markets and restaurants. One of the specialities here is the daily, slightly odd Aquascene Fish Feeding at Doctor's Gulley. At high tide various fish swim onto land to be fed by hand from humans. Wonderful white sand beaches can be found on both sides of the scenic port town of Beagle Gulf.

Since the destruction caused by Tornado Tracy during Christmas of 1974, the city of Darwin has changed dramatically. After the storm, almost nothing was left of the historic 19th-century buildings apart from the Old Navy Headquarters, Fanny Bay Jail, the Court House, Brown's Mart and the Government House with its seven gables. Your journey across the mighty outback ends here, on the coast at the doorstep to Asia.

1 The Arnhem Land Plateau escarpment in Kakadu National Park.

2 Magnetic termite mounds, bizarre yet clever constructions in Litchfield National Park.

3 The Wangi Falls are one of many waterfalls on the edge of the Tabletop Range plateau.

4 Kakadu National Park: The falls cascade into the depths along the 500-km (310-mile) edge of the escarpment.

Top: The goanna, member of the monitor lizard family, is common in northern Australia.
Middle: Woe betides he who falls into the teeth of the attacking salt-water crocodile.
Bottom: The jaribu is Australia's only indigenous stork.

some of which date back as many as 18,000–23,000 years, not only demonstrate the area's climate change, but are also a striking portrayal of the culture of the Aborigines, who have allegedly lived on the continent here for 50,000 years. The best time of year to visit the park is in the dry season from May to November, as the roads are otherwise impassable.

Arguably the most famous Aboriginal rock painting in Australia, in the so-called X-ray style, is Namondjok on Nourlangie Rock in Kakadu National Park. The rock is just one of thousands in the country. Many of the designs symbolize the genesis of life on earth as well as the relationship between humans and their

environment in the mystical context of "dreamtime". The paintings are mostly on rock faces, overhangs and in caves, and the most important materials used were ochre, chalk and wood coal.

Top: The roofs of the Sydney Opera House look like upturned seashells or billowing sails, and are an iconic feature of the city's port. In the shadow of the Harbour Bridge, Dawes Point offers a magnificent panoramic view of the Opera House and Circular Quay, Sydney's historic port.

Bottom: Sydney Harbour Bridge is the city's second great landmark. Opened to traffic in 1932, the bridge was built during the Great Depression. The loan of over six million Australian pounds was finally paid off in 1988. The distinctive arch has a span of 503 m (1,650 ft).

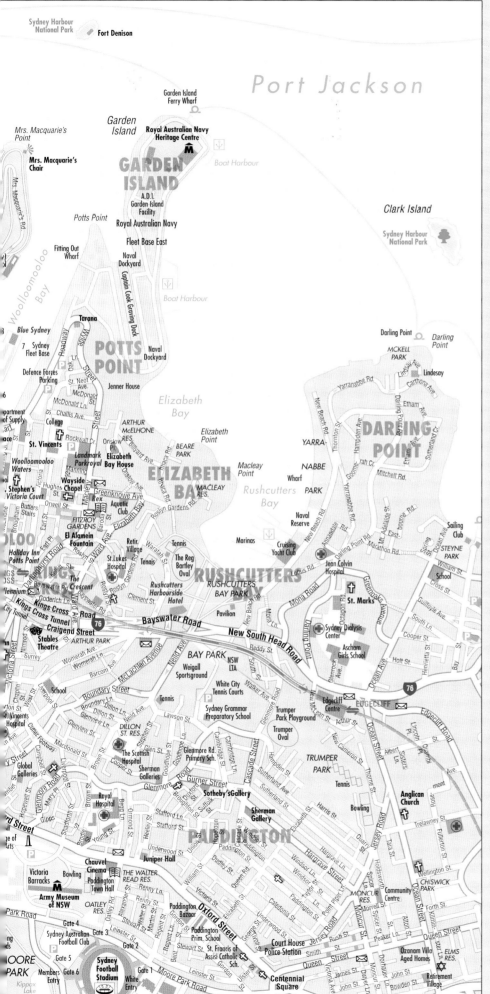

Sydney

The oldest and largest city on the Australian continent, Sydney, the capital of New South Wales, has a population of over four million and is Australia's leading commercial and financial center. Numerous universities, museums and galleries also make Sydney the cultural center of the south-east coast.

In 1788, when the first wave of settlers – mostly convicts and their guards – came ashore under the command of Captain Arthur Phillip, none of them could have imagined that Port Jackson would one day become one of the most beautiful cities in the world. Admittedly, back in those days there was none of the laid-back, almost a height of 134 m (440 ft) and with an span of 503 m (1,650 ft).

The best place to begin your tour of the city is the port, with the Harbour Bridge and the Opera House within striking distance. You could also start by people-watching from one of the many cafés, listening to the street musicians or taking a

Top: Sydney and its Harbour Bridge, one of the most stunning views in Australia.
Middle: Enjoy a walk along the largest natural port in the world.
Bottom: Sydney Tower rises between the roofs of the Sydney Opera House. The viewing platform is 250 m (820 ft) up.

Mediterranean charm of present-day Sydney. Life for convicts and soldiers was rough and tumble. But things began to change towards the end of the 18th century with the first free settlers. Several gold-rushes then followed, the first of which took place in 1851.

Sydney's expansion first began with the arrival of European and then of Asian immigrants, a mixture that characterizes the city's present-day multi-cultural atmosphere. It is also a major financial center, and for most visitors to Australia it is the first stop on their tour of the fifth continent.

From 250 m (820 ft) up on the viewing platform of the 305-m (1,001 ft) Sydney Tower, you get a magnificent view of the skyline, the port, the smart residential suburbs, the Pacific coast and, further inland, the Blue Mountains – not to mention the city's second great landmark, the Harbour Bridge. This amazing construction forms a graceful arc across the bay at

boat trip around the port. The Rocks area is a must for shoppers and pub-goers. From the city center, an elevated railway takes you to Darling Harbour and its myriad attractions. On the somewhat quieter side, the Botanic Gardens feature a cross-section of Australian flora in a tranquil and relaxing setting.

Chinatown is on the south side of town and, like most Chinatowns around the world, has its own unique charm that reflects the relationship and proximity to Asia. Cabramatta, an outlying district some 30 km (18.5 mi) west of the city, is the Vietnamese equivalent of Chinatown.

Other districts worth visiting include Victorian-style Paddington, east of downtown, and the nightclub district, Kings Cross.

Blue Mountains National Park

The Blue Mountains are about 50 km (31 mi) west of Sydney on the western edge of the Cumberland Plain basin. It is an area of outstanding natural beauty and as such attracts no fewer than three million visitors every year.

The Blue Mountains range is actually a sandstone plateau that reaches elevations of over 1,000 m (3,281 ft) in places. Over millions of years, its rivers have eroded and dug their way into the rock to depths of hundreds of meters. The signs of these geological processes are unmistakable: gigantic gorges, precipitous cliffs, pounding waterfalls and a huge variety of flora and fauna including more than one hundred species of birds, eucalyptus trees, mosses, ferns and beautiful wild flowers. The Blue Mountains take their name from the bluish haze that often envelops them and is caused by the release of essential oils from eucalyptus trees.

Blue Mountains National Park covers some 2,700 sq km (1,043 sq mi) and was established in 1959. The park has good facilities and is easy to get around. By car you can reach some spectacular vantage points along the Great Western Highway and Cliff Drive between Leura and Katoomba. Two tourist rail services, the Katoomba Scenic Railway and the Zig Zag Railway, also serve the park. But the best way to explore it is still on foot. Choose from one of the many hikes, among them the Federal Pass Walk, the Prince Henry Cliff Walk or the Grand Canyon Nature Track.

The park's top attractions include the Wentworth Falls, some 300 m (984 ft) high, the Giant Stairway with over one thousand steps at Echo Point,

The 'Three Sisters' tower high above the valley of the Jamison River.

and the Blue Gum Forest (blue gum is a type of eucalyptus) in Grose Valley. The ultimate, must-have photograph is of the 'Three Sisters': three giant rock formations towering high above Jamison Valley.

Try to avoid visiting these places at the weekend and you will have a greater chance of enjoying the wonderful natural landscape in peace.

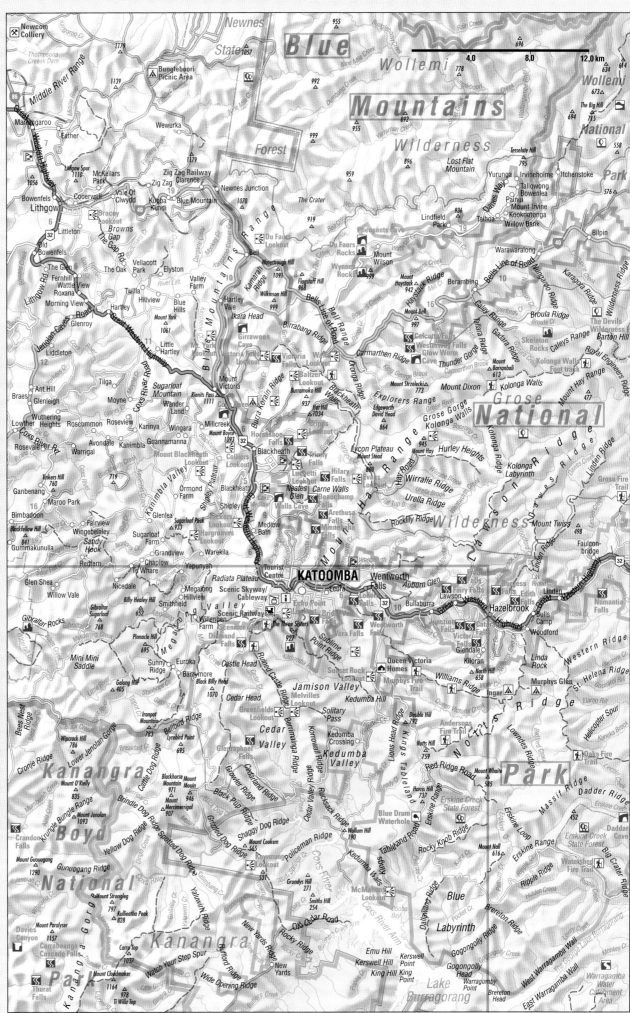

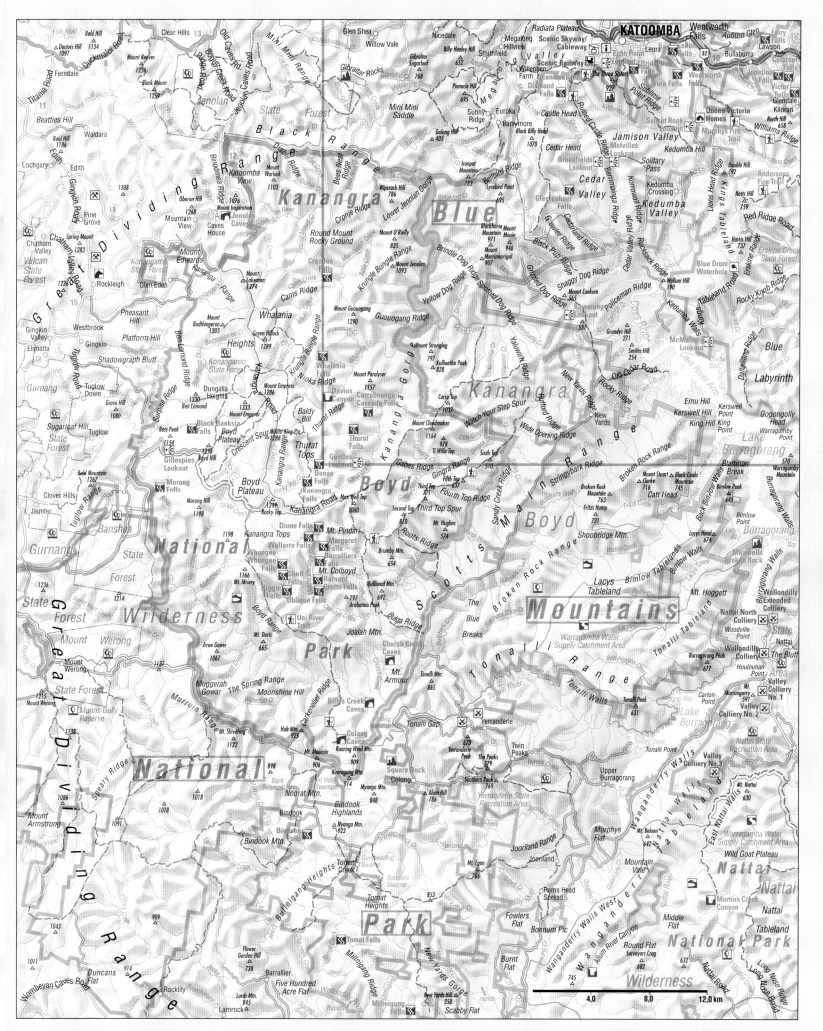

Dorrigo National Park

Picturesque Dorrigo is situated on a plateau bordering a steep escarpment covered in pristine subtropical and cool-temperate rainforest. The entrance to Dorrigo National Park is 4 km (2.5 mi) south-east of the town of Dorrigo. The forest is connected to the New England National Park and, like its neighbour, belongs to the East Coast Temperate and Subtropical Rainforest parks.

The wilderness of the subtropical rainforest and wet eucalypt woodland is an impressive sight, teeming with an abundance of orchids, ferns and mosses. The animal world in this national park is equally colorful and diverse, allowing you the opportunity to see and hear a variety of brightly plumed birds with their shrill songs. Guided tours at night shed careful light on the many nocturnal mammals that roam the park.

The steeply rising terrain attracts heavy rainfall in summer, making a visit to the waterfalls a memorable experience. The visitor center at the entrance to the national park provides much useful information on the native animal and plant life. Nearby is the Skywalk, a wooden

A jungle of ferns in Dorrigo National Park.

walkway that runs 70 m (230 ft) above the treetops and provides some breathtaking views over the rainforest canopy. A number of good tracks lead from two picnic spots, The Glade, a half-mile from the visitor center, and Never Never, in the middle of the park. The trail goes through areas of rainforest and to some of the waterfalls.

If you are interested in the didgeridoo, an Aboriginal musical instrument, the charming nearby hill town of Bellingen is the place to go. These distinctive wind instruments are made from tree trunks hollowed out by termites and fitted with a beeswax mouthpiece. They have a distinctive sound.

At Singleton, north-east of the park, join Highway 15 and head east through the Upper Hunter Valley, a region famous for horse breeding and vineyards, to one of Australia's most famous wine regions, the Lower Hunter Valley.

5 Lower Hunter Valley Cessnock is the main town at the heart of the this wine-producing region. Farms and vineyards are nestled among gently rolling hills, and to the west you can just make out the foothills of the Great Dividing Range.

Grapes have been cultivated in the fertile soil of this region since the 1830s, and there are around 140 wineries in the valley, most of them open to visitors. Among the most famous are Lindemans, Tyrrell's Wines and Wyndham Estate. In stark contrast, the main industries in nearby Newcastle, the second-largest city in New South Wales, are steel, coal and shipping.

Around 40 km (25 mi) north of Newcastle, it is worth making a stop in Port Stephens, the 'dolphin capital of Australia'.

6 Port Stephens Many tourists come to this port to enjoy a trip on a dolphin-watching boat to see the 150–200 dolphins that make Nelson Bay their home. Between May and July, and September and November, pods of whales also swim past the coast here, among them killer whales, minkes and humpbacks.

Port Stephens is also famous for Stockton Beach, some 33 km (21 mi) long, where you can even take your four-wheel-drive for a spin in the sand.

Myall Lakes National Park is 60 km (37 mi) to the north and is the largest lake area in New South Wales.

7 Port Macquarie Founded in 1821 as a penal colony, Port Macquarie is one of the oldest towns in Australia. The Port Macquarie Museum and Courthouse, St Thomas' Anglican Church and the Roto House, all built in the 19th century, are still standing today. Since the 1970s, tourism has boosted the town's fortunes remarkably, and it is also popular among retired Australians, who enjoy the town's relaxed atmosphere. There are plenty of swimming and surfing beaches and a wide variety of other water sports in general on offer.

Heading north along the Pacific Highway, you enter increasingly humid and damp regions, home to dense rainforests. The route then leaves the coastal highway at Kempsey for another detour into the impressive Great Dividing Range. You travel via Bellingen and Dorrigo on the way to New England National Park.

8 New England National Park Covering an area of 300 sq km (116 sq mi), this park is situated on the escarpment of the New England Plateau at an elevation of 1,400 m (4,593 ft). It encompasses one of the largest rainforests in New South Wales and features snow gum trees in the upper regions, temperate rainforest vegetation at the middle elevations, and subtropical rainforest with tree-high ferns at the base of the plateau. Drive up to Point Lookout at 1,562 m

Lamington National Park and Border Ranges National Park

Lamington National Park is a well-developed park first listed as a conservation area in 1915. It is easy to reach from the Pacific Highway. In the middle of the park is the Lamington plateau, which reaches 900–1,200 m (2,952–3,937 ft) and ends in steep cliffs and gorges in the south. The parkland contains more than five hundred waterfalls and a variety of woodlands, ranging from tropical and subtropical rainforest to southern beech forest

(5,125 ft) for a wonderful view of the highland escarpment and the Bellinger Valley.

On the return journey to the coast it is certainly worth making a detour to Dorrigo National Park (see sidebar left). From Dorrigo, the Waterfall Way takes you back to the coast.

Coffs Harbour boasts a series of attractive beaches and is one of the most popular holiday resorts in the state. Banana plantations have been the mainstay of the region's agriculture for more than one hundred years, and reflects the gradual change in climate from subtropical to tropical. Just a few miles north of Coffs Harbour, the Pacific Highway heads inland toward Grafton.

⑨ Grafton This country town, nestled on the banks of the Clarence River, is known as the 'Jacaranda capital of Australia', and its wide, elegant streets are lined with these beautifully fragrant trees. The Jacaranda Festival takes place when the trees bloom in late October or early November.

Grafton was founded by lumberjacks around 1830, with cattle farmers following later. When gold was discovered in the upper reaches of the Clarence River, the town developed rapidly and a busy river port flourished around 1880. Traces of the town's late 19th-century prosperity can be seen in a number of well-preserved buildings on the north side of the river.

A track from Grafton leads to Wooli, the gateway to Yuraygir National Park, about 50 km (31 mi) away.

⑩ Yuraygir National Park This national park encompasses the longest stretch of pristine coastline in New South Wales. It perfectly shows how the coast looked before it became so densely populated and boasts remote sandy beaches, heaths, swamps and lagoons.

The national park has some excellent walking trails and offers perfect conditions for both surfers and anglers.

⑪ Yamba This 19th-century fishing village is about 60 km (37 mi) further north, and has become an angler's paradise. The beautiful beaches offer myriad water sports options, and there are rewarding fishing spots on the Clarence River, in the nearby coastal lakes and along the coast. Angourie Point, just 5 km (3 mi) south of Yamba, is one of the best surfing beaches in the country.

The Pacific Highway now heads north along the seemingly endless string of white-sand beaches toward Byron Bay, about 120 km (75 mi) away.

⑫ Byron Bay This surfer, hippie enclave-cum-holiday resort gets its name not from the famous poet, but from his grandfather,

1 The most powerful lighthouse in Australia is on the Cape Byron headland, 107 m (351 ft) above the ocean.

2 The Lower Hunter Valley has been home to the Lindemans Pokolbin winery since 1870.

Top: A waterfall in Lamington National Park.
Bottom: Subtropical plant life in Border Ranges National Park.

at higher elevations. The park also boasts a rich diversity of animal life, including almost two hundred different species of birds.

Border Ranges National Park, between New South Wales and Queensland, contains the remains of an extinct shield volcano. The park's rainforests are home to gigantic strangler figs, pademelons (small kangaroos) and rare yellow-eared cockatoos.

Although it originated in Hawaii, where Captain Cook first observed locals riding waves on boards in 1778, surfing has become a national pastime in Australia since its introduction at the beginning of the 20th century. The varying sizes of waves along the East Coast offer perfect conditions for the keen surfer. Around

three-quarters of all Australians live no more than an hour from the coast. This photo shows surfers off Burleigh Heads against a backdrop of tourist hotels at Surfers Paradise up on the Gold Coast in Queensland.

The snow-capped summit of Aoraki/Mount Cook is sacred to the Maori.

New Zealand

The South Island: glaciers, fiords and rainforests

Visitors to New Zealand's South Island can expect some absolutely fabulous scenery. You will enjoy one spectacular view after another as you travel along the coast or to the highest peaks in the interior. Some of the more remote regions are difficult to reach, making for a great diversity of plant and wildlife. The island's mountains, lakes and rivers are ideal for those in search of outdoor adventures.

Many consider that New Zealand's South Island embraces the whole range of the world's landscapes in perfect harmony. In the sun-drenched north, the Tasman Sea's large waves pound the shore, while you can relax on the sandy beaches in its sheltered bays. Further south, the agricultural flatlands of Canterbury Plain spread across the eastern side of the island. Although the South Island is much larger than its northern counterpart, it is much less densely populated. Large areas of the interior are almost uninhabited. Only five percent of New Zealand's Maori population lives on the South Island, so there are far fewer Maori sacred sites than on the North Island. On the east coast, you will find two lively, cosmopolitan cities with a distinctly European flavour: Christchurch and Dunedin. Christchurch still boasts colonial buildings and extensive parks and is often described as the most English city outside England, with good reason. As you stroll through the port city of

Brown kiwi.

Dunedin with its many Victorian-Gothic buildings and its lovely parks, you will be reminded of its Scottish heritage: the very name of the city derives from the Gaelic name for the Scottish capital, while the names of some of its streets and quarters will transport you briefly to Edinburgh. Further to the south and west, the plains give way to more hilly country, which rises to form the snow-covered peaks of the Southern Alps. This mountainous region, which forms the backbone of the South Island, is accessible by only a few roads. The highest mountain in the Southern Alps is Aoraki/Mount Cook, originally named after Captain Cook, the British explorer. Five powerful glaciers flow from its summit (3,764 m/12,350 ft) down into the valley. In the Maori language, the mountain is known by its more poetic name Aoraki (Cloud Piercer).

Coastal landscape near Akaroa on the Banks Peninsula, south-east of Christchurch.

Milford Sound, with its steep forest-clad rock faces, is one of the major attractions in New Zealand's South Island.

The south-west of the island is one of New Zealand's most attractive regions, and Queenstown, on the northern shore of Lake Wakatipu, makes a perfect starting point for exploring it. Several fiords, such as the famous Milford Sound, penetrate deep into the island. There are some dramatic waterfalls, Sutherland Falls among them, and a number of impressive dripstone caves. Fiordland National Park at 12,000 sq km (4,632 sq mi) is the country's largest protected area and a designated UNESCO World Heritage Site, a status it certainly deserves. It is home to a wide range of bird species.

This route takes you to a number of large mountain lakes, known collectively as the Southern Lakes Region, which includes Lakes Te Anau, Wakatipu and Wanaka. A little further north, in Westland National Park, fifty-eight glaciers flow down from the mountain tops almost to the west coast. The Franz Josef and Fox Glaciers are the most famous, but the South Island has around three hundred such ice-flows, some of which can be several kilometers long. Owing to the island's high levels of precipitation, the coastal areas are usually covered in jungle-like rainforests.

Following our route northwards along the west coast, you will come across villages that look much the same as they did at the time of the New Zealand gold-rush, which lured many people to seek their fortunes in the area in the 1860s. When it came to an end, some communities, such as Greymouth, switched to coal-mining to sustain their economy. Agriculture continues to play an important role. Although the large majority of the population lives in the towns and cities, farming is vital to the economy of the South Island.

Countless islands, bays and fiords break up the coastline in the north of the South Island.

Lake Wanaka is a long and narrow body of water in the heart of the Southern Lakes district, south-west of Mount Aspiring National Park. The lakebed was created by a glacier during the last ice age. After the ice flow finally melted, the snowmelt collected and filled the basin. The view from one of the mountains

opposite the lake shows how well defined the lakeshore of Wanaka really is: promontories almost completely cut off the small coves. The area surrounding the fourth-largest lake in New Zealand is characterized by dense forest and vegetation.

An unusual view of Mitre Peak (1,692 m/6,437 ft), which is more commonly seen from Milford Sound where it is a familiar landmark. Its jagged, conical peak rises up abrubtly out of the water. This photo was taken from the Milford Track, probably New Zealand's best-known and most beautiful mountain trail.

The Track, which is about 54 km (33 miles) long, starts at Lake Te Anau and follows Mackinnon Pass, past Sutherland Falls to Milford Sound. Time and again, there are breathtaking views along the way.

Aït Ben Haddou is one of the most beautiful examples of architecture in southern Morocco. Although the casbah on the plateau above the *ksar* (fortified village) is in ruins, many of those in Tighremt have been restored. A wall typically "protects" the town, but this one is mostly used as a backdrop in films, for example

in the Hollywood blockbuster *Jewel of the Nile* (1985). Since Ksar Aït Ben Haddou was declared a UNESCO World Heritage Site, preservationists have been trying to protect the ancient structures from ruin.

The Djemma el-Fna – the Square of the Hanged – in Marrakesh comes alive as soon as the sun goes down. During the day, scribes, dentists, soothsayers and water sellers run the massive square on the edge of the souk before night falls and the snake charmers, storytellers and acrobats take over. It is then that

the food stalls get going and the smoke from their fires fills the air, and hundreds or even thousands of people jam the square to watch the performances that continue long into the desert night.

The pyramids of Giza are the only ancient wonder of the world still standing today.

Egypt
A journey through the Kingdom of the Pharaohs

The pyramids of Giza are the most powerful emblem of ancient Egypt. The pharaohs who built them instilled the fabulous structures with dreams of immortality. Egypt's cultural legacy was also influenced by Christianity and Islam. In the desert, time-honoured monasteries are evidence of the religious zeal of the Copts, who are still very much alive today. The various Muslim dynasties gave Cairo its numerous mosques.

Egypt gives visitors an insight into an exotic realm situated at the crossroads of African, Asian and European civilizations, and which is indeed an intersection of myriad cultures. Obviously the monumental tombs and temples are still a subject of fascination today, but their mysterious hieroglyphics and ancients scripts also captivate our curiosities.

The ancient societies of Egypt and the pharaohs began over 5,000 years ago. Most of the monuments from the time of the pharaohs run along the Nile. Along with the pulsating metropolis of Cairo, the 300-km (186-mile) stretch between Luxor and Aswan offers history buffs a multitude of impressive sights. Luxor's attractions include the Valley of the Kings, the tremendous temple complex of Karnak and the funerary temple of the female pharaoh Hatshepsut.

Further south, the temples of Edfu and Kôm Ombo are evidence of the fact that even the Greek and Roman conquerors of

The golden mask of young King Tutankhamun.

Egypt succumbed to a fascination with the Pharaonic culture. Near Aswan, history and the modern world collide. The construction of the Aswan Dam meant the old temples were at risk of being submerged. It was only at great expense that they were relocated in the 1960s. The most famous example of this act of international preservation is the two rock temples of Abu Simbel.

Over 95 percent of Egypt's total surface area is desert that covers more than one million sq km (386,000 sq mi). Only very few of the 75 million inhabitants earn their living in the oases of the western deserts, on the shores of the Red Sea or on Mount Sinai. The vast majority of the population live close together in the Nile valley. As early as the 5th century BC the Greek historian Herodotus wrote that 'Egypt is a gift of the Nile'.

The four colossal figures of Pharaoh Ramses II tower 20 m (65.5 ft) before the facade of the rock temple of Abu Simbel.

The long avenue of ram's-headed sphinxes in front of the temple of the god Amun in Luxor is particularly impressive at dusk.

The hot climate and the Nile's summer floods, which are nowadays controlled by the Aswan Dam, mean that farmers harvest two to four times a year depending on the crop being cultivated. This enables production of the country's basic food supply despite a rapidly increasing population.

In ancient times the Nile delta in the north of Egypt consisted of five branches bringing fertile alluvial soil with the ever plentiful waters. However, over the course of thousands of years the landscape has changed drastically. Today there are only two remaining branches that stretch from the north of Cairo through Lower Egypt to the Mediterranean Sea and water traffic on the river is now divided up with the help of an extensive canal network.

The Nile delta, which covers an area of 24,000 sq km (9,264 sq mi), is Egypt's most important agricultural region producing everything from corn, vegetables and fruit to the famous Egyptian long-fibre cotton. In the 19th century, Alexandria benefited enormously from this 'white gold' and developed into a modern, Mediterranean port city.

Cairo is located at the southern tip of the delta and connects Upper and Lower Egypt. The nation's capital dazzles visitors with the most diverse of sights. The pyramids in Giza in the west tower above the modern city. In the city center minarets, church towers and high-rise buildings vie for the attention of worshippers as Christians and Muslims make their way to prayers. Meanwhile, people of all backgrounds and nationalities stroll along the Nile in this, the 'Mother of the World' as locals have come to call their rich city.

The minarets of Cairo silhouetted in a glowing red-gold sunset.

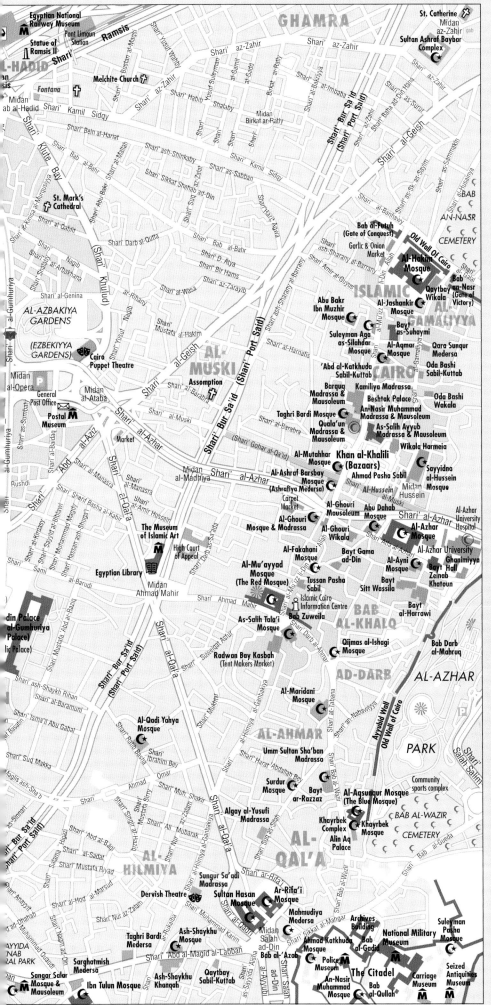

Cairo

The view from the citadel sweeps west over the minarets and the Nile to the silhouettes of the pyramids of Giza – if you're lucky. The Nile city is often hidden from view by the heavy, opaque cloud that floats above it. Humidity from the river, sandstorms from the encroaching desert and pollution from the congested traffic in the inner city are all part of the problem.

A Nilometer at the southern tip of Roda Island is testimony to the Egyptian capital's dignified age. Long before it was given the name of Cairo in the 10th century BC, priests serving ancient Egyptian gods set up wells all over the country to measure the level of the yearly Nile flood and then calculated taxes.

Opposite the island on the eastern bank was one of the country's most important inland ports, Per Hapi en Junu. When the Romans fortified the port, the early Christians made use of the well-protected area to build their first churches here. In the 'Candles Quarter' directly next to the Mari Girgis metro station, the Moallka Church, dedicated to the Virgin Mary,

of the most important institutions in the Islamic world. Bejewelled Islamic architecture was created between the city gates Bab el-Futuh and Bab en-Nasr in the north and Bab es-Suweila in the south.

Over a period of 600 years, Fatimids, Ajjubids, Mamlucks and Osmans had elegant mosques, palaces, commercial establishments, wells and schools built in Cairo. Salah ed-Din, who came to power in AD 1171, had his residence moved to the citadel, but Al-Qahira remained the lively center of the city. Even today, visitors are still fascinated by the bustling bazaars of the Khan el-Khalili. City planners were again kept busy under Mohammed Ali's reign, who used Paris as a model to transform

Top: The skyline at dawn.
Middle: Cairo with the Nile.
Bottom: The muezzin calls the faithful to prayer at the Bussra Mosque.

rises high upon the foundations of the Roman fortress.

In the next neighbourhood is the Ben-Ezra Synagogue where the famous scholar Moses Maimonides presided in the 12th century. It is famed as the location where the pharaoh's daughter rescued the baby Moses from the Nile. Just a few hundred meters north of the synagogue, Africa's oldest mosque gleams after extensive renovations. Amr Ibn el-As had it built in the center of the new capital, Fustat, in AD 642.

Almost 235 years later, Governor Ibn Tulun, appointed by the Abbasids, created an independent entity here on the Nile. His residence must have been magnificent. The enormous courtyard mosque (AD 876–879) is the only structure to have been preserved from this time and is still one of the largest mosques in the world, covering 2.5 ha (6.2 acres). New rulers arrived in Egypt ninety years later – the Fatimid shi'ites, who also needed their own new residence, of course. Surrounded by well-fortified walls they ensconced themselves in the palaces of Al-Qahira. Their Friday Mosque, el-Azhar, was built in AD 969 and is to this day one

Cairo into a modern metropolis in the 19th century. Art-nouveau facades between the Midan el-Opera and the Midan Talaat Harb are evocative of these times.

From here, it's just a stone's throw into modernity at the Midan et-Tahrir, where the first metro station was built, the Arab League has its headquarters and, at the northern end of the square, the treasures of the national museum take you back to the times of the pharaohs.

The sphinx, part human, part lion, was worshiped as a representation of the morning sun god as it crouches in a hollow before the Khafre pyramids. Even back in ancient Egyptian times, people would come to the Western Desert to admire the majestic splendor of these monuments of centuries past. Napoleon is said to

have paused in awe before the figures and instilled a similar sense of admiration in his soldiers as he stood here in 1798. It is still unclear who destroyed the Great Sphinx's nose, but time, sand, wind and pollution from Cairo are certainly taking their toll on this timeless structure in Giza.

The golden throne from the tomb of Tutankhamun portrays the young pharaoh with his wife still bathed in the rays of the sun god, Aten, who was elevated to the status of sole deity by Tutankhamun's predecessor, Akhenaten. It was not until the reign of Tutankhamun that the Egyptians returned to the former system of belief.

Tutankhamun rests in grave no. 62 in the Valley of the Kings, in one of three gold coffins inside a sarcophagus made of red quartzite. He is the only one of the great pharaohs who still lies in his original resting place. The chamber is also adorned with wall paintings.

Only one obelisk now rises before the pylon at the Temple of Amun in Luxor. Thanks to the Egyptian francophile Mohammed Ali, its counterpart has stood on the Place de la Concorde in Paris since 1836. The statues, which were placed before the pylon as decorative elements, display the great Pharaoh Ramses II.

Top: The evening lights create a wonderful ambience at the Temple of Amun in Luxor. The Avenue of Sphinxes leads to the pylon, which is dominated by one of two original obelisks placed here. Bottom: In the rear section of the temple are the imposing papyrus columns from the time of Amenhotep III.

There are almost too many elephants now in Etosha National Park. The pachyderms are best seen at the southern edge of the Etosha Pan where they come to drink, wallow in the mud, spray themselves with water and wash their young. Although the animals are used to vehicles and visitors, you should make sure you

do not get in their way, and retreat slowly if they behave defensively. Cows and bulls can react nervously and aggressively if they are with their young – they have been known to overturn small vehicles when agitated.

Swakopmund

The location selected for Swakopmund was not exactly ideal: the surf was fierce and the coast offered no natural protection for a harbor. Ships could only anchor far offshore, and goods and people had to be transported to the shore with landing boats. Although a breakwater eventually made the landing boats unnecessary, it could not stop the town's decline. The port was closed in 1919. Over the following decades, however, Swakopmund developed into an

This lighthouse is the icon of Swakopmund.

attractive seaside resort, and the town is today a popular holiday destination for Namibians from the highlands. The numerous German colonial buildings have been restored and give the town a nostalgic flair. The red-and-white striped lighthouse blinks between the palms, a luxury hotel has taken over the Art Nouveau train station, and the Imperial District Court is used as a presidential palace.
Walking through town you'll see the Hohenzollern House with the figure of Atlas supporting the world up in the gable; the Woermann House, where the shipping line owner would watch over his fleet from the tower; and the Princess Rupprecht Home, a former military hospital. After browsing the shops downtown, take a detour to the museum and try a German apple pie (Apfelstrudel) at Café Anton.

16 Moon Valley und Welwitschia Plains The Namib Desert starts right at the edge of the town of Swakopmund. It is part of the Namib Naukluft National Park, and those wanting to explore the park off of the main roads can only do so with a special permit from the Ministry of Environment and Tourism. The northern reaches of the park are dominated by the so-called Gravel Namib, sprawling gravel plains that occasionally feature granite formations or inselbergs (monadnocks).
The peculiar ecology of this gravel desert unfolds along the nature trail, Welwitschia Drive (only allowed with a permit). The route turns south from the B2 onto the C28 about 3 km (2 mi) east of Swakopmund, and the rest of the route is well signposted. Information boards explain particularities such as lichen that can emerge after years without a drop of water to then flourish during the next rains. About 18 km (11 mi) down the road you reach the Moon Valley lookout. The black stone in the valley has eroded into some bizarre formations and really does look like a lunar landscape. Another highlight of the park is the Welwitschia Plains, a UNESCO World Heritage Site. The *Welwitschia mirabilis*, a desert plant that looks more like an untidy clump of leaves, is par-

ticularly prevalent in this part of the Namib. The largest specimen, which is protected by a fence, is said to be over 1,500 years old. From Swakopmund, it's just 31 km (19 mi) along the coast to Walvis Bay.

17 Walvis Bay This settlement was founded by the Dutch in 1793. As the only deep-sea port on Namibia's coast until 1994, it actually remained a South African enclave in Namibian territory. The town, with its flat bungalows surrounded by gardens, is home to a commercial port and its inhabitants live off fishing and sea salt extraction. Up to 120,000 birds live in the large lagoon to the north of town including flamingos, peli-

cans and a number of other migratory birds.
From here, the C14 leads you through the flat, monotonous landscape of the Namib Desert. The road follows the steep escarpment and continues into the mountains along a winding track. You reach the turnoff to the Kuiseb Canyon after about 130 km (81 mi).

18 Kuiseb Canyon The Kuiseb is one of several rivers that only runs at certain times of the year. The water originates in the Namibian highlands and crosses the Namib on its way towards the Atlantic.
Around one million years ago, the Kuiseb cut a narrow gorge into the foothills of the escarp-

ment that became famous for a report by German geologists Henno Martin and Wolfgang Korn who hid from the South African authorities here for nearly three years when World War II broke out.
The C14 climbs the foothills of the escarpment over the Kuiseb Pass before heading south and passing through the fantastic scenery of the Namib and arriving in the Naukluft. At the Büllsport guest farm about 145 km (90 mi) away, the D0854 turns off towards the entrance of the Naukluft, part of the national park of the same name.

19 Naukluft This massif, with peaks up to 2,000 m (6,562 ft), appears craggy and precipitous,

Lüderitz and Kolmanskop

In 1883, Bremen businessman Adolf Lüderitz sent his delegate, Heinrich Vogelsang, to the Nama people of Bethanie to acquire land from them. Vogelsang bought the bay and part of the Namib Desert, founded a settlement and named it Lüderitz Bay in honor of his sponsor. Adolf Lüderitz then succeeded in having the land placed under German protection, and German South-West Africa was born. Today, Lüderitz is the country's second most important port after Walvis Bay. Worth seeing here are the well-preserved colonial villas, such as the Goerkehaus, and the rock church, consecrated in 1912. The waterfront is the place to be in the evening, where numerous restaurants and pubs serve fresh seafood.

The Namib has taken Kolmanskop back for itself.

A detour to Bartolomeu Diaz's Padrão takes you 22 km (14 mi) north to a stone cross sitting atop the surf at Diaz Point, where the Portuguese sailor placed it in 1488.

The main attraction here, however, is the diamond mining ghost town of Kolmanskop, founded in 1908, after the first diamond finds were made in the desert. It grew to become a city of fortune hunters and prospectors, with a casino, bowling alley, theater and prestigious villas. The mine sites were exhausted by 1930, and the town itself was abandoned by 1950.

Kolmanskop can only be visited as part of a guided tour organized by Lüderitz Bay Safaris & Tours. Today, sand blows through open windows, the lanes in the bowling alley no longer shine, and the pommel horse and parallel bars in the gym appear to be waiting for the gymnastics team to return.

killed there two years later. The castle today serves as a museum with original furnishings.

Following the D0826 and D0831 for 43 km (27 mi) you will reach the C14. Continue along it for another 137 km (85 mi) until you reach Bethanie.

㉒ Bethanie It is worth making a stop at the Schmelen House in this sleepy little town. The house was built in 1814 by a missionary, Heinrich Schmelen, who lived here among the Nama people in an effort to evangelize and convert them. About 22 km (14 mi) further on, the road meets the B4, which you follow westward for roughly 222 km (138 mi) as far as Lüderitz. The area near Garub train station is home to wild horses that are probably descendents of German soldiers' horses. The Namib Desert on the left of the road is a restricted area for diamonds. On the right you is the southern edge of the national park.

Shortly before Lüderitz on the left-hand side is the former

but thanks to several springs, vegetation thrives in its valleys, and numerous species of birds nest in its mountains. The most striking inhabitant is the endangered Hartmann's mountain zebra. Multi-day hikes lead through the wilderness, and also include a 4x4 trail.

Back at Büllsport farm you reach Solitaire, 50 km (31 mi) north on the C14. On the C19 it is another 80 km (50 mi) to Sesriem, the starting point for trips into the Namib dunes, which stretch over 300 km (186 mi) from Kuiseb in the north to Koichab in the south, and 140 km (87 mi) into the country's interior.

⓴ Sossusvlei Sesriem is an elegant lodge near the deep,

narrow Sesriem Canyon, and also the gateway to that part of the Namib Naukluft Park, where the famous dunes surround the Sossusvlei.

From Sesriem, an asphalt road initially heads along the mostly dry bed of the Tsauchab River. Here, the dunes soar out of the plain to heights of up to 170 m 558 ft). The road ends after about 60 km (37 mi), and the next 5 km (3 mi) to the Sossusvlei through deep sand are either covered on foot or with a four-wheel-drive vehicle. A wall of star dunes surrounds the Vlei, which only contains water after good rainy seasons. Adventurous folks can climb the dunes along the ridge to get a fantastic panorama of the desert.

Follow the same road back to Sesriem and then turn to the south onto the D0826. On the right, the road is lined by the Namib dunes, and on the left by the Zaris Mountains. After 135 km (84 mi), the D0826 turns to the east. About 20 km (12 mi) later, a medieval knights' castle under palm trees appears as if out of the blue.

㉑ Duwisib Castle This castle was designed by architect Wilhelm Sander in 1909, who had erected many colonial buildings in south-western Africa. A German aristocrat, Hansheinrich von Wolff, originally wanted to breed horses here, but was called to the front after the outbreak of World War I and was

1 Covering roughly 5 million ha (12 million acres), Namib Naukluft Park is Africa's largest nature reserve.

2 Flamingos find plenty of food in the Walvis Bay lagoon.

3 Gemsbok or oryx antelope are national animal of Namibia.

Top: The Tsauchab River starts in the highlands and ends in the Dune Namib. In good rainy seasons, it runs with so much water that it bursts through the dunes and fills the basins (known as vleis) with water. Wild ducks then caวort on the lake between the dunes, while springboks and oryx antelope come to drink.

Bottom: The dunes on the edge of the Sossuvlei and the nearby Dead Vlei reach heights of up to 350 m (1,148 ft) and are some of the highest star dunes in the world. While the sickle dunes on the coast migrate up to 75 m (82 yds) a year, the star dunes in the central Namib only shift about 10 m (11 yds).

For a long time, the area around East Pier in Cape Town port seemed destined t̶o̶ ̶r̶u̶i̶n̶, but at the end of the 1980s it was converted into a shopp̶i̶n̶g̶ ̶a̶n̶d̶ leisure district called the Victoria & Alfred Waterfront, based on the concept of San Francisco's Fisherman's Wharf. With its myriad stores, theaters, outdoor cafes,

restaurants and hotels it has become a major draw for tourists in the city, which does not suffer from any shortage of attractions as it is. The yachts and fishing boats in the marina also contribute to the charm of the waterfront.

The colorful beach huts in Muizenberg give this seaside town a nostalgic, Scandanavian feel and fit in well with the Victorian-style houses of the region. They managed to survive from the 19th century and are now rented not on a daily, but rather on a seasonal basis for the entire summer. Here on the western

fringes of False Bay, the coast drops gently into the ocean and the bright, flat beach is much safer and more relaxed than the Atlantic west coast of the country, with its rocky cliffs and strong currents.

Cape vineyards

Even if you aren't a huge wine fan, you should not miss the opportunity to try and perhaps buy some of the Cape's more precious offerings.

Cape Dutch-style winery, surrounded by endless vineyards.

Wine has been grown in the Cape region for nearly 300 years now. The conditions are ideal for red wines, with plenty of sunshine and no frosts. Numerous signposted wine routes make exploration easy. The oldest of these runs around Stellenbosch. The smallest and most exclusive is the 'Constantia' wine route connecting three wineries built in Cape Dutch style.

The wine-growing town of Franschhoek, founded in the late 17th century by French Huguenots, is also worth a visit, as is a tour of the vintner's co-operative KWV in Paarl, whose cellars contain what are supposedly the world's largest casks.

Tulbagh follow the narrow, winding R44 via the jagged Bain's Pass. It is the industrial center of the wine-growing region and the seat of the wine-growers' co-operative KWV, which was founded in 1918 and now looks after more than 5,000 individual vintners.

It stores more than 300 million litres (66 million gal) of wine, and more than three times this amount is processed here every year. There are guided tours that take you to five wine barrels alleged to be the largest in the world. Each of them holds more than 200,000 litres (909,000 gal), was made without nails and weighs 25 tonnes (27.5 tons). The town was named after 'The Pears' ('De Paarl'), giant granite summits that sparkle in the sunlight after it rains. On one slope of Paarl Mountain, 600 m (1,970 ft) high, the Tall Monument, an imposing granite needle, commemorates the development and spread of Afrikaans, the Boer language. Local vineyards such as Nederburg, Rhebokshof, Fairview, Backsberg or Kanonkop are considered the very best by wine enthusiasts.

⑱ Franschhoek This wine-growing town has some extensive vineyards with their typically large mansions. Huguenots fleeing from religious persecution in Europe at the end of the 17th century came to South Africa

and settled in this picturesque valley. Farm names such as Dieu Donné, La Provence or Mont Rochelle testify to the pioneers' provenance.

A large monument at the exit of the village commemorates their achievements. The unusually large number of first-class restaurants, bistros and small inns also hints strongly at the town's French heritage.

⑲ Stellenbosch Nicknamed 'Boer Oxford' because of its venerable elite university, this town is the cultural heart of the winelands. In 1679 the governor Van der Stel established a border settlement on Eerste River. A stroll across the De Braak central square and along Dorp Straat, with its long rows of bright white, partly thatched buildings in classic Cape Dutch style, testify to its rank as South Africa's second-oldest town.

The Burgerhuis with its small town museum is worth a visit, as are the old stagecoach house, the Rhineland missionary church and the beautifully restored mansion of Libertas Parva, which houses an interesting wine museum as well as an art gallery. Well-manicured lawns, shaded oak lanes and the botanical gardens right next to the university campus are definitely worth a leisurely stroll.

The hiking and bicycle trails through the surrounding vineyards are very well-signposted

and nothing if not idyllic. They are certainly a safer option than driving if you have enjoyed some of the local wine!

There are two routes back into Cape Town: either take the N1 back directly, or follow the road south to Somerset West and turn onto the N2 at the starting point of this journey.

1 The Stellenbosch vineyards grow some renowned high-quality wines.

2 It does not get more picturesque than this – the winery at Boschendal is attractive not only because of its excellent wines, but also because of its excellent cuisine and meticulously maintained Cape Dutch architecture.

Cape flora

Botanists have divided the earth's plants into seven floral kingdoms. The smallest but by far the most varied of these is the Cape floristic region. On roughly 70,000 sq km (27,000 sq mi) of space there are approximately 8,600 species of flowering plants. A third of these are native to just the Cape Peninsula, an area measuring only 518 sq km (200 sq mi).

The most characteristic element of the local flora is the so-called fynbos vegetation, which primarily consists of heather and protea plants. The coastal regions receive high levels of rain during the colder months. By contrast, the

Drake meant. The Cape of Good Hope is actually a few kilometers to the west, but the view is much less spectacular from there.

Your return journey goes along a wild, rocky coastline via Simon's Town with its pretty Victorian center and the fishing ports of

Fish Hoek and Kalk Bay. In the surfers' paradise of Muizenberg beach, the colourful huts recall times gone by.

After 20 km (12 miles) or so eastbound on Baden Powell Drive, which runs in a large arc along the flat beaches of False Bay, you get back to the N2. But at Somerset West you leave it behind again. For 60 km (40 miles) you then drive along the so-called Whale Route at the base of the Koeeberg mountains where lovely coastal scenery, and possibly some majestic marine mammals, will accompany you via Kleinmond to Hermanus.

❸ Hermanus This picturesque town, founded by fishermen in 1855, is located on the northern shore of Walker Bay between Kleinrivierberge and the sea. It is famous not only for its many wild flowers, magnificent beaches and outstanding water-sports

options, but also for its deep-sea fishing.

Many people from Cape Town come to spend their weekends in this holiday village where fishing boats, dreamy cottages and the old port give it the feel of an open-air museum.

During the winter, from July to November, Hermanus is a hot spot for whale-watchers from all around the world. They even have a bellman employed at the beach to ring when humpbacks, right whales or even orcas are

1 Fishing ports like Kalk Bay dot the rocky western shore of False Bay.

2 Rocky coastline in the Cape Province.

3 The Cape of Good Hope – every globetrotter's dream.

4 Penguin colonies swimming in the ocean near Table Mountain.

Top: There are more than 100 species of heather (Ericaceae) on the Cape Peninsula.
Middle: The King Protea is South Africa's national flower.
Bottom: Blood flowers bloom from December to April.

inland Karoo steppe is semi-arid with vegetation mostly made up of succulents – herbs and shrubs with fleshy leaves and magnificent flowers. Large forests like the ones near George are relatively rare in South Africa.

Chapman's Peak Drive

It may only be a drive of 10 km (6 miles), but you will never forget this scenic road cut directly into the steep coastal rock faces south of Hout Bay by Italian prisoners-of-war during World War II. Starting in an idyllic fishing port, the road winds its way around the colourful cliffs up to Noordhoek. From its highest point at 600 m (1,970 ft) above Chapman's Bay there is a breathtaking view across to Hout Bay, a rocky outcrop called 'The Sentinel' and the hills around Constantia.

The colorful beach huts in Muizenberg give this seaside town a nostalgic, Scandanavian feel and fit in well with the Victorian-style houses of the region. They managed to survive from the 19th century and are now rented not on a daily, but rather on a seasonal basis for the entire summer. Here on the western

cacy. Because Great Whites do not reach sexual maturity until they are twelve to eighteen years of age, however, and only reproduce every two to three years, we shall soon only be able to see this magnificent creature in movies if drastic measures are not taken immediately to stop its eradication.

Detour

Addo Elephant National Park

The addo elephants that live here are only a small relic of the giant herds that once roamed freely across the Eastern Cape. However, an encounter with one of them is still a very impressive experience. About 200 of these reddish and slightly smaller variants of the true African elephants live in this national park, which is located just 70 km (43 miles) north of Port Elizabeth. When the first settlers arrived in the area near the Sunday River in the 1820s, a peaceful coexistence of humans and elephants proved to be impossible. The giant animals continuously devastated local harvests. In 1919, the farmers hired a game hunter to put an end to the problem. The man did a very

As well as elephants, the Addo Elephant National Park is home to mountain zebras (top) and warthogs (bottom).

thorough job. Only around a dozen addo elephants survived.

In 1931, in order to protect the remaining specimens, some farmers established a reserve measuring 86 sq km (33 sq mi) and providing the herbivorous animals with ideal conditions for their survival. Today, a total of 45 km (28 miles) of roads and tracks criss-cross the national park.

Artificial watering holes make popular observation points where along with the elephants you can see lions, leopards, antelopes, buffalo and perhaps even a specimen of the extremely rare black rhino.

forests nearby that have provided generations of local people with the economic base for a thriving timber industry. The forests are also home to a small herd of free-roaming elephants. A regional speciality is handcrafted hardwood furniture made from yellow wood, iron wood and stink wood.

The town's landmarks are two giant sandstone cliffs called 'The Heads', which tower above the small canal connecting the lagoon to the open ocean. West of Knysna is the Featherbed Nature Reserve, home to the rare blue duikers and a host of other rare bird species.

The most magnificent beaches in the area are called Brenton and Noetzie. The Elephant Nature Walk in Diepwalle State Forest offers some truly outstanding hiking. You get to it along the N9, which branches off inland a few miles after Knysna heading towards Prince Alfred's Pass and Avontour.

⑩ Plettenberg Bay There are some ideal opportunities for hiking in the forests of Kranshoek and Harkerville, approximately 30 km (18 miles) east of Knysna. A few minutes after that in the car take a look to your right off the N2 to see some truly fantastic scenery.

Plettenberg Bay, with its almost 10 km (6 miles) of immaculate sandy beaches and crystal blue waters, really is the essence of the 'South African Riviera'. From July to September there are whales calving within sight of numerous exclusive hotels.

⑪ Tsitsikamma National Park This national park, covering 5,000 ha (12,350 acres) of land, has everything that naturelovers may desire – bizarre cliffs, lonely beaches, steep gorges and luscious vegetation if you make it further up country. Founded in 1962, the area also includes the rich coastal waters.

The Otter Trail, which starts in Nature's Valley and runs along the rocky shore for 42 km (26 miles) right up to the mouth of the Storms River, is one of the country's most attractive longdistance hiking trails. To do it you first have to acquire a permit – only the first 3 km (2 miles) from the eastern entrance are open to those without one. However, even within that distance you are fortunate enough to be able to visit the huge waterfalls and a spectacular hanging bridge that stretches 190 m (623 ft) over the chasm at

a height of 130 m (427 ft). If you are into snorkelling, there is an underwater nature trail where you can go exploring the large variety of marine plants and animals.

⑫ Cape St Francis Near Humansdorp a road turns off to Cape St Francis on your right. This jaunt towards the coast is about 60 km (40 miles) and is well worth doing for a few reasons. First is that the village at the end of the cape really does have a charm of its own with its whitewashed houses and black rooftops. Second is that the long beaches towards Oyster Bay and Jeffrey's Bay to the east are among the most beautiful in South Africa. The third reason has to do with the waves that break here.

In the 1960s Jeffrey's Bay was made legend in the movie *The Endless Summer*, and the waves

still break perfectly here, sometimes for hundreds of yards from the point into the bay. Watching the surfers on this world-famous wave is an enjoyable way to spend a day at the lovely beach. Back on the N2 it is only 70 km (43 miles) to Port Elizabeth.

⑬ Port Elizabeth P.E., as the locals call this important port city, has the gold and diamond trade to thank for its rise. These days the heart of the South African car industry beats a little upriver in Port Elizabeth's 'twin city' of Uitenhage on the banks of the sizeable Swartkops River.

1 An especially spectacular stretch of coastline in Tsitsikamma National Park.

2 Subtropical climate and vegetation – the rain-forests in Tsitsikamma National Park.

Scene at a watering hole in Addo Elephant National Park. 100 years ago these elephants were almost extinct. Today nearly 200 of the giants live on 9,000 ha (22,000 acres) of reserve land. The elephant population density at this park is four times that of Kruger National Park.

Although 'Cape Detroit' is definitely not known for its scenic beauty, this port metropolis with its one million inhabitants still exudes its own personal brand of Victorian charm.

Its lively center and the starting point for guided tours is called Market Square, where the town hall is magnificent and the 'campanile' tower (52 m/170 ft) even has a viewing platform. From Park Donkin Reserve, you have a magnificent view over Algoa Bay and there are some beautifully restored houses from the Victorian era as well as an old lighthouse.

The Museum Complex includes a snake park, dolphin shows in the Oceanium and a regional museum that promise a good variety of entertainment. Close by there are some exquisite beaches such as Kings Beach and Humewood Beach.

Instead of taking the same coastal route back towards Cape Town, we recommend driving the N62/60, which takes you further into the heartland of South Africa. This inland route branches off about 20 km (13 miles) west of Humansdorp, winding its way westwards past Joubertina, Avontour, Uniondale and De Rust – all of which are smart and tidy but otherwise unremarkable agricultural towns.

The landscape of the Little Karoo, as this interior plateau is called, extends over 250 km (155 miles) over a swathe of land about 60 km (40 miles) wide and is strikingly different to the coastal areas. This area, sandwiched between the Kouga and Swart Ranges to the north and the Outeniqua and Langeberg Ranges to the south, gets very little rain. There are colourful rock formations on either side of the road and large areas of the abundant fertile soil are irrigated. Over the years, ostrich farms have developed into a hugely important impetus for the local economy.

⑭ Oudtshoorn This provincial town with 50,000 inhabitants is the 'urban center' of the Little

Karoo. You can hardly imagine it these days, but in the late 19th century it was even a fashion hub and, at one point, a group of inventive farmers decided on a new tack for the fashion scene. They started large-scale ostrich breeding operations in this dry valley and subsequently managed to convince the haute couture of Vienna, Paris and New York that feather boas, capes or fans made from ostrich plumes were indispensable accessories for the fashionably up-to-date. At the height of the resulting boom around 750,000 birds were delivering 500 tonnes of feathers a year. Having become rich overnight, these ostrich 'barons', as they now called themselves, erected decadent mansions of stone and cast iron, the so-called 'feather palaces'. After a downturn lasting several decades, the ostrich business has recently regained some momentum in the wake of the low-cholesterol craze. Ostrich meat is now exported on a large scale,

as is their leather. On some farms, you can try out specialities such as ostrich steaks and omelettes made from the birds' giant eggs, watch ostrich races or even risk a ride on one.

Located 30 km (18 miles) north of the town is an absolute five-star attraction – the Cango Caves. These are some of the world's most terrific stalactite caves and you get to see all their beauty during the course of a two-hour guided tour.

Ostrich farms and other plantations, neat towns with names such as Calitzdorp, Ladismith or Barrydale, and an imposing backdrop of mountain ranges accompany you through this charming region. After passing Montagu, a charming center for growing fruit and wine at the western end of Little Karoo Valley with numerous historic buildings, the road winds its way up more than 6 km (4 miles) to Cogmanskloof Pass. It then goes through a tunnel under a jagged barrier called 'Turkey Rock' and

carries on down into the wide and fertile Bree Valley.

⑮ Robertson This small town is blessed with a wonderfully mild climate and extremely fertile soil. High-quality apples, apricots and above all grapes grow here in luscious abundance. Wild roses, old oak trees and jacaranda trees grow by the roadside. A long sandy beach along the riverbank is reminiscent of the French Riviera.

The area also has a plethora of accommodation in the form of holiday apartments or campsites. Sheilam Cactus Garden is a must for hobby botanists. It is located 8 km (5 miles) outside the town and has one of the most comprehensive cactus collections anywhere in the world. The next main town on the N60 is Worcester, which has few attractions apart from its botanic gardens and Kleinplasie Farm Museum, which invites you to take a touching journey back in time to the daily routine of an 18th-century farm.

There is a worthwhile detour here via Wolseley to the small town of Tulbagh, which is 70 km (43 miles) north of our route.

⑯ Tulbagh Also surrounded by extensive orchards and vineyards, Tulbagh was devastated by an earthquake in 1969 but has since been fully restored. The town center around Church Street is considered to be the most complete collection of Cape Dutch architecture in the country. The town's oldest building is Oude Kerk (Old Church), which was built in 1743.

⑰ Paarl To reach this small town on the Berg River from

1 Scenic Karoo landscape.

2 Ostrich plumes, meat and leather are sought-after export goods.

3 In many places, irrigation turns the Little Karoo into a Garden of Eden.

Cape vineyards

Even if you aren't a huge wine fan, you should not miss the opportunity to try and perhaps buy some of the Cape's more precious offerings.

Cape Dutch-style winery, surrounded by endless vineyards.

Wine has been grown in the Cape region for nearly 300 years now. The conditions are ideal for red wines, with plenty of sunshine and no frosts. Numerous signposted wine routes make exploration easy. The oldest of these runs around Stellenbosch. The smallest and most exclusive is the 'Constantia' wine route connecting three wineries built in Cape Dutch style.
The wine-growing town of Franschhoek, founded in the late 17th century by French Huguenots, is also worth a visit, as is a tour of the vintner's co-operative KWV in Paarl, whose cellars contain what are supposedly the world's largest casks.

Tulbagh follow the narrow, winding R44 via the jagged Bain's Pass. It is the industrial center of the wine-growing region and the seat of the wine-growers' co-operative KWV, which was founded in 1918 and now looks after more than 5,000 individual vintners.
It stores more than 300 million litres (66 million gal) of wine, and more than three times this amount is processed here every year. There are guided tours that take you to five wine barrels alleged to be the largest in the world. Each of them holds more than 200,000 litres (909,000 gal), was made without nails and weighs 25 tonnes (27.5 tons). The town was named after 'The Pears' ('De Paarl'), giant granite summits that sparkle in the sunlight after it rains. On one slope of Paarl Mountain, 600 m (1,970 ft) high, the Tall Monument, an imposing granite needle, commemorates the development and spread of Afrikaans, the Boer language.
Local vineyards such as Nederburg, Rhebokshof, Fairview, Backsberg or Kanonkop are considered the very best by wine enthusiasts.

18 Franschhoek This wine-growing town has some extensive vineyards with their typically large mansions. Huguenots fleeing from religious persecution in Europe at the end of the 17th century came to South Africa

and settled in this picturesque valley. Farm names such as Dieu Donné, La Provence or Mont Rochelle testify to the pioneers' provenance.
A large monument at the exit of the village commemorates their achievements. The unusually large number of first-class restaurants, bistros and small inns also hints strongly at the town's French heritage.

19 Stellenbosch Nicknamed 'Boer Oxford' because of its venerable elite university, this town is the cultural heart of the winelands. In 1679 the governor Van der Stel established a border settlement on Eerste River. A stroll across the De Braak central square and along Dorp Straat, with its long rows of bright white, partly thatched buildings in classic Cape Dutch style, testify to its rank as South Africa's second-oldest town.
The Burgerhuis with its small town museum is worth a visit, as are the old stagecoach house, the Rhineland missionary church and the beautifully restored mansion of Libertas Parva, which houses an interesting wine museum as well as an art gallery. Well-manicured lawns, shaded oak lanes and the botanical gardens right next to the university campus are definitely worth a leisurely stroll.
The hiking and bicycle trails through the surrounding vineyards are very well-signposted

and nothing if not idyllic. They are certainly a safer option than driving if you have enjoyed some of the local wine!
There are two routes back into Cape Town: either take the N1 back directly, or follow the road south to Somerset West and turn onto the N2 at the starting point of this journey.

1 The Stellenbosch vineyards grow some renowned high-quality wines.

2 It does not get more picturesque than this – the winery at Boschendal is attractive not only because of its excellent wines, but also because of its excellent cuisine and meticulously maintained Cape Dutch architecture.

The Twelve Apostles The coastal road between Cape Town and Llandudno is also called Cape Riviera. The Twelve Apostles make a charming backdrop to any beach holiday on Camps Bay.

Paarl The largest town away from the coast is said to be the cradle of Afrikaans, the Boer language. Alongside its museum and many historical buildings, the cellars of the KWV vintner's co-operative and the magnificent wineries in the surrounding area are well worth a visit.

Addo Elephant National Park This protected area houses 200 addo elephants, which were nearly wiped out 100 years ago. It is also home to the last Cape buffalo herd.

Cango Caves The stalactite caves in the Swart Mountains are among the world's most impressive. The 'Big Hall' is 107 m (351 ft) long and 16 m (52 ft) high.

Cape Town Globetrotters say that this city, founded in the 17th century, is one of the world's most beautiful. Its port, its hillside houses and Table Mountain itself make a stunning sight.

Franschhoek This wine-growing town located in a picturesque valley was founded by Huguenots some 300 years ago. The French heritage is visible not only in an interesting museum and monument, but also in a large number of excellent restaurants and wineries.

Port Elizabeth This port city with its Victorian charm has gold and diamonds to thank for its rise. The museum compound includes a snake park and the regional museum is well worth visiting.

Chapman's Peak Drive The coastal road between Noordhoek and Hout Bay is one of the most spectacular in the world, with breathtaking views, such as this one looking east.

Kogelberg Nature Reserve This protected area west of Hermanus is the heart of the Cape floral kingdom.

Wilderness National Park East of George there is an extensive area of freshwater and saltwater lakes that are home to innumerable birds. Some of the lakes are connected via the Serpentine.

Outeniqua Choo-Tjoe Train A ride on this nostalgic steam train from George to Knysna across the Knysna lagoon is one of the highlights of the magnificent Garden Route.

Cape of Good Hope A visit to the southern tip of the Cape Peninsula is a must for any visitor to South Africa. Once seafarers had passed the 'Cape of Storms', they were safely on their way home.

Swellendam This small town was founded in 1745 and still exudes the pioneer spirit with its Cape Dutch buildings.

Bontebok National Park These days there are around 300 of the once-endangered pied buck roaming the park.

Tsitsikamma National Park This park of 5,000 ha (12,350 acres) has some bizarre cliffs, lonely beaches and a heartland rich in abundant vegetation.

Icebergs floating on Lynn Canal (145 km/90 miles) between Skagway and Juneau.

Route 39

Alaska

Far North on the Alaska Highway

Americans like to call their 49th state 'The Last Frontier'. In Alaska, sea-shores, rivers, forests, mountains and glaciers remain almost untouched, brown bears fish for salmon, sea lions fight for territory, and herds of cari-bou trek across the tundra. But even this far north the cities are expanding, oil production is becoming a hazard for the wilderness and civilization is encroaching slowly but steadily on the pristine landscape. Fortunately, sev-eral national parks have been established, and this route takes you there.

When William Seward, the US Secretary of State, bought Alaska from the Russians for two cents per acre in 1867, this vast empty expanse of land was quickly derid-ed as 'Seward's folly'. But the billions of barrels of oil that have since flown through the Alaskan Pipeline have more than earned the initial purchase price he paid.

In Alaska, there are eight national parks protecting the state's valuable natural

resources. By area, the Alaskan peninsula in the north-west of the American conti-nent is the largest state in the US. It meas-ures 1.5 million sq km (1.3 sq mi), easily big enough to fit Western Europe into it. From the Canadian border, which is 2,500 km (1,550 miles) long, the peninsu-la stretches nearly 4,000 km (2,480 miles) to the furthest of the Aleutian Islands on the western tip of the state. To the north of Alaska is the Beaufort Sea, to the west

A walrus herd on the Alaskan coast.

the Bering Straits, and to the south the Pacific Ocean.

The Pacific coast is broken up into innu-merable islands, peninsulas and deep fjords that reach far into the interior. Mount McKinley is North America's high-est mountain at 6,194 m (20,323 ft), and Juneau is the only state capital that is accessible only by boat, via the Alaska Marine Highway, or by plane. Of its highland plains, 40,000 sq km (15,000 sq mi) are covered by glaciers. North of the Arctic Circle, the permafrost soil only thaws to a maximum depth of half a meter, but agriculture is still possible in the Matanuska Valley.

Until 1942, there was no way to get to Alaska by land, and only when the Japan-ese threatened to close in on Alaska did the US government decide to build a road connection through Canada. On 9 March

Mount Wrangell (4,317 m/14,164 ft) is an extinct volcano clearly visible from Glenn Highway, which connects Tok Junction with Anchorage.

Carved out by glaciers, Wonder Lake provides an impressive reflection of Mount McKinley, North America's highest mountain.

1942, a total of 11,000 people began construction on this road, about 2,300 km (1,430 miles) long, between Dawson Creek in Canada to the south and Delta Junction to the north. Despite the huge difficulties encountered, this pioneer route was in use by 20 November 1942 after an impressively short construction period of only eight months.

After the war it was handed over to the civil authorities and gradually improved. Today it is open year-round and in all weather conditions. It remains the only land connection between the USA and Alaska, and despite a tarmac surface along its entire length, the highway is indeed still a challenge. Be prepared for summer snowstorms, mud-slides and washed-out bridges.

The challenge has its rewards, however. Unforgettable scenery awaits you, often right by the roadside, where you occasionally see bears with their cubs, or elks with giant antlers.

Fairbanks and Anchorage are modern cities, but even here the wilderness comes right to your doorstep. A trip into Denali National Park with the mighty Mount McKinley (6,194 m/20,323 ft) is a challenging and unique experience for any visitor. If you want to get even closer to the 'real' Alaska, you can fly from Anchorage to King Salmon in the west and then take a hydroplane to Katmai National Park and Preserve. In July you can watch bears catching salmon from incredibly close range, a world-class sight. Or pay a visit to Kodiak Island with its massive Kodiak bears that weigh up to 500 kg (1,100 lbs) and reach heights of up to 3 m (10 ft). Wilderness in its purest form.

The Arctic tundra is home to small herds of shaggy musk oxen.

Alaska's Whales

'Whale ahead!' That cry means it is time to pay attention. Whale-watching is a truly impressive spectacle. The fountains of water that they blast from their blowholes and the grace of their dorsal fins sliding through the surface of the water as they prepare to dive is something to behold.

Off the Alaskan coast, whale-watching is possible from early summer through to September. During this time, humpback whales come here from their winter quarters off the Mexican coast or from Hawaii, 4,500 km (3,000 miles) away. They come to feed on the large shoals of herring and other fish that abound in these cold waters.

Only rarely do humpback whales make their own rainbow.

These dark grey whales can grow to 16 m (52 ft) in length and weigh up to 40 tons. Their flukes are their individual 'fingerprints'. Each whale has its own unique pattern that does not recur anywhere else in the entire population. These patterns are used by scientists to help identify and study individuals.

Studies have shown that male whales are quite 'musical'. Swimming at 30–50 m (100–150 ft) below the surface, they perform bizarre 'solos' composed of intricate, recurring patterns of sound in hopes of attracting females. Whales give birth to their young in their winter quarters just off the Californian and Mexican coasts. At birth, baby whales already weigh as much as 1.65 tonnes (1.5 tons).

Many places in the south-east of Alaska are good for whale-watching. Some can be reached by boat from Juneau or Haines, including the Inside Passage (Alaska Marine Highway) with its abundance of fish, Sitka, Chatham Straits, Glacier Bay and Frederick Sound.

Our Alaskan dream route begins in Juneau, the capital. After a boat trip across to Haines we take the Haines Highway to the Alaska Highway as far as Border City Lodge where the route actually goes through Canada. Back in Alaska via Fairbanks and Anchorage, the route takes us to Homer on the Kenai Peninsula.

❶ Juneau Alaska's capital is located on a narrow stretch of coastal plain between Gastineau Channel and the steep slopes of Mount Juneau (1,091 m/3,580 ft). Right outside town are the towering Coast Mountains with spectacular glaciers.

In 1880, gold diggers Joe Juneau and Dick Harris first found gold in what is now the town's river. By World War II more than 150 million dollars' worth of the precious metal had been discovered in the area.

As early as 1906 the Alaskan state government was moved to this northern El Dorado. The mines have long been shut down now, and Juneau has become a quiet governmental town. More than half the town's population is involved in running the state.

Both of the town's most important sights are located on

Travel information

Route profile
Length: approx. 3,000 km (1,850 miles), excluding detours
Time required: 3 weeks
Start: Juneau
End: Homer
Route (main locations): Juneau, Glacier Bay National Park, Skagway, Haines, Haines Junction, Whitehorse, Kluane National Park, Tok Junction, Delta Junction, Fairbanks, Denali National Park, Eklutna, Anchorage, Portage, Seward, Kenai, Homer

Traffic information:
Drive on the right in the USA. Speed limits in towns are 25–30 mph (40–48 km/h), and outside towns 65 mph (105 km/h). You must stop when you see a school bus with the indicators on. In Canada, distances are indicated in kilometers, in Alaska in miles. Side roads are commonly unsurfaced – watch out for airborne gravel.

When to go:
The best time to go is from mid-May to late September.

The road into Denali National Park is only open from mid-June.

Information:
Alaska general:
www.alaska.com
www.travelalaska.com
Ferries in Alaska:
Alaska Marine Highway
www.dot.state.ak.us/amhs
Alaska Ferry
www.akferry.org
National Parks:
www.us-national-parks.net

Totem poles – 'history books' carved in cedar trees

The north-west coastal Indians were real masters of the art of wood carving. From Vancouver to Prince Rupert to Ketchikan you can find their characteristic totem poles depicting Indian myths and legends.

The Tlingit Indians on Alaska's southern coast were particularly expressive,

On Canada's west coast and in Alaska, there are many Indian totem poles and long houses with fascinating patterns.

carving important images from their spiritual universe right into the cedar trees. The depictions cover events such as the births, marriages and deaths of local chieftains, or they illustrate entire mythologies.

The most prevalent images are human faces and indigenous animals such as eagles, bears, salmon, whales and frogs. Ravens are a very common theme. To the Indians, these birds were the ancestors of all humankind. Indian totem poles often represent a clan's mythical family tree.

The animals serve to recall the stories of achievements and character traits of important clan members, as well as record legendary events such as storms or battles. They also indicate the privileges and social standing of individual families.

The largest number of these elaborate totem poles can be found in Ketchikan in Alaska's southern regions. At the Totem Heritage Center, a total of thirty-three poles have been resurrected. A further thirteen poles have been put up in a totem park near a beautifully carved and painted Potlatch house, a place where ceremonies were held.

Haines or Skagway you can also take scenic flights over Glacier Bay. The first leg on our route to the north is completed by boat.

❸ Haines This town at the northern end of Lynn Canal used to be a Chilkat settlement. The Chilkats are a sub-tribe of the Tlingit Indians. Worth seeing are the old military outpost 'Fort William H. Seward', the Chilkat Center and a reconstructed Tlingit tribal house.

Before carrying on, you should take the ferry across to Skagway (1 hour) at the end of Taiya Inlet and visit the former gold-diggers' settlement there.

❹ Skagway When gold was discovered on the Klondike River in October 1897, the population of Skagway grew to more than 20,000 almost overnight as

1 Mendenhall Glacier feeds off the massive Juneau Icefield (10,000 sq km/ 3,860 sq mi). Its glacial tongue is 2.5 km (1.6 miles) wide.

2 Haines is located at the end of Inside Passage, where the Chilkat River flows into Lynn Canal, a fjord that stretches 145 km (90 miles).

3 In Glacier Bay National Park, glaciers have carved out some inviting beaches that are now popular with walruses.

Franklin Street, the town's main road. One of them is the Red Dog Saloon, which was already infamous during the gold rush. The other is the Russian Orthodox Church of St Nicholas, which keeps a close watch over the moral fibre of the townsfolk. The church was erected by Russian fur traders in 1894, making it the oldest Russian church in the south-eastern part of Alaska. Another must-see is the Alaska State Museum on Whittier Street, with an exhibition of indigenous Indian culture and a bit of history of the white settlements in the area.

The terrace on the State Office Building offers the best view of Juneau, the straits and Douglas Island just off the coast. An excursion to Mendenhall Glacier, about 20 km (13 miles) north of town, is a must. This glacier calves out of the 10,000-sq-km (3,650-sq-mi) Juneau Icefield, with a face 2.5 km (1.6 miles) long where it breaks off into the lake.

The visitor center offers comprehensive documentation on the glacier, and you can go hiking along its edges.

❷ Glacier Bay National Park You should not leave Juneau without taking a boat or plane trip to this national park 85 km (53 miles) away. Giant glaciers detach themselves directly into the sea here, and giant ice flows descend from mountains that tower above 4,000 m (13,000 ft). No fewer than sixteen glaciers terminate in this large bay, which was completely covered in pack ice as recently as 100 years ago. Since then, the ice has receded by more than 100 km (62 miles), faster than anywhere else on earth.

These days, seals lounge on the ice floes of Glacier Bay, and humpback whales and orcas ply the chilly waters, breaching, hunting and carrying on.

From mid-May to mid-September you can take day trips and longer excursions both by boat and by air from Juneau to Gustavus, a small settlement at the entrance to this huge bay. From

Glacier Bay gives you a view into the history of the North American continent. Just one hundred years ago, the giant bay in which sixteen glaciers calve was completely covered in ice. Since the end of the 19th century, however, the ice sheet has been retreating rapidly, as it did at the end of the Ice Age – but over a

significantly shorter time span. Today, the bay is a meeting place for humpbacks, killer whales, walruses and seals. To experience the true raw beauty of the region, charter a boat or plane from Juneau.

The fauna of the Alaskan mountains

In addition to the state's fabulous natural scenery, the animals of Alaska are among the chief attractions of 'The Last Frontier'. Of all the Alaskan animals, bears and moose are the most impressive, but caribou, elk, mountain sheep and mountain goats can be just as fascinating, as can the various wolves and foxes.

You will certainly never forget seeing the gleaming eyes and pointed ears of a lynx next to your camper at dusk, or watching a moose cow with her young cross the highway right in front of you. But it is easy to forget that there are so many other kinds of furry creatures here, like martens, minks, ermines, beavers, wolverines and foxes.

Dall sheep (top) and Rocky Mountain goats (bottom) live in Alaska's mountainous regions.

Dall sheep and Rocky Mountain goats are natural rock-climbers, living at altitudes of up to 3,000 m (10,000 ft). If you are lucky, you'll see small herds of females with their young scouring the slopes for food.

The variety of bird species here is difficult to appreciate initially, but Alaska's extensive wetlands are home to countless waterfowl. Among them are a number of species of wild geese and ducks, as well as the endangered whooping crane.

most gold seekers landed here before hiking along the Chilkoot Trail to the Yukon River. Between 1897 and 1898, a Wild-West-style town developed that has remained almost intact to this day. The town's Broadway Street is now an historical park. You can't miss the impressive Arctic Brotherhood building, with more than 20,000 wooden sticks decorating its facade, or the Red Onion Saloon, where the floor is still covered in sawdust. Every evening a play is performed in Eagles Hall, bringing the time of the gold diggers to life.

Although the gold rush was past its peak by then, the year 1900 saw the construction of a narrow-gauge railway across White Pass, between Skagway and Whitehorse. The most scenic stretch up to White Pass at 889 m (2,917 ft) is now maintained as a heritage railway and will give you some unforgettable views of this wild and romantic landscape. The different climate zones produce myriad vegetation, from wet coastal forests right up to alpine tundras at the top of the pass.

⑤ Haines Highway/Haines Junction From Haines, the Haines Highway winds its way across the foothills of the Alsek Range. At Porcupine it crosses the border into Canadian British Columbia, and just after that you get to Chilkat Pass at an altitude of 1,065 m (3,494 ft) West of the road, the Tatshenshini-Alsek Preserve connects Glacier Bay National Park to the south and Kluane National Park in the north.

Heading north, the nature reserve joins Wrangell-St Elias National Park back in Alaska. People on both sides of the border have worked together to create this park, the largest protected area on the North American continent. As the crow flies, it stretches more than 700 km (435 miles) from Gustavus at the southern tip of Glacier Bay National Park to Richardson Highway in the north. There are no roads anywhere in the park, but mountains up to 6,000 m (19,500 ft), massive glaciers and pristine forests.

The town of Haines Junction has 500 inhabitants and originally developed from what was once a soldiers' camp during the construction of the Alaska Highway. Here, the Haines Highway meets the Alaska Highway coming from Whitehorse, which itself is also worth an extra detour (111 km/69 miles).

⑥ Whitehorse This is where the exhausted gold diggers would arrive after crossing White Pass. Downriver from the large rapids they were able to

Logan is Canada's highest mountain. Down at more 'moderate' altitudes there are large populations of black bears, brown bears, wolves, mountain sheep, caribou and elk. Further to the west are the inaccessible Icefield Ranges. From the air these look something like a giant lunar landscape made of ice and snow. Given its extraordinary dimensions, it is hardly surprising that Kluane National Park was declared a UNESCO World Heritage Site as early as 1980, alongside Wrangell-St Elias Park, which borders it to the west.

There are very few places on the Alaska Highway to access Kluane National Park on foot, and you can never go any further than to the foot of the icy giants. As an alternative, it is well worth taking a scenic flight across this breathtaking mountain landscape. Small aircraft take off from the town of Burwash at the northern end of Lake Kluane.

Or maybe you are into old ghost towns? At the eastern end of Lake Kluane, a short access road takes you down to Silver City on the lakeshore. This old trading post, long since abandoned, really does give you that 'ghost-town' feel.

From Burwash Landing, the Alaska Highway winds its lonely way through a largely pristine landscape of mountains, forests and tundra all in seemingly endless repetition. Towards the west there are some impressive views of the mighty St Elias Mountains, Canada's highest mountain range. The road first crosses Donjek River, then White River and finally, just before you get to the Alaskan border, there is Beaver Creek, Canada's westernmost settlement with roughly 100 inhabitants.

In October 1942 the last section of the Alaska Highway was completed here.

❽ Tok Junction Our first stop back in Alaska is Tetlin Junction, and after another 19 km (12 miles) you get to the small town of Tok.

Founded in 1942 as a soldier's camp when the Alaska Highway was being built, Tok is considered to be the gateway to Alaska. From here, Fairbanks

❶ The icy world of Wrangell-St Elias National Park is only visible from a helicopter or glacier plane.

❷ A reflection of Mount Huxley (3,828 m/12,560 ft) in a temporarily ice-free pond in Wrangell-St Elias National Park.

❸ Ice on lakes such as Kathleen Lake in Kluane National Park does not melt until late in the spring.

take a paddle steamer further north along the Yukon River. When the Alaska Highway was being built, Whitehorse developed into the largest settlement in the territory.

Today, at the McBride Museum, you can see old gold-digging and mining equipment as well as Indian arts and crafts. Old Log Church, built in 1900, houses an exhibition on the Yukon Territory's missionary history. The paddle steamer permanently

moored at the southern end of Second Avenue is called the 'SS Klondike'. During the gold rush, it regularly plied the Yukon between Whitehorse and Dawson City.

Back at Haines Junction you take the Alaska Highway to Kluane Lake at the eastern end of Kluane National Park.

❼ Kluane National Park North of Haines Junction the road rises up to Bear Creek

Summit at 997 m (3,271 ft) shortly before coming to Boutillier Summit at 1,000 m (3,281 ft). Just beneath the pass is Kluane Lake, the largest lake in the Yukon Territory at 400 sq km (155 sq m). The highway runs along its western shore.

The national park covers an area of 22,000 sq km (8,492 sq mi) and has plenty of untouched nature including high peaks, huge glaciers and sub-Arctic vegetation. At 5,959 m (19,551 ft), Mount

Wonder Lake is right in the center of Denali National Park. It is 6 km (4 mi) long and 85 m (280 ft) deep, and has a wealth of fish including lake trout, pike and eels. The imposing Mount McKinley in the background rises 6,194 m (21,320 ft) into a cloudless blue sky above the lake. It is not only the highest

mountain in North America; it is a full 5,500 m (18,000 ft) above the plateau from which it rises, far higher than Mount Everest, the tallest mountain in the world, rises above its base. Native Americans call it Denali – the Great One.

Vegetation only has a short period of growth in this treeless, sub-polar zone that makes up a large part of Alaska's total area. Wherever the ice and snow allow it, the earth springs into action with plant life of breathtaking variety. Even in places where the soil is less than one meter deep above the permafrost, the

tundra is still home to countless wildflower species and shrubs that provide moose and caribous with fresh greens. Come autumn, berry bushes overloaded with fruit provide the bears with a final feast before the harsh winter kicks in.

Alaska's bears

In addition to numerous black bears, there are between 30,000 and 40,000 brown bears in Alaska. They populate the entire state, from coastal forests up to the northern tundra.

Depending on food supplies, these adaptable creatures can vary greatly both in fur colour and in size. Let's face it – if all you get to eat is berries and gophers, you're just not going to grow as tall as your coastal cousin who can gorge on salmon.

The largest brown bears are usually found in Katmai National Park and on Kodiak Island where they grow to 3 m (10 ft) tall and weigh up to 500 kg

Top: In Alaska, polar bears can only be seen on the Arctic Ocean coast.
Middle: Grizzlies are Alaska's largest beasts of prey.
Bottom: Black bears are all over Alaska.

(1,100 lbs). Kodiaks and grizzlies are the largest terrestrial predators on the planet. If you think you can outrun one, be warned – bears can run at top speeds of 60 km/h (40 mph) and they really are outstanding climbers!

1

and Anchorage are the same distance away.

The visitor center at the crossroads has an interesting exhibition of stuffed animals from Alaska, and Tok is also a center for husky breeding. Dogs-led races start here in winter and in the summer you can see teams practising on a 20-km (12-mile) track that runs parallel to the Alaska Highway.

From Tok Junction, the remaining 111 m (69 miles) of the Alaska Highway follow the mighty Tanana River. The broad flood plains on either side of the road remind us that the glaciers of the Alaska Range once extended all the way down to here.

9 Delta Junction We have now reached the northern end of the 2,300-km (1,430-mile) Alaska Highway. The terminus is located at the junction with Richardson Highway, where a visitors center offers all kinds of information about the construction of the highway and the Trans-Alaska Pipeline.

At Delta Junction the pipeline crosses the Tanana River in a wide arc and it is quite a sight in its own right. Its construction became a necessity when, in

2

1968, the USA's largest oil fields were discovered north of the Brooks Range in Prudhoe Bay. Starting in March 1975 about 22,000 workers were involved in the two-year construction of the line, which now extends 1,280 km (795 miles) straight through the heart of the peninsula and down to the port city of Valdez.

Half the pipeline was installed underground and the rest, nearly 700 km (435 miles) of it, is supported by a system of 78,000 stilts. The pipeline has to be continuously cooled in order to keep the 60°C (140°F) oil from destroying it. Another 153 km (95 miles) down Alaska's oldest highway, the Richardson Highway, you come to Fairbanks.

10 Fairbanks This city on the Tanana River owes its existence to the 1903 gold rush. Within seven years 11,000 people had set up shop on its primitive campsite. In World War II, large military settlements and the construction of the Alaska Highway fostered an economic boom in the town. After 1974 the construction headquarters of the

At the park headquarters you can visit the dog pens where the park rangers breed huskies. During the summer they train them as sled dogs for winter when that is the only mode of transport allowed in the park.

The George Parks Highway now takes us towards Anchorage. Roughly halfway along it you get to the picture-book town of Talkeetna. You get yet another view of Denali from here. It is also the take-off point for scenic flights around the national park.

12 Eklutna About 33 km (20 miles) outside Anchorage you pass the Indian village of Eklutna. The St Nicholas Russian Orthodox Church is oddly located right in the middle of an Indian Cemetery. There is also a Siberian chapel.

Bright wooden houses are set on the graves here, their eaves

Fairbanks: Pioneer Park Open-Air Museum

Pioneer Park (18 ha/45 acres) provides a good introduction to the 100 years of

Timber houses from the 19th century.

Fairbanks' history. In total, twenty-nine houses have been rebuilt to create 'Gold Rush Town', an historic gold-digger settlement. The First Presbyterian Church and the Pioneer Museum are also worth visiting here.

Crookes Creek & Whiskey Island Railroad is a reconstructed miniature train engine that used to transport food to Fairbanks and now takes visitors through the park. HMS *Nenana* is Alaska's only stern-wheeler and is made entirely out of wood.

Trans-Alaska Pipeline were relocated here. Today, Fairbanks is a modern city. The Otto William Geist Museum tells you everything about the history and culture of Alaska's indigenous people.

Before carrying on, take the opportunity to relax and enjoy Chena Hot Springs about 100 km (62 miles) east of the city.

11 Denali National Park Our next destination is the highlight of the entire trip – Denali National Park. To get there take the George Parks Highway from Riley Creek. If you want to see the 24,000 sq km (9,265 sq mi) of the park and the highest mountain in North America (Mount McKinley), you have to take one of the shuttle buses operated by

the park authority. These regularly run the 140 km (87 miles) into the park to Kantishna at Wonder Lake. The trip takes eleven hours, and if you picked a sunny day, you will even get a glimpse of Denali, the High One, at a glorious 6,194 m (20,323 ft). The road runs through some hilly tundra with mountains in the 2,000 m (6,560 ft) range.

1 Denali (Mount McKinley), has a higher rise than Everest: 5,500 m (18,000 ft). The peak is at 6,194 m (20,323 ft) above sea level.

2 A solitary grizzly bear roaming the autumnal tundra in search of food.

The grizzly bear, a subspecies of brown bear, is the undisputed king of Alaska, roaming freely through the tundra and taiga. Grizzlies get their name from the lightly shimmering gray coat on their necks, and they are larger and heavier than black bears. It is only with extreme caution that you should observe these large

bears when they are lurking in the brush. Due to their poor eyesight, however, it is possible to get quite close if you approach them quietly from downwind. But if they are startled, things can quickly turn for the worse. Whatever you do, don't get as close as this photo suggests.

1

In the land of the bears – Katmai National Park and Preserve and Kodiak National Wildlife Refuge

Few national parks in Alaska are accessible by car. Most can only be reached by plane or boat. In the south-west of the state, Katmai National Park and Preserve and Lake Clark form the Alaskan section of the Pacific Ring of Fire, where active volcanoes are as much a part of the scenery as brown bears and salmon.

In the south-east, whales, sea lions and giant flocks of seabirds liven up the coastal areas around Glacier Bay. Weather conditions in Wrangell-St Elias National Park are so hostile that some of its summits and glaciers remain nameless to this day.

Katmai National Park and Preserve
Located in the northern part of the Aleutian Range, this park measures 16,500 sq km (6,370 sq mi). It is home to approximately 1,000 brown bears, innumerable moose, caribou, wolves and foxes. The rivers are famous for their salmon, hence the name on the park gate – King Salmon. The entrance to the park is 465 km (289 miles) from

Anchorage and only accessible by scheduled flight. From early June to mid-September, there are daily seaplane connections to the park's visitor center at Brooks Camp, another 53 km (33 miles) down the road.

Alternatively, from King Salmon you can take a taxi to Lake Camp 15 km (9 miles) away. From here, a motorboat takes visitors across to Brooks Camp, to the Bay of Islands and to other destinations on Naknek Lake. The hub for all activities in the park is Brooks Camp. Everything meets up here – humans, bears, boats, fish and aircraft. In theory, the park is accessible year-round, but you'll need dogs-leds and skis from mid September to late May. At higher altitudes, the snow may hang around well into July. The best time for those spectacular bear snapshots is July, when the red salmon come up the rivers to spawn and the bears go fishing in the rapids.

Volcanoes and bears are the two defining features of the national park.

2

Fifteen of the former are still active since the tremendous 1912 eruption. The results of this monstrous outburst can still be seen in the Valley of Ten Thousand Smokes where a number of hissing, steaming and smoking fumaroles remind us that the earth's crust is really quite fragile.

Throughout the summer the valley can be reached by bus from Brooks Camp. If you want to go hiking in the valley, you can stay overnight at the Baked Mountain Cabin and (provided you have the necessary equipment) climb some of the mountains in the area.

If you have only come to see the bears, things are much easier. From Brooks Camp there is a trail just under 1 km

(0.6 miles) long that leads to Brooks Falls and a viewing platform right above the rapids. When the salmon come upriver, the fishing bears just stand in the river and lazily yet skilfully build up their winter layers. Dumpling Mountain Is also quite easy to get to. It takes less than two hours to climb the 744 m (2,441 ft) to its summit. From there you have some terrific views over the tundra, Naknek Lake and the surrounding mountains.

The absolute highlight of a visit to Katmai National Park, however, is a scenic flight above those areas that are not accessible on foot. The standard flight takes you via the Valley of Ten Thousand Smokes, through Katmai Pass,

along the shore of Katmai Bay up to Swikshak Bay, and then via Kaguyak Crater and Savonoski River back to Brooks Camp.

Kodiak National Wildlife Refuge
Kodiak Island is located in the south of Katmai National Park. The indigenous people of the Aleutian Islands inhabited this area as early as 6,000 years ago. In 1784, Russian trappers and fur traders made Kodiak the first capital of Russian America. To this day, several Russian Orthodox churches bear witness to this period.

Kodiak is the largest island in Alaska and the second-largest in the United

Visitors to the reserve can find valuable information at the visitor center, which is just about 8 km (5 miles) south of the small town of Kodiak. The island can be reached by plane from Anchorage or by ferry via the Alaska Marine Highway. As there are no roads in the reserve, you will need a boat or seaplane. If you want to go fishing for a day, keep your ear to the ground in Kodiak. It is relatively affordable to get yourself taken to the fishing grounds by plane in the morning and be picked up again in the evening.

If, however, you would like to explore the reserve on foot, you are largely left to your own devices. Overnight stays are possible in designated spots, but only in your own tent. For your own safety, you'll need more than just respect for the ubiquitous bears. Never set off without a 'bear bell' attached to your trousers or backpack. As bears are better at hearing than at seeing, these bells serve to forestall any nasty surprises. If you get too close to a bear by mistake, it can easily feel threatened and you will not be able to run away. At 60 km/h (40 mph) bears are always going to be faster!

It is essential to wrap your food in airtight containers. Do not take anything smelly into the tent. Neither cook nor eat in your tent as bears can detect the smell of food for days afterwards. A bar of chocolate in your coat pocket is enough to attract an unwanted visit. There are 'bear gallows' in the designated campsites, gates 4 m (13 ft) high with posts wrapped in sheet metal. You hang your food here overnight, securely fastening the pack high up in the air. If you keep these basic rules in mind and keep a healthy distance between yourself and the bears, you can move around their Kodiak Island in relative safety, and enjoy wilderness in its purest form.

1 Salmon-fishing brown bears at Katmai National Park.

2 The 1912 eruption of the Novarupta volcano gave Katmai National Park its current shape.

3 Karluk Bay on Kodiak Island.

4 In 1784 the Russians founded the first permanent settlement on Kodiak Island.

States at 6,000 sq km (2,315 sq mi). It is characterized by deep fjords, forests and alpine tundra. The climate is moist and cold throughout the year. Today the south-western part of the island is a protected wildlife refuge that is home to numerous brown bear populations as well as 250 bird species. The bald eagles are abundant here, as are the millions of seabirds who spend the winters on Kodiak. They find plenty of food in the shallow coastal waters.

Bald Eagles

In 1782, the bald eagle was chosen as the national animal of the United States. These huge birds of prey can have wingspans of more than 2 m (6.5 ft), helping them glide majestically through the air. Their dark-brown, airfoil-like wings have hundreds of individual feathers that aerodynamically increase wingspan. Their stout heads with pronounced beaks are white, as are their broad tail feathers. Bald eagles are monogamous and use the same nesting tree throughout their lives. Every year they redo the nest for the new brood. Old nests can weigh up to a tonne!

Bald eagles have wingspans of more than 2 m (6.5 ft).

In Katmai National Park alone there are more than 600 breeding pairs of these regal birds. Eagle-watching is particularly good on the Chilkat River near Haines and on the Ninilchik River on the Kenai Peninsula. At the peak of the salmon season, it is not uncommon to see several hundred eagles gathering in both these places to catch fish.

lavishly decorated with wood-carvings. The Indians believe they house the spirits of the dead.
Just south of Eagle River, it is worth taking a 20-km (13-mile) detour to visit Chugach State Park. From here you can do day hikes to the glaciers further up country.

13 Anchorage This city owes its existence to the construction of the railway line between Fairbanks and the ice-free port of Seward on the Kenai Peninsula. Originally a builders' settlement established in 1914, Anchorage eventually developed into a modern aviation hub. It is now home to half of Alaska's entire population. As you enter the city via Glenn Highway you'll see thousands of small- and medium-size aircraft parked at Merill Field. Lake Hood is one of the largest hydroplane airports in the world.

14 Portage After 60 km (37 miles) on Seward Highway, you come to this town at the end of Turnagain Bay. At Girdwood,

just before you get to Portage, is Alaska's northernmost alpine ski resort at Mount Alyeska (1,201 m/3,940 ft). Take a chairlift up to 610 m (2,000 ft) and enjoy a view of the Chugach Mountain Range glaciers.
At the end of the bay is Portage Lake. There are usually some oddly shaped ice floes bobbing on its deep-blue waters. On the far side, Portage Glacier drops into the lake like a giant wall.

15 Seward The natural deep-water port here is the economic engine of this town. The most important annual event is the Silver Salmon Derby in August, a salmon-fishing competition. You'll most likely want to check the Kenai Fjords National Park Visitor Center for information on the 780-sq-km (300-sq-mi) Harding Icefield.
Leaving Kenai you first take Seward Highway back towards Anchorage before turning onto Sterling Highway at Moose Pass.

16 Kenai In 1791 the Russians built their second Alaskan settlement here. After 1846 it became

the center of the Russian Orthodox Church in Alaska. The Holy Assumption Church and its three onion-domed spires are icons of the period, along with an old bible. The bible, like the other equipment in the church, was brought to Alaska from Siberia.

17 Homer Down on the south-west side of the Kenai Peninisula is the 'Halibut Capital', Homer. In this town at the end of Sterling Highway, it's all about fish. A giant fleet of vessels is always ready to set off for the next

catch. If you are into fishing, rent a boat here or book one of the numerous deep-sea fishing tours.

1 Portage Glacier calving into the lake of the same name.

2 The snowy mountains behind the Anchorage Skyline. The wilderness starts right outside the city.

3 Lakes are typical of the Kenai Peninsula, most beautiful during the Indian summer.

Kodiak Island This island is home to the famous Kodiak brown bears, the largest carnivorous land animal in the world. They can weigh up to 500 kg (1,100 lbs).

Kenai Peninsula There are some large lakes on this mountainous peninsula that extends 200 km (135 miles) into the Gulf of Alaska.

Homer This port town on the Kenai Peninsula at the end of Highway 1 is a mecca for deep-sea fishermen.

Denali National Park The center of this park (24,000 sq km/9,265 sq mi), is Denali (Mount McKinley) at 6,194 m (20,323 ft). There are about 430 species of wild flowers here along with grizzlies, moose and caribou.

Anchorage The skyline of this boom town looks a lot like other American cities. Half of Alaska's population lives here and its airport is the eighth largest in the USA. Planes are an indispensable mode of transport in the remote regions here. Many people even have their own.

Chena Hot Springs This oasis of relaxation is located 100 km (62 miles) east of Fairbanks on Steese Highway amid the dense forests of the Chena Valley. A small access road takes you to the sulphur springs where you can enjoy the healing waters. But be careful of any black bears that might be in the car park.

Portage Glacier This glacier south of Anchorage has a giant wall calving right into Portage Lake. Below the green mountains, bizarrely shaped ice floes with a bluish hue float aimlessly on the lake.

Kluane National Park Huge glaciers, sub-Arctic vegetation, bears, wolves, caribou and moose are all integral elements of this park in the Yukon Territory around Mount Logan (5,959 m/19,551 ft).

Wrangell-St Elias National Park Two mountain ranges are protected by this park – the volcanic Wrangell Mountains and the St Elias Mountains with the striking Mount St Elias (5,489 m/18,009 ft).

Glacier Bay National Park In Alaska's southernmost national park there are no fewer than sixteen glaciers terminating in Glacier Bay. The bay is over 100 km (62 miles) long and has only been free of ice for the last 100 years.

Mendenhall Glacier This glacier, which is 20 km (13 miles) north of Juneau, Alaska's capital, is part of the gigantic Juneau Icefield, which measures almost 10,000 sq km (3,860 sq mi). The glacier tongue calves at a width of 2.5 km (1.6 miles) into Mendenhall Lake.

Haines This town at the mouth of the Chilkat River is an area where the Indians are famous for their totem poles.

Route 40

Canada

There are over 2,000 lakes in the 7,861-sq-km (3,034-sq-mi) Réserve Faunique des Laurentides north of Québec.

On the Trans-Canada Highway from the Great Lakes to the Atlantic

Eastern Canada is the country's historic core and heart of the nation. The French founded North America's first cities in Québec province, while modern Canada was launched on Prince Edward Island, which means that a trip through Canada's eastern reaches is also a journey through 250 years of history, not to mention some fascinating scenery.

When traveling from west to east through south-eastern Canada, you cross three vast and diverse regions. Initially you pass through the southern edge of the Canadian Shield, consisting of Pre-cambrian volcanic rock interspersed with myriad lakes and smooth granite domes. The stone is up to 3.6 million years old, and owes its present-day appearance to glacial activity during the Ice Age. The St Lawrence Lowlands, which start near the Great Lakes in southern Ontario and stretch as far as the mouth of the

St Lawrence River into the Atlantic, were also shaped by the Ice Age. The eastern-most reaches of this vast and distinctive area are formed by the Appalachian Mountains. They are the reason the coast-lines of Nova Scotia and Cape Breton Island have so many tiny bays and cliffs reminiscent of places like the west coasts of France and England.

European fishermen came to the east coast and to the St Lawrence River as early as the end of the 15th century to take advantage of the summer catch, but

A grazing moose in Cape Breton Highlands National Park in Nova Scotia.

The thundering torrent of water at Horseshoe Falls, the Canadian side of Niagara Falls.

Ottawa's Parliament Building, the "Canadian Westminster", sits proudly over the Ottawa River, which is spanned by the Alexandra Bridge.

it was not until 1534 that Jacques Cartier flew the French flag in present-day Montréal. It was actually the beaver, or more precisely its fur, that inspired the real development of permanent settlements in this region. Since every fashionista in Europe in those days wanted to wear a beaver-fur hat, Québec was founded as a fur trading center in 1608, and France's Finance Minister Colbert finally arranged New France as a royal colony modeled on the mother country.

As is often the case, however, the success attracted competition. In 1670, the British circumvented the sovereign French territory on the St Lawrence and founded the Hudson's Bay Company in the north. It soon became the most famous fur-trading company on the continent. After the Seven Years War, the Paris Treaty of 1763 forced France to cede New France to England. Since then, French is still spoken along the St Lawrence, but the French no longer had influence over Canada's political structure.

Today, although there are ongoing attempts in French-speaking parts of Canada, i.e. in Québec province and the adjacent regions of Ontario and New Brunswick, to secede, they are actually only a means of strengthening their own position. The accomplishments of secessionists thus far include a successful campaign to ensure French was declared the only official language in Québec in 1977. For visitors coming from the west, it is always fascinating to observe how the first French traces suddenly appear in Ontario. Place names suddenly sound French and, when in the Old Town quarter of Québec, you feel as if you're no longer in North America.

The 14-m-high (46-ft) Big Tub Lighthouse is on the Bruce Peninsula not far from Tobermory.

The Toronto TV tower

The television tower in Toronto was originally built by Canadian National, a railway company, in 1976. It was the highest free-standing building on land in the world until 2007, measuring

The Toronto CN Tower was once the world's highest building.

553.33 m (1,815 ft). The Skypod sits at a height of 351 m (1,152 ft) and has the largest revolving restaurant on earth. Those brave enough can even go higher: Four glass, outdoor cabins rise up to the 447-m-high (1,467 ft) Space Deck in fifty-eight seconds.

The journey from the west bank of Lake Huron along the St Lawrence River to Nova Scotia is a journey through the land of "shimmering water" and heads beyond Québec to the craggy cliffs on the stormy North Atlantic. Although the trip passes through the most densely settled regions of Canada, the wilderness is never far away.

1 Sault Ste Marie This "twin city" is located in both Canada and the United States, on a narrow promontory between Lake Superior and Lake Huron on the St Mary's River. The height difference between the two lakes is overcome by two locks from 1887 that are today listed as historic monuments.

After a small detour to Tahquamenon Falls National Park in the west, your route follows the coast of the North Channel. At Sudbury, the Trans-Canada Highway branches off: Highway 17 heads directly to Ottawa while the south-western branch (Highway 69) runs along the east coast of Georgian Bay.

2 Midland This small town has three main tourist attractions. One is Sainte-Marie among the Hurons, a Jesuit missionary station established in 1639 for the purpose of Christianizing Huron Indians. Laid out in the style of European monastic settlements, the mission has been restored to its original state. The second is

Penetanguishene Discovery Harbour, a marine base that has also been partially restored. The third is Georgian Bay Islands National Park in the middle of the Thirty Thousand Islands (visitor center is in Honey Harbour). A worthwhile detour now takes you from Midland around the southern tip of Georgian Bay to the Bruce Peninsula National Park (Hwy 6). For Toronto, leave the Trans-Canada Highway and take Highway 400.

3 Toronto (see page 582) From Toronto you should make the day trip to Niagara Falls, about 130 km (81 mi) away on the U.S.-Canadian border. Take Highway 400 to get there.

4 Niagara Falls The Niagara River plunges 50 m (164 ft) over a 675-m-long (2,215-ft) fracture line on the Canadian Side; on the U.S. side it is 330 m (1,083 ft) wide. Good observation points are Table Rock, to the west near the horseshoe-shaped waterfall, or the Minolta Tower. Once back

in Toronto, the route heads along highways 401 and 115 to the Trans-Canada Highway 7.

5 Peterborough The biggest attraction in this city on the Kawartha lakes is the Hydraulic Lift Lock from 1904. The lock is made out of a lock basin that can be pushed up or lowered 20 m (66 ft) together with the vessel. The Lang Pioneer Village is a reconstructed 19th-century pioneer village, while the Petro-

glyph Provincial Park features more than nine hundred Indian rock drawings that are between five hundred and one thousand years old.

6 Ottawa Canada's capital is happily mocked as the "Westminster in the Wilderness". The parliament building in English neo-Gothic style is the dominant edifice in Ottawa, and its 90-m (295-ft) Peace Tower has a carillon made up of fifty-three bells.

Travel information

Route profile
Length: approx. 3,500 km (2,175 mi)
Time required: 3 weeks
Start: Sault Ste Marie
End: Halifax
Route (main locations):
Sault Ste. Marie, Toronto, Ottawa, Montréal, Québec, Charlottetown, Halifax

Traffic information:
Two different lines of the Trans-Canada Highway (TCH) run through northern Ontario: the northern line, which connects the most important mining and resource centers, and therefore leads through the breathtaking scenery of the Canadian Shield, with wild

rivers, untouched lakes, numerous small pioneer settlements, and endless forests with their wealth of wildlife; and the southern line, which runs largely parallel to the US border along the Great Lakes (Lake Huron, Lake Superior).

Information:
Here are some websites to help you plan your trip.
Ontario:
www.ontariotravel.net
Québec:
www.bonjourquebec.com
New Brunswick:
www.tourismnbcanada.com
Nova Scotia:
www.novascotia.com
Prince Edward Island:
www.gov.pe.ca

Detour

Bruce Peninsula

The forested Bruce Peninsula is about 100 km (62 mi) long and almost completely separates Georgian Bay from Lake Huron. While beautiful sandy beaches (Dorcas Bay) can be found on the western side, the eastern side is primarily known for its rugged coastline. This is due to the Niagara Escarpment, which creates interesting rock formations and up to 60-m-high (197 ft) cliffs.

Two national parks protect this ection of the western St Lawrence Lowlands: the Bruce Peninsula National Park, which protects the northern tip, and the Fathom Five National Marine Park, which protects the islands. Both parks can be accessed through Tobermory at the northern tip of the peninsula. Ferries set off from the port town to Manitoulin Island and the Fathom Five National Marine Park. The park's visitor center is also located at the port.

Bruce Peninsula is easy to explore on footpaths, the most beautiful of

The Big Tub Lighthouse safeguards entry into Tobermory's port.

which start at Cyprus Lake. "Head of Trials" leads to the caves at Halfway Rock. Stop at the stone arches and Indian Head Cove on the way. From there, you can walk up to 60-m-high (197 ft) rock cliffs at Georgian Bay.

Fathom Five was Canada's first marine park. The best attraction is Flowerpot Island with its two bizarre, 10- and 17-m-high (33- and 56-ft) sandstone pillars.

The tower's impressive observation deck makes the city look like a miniature of itself. The second icon of Ottawa is the Château Laurier Hotel, built in 1912 by Grand Trunk Railway. The most fascinating technicological attraction here is the lock staircase of the Rideau Canal, with a height difference of 25 m (82 ft). The Musée Canadien des Civilisations is also must.

7 Parc de la Gatineau This vast park, with sixty species of tree, is on the north-western edge of Hull. You can take beautiful walks here during the Indian summer, and 200 km (124 mi) of cross-country ski trails attract visitors in winter. Continuing along Highway 7, with a constant a view of the Ottawa River, you arrive in Montréal after roughly 200 km (124 mi).

8 Montréal (see page 583) Québec is 250 km (155 mi) from Montréal, and Autoroute 20, part of the Trans-Canada High-

1 Toronto: View of the Skydome and CN Tower.

2 From the air you can see the Niagara River, Horseshoe Falls and Niagara Falls.

3 Old Town Montréal: the dome of the Marché de Bonsecours at the St Lawrence River,

Toronto

This metropolis on the northern shores of Lake Ontario owes its cosmopolitan character to the large number of immigrants who came here after World War II, and who gave the city its European-Asian composition.

Toronto is an extraordinarily lively city. Bustling Yonge Street is considered a shopping paradise and bold construction projects signal dynamic development, while traditional buildings such as the Holy Trinity Church are listed historic monuments.

Be sure to see: Ontario Place, a futuristic recreation center on Lake Ontario with varying exhibitions, an IMAX cinema and a ultra-modern children's playground; the Harbourfront Center; the converted warehouses on the piers with shops, restaurants, waterfront cafés, art galleries and theaters; and Queen's Quay and York Quay boardwalks.

Toronto Islands, connected to the city via a ferry, is a quiet refuge with

Toronto: looking out over the modern skyline by night.

tranquil canals, footpaths and a historic amusement park for children. The CN Tower was the highest freestanding building in the world until 2007. Its viewing platform provides a spectacular view from 447 m (1,467 ft). The dream-like and particularly interesting museums in town include the Art Gallery of Ontario, a modern art museum with the most famous works by Canadian artists, the Henry Moore Sculpture Center and classic paintings from Europe. There is also the Royal Ontario Museum, the country's largest museum with a wide variety of international exhibitions and a replica of a bat cave. The George R. Gardiner Museum of Ceramic Art specializes in pottery and porcelain, and is the only one of its kind in North America.

Other highlights are the BCE Place, a daring high-rise building with a bright atrium; the Eaton Center, one of the largest shopping malls in the country; the Holy Trinity Church, a 19th-century Catholic church; and Yorkville, the "Greenwich Village" of Toronto.

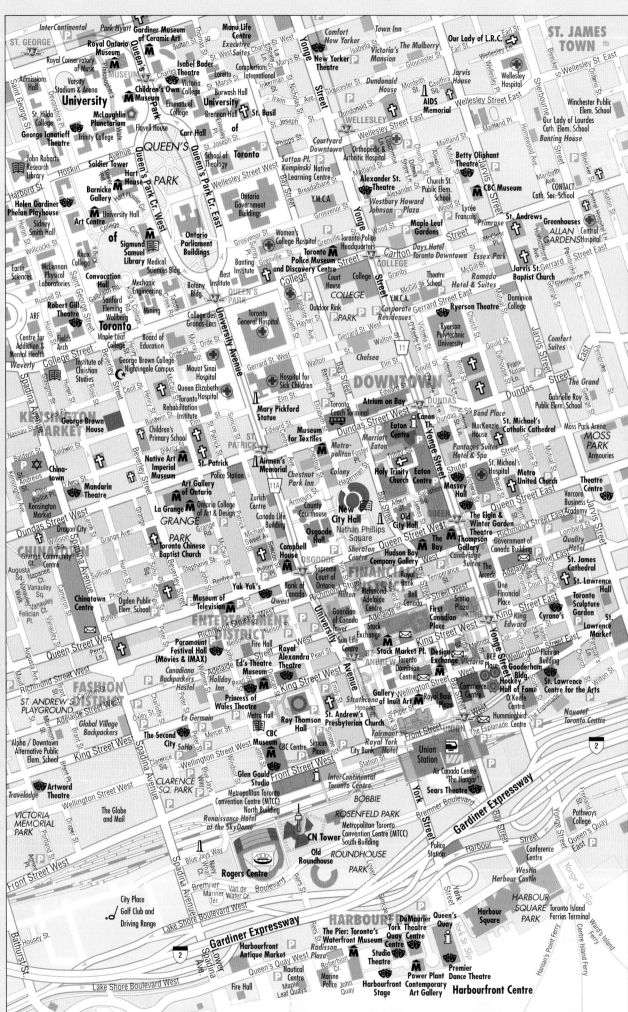

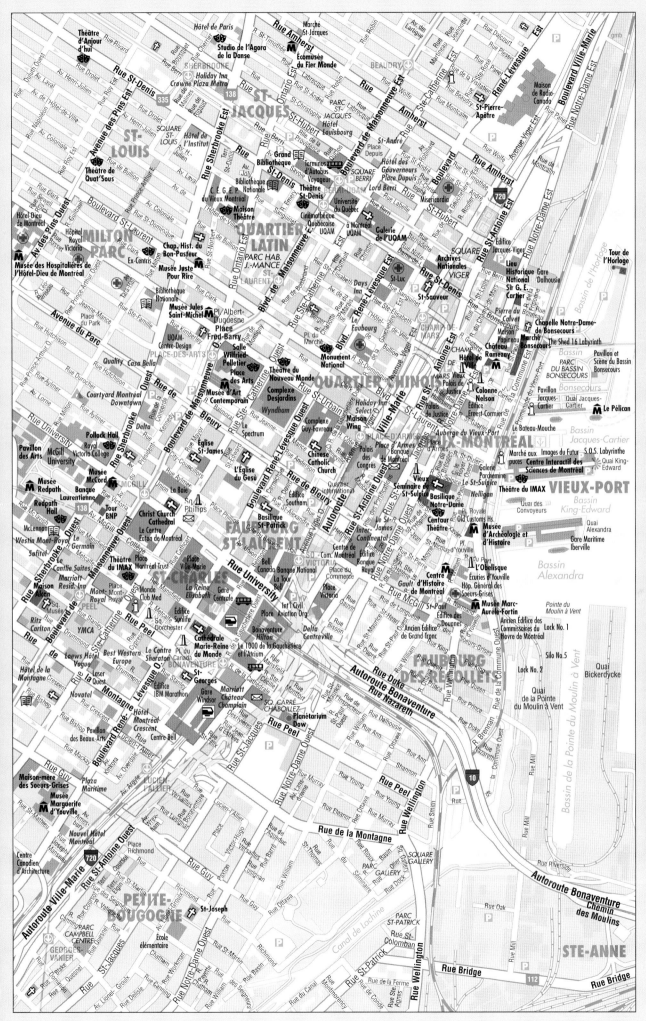

Montréal

Canada's second-largest city was founded by French Catholics in 1642. Due to its ideal location at the confluence of the St Lawrence and Ottawa rivers, Montréal rapidly grew to become a bustling trade center.

Vieux-Montréal, the picturesque Old Town quarter, has numerous historic buildings and narrow alleyways situated on the southern slope of Mont Royal that visibly remind you of the city's distinctly French character.

In winter, locals flee to the Ville souterraine, the underground city with a network of tunnels, passages and shopping centers. You can reach most of the inner-city hotels from the central train station without even having to go outside.

Sights worth visiting here include the Catholic Basilique Notre-Dame, an ornate church actually built by a Protestant Irish-American architect named James O'Donnell around 1829; the Pointe-à-Callière with the Musée d'Archéologie et d'Histoire, which remembers the site of the first settlement; and the Hôtel de Ville, the town hall built in French Empire Style, dating back to the year 1872.

The Notre-Dame-de-Bonsecours Chapel Is, as the Interiors of many model ships indicate, the sailors' church. The Musée des Beaux-Arts was opened as a museum for fine arts back in 1912, while the Biodome de Montréal, a museum dedicated to the environment is housed in the former Olympic velodrome and provides information on various ecosystems.

The Jardin Botanique, created in 1931, is an impressive botanical garden with

View of Montréal's skyline from the port.

26,000 species of plants. Other attractions include the award-winning Musée d'Art Contemporain, the only Canadian museum exclusively dedicated to modern art, and the Place des Arts, which houses concert halls and a theater in one giant complex.

Detour

Réserve Faunique des Laurentides

The southernmost foothills of the Canadian Shield begin just north of Québec city limits. In this densely

Pikauba River in the Laurentides nature reserve.

wooded landscape you will be amazed by the many lakes and free-standing granite domes as the highway quickly trails away into seemingly endless forests.

You arrive at the border of the Réserve Faunique des Laurentides after just 50 km (31 mi). It stretches north over almost 200 km (124 mi) and its central area is not accessible via paths. In this pristine forest region, which has been left in pristine condition, wild bears, lynxes, moose, caribou and wolves are the masters, and only those who are well equipped and who enjoy finding their way through dense, unmarked forests can really survive. You can enter at Pikauba River, Lac Picauba, Rivière Chicoutimi River and Lac Jacques Cartier.

way, heads along the southern side of the St Lawrence River.

❾ Québec (see page 585) From Québec, Autoroute 20 runs parallel to the St Lawrence River before the 185 branches off to the south at Rivière-du-Loup and becomes the Trans-Canada Highway 2 in New Brunswick. The lovely scenic route initially follows the St John River Valley where fields and pastures characterize the landscape. Arriving at Grand Falls, west of Mount Carleton Provincial Park, the St John crashes 25 m (82 ft) over a precipice.

The next stop is the Hartland Covered Bridge, the world's longest covered bridge, measuring 390 m (1,280 ft).

❿ Kings Landing The open-air museum at the St John River displays 19th-century life using thirty reconstructed buildings. Apart from various farmhouses and residential homes, there is a print shop, sawmill, blacksmith's shop, mill and a theater.

You arrive in the capital of New Brunswick 40 km (25 mi) later.

⓫ Fredericton This tranquil regional town at the lower reaches of the St John River was founded by French immigrants in 1732. The most important public buildings and the most beautiful Victorian houses are clustered around Queen Street and King Street. Learn about its history in the York-Sunbury Historical Society Museum.

Follow Highway 2 to the east until Route 114 branches off south toward the Bay of Fundy just beyond Sussex.

⓬ Fundy National Park The Bay of Fundy extends nearly 300 km (186 mi) into the country's interior and separates New Brunswick from Nova Scotia. Its unusual funnel shape produces the world's largest tidal range, which can shift up to 16 m (52 ft)

at the end of Cobequid Bay. At the northernmost arm of the Bay of Fundy is the national park of the same name, with its jagged coast cliffs. The sandstone formations at Cape Enrage are especially beautiful.

Back on Highway 2, you pass through Moncton and reach the star-shaped complex of Fort Beauséjour (Exit 513A at Aulac) at the northern edge of the Cumberland Basin wetland

1 The first-class Hotel Château Frontenac, perched high above the St Lawrence River, is the icon of Québec and one of the city's best addresses.

2 At 390 m (1,280 ft) in length, the Hartland Covered Bridge is the longest covered wooden bridge in the world.

3 High tide in Fundy Bay has formed the sandstone cliffs at Shepody Bay Beach.

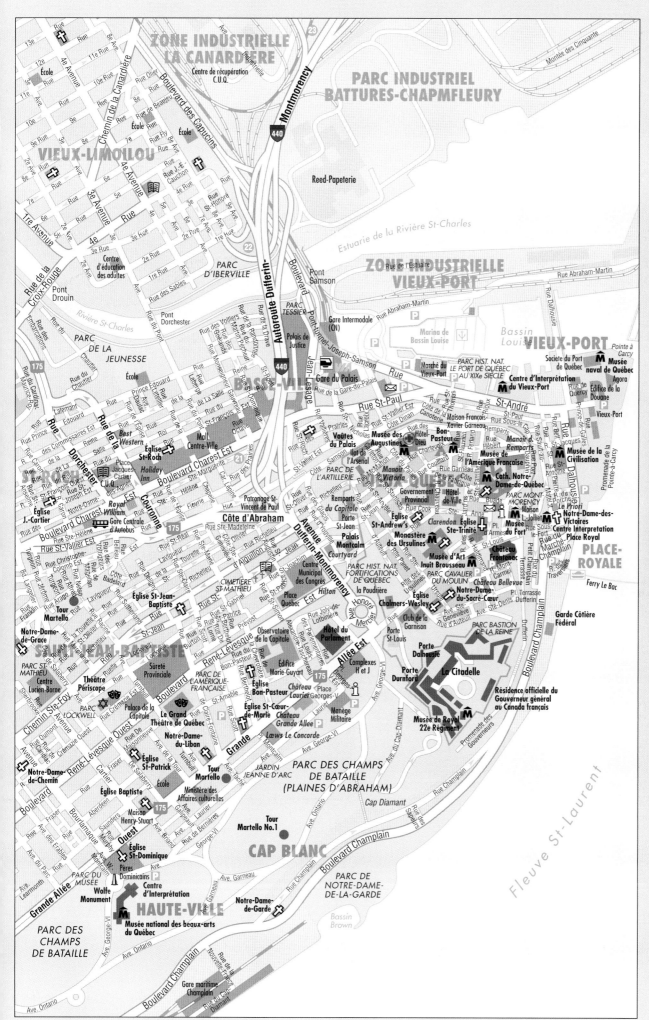

Québec

The capital of the province of the same name is the heart of francophone Canada. More than 90 percent of its 167,500 inhabitants speak French, and the townscape has also maintained its European flair.

Québec City is the only North American metropolis with a city wall, and the Old Town quarter's narrow alleyways even evoke a few memories of old Paris. Québec City has in fact been a UNESCO World Heritage Site since 1985. The settlement was founded here on the banks of the St Lawrence River back in 1608.
After the houses under Cap Diamant were repeatedly burned down, citizens of Quebec retreated to the hill and created the "Haute-Ville", the "Upper town". The upper and lower towns are connected by a cog railway.

Québec at dusk.

Worth seeing here: the Escalier Cass-Cou, or "Breakneck Staircase", which connects the Haute-Ville with the Quartier Petit-Champlain in Basse-Ville, and Place Royale, the former marketplace in the lower town. The Musée de la Civilisation provides an insight into the city's development.
At the eastern end of the city wall in Haute-Ville is La Citadelle from the early 19th century. Since 1920, it has been home to the Royal 22ième Régiment, the only French unit in the Canadian army. The Cathédrale Notre-Dame was built in 1647, and reminds visitors of French rule, while the Maison Chevalier shows how the wealthy families of the 18th and 19th century lived in Quebec.
The luxury hotel Chateau Frontenac, built in 1893, looks like a large European castle. The Parc des Champs-de-Bataille, once the scene of a battle between the British and French on September 13, 1759, is today one of the largest parks in North America, and the tiny Rue du Trésor alleyway brings Parisian charm to Canada.

The Cape Enrage Lighthouse sits atop a high sandstone cliff and helps to secure navigation in the Bay of Fundy. The beacons are particularly necessary here, because the colossal, 300-km-long (186 mi) bay between New Brunswick and Nova Scotia not only looks like a funnel, but also acts like one at the shifting of

the tide. Heading north-east, the bay becomes increasingly narrow and flat. During the rising tide, around 100 billion tonnes (110 billion tons) of water surge into the bay through the broad opening and raise the level by up to 16 m (52 ft) – the highest tidal change in the world.

Lunenburg

In 1753, settlers from Lüneburg, Germany founded this small town in Nova Scotia. With its vibrantly colored old wooden houses and pic-

Lunenburg port

turesque fishing port, it has been listed as a UNESCO World Heritage Site. The townscape includes captain's quarters from over two centuries that are sometimes adorned with Victorian turrets.

about 55 km (34 mi) away. The next stop is the Confederation Bridge, roughly 60 km (37 mi) down the road.

⑬ Confederation Bridge This bridge opened in 1997 and connects Prince Edward Island, also referred to as "P.E.I.", to the Trans-Canada Highway. It is the world's longest bridge over an ice-covered waterway at 13 km (21 mi). At a height of 60 m (197 ft) the crossing takes roughly ten minutes.

⑭ Charlottetown This hilly island is almost treeless, but green pastures and fertile farmland line the road. Charlottetown is considered the "Cradle of the Confederation", as it was here that the decision to unite Canada was made in 1864. The small regional town exudes Victorian charm with its old wooden and half-timbered houses.

⑮ Prince Edward Island National Park The country's smallest national park is 24 km (15 mi) north of Charlottetown. As the St Lawrence River is only 15 m (49 ft) deep here until far out in the sea, the water along the 40-km (25-mi) park coast is a pleasant temperature.

Sault Ste. Marie This town is an important stop on the St Lawrence Seaway. The numerous cataracts to Lake Huron are navigated these days by large locks.

Tahquamenon Falls National Park The Tahquamenon River crashes down roughly 20 m (66 ft), making it the highest waterfall in Michigan.

Toronto The skyline of Canada's largest city is dominated by modern architecture, the most striking feature of which is the 553-m-high (1,814-ft) CN Tower.

Flowerpot Island A bizarre rock on Lake Huron.

Big Tub Lighthouse This lighthouse is the symbol of Bruce Peninsula National Park.

Niagara Falls The 50-m-high (164-ft) waterfalls comprise the American Falls and the Canadian Horseshoe Falls. Goat Island is tucked in between them.

Lake Ontario Covering an area of 20,000 sq km (7,720 sq mi), the easternmost of the Great Lakes is also the smallest. Its most famous city is Toronto.

Montréal Two thirds of the population in Canada's second largest city are French Canadians and continue to speak French today. The Île de Montréal island in the St Lawrence River forms the center of the metropolis.

Ottawa Canada's capital is also referred to as the "Westminster in the Wilderness". The neo-Gothic government buildings are the pride of the city.

Less then 30 km (17 mi) east of Charlottetown, you can learn all about the lifestyle of European immigrants in the 19th century at the Orwell Corner Historic Village. From Wood Islands you head back to Caribou, Nova Scotia, on the mainland by ferry and from there along Highway 104 to the Canso Causeway, the road connection to Cape Breton Island.

Highway 105 crosses the island, and from Sydney it's another 45 km (28 mi) to Louisbourg.

16 Louisbourg This small town on the east coast was the first French center of power in the New World. Tucked behind the 8-m-high (26-ft) walls of Fortresse de Louisbourg are around fifty historic buildings, from the governor's house to the soldiers' barracks. The road then heads along the coast past Sydney and St Ann's through the mountains of the island's north-west and into the most beautiful national park of the Atlantic provinces.

17 Cape Breton Highlands National Park This impassable mountainous region with peaks up to 554 m (1,818 ft) immediately evokes images of Scotland. For hikers and mountaineers

there are numerous trails and routes, while the 300-km-long (186-mi) Cabot Trail, a spectacular coast road around the peninsula is a joy for drivers.

Back on the mainland you follow Highway 104 and then Highway 102 from Truro to Halifax.

18 Halifax The Port of Halifax is the most important in the Atlantic provinces, and the Province House, completed in 1819, is the seat of parliament. Perched high up in the west is the old citadel, whose forts were built until 1856. The city's main landmark, however, is the clock tower from 1795.

1 A fishing village on Prince Edward Island. With the Gulf of St Lawrence, the best fishing grounds are literally at your doorstep.

2 The Cabot Trail opens up the north of Cape Breton Island.

3 The fort of Louisbourg, built by the French around 1740, has been restored to its original condition.

4 The Canadian Coastguard Lighthouse on Cape Breton Island.

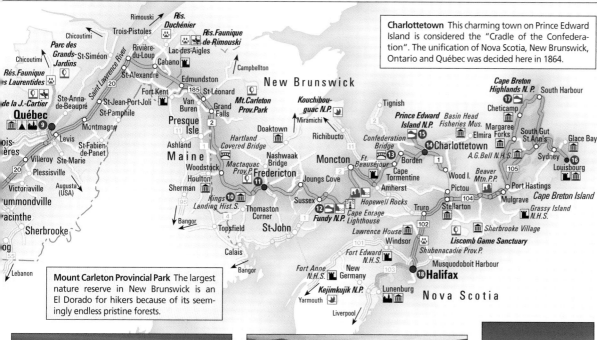

Charlottetown This charming town on Prince Edward Island is considered the "Cradle of the Confederation". The unification of Nova Scotia, New Brunswick, Ontario and Québec was decided here in 1864.

Cape Breton Highlands National Park This huge park is home to moose, beavers and over 250 species of birds.

Hartland Covered Bridge Built in 1901, this bridge is 390 m (1,280 ft) long and spans the St John River. It is the world's longest covered bridge.

Mount Carleton Provincial Park The largest nature reserve in New Brunswick is an El Dorado for hikers because of its seemingly endless pristine forests.

Québec This most recognizable icon of Québec city is the Château Frontenac with its many turrets and verdigris roofs. It was built on the site of the former governor's palace in 1893.

Réserve Faunique des Laurentides You can still spot moose, beavers and caribous in the mountainous region north of Montréal.

Cape Enrage Bizarre sandstones and a lighthouse characterize the cape in Fundy National Park.

Lunenburg This small town on the Atlantic was founded by Germans and Swiss in 1753, and is characterized by the old captain's quarters.

Old farmhouse in Grand Teton National Park in the north-west of the state of Wyoming.

Route 41

Canada and the USA

On the Pan-American Highway from British Columbia to New Mexico

A journey through the North American West is a journey of contrasts. The route passes through mountain landscapes and open plains, pine forests and vast deserts, mining villages and megacities, and illustrates the impressive diversity of this enormous continent.

The full diversity of North America reveals itself in its entirety along the wide open stretches of the Pan-American Highway. From its begining on the Canadian Pacific coast to its end near the border between the USA and Mexico, this route initially travels in a south-easterly and then southerly direction. The roads on this long route are in exceptionally good condition but some of the side roads can be closed during the colder times of the year, especially in the north.

The northern section takes you through the Canadian provinces of British Columbia and Alberta as well as the US state of

Montana. Larger towns are the exception here and the individual towns are often separated by large distances. Newer settlements originally developed from either trading posts or supply centers for the white fur hunters. There are also a number of old gold-digging locations along the Pan-American Highway, where visitors are taken back in time to the gold rush of the 19th century. In some places there are also remnants of Native American Indian cultures, such as the impressive totem poles, longhouses and pueblos.

The Canadian part of the route is loaded with absolutely breathtaking natural

Mount Assiniboine after the first snow.

landscapes. Majestic, snowy mountains reflect in the shimmering turquoise hues of Rocky Mountain lakes. To the east of the highway Mount Robson rises to 3,954 m (12,973 ft) above sea level, the highest peak in the Canadian Rocky Mountains. Glaciers and waterfalls drop powerfully to great depths from high cliffs. The Pan-American Highway is also lined with vast expanses of forest. In a number of areas such as Banff National Park, the oldest National Park in Canada, the natural environment is protected from development.

Further south the scenery changes. In the distance you see the skyscrapers of Calgary, a modern metropolis built on wealth generated by oil and natural resources, and given a makeover for the 1988 Winter Olympics. Some three hours from Calgary are the spectacular lakes

Banff National Park will show you everything that makes the Canadian Rocky Mountains such an attraction – rugged peaks, dense forests, vast open spaces and scenic lakes like Moraine Lake, shown here.

Sunset over Jackson Lake and the granite mountains of the Teton Range.

and mountains of Waterton-Glacier International Peace Park, a union of Glacier and Waterton National Parks.

The route continues through Idaho, Wyoming, Utah and Arizona. There are a number of remarkable contrasts here as well. Remnants of Native American cultures and the Spanish colonial era mix with modern cities and skyscrapers, and extensive forest areas stand in contrast to desert landscapes.

A major highlight of this particular section of North America is Yellowstone National Park in Wyoming. Salt Lake City, the capital of Utah and the center of Mormonism, is also an Olympic city, having hosted the 2002 winter games. In the vast desert expanses of Utah and Arizona the light and landscape change dramatically with the movement of the sun, producing impressive interplays of colours and shad-

ows, and the rocky landscape of the Colorado Plateau is also impressive in places like Bryce Canyon National Park. The Grand Canyon, stretching over 350 km (217 miles) of magnificent desert, is one of the most visited sightseeing attractions in the USA – some 4 million people come here every year.

Sunset Crater, the youngest of Arizona's volcanoes, can be seen near Flagstaff and is today a training area for astronauts. In the adjoining 'Valley of the Sun' to the south the towns appear like oases in the desert. The exclusive golf courses and fields exist only due to artificial irrigation. Phoenix, the capital of Arizona, still has a slight touch of the Wild West to it, but as a center for the aircraft construction and high-tech industries, the city is part of the modern world. Tucson, the 'City of Sunshine', has 350 days of sunshine a year.

Spirit Island in Maligne Lake in Jasper National Park – postcard views par excellence.

Broad plains stretch between the mountain ranges of Banff National Park, and lush vegetation thrives in the summer wherever the landscape is protected from the cold winds of the north. But the growth period is short in these high mountains – the first snow often cuts autumn short in September.

Visitors to Banff National Park can choose between a hike to Mount Tuzo (top), to Vermillion Lake (2nd from top) or a drive along Icefields Parkway (2nd from bottom). Bottom: A popular photograph in Banff is of snow-capped peaks reflected in one of the many lakes (here, Herbert Lake).

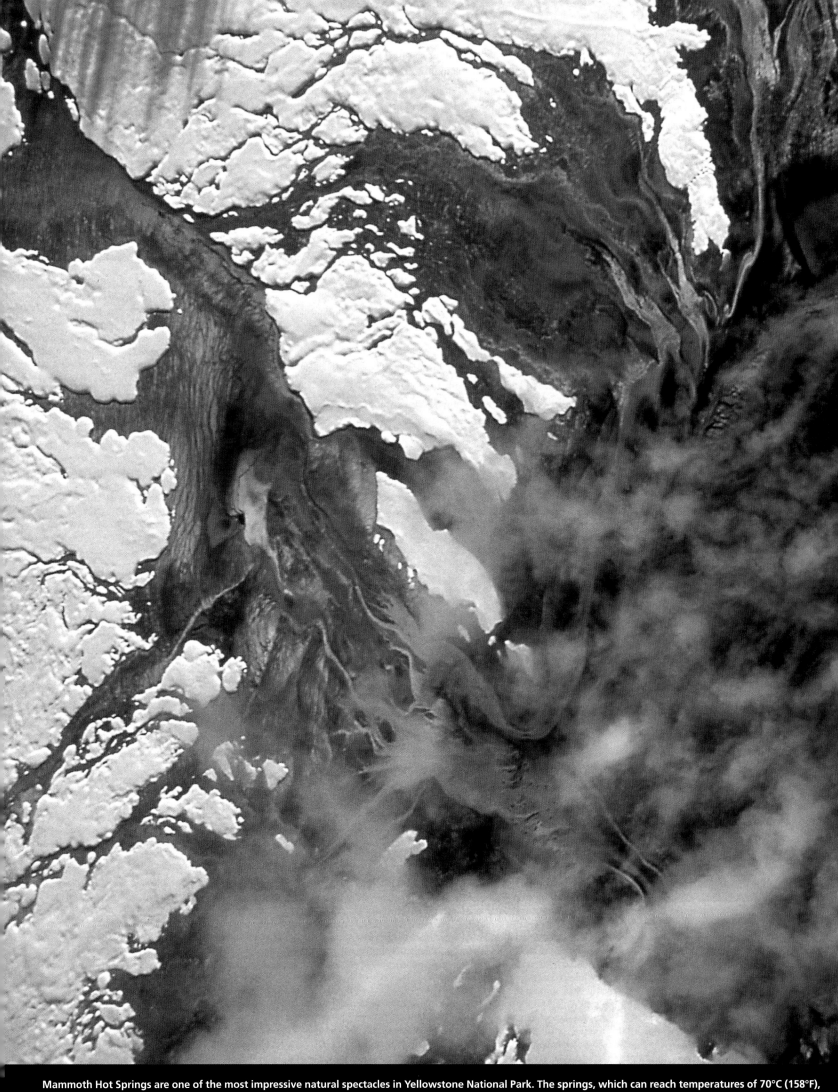

Mammoth Hot Springs are one of the most impressive natural spectacles in Yellowstone National Park. The springs, which can reach temperatures of 70°C (158°F), have created a landscape with of bizarre colors when seen from the sky. After the water reaches the surface, the minerals contained in it are deposited on the

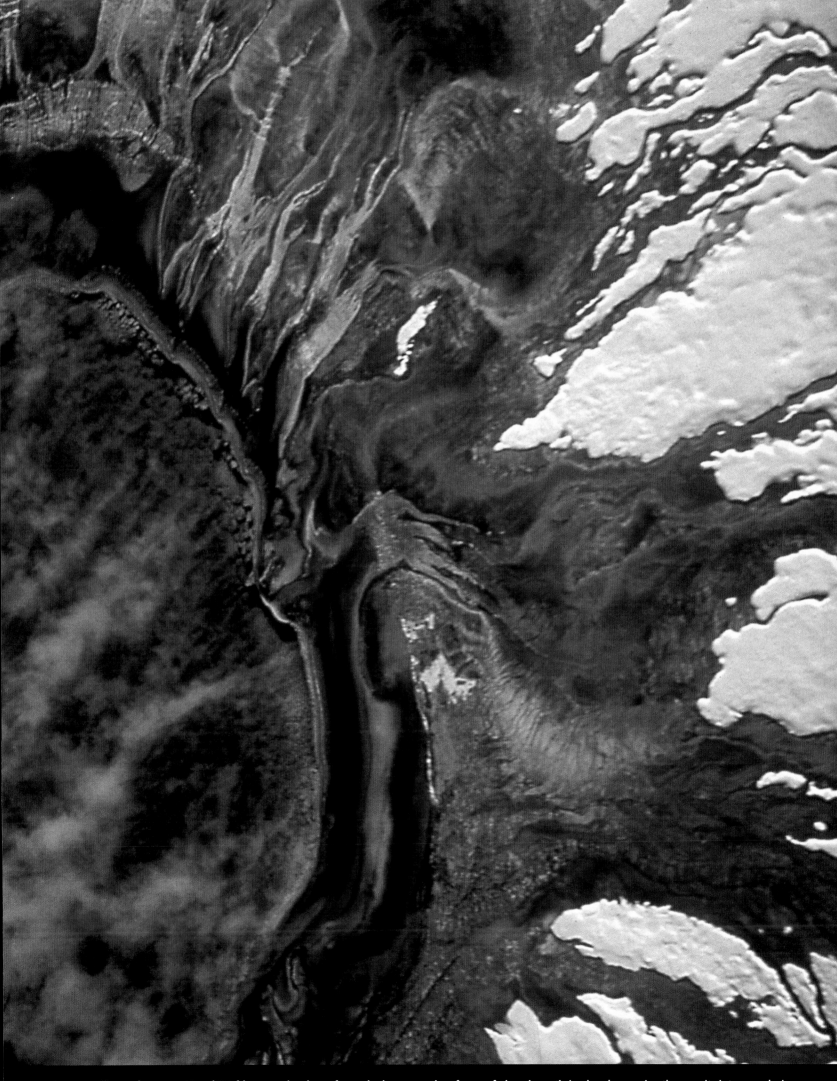

ground. Over millions of years, a 90-m (295-ft) terrace has been formed where countless forms of algae have thrived and now give the area its intense coloring. During twilight the spectacle is at its best as the colors constantly change with the evening light.

Geysers in Yellowstone National Park

The earth displays its powerful forces in a fascinating array of ways in Yellowstone National Park – not with destructive earthquakes or violent volcanic eruptions, but with natural water fountains called geysers that visitors can observe from close up.

The geysers erupt when water boils below the earth's surface, blasting steam and water from their deep shafts. Some of them are incredibly consistent, others erupt at irregular intervals. The forces involved sometimes push the fountains to heights as tall as trees or even buildings. The highest geyser, which only erupts from time to time, is Steamboat. Its blasts sometimes reach 120 m (394 ft), each eruption releasing several thousands

Castle Geyser in Yellowstone National Park.

of litres of water. But its full force is only released every ten years or so.

Geysers are only found in areas with volcanic activity and are subject to specific conditions. What is important is a network of caves in the rock that works its way to the earth's surface. The groundwater collects in this tunnel system and is warmed by the heat of the earth. When the pressure is released the water is forced out. There are only a few places on earth where this natural spectacle occurs as impressively as it does in the Yellowstone National Park. Old Faithful Geyser is the first one in the park to receive a name.

The journey then continues via Browning to Shelby. From here it is a further 82 km (51 miles) on Highway 15 to Great Falls.

⑪ Great Falls The city's sightseeing attractions include the Giant Springs, one of the largest freshwater springs in North America, and the Lewis and Clark National Forest, named after the explorers who traversed much of western North America at the start of the 19th century.

About 44 km (27 miles) northeast of the city is Fort Benton, founded in 1846 as a trading post on the upper reaches of the Missouri River. Continuing south you pass more springs, including White Sulphur Springs. Continuing to Yellowstone National Park it is worth taking a detour near Livingston to the battlefield of Little Bighorn 110 km (68 miles) away.

⑫ Yellowstone National Park From Montana you continue

along the Pan-American Highway to the state of Wyoming, which boasts one of the continent's main attractions. Yellowstone National Park is indeed in a league of its own, not least because it is the oldest and largest in the USA. It receives around 3 million visitors a year, and it is easily accessible by car, although some roads are closed between November and April. The Grand Loop Road meanders 230 km (143 miles) through the park.

If you are approaching from the north it is worth making a short stop at Mammoth Hot Springs where information material and updates on the passability of the side roads are available from the park office.

The significance of the reserve (8,983 sq km/5,582 sq mi) in the midst of the Rocky Mountains and the Grand Tetons was recognized early on as a natural treasure and was declared a national park in 1872. Mother Nature shows her most spectacular side

Animals of Yellowstone National Park

For European visitors, bison in the wild are a special experience and sometimes even cause real traffic jams on the Grand Loop Road. Other animals

Bison fighting for territory.

on this high plateau, which ranges from 2,100 to 2,400 m (6,890 to 7,874 ft). The forces of the earth's core come to the surface in the Yellowstone National Park where the world's most impressive and powerful geysers can be seen. The highest of the roughly 300 geysers is Steamboat.

Approaching from the north you first reach the Norris Geyser Basin where, in addition to the Steamboat, the Echinus Geyser also puts on a show from time to time. A short distance further on to the south-west you reach the Fountain Paint Pot, a basin of bubbling red-brown mud. Upper Geyser Basin has the most geysers in the whole of the national park. It is therefore no surprise that this is where the highest number of visitors will be found. You can even set your watch by some of the geysers and can plan your arrival accordingly.

Old Faithful is one of the most 'punctual', displaying its skills almost every 80 minutes for a few minutes at a time, sending huge quantities of water about 50 m (164 ft) into the air. Other well-known geysers are Giant Geyser and Castle Geyser. And it's not just a visual experience. The accompanying noises as you approach are also fascinating. Make sure you stick to the marked pathways at all times as the unstable ground bubbles and hisses at many places in the park. Steam clouds sometimes even reach as far as the Grand Loop Road.

1 Yellowstone River near the 94-m-high (308-ft) Lower Falls.

2 The tranquil river landscape is ideal bison territory.

3 In summer bison graze on the wide open spaces of the park.

4 Old Faithful Geyser in Yellowstone National Park.

5 A 34-km (21-mile) shoreline road provides access to Yellowstone Lake in the south-west of the park.

such as elks and mountain goats as well as pumas, coyotes and lynx are also at home here. Wolves have also been successfully reintegrated in recent years. Parts of the pine forests in Yellowstone are subject to recurring forest fires.

At 2,300 km (1,440 mi) in length, the Colorado River is the longest river west of the Rocky Mountains. On its way to the Gulf of Mexico (which it no longer actually reaches), the river cuts through spectacular landscapes, many of which the river itself has created over the millennia. Among the most fascinating of

these natural wonders is Marble Canyon in northern Arizona, where the Colorado has dug out a deep gorge with high, steep walls. In the flatter areas, the river snakes its way through bizarre rock formations.

The awe-inspiring sequoias in Redwood National Park can reach heights of up to 112 m (367 ft).

Route 42

USA

'The American Way of Life' between the Pacific coast and the Sierra Nevada

Sun, sea and tanned surfers. It's a popular cliché image that many people have of California and, as with many such clichés, it has an element of truth to it. But the Golden State on the west coast of the USA has myriad other facets as well – majestic mountains, ancient forests with giant redwood trees, superb alpine lakes, breathtaking deserts and one of the most beautiful coastal roads in the country, Highway 1. On top of that there are lively cities such as Los Angeles, San Francisco and San Diego.

'Go West, young man, and grow up with the country!' Since the middle of the 19th century this call has inspired countless people to seek their fortunes in the promised lands of California. Today, millions of tourists from all over the world are also drawn by the magic of this region on the West Coast. Highway 1, with its magnificent views of the mighty Pacific Ocean, could easily be considered one of the most beautiful roads in the world. Yet the

'hinterland' offers equally spectacular natural wonders, from the rock walls and waterfalls of Yosemite National Park and the bizarre limestone formations of Mono Lake to the glorious giant sequoias (redwood trees) scattered throughout the numerous parks around the state. They flourish wonderfully along the misty Pacific coast as well as in the cool Sierra

Nevada mountains. Then there are arid regions such as the Mojave Desert which, at first glance, seem devoid of almost any life. After the brief, irregular showers of rain, however, the desert produces a magical variety of plant life. Death Valley, somewhat off this tour's path, is surrounded by mountains rising to more than 3,000 m (9,843 ft) and evokes lunar landscapes of spectacular proportions. It also boasts such superlatives as the lowest point in the Western Hemisphere and the highest temperature ever recorded. European travellers are continually overwhelmed by the diversity and beauty of these magnificent natural landscapes. Indeed, Mother Nature has been generous to this Pacific region. Gold discoveries in 1849 brought about the first major wave of settlement. Hollywood, synonymous with the glamorous world of film,

In the late 1980s the famous Santa Monica Pier was restored to its former glory.

San Francisco by moonlight. The 2.7-km (1.7-mile) Golden Gate Bridge, at the entrance to San Francisco Bay, was completed in 1937 and links the city with Marin County to the north.

Population growth in Los Angeles in the mid-1900s depleted water levels in Mono Lake to such an extent that evaporation became faster than inflow. These exposed tufa towers are a result of these developments. Successful efforts are now being made to restore the lake's former state.

has the sunny Southern California climate to thank for its existence. Yet the same sun that draws tourists to the beaches also makes the hugely important agricultural business here a major challenge, one that is really only possible with the help of sophisticated and far-reaching irrigation systems. The Californians have artfully mastered their often tough natural environment and do not even seem too distracted by the San Andreas Fault, repeatedly the cause of disastrous earthquakes here.

A tour through California brings to life the many places linked to the region's Spanish and Mexican legacy, like Santa Barbara, San Luis Obispo or Carmel, all of which play host to mission churches founded by Spanish monks along 'El Camino Real', the Royal Road. San Francisco, often considered the most 'Euro-

pean' city in the USA and a dream destination for people around the world, originally boomed after the discovery of gold in the foothills of the Sierra Nevada. It was only in the 20th century that its rival to the south, Los Angeles, grew to its current sprawling size – life without a car is inconceivable here.

California's open-mindedness has often promoted important subculture movements that have even had global influence – the Beat Generation, the Hippies, the Gay Movement, rural communes, ecological movements and other milieus experimenting with alternative lifestyles. Not to be forgotten is of course Silicon Valley, the pioneer site of the digital revolution in the 20th century.

As a whole, a trip through California reflects a sort of microcosm of what the 'American Dream' is all about.

El Capitan and the Merced River in a wintry Yosemite National Park.

Cypress Point is one of the most popular spots on the California coast between Los Angeles and San Francisco. The gnarled, solitary cypress tree (popularly known as the Lone Cypress) on the tiny rock outcrop has to be one of the most photographed trees in the world. If you want to see this glorious interplay of land and

sea on the Monterey Peninsula, turn off Highway One onto 17-Mile Drive. The panorama road includes the tiny outcrop on which the famous tree has stood for over 250 years as well as vast pine and cypress forests along the spectacular coast.

San Francisco

A unique location overlooking an expansive bay on the Pacific Ocean, historic cable cars, unique neighbourhoods like Chinatown and North Beach, bustling Market Street, Fisherman's Wharf and the Golden Gate Bridge have all made San Francisco, the 'Paris of the American West', into a revered travel destination.

The city was founded by the Spanish in 1776 and named Yerba Buena. Only in 1847 was the name changed to San Francisco after the San Francisco de Asís Mission was founded by Father Junipero Serra.

The city's most turbulent period began in January 1848 when gold was discovered in northern California. San Francisco became a base for many gold diggers heading north. More than 40,000 adventurers and profiteers settled in the city in 1849 alone. It soon grew to become an important trading center, and has remained so even after the massive earthquake destroyed entire neighbourhoods throughout the city in 1906.

Alcatraz lies in San Francisco Bay. The rocky island was discovered by the Spanish and named after the pelicans that used to inhabit the island. In the 19th century the US Army built a fort there, which was converted to a military prison in 1909. The first civil prisoners were brought in 1934 to 'The Rock', at the time considered the most secure prison in the world.

The famous cable cars were developed by Andrew S. Hallidie in 1869, the first of them rolling through town in 1873. By 1880 there were already eight lines and since 1964 they have been protected as part of the city's heritage.

One of the USA's most well-known landmarks, the Golden Gate Bridge, opened for traffic in 1937 following four years of construction. Including its access roads, the bridge is 11 km (9 miles) long, and the pylons extend 228 m (748 ft) out of the water. Following the California gold rush of 1849, Fisherman's Wharf was the primary mooring for commercial boats. Today it is geared toward shopping and tourism.

San Francisco's distinct neighbourhoods are a joy to explore. Chinatown, for example, between Broadway, Bush, Kearny and Stockton Street is the second largest Chinese community in the USA (after New York). The official entrance is marked by a large red-green gate at the junction of Grant and Bush streets. The first Star-Spangled Banner was raised in California in 1846 at Portsmouth Square.

Top: The characteristic triangular shape of the Transamerica Pyramid is clearly recognizable among the skyscrapers.
Middle: With their pastel colours and stylish detail, the so-called Painted Ladies are excellent examples of Victorian architecture.
Bottom: A football game in the university town of Berkeley, across the San Francisco Bay to the east.

At 4,317 m (14,179 ft), Mount Shasta dominates all of the other mountains in the area, and its perfect, snow-capped volcanic peak can be seen from truly vast distances. It is the second-largest mountain in the Cascade Range. The solidified lava flows that are visible under the cover of snow and the smoky haze that occa...

sionally rises from near the peak are proof that the mountain is still active. The main ascent route is on the south side of the mountain. At the base of Shasta is the origin of Cold Creek, one of the headwaters of the mighty Sacramento River, and the lakes in the area are good for walks and boating.

The Big Red Lighthouse was erected by the Dutch in 1847 on southern Lake Michigan when they founded the little town of Holland.

USA

Route 66: The American Myth

The first continuous road link between Chicago and Los Angeles still evokes nostalgia today. It is synonymous with freedom and wide open country, cruisers and 'Easy Rider', neon signs and diners – in short, the symbol of a nation whose identity is characterized by being on the road. The West was all about promises and aspirations, a paradise on earth. 'Go California' was the motto – Route 66 was the way there.

The first link between the Great Lakes and the Pacific Ocean has been a continuing legend and the symbol of the American dream ever since Bobby Troup's 'Get your kicks on Route 66'. It was Horace Greely who popularized the phrase 'Go West, young man, and grow up with the country' in the New York Herald Tribune, and with it created the creed of an entire nation. What came of this creed and the people who later followed it through the Depression and droughts of the 1930s has

nowhere been described as tellingly as in John Steinbeck's *The Grapes of Wrath* in which the Joad family heads out on what later became known as the 'Mother Road' to the West.

The clash between dreams and reality remains part of the Route 66 legend today. What has since become a long forgotten chapter in the history of fast-moving America began less than 100 years ago as cars began to make a show of competition for the railways. The 'National

Route 66 in Arizona.

Old Trails Highway' developed from the first 'highways' in the individual states and thus became the predecessor of Route 66. But the nice name still did not stand for much more than sand, gravel and strip roads. It was only on 11 November 1926 that the eight Federal states of Illinois, Missouri, Kansas, Oklahoma, Texas, New Mexico, Arizona and California completed the uniform 4,000-km (2,486-mile) route between Chicago and Los Angeles, and the highway was officially opened as Route 66.

The start of Route 66 is marked by a signpost at the Michigan Avenue/Jackson Drive intersection in Chicago. The idyllic countryside of Illinois begins directly after the suburban neighbourhoods to the west of town. Remote farms and tranquil villages characterize Abraham Lincoln's home country. The Amish people's rejec-

View of the Chicago skyline by night from Sears Tower. Left in the background is the tapered 344-m-high (1,129-ft) John Hancock Center adorned with two antennae.

In the state of New Mexico Route 66 passes through a stark landscape of bizarre rock formations.

tion of the technological age takes the traveller back into a bygone era. You finally reach the 'Gateway to the West' in St Louis where the road crosses the expanse of the Mississippi and through the 192-m-high (630-ft) steel archway designed by Eero Saarinen.

The gentle hills of the Ozark Mountains and the 'glitter world' of the Meramec Caverns are hard to resist. Upon reaching Oklahoma, the 'Native American State', you are finally in the land of cowboys and Indians with its seemingly never-ending plains. The cowboys are still in charge on the giant cattle ranches in the area, and this applies to the 290 km (180 miles) where Route 66 crosses the narrow panhandle in northern Texas.

In New Mexico there is a whole new world waiting to greet the visitor. The special light in the valleys and canyons glows mysteriously on the red and brown cliffs and gentle mountains. Between Santa Fe and Taos you will experience an enchanted landscape with a harmonious combination of Spanish charm and Indian culture.

Next comes Arizona, which is not only the state with the largest Indian reservations, but also an area of spectacular rock formations in Red Rock Country, Oak Creek Canyon and of course the Grand Canyon. Intoxicated by the beauty of the landscape, you enter California, crossing the daunting Mojave Desert with its cacti as the last obstacle before heading down towards the Pacific.

San Bernardino marks the start of the fertile 'Orange Empire' as Route 66 is slowly swallowed up by Los Angeles' endless sea of buildings. It all finally comes to an end in Palisades Park near Santa Monica.

Mexican children pose in traditional costume in Santa Fe, New Mexico.

Detour

The Big Red Lighthouse

When the Dutch founded the small town of Holland on the southern shore of Lake Macatawa (Lake Michigan) in 1847, they immediately recognized its potential as a port. However, the ships had to pass through a narrow passage – only

The Big Red Lighthouse on the eastern shore of Lake Michigan.

70 m (230 ft) in width – between extensive sand dunes.
In order to ensure their safe passage, a bonfire was lit from 1870 at the end of a long wooden pier. With its increasing importance for shipping, this grew to become a building that took on its current shape by 1956. Its nickname 'Big Red' is due to its red colour.

The first continuous East-West connection in the USA from Chicago to Los Angeles remains something of a legend today. Even though during the course of the 20th century large parts of the original Route 66 gave way to more modern Interstate highways, there are still many original stretches where the legend lives on.

1 Chicago (see pp. 634–635). Before starting off towards the south it is worth taking a detour to the town of Holland 110 km (68 miles) away. This reconstructed village is a memorial to the region's Dutch immigrants.
The journey along the legendary Route 66 begins at the Michigan Avenue/Jackson Drive intersection in Chicago and from there Interstate Highway 55 takes you to Springfield. North of Springfield is the Chautauqua National Wildlife Reserve.

2 Springfield The capital of Illinois still has the aura of an idyllic country town today. A little further north, New Salem was the home of the famous president (Lincoln) who lived here in humble circumstances from 1831–1837. The village has now been reconstructed as an open-air museum with staff in period costume who demonstrate how hard life was here 200 years ago.
In Springfield itself the focus is also on President Lincoln and

his carefully restored house on Jackson Street is open to visitors, as is his law office on Adams Street where he practised as a lawyer from 1843–1853. He found his final resting place in Oak Ridge Cemetery.
Lincoln was a parliamentarian in the Old State Capitol in the Downtown Mall but since 1877 state business has been conducted in the opulent new Illinois State Capitol. Shea's Gas Station Museum imparts true Route 66 feeling.
The journey continues southwards via Interstate Highway 55 toward St Louis.

3 St Louis The largest city in the state of Missouri lies on the western bank of the Mississippi just before the confluence with the Missouri River. The Mark Twain National Wildlife Reserve was established on the river north of the city. The city was founded in 1764 by a French fur trader, Pierre Liguest, and it was fur traders who first brought wealth to the new settlement.

Travel information

Route profile
Length: approx. 4,000 km (2,486 miles), excluding detours
Time required: 3 weeks
Start: Chicago
End: Santa Monica
Route (main locations): Chicago, St Louis, Tulsa, Oklahoma City, Santa Fe, Albuquerque, Flagstaff, Barstow, Santa Monica

Traffic information:
Drive on the right in the USA. Maximum speed limits in built-up areas are 25 to 30 mph (40–48 km/h); on the highways 55–70 mph

(88–115 km/h). Speed checks (with tough penalties) are also conducted from the air. Drink-driving is strictly prohibited in all of the states here, with heavy fines. It is prohibited to carry open or even empty bottles or cans of alcoholic beverages in the car (not even in the boot).

Information:
Detailed information on the historical Route 66 as well as the most important sightseeing attractions can be found at:
www.historic66.com or *www.theroadwanderer.net*

Sears Tower

Chicago's skyline is dominated by one of the tallest buildings in the world, the 443-m (1,453-ft) Sears Tower. Its 108 floors were completed in 1973 following thirty years of construction, making it the tallest building in the world until 1998 when the Petronas Towers were built in Kuala Lumpur, Malaysia. However, there is controversy regarding what 'tallest' means. With its antennae the Sears Tower is still the highest point on any building worldwide (520 m/1,706 ft).

The tower's simple design is based on narrow, quadratic pillars, with nine on the lowest level supporting four, then three and then two right at the top. The facade is made from black aluminium sheets and more than

The Sears Tower in Chicago is adorned by two giant antennae.

16,000 bronze-coloured windows. In the lobby visitors are greeted by 'The Universe', a famous hanging mobile by Alexander Calder.

Of course the giant tower also has record-breaking elevators – as double deckers they are always travelling to the 33rd/34th or the 66th/67th floors simultaneously – at a speed of 8.5 m/sec (29 ft/sec).

The most interesting part for visitors is the Skydeck on the 103rd floor at a height of 412 m (1,352 ft). It has its own entrance on Jackson Boulevard and draws some two million visitors every year.

Large parts of the American west were then settled from here. It was from here that the endless wagon trains began their journey across the prairies and it was to here that the riches of the grasslands and the Rocky Mountains were brought back and traded.

The 192-m-high (630-ft) Gateway Arch designed by the Finn, Eero Saarinen, is St Louis' primary landmark and is purposely visible from great distances. As a symbolic 'Gateway to the West', the arch is a reminder that this is where the great tide of settlers heading for the coast began the often perilous expedition.

A short distance south of the Gateway Arch is the Old Cathedral dating from 1834 with its attractive mosaics and a museum of the city's history in the basement. Market Street begins on the Gateway Arch axis and its notable attractions include the dome of the Old Court House from 1864, the magnificent round building that is the Busch Memorial Stadium and the City Hall, which is based on its counterpart in Paris.

On Lindell Boulevard is the splendid St Louis Cathedral built in 1907 in Byzantine style. It has a spectacular mosaic dome. You leave St Louis via Interstate Highway 44 and make your way towards Stanton.

④ Meramec Caverns A visit to the Meramec Caverns about 5 km (3 miles) south of Stanton is not to be missed. They are among the largest stalactite caves in the USA and include some fascinating formations. Some doubt that the famous bandit Jesse James and his gang used the caves as a hideout, but legends certainly tell of their presence here.

For the onward journey you continue down Interstate 44 to Springfield, Missouri.

⑤ Branson South of Springfield, the third-largest city in Missouri, are the Ozark Mountains, which attract a great number of visitors, particularly in autumn.

The small town of Branson is your specific destination reached via Highway 65. It is known as 'America's Biggest Little Town' and the new Mecca of American country music. As such, it has outdone legendary Nashville, Tennessee.

Traditional handicrafts and nostalgic events are staged in 'Silver Dollar City'. Highway 13 takes you to the Talking Rock Caverns, considered the most scenic of the 5,000 caves in Missouri. Those interested in history can make a detour to the Pea Ridge National Monument.

Back in Springfield continue along Interstate 44 westwards.

⑥ Joplin A part of the original Route 66 turns right from Highway 44 shortly before the small town of Joplin, Missouri. Continue through Joplin and shortly thereafter you reach the little town of Galena where time appears to have stood still. The whole town is like an open-air museum.

The next little village is Riverton where the old Marsh Arch Bridge, an arched concrete suspension bridge, was built in 1923

1 The port and skyline of Chicago. The Sears Tower (second from the left) was the tallest building in the world until 1998.

2 At the height of summer, the St Louis sun sets in the middle of the Gateway Arc.

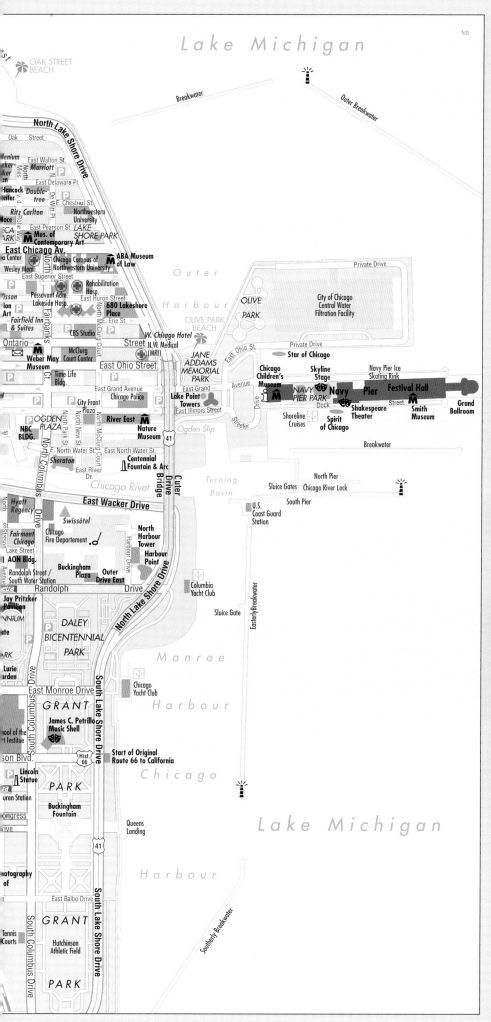

Chicago

Including its outer suburbs, Chicago sprawls over 100 km (62 miles) along the southern shores of Lake Michigan. The city is a fantastic destination for anyone interested in architecture – Downtown Chicago has been highlighted by the works of renowned architects. The city also attracts throngs of visitors with its lively music, museum and multicultural scenes.

Chicago was already an important transport hub and trading center in the 19th century. Cattle and pigs were unloaded here at the largest livestock station in the country and driven to urban slaughterhouses, of which there are only a few remaining.

In the 'Roaring Twenties', the 'Windy City' gained the dubious reputation of being a gangster metropolis, but Al Capone is all but legend now. The skyline of the new Chicago rose up out of the ruins of the old city and is the best proof of the determination and initiative of its residents.

The 'Great Chicago Fire' of 9 October 1871 almost completely destroyed the city. Over 200 people died and more than 90,000 lost everything they had. Today all that remains of the old Chicago is the water tower.

Picasso; 'Flamingo', the bright red giant spider by Alexander Calder in front of the Chicago Federal Center; 'Universe', a gigantic mobile by the same artist in the lobby of the Sears Tower; or 'The Fours Seasons', a 20-m-long (66-ft) mosaic by Marc Chagall in front of the First National Bank.

Then there is also a series of museums worth visiting – the Museum of Science and Industry houses an underground coal mine and a 5-m-high (16-ft) model of a human heart. A reproduction of the largest saurian (dinosaur lizard) in the world awaits you in the Museum of Natural History. The Art Institute of Chicago is renowned for its collection of modern art. The Adler Planetarium, a star-shaped granite building with a copper dome, has a number of surprising special effects. The attractions

Chicago shows off its impressive skyline on both sides of the Chicago River (top). The city established itself as a center of modern architecture at the start of the 20th century. Whether by day (middle) or by night (bottom), the numerous unique skyscrapers are there to be admired on a walk through the streets of Chicago.

State Street is considered the largest pedestrian zone in the world and attracts crowds with its department stores, boutiques, restaurants, cinemas and theaters. Passers-by encounter a number of remarkable artworks on the pavements – a 16-m (52-ft) statue left to the citizens of Chicago by Pablo

in the John G. Shedd Aquarium include a huge coral reef and a shark habitat. There are numerous restaurants and bars to choose from at the Navy Pier. Chicago continues to be a city of jazz and blues and a live concert in one of the very diverse clubs or bars should not be missed.

The Plains Indians

The vast North American plains are the true heart of the country. The land of grass, wind and sunshine extends from Saskatchewan, Canada, in the north more than 3,000 km (1,864 miles) to the south as far as the Rio Grande in Mexico. In total, the plains cover an area of some 2.5 million sq km (1.6 million sq mi). Some of the tribes that dominated this area were the Sioux, the Blackfoot, the Crow and the Cheyenne Indians.

Vast herds of bison grazed on the seemingly endless grasslands and formed the basis of the Indians' livelihood. Before the Europeans came and horses were introduced in the late 600s, Indians hunted bison on foot by driving entire herds to a cliff edge, over which the animals then fell to their deaths. The most famous of these cliff edges in North America is the UNESCO-protected

Top: Shawnee Indians at the Red Earth Festival in Oklahoma. Below: Anadarko – the 'Indian Capital of the Nation'.

Head-Smashed-In Buffalo Jump south of Calgary, Canada.

Some of the Indians lived from hunting and others as resident farmers, with a healthy exchange of goods taking place between the various groups. The beginning of the end of the Plains Indians came in the middle of the 19th century with the white man's massive slaughter of bison. The massacre robbed these hunter Indians of their livelihood, and the inexorable advance of the white man from the east did the rest. The end came in December 1890 with the massacre at Wounded Knee. South-west of Oklahoma City, in Anadarko, an open-air museum with seven Indian villages, the 'Indian Capital of the Nation' commemorates the culture of the Plains Indians.

to span Brush Creek. Route 66 passed over this bridge until 1960. The next stop is Baxter Springs where under no circumstances should you miss a visit to Murphey's Restaurant in the Baxter National Bank, which was closed in 1952. Part of the decor comprises former bank furniture, and old cheques from the 1920s lie on the tables under glass.

7 Miami Here too, little appears to have changed on the outside. Miami developed from a trading station set up in 1890. In 1905 lead and zinc brought a boom to the town. The main attraction is the Coleman Theatre, built in 1929, a cinema with magnificently crafted balconies

and a ceiling lined with gold leaf. On the first floor there is a small exhibition about Route 66 and its history.

8 Tulsa The former 'Oil Capital of the World', Tulsa has long been stripped of this title, but some of the oil barons' art deco villas are still a sign of the city's former wealth.

Waite Phillips' mansion still houses works of art from the Italian Renaissance. The original Route 66 follows Eleventh Street through downtown. Between Tulsa and Oklahoma City you can also travel along lengthy stretches of the historic Route 66, which maintain their rustic charm.

9 Oklahoma City Founded in 1889 – after Indian territories were opened to whites – the capital of Oklahoma owes its wealth to oil. There are still a good 2,000 wells within the city limits today, one of which is directly in front of the Capitol. The spirit of the Wild West is still

alive and well in the National Cowboy Hall of Fame on Persimmon Hill, which includes the replica of an old western town called 'Prosperity Junction'. 'The American Cowboy Gallery' documents the life of the cowboys, and the 'American Rodeo Gallery' is dedicated to that

long-standing western tradition. South-west of the city center is the historic neighbourhood Stockyards City, where you can get a feeling for the way things might have been in the heyday of the cattle business here. South of the city are the Wichita Mountains, a hiking area, and to the north-west is the Washita Battlefield where Custer staged an attack on the Cheyenne Indians in the ongoing and tragic clash of cultures that took place in the area. The journey continues via Interstate 40 westwards to Clinton.

⑩ Clinton The most interesting Route 66 museums on the whole trip are to be found here. Films,

photos and original exhibition pieces document the route's heyday. Beyond Clinton you stay on Interstate 40. Once you get to Amarillo, a detour on Interstate 27 leads to one of the most interesting canyons in the area.

⑪ Palo Duro Canyon State Park This canyon is surrounded by cliffs some 350 m (1,148 ft) high where remote Indian trails lead deep into the canyon to the most spectacular cliff formations. Also called the 'Grand Canyon of Texas', Palo Duro is the second-largest canyon in the USA: 195 km (121 miles) long, 32 km (20 miles) wide and 243 m (797 ft) deep – a good warm-up for the real thing.

⑫ Amarillo Route 66 used to pass along Sixth Avenue in this Texas town, a street lined with some restored buildings from the route's heyday. The American Quarter Horse Heritage Center documents the history of the breeding of the American Quarter Horse.
Cadillac Ranch 15 km (9 miles) to the west is, a bizarre desert exhibition of old Cadillacs. There is a flint quarry further north, Alibates Flint Quarries National Monument. The route continues on Interstate 40 over the border into New Mexico towards Albuquerque.

⑬ Fort Sumner Before reaching the little town of Santa Rosa, it is worth taking a brief detour to the south on Highway 84 to Fort Sumner where 8,000 Navajo and Apache Indians were rounded up in 1864 and forcefully relocated to the fort to survive on their own. Many of them died. The visitor center and adjacent museum tell the story of this gruesome incident.
The town went down in American history a second time as well, as it was here on 16 July 1881 that Pat Garrett shot the famous Billy the Kid. A small museum has been erected in his memory. Back in Santa Rosa, continue to follow Interstate 40. To reach

Santa Fe you need to leave the actual Route 66 at Clines Corners, the intersection of Interstate 40 and Highway 285, then head north toward Santa Fe.

⑭ Santa Fe The second-oldest city in the USA and the capital of New Mexico is characterized by both Indian and Spanish culture. There are eight large museums and a multitude of art galleries, jewellery shops and handicraft stores here. When the Spanish arrived in 1542, there was already a large Pueblo Indian settlement here, which later revolted against the colonials and sent them packing. In the meantime, however, the Spanish made Santa Fe the capital of

1 They're back: nostalgic diners and the cars to match.

2 Some of the buildings in the Old Town of Muskogee, south-east of Tulsa, are reminiscent of the city's early days.

3 Stark cliffs rise 350 m (1,148 ft) in the Palo Duro Canyon.

4 The Oklahoma City National Memorial was erected to commemorate the victims of the attack on the Alfred P. Murrah Federal Building in 1995.

Cadillac Ranch

The Texas town of Amarillo boasts two superlatives. On the one hand, it draws the crowds with the Big Texan Steak Ranch where you can have a 2-kg (4-lbs) steak for free if you can eat it, including side dishes and dessert, in one hour. On the other hand, 15 km (9 miles) west of the city is the Cadillac Ranch where ten old Cadillacs from

Cadillac Ranch: a bizarre reminder of the golden age of the Cadillac.

between 1948 and 1963 are buried halfway in the ground.
This bizarre exhibit is a homage to the American sense of mobility and style. The ten Cadillacs are painted in all the colours of the rainbow and covered in graffiti of all kinds. The front ends are buried in the ground while the rear ends, with the characteristic tail fins, stick up in the air.

The Painted Desert stretches out to the east of Flagstaff, a colorful desert landscape with plateaus, rounded mounds and badlands. The colors come from the minerals embedded in the stone. About 225 million years ago, sediment layers 500 m (1,600 ft) thick settled here below an inland sea. Then, when the

Colorado Plateau rose about sixty million years ago, the top layer eroded, uncovering the myriad tones and sandstone formations. As such, the Painted Desert is a colorful image of a 200-million-year-old world.

Flagstaff Indian Day

A powwow – a colourful Indian gathering – takes place every July in the Coconino County Fairground in Flagstaff where Indian traditions are observed with dancing and singing. The Indians have struggled to retain

Participants at the Flagstaff Indian Day.

their culture, but the songs and dances help keep some of their traditions alive.

Part of the powwow therefore always comprises the large counsel fire where tribal politics are discussed, successes celebrated and losses lamented. The traditional 'giveaway' provides the opportunity to present valuable gifts and to gather money for charity. The dancers are motivated with substantial money prizes and there are also awards for costumes and jewellery. It is a point of honour for everyone to take part – the tribe benefits from a successful powwow the whole year long until the next one.

around 200 million years ago. Today their fractures glimmer with all the colours of the rainbow. The park, which extends both north and south of Interstate 40, is accessed via the 43-km (27-mile) park road and has two information centers, one of which is located at the north entrance, directly accessible from Interstate 40.

Pintado Point, right at the start of the park road, offers the best overview of the Painted Desert. All the colours of the glowing badlands are seen at their best from here.

Blue Mesa Point, reached by the 4.8-km (3-mile) access road, offers a second spectacular overview. Agate House is an 800-year-old Anasazi pueblo, the walls of which are made of petrified wood that glitters in a myriad of colours. The most beautiful of the petrified trees can be found in the southern part of the park. The Giant Logs Trail leads to Old Faithful, a conifer tree that has a diameter of 2.9 m (9.5 ft).

A visit to the Rainbow Forest Museum ought not to be missed either. The exhibition includes a variety of pre-Columbian Indian artefacts fashioned from petrified wood. At the southern end of the park you will reach Highway 180, which will take you directly back to Holbrook and Interstate 40.

20 Winslow About 20,000 years ago a space 'bomb' landed a little further south of the village. The meteorite created a 180-m-deep (591-ft) crater with a circumference of around 1,300 m (4,265 ft). The visitor center has all the details about the meteorite and has pieces of the celestial body on display. It is now a further 70 km (43 miles) on Interstate 40 to Flagstaff.

21 Sunset Crater Before visiting Flagstaff, it is worth making a detour to the north on Highway 89. On the eastern side of the highway is a bizarre volcanic landscape surrounding the Sunset Crater National Monument. The focal point of the volcanic

area is the over 300-m-wide (984-ft) cinder cone of the Sunset Crater. It is the youngest volcano in Arizona and has been active for some 200 years. It first erupted in 1064 and the layer of ash covered an area of over 2,000 sq km (1,243 sq mi). In 1250 the volcano discharged the red and yellow oxidized lava that today still causes the edge of the crater to glow with the colours of a permanent sunset. The area is accessed via Scenic Drive, with spectacular views of the spooky volcanic landscape.

If you take the Sunset Crater National Monument park road a little further north, you soon reach another noteworthy Indian site.

22 Wupatki National Monument There used to be more than 2,000 settlements here that were part of the ancient Indian Sinagua culture. The Indians settled in this region between 500 and 1400. The Wupatki Pueblo, dating back to the 12th and 13th centuries, is relatively well-preserved. The three-storey pueblo had more than 100 rooms, all ventilated by means of a sophisticated system of wall and floor openings. It could also be heated if necessary.

You can learn anything and everything you want to know about the culture of the Sinagua Indians (Sinagua = sine, aqua = without water) in the visitor center.

Detour

Grand Canyon

The canyon landscape created by the Colorado River in north-western Arizona is one of the world's greatest natural wonders. It is here that the Colorado River has carved a 450-km-long (280-mile) path leaving a spectacular gorge landscape in its wake. In places it is up to 1,800 m (5,906 ft) deep.

The canyon walls are sheer rock faces which, at the upper rim of the canyon, are up to 30 km (19 miles) apart. Much of the massive canyon is located within the 4,933-sq-km (3,065-sq-mi) confines of Grand Canyon National Park.

View of the Grand Canyon from Toroweap Point.

The Grand Canyon can be reached from both the north and the south but the southern side offers the most spectacular views (South Rim). This is where most of the tourist facilities are. Due to the volume of visitors, the entire southern rim has now been closed to private cars. A shuttle service brings visitors to the main viewing points.

㉓ **Flagstaff** This city on the southern edge of the San Francisco Mountains was founded in about 1870 when gold diggers followed farmers and ranchers. The railway followed as soon as 1882 and with the completion of Route 66 the transit traffic continued to increase. Flagstaff's sightseeing attractions include the Museum of Northern Arizona with a range of exhibits from the various cultural strata of the Pueblo Indians. Flagstaff's real attraction, however, is its surrounding natural landscape. North of town are the fantastic San Francisco Mountains with the highest point in Arizona. Take a chair lift up the 3,854-m (12,645-ft) Humphrey's Peak.

South-east of Flagstaff is Walnut Canyon, 36 km (22 miles) long and 12 m (39 ft) deep, definitely worth exploring on foot. The canyon conceals around 300 Zinagua Indian cliff dwellings; they lived here from the 10th century and built their dwellings solely under overhanging cliffs. From Flagstaff you can go directly to the Grand Canyon on Highways 89 and 64 or 180 and 64. On Interstate 40 follow the highway as far as Seligman and then take the Highway 66 turn-off. The most scenic stretch of old Route 66, which is still largely in its original condition, takes you to the next stop, Kingman. Access roads lead to the Grand Canyon Caverns and to the

Havasupai Indian Reservation. You then end up in central Kingman after crossing the Interstate Highway 40.

㉔ **Kingman** Between the Cerbat Mountains in the north and the over 2,500-m (8,203-ft) Hualapai Mountains in the south is a traffic interchange in the middle of a desert landscape. Nowhere else on the entire Route 66 has there been a greater investment in nostalgia than here. Old petrol stations and snack bars have been brought back to life, and road signs and signposts have been saved from obsolescence. The entire town is full of unadulterated Route 66 nostalgia. In the

Mohave Museum of History and Arts, with its extensive collection of turquoise jewellery, you learn that the area had already been settled by the Hohokam Indians

1 Sinagua Indian dwellings used to cover the area that is now the Wupatki National Monument.

2 The Wigwam Hotel in Holbrook. An affordable Indian tradition for modern nomads.

3 The 300-m (984-ft) cinder cone of the Sunset Crater is the product of Arizona's youngest volcano.

4 The historic railway station in Flagstaff dates from the 19th century.

The 180-m-deep (595-ft) Barringer Crater south of Winslow was created about twenty thousand years ago when a meteorite from space crashed down in this desert landscape. The visitor center at the crater, which has a diameter of 1,300 m (4,290 ft), tells you everything you need to know about the meteorite.

There are even pieces of the broken celestial monolith on display. On the tour they take you to the rim of the crater where astronauts have trained for their various missions to the moon.

Detour

Joshua Tree National Park

Joshua Tree National Park covers 3,213 sq km (1,997 sq mi) in California and is part of two different deserts – the cooler, slightly more humid and higher Mojave Desert in the north, and the drier Colorado Desert in the south-east. The park, which is ninety percent wilderness, shows very vividly how plants can thrive even in arid regions. In addition to the distinctive Joshua trees, the Colorado Desert is also home to palm groves and cactus gardens as well as the thorny juni bush.

The 'Joshua tree' (*Yucca brevifolia*) is the largest of the yucca trees and grows only in the Mojave Desert, in the northern part of the park. It can reach heights of 18 m (59 ft) and its trunks measure up to 1.2 m (3.9 ft) in circumference. The oldest trees are said to be 900 years old.

The name Joshua tree comes from a group of Mormons who passed through the desert in the middle of the 19th century. The trees reminded them of a story of the prophet Joshua. The rest is history.

The Oasis Visitor Center in Twenty-nine Palms, where two roads begin, is the jumping-off point for excur-

Bizarre rock landscape in Joshua Tree National Park.

sions into the park. One road leads to the north-western part of the park, crosses the Queen and Lost Horse Valleys and provides access to the Jumbo Rocks and the Wonderland of the Rocks. The second road leads to the south-eastern section and provides access to the Cholla Cactus Garden where you will also find the best of the Joshua trees. The best time to go is between March and May when both the Joshua trees and other cacti are in blossom.

If you are planning a visit to the park, make sure that you have a full tank of petrol and sufficient water supplies. In contrast to other national parks, there are neither petrol stations nor hotels or restaurants here. Only two of the basic campsite, Black Rock Canyon and Cottonwood Campgrounds, have water available.

some 1,300 years ago. The museum gives you a history of their work with the precious stones. After Kingman you need to leave Route 66 and Interstate 40 (which goes towards Barstow), to pay homage to the spectacular Hoover Dam and legendary Las Vegas. Both are easy to reach via Highway 93. If you stay on Route 66 you can also visit Lake Havasu south of Kingman.

25 Hoover Dam This dam near Boulder City was once the largest embankment dam in the world. The 221-m-high (725-ft) and 379-m-wide (1,242-ft) construction, which is an amazing 201 m (659 ft) thick at its base, was completed in 1935. The awe-inspiring structure holds back the waters of Lake Mead, a 170-km-long (106-mile) and 150-m-deep (492-ft) body of water. There is a large visitor center on the dam wall where you learn about the dam's fascinating technical details. You can then take a cruise on Lake Mead with the paddle steamer *Desert Princess*.

After 56 km (35 miles) on Highway 93 you then reach Las Vegas.

26 Las Vegas The world's gambling capital is located in the middle of the desert and really only consists of hotels and casinos. No less than fourteen of the

twenty largest hotels in the world are located here. More than 40 million visitors come to Las Vegas each year to seek their fortune and, more often than not, lose their money to the one-armed bandits and casinos. The big casino hotels stage elaborate shows, revues and circuses in order to provide entertainment for the non-gamblers, or perhaps to raise the spirits of those who do try their hands. The individual casinos each have their own theme and these range from 'Stratosphere Tower' to the 'Venetian', complete with Doge

Palace and Campanile, and the 'Luxor', evoking associations with Ancient Egypt with pyramids and pharaohs.

From Las Vegas, Interstate 15 rejoins the old Route 66 at Barstow. But before you reach Barstow, it is worth paying a brief visit to Calico, a ghost town that was once a very successful mining operation at the end of the 19th century due to the discovery of substantial reserves of silver and borax. The minerals here were extracted from more than 500 mines throughout the area. In 1907 Calico was instant-

ly rendered obsolete, a ghost town, when silver and borax prices dropped sharply.

27 Barstow This town to the east of the Edwards Air Force Base is situated in the middle of the desert and serves as a supply center for a huge yet sparsely populated hinterland. The California Desert Information Center is very interesting, providing a plethora of details on the Mojave Desert and its difficult living conditions.

Following Interstate 15 you gradually leave the desert

San Diego

California's southernmost metropolis is directly on the Mexican border. Due to its two protected bays, San Diego has become one of the most important port cities on the west coast.

San Diego was founded in the year 1769 when the Franciscan priest Junipero Serra began construction of a mission. The English first arrived in the village in 1803. Today the small Spanish village has grown into a pulsing metropolis.

The historic center of San Diego is located on Presidio Hill in the north of the town. In Old Town, the San Diego State Historic Park brings Spanish, Mexican and US history to life. Well-restored adobe houses compete with colonial buildings

View over the port of the San Diego skyline.

for attention. The Bazaar del Mundo is full of life.

In downtown San Diego the Gaslamp Quarter is a particular attraction with theaters, bars, restaurants and shops. This area still boasts lovely Victorian buildings from between 1880 and 1910. On the shores of the San Diego Bay, Seaport Village attracts visitors looking for a maritime stroll, while to the north-west is the adjoining San Diego Maritime Museum.

The city's real museum center, however, is the 565-ha (1,396-acre) Balboa Park. Whether you are interested in tropical plants, the Spanish colonial era, the cultural history of the Pueblo Indians, space travel or natural or art history, you will find it all here. The main highlight as far as museums go is the Aerospace Museum and the International Aerospace Hall of Fame. In addition, the San Diego Zoo is an absolute must as it is one of the best zoos in the world. Its counterpart is the Sea World leisure park near Mission Bay.

previously made a living from citrus farming.

If you have plenty of time, it is worth continuing from Anaheim along Interstate 5 to San Diego, 150 km (93 miles) south along the coast.

㉚ Santa Monica In 1935, Route 66 was extended from Los Angeles to Santa Monica and since then has followed Santa Monica Boulevard, terminating at Ocean Boulevard in Palisades Park, where a modest signpost indicates the end of the legendary route, the 'Mother Road' or 'Main Street USA'.

behind and reach the center of the Californian citrus-growing region, San Bernardino County.

㉘ San Bernardino This city, almost 100 km (62 miles) east of Los Angeles, developed from a Franciscan mission founded in 1810. From here you really must do the 'Rim of the World Drive', a panoramic drive through a spectacular high desert and mountain landscape. It passes scenic lakes, reaches an altitude of 2,200 m (7,218 ft) and offers splendid views of the San Bernardino Mountains.

The Joshua Tree National Park is a worthwhile detour from here, if you haven't done it already, and the entrance at Twenty-nine Palms can be reached via Interstate 10 and Highway 62.

The historic Route 66 takes you westwards from San Bernardino, just north of Interstate 10, past Pasadena (Pasadena Freeway) and on towards Los Angeles. Via West Hollywood and Beverly Hills you continue along Santa Monica Boulevard to the famous beach town of Santa Monica. Beforehand, if you want to visit the oldest of Disney's parks, Dis-

neyland, take Interstate 15 and Highway 91 over to Anaheim.

㉙ Anaheim The ending 'heim' is indicative of the German origins of this settlement near the Santa 'Ana' River, where German immigrants settled in about 1857. Anaheim is in Orange County, around 60 km (37 miles) south-east of Los Angeles. The largest attraction is Disneyland, the leisure park founded by Walt Disney in 1955 and which brought an end to the country tranquillity of this once rustic town. Anaheim had

1 South of Kingman are the Hualapai Mountains, over 2,500-m-high (8,203-ft).

2 In 1885 some 1,200 people lived in Calico and sought their fortunes in one of the 500 silver mines. Calico became a ghost town after 1907 and some of the old buildings, here the old school, have been restored.

3 Downtown Los Angeles is characterized by skyscrapers.

4 Despite high temperatures and irregular rainfall, a great diversity of plant and animal species thrives in the Mojave Desert.

Monument Valley glowing red in the evening light

Route 44

USA

The "Wild West": cowboys, canyons and cactus

"Go West, young man…" – It is no coincidence that tourists in America's South-West still follow the old call made to pioneers and settlers. Virtually nowhere else in the world will you find more bizarre rock formations, wilder mountains, more breathtaking canyons, more remote cactus deserts, more impressive caves, or hotter valleys. The remnants of ancient Native American pueblo culture are also unique, and their adobe buildings and handicrafts still fascinate visitors from all over the world.

The American South-West stretches from the southern Rocky Mountains in the east to the Sierra Nevada in the west, and from the northern edge of the Colorado Plateau in Utah to the Mexican border in the south. Six states make up the region: Arizona, Nevada, Utah, Colorado, New Mexico and California.
The north is dominated by the Colorado Plateau, which covers an area of roughly 110,000 sq km (2,460 sq mi) at elevations of 1,000 to 3,000 m (3,281 and 9,843 ft).

The most impressive and most beautiful national parks are found here, including the Grand Canyon, Bryce Canyon, Zion, Arches and Canyonlands. There are a total of eleven national parks in the South-West alone, as well as numerous monuments and state parks. The Organ Pipe Cactus National Monument near Why, Arizona, is even a UNESCO World Nature Heritage Site. Other national monuments are dedicated to ancient and historic Indian settlements. And if that

The "Wild West" was Native American territory.

isn't enough, there are also the national historic parks that are mostly dedicated to the pioneer days, such as the Hubbell Trading Post near Ganado, Arizona.
In the south, the plateau stretches out to the Sonora Desert, which extends deep into Mexico. To the north is the Mojave Desert, home of Death Valley with the lowest point in North America. Temperatures of over 50°C (122°F) in the shade are not uncommon here. But anyone driving into the valley before sunrise will experience an unforgettable interplay of colours on the bizarre rock in places like Zabriskie Point.
The Colorado River is the dominant feature of the entire South-West and runs for over 2,300km (1,429 mi). It originates in the Rocky Mountains, flows through man-made Lake Powell in Utah, continues to whittle away at the Grand Canyon

Delicate Arch in south-east Utah is the symbol not only of Arches National Park, but also of America's entire South-West. The 13.7-m-high (45-ft) sandstone arch glows most impressively in the warm light of the evening sun.

is for many people the epitome of Wild West romanticism.

as it has done for millions of years, and finally peters out before reaching the Gulf of California. The spectacular natural beauty of the American South-West was created over sixty-five million years ago when the pressure of the Pacific Plate formed the Rocky Mountains and the Colorado Plateau was pushed up. Giant fractures allowed stones more than a billion years old to emerge, after which erosion from rivers and the elements created the fantastic worlds of pillars, towers, arches, craters and gorges.

The rugged, mostly arid land was originally exclusively Native American territory, and the oldest traces of their ancient desert culture are some eight thousand years old. About three thousand years ago, sedentary peoples built multi-storey settlements called pueblos. The arrival of the Spaniards in the mid-

16th century, however, marked the beginning of a drastic decline of their civilizations. In the 20th century, cities were built on former Native American lands.

The contrasts in the South-West are therefore remarkable: fascinating remnants of ancient cultures juxtaposed with raucous metropolises, puritan Mormon settlements near the glitz and kitsch of Las Vegas. One journey is really not enough to take it all in, but anyone who follows the dream route laid out before you, starting in Los Angeles, following the Rio Grande northwards through New Mexico, exploring the wonders of Utah and then making a great arch back towards the City of Angels via Las Vegas and Death Valley will experience at least a handful of the highlights. And, at the end of the trip, you will realize that the only option left is to come back and see more.

This Indian chief only wears his full feathered headdress on festive occasions.

Gunslingers and gorgeous landscapes are essential elements in the romance of the Wild West. It is thus no coincidence that John Ford, one of the most famous directors of Westerns, shot *Stagecoach* with John Wayne in the leading role against the stunning backdrop of Monument Valley back in 1939. Location shots for

Billy the Kid, Play Me the Song of Death, Fort Apache and *The Black Falcon* were also filmed here, as well as Walt Disney's legendary nature film *The Living Desert*, which gives you a fast-motion glimpse of desert flowers in bloom.

The multicolored rock formations of Canyonlands National Park are revealed in all their splendor at sunset. The Green River, a major tributary of the mighty Colorado River, flows into the Colorado inside Canyonlands Park. Both rivers have carved gorges up to 600 m deep (1,969 ft) into the sediment stone of the

Colorado Plateau. North of the confluence, visitors can look down into the deep gorges from atop the Island in the Sky District, while the vast wonderland of rock needles unfolds to the south. Numerous traces of Anasazi Indian settlements can also be found here.

White Mesa Arch

Northern Arizona is home to a number of giant sandstone bridges that add considerably to the remarkable charm of America's South-West. These natu-

The 25-m-high (82 ft) White Mesa Arch is made from white limestone.

ral stone arches were created by eons of erosion by the elements. Over time, relentless flows of water loosened the salts contained in the sediment stone and made the stone brittle. The interplay of extreme temperatures then caused the salty stone fragments to fall apart. Only the more resistant stones with a lower salt content remained.

delicately divided escarpments. At the bottom is the Paria Valley with a natural amphitheater shaped like a horseshoe. Erosion has carved deep ditches and furrows into the soft sandstone slopes that have resulted in finely engraved heads, needles and arches. In the early morning, this magical world glows in a spectrum of hues from pale yellow to dark orange. The rock amphitheatre can be accessed via the 27-km-long (17 mile) scenic drive around the upper rim.

East of Bryce Canyon, it's worth visiting the Kodachrome Basin State Park, which you can reach via Highway 12. It is home to splendid rock faces of red-and-white striped sandstone, towering rock chimneys and spindly rock needles that glow in all shades of red, especially at sunrise and sunset. A panorama trail takes you to the most beautiful formations whose rich colors can hardly be surpassed.

Back on Highway 12 and Interstate 89 you will head to nearby Zion National Park.

22 Zion National Park The vertical walls of the Virgin River Canyon break away steeply here at heights of more than 1,000 m (3,281 ft), forming solid pillars and deep recesses. The Mormons saw this as a "natural temple of God" back in the 19th century. Visitors feel like tiny ants but you can walk along the base of the canyon in areas where even the rays of the sun hardly ever shine. Only the southern part of the park (593 sq km/229 sq ft) is open to vehicles along the 29-km-long (18-mi) Scenic Drive. The rest of the park is accessible on more than 160 km (99 mi) of hiking

trails. An absolute must is the Gateway to the Narrows Trail. Along the Weeping Rock Trail, you will pass so-called "Hanging Gardens", a rock overhang covered in ferns.

The best panorama view over the entire canyon can be seen from Angels Landing, a cliff that drops away to a depth of 450 m (1,476 ft) on three sides. Your route follows Highway 89 past Marble Canyon to Wupatki National Monument back in Cameron, Arizona.

23 Wupatki National Monument Roughly 40 km (25 mi) south of Cameron, you come across the ancient pueblo of Wupatki on Highway 89. More than 2,000 Sinagua dwellings dating back to between the 9th and 14th centuries can be found in this arid desert landscape on the western edge of the Painted Desert.

A few miles further south of the pueblo ruins is Sunset Crater National Monument. The focal point here is the 305-m-high (1,001-ft) cinder cone of the Sunset Crater, the result of a massive eruption in 1065, followed by a second in 1250. The region can be accessed on the Scenic Drive with spectacular views over the volcanic landscape. Individual features are explained on the nature trail.

1 The giant craggy rocks and table mountains in Zion National Park impress visitors with their different bands of color.

2 In Zion National Park, gorges are only 4 m (4 yds) wide, as here in Antelope Canyon.

Highways 89 and 64 take you to the Grand Canyon.

24 Grand Canyon National Park This park covers an area of 4,933 sq km (1,904 sq mi) and includes roughly 445 km (277 mi) of the mighty Colorado River, which has carved out a canyon that is up to 1,800 m (5,906 ft) deep with spectacular walls. At its farthest point, the canyon is 30 km (19 mi) wide, and the solid rock formations obviously make for unforgettable photographs. You can enter the Grand Canyon from both the northern and southern sides, but by far the most spectacular views can be seen from the southern side, which is also where the most important tourist facilities are located. Due to the crush of visitors, the entire South Rim has been closed off to individual vehicle traffic and instead there are free shuttle buses which take you to all of the major vista points.

Back on Highway 64 and Interstate 40, you continue on to Kingman, where you take the turnoff to Highway 93 and head towards Hoover Dam.

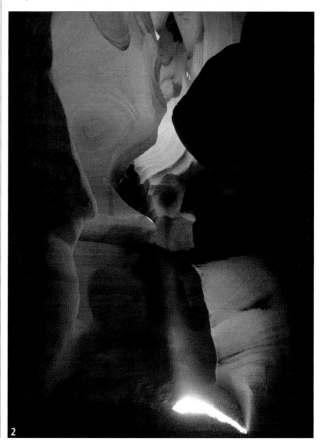

The rock needles in Bryce Canyon National Park, whose colors range from rusty red to yellowish-white, are often reminiscent of human or animal shapes. Over a stretch of around 30 km (19 mi), a giant amphitheater unfolds with rock formations more diverse than you could ever imagine.

The South Rim is an excellent vantage point for looking down into the massive gorges of the Grand Canyon. Although the Scenic Drive has, over time, been closed off to individual traffic for ecological reasons, shuttle buses provide easy access to all of the viewpoints. Anyone really wanting to experience the canyon

however, should do the hike 1,800 m (5,906 ft) down into the gorge. Mules facilitate this adventure to an extent, but even then it is a strenuous undertaking simply because of the high temperatures in the canyon.

Las Vegas This has been the USA's gambling haven since 1931. The countless casinos give their all to outdo each other in an effort to lure more money from gamblers' pockets. Lavish hotel complexes, theaters and erotic shows provide entertainment and luxury around the clock.

Rhyolite Ghost Town This town on the edge of Death Valley reminds us of the Gold Rush. Its main attractions are a house made of beer bottles and a collection of gold-digger utensils.

Grand Canyon The Colorado River has carved a gorge through the Colorado Plateau up to 1,800 m deep (5906 ft), 30 km wide (19 mi) and 445 km long (277 mi). The view from the edge of the canyon sweeps over solid yellow-brown and milky white rock outcrops, pinnacles and towers. The layers in the canyon represent 1.7 billion years of the earth's history.

Death Valley This national park is a desert with impressive rocks, vast sand dunes and temperatures reaching 57°C (135°F). However, springs also allow for extensive flora and fauna. Rock drawings prove that the valley was already settled thousands of years ago.

Sequoia National Park The southern Sierra Nevada is home to a remote high Alpine region with majestic granite peaks, deep gorges, silent mountain lakes, small rivers and impressive forests. The highest peaks are over 4,000 m (13,134 ft) high.

Los Angeles Freeways are the lifeline of Los Angeles, which covers 1,200 sq km (463 sq mi) and comprises many individual towns that have grown together. Stretching from Malibu to Santa Ana, and from Pasadena to Long Beach, the city's highlights include a visit to the film studios in Hollywood.

Organ Pipe Cactus National Monument Many species of cactus bloom in April and May in the habitat of the rare "organ pipe cactus".

Joshua Tree National Park This park south of Twenty-nine Palms is part of the Mojave Desert and is home to dried-up salt lakes and sparse vegetation with cactuses, junipers and yucca palms.

Sonora Desert This desert is full of surprises. The giant saguaro cactuses, for example are up to 150 years old and up to 15 m (49 ft) high. They flower in May. Everything else the desert has to offer is displayed in the Arizona Sonora Desert Museum in Saguaro National Park.

Phoenix The capital of Arizona is in the hottest and driest part of the Sonora Desert, and its warm winter climate has made it one of the most popular holiday destinations in the USA. Retirement communities such as Sun City have been established on its outskirts.

Marble Canyon Formed by the Colorado River, the color of the walls ranges from white to red depending on the position of the sun.

Bryce Canyon National Park This national park in Utah impresses visitors with a tangle of surreal-looking pinnacles and peaks. Here, the rock needles are bathed in the soft yellow and orange hues of the morning sun.

Arches National Park About one thousand freestanding stone arches are clustered here – more than anywhere else in the world – along with mushroom rocks, rock towers, pinnacles and domes of smooth sandstone. In the evening light, the red rocks look as if they are on fire.

Canyonlands National Park The fantastic rock landscape in this national park includes the confluence of the Green River and the Colorado River. The two have carved their way down to depths of 600 m (1,969 ft).

Mesa Verde National Park These historic residential settlements of the Anasazi Indians are set into rock niches and caves. Though protected, many of the rock dwellings and pueblos can be visited.

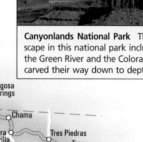

Monument Valley The table mountains and rock pillars formed by the wind are popular film sets. The valley is part of a Navajo reserve, and you can buy handmade Navajo silver jewelry at the Visitor Center.

Taos Pueblo The Pueblo Indians lived in these multi-storey flat-roofed houses more than one thousand years ago.

Acoma Pueblo This beautiful settlement with historic clay-brick buildings and winding alleys sits gracefully atop a plateau.

Albuquerque This city was founded in 1716, and has a lot of Spanish character, with adobe houses and baroque churches in the Old Town. Pictured here is the San Felipe de Neri Church from the early 18th century.

Mission San Xavier del Bac Founded by Spanish priests near Tucson, this church is located on the Tohono O'odham San Xavier Indian Reservation.

Chiricahua National Monument These charming rock landscapes near the Mexican border were once part of Apache hunting grounds.

White Sands National Monument This 600-sq-km (232 sq mi) dune landscape is made of white gypsum sand that glistens like newly fallen snow. Dunes rise to 18 m (59 ft) here. The US Army set off the world's first atomic bomb in the northern part of the desert on July 16, 1945.

The Portland Head Lighthouse on Cape Elizabeth, Maine, was commissioned in 1790 by George Washington, who personally named the first lighthouse attendant in 1791. These days, due to the automation of lighthouse lights, there is no longer an attendant in the lighthouse, but a small museum has been

built and explains some of the history of the location. In the 19th century, poet Henry Wadsworth Longfellow apparently spent a lot of time in the area, which inspired his famous poem, "The Lighthouse".

The fascinating skyline of Manhattan is like a visit to a museum of architecture. You can find all kinds of buildings here, from odd little houses dating from the 19th century and the Art Deco edifices like the Rockefeller Center to New Objectivity works like Mies van der Rohe's Lever House and other

postmodern skyscrapers. And right in the middle of all this architectural genius is one of the largest municipal parks in the world: Central Park, built in 1858 by Frederick Law Olmsted and Calvert Vaux.

Shenandoah National Park in Virginia is home to the river of the same name and includes the most beautiful sections of the Blue Ridge Mountains, part of the eastern range of the Appalachian Mountains. The views from Skyline Drive are particularly breathtaking here as it winds 170 km (560 mi) through the mountain

landscape. The dense forests are famous for their large populations of deer, including red deer, and even an occasional black bear. Hiking through the park it is easy to find some romantic hideaways like this one with a historic water mill built by original settlers.

Williamsburg

Many of the countless colonial-era houses in Williamsburg were built in the 18th century, but when Rich-

The most attractive building in Williamsburg is the Governor's Palace.

mond was declared the capital of the state of Virginia in 1780, the city gradually faded into insignificance. Today Williamsburg resembles an open-air museum. Employees in shops and restaurants often wear 18th-century costumes and on the Fourth of July a parade is staged in historic uniforms. The most impressive buildings are the State House and the British Governor's official residence.

viewing points to take a look at the Shenandoah Valley. The park covers a particularly scenic part of the Appalachians with the panoramic route ending in Waynesboro. From there it is another 60 km (37 miles) to Monticello.

⑱ Monticello This property, which once belonged to Thomas Jefferson (1743–1826), is located to the east of Charlottesville. Jefferson designed the building for the Monticello plantation in Palladian style. Construction began in 1770. After 100 km (62 miles) on Interstate 64 you reach Richmond, the capital of Virginia.

⑲ Richmond The State Capitol on Capitol Square, designed by Thomas Jefferson, is considered to be the first neoclassical building in the USA. Here you will find the only statue for which George Washington modelled in person. The Canal Walk on the northern bank of the James River is ideal for a leisurely stroll. With its Victorian houses the city has retained the flair of the Old South.

⑳ Williamsburg During the 18th century the town was the capital of Virginia. 'Colonial Williamsburg', as the town calls itself, is home to eighty-eight buildings restored as facsimiles of the originals. Parks in the style

of the 18th century complete the scene. Highway 158 leads you to Point Harbor via Hampton, Norfolk and Chesapeake (Highway 64). The port town of Albermarle Sound is the gateway to the Cape Hatteras National Seashore. The nearby Wright Brothers National Monument commemorates the Wright Brothers' attempted flights in 1903.

㉑ Cape Hatteras National Seashore The 210-km-long (130-mile) group of islands off the east coast of North Carolina

is known as the Outer Banks. The only road that goes there is the 150-km-long (93-mile) Highway 12, which connects the islands of Hatteras and Roanoke with each other.

The Outer Banks were once frequently targeted by pirates, and countless ships have been wrecked along the rocky coast. These days the often empty beaches, picturesque lighthouses and other monuments attract nature lovers, recreational sports enthusiasts and even the odd surfer. The majority of the islands are protected areas within the

Cape Hatteras and Cape Lookout National Seashores.

On the return journey to Washington, DC take Highway 13 after leaving Chesapeake. At Salisbury turn off towards Ocean City (Highway 50) via Highway 611 and the bridge over Sinepuxent Bay. There you come to Assateague Island.

㉒ Assateague Island National Seashore Due to its exposure to wind and waves, this island is constantly changing shape. A diverse animal and plant world braves the raw climate here. From the only small road on the island you can even see herds of wild horses roaming this narrow spit of windswept dunes and grass.

The return to Washington takes you via Highway 50. A bridge links the eastern side of Chesapeake Bay with quaint Annapolis, Maryland. Picturesque fishing villages, quaint historic towns and scenic bathing spots line the shores of the bay. The founding of Annapolis, the capital of the state of Maryland, dates back to 1649. From Annapolis you are just a few kilometers away from Washington DC.

1 Not far from the busy American capital there are idyllic spots to be found on Chesapeake Bay.

2 The lighthouse at Cape Hatteras is popular with photographers.

Nantucket Island Prosperity here came in the 18th and 19th centuries from whale hunting, as documented in the Whaling Museum.

Boston The colonial revolt against the English hegemony began with the 'Boston Tea Party'. You still encounter traces of history in many of Boston's neighbourhoods. It is also home to important research institutions and universities such as Harvard University and MIT.

Acadia National Park Mount Desert Island, with its impressive craggy coast, is home to majestic Cadillac Mountain, also part of this striking national park.

New York The heart of this megacity beats loudly in places like Times Square. Every year thousands of people gather here on New Year's Eve to ring in the new year together. Here, in the middle of downtown Manhattan, the impressive skyscrapers rise up into the clouds.

Bath Both the town and its shipyards are rich in tradition. The Maine Maritime Museum and the Bath Iron Works document the history of shipping and shipbuilding in the area.

Philadelphia This is where the Declaration of Independence was signed and the constitution drawn up. Today the metropolis is an important commercial center.

Martha's Vineyard The 'Vineyard' is a popular getaway among East Coast urbanites and plays host to the summer homes of the elite.

Washington The main American political nerve centers are in DC: the White House, the Capitol and the Pentagon, seat of the Dept of Defense.

Atlantic City This East Coast counterpart to Las Vegas attracts visitors with the promise of big winnings and glamorous shows. The boardwalk along the Atlantic is especially scenic.

Shenandoah National Park This beautiful park contains part of the Appalachian Trail, which stretches from Maine to Georgia.

Cape Hatteras Lighthouse The highest lighthouse in the USA has been warning ships of the shallows off Cape Hatteras for more than 100 years.

Monticello This classic Palladian mansion was once the home of Thomas Jefferson, the third President of the United States.

Richmond This defiant granite building was constructed in 1894 and was for a long time the city hall in Virginia's capital.

Cape Lookout The 51-m-high (168-ft) lighthouse at Cape Lookout, built in 1859, rises above the shallows of Core Sound. It is characterized by its unusual decoration – black stripes on a white background.

Williamsburg The many old buildings in Williamsburg, such as the Governor's Palace (1706–1722), bring the colonial history of this coastal town back to life.

Map labels (Route 45):

Woodstock, Maine, Bangor, St.John, Ellsworth, Bucksport, Bar Harbor, Waterville, Belfast, **3** Acadia, Mt.Desert I. N.P., Camden, Penobscot Bay, Augusta, **2** Rockland, Wiscasset, Brunswick, Bath, New Hampshire, North Windham, **1** Portland, Cape Elizabeth, Sanford, Biddeford, Rochester, Sherbrooke, Concord, Portsmouth, Lebanon, Newburyport, Gloucester, **Manchester**, **Lowell**, Salem, Leominster, **BOSTON** **5**, **8** Provincetown, **Worcester**, Cape Cod Nat.Seashore, Massachusetts, Plymouth **6**, Albany, **Providence** **10**, **7** Hyannis, New York, Fall River, Nantucket, **Kingston**, **Hartford** Connecticut, Martha's Vineyard, **Newport** **9**, Catskill Park, New London, Rhode Island, Binghamton, New Paltz, Mystic Seaport, **Newburgh**, New Haven, Orient Point, Scranton, **13** Hudson Valley, Long Island, **Yonkers**, Akron, **Jersey City**, Fire Island Nat. Seashore, Scranton, **Newark**, **12** **NEW YORK**, Statue of Liberty, **Allentown**, New Brunswick, Long Branch, Pennsylvania, Trenton, Lakewood, **PHILADELPHIA**, Island Beach S.P., Lancaster **14**, **New Jersey**, Hammonton, Harrisburg, York, Elkton, Atlantic City, Gettysburg, Wilmington, Ocean City, **BALTIMORE** **15**, Dover, Cape May, Hagerstown, Annapolis, Frederick, **50**, Wincherster, **Arlington**, Delaware, Front Royal, Manassas, **16** **WASHINGTON**, Ocean City, Skyline Caverns, Salisbury, Assateague I. Nat.Seashore, Elkins, Washington, G.Washington Birthplace Nat.Mon., **17** **Shenandoah N.P.**, Fredericksburg, **22**, Harrisonburg, Ruckersville, Modest Town, Waynesboro, Monticello **18**, **Richmond** **19**, Exmore, Charlottesville, Dixie, Williamsburg **20**, Lewisburg, Pocahontas S.P., **64**, Cape Charles Lighthouse, Roanoke, **Virginia** Petersburg, **Virginia Beach**, Lynchburg, Greensboro, **Norfolk** **Chesapeake**, Currituck, Elizabeth City, Point Harbor, Wright Brothers Nat.Mem., Whalebone, North Carolina, Columbia, Waves, Swanquarter, **21** Cape Hatteras Nat.Seashore, Cape Hatteras Lighthouse, Ocracoke Lighthouse, Kinston, Cedar Island, Cape Lookout Nat.Seashore, Kinston, Morehead City, Cape Lookout Lighthouse, Jacksonville, Folkstone, Hubert, Chesapeake Bay, Delaware Bay

Mexico, Guatemala and Belize

Through the Kingdom of the Maya

Culture and beaches all in one – a journey through the Yucatán Peninsula. In the heartland of the Mayan region you can marvel at both ancient pyramids and Spanish-colonial-style baroque towns, while the white sand beaches of the Caribbean offer idyllic relaxation after your adventures.

Mexico: a well-earned siesta in the afternoon.

The name of the peninsula separating the Caribbean Sea from the Gulf of Mexico originally arose from a misunderstanding. When the Spanish conquistadors first set foot on the peninsula at the start of the 16th century they addressed the indigenous people in Spanish. The Maya answered in their language: 'Ma c'ubah than', meaning 'We do not understand your words'. This later became Yucatán. Three countries lay claim to the Yucatán Peninsula: the north and west belong to Mexico, the south-east coast and Barrier Reef to Belize, and the mountainous south-east to Guatemala. Detours from

the route also take you to the most significant ruins in Honduras – Copán. When the conquistadors arrived in Mexico they discovered a uniquely advanced civilization. The Maya had both a precise calendar and their own alphabet. Their massive constructions – pyramids, palaces, places of worship – are all the more astounding given that the Maya had neither the wheel as a means of transport nor iron, metal implements, winches, pulleys, ploughs, or pack or draught animals. Mayan ruins are often located in the midst of tropical rainforests, are often overgrown and have only been partly

uncovered. Sites that are easily accessible for tourists along the route we suggest here are Chichén Itzá, Tulum, Tikal, Edzná and Uxmal. The city of San Cristóbal de las Casas and the surrounding Indian villages in the south-west of the peninsula, Chiapas (Mexico), provide wonderful insight into the present-day life of the descendants of the Maya.

The Indian population of Mexico and Belize makes up around one-tenth of the overall population of each country. In Guatemala, however, half of all citizens are of Indian origin. In Mexico and Guatemala numerous Mayan languages are also still spoken. The Spanish who first landed on the Yucatán Peninsula in 1517 greatly underestimated the scale of Mayan civilization and unfortunately destroyed a large part of their physical culture and records. In their place rose

High above the Caribbean Sea sits Tulum, meaning 'fortress', a mighty wall that once encircled the Mayan town. The original Mayan name was Zama, meaning 'City of Dawn'.

San Miguel is the largest town on the holiday island of Cozumel off the coast of Cancún.

a series of colonial cities from the ruins of older Mayan settlements. The Spanish legacy includes baroque monasteries, cathedrals, palaces and large town plazas. The oldest cathedral in the Americas is in Mérida (1560), Campeche was once the most important port on the Yucatán Peninsula for goods headed to Europe, and there are important monasteries dating back to the 17th and 18th centuries in Antigua, Guatemala.

The route we recommend includes some of the most scenic nature reserves in Central America. On the north-east coast is the Sian Ka'an biosphere reserve (a UNESCO World Heritage Site) covering 4,500 ha (11,120 acres) of jungle and swamp as well as a 100-km-long (62-mile) coral reef. Belize is home to the Blue Hole National Park and the 300-km-long (186-mile) Belize Barrier Reef (also a

UNESCO World Heritage Site). Guatemala is home to the Sierra de Las Minas biosphere reserve. Wild cocoa trees can still be found in the north-east of the peninsula and also in the mountainous regions of the south. Today the east coast, known as the 'Mayan Riviera', is a popular holiday destination – white sand beaches and the splendid reef between Cancún in the north and Tulum Playa in the south provide ideal conditions for both snorkelling and diving.

Yet swimming, diving, snorkelling and relaxing on the 'Mayan Riviera' are just some of the many options for an active holiday on the Yucatán Peninsula. If you go for a hike through the often still pristine tropical rainforests of the national parks and nature reserves in the interior of the peninsula, you will discover an unparalleled wealth of flora and fauna.

'The Old Man from Copán' sculpture in the ruined Mayan town of Copán in the Honduran forest.

Top: The imposing 25-m-high (82-ft) pyramid Temple of Kukulcán in Chichén Itzá is often referred to as "El Castillo". On the summer and winter solstice, the sun shines on the pyramid in such a way that a shadow in the form of a snake falls on the steps, winding down to meet a chiseled snake head at the bottom.

Bottom: The most famous observatory of the Mayans, Caracol, is also in Chichén Itzá. The Mayans charted the exact path of the sun in order to orientate their agricultural efforts to its various angles. The observatory is also called "Las Monjas", or "The Snail", for its shell shape.

Mayan writing

One of the features of an advanced civilization is a distinct system of writing, created once a people have reached a specific level of development. It entails the use of graphic symbols to record and communicate important information.

The Mayans did not invent their writing system themselves. Instead they took it from the original writing of the Olmeken (c. 30 BC). Within 1,000 years they had developed this further and become the only civilization in pre-Columbian America to have a complete writing system comprising of logograms and syllables.

Mayan lettering on a wall panel in Palenque.

The writing, which was very similar to other regional languages, was widespread throughout the entire Mayan lowlands. The oldest complete text was found on pillar 29 in Tikal (AD 292).

The written texts, which are mainly preserved on wall panels, door frames, pillars, ceramic pieces and bark, tell of the lives of rulers – births, coronations, marriages, wars and burials. With only a few exceptions, the block-shape hieroglyphics are read in double columns from left to right and from top to bottom.

The Spanish Franciscan monk Diego de Landa was the first to document Mayan writing in his 'Report on Yucatán' in the 16th century. Their writing remained 'encrypted' to outsiders for centuries until the first images were deciphered in 1820. The majority of the works, however, were decoded only after 1950.

attractive courtyards, facades decorated with stone mosaics and the conspicuous lack of cenotes (natural limestone pools) typical of this style. Indeed, it was the ability to build artificial cisterns that enabled the Mayans to settle in this arid region.

Opposite the entrance to Uxmal stands the 35-m (115-ft) 'Fortune Teller's Pyramid', with its oval foundation, dating from the 6th–10th centuries. The steep, 60° staircase up the pyramid has a safety chain for visitors to hold when climbing.

From Muna it is then around 40 km (25 miles) to the MEX 180.

6 Campeche During the colonial era Campeche became an important port from which the Spanish shipped wood and other valuable raw materials back to Europe. The mighty city wall was reinforced with eight bastions (baluartes) to protect it from constant pirate attacks. From this significant port town on the peninsula we then follow the MEX 180S to Champotón, where we turn onto the MEX 261 towards Francisco Escárcega.

7 Calakmul The detour to Calakmul in the Reserva de la Biósfera Calakmul is around 150 km (93 miles). The reserve protects the largest continuous tropical rainforest area in Mexico and is also host to a number of important Mayan sites – Balamkú, Becán, Xpujil and Calakmul. After around 110 km (68 miles), at Conhuas, a road turns off the two-lane MEX 186 south towards Calakmul. During the rainy season the 60-km (37-mile) surfaced road, first built in 1993, is often passable only with four-wheel-drive vehicles. Although it has not been extensively researched to date, this sprawling settlement, which was continuously inhabited from 500 to 1521, is one of the most important examples of a classic Mayan town and was declared a UNESCO World Heritage Site in 2002. Until the year 1000 Calakmul was the capital of a former kingdom. Thereafter it served merely as a ceremonial center. The 50-m (164-ft) pyramid is the highest in Mexico and from the top is a breathtaking view of these overgrown rainforest ruins. There are around 100 pillars spread around the site, but more valuable archaeological treasures such as the priceless jade masks have been moved to the museum in Campeche.

Back in Francisco Escárcega take the MEX 186 to Palenque.

8 Palenque These ruins, covering an area of 6 sq km (4 sq mi), are about 12 km (7.5 miles) out-

side of town and surrounded by the last sicable area of rainforest on the peninsula. The town, which must have been an important trading center in the region, experienced its heyday between 600 and 800.

One important Mayan ruler is still known by name – Pacal the Great, whose reign coincided

San Cristóbal de las Casas

Founded in 1528, San Cristóbal has fortunately been able to retain much of its originality. The heart of the town is the Zócalo, a grand plaza surrounded by old mansions. The western side of the square is dominated by the Palacio de Municipio while the north

The oldest church in San Cristóbal de las Casas: Santo Domingo.

with one of the most splendid eras in Mayan history. Today only part of the site is accessible to visitors. Try to plan a whole day for it. Inside the most famous temple, the 20-m (66-ft) Templo de las Inscripciones (Temple of the Inscriptions), sixty steps lead 25 m (83 ft) down into the crypt. Similar to the Egyptian pyramids, the step pyramids of Palenque were also the tombs of rulers. The most valuable possessions are now on display in the Museo Nacional de Antropologica in Ciudad de Mexico. Opposite the Temple of the Inscriptions is the El Palacio, where the royal family lived, while other accessible temples are located on the other side of the Otulum River.

One of the most important discoverers of ancient Mexican culture was the American John Lloyd Stephens, who visited the Yucatán between 1839 and 1841. According to his report, when Stephens first visited Palenque, 'a single Indian footpath' led to the archaeological site. He travelled all over the Yucatán with English draughtsman and architect Frederick Catherwood. Stephens recorded his impressions in travel journals while Catherwood captured his in drawings.

On the way from Palenque to San Cristóbal de las Casas it is worth making a stop at the Agua Azul National Park. The more than 500 waterfalls are especially worthy of their name, 'blue water', during the dry period between April and May. They vary in height from 3 m (10 ft) to an impressive 50 m (164 ft).

Beyond Palenque the road climbs gradually into the mountainous area of Montañas del Norte de Chiapas.

9 San Cristóbal de las Casas

This lovely little town at an altitude of 2,100 m (6,890 ft) carries the name of the Spanish Bishop of Chiapas, who was especially committed to the interests of the indigenous peoples. Particularly noticeable are the low-slung buildings in the town, a result of constant fear of earthquakes.

San Cristóbal is the center of one of Mexico's important cocoa-growing areas. The Mayans were already growing the wild plant as a monocrop before the arrival of the Europeans, and even used slave labour to work on their plantations. The striking

terrace-like fields on these steep slopes (sometimes at an angle of 45°) date all the way back to the Mayans who built rows of stones running diagonally over the slope in order to fashion fields of up to 50 by 70 m (164 by 230 ft). The fields were enclosed by walls measuring over 1.5 m (5 ft) high.

Many visitors take trips from San Cristóbal into the outlying villages of the Chamula Indians,

1 Cleared ruins in the north of the Palenque archaeological site.

2 In Palenque, nine terraces lead up to the Temple of the Inscriptions.

3 One of the many waterfalls in the Agua Azul National Park.

side hosts the 16th-century Catedral Nuestra Señora de la Asunción with its baroque facade. The terraces of the Templo de Guadalupe and the Templo de San Cristóbal provide impressive views over the town. Santo Domingo is one of the finest examples of Mexican baroque architecture and an arts and crafts market is held on its terrace. The San Jalobil monastery is involved in preserving the Indian weaving traditions of the surrounding villages.

Guatemala's volcanoes

The Central American land bridge, between North and South America, has only existed for a few million years. The North American plate meets the Caribbean plate in Guatemala, where the tectonic fault line runs from west to east right across the country through Montaguatal. Guatemala also lies directly over a subduction zone where the coconut plate is descending into the earth's mantle below Central America (the North American and the Caribbean plate) at a speed of around 6 cm per year. This causes molten magma to rise to the surface. When its gases reach a certain pressure they are discharged in the form of volcanic eruptions,

Top: The Atitlan volcano (3,535 m/ 11,598 ft).
Below: Eruption of the Pakaja volcano in 1994.

which are often accompanied by earthquakes.

In this tectonically active region, thirty-seven volcanoes can be found in Guatemala alone , most of them in the Sierra Madre, which run parallel to the Pacific coast. The country's highest volcano (and the highest in Central America) is the extinct Tajumulco (4,220 m/13,546 ft) south-west of Huehuetenango. In addition to Acatenango, which last erupted in 1972, there are currently three other active volcanoes. The 3,763-m-high (12,346-ft) Fuego volcano (next to Acatenango) is not far from Antigua Guatemala and last erupted in December 2000. Pacaya, a stratovolcano, has been active since 1965 and last erupted in 1994 when its ash rain fell as far as 30 km (19 miles) away in Ciudad de Guatemala. The stratovolcano Santa Maria (3,772 m/12,378 ft) is located behind Quezaltenango. The youngest and perhaps most dangerous volcano, Santiaguito, last spewed lava and ash from its slopes in February 2003.

for example to San Júan Chamula (11 km/7 miles), or to Zinacantán, where the Tzotzil Indians live (8 km/5 miles).

Another worthwhile excursion from San Cristóbal is to Cañon El Sumidero, with fantastic views of gloriously coloured craggy cliffs that tower to heights of 1,000 m (3,281 ft). With a bit of luck you might even see crocodiles during a boat trip on the river.

From San Cristóbal to Ciudad de Guatemala the route follows the Pan-American Highway, known as the CA1 after the border. Around 85 km (53 miles) southeast of San Cristóbal is Comitán de Dominguez. From there you can take an excursion to the Mayan site of Chinkultic. You will reach the border at Paso Hondo after another 80 km (50 miles). On the Guatemalan side a mountain road leads via La Mesilla through the Sierra de los Cuchumatanes to Huehuetenango. The

roads in the rugged mountainous regions of Guatemala are generally in bad condition and are often full of potholes. Turning off at Los Encuentros, Lago de Atitlan is one of the featured sights in these highlands.

10 Lago de Atitlan Three volcanoes – San Pedro (3,029 m/ 9,938 ft), Atitlan (3,535 m/11,598) and Toliman (3,158 m/10,361 ft) – are reflected in the water of this alpine lake, which lies at 1,560 m (5,118 ft). Alexander von Humboldt wrote of the beauty of this 130-sq-km (81-sq-mi) azure blue lake, describing it as 'the most beautiful lake in the world'. There are fourteen Indian villages located around the lake, some of which already existed prior to the arrival of the Spanish conquistadors.

Today the residents are farmers or make a living from selling traditional handicrafts. The famous Friday market in Sololá, high

above the lake on the northern shore, is even frequented by hordes of Indians from the surrounding areas. The largest settlement is Santiago Atitlan at the southern end of the lake. In 1955 the government declared the lake and surrounding mountains a national park.

At Los Encuentros a narrow road turns off towards Chichicastenango, 20 km (12 miles) further north.

11 Chichicastenango This town, lying at an altitude of 1,965 m (6,447 ft) is characterized by its classic white colonial architecture. In the pre-colonial era the town was an important Mayan trading center. Markets are the main attraction and draw residents from the surrounding areas in their colourful traditional costumes, who come to sell their textiles and carvings. In 1540 a Spaniard erected the oldest building in the town on the

ruins of a Mayan temple, the Santo-Tomás church. Each of the eighteen roads leading to it represents a month in the Mayan calendar, which comprised 18 months each with 20 days.

12 Antigua This village in Panchoytal is situated in a tectonically active region at the foot of three live volcanoes – Agua (3,766 m/12,356 ft), Fuego (3,763 m/12,346 ft) and Acatenango (3,975 m/13,042 ft). In 1541, mud-slides from Agua destroyed the town of Ciudad de Santiago de los Caballeros founded by the Spanish in 1527, but it was rebuilt further north in 1543. Numerous religious orders settled in this Central American capital where monasteries, schools and churches were erected. However, only parts of the Catedral de Santiago (1545) with its five naves have survived the earthquakes of the subsequent centuries. Nuestra

Copán

Copán, the southernmost of the Mayan towns close to the Honduran settlement of Copán Ruinas, lies on a promontory at 620 m (2,034 ft). Densely forested mountains surround the ruins on the Copán River, discovered by the Spaniard Diego Garcia de Palacio in the late 16th century. In 1576 he sent a report of his findings to

Tombstone in Copán.

Señora la Merced is one of the most attractive examples of the Churrigueresque style. Together with the Palacio de los Capitanes Generales and the Palacio del Ayuntamiento, the Capuchin monastery Las Capuchinas is an impressive example of Spanish colonial architecture.

The town was destroyed by strong earthquakes in 1717 and 1773, but the Spanish rebuilt it as La Nueva Guatemala and it later became present-day Ciudad de Guatemala. The previous capital was then simply called Antigua. In 1979 the old city, which in the 18th century was one of the most beautiful baroque ensembles of the Spanish colonial era, and which still retains a great deal of flair today, was declared a UNESCO World Heritage Site.

⑬ Ciudad de Guatemala The rebuilding of the residential town for the Spanish governor took place at a safer distance of 45 km (30 miles). Today, La Nueva Guatemala de la Asunción is still the economic and political center of Guatemala. It lies at 1,480 m (4,856 ft) and is the seat of several universities. The main sightseeing attractions include the cathedral (1782–1809), the National Palace (1939–1943) and the Archaeological Museum. Another important Mayan site is located in Tazumal, not far from Santa Ana in El Salvador, roughly 200 km (124 miles) away.

From the capital it is about 150 km (93 miles) on the CA9 to Rio Hondo where the asphalt

CA10 takes you via Zacapa, Chiguimula and Vado Hondo to the border post at El Florido. About 12 km (7.5 miles) beyond the Guatemala-Honduras border is Copán. On the return journey along the same road, about 70 km (43 miles) beyond Rio Hondo, you reach another UNESCO World Heritage Site – the ruins of Quiriguá.

⑭ Quiriguá This Mayan town on the lower Rio Motagua saw its heyday between 500 and 800. Its layout is very similar to that of Copá, only 50 km (31 miles) away. Explorer John Lloyd Stephens discovered Quiriguá in 1840. Today the archaeological site at the edge of the Sierra del Espiritu Santo is still surrounded by thick jungle, and this is a major part of its attraction. The large mythical creatures carved in stone and the pillars measuring over 10 m (33 ft) in height, which constitute a high point of Mayan sculpture, are among the special attractions here. The highest pillar, E, is 10.5 m (34 ft) high and weighs 65 tonnes (71.5 tons).

Approximately 45 km (28 miles) beyond Quiriguá you leave the CA9 and turn to the north-west towards Lago de Izabal. The lake, 590 sq km (367 sq mi) in size, is surrounded by dense rainforest. Between the largest lake in Guatemala and the Rio Dulce, lined by rainforest, is the Spanish Fort Castillo de San Felipe. The fortress was originally constructed in 1595 to defend the arsenals on the eastern shore

of the lake from the repeated attacks of determined pirates plying the broad river.

The national road CA13 now crosses the foothills of the Sierra de Santa Cruz and continues via Semox into the lowlands of Petén. The small town of Flores on an island in Lago Petén Itzá is a good starting point for a visit to Tikal.

1 The Toliman and San Pedro volcanoes form an impressive backdrop to Lago de Atitlan in the Guatemalan highlands.

2 Universidad de San Carlos (1763) in Antigua.

3 Relief of a high priest in the Quiriguá Archaeological Park, also home to the tallest Mayan pillars.

the Spanish king, Philip II. By the time John Lloyd Stephens wanted to visit the Mayan town of Copán in 1839, none of the residents in surrounding villages was able to answer his questions about the ruins.

Copán appears to have been one of the oldest and most important Mayan religious sites. According to archaeologist estimates, the town had as many as 40,000 inhabitants. Copán's 'Acropolis', said to have been 600-m-long (1,969-ft) and 300-m-wide (1,086-ft) included pyramids, temples and plazas. The pillars, some of which were as high as 3 m (11 ft), are among the most impressive examples of Mayan sculpture. Copán had already been abandoned 500–600 years prior to the Spanish, but the reasons are unclear. Skeletons found in Copán indicate malnutrition and chronic illness.

The god kings who ruled Mayan cities were honored with ornate columns. Even during their lifetime they took on not only the status of worldly rulers, but also the status of gods. The columns, which often recorded the date of birth, death and ascension to the throne, made it possible for researchers to follow

precisely the dynastic orders of the many city states, including here in Copán. The weaving motif was a popular one in Mayan art. It symbolized the woven mats on which the rulers sat.

⑮ Tikal National Park This 576-sq-km (358-sq-mi) national park is surrounded by dense forest and includes one of the most important Mayan sites on the peninsula. Together, the park and rainforest, one of the largest continuous forests in Central America with over 2,000 plant varieties, has been declared a UNESCO World Heritage Site. Between 600 BC and AD 900 as many as 55,000 people lived in Tikal. Today, many of the 4,000 temples, palaces, houses and playing fields are buried under the encroaching forest.

A climb up one of the pyramids, the most important of which are on the Gran Plaza, gives visitors an impressive view of the 16-sq-km (10-sq-mi) Tikal National Park. The Jaguar Temple, some 45 m (148 ft) high, houses a burial chamber where the ruler Ah Cacao lies at rest. From Flores it is about 100 km (62 miles) to the border with Belize, and from there it is another 50 km (31 miles) to Belmopan, which has been the capital of Belize since 1970.

⑯ Guanacaste National Park 3 km (2 miles) north of Belmopan

is the 20-ha (49-acre) national park named after the large Guanacaste tree (Tubroos). It grows in the south of the park and is one of the largest tree types in Central America. The many tree species in the park also include mahogany, the national tree of Belize. South of Belmopan is the Blue Hole National Park, on the road to Dangriga.

⑰ Blue Hole National Park This 2.3-ha (5.7-acre) national park is a popular leisure area for the residents of Belmopan. Large areas of the park contain cave formations and are covered by dense rainforest. Sightseeing attractions include the 33-m (108-ft) collapsed crater that feeds a tributary of the Sibun River. It flows briefly above ground before disappearing into an extensive underground cave system. The 7.5-m (25-ft) 'blue hole' takes its name from its sapphire blue colour. Also within the park is St Herman's Cave, also used by the Mayans as evidenced by the ceramics, spears and torches that have been found inside.

⑱ Belize City Until 1970, Belize City was the capital of the for-

mer British Honduras. Today it is still the largest city in the country as well as an important seaport. St John Cathedral, the oldest Anglican cathedral in Central America, was built in 1812 from bricks that sailing ships from Europe had used as ballast.

The British Governor lived at Government House starting in

1814 (today it is the House of Culture museum). The city is an ideal base for excursions to the Belize Barrier Reef, a renowned diving paradise.

⑲ Belize Barrier Reef System The 300-km (186-mile) Barrier Reef is one of the longest in the northern hemisphere. The many islands and cays off the coast are

1 Guanacaste National Park: The jaguar is the most well-known wild cat on the Yucatán Peninsula.

2 Tikal: Temple 1 is one of the most attractive pyramid tombs of the late classic Mayan period. It rises about 45 m (148 ft) above the central square. Around 55,000 people lived here in the town's heyday. It was abandoned in the 10th or 11th century.

Spectacular diving territory: the Blue Hole in Belize's Barrier Reef is 80 km (50 miles) east of Belize City. Charles Darwin had already provided a description of the reefs back in 1842. About 10,000 years ago a cave collapsed here as land sank into the sea. The hole has a diameter of 300 m (984 ft) and is 125 m (410 ft) deep.

Hidden in the lowland mist is the mysterious outline of a Mayan temple pyramid in Petén. Located in the evergreen rainforests of what is now north-eastern Guatemala, Petén was one of the most important cities in pre-Columbian (before Columbus) Mayan culture. Of the roughly 4,000 buildings that once filled

this metropolis, only a few have been preserved, or even found – the tropical forests have covered most of it in centuries of dense vegetation. The so-called Temple II with its high roof ridge sits atop a pyramid out on the Gran Plaza (above).

Detour

Reserva de la Biósfera Sian Ka'an

This biosphere reserve on the east coast of the Yucatán Peninsula close to Tulum (declared a UNESCO World Heritage Site in 1987) covers

At home in the biosphere reserve – the bottlenose dolphin.

around 100 km (62 miles) of beach as well as coral reefs, bays and lagoons. In the Mayan language the name Sian Ka'an means 'the origin of the heavens'. Tropical rainforest, mangroves and swamps are all close together here and there is a large reef off the coast. Beyond the underwater world, there are numerous bird and reptile species to be observed as well.

covered with mangroves and palms. The cays that are within reach include Ambergris Cay some 58 km (36 miles) north of Belize City as well as the Turneffe Islands. The reef's main attraction is its underwater world, with visibility of up to 30 m (98 ft), the bird reserve, Half Moon Cay and the Blue Hole, a massive collapsed cave.

20 Altun Ha The ruins of Altun Ha are close to the village of Rockstone Pond. It is postulated that this Mayan ceremonial center was originally settled over 2,000 years ago. The Mayans built up much of their trading around Altun Ha. The most valuable finds from Altun Ha include a jade head of the Mayan Sun god that weighs 4.5 kg (9.9 lbs). Via Orange Walk the road continues through the lowlands of Belize to the Mexican port town of Chetumal and along the second largest lake in Mexico,

Laguna de Bacalar (MEX 307), to Felipe Carrillo Puerto. Here an access road branches off to the Sian Ka'an biosphere reserve.

21 Tulum This ancient Mayan town is a popular destination on the peninsula, primarily due to its spectacular location on a cliff overlooking the sea. The conquistadors were impressed by its imposing and protective walls. Five narrow gates opened the way into town. Outside the walls there were two ancient Mayan temple sites north of town.
Tulum has always had a safe port from which pilgrims in the pre-Columbian era once travelled to the island of Cozumel to honour the Moon god Ixchel with sacrifices.
After 1540 Tulum was engulfed by tropical vegetation and forgotten until 1840. From Tulum there is a road leading to the small fishing village of Punta Allen in the Reserva de la Biós-

fera Sian Ka'an. In the forest 48 km (30 miles) north-west of Tulum you can visit another ruins complex – Cobá.

22 Cobá You can reach the site of the ruins on the well-made road in half an hour. US archaeologists began the first excavations of the complex (210 sq km/130 sq mi) in the 1920s, and further excavation projects that are still going on today began in the 1970s. Cobá also has a pyramid. From the top you can see smaller pyramids, temples, a series of procession streets, a playing field, pillars with life-size images of kings and queens, and of course dense forest. In Cobá you can see peccaris (wild pigs), iguanas, tortoises and the colourful toucan.
The 130-km (81-mile) stretch of coast between Tulum and Cancún is also known as the 'Mayan Riviera'. Small villages

and bays such as Puerto Morelos provide swimming and diving opportunities for water enthusiasts. The seaside resort of Playa del Carmen is only a few kilometers south of the more upmarket Cancún, which is the start and end point of this round trip through the Yucatán Peninsulua.

1 Belize's main attraction is the Barrier Reef. At just less than 300 km (186 miles) in length, it is the longest barrier reef in the western hemisphere. Divers will find unique coral, good visibility and more than 350 types of fish. Hundreds of small islands (cays) are scattered along the length of the reef.

2 Never-ending white Caribbean beaches with crystal-clear water characterize the north-east coast of the Yucatán Peninsula, also known as the 'Mayan Riviera'.

Mérida The 'white town' was founded in the 16th century. At its center are the Montejo Palast and the cathedral, one of the first sacral buildings in Mexico.

Chichén Itzá The highlights of the complex in the northern part of the Yucatán Peninsula are the Kukulcán and El Castillo pyramids, probably constructed by the Mayas and the Tolteken. Close by is a deep cenote, an underground limestone well from which water rises and forms a pool.

Cancún With its magnificent beaches and tropical climate the former fishing village in the north-east of the Yucatán has become Mexico's most popular holiday destination. With 20,000 beds and all-night entertainment options, more than 2.5 million tourists visit the giant hotel town each year.

Uxmal The 'Fortune Teller's Pyramid' is a highlight of Mayan architecture. The name dates back to the Spanish era but does not have anything to do with the actual purpose of the construction.

Palenque This archaeological site in the middle of the rainforest is among the most attractive in Mexico. Many of the buildings date from the reign of King Pacal and his son, Chan Balum.

Tulum Situated on a cliff over the Caribbean Sea south of Cancún, the ruins of this Mayan town are easily accessible for even the laziest of beachcombers.

Altun Ha The largest archaeological site in Belize is made up of two plazas with temple and residential complexes. Important jade artefacts have been found here, including a magnificent axe.

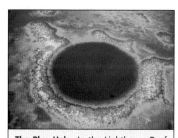

Lago de Atitlan This lake in the highlands of Guatemala (1,560 m/5,118 ft) is tucked between the San Pedro, Atitlan and Toliman volcanoes.

The Blue Hole In the Lighthouse Reef Atoll off the coast of Belize is one of the most beautiful coral reefs in the world. The Blue Hole has a diameter of 300 m (984 ft) and a depth of 125 m (410 ft).

Antigua The Spanish Governor used to rule Central America from this Guatemalan town. A number of baroque churches and palaces from the Spanish colonial era survived the earthquakes of 1717 and 1773, and are definitely worth seeing.

Tazumal Close to Santa Ana in El Salvador is the country's oldest Mayan settlement. The ruins of the 10-sq-km (6-sq-mi) complex with five temples were first cleared only 40 years ago.

Quiriguá The tallest and most artistic Mayan pillars can be found here. Their multitude of shapes evokes associations with the surrounding rainforest.

Tikal These ruins, buried in the jungle in the heart of the Mayan lowlands in present-day Guatemala, have inspired awe in many a visitor. Gustav Bernoulli discovered the ruins in 1877.

Skulls and bones in the Nazca Cemeterio de Chanchilla in Southern Peru.

Peru

With the Panamericana along the Peruvian Pacific coast

Peru was the heart of the Inca civilization, and its riches also made it the center of the Spanish colonial empire. Cuzco, at an altitude of 3,500 m (11,484 ft) in the Andean highlands, was founded as the Inca capital in the 12th century. From here, the Incas continued to expand until their empire reached from Ingapirca in Ecuador to northern Argentina at the start of the 16th century. The Inca themselves had built a road over 5,000 km (3,107 mi) long, setting up stations (tambos) a day's march apart where the travel-weary could stop get refreshments.

The Inca Road was an important communications and transport artery within their extensive dominions. For the most part it ran through the Andes, but there were also shorter, seemingly insignificant, routes along the Pacific coast in what is modern-day Peru.

The Spanish, who had conquered the Inca empire under Francisco Pizarro in 1532, established the capital of their viceroyalty in Lima, on the coast, as early as 1535. However, for a long time Peru's economic heart remained in the country's interior, in the domains of the fallen Inca. Things have changed since then as the focus of power shifted to Lima. In modern times this shift has also been influenced by the Panamericana, which primarily runs along the coast. The ports and coastal towns (Chiclayo, Trujillo, Chim-

Representation of a Mochican chief.

bote, Lima-Callao or Arequipa) have since become important industrial conurbations. The country's mineral resources, meanwhile, have become the backbone of the economy and are shipped from those ports.

Peru was the wealthiest and most important of Spain's Latin American colonies. The country's gold and silver mines – the most important of which were situated near Potosí, in the heart of the former Inca empire – yielded immeasurable volumes and hence almost every important colonial town boasts resplendent civil buildings and magnificent churches.

Then, as now, Peruvian society was characterized by one element: a highly conspicuous contrast between rich and poor. Impoverished shanties stand next to magnificent palaces – those of the colonial era and those of the industrial age.

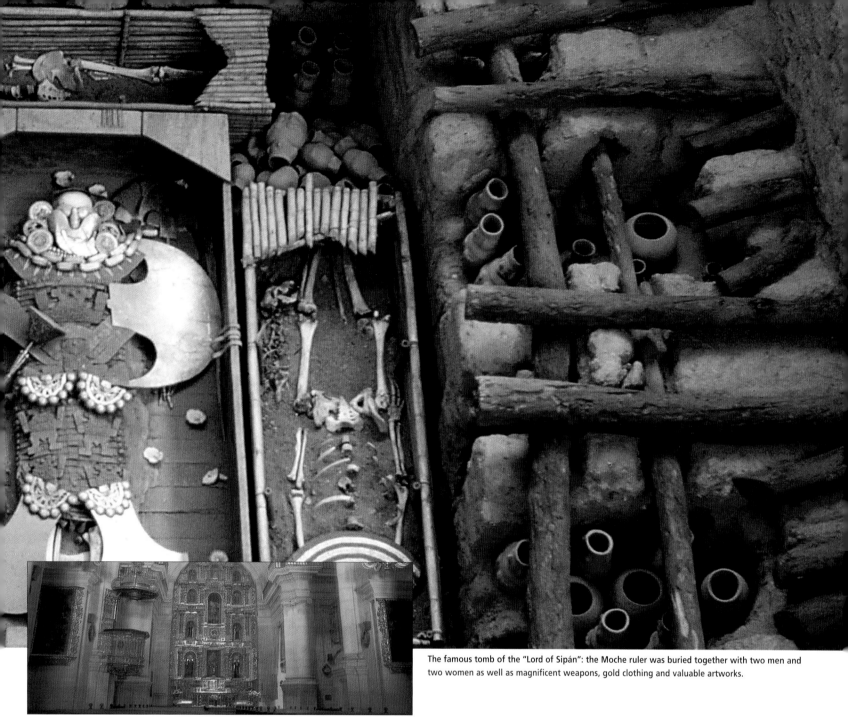

Arequipa, the "White City", is home to numerous baroque monasteries, churches and palaces.

The famous tomb of the "Lord of Sipán": the Moche ruler was buried together with two men and two women as well as magnificent weapons, gold clothing and valuable artworks.

About twenty-seven million people live in Peru, some 70 percent of them in the inhospitable coastal region and 25 percent in the highlands of the Andes. Only 5 percent live in the Selva, the Amazon lowlands. One-third of the population lives within greater Lima alone, and the cities continue to grow.

As in most Latin American countries, Spanish is the official language in Peru but many Peruvians speak a different mother tongue. More than half of the country's inhabitants come from Indian families, so almost one-third of the population speaks Quechua (the language of the Inca empire), and four percent speaks Aymara as their first language. A majority of the poorest people are "indígenas" – indigenous folk. It is estimated that four out of ten Peruvians live in abject poverty.

Peru is the third-largest country in South America after Brazil and Argentina. It is a country of contrasts with arid coastal deserts, impressive peaks in the central Andes region and the Selva, and tropical rainforests in the east that form part of the Amazon lowlands.

The Panamericana follows the coast for almost its entire length, passing mostly through inhospitable scree and sand landscapes. Almost no rain falls here because the humidity coming from the ocean is only released as rain at a height of around 800 m (2,625 ft). The coastal deserts are dotted with occasional river oases where earlier civilizations and later also the Spanish built their towns.

Due to the cold Humboldt Current, however, the entire coast is very rich in fish populations and therefore still a popular area to settle.

View over Huascarán National Park from the statue of Christ in the town of Yungay.

The Moche Civilization

The small village of Moche near the town of Trujillo was eponymous for a civilization that had its religious and political center here, and experienced its golden age from about the start of the Christian calendar through to the eighth century.

Moche civilization reached its greatest size between AD 400 and 600. During this period their realm, which consisted of a number of allied towns, extended from Vicús in the north to Pañamarca in the south. The reasons for the civilization's decline have not yet been fully understood.

Mochican earring depicting a warrior

Experts surmise that the downfall was caused by natural catastrophes: severe earthquakes, including submarine earthquakes, destroyed the sophisticated irrigation system, and a subsequent drought period led to famine and local unrest. The last Moche capital, Pampa Grande, at the mouth of the Lambayeque, was leveled in around AD 700–750.

Since the region is virtually rainless, the Moche devised complicated irrigation systems in order to cultivate cotton, maize, beans, peanuts and chili peppers. Utilizing a network of canals and even the slightest of gradients, huge areas of what had previously been an arid, infertile landscape were converted into productive farmland.

The Moche left numerous artworks for posterity as well which, in addition to the imposing adobe pyramids in Moche, mainly include metal works and ceramics that are impressive in their wealth of shapes and the diversity of motifs.

Following the Panamericana through Peru means that you get to know one portion of the country, but will miss out on some mountain regions and rainforest. But the coastal route does provide an insight into the country's various cultures, which extend from the adobe pyramids of the Moche people to the desert images of the Nazca civilization and Spanish colonial-era buildings.

① Piura The Spanish conquistadors founded this town on the northern rim of the Sechura Desert in 1532, and some of its colonial-era buildings have survived the years. Mostly, though, it is simply a suitable stopover before crossing the desert on the way to Chiclayo.

From Piura you drive through 220 km (137 mi) of bleak sand and stone landscape.

② Chiclayo The fourth-largest town in Peru is the ideal starting point for visiting the region's archaeological sites. You start in Lambayeque 12 km (7.5 mi) to the north-west, which not only has a number of attractive colonial buildings, but also the Museo Tumbas Reales de Sipán. The museum holds wonderful collection of ceramics and textiles from Northern Peru, and exhibits from Sipán, Moche and Chan Chan.

③ Sipán With the tomb of the so-called Lord of Sipán, this town 32 km (20 mi) east of Chic-

layo, the burial site of the Moche warrior, which has been fully reconstructed, is one of Peru's most interesting excavations. The dead ruler lay on the upper level of a 30-m-high (98-ft), six-storey pyramid, beset by a number of decorative items and skeletons.

The landscape becomes more fertile south of Chiclayo, with sugar plantations lining the road before the gray desert begins again at Chicama. It extends as far as Chan Chan about 30 km (19 mi) away.

④ Chan Chan This town was founded in the 12th/13th centuries as the capital of the Chimú realm. The Inca later conquered the Chimú empire in 1460, but its true decline, like many cultures here, came only with the arrival of the Spanish. Chan Chan comprises ten districts, each with a temple pyramid which, like the houses, are built from adobe (clay bricks). From Chan Chan, one of Peru's many UNESCO World Heritage

Travel information

Route profile
Length: about 2,600 km (1,616 mi)
Time required: at least 3 weeks
Start: Piura
End: Tacna
Route (main locations): Piura, Trujillo, Lima, Reserva Nacional de Paracas, Nazca, Arequipa, Tacna

Special note:
Protests and demonstrations with roadblocks have been a regular occurrence in Peru in recent years. Peru also has a pretty high crime rate (drug-related , robbery, kidnapping). Slum areas should be avoided, as should nighttime overland journeys.

The route follows the Panamericana, which runs parallel to the coast, but there are some worthwhile detours to sights in the country's interior. They bring you from Pisco to Ayacucho, from Nazca to Cuzco/Machu Picchu and from Arequipa to Lake Titicaca.

Roads near the coast tend to be well maintained. Farther inland that changes and you may need four-wheel-drive vehicles to get around.

Information:
Here are some websites to help you plan your trip.
travel.peru.com
www.justperu.org
www.peruatravel.com

3

4

Lima

Most visitors to the Peruvian capital leave it again quickly, irritated by the stress, chaotic traffic and the unfortunate poverty that is visible everywhere – and they miss out on some cultural treasures by doing so. A second look at the city reveals that what was once the metropolis of the Spanish colonial empire the Americas, and which actually lost a great deal of its grandeur in the earthquakes of 1687 and 1746, still has a few surprises in store – from carefully restored colonial architectural gems and lovely churches and monasteries, to peaceful courtyards and a number of outstanding museums.

The center of Lima is still the old colonial core (declared a UNESCO World Heritage Site) around the Plaza Mayor. It should really only be visited during the day. The city's most important buildings have stood and still stand around this square, including city hall, the government offices, the cathedral and the bishop's residence.

8 **Chavín de Huántar** It is still not clear today whether Chavín was a town, a temple area or a pilgrimage site. What is clear, however, is that the complex was built around 800 BC and belonged to the Chavín civilization, which extended from Piura to Lake Titicaca between 1400 and 400 BC. At the center of the site is a 5-m (16 ft) monolith depicting a deity with clawed hands and a jaguar's head.

The road now takes you via Callejón de Huaylas back to the Panamericana for the journey to Paramonga.

9 **Paramonga** This Chimú temple stands high up above the coast and affords a splendid

Lima: the cathedral on the Plaza Mayora at dusk.

Most of the buildings date from the 20th century but were built in the colonial style, only the cathedral having been rebuilt at the end of the 18th century following the devastating earthquake of 1746. Even more magnificent are the baroque complex of the nearby Franciscan monastery (completed after 1746), and the Palacio de Torre Tangle, Lima's loveliest secular building. Since it contains the offices of the foreign ministry, however, the inside of the facility is not open to visitors.

There are four museums that are a must in Lima: the Museo Nacional de Arqueología y Antropología which, like the Museo Rafael Larco Herrera and the Museo de la Nación, provides you with an overview of Peru's pre-Columbian (before Columbus) civilizations, and the Museo de Oro with pre-Columbian gold works.

Sites, it just a short distance to the city of Trujillo.

5 **Trujillo** For a city with 1.2 million residents, Trujillo's Old Town has an astonishingly charming colonial feel. Fortunately, many of the 17th- and 18th-century buildings have survived a number of earthquakes: the cathedral with the magnificent choir stalls is one of them, as are the aristocratic houses in the blocks around the central plaza. South of the town center there is a bridge over the Río Moche and 6 km (4 mi) further on you reach the pyramids of Moche.

6 **Moche** The largest of the pyramids at the foot of Cerro Blanco is the Huaca de Sol (pyramid of the sun), built in the 5th century using over 140 million clay bricks. It covers an area of 55,200 sq m (66,000 sq yds), making it one of the largest pre-Columbian structures in all of South America, and has ornately decorated relief walls.

The route now continues south along the Panamericana via Chimbote as far as Casma. Here you leave the coastal road and travel east to Huarás at 3,028 m (9,935 ft) in the Cordillera Negra (Black Range), almost 100 km

(62 mi) away. This town is the gateway to the Huascarán National Park.

7 **Parque Nacional Huascarán** Nevado Huascarán, the highest mountain in the Peruvian Andes, forms the heart of this national park at an elevation of 6,768 m (22,206 ft).

The park contains the core of the Cordillera Blanca (White Range), a snow-capped chain with more than two dozen peaks over 6,000 m (20,000 ft). Chavín de Huántar, yet another UNESCO World Heritage Site, is also within the park.

1 Tucume Moche is about 45 km (30 mi) north of Chiclayo. From Mirador you have a view over twenty-six clay pyramids, unwalled citadels and residential areas.

2 Only a few of the buildings at Chan Chan still bear evidence of the reliefs that once decorated the houses and walls.

3 Huascarán National Park is home to Nevado Huascarán (6,768 m / 22,206 ft), Peru's highest mountain.

4 Paramonga: a temple built of clay bricks, and a Chimú fortress built to defend against the Incas.

The animals of Reserva Nacional de Paracas

The 335,000-ha (827,785-acre) Paracas National Park in the Peruvian coastal desert encompasses land and sea – a peninsula and the pampas. Created in 1975, the park protects a delicate ecosystem with a high level of biodiversity that has developed here due to the cold Humboldt Current. This cold ocean current brings large quantities of plankton with it, while the over three hundred different fish

Pelicans find ideal living conditions on the Paracas Peninsula.

species attract countless sea birds: one hundred fifty bird species have so far been counted, including guano birds, such as the Guanay cormorant, and the very rare blue-footed booby. There are also cormorants, pelicans, flamingos and numerous species of seagull. Tens of thousands of them nest here. The hue and cry is nearly deafening and the stench of the guano is not for the faint of nose.

Giant tortoises have also found a refuge on the Paracas, and the reserve receives sporadic visits from condors, flamingos and parihuanas, a migratory bird from the south. The park's main attraction is its large colonies of sea lions, which pack themselves together tightly on the rocks to bake in the sun, or swim inquisitively around the visiting boats.

Visitors may also encounter the small Humboldt penguins when they are out hunting for food in the cold, clear water. With a bit of luck you will even get to see dolphins.

view of the ocean. Its mighty walls made it impregnable.
After a drive through the coastal desert you reach Lima about 200 km (124 mi) away.

⑩ Lima Lima is Peru's cultural, economic and political center with one-third of the total Peruvian population. The city has twelve universities as well as the oldest college in the Americas, founded in 1551. Lima is also Peru's capital, and is home to the seats of government and administrative offices. The Port of Callao is the country's most important transport hub. As a city, Lima is literally overflowing: the very heavily populated outskirts are full of shanty towns and slums.
After leaving greater Lima you reach Pachacámac after another 30 km (19 mi).

⑪ Pachacámac This excavation site was once the center of the Cuismancu empire, established in around 500 and later subjugated by the Incas. Pachacámac was founded in around 800 and was one of the largest towns in Peru when the Spanish arrived. The Inca built a stepped pyramid around 80 m (262 ft) high over the Cuismancu sanctuary. From the top of the platform you get wonderful panoramic views. The small museum has an interesting

model of the now almost completely derelict town.
The Panamericana stays on the Pacific coast for the next 170 km (106 mi), passing a series of seaside resorts that serve as getaway destinations for residents of Lima during the December to April season and on weekends. Towns such as Punta Hermosa, Punta Negra, San Bartolo, Santa María and especially Pucusana, slightly back from the Panamericana, have great beaches.
San Vicente de Cañete, a small market town surrounded by cotton fields, and Chincha Alta are the next two stops. Chincha Alta is known for its distinctive Afro-Peruvian culture. It is home to many of the descendants of African slaves who were shipped in to work on the plantations in this area.
The road branches off from the Panamericana to Tambo Colorado and Ayacucho, near Pisco.

⑫ Tambo Colorado The Peruvian coast boasts but a few Inca ruins. Tambo Colorado, whose name comes from the traces of red on the walls, is one of the best preserved sites. The ruins are situated at an elevation of 530 m (1,739 ft) about 50 km (31 mi) from the Panamericana. It is not clear whether Tambo Colorado was a sun temple or a military base.

Anyone looking for adventure can continue along the road to Ayacucho, which climbs up into the mountains to an elevation of 4,600 m (15,093 ft) at Castrovirreyna after roughly 70 km (43 mi). The Andes here present a superb panorama.
Back on the Panamericana you soon reach Pisco.

⑬ Pisco The town of Pisco would not be as well known if it were not for the famous marc schnapps. Indeed, the Peruvian national drink, Pisco Sour, has turned the town into a tourist destination even though most of the distilleries are located around Ica, about 60 km (37 mi) further south. The Old Town of Pisco has even developed its own port.

It is now 15 km (9 mi) to Paracas, where the boats sail to the Islas Ballestas.

⑭ Islas Ballestas Because it is a sanctuary for tens of thousands of sea birds, landing on the islands is prohibited. You are only allowed to observe from the boat. The Islas Ballestas, Isla Sangayan and the neighboring Reserva Nacional de Paracas to the south (the Islas Ballestas are not part of the park) boast what is probably the highest density of sea birds in the world. The cliffs of this wild, craggy group of islands, pounded by the foaming blue-green waves of the Pacific, provide ideal nesting grounds – and shelter.
Until the mid-19th century, these sea birds were an indirect source

3000 BC. People here lived primarily from fishing and gathering mussels. In around 1000 BC maize, cassava, cotton and beans were cultivated by a community living here. It is considered the earliest example of a complex society on the southern Peruvian coast. The museum in Paracas details the history of the settlement of the Paracas Peninsula, and displays the archaeological finds excavated on the peninsula since 1925, including mummies, wrapped in woven shrouds.

Both the graves and the mummies had remained almost completely intact due to the location and the dry climate. Based on the burial grounds, the Paracas civilization was divided into two types: the cavernas graves date from the period 600 to 400 BC, while those from the necropolis date from 400 BC to AD 200.

On a slope north-west of the Bay of Paracas (best viewed from the sea) is the 120-m-tall (394-ft) "Candelabra" geoglyph. It is also known as the "Three Crosses", the "Trident" or the "Tree of Life". Its actual meaning remains unclear. Was it a navigational aid for ships? A fetish image? Or a stylized sign of the zodiac? Experts believe that the image derives from the same civilization as the Nazca geoglyphs, while others surmise it was only created in the 19th century.

16 Nazca You can make the comparison yourself with the Nazca Lines (Líneas de Nazca) some 150 km (93 mi) further to the south. They were created in the stony desert soil during the Nazca civilization. The creation involved clearing away the dark gravel of the top layer to a depth of up to 20 cm (9 in) over a width of 1 m (1.1 yds) to form colossal geometric shapes and figures such as a monkey, a 46-m (50-yd) spider, hands and the Colibri, which also often appears on Nazca ceramics. The largest figures measure up to 200 m (219 yds) and some of them are incomplete. There are over one hundred overall and around thirty human or animal images in total. From the viewing platform you get a good

1 The wild, craggy, storm-battered coast of the Paracas Peninsula is a paradise for sea birds.

2 Isla Sangayan is an island off the coast of the Paracas Peninsula inhabited solely by birds and sea lions.

3 Despite its height, the peak of the Chachani Volcano near Arequipa is considered an easy climb at 6,080 m (19,948 ft).

4 The "Candelabra" geoglyph in Paracas, viewed from the ocean.

The Nazca Civilization

The Nazca civilization was established on Peru's southern coast in about 200 BC. Its inhabitants lived mainly in simple mud huts, with only the upper echelons living in adobe houses. Their legacy includes ornate ceramic

The head of a mummy with a woven cap from the Nazca era

works characterized by a variety of shapes and patterns displaying a great deal of similarity to the colossal geoglyphs in the desert near Nazca.

of great wealth for the region: their guano, meaning dung in Quechua, was the best natural fertilizer and fetched high prices on international markets before the rise of artificial fertilizers.

15 Reserva Nacional de Paracas This nature reserve is not just worth a visit for nature lovers, but for anyone interested in ancient civilizations – the peninsula was settled as early as

Detour

Cañón del Colca

The detour to Cañón del Colca is a breathtaking excursion into the Peruvian mountains. The Río Colca canyon, roughly 80 km (50 mi) north-west of Arequipa, is a stunning 70 km (43 mi) long. The journey takes you over plateaus and steep passes, and past lagoons and imposing 6,000-m (20,000-ft) mountains: Volcán Ampato at 6,310 m

The Cañón del Colca is one of the deepest canyons in the world.

(20,703 ft) and Hualca Hualca at 6,025 m (19,768 ft).

You ultimately reach Chivay, the entrance to the canyon and, as you continue west, the canyon gets steeper, narrower and deeper until the drop from the highest cliff's edge at 1,200 m (3,937 ft) is nearly vertical.

look at three of the images: the hands, the lizard and the tree. You are directly on the Panamericana, but even from the platform the lines, which are up to half a mile long, reveal real images. To really grasp their size and beauty, take a short sightseeing flight from the nearby airfield in Nazca. The figures are best seen from the air.

South of Nazca, the Panamericana initially takes you through a desolate desert landscape and past the Cementerio de Chauchilla, where the Nazca dead were preserved in this arid climate with an impressive method of natural mummification.

After 85 km (53 mi), the road reaches the Pacific again near Puerto de Lomas. To Camaná it is another 300 km (186 mi) through a desert of gravel that

skirts the steep coastline. The route takes you up and down hilly stretches, and you roll past a series of bays with beautiful long beaches. There are a number of sleepy fishing villages on the way that only come to life when the regional bus makes a stop here.

17 Camaná With its attractive beaches, this small town has quickly become a popular seaside resort for the residents of Arequipa. Originally founded as the port for Potosí and Arequipa, the goods produced in Camaná are now shipped from the port further south.

18 Arequipa The "White City", or "Ciudad blanca", is the local nickname for Arequipa, and when you arrive at the central

plaza you realize why: the shiny white cathedral and the myriad other white colonial buildings with their two-storey arcades. All of them were built from the white volcanic rock sillar quarried in the region and still used as a building material today.

The Old Town of Arequipa, which was founded in 1540 and experienced its peak in the 17th and 18th centuries, has been perfectly restored, an effort that earned it the title of UNESCO World Heritage Site in 2000. The two most important attractions are buildings of religious significance. The Jesuit church dates from 1698, and the decoration of its façade displays distinct Indian influences, as does Santa Catalina monastery, a "town within a town" with fountains, squares and courtyards. It was expanded in the 17th century to its present size of 20,000 sq m (215,2000 sq ft).

Two volcanoes form the backdrop for Arequipa, at an elevation of 2,370 m (7,776 ft): Volcán Misti (5,835 m/19,145 ft), which is constantly smoking, and the higher but easier to climb Chachaní (6,080 m/19,948 ft).

From Arequipa the route continues through the desert along the Panamericana to the south. Moquegua, a town situated in the river valley of the same name, is worth a short visit and is about 213 km (132 mi) away.

It has a lovely Old Town center around the plaza with a number of well-restored churches and other colonial buildings.

Torota, about 24 km (15 mi) away, also has a scenic Old Town. You then come to Tacna after another 185 km (115 mi).

19 Tacna The last of the larger Peruvian towns before you reach the Chilean border used to belong to Chile, from 1880 to 1929. In 1880, during the so-called Saltpeter War, the Chileans conquered large parts of Peru and Bolivia in order to take control of the salt-producing regions of the desert. Chile gave the town of Tacna back to Peru in 1929 following a referendum. The battlefield from 1880 can be visited on a hill above the town. The town center has two early works by André Gustave Eiffel: the cathedral at the plaza and the fountains.

From Tacna it is then 46 km (29 mi) to the Chilean border at Concordia.

1 Palm-lined Plaza de Armas in Arequipa where the 19th-century cathedral takes up the entire north side of the plaza.

2 Arequipa's volcano, Vocán Misti (5,835 m/19,145 ft) emits clouds of smoke nearly constantly.

Túcume Moche Pirámides Many civilizations have lived in Peru's "Valley of the Pyramids" where twenty-six adobe buildings have been excavated.

Sipán The "Tomb of the Lord of Sipán", the 2nd/3rd-century Moche prince, and his companions is one of South America's most important archeological finds.

Chan-Chan The former Chimú capital is the largest archaeological site in South America. 100,000 people lived in the ten districts here in the 12th/13th centuries.

Parque Nacional Huascarán This reserve is home to the world's largest bromeliad variety. Nevado Huascarán at 6,768 m (22,206 ft) is the highest peak in Peru.

Paramonga This clay brick complex served as a Chimú fortress to defend against the Incas. Pizarro found it nearly completely intact. Seeing the Pacific and the Río Fortaleza from atop the ruins is an overwhelming experience.

Torata This town has a number of colonial buildings worth seeing, including the community church and the stone windmills. In addition to the Sabaya Inca center, Camata, the "Machu Picchu of Moquegua" is particular worth a visit.

Cañón del Colca This massive canyon northwest of Arequipa is 1,200 m (3,937 ft) deep, 70 km (43 mi) long, and is lined with volcanos as high as 6,000 m (19,686 ft).

Volcanos near Arequipa Misti, at 5,835 m (19,145 ft), and Chachani, at 6,080 m (19,948 ft), make for an impressive backdrop.

Lima Despite some disastrous earthquakes, the square-shaped Old Town in Peru's capital, founded in 1535, remains intact. Its unique gems include the Museo de Oro and the cathedral.

Arequipa The "White City" is one of South America's most important cultural and historical sites. Its idiosyncrasies include the Santa Catalina monastery and baroque churches and palaces.

Paracas This peninsula is known for its wealth of fish and birdlife, including flamingos and pelicans. Sea lions and seals also cavort in the cold Humboldt Current.

Reserva Nacional de Paracas The park is the only one of its kind in Peru, and encompasses a marine sanctuary. This picture shows the bird and sea lion island of Sangayan, also part of the reserve.

Nazca The bone-dry landscape is known for its giant geoglyphs. Here: an aerial view of the so-called "Astronaut".

Cementerio de Chauchilla This cemetery in the middle of the desert is a macabre conglomeration of plundered graves and pre-Columbian mummies.

Stone pillars at the sun gate of the ruined city of Tiahuanaca, south of Lake Titicaca.

Peru and Bolivia

The Inca Trail

The Inca Trail connects the capitals of Peru and Bolivia and passes through culturally and historically significant sites in the highlands of the Andes Mountains. Travellers will be amazed by magnificent monuments dating back to early Inca civilization and Spanish colonial times.

The Inca Trail begins in the Peruvian capital of Lima, extends through the western cordilleras (range) of the Andes and runs right across Peru to Lake Titicaca. From there, one of the most spectacular routes in the whole of South America travels over Bolivian territory through the basin scenery of the Altiplano to the south-east and finally terminates in the eastern cordilleras of the Andes, in Sucre, the country's constitutional capital.

A fascinating natural environment, protected in a number of national parks such as the Parque Nacional Manú, provides a stunning backdrop for the region's cultural treasures.

At the beginning of the 16th century, before the arrival of the Spanish, the Inca Empire covered almost the entire Andes region, including parts of the Andean foreland. A large number of the architectural treasures of this advanced civilization have been preserved along the Inca Trail. The architectural highlights include spectacular temples and palaces as well as a series of fortresses built at impressively shrewd locations. Most of these huge buildings, such as the large sun temple at

Highland Indians with their llamas.

Cuzco, were also built without significant technological assistance. A prime example of the strategic locations selected for Inca settlements is Machu Picchu, an extraordinary terraced site and one of the Inca's last places of refuge from advancing colonial troops.

Ironically, the Spanish never actually discovered this well-hidden settlement, which lies at around 2,800 m (9,187 ft). It was an American explorer who first discovered it in 1911. However, the discovery brought with it more riddles than answers regarding Inca culture.

Lake Titicaca, which still has a healthy fish population, straddles the Peru-Bolivia border. It lies 3,812 m (12,507 ft) above sea level and is not only the largest lake in South America, it is also the highest navigable lake in the world. Close to its southern shores is the town of Tiahuanaco (also

A view of the ruins of Machu Picchu, a glorious terraced Inca city in the high Andes.

In Sillustani, a peninsula on Laky Umayo, the Colla cultures buried their important citizens under chullpas, or burial mounds, measuring over 10 m (6 ft) in height and dating back to the 13th century.

known as Tiwanaku) which, up until the 10th century, was the religious and administrative center of an important pre-Columbian civilization. The natural environment in the region around Lake Titicaca is also spectacular. Some of the highest mountains in the Andes are here, including the 6,880-m (22,573-ft) Nevado del Illimani south-east of Bolivia's largest city and administrative capital, La Paz.

Numerous remnants of the Spanish colonial era can also be seen here, in particular in the area around Lago de Poopó. The Europeans were especially interested in the mineral wealth of the 'New World', and many Indians were forced to work as slaves in Spanish mines, many of them losing their lives in the process. At the beginning of the 17th century Potosí was the world's most important center for silver mining. As a result of its historical

significance the town has been declared a World Heritage Site, together with Cuzco, Machu Picchu and the Old Town in Lima. The distinction is intended for both the time-honoured Inca sites and for some of the architectural achievements of the Spanish colonial rulers.

In addition to these cultural and historical features, the diverse natural environment in this South American region has also been given its share of attention – the Manú National Park, in the transition zone between the Amazon lowlands and the middle Andes, has also been declared a UNESCO World Heritage Site.

With its dramatic differences in altitude, the Inca Trail provides a wonderful cross-section not only of Peru and the northern reaches of Bolivia, but also of the history and natural environment of an entire continent.

Women with traditional headwear offer their produce at the market in Cuzco.

Pachacámac

Pachacámac was a popular pilgrimage destination as far back as the 9th century – long before the advance of the Inca. The sites are around 30 km

Remains of a pyramid in Pachacámac.

(19 miles) south-east of Lima and are still shrouded in legend. Pilgrims covered great distances on difficult routes to come and consult the oracle. Interestingly, Pachacámac lost none of its mystery following the Inca invasion in the 15th century. On the contrary, not only did the new rulers take over the existing temples, they also extended the site to include the 80-m-high (262-ft) sun pyramid. Pachacámac subsequently became one of the most important administrative centers in the Inca Empire. The excellent condition of the ruins is particularly remarkable.

The Inca Trail runs from Lima on the Peruvian Pacific coast through countless Andean passes, majestic mountains and high plateaus on its way to Sucre in Bolivia. The route features both desert landscapes and tropical rainforests as well as high mountain lakes. The well-preserved Inca ruins make the journey an unforgettable experience.

❶ Lima Our journey begins in the largest city on the Inca Trail, where traffic is characterized by the expected noise and chaos of a large urban center. Lima was founded by the Spanish in 1535 and they quickly established it as the focal point of their colonial empire in South America. In 1826 Lima replaced Cuzco as the capital and grew into a wealthy metropolis.

Some of the most magnificent buildings from this era – both palaces and churches – have since been beautifully restored to their original glory. The main cathedral (1535–1625) is located on Plaza San Martín in the historic Old Town, which itself has been declared a World Heritage Site in its entirety. The tomb of the conqueror Francisco Pizarro, the founder of Lima, is also said to be somewhere in the city.

Lima is a junction for important transcontinental routes such as the Pan-American Highway. When you leave Lima heading east you will unfortunately encounter few inviting locations. Due to significant migration from the countryside, sprawling slums have developed on the outskirts of the city. Road conditions in the outer areas can be very bad at times. The multi-lane Pan-American Highway runs past these outskirts before heading south towards Pachacámac.

You will soon leave the coastal flats as the road climbs quickly into the Andean foothills toward the market town of La Oroya. There are some steep, winding sections here. From there a detour (64 km/40 miles) heads north to Junín. Several memorials here commemorate the battle of Junín in 1824 between Simon Bolívar's troops and Spanish soldiers, one of many South American battles for independence. The journey then continues through the narrow Mantaro valley towards Huáncayo.

❷ Huáncayo The Mantaro Valley is renowned for its numerous

Travel information

Route profile

Length: approx. 2,000 km (1,243 miles), excluding detours
Time required: 3 weeks
Start: Lima, Peru
End: Sucre, Bolivia
Route (main locations): Lima, Ayacucho, Cuzco, Machu Picchu, Lake Titicaca, La Paz, Cochabamba, Oruro, Potosí, Sucre

Traffic information:

Drive on the right side. Road conditions vary considerably. Heavy rainfall and the resulting landslides can make some mountain routes impassable.

When to go:

The best time for travelling to the Andes is during the southern hemisphere winter (May to September), as the southern summer (December to March) is the rainy season. The temperature range between night and day is considerable.

Information:

Peru travel info:
www.peru.info/perueng.asp
Bolivian travel info:
www.boliviaweb.com
Peruvian and Bolivian embassies around the world:
www.embassyworld.com

Inca architecture

Where they came from is uncertain, but it is beyond dispute that the Inca's architectural legacy is the most magnificent on the South American continent. Their monumental buildings are considered the most important cultural achievements of the Inca, despite the fact that the craftsmen of this advanced Indian civilization had no significant technological aids at their disposal.

Today it still seems barely conceivable that huge blocks of stone could be worked so smoothly without the use of metal tools, much less assembled without the use of joints. And yet it was not just individual houses, temples, palaces and tombs that were built. Whole cities were constructed without even the use of the wheel.

Top: Stone circle in the Inca fortress Sacsayhuamán.
Bottom: The almost seamless stone walls at Sacsayhuamán.

Furthermore, the materials often had to be transported to remote, nearly inaccessible locations at high altitudes, such as Machu Picchu. The remains of Inca architecture can also be found in the beautiful city of Cuzco and a number of other places.

All the sites have in common a high degree of functionality (even the religious buildings) and a simplicity of decoration. One essential function of the monumental buildings was to intimidate enemies. To this end, the Inca secured their settlements with mighty walls. Despite, or perhaps because of the aura of magic that still pervades their architecture today, Inca architecture is among the best researched architecture of the pre-Columbian era.

most important of their kind in South America, drawing visitors from all parts of the country.

❹ **Huari** Approximately 22 km (14 miles) north-east of Ayacucho is Huari, once the center of the culture of the same name (6th–12th centuries). Nearly 100,000 people lived here during the heyday of the Huari Empire in the 9th century. The city was carefully planned and the grid-like layout of the streets can still be seen today. The well-organized Huari armies had a history of subordinating enemy peoples, but the city was ultimately abandoned in the 10th century. Back on the main route we now head east past more Andean peaks towards Cuzco, the red

1 Rooftop view of the Renaissance-style cathedral in Cuzco (17th century).

2 Plaza San Martin, the lively center of the Peruvian capital, Lima.

3 Near Cuzco, a high-altitude basin framed by snow-capped Andean peaks.

4 The Corpus Christi procession is one of the most important religious ceremonies in Cuzco.

pre-Columbian ruins. It ends in Huáncayo, the largest town in the region. Maize, potatoes and vegetables are grown outside the town using irrigation and in some places the allotments seem to stretch beyond the horizon. Huáncayo, at an altitude of roughly 3,350 m (10,991 ft), is an important regional trading center. Today there is little left as a reminder that the town was once a center of the Inca Empire.

It is now characterized by Spanish colonial architecture.
The route now heads along a valley towards the south and the climate becomes milder with the decreasing altitude. Prickly pears grow right up to the roadside, their fruit highly prized by the Peruvians.

❸ **Ayacucho** This city, at an elevation of 2,760 m (9,056 ft), is an interesting combination of

past and present. Ayacucho was at one time the capital of the Huari Empire, one of the first advanced civilizations in the Andes and, as such, a predecessor to the Incas.
The city was discovered and refounded in 1539 by Francisco Pizarro. It is known as the 'City of 33 churches' and religious ceremonies play an important role here. The Holy Week processions (Semana Santa) are among the

Valle Sagrado de los Incas

One of the most revered destinations on a journey through Peru is the Sacred Valley of the Incas, best reached via Pisac. The Spanish name for the central section of the Urubamba Valley, Valle Sagrado de los Incas, refers to its fertile soils – and it's no surprise. The mild climate and the protected location made it possible for the Inca to make incredibly productive use of the land.

It was here, between Pisac and Ollanta, that the foundation for this advanced Indian civilization was formed. It was here that the staple crops were cultivated and the seeds sold for distribution throughout the country. And it is here that evidence still indicates the sophisticated methods used by the Incas to work the land.

Farming (top) and salt mining (bottom) have been carried out in the Sacred Valley of the Incas for centuries.

The steep slopes here were laboriously terraced in order to grow staple crops like potatoes, maize and quinoa, among other things. Land in this region was thus made available for agriculture up to an astounding altitude of about 4,000 m (13,120 ft). The terraces built in hollows are even reminiscent of amphitheaters. These fields are still worked by family groups to this day.

The villages, which seem to have remained untouched by the passing of time, are further testimony to the Sacred Valley's cultural legacy – dusty roads between simple adobe houses, wobbly wooden stands at the markets and people in traditional costumes retain the valley's authenticity. But it was not always so tranquil here. This valley was the scene of bloody battles between the Inca and Spanish invaders, who even managed to take the fortress of Ollantaytambo.

tiled roofs of which can be seen from miles away.

5 Cuzco For many travellers, Cuzco is one of the most important destinations in Peru. With its scenic location in the Andes, relaxed atmosphere, easy access to its attractions, and especially as a base for tours to the Urubamba Valley and Machu Picchu, the city is indeed a highlight along the Inca Trail.

For the Incas, Cuzco was the focal point of their empire and therefore the center of the world as they knew it. They established the city as a political, religious and cultural hub. Upon their arrival the Spanish knew of the city's importance but were dazzled by its wealth and grandeur. Unlike other Inca strongholds, the Spanish destroyed only a few

of the buildings when they invaded Cuzco, and only the most significant structures with political or religious functions were razed. On those foundations the colonial rulers then erected a series of their own buildings, some stately in scale, others of religious importance. The Plaza de Armas, for example, was constructed on the site of the former main square, Huacaypata, at the time 600 m (1,969 ft) long. Santo Domingo monastery was built from the ruins of the Coricancha sun temple. The Jesuit church La Compañía (1571) was constructed on the foundations of the grand Inca palace, Huayna Capac.

In 1950, parts of the city were destroyed by a strong earthquake. Fortuitously, however, the quake actually unearthed

a number of Inca remains that had been previously hidden from view.

Cuzco's importance remains unchanged for the descendants of the Inca. The Quechua-speaking Indians hold colourful ceremonies in the city, in which the customs and traditions of their forebearers are relived, and yet Christian festivals are also celebrated with enthusiasm. The annual Corpus Christi processions in particular attract much attention. In 1983 the Old Town was declared a UNESCO World Heritage Site.

6 Sacsayhuamán Situated above Cuzco – about 3 km (2 miles) north of the city – are the remains of a mighty fortress. Between 1440 and 1532 the Inca built an imposing citadel here

encircled by three concentric walls.

Sacsayhuamán can be reached on foot from Cuzco in just under half an hour. The path leads from the Plaza de Armas via the Calle Suecia, past San Cristobal church and via the old Inca path up to the fortress.

In their time the stone blocks, which are up to 5 m (16 ft) high and weigh 200 tonnes (220 tons), intimidated many a would-be attacker and thus fulfilled their purpose as a demonstration of the power of their owners. The fortress is a main attraction in the Cuzco area. Today it is assumed that the fortress was built to control the most vulnerable entrance to the city. The complex includes a number of store rooms for food and an armory for weapons.

Manú National Park

Some 100 km (62 miles) north of Cuzco is the Manú National Park (15,300 sq km/9,507 sq mi) in the area between the Amazon lowlands and the Andes. Due to the changes in altitude here, from 400–4,000 m (1,312–13,124 ft), the range of habitats extends from tropical lowland rainforest to mountain and cloud forest to highland steppe. The fauna is equally diverse. In addition to some 800 bird, 200 mammal and 120 fish

Top: A colourful scarlet parrot in flight.
Middle: The Manú meanders through the lowlands.
Bottom: The Black Caiman is one of the most striking reptiles in the park.

species, there are also countless insect species. As a result, the area was declared a National Park in 1973 and a UNESCO World Heritage Site in 1987.
To protect its flora and fauna, the national park has only minimal road infrastructure, but it is not empty of people. There are about thirty villages here. Approach the park via Paucartambo and the Acjanacu Pass to the mountain village of Atalaya on the Río Alto Madre de Dios. From here, boats bring visitors to Boca Manú, at the edge of the area open to tourists.

During the Spanish invasion, hundreds of Inca warriors barricaded themselves within the walls of Sacsayhuamán, right up until the bitter end. In addition to the heavy fighting, strong earthquakes have also caused significant damage to the structure. Today only about one-third of the fortress remains.

7 Pisac On a 32-km-long (20-mile) detour to the north you are led along a scenic road via the cult site Kenko, the 'Red Fortress' (Puca Pucara), and the sacred spring of Tambo Machay in the idyllic village of Pisac, which can be reached by a metal bridge. Inca influences clash here with colonial era flair.

Market days in Pisac are full of activity. Souvenirs such as flutes, jewellery, and clothing made from llama wool are traded on the central plaza. Just as attractive, however, are the ruins of an Inca ceremonial site located 600 m (1,969 ft) above the village.

8 Ollantaytambo At the end of the Sacred Valley, 19 km (12 miles) beyond the main town of Urubamba, is the village of Ollanta (2,800 m/9,187 ft), named after Ollantay, an Inca military leader. The fortress, with its spectacular stone terraces, stands on a bluff above the village. The Inca began construction on the well-fortified complex in 1460, but the project took much longer than planned. Ollantaytambo was not yet complete when the Spanish attacked in 1523.

Despite that, residents of Ollanta are still enjoying the benefits of the irrigation system developed back then by the Inca. Even during the dry season there was, and is, enough water available for agriculture.

Costumes worn by local residents are especially eye-catching and have hardly changed from those worn by their forefathers 500 years ago. The last few meters to the fortress have to be covered on foot.

While the landscape in the Cuzco hinterland is characterized by sparse vegetation, the scenery changes drastically as you head towards Machu Picchu. It becomes more tropical and the monotone flora of the highlands gives way to dense rainforest. The road starts to wind pretty heavily now, with tight curves and an occasionally hair-raising climb up to the 'City of Clouds'.

9 Machu Picchu The 'City of Clouds', as Machu Picchu is also known, is about 80 km (50 miles) north-west of Cuzco. Surrounded by imposing mountains and set in the midst of a dense forest is the most significant and fascinating archaeological site in South America. It is spectacularly located on a high mountain ridge nearly 600 m (1,969 ft) above the Urubamba River. There is hardly any other site where the technical and mechanical skills of the Inca are demonstrated more tangibly than Machu Picchu, and it is therefore no surprise that the site was declared a UNESCO World Heritage Site in 1983. It is also no surprise that myths and legends still surround this magical place today. In fact, its very origins remain unknown.

It is assumed that Machu Picchu was built in the 15th century. One theory holds that Machu Picchu served as a place of refuge during the Spanish invasion.

1 The walls of the Inca fortress Sacsayhuamán were intended to command the respect of attackers.

2 Ruins at the Inca ceremonial center of Pisac with the typical trapezoid doors.

3 The sun temple and stone terraces of the Ollantaytambo fortress.

4 View from the strategically situated village of Pisac down into the Sacred Valley of the Incas.

The condor

A lonely figure circling high above the peaks of the Andes – zologically one of the New World vultures, in the old world the condor was considered the symbol of South America. It is one of the largest volant birds in the world

Condor – King of the Sky.

and its wing-span can reach more than 3 m (10 ft). Its black plumage and fluffy white ruff are especially striking. Condors do not build an eyrie. Instead they lay their only egg in a rock crevice. The carcasses of larger mammals are their main source of food.

Another theory supposes that the Inca relocated their political center to this barely visible and even more inaccessible site. One thing remains certain, however – the colonial Spanish were fully unaware of the existence of this city. The site was first discovered in 1911.

The city's structure is still easily recognizable. Stone houses comprise one room only and are arranged around small courtyards. What might appear simple at first is in fact the result of considerable technical and mechanical skill on the part of the builders. The structures are grouped around a central, more or less quadratic formation. The most striking buildings include the temple tower, or Torreon, and the Sintihuatana sun temple, with seventy-eight stone steps leading up to it.

From Machu Picchu you first need to return to Pisac via the same road, where another road then branches off toward Huambutiyo. On a narrow, gravel road you will then come to Paucartambo and Atalaya, jumping-off point for a visit to the Manú National Park.

From Pisac back on the Inca Trail you soon branch off onto a signposted side road heading north to Tipón. The gravel road here is typically in good condition. After

about 4 km (2.5 miles) you will reach the ruins of the old city of Tipón at an altitude of about 3,500 m (11,454 ft).

10 Tipón Especially noteworthy here are the well-preserved terraces, where a sophisticated system of irrigation still enables productive cultivation of the land. It is now surmised that the Inca used the site as an experimental area for acclimatizing plants that otherwise only grew in lower-lying areas. On the onward journey from Tipón towards the south-east you pass

the little village of Andahuaylillas where the 17th-century baroque church is worth a brief visit. The peak of Nudo Ausandate towers 6,400 m (20,998 ft) above you on the left.

11 Raqchi Located at the base of the Quinsachata volcano, this town hosts an important traditional festival every year on the 3rd Sunday of June. From a distance, the temple, which is dedicated to Viracocha, the most important Inca god, resembles a viaduct because of its 15-m-high (49-ft) walls. It provides

an impressive backdrop for the festivities.

1 The ruins of Machu Picchu are even impressive when shrouded in mist. Yet they lay hidden for several centuries without the help of this natural veil. Situated as it is 600 m (1,969 ft) above the Urubamba River on a high mountain bluff, this surprisingly well-preserved Inca ruin is reached only with difficulty.

2 On the Inca Trail, the Nudo Ausandate (6,400 m/20,998 ft) rises out of the high Andean plateau.

It is hard to imagine how the Inca could have transported the stone blocks that were used to build the magnificent structures to Machu Picchu. Both the buildings and the site itself are testimony to their advanced skills and craftsmanship. Sophisticated irrigation systems were constructed for agricultural purposes.

The Sacsayhuamán fort is the most important sight in the area around Cuzco, the historic capital of the Inca Empire. It is presumed that around twenty thousand people were put to work on the 70-year project. The fort protected a number of vital supply routes to the former Inca capital. Because of its strategic importance

Sacsayhuamán was extremely well built and it took a number of heavy battles before the Spanish conquistadors were able to break the resistance of the Inca and take the fort. An earthquake also left its marks here – only a section of the original complex is still standing.

Two panoramic views from the Parque Nacional Lauca: herds of alpacas and llamas make use of the varying vegetation comprising tufts of grass on the more than 4,000-m-high (13,124 ft) plateau. The plano is dominated by a number of magnificent 6,000-m (19,686 ft) peaks, the most famous of which include the

perfectly shaped Pomarape volcano (to the left in the lower picture) and Parinacota (top picture and below right), both of which belong to Bolivia. The Lago Chungara is one of the national park's major attractions – on windless days its blue-green waters reflect the volcanic peaks.

The granite peaks of the Fitz Roy Massif rise almost 3,000 m (9,840 ft) above the plains of Patagonia. The highest of them all, the Cerro Fitz Roy, reaches a height of 3,375 m (11,070 ft); it is considered to be one of the most difficult mountains in the world to climb. You will rarely be lucky enough to have such a

clear view of the peak– as here across Lago Sucia – because of the thick clouds which often obscure the summit. Stormy gusts and fall winds whip across the region, bringing snow and sleet. Anyone hiking in the Los Glaciares National Park must be prepared for sudden changes in weather conditions.

Patagonia's animals

Most visitors to Patagonia will first encouter guanacos and rheas. The guanaco, a dark-brown type of camel and a relative of the llama, live in herds of five to twenty-five animals in the national parks of the south. The steppes of Argentina are also home to

Top: The Pampas hare covers long distances in search of food.
Bottom: The Pampas fox is mostly active at night.

the ostrich-like common rhea or nandu. At the beginning of incubation, the males of the species carve out their territories while the females gad about in groups. Rarer sights are the Pampas hare (maras), the pudu, and the Patagonian huemul, a species of deer about 1.5 m (5 ft) in height. The red fox and the puma are the only predators in this part of the world.

Argentino to such an extent that every few years it completely seals off the Brazo Rico, one of the lake's offshoots.

11 **Puerto Natales** The town, situated on the Ultima Esperanza Estuary, was the last hope of sailors who had got lost in the countless channels of southern Patagonia in their search for an east-west passage. Puerto Natales is the best starting point for a visit to nearby Torres del Paine National Park, and also a worthwhile stop for arranging various excursions.

For example, you could take a boat ride on Seno de la Ultima Esperanza (Last Hope Sound) up to the border of the Bernardo O'Higgins National Park to Cerro Balmaceda (2,035 m/6,676 ft) with its impressive glaciers. Bird lovers should visit the town's old pier in the late afternoon. It's a meeting place for hundreds of cormorants.

12 **Cueva del Milodón** En route to the Torres del Paine National Park, it is well worth taking time to pay a short visit to Cueva del Milodón. To get there, go 8 km (5 miles) north out of Puerto Natales and head west. After 5 km (3 miles) you reach the cave where German immigrant Hermann Eberhard found remains of a huge dinosaur, a 4-m (13-ft) megatherium, in 1896. A replica of the creature by the entrance to the cave shows how it may have looked.

13 **Torres del Paine National Park** The peaks of the Torres del

Paine Massif rise dramatically from the windswept plain. These steep, seemingly impregnable mountains have granite peaks, the highest of which is Cerro Torre Grande at 3,050 m (10,007 ft), surrounded by the peaks of Paine Chico, Torres del Paine and Cuernos del Paine.

This is Chile's adventure paradise. Visitors can choose between embarking on long hiking trails in the park, daylong tours, or a hiking trail around the entire massif. All these trails pass by bluish-white, opaque, glacial lakes with floating icebergs. They include Grey Glacier and the amazing Río Paine, which plummets into Lake Pehoe as a cascading waterfall.

The stunted trees brace themselves against the wind here, but in early summer the plains form a sea of flowers. In addition to guanacos, you will likely spot condors and sundry waterfowl. Remember to take warm clothing.

To the south of Puerto Natales, the route continues straight through the plains. Stubby grass grows on both sides of the road. You'll often see guanacos, rheas and sheep. This is Ruta 9 to Punta Arenas.

Some 34 km (21 miles) before the city, a road branches westwards. After 23 km (14 miles) you reach Otway Sound, home to a large penguin colony.

14 **Monumento Natural Los Pingüinos** There is another

large penguin colony to the north-east of Punta Arenas, right on the Strait of Magellan. In the summer months, some 2,500 Magellan penguins, the smallest of the species, live in this colony. They only grow to between 50 and 70 cm (20 and 28 in) and weigh a mere 5 kg (11 lbs). They can be easily recognized by their black-and-white heads and the black stripe running across the upper part of their torsos.

1 Guanacos, relatives of the llama, in a flowery meadow in the Torres del Paine National Park.

2 Rider on the Patagonian plains north of Punta Arenas.

One of the wonders of nature – a cluster of flowers, mainly lupins, in the Torres del Paine National Park, with snowy peaks in the background. This magnificent sight can be seen only in late spring and early summer.

The Patagonia coast and its marine life

The Patagonian coastal areas are rich in species variety, but the true animal paradise is located far to the east of the route on the Váldes Peninsula, where every year from July through to mid December you can see black-and-white killer whales (orcas) and

Above: Macaroni penguins, recognizable by the feathers over their eyes. Below: The sea lion can weigh up to 320 kg (700 lbs).

loads of southern right whales. In many coastal waters, you can catch sight of sea lions – especially in Tierra del Fuego's Beagle Channel – as well as dolphins, which are crossing the Strait of Magellan. The largest colony of the 70-cm-tall (28-in) Magellan penguins along your route lives at Seno Otway near Punta Arenas.

⑮ Punta Arenas This city, founded in the mid 19th century as a penal colony, grew quickly and was an important port for ships plying the west coast of America until the construction of the Panama Canal in 1914. Patagonia's profitable sheep-farming also made its contribution to the city's success, allowing wealthy inhabitants to build large sheep estancias (ranches) around the city center.

The Palacio Braun-Menéndez, today a museum, shows how the upper class lived in those days: walls covered in fabric imported from France, billiard tables from England, gold-plated fireguards from Flanders and Carrara marble decorations from Italy. Burials were no less regal here. The Punta Arenas cemetery contains the enormous mausoleums of the city's wealthier families. The Museo Regional Mayorino Borgatallo is also worth a visit.

From Punta Arenas you can drive 50 km (31 miles) back to the intersection of Ruta 9 and Ruta 255. Then follow Ruta 255 in a northeast direction until you reach Punta Delgada. From there, Ruta 3, which starts in Argentina, leads south and soon reaches the Strait, where a ferry transports travellers to Puerto Espora in Tierra del Fuego.

⑯ Strait of Magellan/Tierra del Fuego In 1520, Fernando de Magellan was the first to sail through the Strait later named after him. As he skirted the mainland and the islands, he saw fire and smoke, hence the archipelago's name. The island group covers an area of 73,500 sq km (28,378 sq mi). Its main island, the

western part of which belongs to Chile, covers an area of about 47,000 sq km (18,147 sq mi).

It is some 280 km (174 miles) from Puerto Espora to the Río Grande through vast, open countryside. At San Sebastián Bay, you can cross the border into Argentina. South of the Río Grande, the landscape changes – the valleys become narrower, the hills higher, and dense forests come into view. After about 250 km (155 miles), you reach Ushuaia and the adjacent Tierra del Fuego National Park.

⑰ Tierra del Fuego National Park Hikers will enjoy Tierra del Fuego National Park, which begins 18 km (11 miles) west of Ushuaia. It is easily accessible in its southern part but inaccessible in the north, and stretches along the Chilean border offering marshes, rocky cliffs and temperate rainforests.

Ruta 3, the Argentinean part of the southern Pan-American Highway, leads directly into the park and ends picturesquely at the Bahía Lapataia.

⑱ Ushuaia The southernmost city in the world is set between the icy waters of the deep Beagle Channel and the peaks of the Cordillera which, despite being only 1,500 m (4,921 feet) high, are always covered in snow. Originally founded as a penal colony, the city lives most-

ly from tourism these days. The Museo Fin del Mundo has a collection depicting the early and colonial history of the region. If the weather is good, take a boat trip to the glorious 'End of the World', Cape Horn.

1 The Tierra del Fuego National Park entices adventuresome travellers with its expansive steppe, mountainous landscape and impenetrable jungles and rainforests.

2 Punta Arenas port in the Strait of Magellan.

3 View of Ushuaia port, the southermost city in the world. The foothills of the Darwin Cordillera rise up in the background.

Aconcagua The highest mountain in the Americas at 6,963 m (23,000 ft), Aconcagua is near Mendoza on the Chilean border. It was first 'officially' climbed in 1897. Today, 2,000 to 4,000 mountaineers enjoy it every year.

Mendoza This modern city of 600,000 also has a colonial past, though it has largely been destroyed by earthquakes. Mendoza has now become the hub of Argentina's flourishing grape growing and wine industry. It has many wineries and bodegas where visitors can get a taste of the local wine amid some stunning landscape.

Los Alerces National Park Massive alerces trees, some are believed to be over 3,500 years old, grow to a massive height and girth.

Villa el Chocón Jurassic Park in Argentina: dinosaur fossils and models are on show at Neuquén.

Los Glaciares National Park This park consists mainly of two formations, the high mountain landscape in the north, with the FitzRoy Massif, and the inland glaciers in the south, with the Upsala and Perito-Moreno Glaciers.

The Torres del Paine National Park The highest peak in the park is the 3,050-m-high (10,007-ft) Cerro Torre Grande, surrounded by Paine Chico, Torres del Paine and Cuernas del Paine.

Ushuaia This city, the southernmost in Argentina, lies on the Beagle Channel. The Museo del Fin del Mundo (End of the World Museum) displays exhibits from the prehistoric and colonial history of Tierra del Fuego.

Córdoba Argentina's second-largest city (1.5 million inhabitants) is home to the country's oldest university. The picture shows the cathedral and Cabildo in the central plaza of town.

Cueva de las Manos In a sizeable cave in the Río Pinturas Canyon, the original inhabitants of this area left behind the oldest indications of human settlement in South America.

Nahuel Huapi National Park This park near Bariloche has several different landscape zones including the High Andes, rainforest, transitional forest and steppe.

Perito Moreno National Park The national park surrounding Lake Belgrano (the picture shows the broad Belgrano Peninsula) showcases wild and pristine Patagonian nature. Numerous indigenous animals live here, including pumas, guanacos, nandus, flamingos and condors.

Tierra del Fuego National Park This national park, close to Ushuaia in Terra del Fuego, runs to the Chilean border with its lakes, glaciers and rainforests.

Punta Arenas Until the Panama Canal was built in 1914, this port town was of great importance at the tip of South America. Some of the typical houses from that period still remain.

The Los Pingüinos and Seno Otway Penguin Colonies Thousands of Magellan penguins live here near Punta Arenas in the summer. They are the smallest species of penguin in South America.

Map labels:

Cerro Colorado, Laguna Mar Chiquita, Cruz del Eje, Villa del Totoral, La Rioja, Cosquín, CÓRDOBA, Miramar, P.N.Qda. del Condorito, Alta Gracia, Santa Fé, San Juan, La Rioja, Difunta Correa, Villa Dolores, Villa General Belgrano, Villa María, Termas de Villavicencio, Encón, P.N.Sierra de las Quijadas, Quines, Co.Aconcagua 6963, Santiago, Mendoza, San Luis, Río Cuarto, Puente del Inca, San Martín, La Paz, Beazley, La Loma, Rosario, Tunuyán, Pareditas, Villa Mercedes, Monte Comán, San Rafael, Santa Rosa, Molina, Pozo de las Animas, Fuerte San Rafael, General Alvear, El Sosneado, R.N. Gil de Vilches, Fortín Malal-Hué, Bardas Blancas, Cueva de las Brujas, Cerro Payún 3680, Ranquil del Norte, Volcán Tromen 3978, P.N. Laguna del Laja, Chos Malal, Copahue, CHILE, Curacautín, Las Lajas, Añelo, Bahía Blanca, Zapala, Cutral-Có, Neuquén, P.N. Conguillío, P.N.Laguna Blanca, Villa El Chocón, P.N. Huerquehue, La Ofelia, Catán Lil, P.N. Lanín, San Martín de los Andes, Piedra del Aguila, Osorno, P.N.Nahuel Huapi, Paso Flores, P.N.Puyehue, Valle Encantado, Pilcaniyeu, San Carlos de Bariloche, P.N.Lago Puelo, El Maitén, P.N.Los Alerces, Esquel, Futaleufú, Tecka, Pampa de Agnia, R.N.Lago Rosselot, Lago Vintter, P.N.Queulat, Nueva Lubecka, Buen Pasto, Villa Amengual, Alto Río Senguer, Sarmiento, Coihaique, Río Mayo, Bosque Petrificado J.Ormachea, L.Buenos Aires, Bosque Petrificado Victor Szlapelis, Chile Chico, Perito Moreno, Las Heras, Monte San Lorenzo o Cochrane 3706, Bajo Caracoles, Cueva de las Manos, Lago Belgrano, P.N. Perito Moreno, Gobernador Gregores, Monte Fitz Roy 3375, El Chaltén, La Julia, Tres Lagos, P.N.Los Glaciares, Lago Viedma, El Calafate, El Cerrito, P.N. Torres del Paine, Ea.Cerro Guido, Esperanza, Pasada Conaf, Tapi Aike, Cueva del Milodón, Güer Aike, P.N.Pali-Aike, Río Gallegos, Puerto Natales, Morro Chico, Punta Delgada, Strait of Magellan, Puerto Espora, Cullén, M.N., Los Pingüinos, San Sebastián, Punta Arenas, Porvenir, Tierra del Fuego, Río Grande, Fuerte Bulnes, Puerto Arturo, P.N.Tierra del Fuego, Estancia San Pablo, P.N.Alberto de Agostini, Ushuaia, Puerto Toro, Puerto Williams, P.N.Cabo de Hornos, Cape Horn

ARGENTINA

Photo index

Abbreviations:

C: Corbis	DFA: Das FotoArchiv
G: Getty	Hub: Huber
P: Premium	Mau: Mauritius

2–3 top: C_P.Saloutos; 2–3 bot.: P_Sisk; 4 l, P; 4 cen.: ifa; 4 r: P; 5 l : ifa; 5 middle: ifa; 5 r: P, 6/7: ifa.

Route 1: 10 large photo: Getty; cen.: C_center Everton; bot.: C_B.Vikander; 11 cen.: C_center Everton; bot.: C_WildCountry; 12.1: C_K.Schafer; 2: C_B.Vikander; edge: C_C.Karnow; 13.3: C_I.Yspeert; 4: C_C.Karnow; 5: ifa_F.Aberham; top edge: C_H.Stadler; bot.: C_K.Schafer; 14–15: C_W.Kaehler; 16.1: C_B.Krist; 2+3: C_K.Schafer; top edge: C_Y.Artus-Bertrand; cen.: C_W.Kaehler; bot.: ifa_BCI; 17 map (from l to r, from top to bot.): C_I.Yspeert; 2 x C_B.Vikander; C_H.Stadler; C_B.Krist; P; laif_Neuendorf; N.N.; P; C_K.Schafer.

Route 2: 18 large photo: P_ImageState; cen.: P; u+19 cen.: P_Slide File; bot.: P_Nägele; 20.1: P_Pan.Images; edge: laif_Krinitz; 21 t : P; bot.: laif_Krinitz; 22.1: P; 2: P_ImageState/E.Collacott; 3: P_MonTresor/ P.Adams; 4: P_Images Colour; edge: DFA_Riedmiller; 23.5+6: P; edge top + bot.: P; 24–25 t : P_Images Colour; bot.: P; 26.1: ifa_Harris; 2: P_Mon Tresor/C.Blake; 3: P_Pan.Images; edge: P_Japack; 27 map (counterclockwise from top l): C_R.Cummins; C_T.Thomson; P; C_T.Thomson; P_Pan.Images; P_Slide File; P, 2 x C_B.Krist.

Route 3: 28 large photo+center: P; bot.: Getty; 29 cen.: P_StockImage/ B.Ancelot; bot.: ifa_Nägele; 30.1: P_Pan.Images/K.Collins; 2: P_Pan. Images; 3: P_StockImage/Shankar; edge: ifa_Travel Pixs; 31: Huber; 32.1: P_ImageState; 2+3: ifa_J.Arnold Images; top edge: C_R.Antrobus; bot.: C_RM; 33.4: C_WildCountry; in box: C_A.Gyori; top edge: C_J.Richardson; cen.: DFA_Babovic; bot.: C_J.Richardson; 34.1+2+4: ifa_Panstock; 3: P_ImageState; 35.1: ifa_J.ArnoldImages; 2+3+ top edge: P_ImageState; cen.: C_C.Perry; bot.: C_Wild Country; 36–37 t : ifa_TravelPix; bot.+38.1+2: P_Image State; 3: ifa_ J.ArnoldImages; edge: ifa_Walsh; 39 map (counterclockwise from top l): C_WildCountry; P_FirstLight/ centerMcQuay; C_centerEverton; C_S.Vannini; ifa_J.Arnold Images; C_centerLewis; C_D.Croucher; P; C_Wild Country; C_T.Svensson; P_Brown.

Route 4: 40 large photo: P_ImageState; cen.: P; bot.: P_Nägele/Klammet; 41 cen.: C_center Everton; bot.: P_ImageState; 42.1: P_Image State/A.Glass; 2: P_Warren; top edge: C_A.Woolfitt; bot.: C_cen. Listri; 43.3: C_R.Antrobus; 4: C_J.Hawkes; 5: P_Image State/P.Prestidge; top edge: C_J.Hawkes; bot.: C_C. Cormak; 45 t : P_Pan.Images/S.Tarlan; cen. + bot.: P_Pan.Images; 47 top: ifa_IT/tpl; bot.: P_Stock/S.Vidler; 48.1: P_Image State; 2: P_Pan. Images; 3: P_Image State; 4: P_Mon Tresor/P.Adams; edge: C_A.Brown; 49.5: C_A.Brown/ Ecoscene; 6: C_A.Towse; edge: P; 50.1: C_N.Wheeler; 2: C_center Freeman; 51.3: laif_Zielske; 50–51 map (counterclockwise from top l): C_A.Hornak; ifa_Nägele; C_centerDillon; C_A.Hornak; P_Pan. Images; C_P.Libera; P; C_D.Croucher; P_ImageState; P_Images; 2 x ifa_Nägele; ifa_ Gottschalk; C_CordaiyPhoto LibraryLtd.; P_ImagesColour.

Route 5: 52 large photo: C; cen.: C_F.Grehan; bot.: P_Loken; 53 cen.: P_ImageState; bot.: ifa_J.ArnoldImages; 54.1+2: ifa_Panstock; top edge: P; bot.: ifa_J.ArnoldImages; 55.3: P_Loken; 4+Rand top + bot.+56–57: ifa_J.ArnoldImages; 58.1: Klammet; 2: P; in box: C_B.Vikander; edge top + bot.: P_Delphoto; 59.3: P_Woike; 4: C_C.Lisle; edge: Getty; 60.1: Mau_Sipa; 2: ifa_Panstock; 61.3: laif_Galli; 4: ifa_Aberham; 5: N.N.; 62–63: N.N.; 64.1: P_Sittig; 2: C_F.Grehan; 3: ifa_Rose; top edge: ifa_Aberham; bot.: P_Woike; 65 map (from top to bot., from l to r): ifa_IndexStock; ifa_Aberham; Getty; P; ifa_J.ArnoldImages; C_F.Grehan; ifa_Harris; Getty; 2x P; P_Delphoto; ifa_J.Arnold Images; ifa_Opitz.

Route 6: 66 large photo: ifa_F.Chmura; cen.: ifa_Panstock; bot.: ifa_Lahallcomp.; 67 cen.: digitalvision_J.Woodhouse; bot.: P_Mon Tresor/K.Yamashita; 68.1: Klammet; 2: C_H.Stadler; 3: C_cen. Everton; edge: laif_Huber; 69 t : DFA_Schmid; cen.: laif_Huber; bot.: laif_Zanetti; 70.1: ifa_K.Welsh; 2: ifa_Panstock; 3: ifa_Lahall; top edge: C_center Everton; cen.: C_C.Lisle; bot.: ifa_J.ArnoldImages; 71 t : C_H.Strand; bot.: C_B.Krist; 72.1: Pix_Kotoh; 2: Klammet; 3: Nordis_Trobitzsch; 4: Klammet; top edge: ifa_Lahall; bot.: C_center Everton; 73 map (from top to bot., from l to r): ifa_F.Chmura; P_StockImage/K.Stimpson; ifa_K.Welsh; C_cen. Everton; ifa_Nowitz; P_Pan.Images; Klammet; ifa_F.Chmura; C_B.Krist; DFA_Meyer; ifa_Panstock; laif_Huber; C_center Everton.

Route 7: 74 large photo: DFA_Schmid; cen.: ifa_J.Arnold Images; bot.: C_C.Lisle; 75 cen.: ifa_J.ArnoldImages; bot.: ifa_P.Grüner; 76.1: C_J.Rogers; 2: C_C.Lisle; edge top + cen.: DFA_Mayer/ Bauer; bot.: C_C.Lisle; 77: ifa_Lecom; 78.1: P; 2: ifa_J.Arnold Images; 79.3+4: P; 80.1: Nordis_Trobitzsch; 2: C_D.Houser; edge: C_C.Lisle; 81+ 82.1: C_H.Stadler; 2+3: C_S.Widstand, edge: C_D.Houser; 83 map (from top to bot., from l to r): P_Jämsen; P; C_cen. Yamashita; C_C.Lisle; 2xC_H.Stadler; Nordis_Trobiztsch; DFA_Schmid; C_B.Mays; 3x P.

Route 8: 84 large photo: ifa_J.ArnoldImages; cen.: C_G.Schmid; bot.: ifa_J.ArnoldImages; 85 cen.: ifa_Russia; bot.: C_G.Schmid; 86.1: ifa_J.ArnoldImages; edge: P; 87.2: C_center Beebe; 3: P; 4: P_Buss; edge top + bot.: AKG; 89 t : P_Hilger; bot.: ifa_Hollweck; 80.1: Hub_Gräfenhain; 2+edge: C_G.Schmid; 91 map (from top to bot., from l to r): P_Buss; C_W.Kaehler; C_B.Mays; C_T.&G.Baldizzone; C_G.Schmid; P; C_M,Beebe; C_P.Turnley; Hub_Gräfenhain; ifa_J.ArnoldImages; P_Hilger; C_D.Orezzo I

Route 9: 92 large photo: Dr.C.Zahn; cen.: P_Hänel; bot.: P_Hicks; 93 bot.: C_S.Raymer; 94.1: Mau; 2: Huber; edge: Wandmacher; 95.3+5+ top edge: Huber; 4: DFA_Babovic; edge cen. + bot.: Wandmacher; 96+97 top + bot.: Huber; 98.1: Böttcher; 2: BAV_Otto; 3+top edge : Huber; bot.: ifa_Aberham; 99.4: ifa_E.Pott; top edge: DFA_Müller/ Scheibner; bot.: Hub_Schmid; 100–101: DFA_Vollmer; 102.1: Hub_Schmid; 2: P; edge top + cen. + bot.: Freyer; 103.3: DFA_Müller; top edge: laif; cen.: P; bot.: ifa_Tschanz; 104–105: P; 106.1: laif_Kirchner; 2: N.N.; 3: Mau_Vidler; edge: C_P.Giraud; 107.4: ifa_J.ArnoldImages; 5: Mau; top edge: C_L.Kennedy; bot.: C_J.Marshall; 108.1: P; 2: Huber; 109.3:C_T.Bognár; 108–109 map (counterclockwise from top l): P_Hänel; Huber; DFA_Vollmer; Dr.C.Zahn; Hub_Schmid; ifa_J.ArnoldImages; ifa_Aberham; N.N.; P; DFA_Müller; 2x P; 2x Huber.

Route 10: 110 large photo: P_Pan.Images; cen.: ifa_ Panstock; bot.: Bieker; 111 cen.: ifa_Comnet; bot.: ifa_Harris; 112.1+2: Huber; 3: ifa_Comnet; top edge: Monheim; bot.: P_Otto; 113.4: Getty; 5+Rand: Huber; 114–115: Getty; 116.1: P_Hänel; 2: Hub_Gräfenhain; edge: Hub_Schmid; 117.3: C_D.Croucher; edge: Gaasterland_laif; 118.1: ifa_ J.ArnoldImages; 2: Monheim; 3: Huber; edge top + bot.: Herzig; 119.4: Romeis; 5: Bieker; Rand top + bot.: Huber; 121: Huber; 122.1: Mau; 2: Romeis; top edge: Freyer; cen.: Huber; bot.: P_Roda; 123 map (from top to bot.; from l to r): Huber; 2x Getty; ifa_Panstock; 2x Huber; ifa_J.ArnoldImages, Gaasterland_laif; ifa_Krämer; P_Pan.Images; Schilgen; Huber; Romeis; Freyer.

Route 11: 124 large photo: Huber; cen.: Bieker; bot.: Huber; 125 cen.: P; bot.: DFA; 126.1: Romeis; 2: Huber; top edge: Hub_Schmid; bot.: Wackenhut; 127.3: ifa_J.ArnoldImages, top edge: Freyer; bot.: Romeis; 128–129: Freyer; 130.1+2+Rand: Romeis; 3: Hub_Schmid; 131 top + bot.: Romeis; 132.1: Klammet; 2: Romeis; edge: DFA; 133.3+ edge: Freyer; 134.1: Klaes; 2: Romeis; 3: Huber; top edge: ifa_P.Grüner; bot.: ifa_K.Amthor; 135 map (from l to r, from top to bot.): Romeis; Hub_Schmid; Huber; Romeis; 2 x Huber; Bieker; ifa_Panstock; Huber; Freyer; ifa_Fufy; P_S.Bunka; Klammet; P_Buss.

Route 12: 136 large photo: laif_Celetano; cen.: ifa_ Panstock; bot.: P_Wolf; 137 cen.: ifa_Panstock; bot.: P; 138.1: Huber; 2: C_©Royalty-Free; edge: Hub_Damm; 139.3: Wackenhut; top edge: Herzig; cen. + bot.: Schilgen; 141: Böttcher; 142.1: ifa_J.ArnoldImages; 2: P; top edge: ifa_P.Grüner; bot.: ifa_Horinek; 143: ifa_J.ArnoldImages; 144.1: ifa_Chmura; 2: Huber; edge: ifa_IndexStock; 145.3: P_Handl; 146.1: DFA_Riedmiller; 2: ifa_J.Arnold Images; edge: P; 147.3: Westermann; 4: ifa_Lecom; top edge: ifa_Geiersperger; bot.: P; 148.1: stone_Armand; 2: laif; 3: C_V.Rastelli; top edge: Klammet; bot.: ifa_Lecom; 149 t : Mau; bot.: P; 150–151: Huber; 152.1: ifa_PictureFinders; 2: ifa_ISIFA; top edge: Mau; cen.: Huber; bot.: ifa_Kanzler; 153 map (from l to r, from top to bot.): C_©RoyaltyFree; ifa_Panstock; ifa_Glück; Huber; Wandmacher; FAN_Rufenbach; Huber; ifa_P.Grüner; ifa_Chmura; Westermann; DFA_Riedmiller; stone_Armand; C_V.Rastelli; ifa_ISIFA.

Route 13: 154 large photo: ifa_vision; cen.: P; bot.: Huber; 155 cen.: P_Pan. Images/T.Winz; bot.: Mediacolor's; 156.1: P_Pan. Images; 2: ifa_J.ArnoldImages; edge: ifa_Harris; 157.3: Mediacolor's; 4: P_MonTresor/ K.Yamashita; edge: P_Prisma/ Held; 158.1: P_S.Bunka; 2: ifa_J.ArnoldImages; 3: ifa_Sonderegger; edge: P; 159.4 + top edge: ifa_Sonderegger; Rand bot.: ifa_J.ArnoldImages; 160–161: ifa_Lecom; 162.1: ifa_Aberham; 2: ifa_Lecom; edge: Monheim; 163.3 + edge: ifa_U.Siebig; 164.1: P_Pan. Images/W.Marr; 2: ifa_Rose; edge: B.vonGirard; 165 edge: P; 164–165 map (counterclockwise from top l): ifa_Harris; P_Prisma/Held; P_MonTresor/K.Yamashita; ifa_Sonderegger; Monheim; ifa_Siebig; P; ifa_vision; ifa_Lecom; Klammet; 2x mediacolors; Getty; ifa_J.ArnoldImages.

Route 14: 166 large photo: P_Maywald; cen.: ifa_J.ArnoldImages; bot.: C_F.Mayer; 167 cen.: P_Meer; bot.: ifa_P.Graf; 168.1: P_Pan. Images/T.Winz; 2: Monheim_Helle; 3: P_Maywald; top edge: P_Pan. Images/Vladpans; bot.: ifa_J.ArnoldImages; 169.4: P_Martens; 5: P_Pan.Images/ Vladpans; 6: P_S.Bunka; top edge: P_Roda; bot.: C_C.van Leeuwen; 171 top + bot.+172.1: ifa_Panstock; 2: Monheim; 3: C_R.Klune; edge: C_D. Bartruff; 173.4: N.N.; 5: P; edge: C_D.Bartruff; 174–175 top + bot.: P; 177 t : ifa_Stadler; bot.: P; 178.1: C_T.Bognar; 2: Klammet; edge: C_F.Grehan; 179 map (counterclockwise from top l): Monheim; 2x ifa_ J.ArnoldImages, P_Roda; C_D.Bartruff; P_Maywald; N.N.; ifa_Stadler; P_Meer; P; Monheim; P_Martens; P; C_B.Ross.

Route 15: 180 large photo: ifa_Panstock; cen.: DFA_Mayer; bot.+ 181 bot.: ifa_J.ArnoldImages; 182.1+2: ifa_Panstock; edge: ifa_Lescourret; 183.3: ifa_J.ArnoldImages; top edge: C_R.Klune; bot.: C_L.Snider; 184–185: ifa_J.ArnoldImages; 186.1: C_Y.Arthus-Bertrand; 2: C_N.Wheeler; edge: laif_ Linke; 187.3+4: ifa_Diaf; 5: C_R.Bickel; 188.1: C_R.Estall; 2: C_L.Snider; edge: ifa_Diaf; 189.3+Rand: ifa_J.Arnold Images; 188–189 map (from top to bot., from l to r): C_H.Stadler; ifa_Diaf; ifa_J.ArnoldImages; 2x ifa_Panstock; ifa_Diaf; ifa_J.Arnold Images; ifa_Haigh; P; C_H.Stadler; C_R.Estall; Hartmann; C_R.Klune; ifa_J.ArnoldImages; P.

Route 16: 190 large photo: Monheim; cen.: ifa_Panstock; bot.: C_Archivo Iconografico S.A.; 191 cen.: P_Pan. Images/O.Cajko; bot.: C_O.Franken; 192.1: P; edge: C_C.Aurness; 193.2+3: Herzig; 4: P_Pictor; edge: AKG; 195 top + cen.: P; bot.: Hub_Radelt; 197 t : P; bot.: Hub_ Giovanni; 198.1: ifa_Panstock; 2: C_A.Woolfitt; Rand; C_B.Krist; 199.3: C_ArchivoIconografico S.A.; 4: laif_Linke; edge top + bot.: C_C.Loviny; 200.1: C_D.Marsico; 2: P; top edge: C_Y.Arthus-Bertrand; bot.: C_N.Wheeler; 201 top edge: C_R.Holmes; bot.: C_O.Franken; 202.1: laif_Piepenburg; 2: C_G.Mooney; edge: C_F cen. Frei; 203 map (from top to bot., from l to r): Hub_Radelt; Herz; C_A.Woolfitt; P; P_Buss; C_center Busselle; Getty_Waite; C_C.Loviny; C_O'Rear; C_H.Stadler; C_center Setboum.

Route 17: 204 large photo+center: ifa_Panstock; bot.: ifa_J.ArnoldImages; 205 cen.: ifa_TPC; bot.: ifa_J.ArnoldImages; 206.1: P_Sixty Six; 2: ifa_Panstock: 3: Hub_ Gräfenhain; edge: Hub_Radelt; 207.4: ifa_Harris; 5: Hub_ Giovanni; 6: Mau; edge: DFA; 208.1: Hub_Giovanni; 2: ifa_Panstock; edge: ifa_J.Arnold Images; 209: ifa_Diaf; 210+211.1: P; 2+3+4+212 top + bot.: ifa_Panstock; 214.1: ifa; 2: P; edge: ifa_R.Maier; 215.3: ifa_Harris; edge: P_Barnes; 217 t : Huber_Schmid; cen.: G. Schmid; bot.: Mau_Mattes; 218.1: P_Hicks; edge: ifa_Held; 218–219 map (from top to bot., from l to r): ifa_Stockshooter; ifa_TPC; Hub_Giovanni; ifa_Panstock; ifa_TPC; 2x ifa_J.Arnold-Images; ifa_Harris; ifa_J.Arnold Images; P_Barnes; ifa_J.ArnoldImages; ifa_Harris; ifa_J.ArnoldImages; ifa_R.Maier; ifa_Diaf; ifa_Panstock; ifa_TPC.

Route 18: 220 large photo: C_J.Hicks; cen.: ifa_Aberham; bot.: C_B.Harrinton; 221 cen.: C_H.Stadler; bot.: ifa_Barnes; 222.1: ifa_Hauck; 2: C_A.Jemolo; top edge: Hub_Giovanni; bot.: C_O.Franken; 223.3: C_J.Hicks; 4: C_A.Jemolo; top edge: C_V.Noticias; bot.: C_center Bellver; 224.1: C_J.Hicks; 2: C_center Bellver; 3: C_F.Muntada; edge: C_V.Noticias; 225.4: C_J.Hicks; 5: laif_Gonzales; 6: ifa_Barnes; edge: ifa_Fried; 226–227: C; 228.1+2: C_H.Stadler; 3: ifa_Tschanz; top edge: C_O.Alamany+E.Vicens; cen.: C_O.Alamany; bot.: C_center Busselle; 229.4: C_H.Stadler; edge: Getty_Frerck; 230.1: P_SixtySix; edge: ifa_J.ArnoldImages; 231.2: P.; 230–231 map (counterclockwise from top l): 2x ifa_Tschanz; C_O.Alamany+E.Vicens; Getty_Frerck; C_H.Stadler; ifa_Harris; Hub_Giovanni; ifa_Hauck; C_V.Noticias; 2x C_J.Hicks; C_H.Roth; laif_Gonzales; C_V.Noticias; J.Bradley.

Route 19: 232 large photo: P_ImageState; cen.: C_A.Lope; bot.: C_S.Maze; 233 cen.: ifa_Panstock; bot.: ifa_K.Welsh; 234.1: P_Pan.Images/ T.Thompson; 2: C_J.Hicks; top edge: C_A.Woolfitt; bot.: C_N.Wheeler; 235.3: Pix_Silberbauer; 237 t : P; bot.: P_Pan.Images; 238.1: P_SixtySix; 2: C_C.+A.Purcell; top edge: C_ArchivoIconografico,S.A.; bot.: ifa_TPC; 240–241: ifa_K.Welsh; 242.1: P_SixtySix; 2: C_P.Wilson; edge: P_Nägele; 243 map (counterclockwise from top l): Getty_Cornish; C_A.Lope; C_ArchivoIconografico S.A.; ifa_Harris; ifa_Int.Stock; C_cen. Busselle; C_J.Raga; ifa_Aberham; P; C_A.Lope; C_F.Muntada; P.

Route 20: 244 large photo: P_ImageState; cen.: ifa_F.Chmura; bot.: ifa_Kanzler; 245 cen.: P_Vidler/Smith; bot.: P_Otto; 246.1+2: P; edge: C_N.Wheeler; 247: P; 248–249: ifa_Aberham; 250.1: ifa_Kanzler; 2: P; top edge: DFA_Schwerberger; cen.: P; bot.: ifa; 251.3: ifa_J.Arnold Images; edge: ifa_Baier; 252.1: ifa_Held; 2+3: ifa_Harris; edge: N.N.; 253.4: ifa_Harris; 5: ifa_F.Hollweck; 6: ifa_P. Grüner; edge: ifa_K.Welsh; Selbach_laif; 2: Franz Marc Frei; top edge: Mau_AGE; bot.: P; 255 map (from top to bot., from l to r): P_Mon Tresor/K.Yamashita; ifa_Nägele; C_center Chaplow; ifa_J.ArnoldImages; C_O.Alamany& E.Vicens; C_center Everton; 2x ifa_J.ArnoldImages; P_SixtySix; C_center Stephenson; ifa_J.Arnold Images; ifa_K.Welsh; ifa_J.Arnold Images; ifa_K.Welsh.

Route 21: 256 large photo: P_SixtySix; cen.: ifa_Panstock; bot.: ifa_Eich; 257 cen.: P_SixtySix; bot.: P_Buss; 258.1: P_Pan.Images/ T.Winz; 2: P_Pan.Images/Vladpans; 3: P_MonTresor/K.Yamashita; edge: ifa_Arakaki; 259 t : P_Pan.Images/J.Millan, cen.: P_Pan.Images; bot.: P_MonTresor/K.Yamashita; 260.1:P_Pan. Images/R.Frerck; 2: P_Pan. Images/S.Tarlan; edge: C_T.Arruza; 261.3: ifa_J.ArnoldImages; 4: C_D.&J.Heaton; edge: P_Roda; 262.1: C_D.Marsico; 2: ifa_Panstock; edge: P_Wackenhut; 263.3: P_Jessel; 4+5: C_C.O'Rear; edge: C_RoyaltyFree; 264.1: P_SixtySix; 2: ifa_J.ArnoldImages; 3: C_U.Schmid; edge: P_Coleman/J.Clark; 265 map (from top to bot., from l to r): P_Yamashita; P_Roda; C_D.&J.Heaton; ifa_J.ArnoldImages; P_Wackenhut; P_Pan.Images/R.Frerck; C_D.Marsico; P_Yamashita; ifa_Panstock; ifa_Arakaki; P_Jessel; ifa_Panstock;P_SixtySix; C_C.O'Rear.

Route 22: 266 large photo: P_Winz; cen.: P; bot.: Klammet_ Nägele; 267 cen.: P; bot.: laif; 268.1: P_Winz; 2+edge: C_D.Marsico; 269 t : Klammet; bot.: Hub_Giovanni; 270–271: P_Pan.Images/K.Stimpson; 272.1: C_D.Marsico; 2: laif; 3: Getty; edge: Klammet_GK; 273.4: P_SixtySix; edge: Janke; 274.1: P_ImageState; 2: C_E.&P. Ragazzini; edge: ifa_Amadeus; 275 edge: P_Roda; 276–277: ifa_Aberham; 278.1+2: P_Image State; 3: P_NawrockiStock/ cen. Brohm; edge: P; 279 map (counterclockwise from top l): C_D.Marsico; laif; ifa_J.ArnoldImages; C_D.Marsico; P_Pan.Images/K.Stimpson; P; P_ImageState; 3x P; Janke; P; Klammet_GK.

Route 23: 280 large photo: ifa_Panstock; cen.: C_Vanni; bot.: Getty_Frerck; 281 cen.: C_S.Vannini; bot.: Mau_AGE; 282.1: ifa_AlastorPhoto; 2: P_Pan.Images/Cajko; edge: P_Roda; 283.3: Getty_TCL/Layda; edge: P; 285 top + bot. + 286–287: P; 288.1: laif_Ogando; 2: Mau_Torino; in box: ifa_Picture Finders; edge: C_Jodice; 289.3: ifa_J.Arnold Images; edge: C_R.Ressmeyer; 290–291: P; 292.1+ 2: ifa_Harris; top edge: ifa_J.ArnoldImages; bot.: ifa_Keribar; 293.3: C_Heaton; in box: P; edge: C_Orti; 294.1+Rand: C_S.Vannini; 2: Mau_Pigneter; 295 map (from top to bot., from l to r): P_Pan.Images/Cajko; Getty_TCL/Layda; C_F cen. Frei; C_Bettmann; C_J.Heseltine; C_center Jodice; C_A.deLuca; ifa_Panstock; Mau_Torino; C_S.Vannini; C_D.Ball; ifa_J.ArnoldImages; P; ifa_Harris; C_Heaton.

Route 24: 296 large photo: P; cen.: C_J.Hicks; bot.: ifa_G.Aigner; 297 cen.: ifa_F.Aberham; bot.: laif; 298.1: P_ImageState; 2: Klammet; edge: P_Hicks; 299: P; 300: Huber_Giovanni; 301 alle: P; 302.1: C_J.Raga; 2: P_SixtySix; top edge: ifa_Rölle; cen.: ifa_Aberham; bot.: ifa_Strobl; 303.3: C_J.Hicks; edge: Huber; 304.1: C_J.Hicks; 2: Hub_Simeone; top edge: laif_Amme; bot.: P; 305.3: ifa_Aberham; 4: Hub_Puntschuh; top edge: C_B.Brecelj; bot.: ifa_Aberham; 306.1: laif_Sasse; 2: ifa_Kanzler; top edge: C_center Everton; bot.: C_center Listri; 307.3: ifa_Aberham; 4: ifa_Amadeus; edge: ifa_Arakaki; 308.1: P; 2: C_ArchivoIconografico S.A.; Rand top + bot.: Getty; 309 map (from l to r, from top to bot.): C_D.Marsico; P_ImageState; C_N.Wheeler; P; ifa_Aberham; Huber; ifa_J.ArnoldImages; C_J.Heseltine; Huber_Mehlig; Mau_fm; ifa_Aberham; Getty_Rauch; P.

Route 25: 310 large photo: ifa_Aberham; cen.: ifa_ Panstock; bot.: ifa_Alexandre; 311 cen.: C_center Everton; bot.: C_J.Dickman; 312.1: ifa_Aberham; 2: C_K.Westermann; edge: C_J.Dickman; 313 top + bot.: C_H.Stadler; cen.: C_N. Wheeler; 314–315: P_NGS/S.Brimberg; 316.1+2: C_center Everton; top edge: ifa_Strobl; bot.: C_H.Stadler; 317.3: ifa_Tschanz; 4: ifa_Aberham; edge: C_deSelva; 318.1+2: C_H.Stadler; edge: C; 319 map (from top to bot., from l to r): C_H.Stadler; ifa_Aberham; C_L.Nelson; C_N.Wheeler; C_center Everton; C_J.Dickman; ifa_Tschanz; C_center Everton; 2x ifa_Aberham; C_H.Stadler; ifa_Aberham.

Route 26: 320 large photo: P_S.Bunka; cen.: C_P.Souders; bot.: ifa_Index Stock; 321 cen.: ifa_Panstock; bot.: P_ImageState; 322.1: C_P.Saloutos; 2: ifa_Thouvenin; edge: C_Y.Arthus-Bertrand; 323.3: C_J.Hicks; edge: P; 324: P_Souders; 325: C_C.Perry; 326.1: C_J.Hicks; 2: P_Brown; 327.3 + edge top + bot.: C_P.Souders; 328–329: ifa_J.ArnoldImages; 330.1: C_I.Yspeert; 2+ edge: C_ArchivoIconografico S.A.; 331.3: ifa_Aberham; edge: laif_on location; 332.1: laif_Harscher; 2: look_K.Kreder; 3: ifa_W.Otto; edge: laif_Tophoven; 333 map (counterclockwise from top l): P; ifa_Aberham; C_P.Souders; ifa_Panstock; ifa_Picture Finders; ifa_W.Otto; Huber_Mehlig; laif_Caputo; Huber; P_ImageState; ifa_J.ArnoldImages.

Route 27: 334/335: Premium/Tarlan; 334 cen.: IFA; 334 bot.: ifa_J.ArnoldImages; 3353 cen.: 3IFA/Panstock; 335 bot.: P_Stanfield; Rand 336: P_Pictor; 336/337: P_Panoramic Images; 4/336: ifa_Aydogmus; 337/3: N.N.; 337/4: P_Smith; 337: P_Spichtinger; 338/339: P_Spichtinger; 341 t: Mau_ Schwarz; 341 bot.: Hollweck; 342 top edge: laif_Tophoven; 342 Rand cen.: Mau_Hänel; 342 Rand bot.: ifa_Kohlhas; 342 cen.: laif_Müller; 343: ifa_J.Arnold Images; 343 top edge: P; 343 Rand bot.: P; 344 side col.: C_Wheeler; 344/345 t : P_Pictor; 344/345 bot.: ifa_Keribar; 345 top edge: Klammet; 345 Rand bot.: C_ArchivoIconografico; 346/347: ifa_J.Arnold Images; 348 edge: ifa ; 348: C_Vanni; 349/2: ifa_J.Arnold Images; 350/351 map (from l to r): P; Hub_Schmid; 4 x ifa; laif_Tophoven; 2 x C; P; ifa; C; 5 x ifa; C; P; ifa.

Route 28: 352/353 large photo: P, 352/353 bot.: Getty_ Stone/ Allison; 352 bot.: ifa IndexStock: 353: ifa_Index Stock; 354 side col.: C_Freeman; 354.1: ifa_BCI; 355: C_Sutherland; 356/357: C_Bartruff; 359 t : C_Hebberd; 359 bot.: Getty_Wedewarth; 360 side col.: C_Vikander; 360.1: Minden_Mangelsen; 360.2: DFA_Riedm; 361: C_Enock; 362 side col.: C_Zuckermann; 362.1: C_Horner; 362.2: ifa_ J.ArnoldImages; 364 side col.: C_Krist; 364.1: C_Freeman; 364.2: ifa_Aberham; 365 side col.: P_Stock Image; 366 side col.: C_Cumming; 366.1: P; 367 map (counterclockwise from top l): ifa_J.ArnoldImages; ifa_BCI; C_L.Hebbert; Media-color's; P_Pictor; P_Pan. Images, E.Bronsteen; C_Freeman; ifa_J.ArnoldImages; C_Freeman; C_S.Collins; C_Freeman.

Route 29: 368/369 large photo: C_Baldizzone; 368 cen.: Getty_TCL; 368 bot.: C_Rowell; 369 cen.: P_IC; 369 bot.:

C_Rowell; 370 side col. t : K. U. Müller; 370 side col. bot.: C_Heaton; 370.1: P_Philips; 370.2: C_Everton; 371: P_Image State;372/373: P; 374/375: C_Kaehler, 376: P; 377.1: P_ImageState; 377.2: P_Frederiksson; 377 side col.: ifa_J.ArnoldImages; 378.1: C_Rowell; 378.2: P_Image State; 378.3: P_ImageState; 379.4: P_Monteath; 379.5: Hub; 379.6: ifa_J.ArnoldImages; 380 side col. top + bot.: C_Rowell; 380.1: C_Vikander; 380.2: C_Kolisch; 381.3: DFA_Zippel; 381 side col. top + bot.: C_Lisle; 382/383: ifa; 384 side col.: C_Lovell; 384.1 ifa_Koubou; 384.2: ifa_AP&F; 384.3: C_Dean; 385 map (from l to r, from top to bot.): ifa_Schmidt; P_ImageState; P_Philips; C_Kaehler; C_Everton; C_Lovell; P_ImageState; C_Rowell; C_Lovell; C_Wright; C_Rowell; ifa_Int. Stock; C_Lisle.
Route 30: 386/387 large photo: ifa_J. ArnoldImages; 386 cen.: ifa_Panstock; 386 u:. C_Y.Liu; 387 cen.: P_PanoramicImages/ Yamashita; 387 bot.: C_Nowitz; 388 side col.: C_Horner; 388.1: ifa_Panstock; 388.2: P_Panoramic Images/Yamashita; 389.3: C_Tettoni; 389 side col.: ifa_Fried; 390/391: C_Tettoni; 392 side col.: ifa_Jäger: 392.1; ifa Alastor Photo; 392.2: P; 392 in box: ifa_J.ArnoldImages; 393.3: ifa_J.Arnold Images; 393.4: ifa_Siebig; 393 side col. top: ifa_Jäger; 393 side col. cen.: P_PacificStock/D.Perrine; 393 side col. bot.: P_Image State; 395 t : P; 395 bot.: DFA; 396 side col. o: C_Wheeler; 396 side col. bot.: C_Houser; 396.1: ifa_J.Arnold Images; 396.2: C_Everton; 397: ifa_F. Raga; 399: P_Roda; 400 side col.: C_Houser; 400.1: P; 400.2: ifa_IndexStock; 401 map (counterclockwise from top l): C_Horner; P_PanoramicImages/Yamashita; C_Nowitz; P; ifa_F. Raga; P_Roda; 2x ifa_J.ArnoldImages; P; ifa_Panstock.
Route 31: 402/403: Corbis/K. Su; 402 bot.: Zefa/Minden/ Lanting; 403 t : P; 403 bot.: K.-U. Müller; 404/405 t : K. Su_Corbis 405 cen. + bot.: Mau_O'Brien; 406 side col.: Zefa/Minden/Lanting; 406.1: C_Wier; 406.2: C_Gyori; 406.3: C_K. Su; 407/4: C_Robbins; 407/5: P; 407 side col.: Zefa/Anderle; 408 side col.: K. U. Müller; 408/409 t : P_Bunka; 408/2 C_K. Su; 408/409 bot.: C_K. Su; 409/4: C_K. Su; 409 side col.: C_Ergenbright; 410 side col.: K.-U. Müller; 410/411: P_Bunka; 410/2: C_Ergenbright; 411/3: K.-U. Müller; 411 side col.: K.-U. Müller; 412 side col.: C_BohemianNomadPicturemakers; 412/ 413: P_Weld; 412/2: K. U. Müller; 412/3: K.-U. Müller; 413/4: C_K. Su; 414/415: Hub; 416/417: C_K. Su; 418–419 map t (from l to r): C_Westermann; C_K. Su; C_Wier; C_Ergenbright; Zefa/ Minden/Lanting; C_Wishnesky; P; C_Wishnesky; Royalty Free_Corbis; K. Su_Corbis; 418–419 map bot.(from l to r): 2 x K. - U. Müller; C_Ergenbright; Premium; Corbis; Ifa; Corbis_van der Hilst; K.- U. Müller; Corbis_So Hing-Keung.
Route 32: 420/421: C_Souders; 420 cen.: ifa_Panstock; 420 bot.: L_Emmler; 421 cen.: C_Fisher; 421 bot.: P_APL; 422 side col.: Okapia/Watts/Bios; 422.1: C_Nowitz; 422.2: L_Emmler; 423.3: C_Souders; 423 side col.: P_APL; 424/425 t : P; 424/ 425 bot.: P; 426: C_Nowitz; 427.1: C_Clarke; 427.2: C_Mastrorillo; 427 side col.: FAN/Heinrichson; 428/429: Pix_APL/La Motta; 430.1: P; 430.2: C_Allofs; 431.3: P_Watts; 431.4: C_Enock; 432/433: Corbis _Arthus-Bertrand; 434 side col.: C_Tweedie; 434.1: C_Souders; 434.2: ifa_Siebig; 434.3: ifa_Siebig; 435.4: C_RoyaltyFree; 435 side col. t : C_Allofs; 335 side col. cen.: C_Conway; 335 side col. bot.: C_Yamashita; 336/337: Transglobe/Schmitz; 438 map (from top l to bot. r): C_Nowitz; P; C_Mastrorillo; C_Clarke; ifa_PictureFinders; 2x C_Souders; Look_Dressler; L_Emmler; C; 439 map (from top l to bot. r) C_Tweedie; Transglobe_Schmitz; ifa_Siebig; C_Allofs; ifa_Siebig; ifa_IndexStock; ifa_Prenzel; C_Clarke; C_E&D Hosking; C_Sparks; C_Clarke; C_M&P Fogden.
Route 33: 440/441 t: ifa/J. Arnold Images; 441 b: Corbis/ P. Souders; 442 m: ifa/AP&F; 442 b: Premium/Pacific Stock/J. Watt; 442 C: Premium/ APL; 442.1: Premium; 443.2: Corbis/P. Souders; 443 C: Reinhard; 444/445 t+b+ 447 t: ifa/J. Arnold Images; 447 m: Premium/S. Bunka; 447 b: Premium/ APL; 448: C. Emmler; 450 C: Corbis/ T. Allofs; 450.1: Premium/Pan. Images/Vladplans; 450.2: alamy/center Rock; 451 C t: Corbis/B. Ross; 451 C b: Corbis/center Harvey; 452/453: laif/Kreuels; 454.1: Corbis/center Pole; 454.2: Premium/Voigt/ C. Voigt; 455 map CLK starting t le: Corbis/B. Ross, Corbis/center Harvey, Premium/APL, Corbis/Y. Arthus-Bertrand, Corbis/ Reuters, Premium/T. Brakefield, Corbis/B. Ross, Corbis/R. Holmes, Premium/APL, laif/ Emmler, Corbis/T. Allofs.
Route 34: 456 large photo: Getty; cen.: P_ImageState; bot.: P_Minden/T.deRoy; 457 cen.: P_ImageState; bot.: ifa_J. ArnoldImages; 458.1: ifa_J.ArnoldImages; 2: P_S.Bunka; side col.: C_R.Holmes; 459.3: ifa_J.ArnoldImages; 460.1: ifa_J. ArnoldImages; 2: P_ImageState/A.Apse; side col. top + bot.: P_ImageState; 461.3: P; 462–463: ifa_J.ArnoldImages; 465 t+bot: laif/Heeb; 466–467: ifa_IndexStock; 468.1: ifa_Panstock; 2: P_Image State; 3: P_ImageState/ A.Apse; side col.: C_R.Klune; 469.1: P_ImageState/A.Apse; 2: ifa_J.ArnoldImages; side col.: ifa_AP&F; 470.1: ifa_Panstock; 2: ifa_J.ArnoldImages; side col.: C_R.Holmes; 471.3: C_H.Stadler; side col.: P_ImageState/cen. Allen; 472.1+2: P_ImageState/A.Apse; 3: C_H.G.Roth; side col.: C_R.Holmes; 473 map counterclockwise from top l: C_H. Roth; alamy_N.Cleave; 2x ifa_J.ArnoldImages; P_A.Seiden; ifa_J.ArnoldImages; P_K.Wothe; ifa_J.Arnold Images; Hub_Damm; P; C_B.S.P.I.; ifa_J.ArnoldImages.
Route 35: 474/475: ifa_Minke; 474 cen.: P_ImageState; 474 bot.: ifa_Aberham; 475 cen.: P_Vidler; 475 bot.: ifa_Diaf/SDP; 476 side col. top : Mau_Thamm; 476 side col. cen.: C_Osborne; 476 side col. bot.: P_Image State; 476.1: Getty; 476.2: C_Lisle; 477 t : FAN_Schindel; 477 bot.: Getty_Kenward; 478: ifa_Welsh; 479.1: ifa_Steinhardt; 479.2: ifa_Welsh; 479.3: P_Image State; 479 side col.: ifa_Steinhardt; 480 side col. t : P_Prisma; 480 side col. bot.: ifa_Aberham; 480.1: P_Shankar; 480.2: C_Vannini; 481.3: P_Bunka; 481.4: P_Shankar; 481 side col.: C_Schwartz; 482/483: Ifa_Arnold Images; 484 side col. top : ifa_Aberham; 484 side col. bot.: ifa_Thouvenin; 484.1: ifa_Diaf; 484.2: ifa_Everts; 485.3: L_Specht; 485 side col. top : P_Smith; 485 side col. cen.: ifa_J. ArnoldImages; 485 side col. bot.: ifa_J.ArnoldImages; 486/487: P; 488 top : C_Pitamitz; 488 bot.: C_Vannini; 489.1: ifa_J.ArnoldImages; 489.2: ifa_Aberham; 489 side col.: L_Gartung; 490 side col.: L; 490.1: ifa_Koubou; 490.2: C_Landau; 491 t : C_Venturi; 492 bot.: C_Lisle; 492 map (from top left to bot. right): C_Westermann; C_Arthus-Bertrand; C_Ward; C_Holmes; L_Specht; C_Maisant; Getty; C_Osborne; L_Specht; ifa_ Aberham; ifa_Thouvenin; ifa_Diaf; 493 map (top from ln.re. bot.): C_Bennett; C_Lisle; Mau_Thamm; P_Vidler; ifa_Welsh; C_Holmes; P_Hummel; C_Tidman; P_Prisma; P_ImageState; ifa_Aberham; C_Lisle.
Route 36: 494 large photo: Hub; cen. + bot.: P_Janek; 495 cen.: P_StockImage/S.Harris, bot.: ifa_Harris; 496 side col. t : C_O.Lang; bot.: C_H.G.Roth; 1: ifa_W.Grubb; 2: P_Buss; 497.3: P; 4: C_D.Bartruff; side col.: ifa_PictureFinders; 499 t : ifa_Panstock; cen.: DFA_Riedmiller; bot.: laif_Krause; 500–501: P; 502.1: ifa_ShashinKoubou; 2: ifa_J.ArnoldImages; 503.3: N.N.; 504: Hub_Damm; 505: P; 506.1: P_T.Smith; 2: P_NawrockiStock/ S.Vidler; 507.3: ifa_Panstock; 4: ifa_J.ArnoldImages; 508: Getty_ Westmoreland; 509 t : Mediacolor's; bot.: DFA_Riedmiller; 510.1: Hub_Zoom; 2: laif_Krause; 511.3: stone_Press, 512 side col.: P_Boyer; 1: ifa_; 2: P_s.Bunka; 513 map from l to r, from top to bot.: C_P.Nilson; Getty_Armand; ifa_JAI; C_W.Kaehler; ifa_Harris; laif_Emmler; ifa_TPC; Getty_ Westmorland; C_S.Vannini; C_N. Wheeler; ifa_Alexandre; C_W.Forman; Hub_Damm; stone_Press; DFA_A.Buck.
Route 37: 514 large photo: alamy_ImageState; cen.: P; bot.Schapowalow; 515 cen.: P_Plessis; bot.: C.+W. Kunth; 516.1: C_Fogden; 2: ifa; side col.: C_Johnson; 517.3: C_Arbib; 4: ifa; side col.: P_Philips; 518.1+2: C.+W.Kunth; 3: P; 520–521: W.Kunth; 522.1: C_Arbib; 2: P_Plessis, side col.: C_Y.Arthus-Bertrand; 523.3: C_Arbib; 524.1: C_Fogden; 2: ifa_J.Arnold Images; side col.: C.+W.Kunth; 525.3: N.N.; side col.: P_Herzog; 526–527 t : P_Plessis; bot.P_Wolfe; 528.1: P_Delphoto; 2: P_Herzog; side col. top + bot.: König; 530.1: N.N.; 2: C_Johnson; side col.: C_Arbib; 531: P_Stone/ A.Wolfe; 532.1: ifa; 2: P; side col.: ifa_BCI; 533.3+4: P; 534.1: W.Kunth; 2: P; side col.: Mediacolor's_Ehlers; 535.3: P; 536 map from l to r., from top to bot.: P_Plessis; C_Y.Arthus-Bertrand; ifa_B.Fischer; Kunth; C_center &P.Fogden; C_A.Arbib; ifa_J.ArnoldImages; ifa_B.Fischer; P_Delphoto; P_Plessis; ifa_J.ArnoldImages; P_Herzog; 537: mediacolor's_Ehlers; C_P.Johnson; ifa_K.Welsh; ifa_J.ArnoldImages; ifa_Aberham; C_P.Souders; C_G.Thomson; P_Graben; P_Delphoto; C_P.Johnson; C_G.Rowell.
Route 38: 538/539: ifa_Aberham; 538 bot.: ifa_Sohns; 539 cen.: ifa_Sohns; 539 bot.: ifa_Index Stock; 540/541: IFA_J. Arnold Images; 542.1: ifa_J. ArnoldImages; 542.2: ifa_ FischerB.; 542 side col. t : P_ImageState; 542 side col. cen.: ifa_Becker; 542 side col. bot.: P_Digital Vision; 543 in box: P_Kiefner; 543.3: Ifa_Aberham; 543.4: C_Reuters; 543 side col. t : ifa_Sohns; 543 side col. cen.: ifa_Picture Finders; 543 side col. bot.: P_Prisma; 544/545: Corbis_Houser; 547 t: ifa_J.ArnoldImages; 547 top middle: ifa_LDW; 547 side col. cen.: ifa_J.ArnoldImages; 547 side col. bot.: P_Raga; 548 side col.: ifa_J.ArnoldImages; 548.1 DFA/ Tack; 548.2: C_Krist; 549.3: ifa_Aberham; 549 side col.: P_Watt; 550/551: P_Watt; 552 side col. t : Corbis; 552 side col. bot.: ifa_Aberham; 552.1: C_O'Rear; 552.2: ifa_Aberham; 553: P_Lanting/Minden; 554.1: ifa_ J.ArnoldImages; 554.2: ifa_ Sohns; 555.3: L; 556 side col.: P_AnkaAgency/ N.Austen; 556.1 Alamy/D.Sanger; 556.2: ifa_J.ArnoldImages; 557 map (from l to r, from top to bot.): P_Herzog; C_Souders; C_Krist; ifa_LDW; ifa_PictureFinders; P_Hilger; ifa_Aberham; C_Harvey; ifa_Aberham; ifa_Picture Finders; P_Image State; C_Gallo Images/Hosten; C_Harvey; C_Alamany&Vicen
Route 39: 558/559: ifa_Warter; 558 M: P; 558 bot.: P_Wisniewski; 559 cen.: P_Prier; 559 bot.: C_Widstrand; 560 side col.: ifa_Int.Stock; 560.1: P_Schott; 560.2: P_Minden; 561.3: Mau_Rosing; 561 side col.: C_Peebles; 562/563: P; 564 side col. t : P; 564 side col. bot.: P; 564.1: C_Sohm; 564.2: P_Clifton; 565.3: C_Keaton; 566/567: Royalty Free_ Corbis; 568/569: Premium; 570 side col. t : P; 570 side col. cen.: P; 570 side col. bot.: P; 570.1: C_Sohm; 570.2: P; 571 side col.: C_Thompson; 572/573: P; 574.1: ifa_Panstock; 574.2: ifa_Warter; 574.3: C_Cooke; 574.4: C_Cooke; 576 side col.: C_Allofs; 576.1: C_Sohm; 576.2: Corbis; 576.3: ifa_BCI; 577 map (from l to r, from top to bot.): P_Wothe; ifa_BCI; C_Streano; ifa_Kokta; ifa_Peebles; C_Krist; C_Sohm; C_Keaton; C_Johnson; C_Hymans; C_Peebles.
Route 40: 578 large photo: P_OrionPress; cen.: P_Yamashita; bot.: C_Gehman; 579 cen. + bot.: C_Souders; 580 side col.: C_Souders; 1: P_Schwabel; 581.2: P_Bunka; 3: P_Pan. Images; side col.: C_Souders; 582: P_Schwabel; 583: P_Buss; 584 side col.: C_Lewis; 1: P_Yamashita; 2+3: C_Souders; 585: Getty_Marcoux; 586–587: C_Souders; 588 side col.: C_Nowitz; 1: C_Probst; 2: C_Steedman; 589.3: C_Kaehler; 4: C_Mays; 588–589 map from top to bot., from l to r: C_J.Sohm; P_Halling; C_R.Gehman; P_FirstLight/K.Straitton; C_R.Watts; 2x C_P.Souders; P_OrionPress; C_P.Souders; P_S.Bunka; C_cen. Lewis; C_P.Souders; C_B.Rowan.
Route 41: 590/591: P_Stock Image; 590 cen.: ifa_Harris; 590 bot.: P_Wiggett; 591 cen.: C_Ono; 591 bot.: ifa_Lahall; 592 side col.: P_FirstLight; 592.1: P_Watts; 592.2: ifa_Panstock; 593.3 P_S.Bunka; 593.4: ifa_Panstock; 594: P; 595 t , cen. top + bot.: P; bot.: ifa; 596 side col.: P_FirstLight; 596.1: P_Sisk; 596.2: C_Muench; 597.3: ifa_Panstock; 597.4: ifa_J.ArnoldImages; 597 side col.: ifa_J.Arnold Images; 598–599: P_Minden; 600 side col.: ifa_BCI, 600.1: ifa_Harris; 600.2: Pix/ Minden/Mangesen; 600.3: ifa_BCI; 601.4: ifa_Panstock; 601.5: Pix/Minden/ Fitzharris; 601 side col.: P; 602.1: P; 602.2: P_Larson; 602.3: C_Sohm; 604 side col.: ifa_J.ArnoldImages; 604.1: ifa_Panstock; 604.2: ifa_Panstock; 605.3: P_Sisk; 605.4: P_Milbradt; 605 side col.: P_Wittek; 606–607: C_Muench; 608 side col.: C_Lovell; 608.1: P_Sisk; 608.2: ifa_Siebig; 609.3: ifa_Siebig; 609 side col.: C_Mays; 610 map (top from ln.re.bot.): C_Marx; C; P_Image State; ifa_Panstock; C_FirstLight; P_FirstLight/Wiggett; C_Ricca; ifa_J. ArnoldImages; C_Rowell; ifa_Panstock; 611 map (top from l re.Seite) C_Sohm; C_Sohm; C_Randklev; C_Lovell; C_Mays: (rechte Seite) NOK; ifa_NHPA; C_Sedam; C_Huey; P_NGS/ Blair; C_Cummins.
Route 42: 612/613: Getty_Layda; 612 cen.: P_Gilchrist; 612 bot.: P_Hympendahl; 613 cen.: P_Watts; 613 bot.: C_Rowell; 614 side col.: C_Ross; 614.1: P; 614.2: C_Muench; 614.3 C_Muench; 615.4: C_Krist; 615 side col.: C_Muench; 616/617: Corbis_Krist; 619 t : Mau_VisaImage; 619 cen.: C_Saloutos; 619 bot.: C_Sinibaldi; 620 side col. t : C_O'Rear; 620 side col. cen.: C_Tharp; 620 side col. bot.: C_Streano; 620.1: P_Stimpson; 620.2: P_PanoramicImages; 620.3: P_Watts; 621.4: P_PanoramicImages; 621.5: Corbis; 621.6: C_Sohm; 621 Randp.: C_Sedam; 622 t : P_Wheelan; 622 cen.: P_StockImage; 622 bot.: P_Sanford; 624/625: Corbis_O'Rear; 626 side col. t : Mediacolor's; 626 side col. bot.: C_Rowell; 626.1: P; 626.2: P_Sisk; 626.3: P_PanoramicImages; 627.4: P_C.Cliffton; 627 side col.: P; 628 side col.: König; 628.1: P_Winz; 628.2: P_Foott; 629 map (counterclockwise from top l): C_Gulin; C_Bean; C_Sohm; C_Watts; C_Sinibaldi; N.N.; C_Saloutos; P_AGF; C_Schermeister; ifa_Hicks; P_Hicks; P_Winz.
Route 43: 630/631: P; 630 cen.: P_Palmisano; 630 bot.: ifa_ Index Stock; 631 cen.: P_Schwabel; 631 bot.: ifa_Index Stock; 632 side col.: P; 632.1: ifa_Panstock; 632.2: P_Bunka; 633 side col.: Getty_Wells; 635 t : ifa_Panstock; 635 cen.: P_ Schramm; 635 bot.: ifa_Panstock; 636 side col. t : C_Turnley; 636 side col. bot.: C_Hebbert; 636.1: P; 636.2: C_Lehman; 636.3: C_Muench; 637.4: C_Vadnai; 637 side col.: ifa_TPC; 638 side col.: ifa_Koubou; 638.1: P_Frilet; 638.2: C_Cummins; 639.3: C_Huey; 639.4: C_Fleming; 639 side col.: P; 640/641: Ifa; 642 side col.: C_Bean; 642.1: ifa_Siebig; 642.2: ifa_Siebig; 643.3: ifa_Gottschalk; 643.4: C_French; 643 side col.: P_Sisk; 644/645: Corbis; 646 side col.: ifa_Visions OfAmerica; 646.1: C_Muench; 646.2: C_Zaska; 647.3: P_ImageState; 647.4: P_StockImage; 647 side col.: ifa_J.Arnold Images; 648/649 map oben (counterclockwise from top l): C_Faris; C_Bean; C_Lehman; P_Vidler; C; P_Raga; C_Ergenbright; C_Hebbert; C_Lehman; C_Bake; 648/649 map unten (counterclockwise from top l): C_Saloutos; C_Corwin; P_PanoramicImages; ifa_Siebig; C_Huey; C_Fleming; ifa_TPD; C_Muench; C_Cummins; C_Huey; C_Bean; C_Muench; C_Krist.
Route 44: 650 large photo: ifa_Panstock; cen.: P; bot.: ifa_PictureFinders; 651 bot.: Getty_Hiser; 652.1: P; 2: P_Shaw; side col.: DFA_Tack; 653.3: ifa_Panstock; side col. top + bot.: P_Wisniewski; 654: ifa_Siebig; 655.1: ifa_Panstock; 2: C.Heeb; side col.: C_Garanger; 656.1+2: C_G.Huey; side col.: ifa_Siebig; 657.3: ifa_TPC; 4: ifa_Siebig; 5: ifa_Panstock; side col. top + bot.: ifa_Siebig; 658–659 t : P_Schott; bot.: ifa_Panstock; 660.1+2+3: ifa_Panstock; side col. t : Reinhard; cen. + bot.: P; 662–663: ifa_Int.Stock; 664.1: P_Schwabel; 2: P_Delphoto; side col.: ifa_Kokta; 665: ifa_J.ArnoldImages; 666–667: P_Sisk; 668.1: P_Lawrence; 2: P_Watts; 3: P_ImageState; side col.: ifa_Index Stock; 669 top + bot.: ifa_Panstock; 670–671 t : P; bot.: ifa_Panstock; 672–673 map from l to r, from top to bot.: ifa_Panstock; C_center Garanger; stone_Craddock; ifa_Siebig; ifa_JAI; ifa_Panstock; Getty_Sinbaldi; ifa_Panstock; C_G.Huey; ifa_Siebig; C; ifa_DirectStock; ifa_TPC; C_T.Bean; P_Halling; Kolhas; ifa_Panstock; P_J.Cowlin; ifa_Siebig; P_Mahlke; ifa_Panstock.
Route 45: 674 large photo: TheStockMarket/Berenholtz; cen.: C_R.Ono; bot.: AKG; 675 bot.: ifa_PictureFinders; 676.1+2: C_Sohm; side col.: C_Owaki-Kulla; 677.3: C_R.Ono; side col. top + bot.: ifa_Panstock; 678–679: ifa_TPC; 680 t : P_Image State/C.Waite; cen.: C_B.Krist; bot.: C_R.Nowitz; 682.1: C_C.Karnow; 2: C_R.Berenholtz; side col.: C_Bettmann; 683.1: C_Sohm; 2: C_R.Howard; 3+ side col.: C_B.Krist; 684–685: P; 686 t : P_FirstLight/F.Hudec; cen. top + bot.: P; bot.: P_Hicks; 689 t : ifa_IT/tpl; cen. t: C_R.Berenholtz; cen. bot.: C_J.Hicks; bot.: C_A.Schein; 690.1: Hub_Giovanni; 2: P_Pan.Images; side col.: C; 691: Stone/Armand; 692–693: P_Pan.Images; 694.1: C_J.Amos; 2: C_Kulla; side col.: ifa_J.ArnoldImages; 695 map counterclockwise from top l: C_C.Karnow; C_J.Sohm; C_D.Muench; C_R.Berenholtz; C_R.Cummins; ifa_J.ArnoldImages; C_Owaki-Kulla; C_RoyaltyFree; Mau_GFP; C_D.Muench; stone_Armand; P_Schwabel; P_V.Palmisano.
Route 46: 696 large photo: P, bot.: P_StockImage/C.Sarramon; 697 cen.: ifa_LDW; bot.: C_Arthus-Bertrand; 698.1: ifa_Panstock; 2: Kohlhas; side col.: ifa_J.ArnoldImages; 699.3: P_Nawrocki Stock/S.Vidler; side col.: ifa_Held; 700–701 top + bot.: Marr; 702.1: ifa_Panstock; 2: P_Stock Image/J.Brunton; side col.: laif_Eid; 703.3: ifa_AP&F; side col.: ifa_PictureFinders; 704.1: ifa_IndexStock; 2: P_Pan.Images; side col. t : ifa_Int.Stock; bot.: ifa_AP&F; 705.3: C_Lenars; side col.: C_R.A.Cooke; 706–707: NGS/Garrett; 708.1: P; 2: P_ImageState/T.Booth; 709 Huber_Giovanni; 710–711: laif_Tophoven; 712.1: ifa_BCI; 2: ifa_Panstock; side col.: P_Pacificstock/D.Perrine; 713 map counterclockwise from top l: C_center Everton; ifa_Marr; ifa_J.ArnoldImages; P_Buss; C_B.Mays; C_R. Watts; stone_Hiser; C_C.&J.Lenars; C_J.Poblete; 2x ifa_K.Welsh; ifa_Panstock; ifa_Koub.
Route 47: 714 large photo: C_Schafer; cen.: C_Slater; bot.: C_Dagli Orti; 715 cen.: Pix/Raga; bot.: C_Ergenbright; 716 side col.: C_DagliOrti; 1: C_Benn; 2: C_CorralVega; 717.3: laif_Gonzalez; 4: C_Donoso; side col.: C_Schafer; 718 side col.: C_Schafer; 1+2+719.3: C_Y.Arthus-Bertrand; 4: C_Sparshatt; side col.: C_Donoso; 720 side col.: C_Reuters; 1: C_Corral Vega; 2: C_Y.Arthus-Bertrand; 721 map from l to r, from top to bot.: C_Benn; C_K.Schafer; C_CorralVega; laif_Gonzalez; C_J.Donoso; C_Reuters; C_Y.Arthus-Bertrand; P_Roda; Pix_Raga; 3x C_Y. Arthus-Bertrand; C_J.Slater.
Route 48: 722/723: P_PanoramicImages; 722 cen.: C_Stadler; 722 bot.: C_Horner; 723 cen.: C_Stadler; 723 bot.: P_Raga; 724 side col.: C_Donoso; 724.1: C_Vega; 724.2: P_Roda; 725.3: P_Roda; 725.4: C_Vega; 725 side col. t : C_Vega; 725 side col. bot.: laif_Gonzalez; 726 side col. t : C_Stadler; 726 side col. bot.: C_Stadler; 726.1: P_Pecha; 726.2: C_Rowell; 726.3: C_Lovell; 727.4: C_Stadler; 727 side col. t : C_Allofs; 728 side col.: C_Mays; 728.1: C_Vikander; 728.2: C_Lovell; 729 t l: laif_Gonzalez; 729 t re.: laif_Gonzalez; 729 bot. l: laif_Gonzalez; 729 bot.re.: laif_Gonzalez; 730/731: C_Horner; 732 side col.: C_Horner; 732.1: C_Stadler; 732.2: Woodhouse; 733.3: Woodhouse; 733.4 C_Baldizzone; 733 side col. t : ifa_J.ArnoldImages; 733 side col. cen.: C_Houck; 733 side col. bot.: P_Japack; 734 side col. t : C_Stadler; 734 side col. bot.: C_Vega; 734.1: C_Houck; 734.2: C_Wright; 735.3: C_Horner; 735.4: C_Wright; 735 side col.: C_Vega; 735 side col.: P; 735.1: C_Spashatt; 735.2: C_Pepita; 737 map (from l to r, from top to bot.): L_Gonzalez; C_Donoso; P_Roda; C_Horner; Getty_Lanting; L_Gonzalez; C_Johnson; Mau_Vidler; C_Kaehler; Stone_Allison; C_Sparshatt; C_Pepita.
Route 49: 738 large photo: C_Stadler; cen.: digitalvision/ Woodhouse; bot.: C_Allofs; 739 cen.: P_AltitekImages; bot.: C_Stadler; 740 side col. top + bot.: P; 1: C_Stadler; 741.2: C_Stadler; 3: P_Hummel; 742–743 t : C_Lovell; bot.: Getty/ Bavaria; 744.1: digitalvision/Woodhouse; 2: P_Hummel; 3: C_Stadler; 745.4+ side col.: C_Stadler; 746 side col. top + bot.: C_Ressmeyer; 1+2: C_Stadler; 3: ifa_J.Arnold Images; 747.4: C_Everton; 5: C_Stadler; side col.: C_Nowitz; 748 side col.: C_Kaehler; 1: P_Pan.Images; 2: C_Rowell; 749.3: C_Y.Arthus-Bertrand; 4: C_Everton; side col.: C_Stadler; 750 side col.: C_West; 1: C_Stadler; 2: C_Kaehler; 751: C_Peebles; 752 map counterclockwise from top l: C_H.Stadler; C_T.Arruza; C_P.Corral Vega; C_H.Stadler; C_D.Keaton; C_center Everton; C_H.Stadler; ifa_JAI; C_R.Ressmeyer; C_H.Stadler; P_Hummel; 753 map from l to r, from top to bot.: C_C.O'Rear; C_G.Rowell; 2x C_H.Stadler; C_R.Ergenbright; ifa_Hasenkopf; C_center Everton; C_W.Kaehler; P_Pan.Images; C_T.West; C_W.Kaehler; C_A.Schaefer; C_D.Peebles.
Route 50: 754/755: P_PanoramicImages; 754 cen.: P; 754 bot.: C; 755 cen.: Getty-Stone_Klevansky; 755 bot.: C_Stadler; 756 side col. t : Corbis; 756 side col. bot.: C_Stadler; 756.1: C_Johnson; 756.2: C_Y.Arthus-Bertrand; 757.3: C_Y.Arthus-Bertrand; 757.4 C_Picimpact; 757 side col. t : C_Picimpact; 757 side col. bot.: C_Houghton; 758–759: N.N.; 760 side col. t : C_Stadler; 760 side col. bot.: C_Stadler; 760.1: P_Maywald; 760.2: C_Picimpact; 760.3: C_Modic; 761.4: C_Lovell; 761.5: C_Stadler; 761 side col.: C_Stadler; 762 side col. t : P; 762 side col. bot.: P; 762 .1 C_Rowell; 762.2: C_Stadler; 763: C_Rowell; 764 side col. t: P; 764 side col. bot.: P; 764.1: C Picimpact; 764.2: C_Everton; 764.3: C_Schafer; 765 map (from l to r, from top to bot.): C_Keaton; ifa_Koubou; C_Rowell; C_Vo TrungDung; C_Stadler; C_Ergenbright; C_Neden; C_West; C_Rowell; C_Pikamitz; C_Ergenbright; 2x C_Lovell.

This edition is published on behalf of APA Publications GmbH & Co. Verlag KG, Singapore Branch, Singapore by Verlag Wolfgang Kunth GmbH & Co KG, Munich, Germany

Distribution of this edition:

GeoCenter International Ltd
Meridian House, Churchill Way West
Basingstoke, Hampshire RG21 6YR
Great Britain
Tel.: (44) 1256 817 987
Fax: (44) 1256 817 988
sales@geocenter.co.uk
www.insightguides.com

ISBN 978-981-258-993-4

Original edition:
© 2008 Verlag Wolfgang Kunth GmbH & Co. KG, Munich
Königinstr. 11
80539 Munich
Ph: +49.89.45 80 20-0
Fax: +49.89.45 80 20-21
www.kunth-verlag.de

English edition:
Translation: Sylvia Goulding, Emily Plank, Katherine Taylor
Editor: Kevin White for bookwise Medienproduktion GmbH, Munich
Production: bookwise Medienproduktion GmbH, Munich
© Cartography: GeoGraphic Publishers GmbH & Co. KG

Printing and binding in Slovakia

The information and facts presented in this book have been extensively researched and edited for accuracy. The publishers, authors, and editors cannot, however, guarantee that all of the information in the book is entirely accurate or up to date at the time of publication. The publishers are grateful for any suggestions or corrections that would improve the content of this book.